Contents

Language and Gender: A Reader

Language and Gender: A Reader

Edited by Jennifer Coates

Blackwell
Publishing

BLACKWELL PUBLISHING
350 Main Street, Malden, MA 02148-5020, USA
9600 Garsington Road, Oxford OX4 2DQ, UK
550 Swanston Street, Carlton, Victoria 3053, Australia

First published 1998

12   2007

Library of Congress Cataloging-in-Publication Data

Language and gender : a reader / edited by Jennifer Coates.
      p. cm.
    Includes bibliographical references and index.
    ISBN 978-0-631-19594-8 (hbk. : alk. paper) — ISBN 978-0-631-19595-5 (pbk. : alk. paper)
    1. Language and languages–Sex differences. I. Coates, Jennifer.
  P120.S48L338   1998
  306.44 — dc21   97–18909
                                                                          CIP

A catalogue record for this title is available from the British Library.

Set in 10.5 on 12.5 pt Ehrhardt
by Graphicraft Typesetting, Hong Kong
Printed and bound in India by
Replika Press Pvt. Ltd

The publisher's policy is to use permanent paper from mills that operate a sustainable forestry
policy, and which has been manufactured from pulp processed using acid-free and elementary
chlorine-free practices. Furthermore, the publisher ensures that the text paper and cover board
used have met acceptable environmental accreditation standards.

For further information on
Blackwell Publishing, visit our website:
www.blackwellpublishing.com

Contributors

Elizabeth Aries is Professor of Psychology at Amherst College, Massachusetts, USA. Her research and writing have centred on gender and communication and she has published widely on the topic. Recent publications include *Men and Women in Interaction: Reconsidering the Differences* (Oxford, 1996).

Bowman Kim Atkins is Associate Executive Director and Director for HIV programs at the Community Family Planning Council of New York City. He worked with William O'Barr at Duke University on the language and law project in the 1970s, and subsequently carried out fieldwork in Northern Thailand for his own social anthropological research project. His current work includes publishing and presenting research on issues of HIV prevention and treatment for women.

Victoria Bergvall is an Associate Professor of Linguistics at Michigan Technological University, USA. Her present research interests include the coherence of gender as a linguistic variable and the politics of linguistic practice. Besides co-editing *Rethinking Language and Gender Research: Theory and Practice* (1996), she has published recently in *Discourse & Society* and *Natural Language and Linguistic Theory*.

Janet Bing is a professor at Old Dominion University in Norfolk, Virginia, USA. She is author of *Aspects of English Prosody* (1985), *Grammar Guide* (1989) and co-editor of *Rethinking Language and Gender Research* (1996) and of a number of articles in phonology and language and gender.

Ruth Borker, at the time of her death in 1989, was the Coordinator of Women's Studies at Randolph-Macon Woman's College, USA. In the previous fifteen years she had taught anthropology and women's studies at a number of different institutions including Cornell University, UC Berkeley, San Francisco State, Lewis and Clark College, Santa Clara University and Pitzer College. Her major research concerned gender, language, and Evangelical Christianity in Scotland and California.

John Bradley is a lecturer in natural, cultural and resource management at Batchelor College, an institute of Aboriginal tertiary education in the Northern Territory, Australia. He is working on the development of curriculum at tertiary level which deals with issues of ethnobiology. He has been working since 1979 in the south-west Gulf of Carpentaria researching indigenous people's relationships with the environment.

Penelope Brown is an anthropologist at the Max Planck Institute for Psycholinguistics in The Netherlands. She currently does research in the field of cognitive anthropology, specializing in cross-linguistic approaches to child language acquisition. She is co-author with Stephen C. Levinson of *Politeness: Some Universals in Language Usage* (1978), and has published a number of papers on politeness, gender and language, and child language.

Deborah Cameron is Professor of English Language at Strathclyde University in Glasgow, and has also taught in England, Sweden and the USA. A feminist and sociolinguist with particular interests in the study of language, gender, and power, she is the author of *Feminism and Linguistic Theory* (1992) and *Verbal Hygiene* (1995).

Jenny Cheshire is Professor of Linguistics at Queen Mary and Westfield College, University of London. Her research covers several different aspects of sociolinguistics, especially syntactic variation in spoken English. Her most recent publication is *Taming the Vernacular: From Dialect to Written Spoken Language* (Longman, 1997, co-edited with Dieter Stein).

Jennifer Coates is Professor of English Language and Linguistics at Roehampton Institute, London. Her research and writing have centred on two different areas of linguistics: English mood and modality, and language and gender. She has published six books, including *Women, Men and Language* (originally published 1986, 2nd edition 1993) and *Women Talk: Conversation Between Women Friends* (1996).

Victoria Leto DeFrancisco is an Associate Professor in Communication Studies and Director of Women's Studies at the University of Northern Iowa, USA. Her research interests include the study of gender dynamics in interpersonal relations, women, self-esteem and the role of education, feminist theory and methodology, and multicultural education. She is co-author of *Women's Voices in Our Time: Statements by American Leaders* (1993), and guest-edited a special issue of *Women's Studies in Communication*.

Tamra DiBenedetto is an Assistant Professor of English at Riverside Community College, Southern California, where she teaches composition, critical thinking and creative writing, and is adviser for the literary magazine *The Muse*. She is currently at work on a collection of poetry.

Penelope Eckert is a sociolinguist who combines ethnographic work with quantitative studies of variation in the study of the relation between variation and social practice and identity. Her work focuses on preadolescents and adolescents in the USA. She is Professor of Linguistics at Stanford University and Research Scientist at the Institute for Research on Learning, Menlo Park, California.

Edina Eisikovits is a Lecturer in Linguistics at Monash University, Melbourne, Australia. Her major research interests are in Australian English, adolescent speech, literacy development, and bilingual education. She is currently working on two research projects, one on ethnolects in Australian English, the other on the development of biliteracy in the primary school.

Susan Gal is Professor of Anthropology at the University of Chicago and is working on a book about the making of memory and political rhetoric in Eastern Europe after socialism. Her interests include the relationship of language to gender, politics and nationalism.

Marjorie Harness Goodwin is Professor of Anthropology at the University of California, Los Angeles. Her research interests include children's social organization, language and gender, workplace ethnography, conversation analysis, and the discursive organization of affect and aphasia in its social milieu. She is author of *He-Said-She-Said: Talk as Social Organization Among Black Children* (Indiana U.P., 1990).

Susan Herring is an Associate Professor of Linguistics at the University of Texas at Arlington. One of the first scholars to study gender differences in computer-mediated communication, she is also the editor of *Computer-Mediated Communication: Linguistic, Social and Cross-Cultural Perspectives* (John Benjamins, 1996) and *Computer-Mediated Discourse Analysis* (special issue of the *Electronic Journal of Communication*, 1996).

Janet Holmes holds a personal Chair in Linguistics at Victoria University of Wellington. She has published on a range of topics, including New Zealand English, language and gender, sexist language, pragmatic particles and hedges, compliments and apologies. Recent books include *An Introduction to Sociolinguistics* (1992) and *Women, Men and Politeness* (1995).

Deborah A. Johnson is Coordinator of the Pre-Graduate Intensive English Program at the University of Texas at Arlington, where she is also pursuing a PhD in Humanities. Her primary research interests are in women's spoken discourse, especially political discourse and politicians' speeches.

Fern L. Johnson is Professor of English and core faculty member in the Women's Studies and the Communication and Culture programs at Clark University in

Worcester, Massachusetts (USA), where she served as Provost and Vice President for Academic Affairs from 1988 to 1994. She studies the discourses of gender and race in cultural context, and has published numerous articles and book chapters on these topics.

Koenraad Kuiper is currently Associate Professor and Head of the Department of Linguistics at the University of Canterbury, New Zealand. He is author of two recent books: *Smooth Talkers* (Erlbaum, 1996) and, with W. Scott Allan, *An Introduction to English Language: Sound, Word and Sentence* (Macmillan, 1996).

Daniel Maltz is an independent scholar living in Lynchburg, Virginia. Trained as an anthropologist at Cornell University and the University of California at Berkeley, his research interests include gender, religious language, and community identity. He is presently involved in an ethnographic reconstruction of the world of his own childhood in the 1950s suburbs of Washington, DC.

Sally McConnell-Ginet is Professor of Linguistics at Cornell University, where she has also been very active in Women's Studies. Although her training and many of her publications are in formal semantics, she began work on language and gender in the early 1970s and has a number of publications in this area. Much of her recent work on language and gender has been carried out in collaboration with Penelope Eckert, her co-author in this volume.

Bonnie McElhinny is Assistant Professor of Anthropology at the University of Toronto. Her work focuses on language, gender, and political economy. She has published widely and is currently completing a linguistic ethnography, tentatively entitled *Policing Gender*, based on her fieldwork with the Pittsburgh police department.

Marie Wilson Nelson was formerly Director of the Composition Tutorial Center, based in the English Department of George Mason University, Fairfax, Virginia, USA.

Patricia Nichols is Professor of Linguistics and Language Development at San Jose State University in California, where she teaches classes in sociolinguistics, English grammar, and teacher education. Her research focuses on language contact between African, European, and Amerindian languages in early South Carolina and between Spanish and English in contemporary California.

William M. O'Barr holds joint appointments at Duke University in the departments of Cultural Anthropology, Sociology and English, and is Adjunct Professor of Legal Anthropology at the University of North Carolina at Chapel Hill. In recent work he has collaborated with John M. Conley on a series of studies involving language in the courtroom, small claims and pension funds and institutional investment. Recent books (with Conley) include *Roles versus Relationships: The Ethnography of Legal Discourse* (1990) and *Fortune and Folly – The Wealth and Power of*

Institutional Investing (1992). He is currently working on a new book, *Discourse and Dominance: Studies in Law, Language and Power*.

Jane Pilkington studied linguistics at Victoria University, Wellington, New Zealand, where she became interested in language and gender issues. She recently completed her MA, which looks at gender and gossip in more depth, and is now working as an editor with a legal publishing firm.

Katsue Akiba Reynolds is Professor in Japanese and Sociolinguistics in the Department of East Asian Languages and Literatures at the University of Hawaii, Honolulu, and Professor in Comparative Language and Culture at Josai International University, Japan. She has translated major works by Robin Lakoff and Dale Spender into Japanese. Besides publishing articles on Japanese women's language, she edited *Onna to Nihonngo* ('Women and Japanese') in 1993.

Joan Swann is a senior lecturer in the School of Education at the Open University, where her work includes the preparation of multimedia teaching materials on sociolinguistics and education. Her teaching and research reflect a long interest in language and gender. Books in this area include *Gender Voices* (1989, Blackwell, with David Graddol) and *Girls, Boys and Language* (1992, Blackwell).

Deborah Tannen is University Professor and Professor of Linguistics at Georgetown University. Her fifteen books include *Talking from 9 to 5* (1996) and *You Just Don't Understand: Women and Men in Conversation* (1990). Best known for her writing on communication between women and men, her research interests have included spoken and written language, cross-cultural communication, modern Greek discourse, and the relationship between conversational and literary discourse.

Senta Troemel-Ploetz is an independent scholar living in Lancaster, Pennsylvania. She was a Professor of Linguistics at the University of Konstanz 1980–4, and has held guest professorships in Europe and the USA. Her chief research interests are psychotherapeutic discourse and language and gender. Recent publications include *Vatersprache – Mutterland: Beobachtungen zu Sprache und Politik* (1992) and *Frauengespräche: Sprache der Verständigung* (1996).

Peter Trudgill is Professor of English Language and Linguistics at the University of Lausanne. Before moving to Switzerland, he taught at the Universities of Reading and Essex. His publications include *Sociolinguistics: An Introduction to Language and Society* (Penguin, 1983), *Dialects in Contact* (Blackwell, 1986) and *Dialects of England* (Blackwell, 1990).

Candace West is a Professor of Sociology at the University of California, Santa Cruz. Her recent articles focus on talk as part of the interactional scaffolding of social structure: 'Goffman in feminist perspective' (*Sociological Perspectives*, 1996),

'Ethnography and orthography: A modest methodological proposal' (*Journal of Contemporary Ethnography*, 1996), 'Doing difference' (with Sarah Fenstermaker, *Gender & Society*, 1995) and 'Women's competence in conversation' (*Discourse & Society*, 1995).

Patricia J. Wetzel is Professor of Japanese at Portland State University. She specializes in the sociolinguistics and pragmatics of Japanese honorifics and Japanese politeness, and has published many papers in this area. She is currently working on a book about the Japanese language 'how-to' industry and vernacular accounts of linguistic convention.

Don H. Zimmerman is Dean of the Division of Social Sciences and Professor of Sociology at the University of California, Santa Barbara. His chief research interests are the organization of conversational interaction and talk in institutional settings. He is currently working on a book, *9–1–1 Emergency: The Social Organisation of Calling for Help* (with J. Whalen and D. Whalen), to be published by Lawrence Erlbaum.

Editor's Note

Some papers in this Reader appear in their original form: Cameron; Coates; DeFrancisco; Eckert and McConnell-Ginet; Holmes (Part VIII); Kuiper; Maltz and Borker; Nichols; Tannen; Troemel Ploetz; West and Zimmerman.

The majority of papers in the Reader have been edited and abridged, in consultation with the authors(s): Bradley; Brown; Cheshire; Eisikovits; Gal; Goodwin; Holmes (Part II); Johnson and Aries; McElhinny; Nelson; O'Barr and Atkins; Pilkington; Reynolds; Swann; Trudgill; West (Parts V and VI); Wetzel. Where sentences or paragraphs from the original have been cut, this has been marked with the following symbol: [. . .].

Two papers have been revised especially for the Reader by their authors: Bing and Bergvall; Herring, Johnson and DiBenedetto. The paper by Penelope Eckert was written specifically for this Reader.

I would like to thank all these writers for their generosity in allowing me to reproduce their work in this Reader.

JETC

Acknowledgements

The editor and publishers would like to thank the following copyright holders for permission to reprint material:

Ablex Publishing Corporation for 'Cooperation and competition across girls' play activities' by Marjorie Goodwin (from Alexandra Dundas Todd and Sue Fisher (eds) *Gender and Discourse: The Power of Talk*) and 'Women's ways: interactive patterns in predominantly female research teams' by Marie Wilson Nelson (from Barbara Bate and Anita Taylor (eds) *Women Communicating: Studies of Women's Talk*); Addison Wesley Longman for 'Gossip revisited: language in all-female groups' by Jennifer Coates and 'Talk control: an illustration from the classroom of problems in analysing male dominance of conversation' by Joan Swann (both from J. Coates and D. Cameron (eds) *Women in Their Speech Communities*), extract from 'What a lovely tie' by Janet Holmes (from Janet Holmes, *Women, Men and Politeness*), and extract from 'The question of questions' by Janet Bing and Victoria Bergvall (from V. Bergvall et al. (eds) *Rethinking Language and Gender Research: Theory and Practice*); Arnold Publishers for 'Linguistic variation and social function' by Jenny Cheshire (from S. Romaine (ed.) *Sociolinguistic Variation in Speech Communities*); *Australian Journal of Communication* for 'Women's talk: the question of sociolinguistic universals' by Janet Holmes; Berkeley Women and Language Group for 'Communities of practice: where gender, language and power all live' by Penelope Eckert and Sally McConnell-Ginet, 'Participation in electronic discourse in a "feminist" field' by Susan Herring, Deborah Johnson and Tamra DiBenedetto, '"I don't smile much anymore": affect, gender and the discourse of Pittsburgh police officers' by Bonnie McElhinny, 'Female speakers of Japanese in transition' by Katsue Reynolds; Blackwell Publishers for 'Performing gender identity: young men's talk and the construction of heterosexual masculinity' by Deborah Cameron (from Sally Johnson and Ulrike Meinhof (eds) *Language and Masculinity*), and extract from 'Sex and covert prestige: linguistic change in the urban dialect of Norwich' by Peter Trudgill (from P. Trudgill, *On Dialect*); Cambridge University Press for 'Peasant men can't get wives: language change and sex roles in a bilingual community' by Susan Gal (from *Language in Society*, 7), 'Are "powerless" communication strategies the Japanese norm?' by Patricia Wetzel (from *Language in Society*, 17, 4), 'Sporting formulae in New Zealand English: two models of male solidarity' by Koenraad Kuiper (from J. Cheshire (ed.) *English around the World*), 'A cultural approach to male–female miscommunication' by Daniel Maltz and Ruth Borker (from J. Gumperz (ed.) *Language and Social Identity*); Elsevier Science Ltd, Oxford, England, for 'The talk of women friends' by Fern Johnson and Elizabeth Aries (from *Women's Studies International Forum*, 6, 4, 1983); Greenwood Publishing Group, Inc., Westport, CT, for 'How and why are women more polite' by Penelope Brown and extract from ' "Women's language" or "powerless language"?' by William O'Barr and Bowman Atkins (both from S. McConnell-Ginet et al. (eds) (1980) *Women and Language in Literature and Society*); JAI Press Inc. for 'When the doctor is a lady' by Candace West (from *Symbolic Interaction*, 7, 1984); *Journal of Aboriginal Linguistics* for 'Yanyuwa: "Men speak one way, women speak another" ' by John Bradley; Mouton Publishers for 'Black women in the rural south: conservative and innovative' by Patricia Nichols (from B. L. Dubois and I. Crouch (eds) *American Minority Women in Sociolinguistic Perspective*); Rhoda Weyr Agency for extract from *That's Not What I Meant* by Deborah Tannen, Ballantine Books, New York (1986); Sage Publications Ltd for 'The sounds of silence: how men silence women in marital relations' by Victoria DeFrancisco (from *Discourse and Society*, 2, 4), 'Selling the apolitical' by Senta Troemel-Ploetz (from *Discourse and Society*, 2, 4), and ' "Not just doctors' orders": directive–response sequences in patients' visits to women and men physicians' by Candace West (from *Discourse and Society*, 1, 1); University of California Press for 'Women's place in everyday talk' by Candace West and Don Zimmerman (from *Social Problems*, 24); University of Queensland Press for 'Girl-talk/boy-talk: sex differences in adolescent speech' by Edina Eisikovits (from Peter Collins and David Blair (eds) *Australian English*); *Wellington Working Papers in Linguistics* for ' "Don't try and make out that I'm nice": the different strategies women and men use when gossiping' by Jane Pilkington.

Every effort has been made to obtain permission to reproduce copyright material. If any proper acknowledgement has not been made, or permission not received, we would invite copyright holders to inform us of the oversight.

Transcription Conventions 1

These transcription symbols (as used in the papers by Goodwin; DeFrancisco; West; West and Zimmerman) are based on those devised by Gail Jefferson in the course of research undertaken with Harvey Sacks (see H. Sacks, E. Schegloff and G. Jefferson (1974) 'A simplest systematics for the organization of turn-taking for conversation', *Language*, 50, 696–735, pp. 731–3).

A: I had [them] B:　　　[Did] you	Brackets around portions of utterances indicate that the portions bracketed overlap one another.
//them	Double slashes provide an alternative method of marking overlap.
A: 'swhat I said= B: =But you didn't	Equals signs indicate 'latching': there is no interval between the end of a prior turn and the start of a next piece of talk.
THIRteen	Capital letters mark speech that is much louder than surrounding talk.
°thirteen	A degree sign marks speech that is much quieter than surrounding talk.
thirteen	Italics indicate some form of emphasis.
?,!.	Punctuation symbols are used to mark intonation, not grammar.
(0.5)	Numbers in parentheses mark silences in seconds and tenths of seconds.
(.)	Parentheses around a period/full stop indicate a pause of one-tenth of one second.
(#)	Parentheses around the symbol '#' indicate a pause of one second or less that it wasn't possible to discriminate precisely.

we:::ll	Colons indicate that the sound just before the colon has been lengthened.
but-	A hyphen marks an abrupt cut-off point in the production of talk.
((chanting))	Double parentheses enclose transcriber's comments or descriptions.
(only)	Material in parentheses indicates that the transcriber was uncertain of the exact word(s) heard.
.hh	A series of 'h's preceded by a dot marks an inbreath.
hhh	A series of 'h's with no dot marks an outbreath.
eh-heh-heh engh-hengh	These symbols mark laughter syllables (inhaled when preceded by a dot).
(x)	Parentheses enclosing an 'x' indicate a hitch or stutter on the part of the speaker.
(xxxx)	Parentheses enclosing several 'x's indicate untranscribable material.
10/19/70/15 *or* (T15:50−60)	The citation preceding an example locates the transcript where the original data can be found.

Transcription Conventions 2

These symbols are used in the papers by Cameron and by Coates.

. . . .
```
A: newspapers and stuff/
B:                    yes/
```
. . . .

A dotted line marks the beginning of a stave and indicates that the words enclosed by the lines are to be read simultaneously (like a musical score).

. . . .
```
A: papers and ⌈stuff/
B:             ⌊yes/good/
```
. . . .

Brackets around portions of utterances indicate the start of overlap.

. . . .
```
A: they're meant to be=
B:                  =adults/
```
. . . .

Equals signs indicate 'latching': there is no discernible gap between the two chunks of talk.

she pushes him to the limit/

A slash (/) indicates the end of a tone group or chunk of talk.

pregnant?

A question mark indicates the end of a chunk of talk which is being analysed as a question.

he's got this twi- twitch/
I was- I was stopped by a train/

A hyphen indicates an incomplete word or utterance.

he sort of . sat and read

Pauses are indicated by a full stop (short pause – less than 0.5 seconds) or a dash (long pause).

((mean))

Double round parentheses indicate that there is doubt about the accuracy of the transcription.

((xxxx))	Double round parentheses enclosing several 'x's indicate untranscribable material.
\<LAUGHING\> I can't help it \<WHINEY\>	Angled brackets give clarificatory information, relating either to that point in talk or to immediately preceding underlined material.
MEXICO	Capital letters are used for words/syllables uttered with emphasis.
Mexico	Emphatic stress on italicized item.
%bloody hell%	The symbol % encloses words or phrases that are spoken very quietly.
.hhh	This symbol indicates that the speaker takes a sharp intake of breath.
[. . .]	This symbol [. . .] indicates that material has been omitted.

Introduction

This Reader is designed to introduce students to some of the main topics in the area of Language and Gender. It is also designed to give you access to a selection of key papers. Publications in the language and gender area are now legion, and access to these publications is not always easy: some papers are published in obscure academic journals or in journals published outside Britain and the USA; others were first published in edited collections which are now out of print. It is one of the aims of this Reader to make a selection of these papers accessible by bringing them together in one volume.

In this Reader I shall not be concerned with issues of sexism in language (for which see Cameron 1992). Nor should the Reader be confused with one of the many edited collections which present contemporary work on language and gender from a particular point of view or with a particular theme at a particular time. (Good recent collections of papers are Bergvall, Bing and Freed 1996; Coates and Cameron 1989; Hall and Bucholtz 1995; and Tannen 1993.) By contrast, the focus of this book is gender-differentiated language use, and my aim is to be comprehensive.

The papers included here have been selected for various reasons. First, they cover the spectrum of language and gender research since the mid-1970s, years which have been extraordinarily productive in this area. This coverage will allow you to develop some understanding of the way the field has developed during this time. Secondly, papers have been chosen to represent a variety of sub-topics within the field, to give you a sense of the breadth of research going on in this area. Thirdly, the papers have been chosen to represent a variety of theoretical and methodological approaches. Fourthly, they have been selected to illustrate gender-related variation in a range of languages and cultures (though research in English-speaking communities inevitably predominates).

I have tried to cover research in language and gender which focuses on the whole range of women and men, in terms of age, social class and ethnicity. But the bias of sociolinguistic research to younger, white speakers is unavoidably reflected in the book. (And the variable of sexual orientation is not represented because it has been largely ignored in research. However, the first collection of papers dealing with the co-variation of language and sexual orientation is about to appear (Livia and Hall 1997).)

This book has several aims, not all of which are compatible. One aim is to introduce you to some of the best work in the field. Another is to give an idea of the breadth of the area, and to illustrate particular topics from as wide a range of material as possible. Some of the papers included are classics, or deserve to become so: they discuss innovative research and present their findings in ways that have had a profound influence on the language and gender field and in sociolinguistics generally. All the papers included in the Reader provide important insights into the complex interrelationship of language and gender.

Collections of papers such as this Reader exist to provide key material in a parti-cular area, to accompany study in that area, or to be read for their own sake. With the growing use of introductory texts which summarize extant research, there is a danger that students do not have first-hand contact with original work. It is very probable that you will use this Reader alongside a general introduction to the subject (such as Graddol and Swann 1989 or Coates 1993). To get a true feel for the subject, it is important not to rely solely on such texts, which are essentially second-hand accounts, but to go back to the original research. That is what a Reader allows you to do.

Language and Gender

Interest in the way women and men talk has grown astronomically since the mid-1970s, and sociolinguistic research carried out in many different cultures means that we now know far more than we did about the ways in which women and men inter-act and about the ways in which their patterns of talk differ. We also know that in all known societies it is the way men speak that is held in high esteem, while women's ways of talking are compared unfavourably with men's. These cultural beliefs are collectively known as 'folklinguistics' (see Coates 1993: 16–37). There is now con-vincing evidence that many of our folklinguistic beliefs are false. For example, the notion that women are chatterboxes has not survived scrutiny: research in a range of different social contexts – in the workplace, in the classroom, in television discussion programmes, in electronic discussions via computer, for example – has revealed that in mixed groups male speakers talk more than female speakers. (See Part III for papers exploring this topic.)

Research since the 1970s has begun to replace folklinguistic myths with sociolin-guistic 'facts' (I have placed the word 'facts' in scare-quotes to indicate that the term should be read with care: the 'facts' of one generation of sociolinguists are often con-tradicted or overturned by the 'facts' revealed by the next generation). Early research on gender differences in language tended to focus on mixed talk, that is, talk involving both women and men. Initially, researchers concentrated on what were seen as core features of language: phonetics and phonology, syntax and morphology. Then re-searchers began to turn their attention to broader aspects of talk, the conversational strategies characteristic of male and female speakers. More recently, researchers have begun to look at single-sex interaction and to ask questions such as: how do speakers 'do gender', and is gender performed differently in single-sex groups?

These changes in focus have been accompanied by shifts in theoretical perspective. In the early years (the 1960s and 1970s), research into the interaction of language and gender relied on a predominantly essentialist paradigm which categorized speakers primarily according to biological sex, and used mainly quantitative methods. Next, in the 1970s and 1980s, came a period which recognized the cultural construction of categories such as gender; during this period, more qualitative, ethnographic approaches predominated. In recent research, a more dynamic social constructionist approach has emerged which makes possible the combination of quantitative and qualitative research.

The Reader to some extent retraces this historical route, in terms of both subject matter and approach. It starts with work focusing on pronunciation and grammar and drawing on a quantitative paradigm (Part I). It then moves on to work focusing on conversational strategies and drawing on a more ethnographic paradigm (Part II). The concentration of earlier research on mixed talk inevitably led to an interest in conversational dominance, that is, in the ways male speakers employ particular strategies in conversation to dominate talk. Papers exploring conversational dominance are represented in Part III. The Reader then moves on to single-sex talk (Part IV), looking at both all-female and all-male interaction. Interest in all-female talk has led researchers to ask whether women are able to use the speech patterns typical of women's talk in the private domain as they take up careers in the public domain (Part V). The papers in these opening five sections raise many questions, and two of the major debates in the field form the basis for Parts VI and VII. Part VI focuses on the question 'is the salient variable gender or power?' while Part VII assesses the value of the two main theoretical frameworks adopted by researchers, the difference (or two cultures) model and the dominance model. The final section (Part VIII) is devoted to three recent papers which provide an overview of the field and raise important questions about the future of language and gender research.

Notes on How to Use the Reader

I have ordered the eight sections to give some feel for the historical unfolding of the subject, and for the development of different theoretical frameworks to make sense of research findings. The first section is devoted to papers reporting on sociolinguistic research carried out in the late 1970s and 1980s (apart from the original paper by Penelope Eckert which closes the section). In several cases, the papers reprinted here arose out of research whose initial focus was on social class or age rather than gender. As gender emerged as a key variable, so research broadened to explore variation in the entire gamut of linguistic strategies, moving from the micro-level of phonetic features to the macro-level of turn-taking practices. At the same time, researchers began to draw on a wider range of theoretical approaches, moving from the purely quantitative to more qualitative, ethnographic approaches. So you will find that some of the older papers are to be found in the early sections of the Reader, with the most recent appearing in the final section. The final section is designed to act as a springboard into the present, to give you a feel for the way contemporary researchers are thinking about language and gender now. Each Part begins with a brief introduction, which discusses the topic or theme of that section, and then summarizes the papers included in it.

You can choose to follow the Reader step by step, section by section: this would give you a clear idea of the way the field has developed, and would organize your reading into a number of coherent topics. But there are many other possibilities. You could equally well start with the last section (Part VIII), to get a feel for what's going on in language and gender *now*. Or you could construct your own topics or themes by picking out papers from existing sections. For example, the Reader does not contain a separate section on gender differences in children's talk, but you could pick out the papers by Cheshire (Part I), Eisikovits (Part I), Goodwin (Part II) and Swann (Part III), all of which deal with gender differences in the language of children and adolescents. Or you could choose to focus on gender differences in non-English-speaking cultures, picking out papers such as those on an Australian Aboriginal community (Bradley, Part I), on two black communities in South Carolina (Nichols, Part I), on a Hungarian/German bilingual community in Austria (Gal, Part II), on a Mayan community in Mexico (Brown, Part II) or on Japan as a speech community (Reynolds, Part V; Wetzel, Part VI).

Sociolinguistic research is always concerned with language change, and this theme also runs through the Reader. In particular, the link between gender-differentiated language use and language change is a significant part of discussion in papers included in Part I (gender differences in pronunciation and grammar) and also in Part V, which focuses on the phenomenon of women's language in the public domain, and which asks the question: do women have to change their speaking practices to be successful in the workplace?

Another question at the heart of sociolinguistic work is that concerning the relationship between language and identity. This is again a theme that can be followed throughout the Reader, both in terms of the ways in which women and men perform gender through differentiated language practices, but also in terms of the complex intersection of gender with age, class, ethnicity and other non-linguistic variables. In other words, by using the cross-section of papers included in the Reader, you can attempt to tease out some of the questions raised in the concluding papers: is gender more salient than social status to our sense of who we are? Is it important to pay attention to the ways in which male and female speakers are *similar* as speakers, as well as the ways in which we differ? If the work of identity construction is ongoing, then is it better to conceptualize gender as fluid rather than fixed?

Conclusion

As I hope I have demonstrated, there are many ways to use this book. However you choose to map out your journey through the vast territory of language and gender research, the papers included here should provide you with more than enough material to enrich your understanding of the co-variation of language and gender, and of the ways in which women and men in the late twentieth century construct themselves *as* women or men.

REFERENCES

Bergvall, Victoria, Bing, Janet and Freed, Alice (eds) (1996) *Rethinking Language and Gender Research: Theory and Practice*. London: Longman.

Cameron, Deborah (1992) *The Feminist Critique of Language*. London: Routledge.

Coates, Jennifer (1993) *Women, Men and Language* (2nd edn). London: Longman.

Coates, Jennifer and Cameron, Deborah (eds) (1989) *Women in Their Speech Communities*. London: Longman.

Graddol, David and Swann, Joan (1989) *Gender Voices*. Oxford: Blackwell.

Hall, Kira and Bucholtz, Mary (eds) (1995) *Gender Articulated*. London: Routledge.

Livia, Anna and Hall, Kira (eds) (1997) *Queerly Phrased*. Oxford: Oxford University Press.

Tannen, Deborah (ed.) (1993) *Gender and Conversational Interaction*. Oxford: Oxford University Press.

Part I

Gender Differences in Pronunciation and Grammar

This section includes a range of papers which look at the way women's and men's speech varies in terms of pronunciation and grammar. As long ago as the seventeenth century, differences in the language used by women and men were remarked upon in anthropological writings. Missionaries and explorers came across societies where they claimed to find distinct languages for male and female speakers. In fact, their accounts exaggerated the reality: what we find in some languages are phonological, morphological, syntactic or lexical contrasts where the speaker's gender determines which form is chosen. The first paper in this section, John Bradley's 'Yanyuwa: "Men speak one way, women speak another"', describes an Australian aboriginal language in which the choice of particular case-marking suffixes depends on the gender of the speaker.

Gender-exclusive differences of this kind mean that speakers who use a form inappropriate to their gender will be strongly reprimanded, as Bradley's paper makes clear: he quotes a Yanyuwa male who reminisces as follows: 'I spoke like a woman and [my mother] yelled at me, "Hey! you are a man, you have no foreskin, why do you talk like a woman? . . .". I was shamed.' Such linguistic differences clearly function to keep gender roles distinct. However, most of the linguistic variation associated with gender found today involves *gender-preferential* rather than gender-exclusive differences. This means that, rather than there being linguistic forms associated exclusively with one gender, there is instead a tendency for women or for men to use a certain form more frequently. The difference between gender-exclusive and gender-preferential usage seems to correlate with differences between non-industrialized societies, such as the Yanyuwa, and industrialized societies, such as Britain and the USA. Non-industrial societies tend to have clearly demarcated gender roles, whereas in modern industrialized societies gender roles are much less rigidly structured.

Modern industrialized societies are the setting for the other five papers in this section, which report on sociolinguistic research carried out in Britain, the USA and Australia into gender-preferential differences in usage. They all use a quantitative approach, that is, results showing phonological or grammatical differences are presented in terms of either raw numbers or percentages, and statistical tests are used to demonstrate the significance of these findings. This approach is common throughout the sciences and social sciences, and it has proved a valuable tool for sociolinguists exploring gender-preferential differences (as it can demonstrate gender difference despite the fact that women and men are using the same linguistic forms). This approach was developed by William Labov in his pioneering book *Sociolinguistic Patterns* (1972), and it has provided sociolinguists with a model for work on linguistic variation; the model is often referred to as the Variationist Paradigm.

Peter Trudgill's paper, 'Sex and Covert Prestige', focuses on gender differences in pronunciation, and draws on his research into phonetic and phonological variation in the English town of Norwich. Trudgill shows how variation is correlated not only with the social class of speakers (with middle-class speakers using forms closer to Received Pronunciation than working-class speakers) but also with speaker's gender. Male speakers, in Trudgill's sample, were more likely than female speakers to use non-standard forms. Trudgill, following Labov, accounts for this pattern by appealing to the notion of 'covert prestige'. 'Covert' prestige is hypothesized to inhere in vernacular variants, just as 'overt' prestige inheres in standard variants. Trudgill carried out self-evaluation tests (which asked speakers to say which pronunciation of particular words was closest to their own) – the results of these tests showed that men tended to claim that they used non-standard forms when recordings of their speech proved this was not the case, while women tended to over-report, that is, to claim that they used more standard forms than they actually did. These results suggest that covert prestige is a powerful force in the speech community of Norwich.

The next two papers focus on grammatical, not phonological, variation, and explore the everyday interaction of adolescents. Jenny Cheshire's paper, 'Linguistic Variation and Social Function', is based on her research into the grammatical usage of young people in Reading, England, research which revealed significant gender differences. Cheshire collected her data through participant observation rather than through sociolinguistic interviews. Participant observation involves the researcher in long-term research: as the term suggests, the researcher becomes, as far as possible, a participant in the social group under scrutiny. The advantage of this research method is that large amounts of spontaneous speech can be collected over time, as participants become familiar with the researcher and lose self-consciousness about the presence of a tape-recorder. Cheshire spent nine months hanging around the adventure playgrounds where groups of young people collected after school or during school hours when they played truant. Her results revealed that non-standard grammatical forms were used less often by the girls than by the boys (apart from non-standard *do*), a finding which has been widely replicated in variationist studies.

What is particularly interesting about Cheshire's work is her use of Social Network Theory. This was first applied to sociolinguistic research by James and Lesley Milroy in their work on linguistic variation in Belfast, Northern Ireland (see Milroy and Milroy 1978; Milroy 1980). At the heart of Social Network Theory is its claim that members of a speech community are connected to each other in social networks, and that dense and multiplex networks reinforce vernacular norms. (Dense networks are those where everyone knows everyone else; multiplex networks are those where connections between people are of many different kinds – they may, for example, know each other as friends and as workmates and as neighbours.) In other words, social networks operate as norm enforcement mechanisms. In the case of language, this means that a closely knit group will have the capacity to enforce linguistic norms. Cheshire's research demonstrates that young people in Reading belong to social groups that are organized in terms of gender – the boys hang about with boys, the girls with other girls – and that membership of these close-knit single-sex groups results in different patterns of linguistic usage for boys and girls.

This was also the chief finding of Edina Eisikovits' research. Eisikovits' paper, 'Girl-talk/Boy-talk', arose from her study of the grammatical patterns typical of adolescents aged 13 and 16 living in working-class areas of Sydney, Australia. The adolescents were interviewed in self-selected pairs, to encourage informality. Eisikovits' findings for her 16-year-old informants correspond to the expected pattern, with female speech closer to the standard, and male speakers consistently using a higher proportion of non-standard forms. But, interestingly, this pattern was *not* apparent in the speech of the younger adolescent speakers she interviewed. In fact, the 13-year-old girls used a higher proportion of non-standard past-tense verb forms than any other group. It seems that many of the non-standard features of Sydney vernacular speech have prestige for young adolescents of both sexes. But as they get older, girls learn to modify their speech in the direction of the standard, while boys seem to consolidate their perception of non-standard forms as having positive value. By the age of 16, young speakers have adjusted their speech to be more congruent with adult usage.

The next paper in this section, Patricia Nichols' 'Black Women in the Rural South: Conservative and Innovative', is again about grammatical variation, but this time the research focuses on adult speakers. Nichols carried out fieldwork in two black communities in South Carolina, USA, one on the mainland and one on a nearby island, in order to investigate the shift from an English creole known as Gullah to a more standard variety of English. Nichols found that the women in her sample did not behave uniformly. Older mainland women were the heaviest users of Gullah variants, but young and middle-aged island women, by contrast, were the most advanced in the shift to Standard English. Nichols explains this finding in terms of local job opportunities. Men of all ages in the area work in the construction industry, while older women work in domestic and agricultural jobs. These speakers have little incentive to speak Standard English. The younger island women, on the other hand, have different work opportunities in white-collar and service jobs. These jobs require Standard English and bring the younger women into contact with Standard English speakers. The younger black women therefore have both the incentive and the opportunity to acquire the standard variety.

The last paper in this section is Penelope Eckert's 'Gender and Sociolinguistic Variation'. Eckert's data was obtained through participant observation: her subjects were students at Belten High, a high school in the suburbs of Detroit. The students she focuses on belong to two dominant groups in the school: 'jocks' and 'burnouts'. 'Jocks' are students who participate enthusiastically in school culture and aim to go on to college; 'burnouts' are students who reject the idea of the school as central to their lives, and who are more interested in activities outside school. To put it simply, the jocks constitute a middle-class culture, the burnouts a working-class culture. Eckert studied phonological variation in the speech of these students: her analysis reveals the complex correlation between pronunciation, gender and social category (jock or burnout). There is not a simple male–female divide in her findings; rather, jock girls are the most conservative group, while burnout girls are the most advanced speakers in terms of new vernacular forms. In other words, the girls' usage is more polarized than the boys'. Eckert argues that girls have to work harder at being good jocks or good burnouts, because, as females, they are marginalized in the linguistic 'marketplace'. I have placed this paper at the end of the section because it shows very clearly how variationist studies have progressed. Eckert is concerned to demonstrate that there is no neat one-to-one correlation between language use and gender. She also draws on a theoretical framework (Bourdieu and Boltanski's notion of a symbolic market) which illustrates the increasing influence that European social theory is having on sociolinguists.

The six papers in this section deal not just with differences in linguistic usage between male and female speakers, but also with explanations for these differences. Explanations draw on a range of concepts: covert prestige – that is, the positive value assigned to vernacular forms by working-class and male speakers although this might be denied in interview (Trudgill; Eisikovits); social networks – that is, the power of social groups to enforce group norms (Cheshire); economic factors – that is, the pressures exerted by the job market which bring some speakers, but not others, into contact with more standard speech forms (Nichols); the linguistic market – that is, the idea that female speakers have to use more standard (or more vernacular) speech because they are marginalized in the linguistic marketplace (Eckert). All these explanations seek to clarify our understanding of why male and female speakers use language differently. Some additionally try to clarify why many studies find a pattern of female speakers using linguistic forms closer to the standard. But this pattern is not invariant; moreover, it is certainly not the case that male speakers invariably use more vernacular forms more frequently than women. Eckert's research shows the converse, as does Beth Thomas's work on language use in a small Welsh community (Thomas 1989).

The papers in this section reveal that there can be many different patterns of usage. Speakers' usage may vary in relation to age or social class or a whole host of other variables, as well as in relation to gender. In terms of explanations, there is now a strong feeling that it is inadvisable to treat 'women' or 'men' as monolithic categories. (For a critique of current sociolinguistic explanations, see Cameron and Coates 1989, and Cheshire and Gardner-Chloros 1998; see also the papers in the final section of the Reader.)

REFERENCES

Cameron, Deborah and Coates, Jennifer (1989) 'Some problems in the sociolinguistic explanation of sex differences', pp. 13–32 in Jennifer Coates and Deborah Cameron (eds) *Women in Their Speech Communities*. London: Longman.

Cheshire, Jenny and Gardner-Chloros, Penelope (1998) 'Code-switching and the sociolinguistic gender pattern', in Beverly Hill and Sachiko Ide (eds) 'Women's languages in various parts of the world', *International Journal of the Sociology of Language*, Special Issue.

Labov, William (1972) *Sociolinguistic Patterns*. Philadelphia: University of Pennsylvania Press.

Milroy, James and Milroy, Lesley (1978) 'Belfast: change and variation in an urban vernacular', in Peter Trudgill (ed.) *Sociolinguistic Patterns in British English*. London: Arnold.

Milroy, Lesley (1980) *Language and Social Networks*. Oxford: Blackwell.

Thomas, Beth (1989) 'Differences of sex and sects: linguistic variation and social networks in a Welsh mining village', pp. 51–60 in Jennifer Coates and Deborah Cameron (eds) *Women in Their Speech Communities*. London: Longman.

RECOMMENDED FURTHER READING

Cameron, Deborah and Coates, Jennifer (1989) 'Some problems in the sociolinguistic explanation of sex differences', pp. 13–26 in Jennifer Coates and Deborah Cameron (eds) *Women in Their Speech Communities*. London: Longman.

Cheshire, Jenny (1982) *Variation in an English Dialect*. Cambridge: Cambridge University Press.

Coates, Jennifer and Cameron, Deborah (eds) (1989) *Women in Their Speech Communities*. London: Longman.

Eckert, Penelope (in press) *Variation and Social Practice: The Linguistic Construction of Social Meaning in Belten High*. Oxford: Blackwell.

Labov, William (1990) 'The intersection of sex and social class in the course of linguistic change'. *Language Variation and Change*, 2, 205–57.

Milroy, Lesley (1980) *Language and Social Networks*. Oxford: Blackwell.

1

Yanyuwa: 'Men speak one way, women speak another'

John Bradley

This paper describes briefly the apparently unique system within the Yanyuwa language of having separate dialects for male and female speakers. I will highlight some of the social and ethnographic features of language as it is used in day-to-day speech and in such specific examples as song and ritual. The system is pervasive and distinctly marks the way in which men and women must speak. As a result the roles of men and women in Yanyuwa society are not only contrasted by their social roles, such as ritual life, hunting and nurturing, such as can be found in other Aboriginal communities, but also explicitly by the use of different dialects by male and female speakers. The sex of the hearer has no relevance to the way the language is spoken: men speak their dialect to women and women speak their dialect to men.

The Yanyuwa people today are centred around the township of Borroloola some 970 kilometres south-east of Darwin. Traditionally the Yanyuwa people occupied the Sir Edward Pellew Group of Islands and the lower reaches of the McArthur River delta system and the Wearyan River. Today Yanyuwa speakers number approximately 90 to 150, ranging in age from the late twenties upwards. The younger generation have grown up speaking English with some influence from Kriol, though many have obtained a passive knowledge of Yanyuwa. The reasons for the decline in the language are many, varied and complex and have been described by Jean Kirton (1987). She has been working with the Yanyuwa since 1963 and has been in a position to document the language in considerable detail (see bibliography).

There have been a number of languages recorded throughout the world that have some sex differences. Edward Sapir (1923: 263–285) documented the now extinct Indian Yahi language, a dialect of the Yanna group in Northern California. Sapir noted dialect differences relating to sex and found that in Yana the male form was longer than the female form and included a final syllable as the root; dialectal differences occurred more in complete words than in suffixed elements. There was also a further non-structural distinction in pronunciation whereby men when talking to men spoken fully and deliberately and when speaking with a woman preferred a 'clipped' style of speaking. Three examples of the Yana speech are given below.

	male	female
'grizzly bear'	*t'en'na*	*t'et*
'see me'	*diwai-dja*	*diwa-tch*
'Yana'	*Yana*	*Yah*

Sapir concludes that there are or have been few if any languages in the world in which the split in a dialect has been so pervasive or so thorough: The sex-based dialect differences in Yanyuwa are at least as far-reaching. The following text illustrates the extent of divergence between the two dialects (see Kirton 1988 for a full discussion of the grammatical differences). Note that the same word stems are used in both dialects, but it is the class-marking prefixes on the noun classes, verbs and pronouns which are affected. (N.B. Yanyuwa has seven classes of common nouns: male (M); female (F); masculine (MSC); feminine (FEM); food (non-meat) (FD); arboreal (ARB); and abstract (ABS); and four cases: nominative (NOM); dative (DAT); ergative-allative (ERG/ALL) marking transitive subject and 'to' a person or location; and ablative (AB).)

Women's Dialect
Nya-ja nya-wukuthu nya-rduwarra   niya-wini nya-Wungkurli   kiwa-wingka
This-M M-short   M-initiated man his-name M-personal name he-go
wayka-liya ji-wamarra-lu   niwa-yirdi na-ridiridi   ji-walya-wu
down-wards MSC-sea-ALL he-bring   ARB-harpoon MSC-dugong/turtle-DAT

Men's Dialect
Jinangu ɸ-wukuthu ɸ-rduwarra   na-wini   ɸ-Wungkurli   ka-wingka wayka-liya
This   short   initiated man his-name personal name he-go   down-wards
ki-wamarra-lu   na-yirdi na-ridiridi   ki-walya-wu
MSC-sea-ALL he-bring ARB-harpoon MSC-dugong/turtle-DAT

'The short initiated man whose name is Wungkurli, went down to the sea, taking a harpoon with him for dugong or sea turtle.'

The reason behind this dialect distinction is today unknown and the reason why a male and female dialect arose can only be left to the realms of speculation. The Yanyuwa themselves give no definitive answer as to why there are two dialects, and there is no mythological account for the distinction. In their mythology the female Creator Beings speak the women's dialect and the male Creator Beings speak the men's dialect. The Yanyuwa give no special terms for the two dialects and refer to them simply as *liyi-wulu-wu* 'for the men' and *liyi-nhanawaya-wu* 'for the women'. The most common statement given by the Yanyuwa people in relation to their language is as follows:

'Men speak one way, women speak another, that's just the way it is!' (Annie Karrakayn, 1986)

When I first asked why men and women had different dialects, people deferred to the knowledge of the elders who also readily admitted they did not really know, and thought that the question was a little peculiar. As one of the older Yanyuwa men put it:

> 'I am ignorant why there are languages for the men and women, maybe the Dreamings made it that way. I don't know, the old people spoke that way and we follow them. What about him, that "whitefella boss man" (scientist), he might know you should go and ask him.' (Old Tim Rakuwurlma, 1985)

Other people who profess a belief in Christianity believe that their language was given to them by God because that is the way He wanted the Yanyuwa people to speak. Only a few individuals offered opinions which were different from that of the general community.

> 'I don't really know, but I was thinking that men and women have to respect each other, so we talk different ways and so we show respect for each other, just like ceremony; you know men have their ceremony and their language well same way women have their own ceremony and their own language.' (Mussolini Harvey, 1986)

Two women, on hearing of Mussolini Harvey's comment, said they would do more thinking on the question and eventually came up with the following statement.

> 'Look at you, you're different you don't have *na-wunhan* [breasts] and you are a man, well same way you can't have woman's parts [vagina] so you see we're different, different body, different job, different language, that's why I can't talk like a man and you can't talk like us ladies.' (Amy Friday with Bella Charlie, 1986)

It is obvious then that some Yanyuwa people see the system of two dialects as a natural off-shoot of differing sex roles within their community, in terms of such matters as ritual divisions of labour and other more daily activities such as child nurturing, hunting, social and group dynamics.

Unfortunately the younger generation of Yanyuwa people no longer speak Yanyuwa, so it is very difficult to discuss the way in which the Yanyuwa language was acquired by children. However, conversations with the older Yanyuwa people have enabled at least a partial, albeit fragmentary, reconstruction. It appears that in very early childhood children spoke a form of neutral Yanyuwa, that is, the dialectal markers were removed from words, so that 'at or with the fire' became *buyuka-la* rather than the correct *ji-buyuka-la* for women and *ki-buyuka-la* for men. As the children grew up they were reared in a predominantly female atmosphere surrounded by grandmothers, mothers and aunts, so that the language for the children of both sexes was predominantly the women's dialect.

In early adolescence boys were, and still are, initiated through a series of rituals which culminated in circumcision, after which they were considered men and from which time onwards they were expected to speak the men's dialect. However, it was no smooth transition. For at least 10 years the boys had been speaking a predominantly female form of Yanyuwa and only passively hearing the men's dialect. As a consequence, for a short while after initiation they spoke a form of Yanyuwa which was a mixture of both men's and women's dialects. This was a situation which the older Yanyuwa apparently did not tolerate and the young men were disciplined for speaking incorrectly. A middle aged man gave the following account of such a situation.

> 'I was only a newly initiated man, and I asked my mother where Douglas [male cousin] was. I spoke like a woman and she yelled at me, "Hey! you are a man, you have no foreskin, why do you talk like a woman? Speak like a man, you are not a small child!" I was shamed, it was not easy to get the men's words right straight away.' (D.M. 1986)

Another man remembers asking to go dugong hunting with his uncle using the female dialect.

> 'When I spoke like a woman my father said to me, "Where are your breasts and woman's parts [vagina]?" I was really shamed. I was very careful for a while after that to speak the men's words.' (J.T. 1986)

To the Yanyuwa the two dialects are socially very important and after maturity it is considered only proper to speak the dialect of the sex to which one belongs.

Today most young people are more familiar with the female form of the language because of their frequent association with female company, for example at meal times and shopping trips to the store. Consequently when on the odd occasion a young Yanyuwa male uses Yanyuwa he often speaks the women's dialect, for which he is then disciplined. The following example is typical of such a situation.

SON: Mum, did you buy *ni-warnnyi* [meat]?
MOTHER: Hey! Are you a man or woman? Man got to talk *na-warnnyi* not *ni-warrnyi* that's women's talk, you got to talk properly, you not little kid you know.
SON: Hey look you complain because young people don't talk language and when we do you got to laugh at us, man may as well not even bother.
MOTHER: Well, you just got to learn to talk proper way just like we did.
(A.I. and D.I. 1985)

It would appear that the system of having separate dialects for men and women invokes strong feelings about speaking correctly, which in itself creates a system where slovenliness of speech is not acceptable social behaviour. If individuals wish to speak Yanyuwa then they are expected to speak the dialect which is associated with their sex – there is no other alternative.

The groups neighbouring the Yanyuwa, such as the Mara, Garawa and Kurdanji, all say that Yanyuwa is 'too rough to learn', that is, the sex-differentiated dialects are somewhat obstructive to the understanding and learning of the language for a person of non-Yanyuwa descent. Only a few Garawa and Mara speakers today speak Yanyuwa with an easy fluency, while the Yanyuwa declare that Garawa and Mara are easy languages and the fact that many Yanyuwa people today have Mara and Garawa as second and third language is proof of this for the Yanyuwa.

There are occasions when the Yanyuwa men and women do speak each other's dialects, such as when they are relating a story where people of the opposite sex to the speaker have spoken, in which case the quotation will normally be in the dialect which relates to the sex of the person who has spoken. However, there are times especially in rapid general conversation where the distinctions are not highlighted and one must rely on other contextual clues to find out the sex of the speakers involved.

On rare occasions, men and women utilize the dialectal differences in Yanyuwa to draw attention to themselves. Once an elderly man in charge of certain public funeral rituals was not pleased with the way the performances were developing. He began orating his displeasure. At first people paid little attention until a woman pointed out that he was using the female dialect. When this was realized people listened to what was being said. I have witnessed such an occurrence once in eight years of fieldwork, though people present at the time said it had occasionally happened in the past. It is more common for both sexes to be somewhat hesitant to speak the dialect of the other sex unless it is for a specific reason, such as working for anthropologists or linguistic researchers, and on some occasions male Yanyuwa speakers have difficulty constructing the female form of the language and often defer to their wives or ask what they have stated to be checked with a female speaker; the women's dialect is the more complex of the two.

Both men and women will use the dialect of the opposite sex quite freely in joking situations, more specifically in situations relating to male and female relationships and sexual encounters. These situations are somewhat ribald and risqué and full of humour to the Yanyuwa. Amongst the men such occurrences take place after certain ceremonial performances, for example where a male dancer impersonates a woman, after which he will tease his brothers-in-law as if they are his prospective wives. An example is given below.

Female Dialect spoken by Male Speaker
Nya-ngatha nya-Nyilba   nya-yabi yinda   nya-marringaya nda-wuna
M-for me   M-pers.name M-good you:sg M-beautiful   your:sg-buttocks
'My Nyilba, you are too good, you have beautiful buttocks.'
(T.F. 1986)

Another unusual occurrence is the use of the female dialect form within the song cycles used by the Yanyuwa men during ceremonial performance. Many of the male mythological species are marked with the female dialect marker *nya-*. In everyday spoken Yanyuwa the men do not use the names of these creatures with this prefix. Examples are *nya-Yilayi*, Spotted Nightjar, *nya-Walungkanarra*, Rainbow Serpent, and *nya-Wurrunkardi*, the personal name of the Dingo Dreaming.

Within the song cycles, there are also female dialectal markers on common nouns and a number of verb stems from the female dialect. Two examples are given below:

Song Verse

Manankurra	'At Manankurra
kiya-alarri	He (a Shark Dreaming) stood.'

Manankurra
place name

kiya-alarri
he: stand

The prefix *kiya-* in the second line of the above verse is a women's dialect prefix, while in the men's dialect it is *ka-*.

Song Verse

Warriyangalayani	'The Hammerhead Shark
ni-mambul ni-ngurru	makes spray with its nose.'

Warriyangalayani
Hammerhead shark

ni-mambul ni-ngurru
its:spray   its:nose

The prefix *ni-* in the second line is the female masculine form. In the male dialect it would be *na-*.

When the men were questioned as to why the female dialect forms were found in song cycles, especially when some song cycles deal with male figures, they could give no answer and did not appear to be particularly disturbed. They classed such occurrences as 'That's just the Dreaming, they're different'. It is tempting to hypothesize that the female dialect may be the more archaic of the two, but without sufficient evidence such a hypothesis remains very tentative. The occurrences of feminine dialect forms in the song cycles are too irregular to form any definite conclusions.

A hypothesis put forward by Dixon (1968) suggests that in some Aboriginal languages there is evidence of an underlying logic in apparent exceptions. He puts forward rules which apply to transfer of class membership in Australian languages. He believes irregular occurrences are in fact a purposeful class transference which classifies according to mythological characteristics rather than observable ones or which mark some important property, quite often danger. Dixon's hypothesis may be relevant to the unusual prefixing which occurs in Yanyuwa song cycles.

There are other examples of unusual language usage which fit more into the mundane social life of the Yanyuwa. Two such examples are where root words are given irregular male and female prefixes:

nya-bardibardi
M-old woman

This word is used by women to refer to older men who associate with women, especially widows, and who constantly demand food or money from them.

rra-malbu
FEM-old man

This word is used by men to refer to older women who are said to associate with men too much, especially in relation to aspects of Yanyuwa life in which they should only be minimally involved. Both of the above terms are not regularly used and are meant to be somewhat insulting in their intent.

The Yanyuwa language also has complex avoidance and kinship terms, both of which are affected by the men's and women's dialects. This has been described by Kirton (1982, 1988).

In any given culture there will be differences in the way men and women speak, for example, in terms of address and the use of expletives, but it would appear that in Yanyuwa the speech differences of male and female speakers are so extensive that the two forms of speech have become dialects of the one language.

In Yanyuwa society the system of two dialects is all pervasive; in day to day usage the two dialects are an intrinsic part of the language. The Yanyuwa continually stressed when asked why there were separate dialects: 'It's just the way it is, no other reason.' In fact many of the Yanyuwa thought, and probably still think, the question a trifle stupid. None of the neighbouring languages share this feature, and in fact some of these people, such as the Garawa, Mara and Kurdanji, see Yanyuwa as a language too difficult to learn because of the separate dialects. Even though the Yanyuwa take for granted their system of male and female dialects they still place much importance on speaking correctly.

The reasons as to why two distinct dialects for female and male speakers have developed are lost in time. This feature has however served to make Yanyuwa a language unique within Aboriginal Australia, if not the world.

REFERENCES

Dixon, R. M. W. 1968. Noun classes. *Lingua* 21, 104–24.
Grimes, B. J. ed. 1984. *Index to Tenth Edition of Ethnologue: Languages of the World*. Texas: Wycliffe Bible Translators.
Heath, J. 1981. *Basic Material in Mara Grammar, Texts and Dictionary*. PL.
Kirton, J. F. 1970. Twelve pronominal sets in Yanyuwa. *PL* series C, 13, 825–44.
Kirton, J. F. 1971. Complexities of Yanyuwa nouns. *PL* series A, 27, 15–70.
Kirton, J. F. 1987. Yanyuwa – a dying language. *Work Papers of SIL-AAB* Series B, 13, 1–19.
Kirton, J. F. 1988. Men's and women's dialects. *Aboriginal Linguistics* 1.
Kirton, J. F. & B. Charlie. 1978. Seven articulatory positions in Yanyuwa consonants. *PL* Series A, 51, 179–98.
Kirton, J. F. & N. Timothy. 1977. Yanyuwa concepts relating to 'skin'. *Oceania* 47, 320–22.

Kirton, J. F. & N. Timothy. 1978. Yanyuwa verbs. *PL* Series A, 51, 1–52.

Kirton, J. F. & N. Timothy. 1982. Some thoughts on Yanyuwa language and culture. *Work Papers of SIL-AAB* Series B, 8.

Kramer, C. 1975. Sex related differences in address systems. *Anthropological Linguistics* 17, 198–210.

Kroskrity, P. V. 1983. On male and female speech in the Pueblo South West. *IJAL* 49, 88–91.

Sapir, E. 1923. Text analyses of three Yana dialects. *America Archaeology and Ethnology* 20, 263–85.

Taylor, D. 1954. Diachronic note on the Carib contribution to Island Carib. *IJAL* 20, 28–33.

2

Sex and Covert Prestige

Peter Trudgill

In this paper we present some data which illustrate quite clearly the phenomenon of sex differentiation in language in one variety of British English. We then examine an explanation for this differentiation. [. . .]

The results from which the following figures are taken are based on an urban dialect survey of the city of Norwich carried out in the summer of 1968 with a random sample, 60 in number, of the population of the city, and reported in detail in Trudgill (1974). This sociolinguistic research was concerned mainly with correlating phonetic and phonological variables with social class, age, and stylistic context. Some work was also done, however, in studying the relationships that obtain between linguistic phenomena and sex.

In order to relate the phonological material to the social class of informants and the other parameters, a number of phonetic and phonological variables were developed, and index scores calculated for individuals and groups in the manner of Labov (1966a) [. . .]. The first of these variables that I wish to discuss is the variable (ng). This is the pronunciation of the suffix *-ing* in *walking, laughing,* etc., and is a well-known variable in many types of English. In the case of Norwich English there are two possible pronunciations of this variable: [ɪŋ], which also occurs in the prestige accent, RP, and [ən ~ n̩]. The former is labelled (ng)-1 and the latter (ng)-2.

Index scores were developed for this variable by initially awarding 1 for each instance of (ng)-1 and 2 for each instance of (ng)-2. These scores were then summed and divided by the total number of instances, to give the mean score. Indices were finally calculated by subtracting 1 from the mean score and multiplying the result by 100. In this case, this gives an index score of 000 for consistent use of RP (ng)-1, and 100 for consistent use of (ng)-2, and the scores are equivalent to the simple percentage of non-RP forms used. (For variables with more than two variants this simple relationship, of course, does not apply.) Indices were calculated in the first instance for individual informants in each contextual style and subsequently for each group of informants. The four contextual styles:

> word list style: WLS
> reading passage style: RPS
> formal speech: FS
> casual speech: CS

are equivalent to the styles discussed by Labov (1966a) and were elicited in a similar manner. Indices for other variables were calculated in the same way.

Table 1 shows the average (ng) index scores for informants in the five social class groups obtained in the survey, in the four contextual styles. The social class divisions are based on an index that was developed using income, education, dwelling type, location of dwelling, occupation, and occupation of father as parameters. The five classes have been labelled:

> middle middle class: MMC
> lower middle class: LMC
> upper working class: UWC
> middle working class: MWC
> lower working class: LWC

The table shows very clearly that (ng) is a linguistic variable in Norwich English. Scores range from a high of 100 per cent non-RP forms by the LWC in CS to a low of 0 per cent by the MMC in RPS and by the MMC and LMC in WLS. The pattern of differentiation is also structured in a very clear manner. For each of the social classes, scores rise consistently from WLS to CS; and for each style scores rise consistently from MMC to LWC.

Table 1   (ng) Index scores by class and style

	Style				
Class	*WLS*	*RPS*	*FS*	*CS*	*N*
MMC	000	000	003	028	6
LMC	000	010	015	042	8
UWC	005	015	074	087	16
MWC	023	044	088	095	22
LWC	029	066	098	100	8

In his study of this same variable in American English, Fischer (1958) found that males used a higher percentage of non-standard [n] forms than females. Since we have shown that (ng) is a variable in Norwich English, we could expect, if sex differentiation of the type we have been discussing also occurs here, that the same sort of pattern would emerge. Table 2 shows that this is in fact very largely the case. In 17 cases out of 20, *male* scores are greater than or equal to corresponding *female* scores. We can therefore state that a high (ng) index is typical not only of WC

Table 2 (ng) Index scores by class, style and sex

Class	Sex	Style WLS	RPS	FS	CS
MMC	M	000	000	004	031
	F	000	000	000	000
LMC	M	000	020	027	017
	F	000	000	003	067
UWC	M	000	018	081	095
	F	011	013	068	077
MWC	M	024	043	091	097
	F	020	046	081	088
LWC	M	060	100	100	100
	F	017	054	097	100

speakers in Norwich but also of *male* speakers. This pattern, moreover, is repeated for the vast majority of the other nineteen variables studied in Norwich.

[. . .] In this paper we seek an explanation for this phenomenon in terms of the fact that WC speech, like other aspects of WC culture, appears, at least in some western societies, to have connotations of masculinity (see Labov, 1966a: 495), probably because it is associated with the roughness and toughness supposedly characteristic of WC life which are, stereotypically and to a certain extent, often considered to be desirable masculine attributes. They are not, on the other hand, widely considered to be desirable feminine characteristics. On the contrary, features such as 'refinement' and 'sophistication' are much preferred in some western societies.

As it stands, this argument is largely speculative. What it requires is some concrete evidence. This need for evidence was discussed by Labov (1966b: 108) who wrote that in New York

> the socio-economic structure confers prestige on the middle-class pattern associated with the more formal styles. [But] one can't avoid the implication that in New York City we must have an equal and opposing prestige for informal, working-class speech – a covert prestige enforcing this speech pattern. We must assume that people in New York City want to talk as they do, yet this fact is not at all obvious in any overt response that you can draw from interview subjects.

It is suspected, in other words, that there are hidden values associated with nonstandard speech, and that, as far as our present argument is concerned, they are particularly important in explaining the sex differentiation of linguistic variables. Labov, however, has not been able to uncover them or prove that they exist. We can guess that these values are there, but they are values which are not usually overtly expressed. They are not values which speakers readily admit to having, and for that reason they are difficult to study. Happily, the urban dialect survey carried out in Norwich provided some evidence which argues very strongly in favour of our hypothesis, and which managed, as it were, to remove the outer layer of overtly expressed values and penetrate to the hidden values beneath. That is, we now have some objective data which actually demonstrates that for male speakers, WC non-standard speech is in a very real sense highly valued and prestigious.

Labov has produced evidence to show that almost all speakers in New York City share a common set of linguistic norms, whatever their actual linguistic performance, and that they hear and report themselves as using these prestigious linguistic forms, rather than the forms they actually do use. This 'dishonesty' in reporting what they say is of course not deliberate, but it does suggest that informants, at least so far as their conscious awareness is concerned, are dissatisfied with the way they speak, and would prefer to be able to use more standard forms. This was in fact confirmed by comments New York City informants actually made about their own speech.

Overt comments made by the Norwich informants on their own speech were also of this type. Comments such as 'I talk horrible' were typical. It also began to appear, however, that, as suggested above, there were other, deeper motivations for their actual linguistic behaviour than these overtly expressed notions of their own 'bad speech'. For example, many informants who initially stated that they did not speak properly, and would like to do so, admitted, if pressed, that they perhaps would not *really* like to, and that they would almost certainly be considered foolish, arrogant or disloyal by their friends and family if they did. This is our first piece of evidence.

Far more important, however, is the evidence that was obtained by means of the Self-Evaluation Test, in which half of the Norwich informants took part. This is particularly the case when the results of this test are compared to those obtained by a similar test conducted by Labov in New York. In the Norwich Self-Evaluation Test, 12 lexical items were read aloud, to informants, with two or more different pronunciations. For example the word *tune* was read with two different pronunciations: (1) [tjuːn] (roughly, 'tyoon'); (2) [tuːn] (roughly, 'toon'). Informants were then asked to indicate, by marking a number on a chart, which of these pronunciations most closely resembled the way in which they normally said this word.

The corresponding Self-Evaluation Test in New York for the variable (r) – presence or absence of post-vocalic /r/ (a prestige feature) – produced the following results. Informants who in FS used over 30 per cent /r/ were, very generously, considered to be (post-vocalic) /r/-users. Seventy per cent of those who, in this sense, were /r/-users reported that they normally used /r/. But 62 per cent of those who were *not* /r/-users *also* reported that they normally used /r/. As Labov says (1966a: 455): 'In the conscious report of their own usage . . . New York respondents are very inaccurate'. The accuracy, moreover, is overwhelmingly in the direction of reporting themselves as using a form which is *more* statusful than the one they

Table 3   Self-evaluating of (r) – New York

Used	Percentage reported		
	/r/	φ	
/r/	79	21	= 100
φ	62	38	= 100

Table 4   Self-evaluation of (yu)

Used	(yu) Percentage reported		
	1	2	
1	60	40	= 100
2	16	84	= 100

actually use. Labov (1966a: 455) claims that 'no conscious deceit plays a part in this process' and that 'most of the respondents seemed to perceive their own speech in terms of the norms at which they were aiming rather than the sound actually produced'.

The full results of this test are shown in table 3. It shows that 62 per cent of non-/r/-users 'over-reported' themselves as using /r/, and 21 per cent of /r/-users 'under-reported', although in view of Labov's 30 per cent dividing line, the latter were very probably simply being accurate.

In the Norwich test, the criteria used were much more rigorous. In comparing the results obtained in the Self-Evaluation Test to forms actually used in Norwich, *casual speech* was used rather than *formal speech*, since CS more closely approximates everyday speech – to how informants normally pronounce words, which is what they were asked to report on. Moreover, informants were allowed *no* latitude in their self-evaluation. It was considered that the form informants used in everyday speech was the variant indicated by the appropriate CS index for that individual informant. For example, an (ng) index of between 050 and 100 was taken as indicating an (ng)-2 user rather than (ng)-1 user. In other words, the dividing line is 50 per cent rather than Labov's more lenient 30 per cent. If, therefore, the characteristics of the Norwich sample were identical to those of the New York sample, we would expect a significantly *higher* degree of *over-reporting* from the Norwich informants.

The results, in fact, show the exact reverse of this, as can be seen from table 4. This table gives the results of the Self-Evaluation Test for the variable (yu), which is the pronunciation of the vowel in items such as *tune, music, queue, huge*. In Norwich English items such as these have two possible pronunciations: (yu)-1 has [j] as in RP-like [kjuː ~ kjʉː]; (yu)-2 omits [j] as in [kʉː ~ kɜʉ], *queue*.

Table 4 provides a very striking contrast to the New York results shown in table 3 in that only 16 per cent of (yu)-2 users, as compared to the equivalent figure of 62 per cent in New York, over-reported themselves as using the more statusful RP-like variant (yu)-1 when they did not in fact do so. Even more significant, however, is the fact that as many as 40 per cent of (yu)-1 users actually *under*-reported – and the under-reporting is in this case quite genuine.

A further breakdown of the scores given in table 4 is also very revealing. Of the 16 per cent (yu)-2 users who over-reported, *all* were women. Of the (yu)-1 users who under-reported, half were men and half women. Here we see, for the first time, the emergence of the hidden values that underlie the sex differentiation described earlier in this paper. If we take the sample as a whole, we have the percentages of speakers under- and over-reporting shown in table 5. Male informants, it will be noted, are strikingly more accurate in their self-assessment than are female informants.

Table 5   Percentage of informants over- and under-reporting (yu)

	Total	*Male*	*Female*
Over-r	13	0	29
Under-r	7	6	7
Accurate	80	94	64

The hidden values, however, emerge much more clearly from a study of the other variables tested in this way, (er), (ō) and (ā), illustrated in tables 6, 7, and 8, respectively. The variable (er) is the vowel in *ear, here, idea*, which in Norwich English ranges from [ɪə] to [ɛː]; (ō) is the vowel in *road, nose, moan* (but not in *rowed, knows, mown*, which are distinct) and ranges from [ɵu] through [uː] to [ʊ]; and (ā) is the vowel in the lexical set of *gate, face, name*, which ranges from [eɪ] to [æi].

Table 6   Percentage of informants over- and under-reporting (er)

	Total	*Male*	*Female*
Over-r	43	22	68
Under-r	33	50	14
Accurate	23	28	18

Table 7   Percentage of informants over- and under-reporting (ō)

	Total	*Male*	*Female*
Over-r	18	12	25
Under-r	36	54	18
Accurate	45	34	57

Table 8 Percentage of informants over- and under-reporting (ā)

	Total	Male	Female
Over-r	32	22	43
Under-r	15	28	0
Accurate	53	50	57

For each of these variables, it will be seen, there are more male speakers who claim to use a *less* prestigious variant than they actually do than there are who over-report, and for one of the variables (ō), the difference is very striking: 54 per cent to 12 per cent. In two of the cases, moreover, there are more male speakers who under-report than there are who are accurate.

Although there are some notable differences between the four variables illustrated here,[1] it is clear that Norwich informants are much more prone to under-report than New York informants, and that – this is central to our argument – *male* informants in Norwich are much more likely to *under*-report, *female* informants to *over*-report.

This, then, is the objective evidence which demonstrates that male speakers, at least in Norwich, are at a subconscious or perhaps simply private level very favourably disposed towards non-standard speech forms. This is so much the case that as many as 54 per cent of them, in one case, claim to use these forms or hear themselves as using them *even when they do not do so*. If it is true that informants 'perceive their own speech in terms of the norms at which they are aiming rather than the sound actually produced' then the norm at which a large number of Norwich males are aiming is *non-standard WC speech*. This favourable attitude is never overtly expressed, but the responses to these tests show that statements about 'bad speech' are for public consumption only. Privately and subconsciously, a large number of male speakers are more concerned with acquiring prestige of the covert sort and with signalling group solidarity than with obtaining social status, as this is more usually defined. [. . .] By means of these figures, therefore, we have been able to demonstrate both that it is possible to obtain evidence of the 'covert prestige' associated with non-standard varieties, and that, for Norwich men, working-class speech is statusful and prestigious.

[. . .]

NOTE

1 These differences may be due to a skewing effect resulting from the necessity of using only a small number of individual lexical items to stand for each variable in the tests. (Informants' reports of their pronunciation of *tune*, for example, do not *necessarily* mean that they would pronounce or report *Tuesday* or *tube* in the same way.)

REFERENCES

Fischer, J. L. (1958) 'Social influences on the choice of a linguistic variant'. *Word* 14, 47–56.

Labov, W. (1966a) *The Social Stratification of English in New York City*. Washington, DC: Center for Applied Linguistics.

Labov, W. (1966b) 'Hypercorrection by the lower middle class as a factor in linguistic change', in W. Bright (ed.) *Sociolinguistics*. The Hague: Mouton.

Trudgill, P. (1974) *The Social Differentiation of English in Norwich*. London: Cambridge University Press.

3

Linguistic Variation and Social Function

Jenny Cheshire

The fact that linguistic variation is correlated with a wide range of sociological characteristics of speakers has been extensively documented over the last 15 years by the many studies that have been inspired by the work of William Labov. It is well established, for example, that the frequency with which speakers use non-standard linguistic features is correlated with their socioeconomic class. More recently, studies involving speakers from a single socioeconomic class have been able to reveal some of the more subtle aspects of sociolinguistic variation. It has been found, for example, that the frequency of use of non-standard phonological features in Belfast English is correlated with the type of social network in which speakers are involved (see Milroy and Margrain 1980). This paper will show that the frequency with which adolescent speakers use many non-standard morphological and syntactic features of the variety of English spoken in the town of Reading, in Berkshire, is correlated with the extent to which they adhere to the norms of the vernacular culture. It will also show that linguistic variables often fulfil different social and semantic functions for the speakers who use them.

The paper will consider nine non-standard features of Reading English:

1 the present tense suffix with non 3rd person singular subjects
    e.g. we *goes* shopping on Saturdays
2 *has* with non 3rd person singular subjects
    e.g. we *has* a little fire, keeps us warm
3 *was* with plural subjects (and singular *you*)
    e.g. you *was* outside
4 multiple negation
    e.g. I'm *not* going *nowhere*
5 negative past tense *never*, used for standard English *didn't*
    e.g. I *never* done it, it was him
6 *what* used for standard English *who*, *whom*, *which*, and *that*
    e.g. there's a knob *what* you turn
        are you the boy *what*'s just come?

7   auxiliary *do* with 3rd person singular subjects
e.g. how much *do* he want for it?
8   past tense *come*
e.g. I *come* down here yesterday
9   *ain't*, used for negative present tense forms of *be* and *have*, with all subjects
e.g. I *ain't* going
I *ain't* got any

Many, though not all, of these features function as markers of vernacular loyalty for adolescent speakers in Reading, though some are more sensitive markers than others. *Ain't*, in particular, is able overtly to symbolize some of the important values of the vernacular culture. Furthermore, some features are markers of loyalty to the vernacular culture for adolescent boys but not for adolescent girls, and vice-versa.

The Data

The analysis is based on the spontaneous, natural speech of three groups of adolescents, recorded by the method of long-term participant-observation in adventure playgrounds in Reading. The aim was to record speech that was as close as possible to the vernacular, or most informal style, of the speakers. Thirteen boys and twelve girls were recorded over a period of about eight months.

Some of the speakers were subsequently recorded at school, by their teacher, with two or three of their friends. The fieldwork procedures are discussed in detail in Cheshire 1982.

The Vernacular Culture Index

Labov (1966) maintains that the use of non-standard features is controlled by the norms of the vernacular subculture, whilst the use of standard English features is controlled by the overt norms of the mainstream culture in society. Any analysis of variation in the occurrence of non-standard features needs to take this into account, for it means that an adequate sample of non-standard forms is more likely to be found where speakers conform more closely to vernacular norms than to the overt norms of the dominant mainstream culture. The speakers who were chosen for the present study were children who often met at the adventure playgrounds when they should have been at school, and the boys, in particular, were members of a very well-defined subculture. In many respects this culture resembled a delinquent subculture (as defined, for example, by Andry 1960; Cohen 1965; Downes 1966; Willmott 1966 and many other writers). Many of the boys' activities, for example, centred around what Miller (1958) calls the 'cultural foci' of *trouble, excitement, toughness, fate, autonomy* and *smartness* (in the American English sense of 'outsmarting').

Since the vernacular culture was in this case very clearly defined, it was possible to isolate a small number of indicators that could be used to construct a 'vernacular culture index', in the same way that socioeconomic indices are constructed. It seemed reasonable to assume that those aspects of the peer-group culture that were sources of prestige for group members and that were frequent topics of conversation were of central importance within the culture. Six factors that met these requirements were selected. Four of these reflect the norms of trouble and excitement; three directly, and one more indirectly. *Skill at fighting, the carrying of a weapon* and *participation in minor criminal activities*, such as shoplifting, arson, and vandalism, are clearly connected with trouble and excitement. Though interrelated, they were treated as separate indicators because not all boys took part in all the activities to the same extent. The job that the boys hoped to have when they left school was also included as a separate indicator, for the same reason. Again, acceptable jobs reflect the norms of trouble and excitement, though perhaps more indirectly here, and the job that the boys hoped to have when they left school (or, in a few cases, that they already had) was an important contributing factor to the opinion that they formed of themselves and of other group members. Some jobs that were acceptable were slaughterer, lorry driver, motor mechanic, and soldier; jobs that were unacceptable were mostly white-collar jobs. A fifth indicator was 'style': the extent to which dress and hairstyle were important to speakers. Many writers stress the importance of style as a symbolic value within adolescent subcultures (see, for example, Cohen 1972; Clarke 1973), and for many of the boys in the group it was a frequent topic of conversation.

Finally, a measure of 'swearing' was included in the index, since this appeared to be an extremely important symbol of vernacular identity for both boys and girls. Swearing is, of course, a linguistic feature, but this does not affect its use as an indicator here, since it involves only a few lexical items which could not be marked for any of the non-standard features of Reading English. [. . .]

The boys were then given a score for each of the indicators, and were divided into four groups on the basis of their total score. Group 1 consists of those boys who can be considered to adhere most closely to the norms of the vernacular culture, whilst group 4 consists of boys who do not adhere closely to vernacular norms. Groups 2 and 3 are intermediate in their adherence, with group 2 adhering more closely than group 3.

Linguistic Markers of Adherence to the Vernacular Culture

Table 1 shows the frequency of occurrence of the nine non-standard features in the speech of the four groups of boys.

The features are arranged into three classes, which reflect the extent to which they mark adherence to the vernacular culture. Class A contains four features whose frequency is very finely linked to the vernacular culture index of the speakers. The most sensitive indicator is the non-standard present tense suffix, which occurs very frequently in the speech of those boys who are most firmly immersed in the vernacular

Table 1   Adherence to vernacular culture and frequency of occurrence of non-standard forms

		Group 1	*Group 2*	*Group 3*	*Group 4*
Class A	non-standard –s	77.36	54.03	36.57	21.21
	non-standard *has*	66.67	50.00	41.65	(33.33)
	non-standard *was*	90.32	89.74	83.33	75.00
	negative concord	100.00	85.71	83.33	71.43
Class B	non-standard *never*	64.71	41.67	45.45	37.50
	non-standard *what*	92.31	7.69	33.33	0.00
Class C	non-standard aux. *do*	58.33	37.50	83.33	—
	non-standard *come*	100.00	100.00	100.00	(100.00)
	ain't=aux *have*	78.26	64.52	80.00	(100.00)
	ain't=aux *be*	58.82	72.22	80.00	(100.00)
	ain't=copula	100.00	76.19	56.52	75.00

NB. Bracketed figures indicate that the number of occurrences of the variable is low, and that the indices may not, therefore, be reliable. Following Labov (1970) less than 5 occurrences was considered to be too low for reliability.

Table 2   Frequency indices of group 1, groups 2 and 3, and group 4

	Group 1	*Groups 2 & 3*	*Group 4*
non-standard *never*	64.71	43.00	37.50
non-standard *what*	92.31	18.00	0.00

culture (group 1), progressively less frequently in the speech of groups 2 and 3, and rather infrequently in the speech of boys who are only loosely involved in the culture (group 4). This feature, then, functions as a powerful marker of vernacular loyalty.

The features in Class B (non-standard *never* and non-standard *what*) also function as markers of vernacular loyalty, but they are less sensitive markers than the features in Class A. Significant variation occurs only between speakers in Group 1 and speakers in Group 4, in other words, between the boys who adhere most closely to the vernacular culture, and the boys who adhere least closely. This type of sociolinguistic variation is not unusual: Policansky (1980) reports similar behaviour with subject–verb concord in Belfast English, where significant variation is found only between speakers at the extreme ends of the social network scale (cf. also Jahangiri and Hudson, 1982).

The fact that there is some correlation between the vernacular culture index and the frequency of use of Group B features can be clearly seen if the speakers in Groups 2 and 3 are amalgamated into a single group. Table 2 shows that non-standard *never* and non-standard *what* now show regular patterns of variation. These features, then, do function as markers of vernacular loyalty. But they are less sensitive markers than the features in Class A, showing regular patterning only with rather broad groupings of speakers.

Features in Class C, on the other hand, do not show any correlation with the speakers' vernacular culture index. For the most part, figures are completely irregular. All these features, however, are involved in other, more complex, kinds of sociolinguistic variation, and this could explain why they do not function as straightforward markers of vernacular loyalty. There is convincing evidence, for example, that non-standard auxiliary *do* is undergoing a linguistic change away from an earlier dialect form towards the standard English form (see Cheshire 1978. See also Aitchison 1981 for some interesting ideas concerning the mechanism of the change). Some forms of *ain't* appear to function as a direct marker of a vernacular norm, as we will see. We will also see that the use of non-standard *come* bears an interesting relation to the sex of speakers: it functions as a marker of vernacular loyalty for adolescent girls, but for boys it is an invariant feature, occurring 100 per cent of the time in their speech, irrespective of the extent to which they adhere to the vernacular culture.

Stylistic Variation

We will now consider what happens to the frequency of occurrence of these linguistic features when the boys are at school. The Labovian view of style shifting is that formality–informality can be considered as a linear continuum, reflecting the amount of attention that speakers give to their speech. As formality increases, the frequency of occurrence of some non-standard linguistic features decreases (see Labov 1972, chapter 3). This approach has been questioned by a number of scholars. L. Milroy (1980) and Romaine (1980), for example, found that reading, where attention is directly focused on speech, does not consistently result in the use of fewer non-standard features. And Wolfson (1976) points out that in some situations speakers will monitor their speech carefully to ensure that they use *more* non-standard features, in order to produce an appropriately informal speech style.

The present study also found difficulties in applying the Labovian approach to the analysis of style, for the ability of some linguistic features to signal vernacular loyalty affects the frequency with which they occur in different speech styles.

The recordings made at school were clearly made in a more formal setting than the recordings made in the adventure playgrounds. The speakers were in school, where the overt norms of mainstream society are maintained (see, for example, Moss 1973), the teacher was present, the speaker knew that he was being recorded, and there had been no 'warm-up' session with the tape-recorder before the recording was made. On the other hand, the speaker did have two (at least) of his friends present. This was in an attempt to stop him 'drying up', as he may have done in a straightforward interview situation, and although the intention was to make the situation somewhat more relaxed, it nevertheless clearly represents a more formal setting than the adventure playground.

Table 3   Stylistic variation in the frequency of occurrence of non-standard forms

		Vernacular style	*School style*
Class A	non-standard -*s*	57.03	31.49
	non-standard *has*	46.43	35.71
	non-standard *was*	91.67	88.57
	negative concord	90.70	66.67
Class B	non-standard *never*	49.21	15.38
	non-standard *what*	50.00	54.55
Class C	non-standard *do*	—	—
	non-standard *come*	100.00	100.00
	ain't=aux. *have*	93.02	100.00
	ain't=copula	74.47	77.78

Unfortunately only eight of the thirteen boys could be recorded at school. Four boys had recently left school, and the fifth was so unpopular with the teacher that she could not be persuaded to spend extra time with him.

Table 3 shows the frequency of occurrence of the non-standard linguistic features in the vernacular style and in the school style of these eight speakers. We can see that those features that are sensitive markers of vernacular loyalty (Class A) all occur less often in the boys' school style than in their vernacular style, though the difference in frequency is very small in the case of non-standard *was*.

Non-standard *never*, in Class B, also occurs less often in the school recordings. Non-standard *what*, however, does not decrease in frequency; instead, it increases slightly in occurrence. The remaining features in the table do not decrease in frequency in the school style, either. Non-standard *come* remains invariant, and *ain't* increases in frequency by quite a large amount. (There were no occurrences of third person singular forms of auxiliary *do* in the school recordings.)

So far, of course, this is quite in accordance with the Labovian view of the stylistic continuum. Labov classifies linguistic variables into 'indicators' and 'markers', which differ in that indicators show regular variation only with sociological characteristics of speakers, whereas markers also show regular correlation with style. We could, therefore, class the linguistic variables in Class A, together with non-standard *never*, as markers in Reading English, and class the other variables as indicators. But this would be oversimplistic. As we will see, there are some more complex factors involved in stylistic variation, which only become apparent if we compare the linguistic behaviour of individual speakers, rather than of groups of speakers.

Table 3 expressed the frequency of occurrence of the non-standard features in terms of group indices; in other words, the speech of the eight boys analysed together, as a whole. There are many practical advantages to the analysis of the speech of groups of speakers, particularly where morphological and syntactic variables are concerned. One advantage is that variables may not occur frequently

Table 4   Frequency of occurrence of non-standard present tense verb forms

	Vernacular style	School style
Noddy	81.00	77.78
Ricky	70.83	34.62
Perry	71.43	54.55
Jed	45.00	0.00
Kitty	45.71	33.33
Gammy	57.14	31.75
Barney	31.58	54.17
Colin	38.46	0.00

enough in the language of an individual speaker for a detailed analysis to be made, whereas the language of a group of speakers will usually provide an adequate number of occurrences of crucial forms (cf. also the discussion in J. Milroy 1982).

The school recordings consisted of only about half an hour of speech for each boy. This did not provide enough data for an analysis in terms of individual speakers, and in most cases it did not even provide enough data for a group analysis. There was one exception, however. Present tense verb forms occur very frequently in speech, so that even within a half hour recording there were enough forms for an analysis of their use by individual speakers to be made. This enables us to investigate some of the more subtle aspects of sociolinguistic variation, that would be overlooked in a group analysis.

Table 4 shows the frequency of occurrence of non-standard present tense verb forms in the speech of each of the eight boys, in their vernacular style and in their school style. Noddy, Ricky and Perry are Group 1 speakers, with a high vernacular culture index; Kitty, Jed and Gammy are Group 2 speakers, and Barney and Colin are in Group 3.

There are considerable differences in the use of the non-standard forms by the different speakers. Noddy's use of the non-standard form, for example, decreases by only 3.22 per cent in his school style, whereas the other Group 1 speakers (Ricky and Perry) show a much greater decrease. Jed (a Group 2 speaker) does not use the non-standard form at all in his school style, although the other Group 2 speakers (Kitty and Gammy) continue to use non-standard forms, albeit with a reduced frequency. Colin, like Jed, does not use the non-standard form in school style; Barney's use of the form, on the other hand, actually increases, by quite a large amount.

Present tense verb forms are sensitive markers of vernacular loyalty, as we have seen; and a group analysis of their occurrence in different speech styles showed that they were also sensitive to style. We saw that the feature could be classed as a marker, in the Labovian sense. Individual analyses, however, reveal that two speakers do not show the decrease in frequency that we would expect to find in their school style: Noddy, as we have seen, shows only a slight decrease, unlike the other boys in his group, and Barney's frequency actually increases. Their linguistic behaviour does not seem to be related to the vernacular culture index, for Noddy is a Group 1 speaker, showing strong allegiance to the peer-group culture, whilst Barney is a Group 3 speaker. One factor that could explain Noddy's behaviour is age: Noddy was only 11, whilst the other boys were aged between 13 and 16. Noddy may, therefore, have simply not yet acquired the ability to style shift. Labov (1965) suggested that children do not acquire this ability until the age of about 14, and there is some empirical evidence to support this (see Macaulay 1977). Other recent studies, however, have found evidence of stylistic sensitivity at a rather younger age (see Reid 1978; Romaine 1975), so that we cannot conclude with any certainty that this is a relevant factor here. In any case, Barney's behaviour cannot be explained this way, for he was 15, and old enough to show some signs of stylistic sensitivity. We need to explore further, then, to discover an explanation for this irregular behaviour.

Barney was recorded with Noddy and Kitty, by their teacher. The teacher was asking them about their activities outside school, and the boys were talking about a disco that they were trying to organize. The teacher was making valiant efforts to understand the conversation, but was obviously unfamiliar with the kind of amplifying equipment and with the situation that the boys were telling him about. It is worth noting that Barney and Noddy hated school and made very derisory remarks about their teachers. Barney had only just returned to school after an absence of a whole term, and Noddy attended school only intermittently. Kitty, on the other hand, attended school more regularly – his father was very strict, and he did not dare to play truant as often as his friends did.

These factors suggest an explanation for the boys' linguistic behaviour. A great deal of insight into linguistic behaviour has been gained from recent research by social psychologists, working within the framework of speech accommodation theory. It has been shown that speakers who are favourably disposed towards each other and who are 'working towards a common goal' adjust their speech so that they each speak more like the other, whereas speakers who are not working towards a common goal may diverge in their linguistic behaviour. One way in which speech convergence is marked is the frequency of occurrence of certain linguistic variables (see Thakerar, Giles and Cheshire 1982).

An explanation along these lines gives some insight into the behaviour of Noddy, Kitty and Barney in the school situation. Kitty knows the teacher, attends school fairly regularly, and we can imagine that he accepts the constraints of the situation. As a result his speech converges towards the teacher's, and he uses fewer non-standard linguistic forms than he does normally. Noddy, on the other hand, hates school and dislikes the teacher; as a result he asserts his allegiance to the peer-group culture rather than to the school, by refusing to acknowledge the situational constraints. The frequency with which he uses the non-standard form, therefore, does not change (or changes only slightly). Barney, who has only recently returned to school, asserts his total independence and hostility to the school by using more non-standard forms than he does usually. This is a very clear example of speech divergence. As we saw earlier, Barney is not closely involved in the vernacular culture, and this is reflected in his speech by a relatively low use of non-standard present tense forms. When he wants to assert his independence from the school culture, however, he is able to exploit the resources of the language system, by choosing to use a higher proportion of non-standard forms than he does usually.

Can an explanation in these terms account for the linguistic behaviour of the other boys in this study? For at least three of the boys, it seems that it can.

Ricky, Perry and Gammy were recorded together, by a teacher that they knew and liked. He had taken them on camping and fishing weekend expeditions, with some of their classmates. The conversation was initially about one of these weekends, and then moved on to racing cars and motorbikes, subjects that interested both the teacher and the boys. Speech accommodation theory would predict that in this situation the linguistic behaviour of the boys would converge towards that of their teacher (and, of course, vice-versa). This is precisely what happens – all three boys use a lower proportion of non-standard present tense forms here than they do in their vernacular speech style. The fact that they continue to use *some* non-standard forms, however, means that they are still able to show their allegiance to the vernacular subculture.

Jed and Colin behave rather differently from the other boys, for in their school recordings they do not use any non-standard forms at all. This is surprising, particularly in the case of Jed, who is a Group 2 speaker, like Kitty and Gammy. There are, however, some striking similarities between the linguistic behaviour of these two boys, and the situations in which the school recordings were made. They were recorded at different times, with a different speaker, but both recordings were made in a classroom situation, with about 20 pupils and the teacher. Both Jed and Colin participated a great deal in the discussions, partly because the teacher had purposely chosen topics on which they had strong views (football hooliganism, in Jed's case, and truancy, in Colin's case), and partly because they were encouraged to take part by the teacher. It is possible, though, that the situation was so drastically different from the situation in the adventure playground that the overall formality overrode the option of displaying linguistically their allegiance to the vernacular culture. Or perhaps the fact that no other members of the peer-group were present meant that the boys were more susceptible to the pressures of the norms of the school culture.

It seems, then, that a simple analysis in terms of the formality or informality of the situation cannot fully explain stylistic variation here. A better explanation can, perhaps, be achieved if we think in terms of situational constraints on exploiting the resources of the linguistic system. The non-standard present tense suffix is a powerful indicator of vernacular loyalty, and in some cases this function overrides other situational constraints on linguistic behaviour (as in the speech of Noddy and Barney, for example). In other cases (as with Jed and Colin), the situational constraints exclude the possibility of using the feature in this way.

The Linguistic Behaviour of Adolescent Girls

Many surveys of non-standard English have found that female speakers use non-standard speech forms less frequently than male speakers do. Table 5 shows that an

Table 5   Linguistic variation and sex differences

	Frequency indices for non-standard features in boys' speech	Frequency indices for non-standard features in girls' speech
non-standard –*s*	53.16	52.04
non-standard *has*	54.76	51.61
non-standard *was*	88.15	73.58
negative concord	88.33	51.85
non-standard *never*	46.84	40.00
non-standard *what*	36.36	14.58
non-standard *do*	57.69	78.95
non-standard *come*	100.00	75.33
ain't=aux *have*	92.00	64.58
ain't=aux *be*	74.19	42.11
ain't=copula	85.83	61.18

analysis of the use of non-standard forms by girls and by boys confirms this pattern of behaviour.

Only non-standard auxiliary *do* is used more often by girls than by boys. As we have seen, this feature is involved in an on-going linguistic change, and has several irregular characteristics. The other non-standard features are all used less often by girls than they are by boys. In some cases the difference in frequency is very small (non-standard present tense verb forms, for example), but for most features the difference in frequency is more striking. This kind of analysis, however, again conceals the ways in which linguistic features function as symbols of vernacular identity.

It was not possible to construct a vernacular culture index for the girls, as it was for the boys. The girls did not form structured peer-groups in the way that the boys did and, partly as a result of this, the norms of their vernacular subculture were less well-defined. It was possible, however, to divide the girls loosely into two groups, for three of the girls were clearly different from the others. They did not swear, steal, or set fire to the playground. They attended school regularly, and their parents did not approve of the adventure playground, because the children that their daughters met there were 'common' and 'rough'.

Table 6 shows the frequency of use of the nine non-standard features in the speech of these three girls, and also in the speech of the other girls in the group. This division of speakers is, of course, not ideal, since we are comparing the speech of a group of only three speakers with the speech of a group of nine speakers, but it can, nevertheless, give us an idea of the different ways in which linguistic features can function as markers of vernacular loyalty.

It can be seen from the table that some linguistic features appear to mark adherence to the vernacular culture, in that they are used less often by the 'good' girls than

Table 6 Use of non-standard features by 'good' girls and by other girls

	Frequency index: 'good' girls	Frequency index: other girls
non-standard *-s*	25.84	57.27
non-standard *has*	36.36	35.85
non-standard *was*	63.64	80.95
negative concord	12.50	58.70
non-standard *never*	45.45	41.07
non-standard *what*	33.33	5.56
non-standard *come*	30.77	90.63
ain't=copula	14.29	67.12

(There are no data for non-standard auxiliary *do*, nor for *ain't* as auxiliary *be* or as auxiliary *have*.)

by the others. Other features, however, do not behave in this way. And if we compare table 6 with table 1, which showed those features that mark vernacular loyalty in the boys' speech, some interesting differences emerge.

Features 1–4, for example (non-standard *-s*, non-standard *has*, non-standard *was* and negative concord), all function as sensitive markers of vernacular loyalty for boys. Three of these features function in the same way for girls, as table 6 shows. Non-standard *has*, however, is used with approximately the same frequency by both 'good' girls and the other girls. This feature does not, therefore, function as a marker of vernacular loyalty for girls.

Non-standard *never* and non-standard *what* functioned only loosely as markers of vernacular loyalty for the boys. For girls, they do not appear to fulfil any symbolic function at all: the 'good' girls use them, in fact, more often than the other girls.

On the other hand, non-standard *come* and *ain't* appear to function as markers of vernacular identity for girls, although they do not for boys. Non-standard *come* is an invariant feature of the dialect for boys, occurring 100 per cent of the time in the speech of all speakers, in both speech styles (including those speakers who adhere only loosely to the norms of the vernacular culture). 'Good' girls, however, use non-standard *come* relatively infrequently (30.77 per cent of the time), whilst the other girls use it much more often (90.63 per cent of the time). Similarly, *ain't* is used much less often by the 'good' girls than it is by the other girls.

We can conclude, then, that male and female speakers in Reading exploit the resources of the linguistic system in different ways. Some linguistic features are markers of vernacular loyalty for both sexes (non-standard present tense verb forms, non-standard *was*, and negative concord). Some features function in this way for boys only (non-standard *never* and non-standard *what*). And others fulfil this function only for girls (non-standard *come* and *ain't*).

[. . .]

Conclusion

This paper has focused on the social function of linguistic variation in the speech of adolescent peer-groups. We have seen that non-standard linguistic features function in a number of different ways. Some are very sensitive markers of vernacular loyalty, showing a regular correlation in frequency with the extent to which speakers adhere to the vernacular culture. Others are less sensitive markers of vernacular loyalty. Finally, we have seen that the social function of non-standard features can vary with the sex of the speaker, and that this social function can sometimes override the constraints imposed on speakers by the formality of the situation. [. . .]

REFERENCES

Aitchison, J. (1981) *Language Change: Progress or Decay?* London: Fontana.

Andry, R. G. (1960) *Delinquency and Parental Pathology.* London: Methuen.

Cheshire, J. (1978) 'Present tense verbs in Reading English', in P. Trudgill (ed.) *Sociolinguistic Patterns in British English*, pp. 52–68. London: Edward Arnold.

Cheshire, J. (1982) *Variation in an English Dialect: A Sociolinguistic Study.* London: Cambridge University Press.

Clarke, J. (1973) *The Skinheads and the Study of Youth Culture.* Occasional paper. Birmingham: Centre for Contemporary Cultural Studies.

Cohen, A. K. (1965) *Delinquent Boys.* New York: The Free Press.

Cohen, P. (1972) *Subcultural Conflict and Working-Class Community. Working Papers in Cultural Studies, 2.* Birmingham: Centre for Contemporary Cultural Studies.

Downes, D. (1966) *The Delinquent Solution.* London: Routledge & Kegan Paul.

Jahangiri, N. and Hudson, R. (1982) 'Patterns of variation in Tehrani Persian', in S. Romaine (ed.) *Sociolinguistic Variation in Speech Communities.* London: Edward Arnold.

Labov, W. (1965) 'Stages in the acquisition of Standard English', in R. Shuy (ed.) *Social Dialects and Language Learning. Proceedings of the Bloomington, Indiana, Conference 1964.* Champaign, IL: National Council of Teachers of English.

Labov, W. (1966) *The Social Stratification of English in New York City.* Washington, DC: Center for Applied Linguistics.

Labov, W. (1970) 'The study of language in its social context'. *Studium Generale*, 23, 30–87.

Labov, W. (1972) *Sociolinguistic Patterns.* Philadelphia: Pennsylvania University Press.

Macaulay, R. K. S. (1977) *Language, Social Class and Education: A Glasgow Study.* Edinburgh: Edinburgh University Press.

Miller, W. B. (1958) 'Lower-class culture as a generating milieu of gang delinquency'. *Journal of Social Issues*, 14, 3, 5–19.

Milroy, J. (1982) 'Probing under the tip of the iceberg: phonological "normalization" and the shape of speech communities', in S. Romaine (ed.) *Sociolinguistic Variation in Speech Communities.* London: Edward Arnold.

Milroy, L. (1980) *Language and Social Networks.* Oxford: Blackwell.

Milroy, L. and Margrain, S. (1980) 'Vernacular language loyalty and social network'. *Language in Society*, 9, 43–70.

Moss, M. H. (1973) *Deprivation and Disadvantage?* Open University Course Book E 262:8. Milton Keynes: The Open University Press.

Policansky, L. (1980) 'Verb Concord Variation in Belfast Vernacular.' Paper delivered to the Sociolinguistic Symposium, Walsall.

Reid, E. (1978) 'Social and stylistic variation in the speech of children: some evidence from Edinburgh', in P. Trudgill (ed.) *Sociolinguistic Patterns in British English*, pp. 158–73. London: Edward Arnold.

Romaine, S. (1975) 'Linguistic Variability in the Speech of some Edinburgh School-Children.' University of Edinburgh, M. Litt thesis.

Romaine, S. (1980) 'Stylistic variation and evaluative reactions to speech: problems in the investigation of linguistic attitudes in Scotland'. *Language and Speech*, 23, 3, 213–32.

Thakerar, J. N., Giles, H. and Cheshire, J. (1982) 'Psychological and linguistic parameters of speech accommodation theory', in C. Fraser and K. R. Scherer (eds) *Advances in the Social Psychology of Language*. Cambridge: Cambridge University Press.

Willmott, P. (1966) *Adolescent Boys of East London*. London: Routledge & Kegan Paul.

Wolfson, N. (1976) 'Speech events and natural speech: some implications for sociolinguistic methodology'. *Language in Society*, 5, 2, 189–211.

4

Girl-talk/Boy-talk: Sex Differences in Adolescent Speech

Edina Eisikovits

[. . .]

Given the rigid sex divisions in Australian society (see Encel, McKenzie, and Tebbutt 1974) and especially the strong working class ethic of "Ockerism", the role of sex differences as a factor in determining linguistic behaviour in Australian English would seem to be an important area for investigation. Indeed, Mitchell and Delbridge's work on phonology (1965, 38) suggests that sex is a strong determinant of variation in Australian English:

> The distribution of boys in the vowel spectrum is significantly different from that of girls . . . These figures strongly suggest that the sex differences must be an important, perhaps an overriding influence in the distribution of the varieties of Australian speech.

Moreover, Shopen (1978, 44) in his study of the variable *-ING* in Canberra points out that "the most important distinction emerges as that between men and women in their roles both as speakers and listeners . . .". Horvath (1985) similarly identifies sex as a major variable in Australian English.

This chapter will look at sex differences from a developmental perspective, focusing on grammatical variation in a sample of adolescent speakers. Most past studies have tended to treat age and sex as separate categories, so we have little information about whether adolescent females behave like adults and if not when such behaviour is learnt.

On the other hand, we do know that adolescence is the period in which the use of non-standard forms is at its peak and that this usage tends to decline with increased age (Wolfram and Fasold 1974, 90 ff). It is also the period during which social perceptions affecting linguistic behaviour are developed. The identification of when – if at all – these perceptions and hence changes in linguistic behaviour become evident is one of the goals of this chapter.

Methodology

The data for this study consist of more than fifty hours of tape-recorded conversation. The sample of informants was made up of twenty males and twenty females, equally divided into two age groups, a younger group in year 8 of secondary school, average age thirteen years eleven months and an older group in year 10, average age sixteen years one month. All were Australian-born of Australian-born parents and were long-term residents of inner-Sydney working class suburbs such as Glebe, Petersham, and Annandale. Their parents had occupations relatively low in social status; for example, cleaner, canteen assistant, truck driver. The informants were interviewed in pairs with the view of obtaining as broad a picture of their natural language as is possible within the limitations of a tape-recorded situation. In addition, those of the younger group in year 8 still at school two years later were interviewed a second time in year 10, thereby providing a small developmental group against which changes over apparent time could be compared.

In all, twelve grammatical variables were examined in the larger study of Inner-Sydney English (ISE) from which these data were drawn (Eisikovits 1981), but for the purposes of this chapter, three highly stigmatised variables have been isolated for consideration. It should be noted, however, that the patterns evident with respect to these three variables were similarly evident with respect to other grammatical variables examined in the larger study.

The three variables to be considered in detail here are:

1 non-standard past tense forms such as *seen* and *done*, as in:
   He woke up and seen something.
2 multiple negation; for example,
   They don't say nothing.
3 invariable *don't*; for example,
   Mum don't have to do nothing.

The occurrence of these forms is quantified using the paradigmatic Labovian model, that is:

$$\% \text{ frequency} = \frac{\text{number of occurrences of non-standard form}}{\text{total number of potential occurrences}}$$

Results

Non-standard past tense forms

Table 1 shows the frequencies of occurrence of non-standard past tense forms for each of the age/sex groupings in this study.

Table 1   Non-standard past tense forms for age/sex

Younger girls (N = 10) Occurrences: 134/313 % : 42.8 $\chi^2 = 14.79$ p < .001	Older girls (N = 10) Occurrences: 86/307 % : 28.0
Younger boys (N = 10) Occurrences: 138/481 % : 28.9 $\chi^2 = 2.04$ p > .001	Older boys (N = 10) Occurrences: 137/411 % : 33.3

Table 2   Occurrence of non-standard past tense forms of five verbs among male speakers

	Younger boys	*Older boys*
seen	58.9 (33/156)	67.9 (36/13)
done	65.5 (19/29)	61.3 (19/31)
come	55.8 (58/104)	75.9 (66/87)
give	4.8 (1/21)	14.3 (4/28)
run	23.1 (6/26)	0 (0/16)

From this table it can be seen that males and females differ considerably in their use of these forms. Among the female speakers there is a significant decline in use with age ($\chi^2 = 14.79$; p < .001). This pattern may be observed even more dramatically in the case of individual verbs, especially past tense *done* and *come*. With *done*, the almost categorical use of this form among the younger girls (94.4 per cent) may be contrasted with the significantly lower frequency of usage – 45.2 per cent – among the older females. Similarly, past tense *come* decreases from 93.3 per cent among the younger girls to 52.9 per cent among the older girls.

Among the males, no such decline is apparent. Not only is a comparison of overall group results not significant ($\chi^2 = 2.04$; p > .001), but also when the pattern of usage of the five most frequently occurring individual verbs is examined among the two male groups, only one – *run* – declines significantly. The remaining four occur in both groups with either a very similar or an increased frequency (see table 2). Indeed, for one verb, past tense *come*, there is a significant increase in the use of the non-standard form with increased age ($\chi^2 = 8.36$; p < .01).

The same pattern may be observed in individual cases in the speech of the five male informants interviewed twice, once in year 8 and then again two years later in year 10. In almost all cases, these informants evidence either a very similar or an

Table 3 Frequencies of occurrence of non-standard past tense forms among male developmental group

Informant:	1B		2B		4B		5B		6B	
	Year 8	Year 10	Year 8	Year 10	Year 8	Year 10	Year 8	Year 10	Year 8	Year 10
seen	90	100	100	0	0	25	0	100	0	33.3
done	100	100	100	100	33.3	50	0	0	0	76.9
come	27.3	46.7	100	100	88.2	90.5	20	0	0	50
give	0	0	0	0	0	0	0	0	0	0
run	33.3	0	50	0	0	25	0	0	0	0
				(0/1)						

Table 4 Multiple negation within the clause for age/sex

Younger girls (N = 10)	Older girls (N = 10)
Occurrences: 56/115	Occurrences: 42/192
% : 48.7	% : 21.7
$\chi^2 = 24.72$	
p < .001	

Younger boys (N = 10)	Older boys (N = 10)
Occurrences: 54/107	Occurrences: 56/127
% : 50.5	% : 44.1
$\chi^2 = 0.94$	
p > .001	

increased frequency in the use of non-standard past tense forms with increased age (see table 3). Informant 6B provides a dramatic example of this. Whereas in year 8 none of his past tense forms of *see*, *do* have the *seen/done* form, in year 10 there are eleven occurrences of *seen/done* compared with only five *saw/did*.

Multiple negation

A similar pattern of variation occurs with the use of multiple negation (see table 4). Again among the female speakers there is a significant decline in use of this form with age ($\chi^2 = 24.72$; p < .001). This pattern can be observed in individual cases in the speech of two girls, 1A and 6A, who were interviewed twice, once in year 8 and again two years later in year 10. Both of these speakers evidence a sharp decline in their use of multiple negation. Speaker 1A drops from a frequency of 30.8 per cent

Table 5   Multiple negation within the clause among male developmental group

Speaker	% frequency year 8	% frequency year 10
1B	62.5	52.9
2B	68.4	75
4B	40.9	52.4
5B	—	12.5
6B	—	7.1

Table 6   *Don't/Doesn't* for age/sex

Younger girls (N = 10) Occurrences: 3/63 % : 4.8	Older girls (N = 10) Occurrences: 5/77 % : 6.5
Younger boys (N = 10) Occurrences: 13/78 % : 16.7 $\chi^2 = 19.23$ p < .001	Older boys (N = 10) Occurrences: 31/60 % : 51.7

in year 8 to 12.5 per cent in year 10 while 6A declines even more dramatically from 87.9 per cent in year 8 to 42.9 per cent two years later in year 10. This is especially interesting for 6A in that in the earlier year 8 interview she evidences the highest frequency of use of this form (87.9 per cent) of all speakers in the sample.

Among the male speakers, no such decline is apparent. Not only is a comparison of overall group results again not significant ($\chi^2 = 0.94$; p > .001) but also, when the results of the five male speakers in the developmental group are examined, only one declines. The remaining four use either a very similar or an increased frequency of this variable (see table 5). This is especially interesting for the two speakers, 5B and 6B, who appear to have acquired this feature from year 8 to year 10. Note that it was 6B who also acquired the *seen/done* past tense forms in this period.

Invariable *don't*

This movement towards an increase in the use of non–standard forms among the male group is markedly apparent when we consider the use of invariable *don't* (see table 6).

The trends here are consistent with those evident with respect to other variables examined so far but they are not altogether parallel. With both of the other variables, it is the females who decline significantly in their use of the non–standard form with age whereas here it is the male group which significantly increases its usage with age ($\chi^2 = 19.23$; p < .001). Among the girls on the other hand the use of *don't* is never favoured. The low frequency evident among the girls remains relatively constant with age, suggesting that this variable is heavily sex-marked.

Discussion

The existence of such different patterns of usage of non–standard forms among the two sex groups poses an obvious problem: why should an increase in age bring about such different patterns of usage among male and female speakers? Why is it only the girls who decline in their use of such forms as they grow older whereas, if anything, the boys increase their usage of such forms? If such forms are seen simply as developmental features we would expect a consistent decline with age among both groups. Clearly, at least two separate but intersecting factors are involved here: one developmental and the other relating to sex differences. Studies of sex variation in phonology in the past (Labov 1966; Shuy, Wolfram, and Riley 1966; Trudgill 1972, revised version reprinted in this volume, p. 21) have tended to suggest that women regularly use more socially prestigious speech than men. Such sensitivity among female speakers is particularly evident in lower middle class and upper working class speech (compare Wolfram 1969).

In addition, women have been shown to evidence greater stylistic variation than men. Studies by Wolfram (1969), Labov (1972a), and Trudgill (1972), have shown that lower middle class women – especially younger females in the process of social mobility – are likely to evidence particular sensitivity to prestige norms in more formal speech situations.

Such sensitivity to social and stylistic variation is acquired by the child in various stages. Labov (1964, 81) presents a tentative model of language acquisition which incorporates the child's growing awareness of and control over variation in language. He specifies six levels of development; (i) the basic grammar, (ii) the vernacular, (iii) social perception, (iv) stylistic variation, (v) the consistent standard and finally, (vi) the acquisition of the full range. These stages are not entirely separate entities but are markers along a continuum of change. From Labov's model we would expect the informants in this study to be at stages (iii) and (iv); that is, initially at the stage of perceiving the social significance of speech and then gradually learning to modify their own speech in line with these perceptions. Such a view would account for the particularly high frequency of non–standard forms among the younger female group as well as for the decrease with age apparent in the use of such forms by the female informants. However, if this model is used to account for the use of non–standard forms here, we would expect a consistent decline with age among both the male and female groups. Hence, we are still left with the problem of accounting for the usage of the male speakers who, unlike their female counterparts, do not appear to modify their speech in the direction of the prestige standard.

One possible explanation for this is that the two groups do not share the same prestige standard; that is, forms perceived positively by one group are not similarly viewed by the other. Smith (1985, 83), citing research evidence from Labov (1966) and Trudgill (1972), suggests that such a difference in prestige norms may be widespread:

> Given the fact that men and women typically occupy quite different social niches, and are often clearly differentiated even in those they share, it would not be surprising to find that the sexes are habituated to different sets of context-dependent speech norms, and that their speech, and their impression of others' speech, reflect these differences.

Certainly, the attitudes and perceptions evidenced by the two sex groups in this study show some striking differences. Although both boys and girls were interviewed at similar points in their lives – the two older groups were at the conclusion of their high school education so that they were all looking outwards to the broader community – their orientations and "world views" differ significantly.

Among the older girls there is a serious and conservative acceptance of the responsibilities of adulthood. All are concerned with fitting in with society and its expectations rather than, as two years earlier, with the conflicts with it. No longer are they rebellious in their attitudes towards family, school, and society in general. All see themselves as having "grown up" – a process which for the girls means "settling down". This change is aptly summed up by 1E: "I think I've settled down a lot. It's better not being in trouble anyway."

A similar response comes from 1C, replying to the interviewer's question; "Do you feel a lot older than you did say two years ago?"

> That was funny you said that because, see I keep a diary an I was reading over what I'd written before and just from the beginning of the year you can see that what you've written, how stupid you must've been then to do that sort of thing, you know, 'cause whatever you've said or done or something you wrote, I've written it down, you know, the fights I've had with Mum an that. Then, like when you read it through you think, "Yeah, that was ridiculous. Mum was right all the time," or summat like that, you know. Yeah, you notice how you do change an that. You realise your mistakes.

That this new conservatism is extended to attitudes to language may be seen in 1E's changed view of swearing. Asked what her fights with her boyfriend are about, she replies:

> Oh, petty things. Like, oh, sometimes he swears at me and I don't like swearing anymore. An he'll swear at me so we have a fight about that.

Even more telling are her later comments:

1E: We went – I've seen "One Flew Over the Cuckoo's Nest" – can't even say "cuckoo" properly. That was a good show. The only thing is they swear a lot in it.

INT: And that really bothers you?

1E: Mm. Sometimes, like, sometimes I'll be in the mood for it an other times I'll think, you know, "I don't wanna say that." Cause when you listen t'other people it sounds terrible, you know . . .

INT: You don't think about that when you're 13 or 14 doing it yourself.

1E: No, you don't. When you get older, you think, "Oh Jesus, what did I ever say that for?"

Among the boys, however, a rather different perception emerges. They, too, see themselves as having grown up, but for them this does not necessarily mean settling down or conforming to family or societal expectations of "good" behaviour. Instead, it is more usually seen as a movement towards self-assertion, "toughness" and an unwillingness to be dictated to. Again, some typical comments to illustrate this change:

9D: They said juniors are definitely not allowed to drink. We still drink though. They can't stop us really.

1D: I was pulled up by the police about 20 yards from me front door. They said, "Where do ya live?" That made me feel real good. I said, "Right there." You know you can give 'em cheek, bit a cheek back an they can't say nothing.

INT: Your Mum and Dad didn't try to push you into anything? [a job]

5F: No. If they did, I'd push 'em back.

Many spoke about on-going conflict with the police, the school, teachers, and to a lesser extent, parents, relating these stories with defiance and bravado. Incidents in which they were able to outwit authority were recounted with pride as evidence of toughness and skill. Never was there any admission of earlier errors as foolishness as there was among the older girls. Indeed, where family conflicts had diminished, this was because of reduced parental controls on the boys' actions rather than any recognition on their parts, as with the girls, of the validity of their parents' viewpoints. Consider, for example, the following dialogue:

INT: What sort of things do you have rows with your Mum and Dad about?

2D: Oh, we useta have rows. That was before I was 16. Useta have rows about comin home too late, early in the mornin an that. But now, it's just when I get in trouble off the police or something, you know. I just get in trouble for that . . . I don't stick around when they go off their heads.

INT: What happens if you come home really smashed?

2D: I do every week. But Dad doesn't mind.

INT: They don't nag you about stuff like that?

2D: Oh, me Mother used to. She still does a bit cause, you know, you're supposed to be a certain age to drink in a pub an if you're in there, you know, you get fined or sumpin, you know. But you can get away with it easy.

INT: What about homework?

1D: If I wanna do it, I do it. If I don't Mum don't care.

2D: They make me sisters an that do their homework.

This extract would suggest that not only are the older boys less conformist than their female counterparts but also that this independence is given tacit support by their parents and the community at large. Unlike the girls, they are encouraged to be independent and tough. Clearly, different behavioural norms as well as different social perceptions exist for the two sexes. Given these differences, it is hardly surprising that the two groups differ in their attitudes to and use of language. We have already seen the growing conservatism of the girls in their attitude to swearing. The boys on the other hand tend to move in a contrary direction:

INT: Did you used to get beltings when you were a kid?
6D: Oh, swore once when I was about five an I was belted off me mother. Tried to wash me mouth out with soap.
5D: Yeah, that's what they always say.
INT: You were in trouble for the same thing?
5D: Yeah, for swearing.
INT: What did they do to you?
5D: Oh, they just took me inside an smacked me. That's all.
INT: What about now?
5D: If I swear in front of me mother now she don't say nothing.

Such different social and linguistic perceptions may provide an explanation for the two groups' differing usage of non-standard forms here. That is, while the girls are increasingly ready to accept external social norms – a conformity mirrored in their readiness to modify their speech in line with external prestige norms – the boys are not so accepting. Indeed, they are learning to assert themselves, to express their opposition to authority and the middle class establishment – an opposition similarly mirrored in the maintenance/increase in their use of non-standard forms.

This increased use of non-standard forms among the males would suggest that for this group these forms carry their own prestige as a marker of masculinity and toughness, so that as the boys grow older and identify more strongly with their own class and sex their use of these forms is favoured.

That such prestige value is attached to non-standard forms by the males in this study may be seen from the direction of their self-corrections. Unlike the older females who self-correct towards standard forms, for example:

Our Deputy-Principal was really nice and he sort of let my group, the kids I hang – hung around with, get away with almost anything.

An me and Kerry – or should I say, Kerry and I – are the only ones who've done the project.

the older males self-correct in the opposite direction, favouring the non-standard over the standard form. For example:

I didn't know what I did – what I done.

He's my family doctor. I've known im ever since I was a kid. An 'e gave – give it to me an 'e said, "As long as it's helping you, I'll give it to you" you know.

That such consciousness of external prestige norms is only just developing among the older girls is evidenced in the contrary direction among the younger girls who self-correct in line with the males, for example:

It don't work out anyway – it don't work out noways.

[. . .]

Conclusions

What all this would suggest is that for the girls the norms which they become increasingly aware of are in line with those of external social usage. [. . .] The boys, however, [. . .] appear to use non-standard forms to affirm their own masculinity and toughness and their working class anti–establishment values.

Some anecdotal evidence of the boys' orientation may be drawn from the practice of individual speakers. Speaker 7D, for example, uses the non-standard forms, double negatives and invariable *don't*, in speech in which he is seeking in some way to affirm his own strength as a male in situations dominated by women or women's values. For example, in describing his part in housekeeping (he is the eldest of five children in a single parent family):

So I make sure the housework's done so Mum won't have to do nothing . . . All I have to do is put em clothes in the machine and turn the dial round and it goes for 40 minutes, then I just hang it up, so Mum don't have to do nothing.

Later, discussing his part in a fight with a girl:

She started hitting me again and again and I didn't do nothing then cause she was one of me friends.

Similarly with 1D, use of the double negative seems to be associated with the expression of anti–establishment values. Describing a confrontation with the police in which he outwits authority, he says:

That made me feel good . . . you know, you can give 'em cheek, bit a cheek back 'n they can't say nothing.

Again in a narrative recounting how he manages to drink in pubs though underage, he says:

Oh, it's pretty easy to get away with. Go down town, pubs down there. They don't say nothing to ya.

For 5D, the expression of his toughness and growing independence from his family, especially his mother, is couched in the use of non-standard forms. Having just described how in his childhood he was severely disciplined for swearing, he concludes:

> If I swear in front of me mother now she don't say nothing.

Similarly for 6D, his attempt to assert himself in describing his relationship with his older sister is suggested in his comment:

> Me sister don't boss me around.

That his assertiveness is still tempered by some dependence is evident as he continues:

> Me brother, I don't worry about him much, but me Father is real strict. Doesn't like bad manners or talking at the table . . .

For other male speakers, the "them and us" attitude to society – school and teachers, employers and migrants – is suggested in their use of non-standard forms. Speaker 10D, for example, expresses his criticism of an authoritarian schoolmaster as follows:

> He's always patrolling round, seeing what you're doing. Like he don't trust us . . .

Later, describing an unpopular migrant group, he concludes:

> Everybody don't like 'em.

Similarly, 1D, discussing the attitude of the peer group to work, comments:

> Half of 'em don't wanna work anyway. There's one kid, Roger, he don't wanna work so he told 'em down the Dole office he wanted to be an elephant trainer.

What we have then is very strong evidence for age and sex differences in this variety of Australian adolescent speech – differences which reflect different social and linguistic norms held by the two sex groups. The extent to which these norms are held by Australian adolescents in general and not just residents of the inner-city area of Sydney is a question well worthy of future investigation.

REFERENCES

Adelman, C. 1976. The language of teenage groups. In *They don't speak our language*, ed. S. Rogers, pp. 80–105. London: Edward Arnold.

Bourhis, R., and H. Giles. 1977. The language of intergroup distinctiveness. In *Language, ethnicity and intergroup relations*, ed. H. Giles, pp. 119–35. European Monographs in Social Psychology, 13. London: Academic Press.

Cheshire, J. 1982. *Variation in an English dialect*. Cambridge: Cambridge University Press.

Delbridge, A. 1977. The only known exception is Australia: A study in dialect variation (mimeograph).

Eisikovits, E. 1981. *Inner-Sydney English: An investigation of grammatical variation in adolescent speech*. Unpublished Ph.D. thesis, University of Sydney.

Eisikovits, E., and J. Dixon. 1982. Learning to tell stories. *Developments in English Teaching* 1(1): 25–30.

Encel, S., N. McKenzie, and M. Tebbutt. 1974. *Women and society: An Australian study*. Melbourne: Cheshire.

Ervin-Tripp, S. 1964. Interaction of topic, listener and speaker. In *The ethnography of communication*, ed. S. Gumperz and D. Hymes, pp. 86–102. *American Anthropologist 66(6)*, Part 2.

Fasold, R. 1972. *Tense marking in Black English: A linguistic and social analysis*. Urban Language Series, 8. Arlington, Virginia: Center for Applied Linguistics.

Feagin, C. 1979. *Variation and change in Alabama English: A sociolinguistic study of the White community*. Washington, D. C.: Georgetown University Press.

Giles, H. 1973. Accent mobility: A model and some data. *Anthropological Linguistics* 15: 87–105.

———. 1977. Social psychology and applied linguistics. *ITL: Review of Applied Linguistics* 33: 27–42.

Horvath, B. 1985. *Variation in Australian English: The sociolects of Sydney*. Cambridge Studies in Linguistics, 45. Cambridge: Cambridge University Press.

Labov, W. 1964. Stages in the acquisition of Standard English. In *Social dialects and language learning*, ed. R. Shuy. Champaign, Illinois: National Council of Teachers of English.

———. 1966. *The social stratification of English in New York City*. Washington, DC: Center for Applied Linguistics.

———. 1970. The study of language in its social context. *Studium Generale* 23(1): 30–87.

———. 1972a. *Language in the inner-city: Studies in the Black English vernacular*. Philadelphia: University of Pennsylvania Press.

———. 1972b. Some principles of linguistic methodology. *Language in Society* 1: 97–120.

Milroy, L. 1980. *Language and social networks*. Oxford: Blackwell.

Mitchell, A., and A. Delbridge. 1965. *The speech of Australian adolescents: A survey*. Sydney: Angus & Robertson.

Romaine, S. 1984. *The language of children and adolescents: The acquisition of communicative competence*. Language in Society, 7. Oxford: Blackwell.

Romaine, S., and E. Reid. 1976. Glottal sloppiness? A sociolinguistic view of urban speech in Scotland. *Teaching English* 9(3): 12–16.

Sankoff, G., and H. Cedergren. 1971. Some results of a sociolinguistic study of Montreal French. In *Linguistic diversity in Canadian society*, ed. R. Darnell. Edmonton and Champaign: Linguistic Research Inc.

Shopen, T. 1978. Research on the variable (ING) in Canberra, Australia. *Talanya* 5: 42–52.

Shopen, T., W. Wolfram, and W. Riley 1976. Linguistic correlates of social stratification in Detroit speech. Final Report. Co-operative Research Project 6–1347. Washington, DC: US Office of Education, Department of Health, Education and Welfare.

Shuy, R., W. Wolfram, and W. Riley, 1966. *A study of social dialects in Detroit*. Final report. Project 7–1347. Washington, DC: US Office of Education, Department of Health, Education and Welfare.

Smith, P. 1979. Sex markers in speech. In *Social markers in speech*, ed. K. R. Scherer and H. Giles, pp. 107–46. Cambridge: Cambridge University Press.

——. 1985. *Language, the sexes and society*. Language in Society, 8. Oxford: Blackwell.

Trudgill, P. 1972. Sex, covert prestige and linguistic change in the urban British English of Norwich. *Language in Society* 1: 179–95. Reprinted in B. Thorne and N. Henley, eds. 1975. *Language and sex: Difference and dominance*. Rowley, Mass: Newbury House.

——, ed. 1978. *Sociolinguistic patterns in British English*. London: Edward Arnold.

Wolfram, W. 1969. *A sociolinguistic description of Detroit Negro speech*. Urban Language Series, 5. Washington, DC: Center for Applied Linguistics.

Wolfram, W., and D. Christian. 1976. *Appalachian English*. Arlington, Virginia: Center for Applied Linguistics.

Wolfram, W., and R. Fasold. 1974. *The study of social dialects in American English*. New Jersey: Prentice-Hall.

5

Black Women in the Rural South: Conservative and Innovative

Patricia C. Nichols

Recent sociolinguistic studies have discovered sex as an important variable in language use. Prior to the 1950s little attention was given to the speaker's sex when describing linguistic systems, except in a few European studies and some descriptions of more exotic languages. This paper will examine briefly the orientation of several sociolinguistic studies which have looked at sex-related language differences, and will present data from a more recent study of a black population in rural South Carolina. I will suggest both culture-specific and crosscultural reasons for the linguistic differences which have been found for men and women.

One of the first studies to recognize the importance of studying differences in speech behavior between members of a small group who engaged in frequent face-to-face interaction was Fischer's 1958 comparison of boys' and girls' use of *ing/in* participle endings. This study of playmates in a semi-rural New England village revealed that girls consistently used more of the standard-prestige *-ing* ending than boys. Labov later found similar patterns for men and women in the much larger and more diverse population of New York City. His 1966 dissertation found, however, that women's linguistic behavior differed from that of men's in two general ways: in careful speech women used fewer stigmatized forms, but in shifting between casual and careful styles, women showed sharper shifts from stigmatized forms to prestige forms than did men. Lower middle-class women showed the most extreme style shifts. Studies in Detroit confirmed women's greater use of prestige forms. Shuy, Wolfram and Riley (1968) found women using the prestigious *-ing* ending more than twice as often as men among the general urban population of Detroit, while Wolfram (1969) found that, for the black speakers of that city, females within each social class used forms closer to standard norms than did males. A study of the black working-class population of Washington, D.C., however, did not find females to use more standard forms than males; Fasold (1972) reported either no difference or slightly more use of standard forms by males. Other studies of whites in urban centers have found women to use more prestigious forms than men. In North Carolina, Levine and Crockett's study (1967) of a Piedmont community found equal use of the postvocalic *r*, a prestige form for that region, for both men and women in reading sentences. In a more formal word-list style, women used the feature more frequently than men. Sankoff and Cedergren (1971) found women in Montreal using the standard Canadian French liquid *l* more frequently than men generally, although younger professional women used it less than older women within their class. In Norwich, England, Trudgill (1972, revised version reprinted in this volume, p. 21; 1974) found women to use the standard-prestige *-ing* ending more frequently than men.

Besides these studies of sex differences in use of prestige features which show women to exhibit more conservative linguistic behavior than men generally, studies of sound changes have been made which indicate that women exhibit innovative behavior and are far ahead of men in this portion of the language. Labov, Yaeger and Steiner (1972) have found women more advanced than men for several sound changes in a variety of U.S. communities. How are we to explain these two tendencies of women speakers, both the use of standard-prestige features and the spread of new sounds?

Several explanations have been advanced. Labov and Trudgill have suggested that women are 'linguistically insecure'. Trudgill elaborates on this point by observing that women achieve status in western societies more on the basis of how they look than on what they do. Use of prestigious language might be seen as one of women's limited means of achieving and signaling status, particularly in more formal situations. More recently, Labov (1972: 304) has postulated that the wide expressive range exhibited by women may be understood in terms of linguistic behavior considered more appropriate for one sex than for the other. Shuy (1970: 856) expresses general despair at arriving at some satisfactory explanation, with the comment, 'Women continue to be one of the mysteries of the universe.'

In addition to the general problem of failing to find convincing explanations for the seemingly paradoxical behavior of women speakers, most of these previous sociolinguistic studies exhibit three serious methodological problems. The most serious is that of methods used to assign women to particular social classes. In examining methods currently used for social stratification, some sociologists recently have maintained that no present method permits accurate classification of women in modern societies (Watson and Barth 1964; Acker 1973). Typically, occupation is the measure most heavily used as a major index of social class, and the family is arbitrarily taken to be the primary social unit. Most of the sociolinguistic studies discussed here have followed this practice, using the occupation of head of household as a major index of an entire family's social class. Problems are raised by the presence of unmarried women and widows. Some of the studies assign widows the occupation of their dead husbands. Single women are variously assigned their own occupations (typically low-status), their father's occupations, or are systematically eliminated from the study because of the problems they pose for classification (see Levine and Crockett 1967). Obvious problems are raised when trying to compare the speech of women in one study with that of women in another, particularly for single women. In addition, there is actually little or no evidence to support the general assumption that married women belong to the same social class as their husbands (Acker 1973). The social stratification procedures used raise questions about the validity of comparing men's and women's speech both within classes and from study to study. No sociolinguistic research has overtly dealt with these issues.

Related to the problem of social stratification is the seriousness with which sex is treated as a variable. Most studies have not taken care to match speakers for age and sex, as well as for social class. Those studies with a disproportion of one sex in some age groups, such as Fasold's (1972), have reported difficulties in drawing valid conclusions about sex differences in language use. While Labov has been in the forefront of recognizing the importance of sex differences as a factor in linguistic change, his New York study included far more women than men overall; his lowest class contained more than twice as many women as men, while his highest class contained almost twice as many men as women. His more recent studies have concentrated on speech used in male social groups. Trudgill uses an equal number of male and female speakers, but does not give figures on their distribution by social class. The studies of Fischer (1958) and of Sankoff and Cedergren (1971) are exceptions to the general failure to match speakers for both sex and age, within larger social groups.

A final methodological problem has been the general lack of discussion about community norms for language use. Labov has been an exception on this point, taking care to establish from his data the norms for a social group. Little discussion has been devoted to the problem of comparing linguistic behavior from group to group for the two sexes. Use of a given feature may represent conservative linguistic behavior within one social group and innovative behavior within another. To take only one obvious example, use of the *-ing* ending may mean preservation of an older form for a white middle class group, but introduction of a new form for a black working class group. The question of differences in community norms needs much fuller examination in order for sex differences in language use to be characterized accurately.

For the rural black population which I studied in coastal South Carolina for a five-month period in 1974–75, the use of standard-prestige features was innovative behavior. The language variety spoken by blacks in Georgetown County has been variously called 'Gullah', 'Geechee', or 'Sea Island Creole'. It has developed historically from a pidgin based on both English and West African languages, spoken by the earliest African immigrants to this region. The language now used by blacks in this region constitutes a post-creole continuum (see DeCamp 1971) which encompasses creole, non-standard, and standard varieties of English. The three syntactic variables chosen for study and their Gullah realizations were:

(1) the *for-to* complementizer
   'I come *for* get my coat.'

(2) the static-locative preposition *at*
   'Can we stay *to* the table?'

(3) the third person singular pronoun *it*
   'Well, *ee* was a fun to me.'
   'Over there, they call *um* over the island.'

Based on previous studies of Gullah (Turner 1949; Cunningham 1970), the use of standard forms for these variables would be innovative for most black speakers in the isolated rural area I chose for study. Use of creole variants would be maintenance of archaic forms. More detailed linguistic analysis of these variables is provided elsewhere (Nichols 1976).

In order to become familiar with the natural age and social groups within the community I had initially selected, I obtained an unpaid job in the elementary school. Influenced by the concept of 'action anthropology', as discussed by Piddington (1960) and others, I sought to act in some functional capacity within the community under study. After several months of observing the language used by school children and participating in varied community activities, I recognized three subgroups within the black population, which constituted approximately half of the total county population. The all-black community of a river island accessible only by boat remained the primary focus of my study, but I recognized that two distinct mainland groups existed within the total black population. One of these groups was composed of the educated elite of the black community and included teachers, preachers, political figures, businessmen, and school board members; most of these families had owned land for several generations. The second mainland group had far less education (often none for older members), held laboring jobs, and usually had not owned land for more than one generation. The island community fell somewhere in between the two mainland groups, having kinspeople in both, with educational and economic levels about those of the lowest group but with no professional jobs among island residents. I subsequently included older members from the lower mainland group in my study, along with adults in three age groups from the island community.

The population of the river island was approximately two hundred, composed of several large families who owned land there and contributed to the support of a community church which was the center of much of the social life of the island. Residents engaged in frequent face-to-face interaction in church activities, meetings and parties in the abandoned schoolhouse, daily boat rides to mainland jobs and to mainland schools, and constant walks from the boat landing to homes at the interior of the island. The standard of living has been steadily rising since the forties, when subsistence rice farming was abandoned with the availability of motorized transportation. Daily commuting to mainland jobs is now the practice, with most families having at least two working members. Some jobs, particularly for women, are seasonal in nature, however. Electricity became available in the last decade, and a telephone cable was installed three years ago, bringing closer ties with the mainland. The level of education has risen since the county provided bus and boat transportation to county secondary schools about two decades ago.

Recordings of language used in the island community and one mainland group were made after I had become fairly well known and had observed daily life in both groups for several months. I taught a volunteer composition class on the island one night a week, which gave me the opportunity to be in that community regularly in a functional capacity and brought me into contact with younger adults of high school

Table 1 Non-standard variants used for *for-to*, *at*, and *it*

	Speakers	Non-standard variants used for:					
		for-to		at		it	
		NS/tot	%NS	NS/tot	%NS	NS/tot	%NS
65–90 yrs mainland	f. SS	8/12	(.66)	7/7	(1.00)	6/10	(.60)
	f. SG	17/26	(.65)	17/20	(.85)	32/37	(.85)
	m. BD	1/5	(.20)	7/10	(.70)	12/20	(.60)
	m. MW	0/3	(.00)	2/4	(.50)	5/6	(.83)
65–90 yrs island	f. MC	3/7	(.43)	3/6	(.50)	4/30	(.13)
	f. MN	0/8	(.00)	3/5	(.60)	0/16	(.00)
	m. JW	3/28	(.11)	7/10	(.70)	21/77	(.27)
	m. JH	2/30	(.06)	9/11	(.82)	13/31	(.41)
30–50 yrs island	f. TW	0/7	(.00)	0/1	(.00)	0/5	(.00)
	f. GF	0/7	(.00)	1/3	(.33)	0/32	(.00)
	m. GW	0/24	(.00)	4/7	(.57)	13/75	(.17)
	m. JT	0/11	(.00)	6/7	(.86)	2/5	(.40)
15–25 yrs island	f. CW	0/3	(.00)	2/2	(1.00)	0/5	(.00)
	f. JTTT	0/36	(.00)	0/13	(.00)	0/57	(.00)
	m. JW	2/11	(.18)	3/4	(.75)	2/5	(.40)
	m. JTT	2/11	(.18)	0/1	(.00)	5/47	(.11)

age and slightly older. I determined that the ages fell into natural groups of older adults who no longer worked outside the home and remained on the island most of the time; middle-age adults, with growing families, who commuted off the island daily; and young adults, not yet married, who engaged in social or school activities with each other. From each of these three groups I chose two men and two women to record in unstructured conversations of less than thirty minutes each. I was a participant in all of the conversations, together with other family members who happened to be present. All recordings were made with the knowledge of the participants, in their own homes. Subject matter with older residents was primarily history and customs; with middle-age, history and child-rearing practices; with younger adults, future plans and comparison of their childhood and their siblings'. No formal questionnaire was used, but efforts were made to learn the approximate age of the speaker and the amount of traveling he or she had done. For the mainland group, recordings were made of two men and two women in the older group only. Table 1 shows the frequency with which each variable was used by each speaker, according to sex and age, for the three island groups and the one mainland group. For each variable, the number of times non-standard variants were used is compared with the total possible times they could have been used; the figure in parentheses is the percentage of non-standard variants used.

Comparison of the figures for the oldest adults in both mainland and island communities indicates that women from the mainland group show more conservative linguistic behavior than mainland men, while those from the island are more innovative than the men. Mainland women use more archaic forms for the two variables *for-to* and *at*, while the two sexes are about the same for the other variable. Island women use fewer archaic forms than island men for variables *at* and *it*. One island woman, MC, uses more archaic forms for the variable *for-to* than either island man, but fewer nevertheless than both mainland women. MC is perhaps a transitional figure for island women, since she was confined to the island for most of her young life and engaged in work off the island only later in her life, when motor boats became more widely used. MN, the other island woman in the oldest age group, lived off the island for a portion of her young married life. In addition, both her mother and an aunt had some college education, although she herself had not. The two island men had worked and lived off the island for brief portions of their young adulthood, before and after marriage, with JW spending a five-year period away on a shipyard job during World War II. JH was the only island adult I encountered who had had no schooling. For the mainland group, both educational levels and mobility were lower. Only the man, BD, had attended school in this group; he had also lived outside the area for a time and had held better jobs than the other three mainland adults. The two older women in this group had done domestic work all their lives, and both were now caring for 'grands' for assorted relatives who either worked in the area or lived out of state. SS was the daughter of a former slave and had worked for one family, on the same plantation, all her life. The other older man, MW, had moved into the area as a young man and had worked on the same plantation for fifty years of his life; he had relatives on the river island.

In other age groups, island women were also more linguistically innovative than island men. For the middle-age group, women used more standard forms for *at* and *it*, while neither sex used archaic variants for the *for-to* complementizer – perhaps the most stigmatized of the three variables. In the youngest age group, males used non-standard forms for *for-to* and *it*, while females used none. Use of *at* was about the same for both sexes in this group. (*At* is probably the least stigmatized of the variables, since at least one member of both sexes in every age group uses some non-standard variant of it.) JTT and JTTT, a brother and sister who have jobs entailing conversation with diverse people, use no non-standard variants for *at*, while CW and JW, another brother and sister still in high school, both use some. In three different age groups for the island community, then, linguistic variation on selected syntactic forms suggests that women are moving toward standard-prestige forms faster than island men.

Both culture-specific and crosscultural explanations can be suggested for these differences in language use for the two sexes. For the particular communities in which these people live, the two sexes have very real differences in occupational opportunities. All island women work outside the home at some time during their lives, as do most black women in the area. Two of the top five occupations open to black women in the state are white-collar and require use of the standard language variety, while all of the top occupations open to black men are blue-collar and require few language-related tasks. Since the median salary for black women in the state for 1970 census figures is less than half that for black men, there is incentive for women to train for the available higher paying jobs. With good clerical skills or with a college education, a woman can make almost as much as some blue-collar construction workers; hence, many families invest in higher education for their daughters rather than for their sons, since the job choices for women have been basically domestic work or teaching. Island men sometimes attend trade school, but never college; most middle-age men work at good-paying jobs in the construction industry. In the mainland group studied, the low level of education characteristic of this group limits women to domestic or other low-paying jobs involving physical labor. Men in this group work at both unskilled labor within the community or at factory jobs in town, which entail some interaction with a more diverse population than that encountered by women in their group. Thus, for both groups studied, differences in occupational choices available to the sexes are associated with differences in linguistic experiences, though in different directions for each community. The standard language used by island women reflects their attraction to occupations requiring language-related tasks, as well as their membership in an economically mobile community. Mainland women, who have had no similar opportunities for change, maintain more archaic forms than the relatively more mobile men in their group.

On a crosscultural level, recent anthropological analyses have pointed out that men and women universally occupy different positions within their cultural and social groups, in terms of public authority and central cultural values of the group (Rosaldo 1974; Ortner 1974). Rosaldo has observed that women are considered anomalous figures by many societies. For both social groups studied here, women occupy lower relative positions than men in terms of earning power, occupational choices, and geographic mobility. Men hold more authority within their families, churches, and local government, while women are in charge of the domestic sphere and assume less public authority than men of their age. While women in one group hold higher status jobs than men, and lower status jobs than men in the other group, linguistic patterns are similar in that the sexes speak differently in both cases. Linguists have long understood that the interaction of language and social life has important consequences for linguistic behavior (Ferguson 1959; Hymes 1967, 1973). Hymes observes that inequality among speakers arises because some speakers participate in social situations not available to other speakers. If women are universally limited in their exercise of public authority, as Rosaldo suggests, we must expect certain linguistic consequences to follow from the different life experiences of the two sexes. Men and women will speak differently from each other in every social group.

A more adequate sociology of women will enable us to understand the linguistic behavior of women as a reflection of their peripheral status within their communities. The present study suggests that women lag behind men in the adoption of new forms within traditional, relatively stable societies. In more mobile groups, like that of the island community here, we might expect women to be in advance of men. Perhaps in transitional groups, women will exhibit both conservative and innovative behavior. Whatever the particular pattern, language used by women must be dealt with in terms of the social roles available to women rather than dismissed as one of the great mysteries of the universe.

REFERENCES

Acker, Joan (1973), 'Women and social stratification: A case of intellectual sexism', *American Journal of Sociology* 78: 936–45.

Cunningham, Irma (1970), 'A syntactic analysis of Sea Island Creole ("Gullah")'. Unpublished University of Michigan dissertation.

DeCamp, David (1971), 'Toward a generative analysis of a post-creole speech continuum', in D. Hymes (ed.), *Pidginization and Creolization of Languages*. Cambridge, Cambridge University Press.

Fasold, Ralph (1972), *Tense Marking in Black English: A Linguistic and Social Analysis*. Washington, D.C., Center for Applied Linguistics.

Ferguson, Charles A. (1959), 'Diglossia', *Word* 15: 325–40.

Fischer, John L. (1958), 'Social influence in the choice of a linguistic variant', *Word* 14: 47–56.

Hymes, Dell (1967), 'Models of the interaction of language and social setting', *Journal of Social Issues* 23: 8–28.

——(1973), 'On the origins and foundations of inequality among speakers', *Daedalus* 102: 59–86.

Labov, William (1966), *The Social Stratification of English in New York City*. Washington, D.C., Center for Applied Linguistics.

——(1972), *Sociolinguistic Patterns*. Philadelphia, University of Pennsylvania Press.

Labov, William, Yaeger, Malcah, and Steiner, Richard (1972), *A Quantitative Study of Sound Change in Progress*. Philadelphia, U.S. Regional Survey.

Levine, Lewis, and Crockett, Harry J., Jr. (1967), 'Speech variation in a Piedmont community: Postvocalic r', in S. Lieberson (ed.), *Explorations in Sociolinguistics*. Bloomington, Indiana University.

Nichols, Patricia C. (1976), 'Linguistic change in Gullah: Sex, age, and mobility'. Unpublished Stanford University dissertation.

Ortner, Sherry (1974), 'Is female to male as nature is to culture?', in M. Rosaldo and L. Lamphere (eds.), *Women, Culture and Society*. Palo Alto, Stanford University Press.

Piddington, Ralph (1960), 'Action anthropology', *Journal of the Polynesian Society* 69: 199–213. In J. Clifton (ed.), *Applied Anthropology: Readings in the Use of the Science of Man*. Boston, Houghton Mifflin Co. (1970).

Rosaldo, Michelle Zimbalist (1974), 'Women, culture, and society: A theoretical overview', in M. Rosaldo and L. Lamphere (eds), *Women, Culture and Society*. Palo Alto, Stanford University Press.

Sankoff, Gillian, and Cedergren, Henrietta (1971), 'Some results of a sociolinguistic study of Montreal French', in R. Darnell (ed.), *Linguistic Diversity in Canadian Society*. Edmonton, Linguistic Research, Inc., 61–87.

Shuy, Roger (1970), 'Sociolinguistic research at the Center for Applied Linguistics: The correlation of language and sex', *International Days of Sociolinguistics*. Rome, Instituto Luigi Sturzo, 849–57.

Shuy, Roger, Wolfram, Walt, and Riley, William K. (1968), *Field Techniques in an Urban Language Study*. Washington, D.C., Center for Applied Linguistics.

Trudgill, Peter (1972), 'Sex, covert prestige and linguistic change in the urban British English of Norwich', *Language in Society* 1: 179–95.

——(1974), *The Social Differentiation of English in Norwich*. Cambridge, Cambridge University Press.

Turner, Lorenzo (1949), *Africanisms in the Gullah Dialect*. Chicago, University of Chicago Press.

U.S. Bureau of the Census (1973), 'Subject reports: Negro population'. *1970 Census of Population*.

Watson, Walter, and Barth, Ernest (1964), 'Questionable assumptions in the theory of social stratification', *Pacific Sociological Review* 7: 10–16.

Wolfram, Walt (1969), *A Sociolinguistic Description of Detroit Negro Speech*. Washington, D.C., Center for Applied Linguistics.

6

Gender and Sociolinguistic Variation

Penelope Eckert

Sociolinguistic Variation

We generally think of language as a means of communicating referential meaning – for telling each other what we think, what we want, what we see. The linguistic system is also constructed in such a way as to create resources for the expression of social meaning – nuances of emotion, attitude, social identity – without actually stating it in so many words. One of the subtlest of these resources is what is referred to as *sociolinguistic variation*, particularly phonological variation, or what is commonly referred to as "accent." Phonological variation, or nuances of pronunciation, can signal important information about aspects of speakers' social identity – about such things as class, age, ethnicity and gender. This chapter will explore the manifestations of gender in phonological variation, and the interactions between gender and some other aspects of identity.

I begin with a very brief description of phonological variation, taking as an example a well-known instance from American English. In the midwest, as in many parts of the United States, the vowel in *bad*, *ham* and *rag* can be pronounced as [æ] – the way it is pronounced in RP, or by careful newscasters in the US. It can also be pronounced as a high front vowel [e] or as a diphthong [eᵊ] or even [iᵊ], sounding much like the vowel in *beer*. This variability does not change the identity of the word – it has no effect on its referential meaning. A [hiᵊm] is every bit as much a smoked (or salted) pig's thigh as a [hæm], but the difference in pronunciation carries social meaning. The nature of this social meaning, particularly with respect to gender, is the subject of this chapter.

The most common approach to variation is to view variables as constituting a continuum between "standard" and "vernacular" language. [hæm] is what we call the "standard" pronunciation in American English, whereas [hiᵊm] is called "non-standard" or "vernacular." Standard pronunciations are part of the standard language – the variety of language that is associated with education, central government, and other institutions of national or global power. In opposition to the standard is what is commonly called the vernacular, the language of locally based communities – most people's everyday language. The vernacular has local and regional features – features that are muted in the standard. The closer a person's speech is to the standard the more difficult it is to tell where he or she is from; the closer to the vernacular, the stronger and more identifiable their regional or local accent. The difference between standard and vernacular is not abrupt, but a matter of degree. The phonetic continuum between [æ] and [iˀ], for example, offers a range of possible pronunciations that lie somewhere in between the most standard and the most vernacular pronunciation. All speakers use a range of these pronunciations, varying in their use depending on who they're talking to, the topic, the degree of formality, etc. At the same time, the range of variants that a given speaker uses in this way reflects where she or he falls in the social matrix.

While the standard variety is associated with the people, settings and institutions of social and economic power, the non-standard variety is associated with locally based communities. The heart of these communities is in the working class and the lower middle class – in social networks based in local neighborhoods and workplaces (see Milroy 1980 for a thorough discussion of the relation between social class, social networks, and the use of the vernacular). The local vernacular has all the flavor of the community, and it both constructs and evokes solidarity among the community's members.

Since there is a relation between such broad social categorizations as socioeconomic class and the extent to which one's life is based in local networks, sociolinguistic variation is associated simultaneously with broad social categories like class, and with nuances of local meaning within communities. For example, in a study of Martha's Vineyard, an island off the coast of Massachusetts, William Labov (1972) found a relation between the use of vernacular features and local identity. Speakers who identified with the local traditional fishing culture used more of the vernacular features than people who identified with the emerging mainland-oriented tourist economy. Thus, the vernacular can be associated not simply with place, but with quite local issues.

Quantitative studies of correlations between linguistic variables and the social characteristics of speakers have shown a set of patterns that recur from community to community in the industrialized world. The best-known set of findings in this correlational enterprise has been class stratification. Predictably, as one moves up the socioeconomic hierarchy, people produce an increasing percentage of standard pronunciations (see, e.g., Labov 1966; Macaulay 1977; Trudgill 1974). But while the study of variation has traditionally focused on socioeconomic class, it has emerged that gender is at least as powerful a force in patterns of sociolinguistic variation. The traditional focus on class, however, has led many researchers to treat gender as secondary, and as independent of other social variables. This is not only a result of a particular academic practice, but of popular thought about gender. It is traditional to think of gender as oppositional – indeed, the expression "the opposite sex" is the only colloquial way to refer to the other sex. Gender is commonly thought of, therefore, as independent of other aspects of identity as well, so that being male or female is commonly thought to have the same effect on people's behavior, identities, etc. regardless of age, ethnicity, social class etc. But (as emphasized by Eckert and McConnell-Ginet in this volume, p. 484) gender practices differ considerably from culture to culture, from place to place, from group to group, living at the intersection of all the other aspects of social identity. Nonetheless, it has become commonplace to speak of "men's speech" and "women's speech" – even of "men's language" and "women's language." Because gender is viewed as independent of other aspects of identity, it has been common practice to generalize on the basis of observations in a restricted population, and it has also been common practice to interpret gross statistical gender differences as reflecting a pure gender effect. The use of statistics in an area as understudied as gender can lead researchers down a garden path of naive assumption, encouraging them to attribute things to gender that may well be more closely related to other aspects of identity. One particular difficulty with a heavy-handed use of statistics is that explanations frequently lie in the exceptions, which are just the cases that statistical studies tend to ignore.

Is Women's Speech More Conservative?

One of the most popular generalizations about male and female speech is the common claim that women's speech is more conservative than men's. And connected to this popular generalization is a series of popular explanations for it: e.g. women are status-conscious or polite, men are rough and down-to-earth. Since the generalization that women's speech is more conservative than men's is not entirely accurate, it is important to examine the ways in which it is true and false, and to consider the nature of possible explanations for the patterns that do emerge.

The patterns in phonological variation are quite heterogeneous. However, there is one fairly general observation that can be made (Labov 1991). Certain sociolinguistic variables have been around for generations: the so-called "stable" variables such as the variation between *walking* and *walkin'*, or between *this* and *dis*, *that* and *dat*. Women tend to be more standard overall in their use of these variables than men. Other variables are a reflection of the progress of linguistic change (the raising of (ae) discussed above is one such variable). Men are frequently more conservative than women in their use of these variables. As we move away from phonological variation to the use of grammatical variables, such as negative concord (e.g. *I didn't do anything* vs. *I didn't do nothing*), women's usage is considerably more standard, or conservative, than men's. It is significant that these grammatical variables are quite clearly consciously recognized and stigmatized, and far more so than the phonological variables. These differences suggest that conservatism is not an all-or-nothing phenomenon. A variety of explanations have been proposed for women's more conservative usages.

One important factor in people's use of variation is their relation to linguistic "markets." The notion of a symbolic market, developed by Pierre Bourdieu and Luc Boltanski (1975) and extended to the study of variation by David Sankoff and

Suzanne Laberge (1978), builds on the importance of symbolic capital for success in functioning in different parts of society. One will have little chance of succeeding in the diplomatic corps if one does not possess a range of knowledge that marks one as the "right kind" of person: the right table manners, the right style of dress, the right ways of entertaining guests, the right language. While the work of Bourdieu focuses on the symbolic capital of elites, this is equally true if one is to be accepted in a peasant village or in an urban ghetto (Woolard 1985) – what is "right" depends on the market in which one is engaged.

From the start, women and men overall stand in very different relations to linguistic markets. Peter Trudgill's account (1972, revised version reprinted in this volume, p. 21) of gender differences in the pronunciation of English in Norwich found women overall to be more conservative in their use of almost all variables. He speculated that this was because of women's exclusion from the workplace. According to Trudgill, because women's position in society is generally subordinate to men's, and because women have fewer opportunities to secure their positions through occupational success or other abilities, they find it necessary to use symbolic means to enhance their position.

While overall exclusion from the workplace may throw women onto symbolic means of establishing a place in the world, the workplace itself also has a variety of ways of constraining women to use more standard language. While standard language is crucial to performing many white-collar jobs, it is more generally crucial to the kinds of jobs that Sankoff et al. (1989) refer to as "technicians of language" – writers, academics, secretaries, receptionists. The earliest white-collar employment of women as teachers puts women's work squarely in the standard language market. But outside of education as well, many women's jobs require standard language by virtue of the function of these jobs as "front end" workers. Secretaries, receptionists, flight attendants and hostesses all make their living by representing an organization to its clients. In some important sense, they are part of the organization's symbolic capital. Thus for women, the need for standard language is not restricted to prestigious or higher paid occupations.

And what of women in the more prestigious occupations? To the extent that men dominate institutions, and particularly elite institutions, one might think of them as more engaged in the standard language market. However, one might also consider that to the same extent, men have greater legitimacy in these institutions, while women moving into them are generally seen as interlopers, and are at greater pains to prove that they belong. One means for proving worthiness is meticulous attention to symbolic capital – hence the millions made in self-help books to help professional women "dress for success." The more meticulous use of standard language, by the same token – "talking for success" – could make women's speech more conservative than their male peers'.

Margaret Deuchar (1989) argues that women's place in society more generally makes them more vulnerable to criticism, and that the more meticulous use of standard language could be seen as a way of being "beyond reproach." This has particular meaning in the light of Walt Wolfram's findings in his study (1969) of variation in the Detroit African American community. Wolfram found women at all socioeconomic levels to be more conservative in the use of features of African American Vernacular English (AAVE) than men. This gender pattern is overwhelmingly consistent, and more consistent than has been found in any other speech community. It is worth considering that among women in our society, African American women are the most subject to denigration, and that their very systematic use of standard language may well be a response to their greater social vulnerability. This argument is related to Penelope Brown's analysis (1980, reprinted in this volume, p. 81) of women's politeness in a Mayan community, in which she argues that women employ forms of politeness towards men as a strategy to avoid physical abuse.

In the above cases, we are focusing on women's place with respect to the standard language market. But women are vernacular speakers as well. Nonetheless, description of the social meaning of the vernacular has commonly focused on the relation between the vernacular and masculinity. Peter Trudgill (1972) has argued that men's use of the vernacular is associated with the general value among men of the toughness or physical prowess associated with working-class masculinity. But working-class culture and the local marketplace has to do with much more than toughness and masculinity. Perhaps more important is the role of know-how in locally based networks. The vernacular is commonly associated with blue-collar professions – not only people who work on the factory floor, but people who keep the infrastructure operating: mechanics, electricians, plumbers, construction workers. These are people whose skills are essential to the well-being of our day-to-day physical environment. The vernacular is associated, then, with a range of capabilities for functioning in the physical world – capabilities that include, but extend well beyond, physical power. And many of these capabilities are shared by men and women. It is notable, though, that the occupations traditionally available to, and associated with, women in the local market – such as cleaning, sewing, cooking and childcare – are as essential and often as skilled as men's work in the equivalent market, but not equally valued. Thus in the vernacular market, as in the standard language market, women's pursuits are marginalized, hence marginalizing women's claims to social centrality. If marginalization in the standard language market leads women to use more standard language, one might expect marginalization in the local market to lead women to use more vernacular.

This relatively abstract discussion of gender and the linguistic market makes it clear that we cannot understand the relation between variation and gender unless we explore quite concrete situations. To this purpose, the following discussion will examine some patterns of variation in a well-defined adolescent population, with the purpose of seeing the linguistic relation between gender and other aspects of social identity.

Belten High

Belten High is a comprehensive public high school in the suburbs of Detroit, serving 2,000 predominantly white students from families ranging from working-class through upper middle-class. In most social science studies, children are assigned their parents' (usually their fathers') socioeconomic status. But adolescents are not just their parents' children – they are moving into their adult identities. The transition from parents' class to one's own commonly begins in school, and is articulated through one's forms of participation in the school. In Belten High, as in many high schools across the US, two class-based social categories dominate discourses of adolescent identity. Some students, primarily college-bound, participate enthusiastically in school, particularly in the extracurricular sphere; others, primarily bound for the blue-collar workplace, reject the school's pretentions to be a total institution, and base their lives and activities outside of school in the neighborhood and in the broader local urban–suburban area. These categories commonly have names, and in Belten High, as in high schools throughout the Detroit suburbs in the 1980s, the members of the school-oriented category were referred to (and referred to themselves) as *jocks* while the locally oriented category were referred to (and referred to themselves) as *burnouts*. The jocks constitute a middle-class culture, oriented to the global market that the school and its college- and career-bound emphasis represents. Spending most of their time in school, and engaged in the institutional enterprise, the jocks are very much in the standard language marketplace. The burnouts constitute a working-class culture, engaging in the school's downplayed vocational curriculum but minimizing their time in school in favor of independent engagement in the local and urban scene.

The jocks and the burnouts, together accounting for just less than half the students in the school, constitute mutually opposed and relatively hostile categories. This opposition is constructed through a broad range of symbolic means, from territory to clothing, hairdo, substance use, musical tastes and friendship patterns (for a full account of these categories, see Eckert 1989). And while many people are neither jocks nor burnouts, the importance of these two categories is underscored by the fact that almost all students in the school who are neither jocks nor burnouts are referred to (and refer to themselves) as *in-betweens*, and describe themselves in relation to those two categories.

Each of these categories is composed of several social network clusters, and roughly equal numbers of boys and girls. The categories began in late elementary school as two separate, and somewhat rival, heterosexual crowds, surfacing in junior high school as full-blown opposed social categories. The jocks and the burnouts constitute communities of practice, based in very different (and class-based) responses to the school institution. They are distinguished not simply by their attitudes towards school, but by a range of differences in social practice, some of them quite profound. The jocks and the burnouts are continually engaged in a mutual process of meaning-making, as individuals engage among themselves in making sense of who they are, why they're together, and what their place is in the world.

Eckert and McConnell-Ginet (1995) discuss at some length the complexities of the interactions among gender and social category in Belten High. The resources and constraints for girls' and boys' actions and construction of identities are radically different. Just as women are marginalized in the adult marketplace, so are girls in the adolescent marketplace. Most specifically, boys' actions and roles are defining of the jock and burnout categories, just as men's actions and occupations are defining of the adult professional and blue-collar worlds. While a boy can build a highly valued jock identity through athletics, a girl cannot (or could not in the early 1980s, when this work was done). And while a boy can build a highly valued burnout image by rumbling in the streets of Detroit, with dirt biking or working on his car, a girl cannot. Jock girls can gain status only through participation in the school social sphere – student government, cheerleading, organizing dances – all of which are seen as secondary, or even auxiliary, to boys' varsity athletics. Legitimized activities are harder for burnout girls to find, since there are relatively few interesting non-school activities open to girls. Rather, burnout girls gain status through their social skill, their networks, and their reputation for daring and fun. Furthermore, while a boy can gain importance and popularity without good looks, a girl cannot; and while a boy can experiment with quasi-legal behavior and maintain (perhaps even enhance) his status as a jock, a girl who does risks not only her status as a jock but her closest friendships. There is little latitude for jock and burnout girls to stray into each other's territories – a jock girl who behaves in the least like a burnout will be labelled a "slut," while a burnout girl who behaves in the least like a jock will be labelled a "snob." The relation between female jocks and burnouts, then, is truly a relation of opposition and avoidance. On the other hand, the relation between male jocks and burnouts is more one of competition around physical prowess. While the jocks establish their physical prowess through school sports, the burnouts establish theirs sometimes through independent sports, but more saliently through fighting ability and urban know-how. Jock and burnout boys, therefore, represent something of a mutual threat, since each is recognized for a different and important aspect of masculine physical capability.

Sociolinguistic Variation in Belten High

Virtually all of the students of Belten High speak a local version of white Anglo American English. To illustrate the range of gender dynamics in variation, I will focus on three vowels that show flux in this dialect: (ae) as in *bad*, (uh) as in *cut*, and (ay) as in *fight*.[1] As described above, the variable (ae) ranges from a conservative pronunciation [æ] to a raised variant [e], so that *bad* sounds more like *bade*. (uh) ranges from its conservative pronunciation [ʌ] to a backed pronunciation [ɔ], making *cut* sound more like *caught*. Finally, the diphthong (ay) monophthongizes to [a:] so that, for example, *right* sounds like a drawn-out pronunciation of *rot*. All speakers in Belten High produce a range of variants for each of these three variables. What differs from speaker to speaker, or from group to group, is the frequency with which they produce the different variants. In the following discussion, I will refer to raised (ae), backed (uh) and monophthongized (ay) as advanced (vernacular) variants.

Just as jocks and burnouts differ in their relation to the urban area, so do the linguistic variables. Belten High sits in the midst of the urban sprawl that surrounds

Table 1   Correlations of three phonological variables with gender and social category as independent variables

Variable	Girls	Boys	Burnouts	Jocks	Input	Significance
(ae)	0.573	0.438	—	—	0.371	0.000
(ay)	0.426	0.555	—	—	0.072	0.006
(uh)	—	—	0.571	0.437	0.494	0.000

Detroit, a vast social landscape, and as discussed above, an important part of social practice in the urban–suburban continuum involves orientation towards the city of Detroit. An important aspect of the social meaning of variables, therefore, is to be found in the distribution of uses of variants in the urban–suburban area. The backing of (uh) and the monophthongization of (ay) are considerably more advanced as one moves closer to Detroit, while the raising of (ae) is more advanced as one moves away from Detroit (Eckert forthcoming). Thus while (ay) and (uh) can be associated with urban white speech, (ae) is more closely related to the suburbs. For this reason, I refer to (ay) and (uh) as urban variables, and (ae) as a suburban variable.

As shown in table 1, these three variables show different statistical patterns across the population of jocks and burnouts in Belten High. The figures in this table represent the results of a variable rule analysis,[2] indicating the relative rates of use of advanced variants by categories of speakers.[3] Table 1 treats gender and social category as independent variables, following a common statistical approach to gender and variation. This mode of analysis assumes that gender and social category membership have completely independent effects on language use – that gender and social category are separable. Each of these three variables shows a quite different pattern of correlation with gender and social category. In the case of (ae) and (ay), only gender correlates significantly with the use of advanced variants, with opposite effects: girls lead in the raising of (ae) and boys lead in the monophthongization of (ay). In the case of (uh), only social category shows a significant correlation, with burnouts leading jocks in the use of advanced variants. On the basis of table 1, one might be tempted to say that (ae) is a "female marker", (ay) is a "male marker", and (uh) is a "burnout marker." If we assume that social category and gender are inseparable, though, we might do well to examine the behavior of male and female jocks and burnouts separately, as shown in table 2. The figures shown in table 2, and displayed graphically in figure 1, paint a very different picture of the use of these variables. There is a clear and quite complex interaction between gender, social category, and local orientation. While the gender differentiation of (ae) and (ay) is overwhelming and clearly greater than the social category differentiation, it is also clear that these variables are not simply gender markers. Particularly, there is an apparent relation between gender, social category, and urban–suburban orientation. Not only do boys lead in the use of the urban variable (ay), but burnouts lead jocks in its use among the girls (the jock–burnout difference among the boys is not

Table 2 Correlations of three phonological variables with gender and social category as interacting variables

| Variable | Girls | | Boys | | Input | Significance |
	Burnouts	Jocks	Burnouts	Jocks		
(ae)	0.611	0.535	0.386	0.466	0.371	0.000
(ay)	0.483	0.336	0.579	0.545	0.070	0.008
(uh)	0.619	0.418	0.532	0.450	0.494	0.000

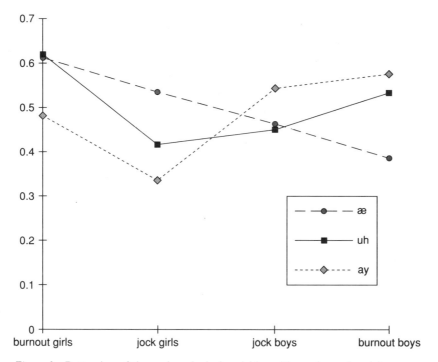

Figure 1 Patterning of three phonological variables with gender and social category

statistically significant). And not only do girls lead in the use of the suburban variable (ae), but jocks lead burnouts in its use among the boys. This makes a complex association among masculinity, burnout affiliation and urban-ness on the one hand, and femininity, jock affiliation and suburban-ness on the other. In the case of (uh) backing, gender gives way to a more straightforward relation between urban orientation and burnout affiliation.

Another, more general way of considering these data is in terms of the overall accent. The burnout girls lead the jock girls in the use of all three variables, and indeed they lead the entire population in the use of (ae) and (uh). This means that their local accent is the strongest of all the four categories of speakers. Following the burnout girls in the localness of their overall accent are the burnout boys. However, the burnout boys' extremely low values for the suburban variant (ae) leave them with a specifically urban accent. The jocks, male and female, emerge as relatively con-servative, but with the boys making greater use of the urban variables (uh) and (ay) and the girls making greater use of the suburban variable (ae). The jock boys' accent is more suburban than the burnout boys', and less than the jock girls'. The question of who is more conservative in this population, then, does not have a simple answer. But perhaps what is most striking is that the girls describe the overall envelope of variation in this community. The burnout girls are the most advanced speakers in the community overall, and the jock girls are the most conservative – if only margin-ally more conservative than the jock boys. This is consonant with the observations from earlier studies made above. The constraints on girls to conform to an exagger-ated social category type are clearly related to their diminished possibilities for claiming membership or category status. In Eckert (1990), I argued that to the extent that men control material capital, women are constrained to accumulate symbolic capital. Thus while men develop a sense of themselves and find a place in the world on the basis of their actions and abilities, women have to focus on the production of selves – to develop authority through a continual proof of worthiness. Thus the jock and the burnout girls are continually working on their jockhood and their burnouthood, refining and elaborating their mutual differences, focusing on being good jocks or burnouts, just as later in life they will no doubt be focusing on being good mothers, wives, friends – focusing on how they are, while their male peers will be focusing on what they do.

Conclusions

One important lesson from these correlations is that across-the-board differences taken alone can seriously misrepresent the social meanings of variables. We clearly cannot talk about gender independently of other aspects of social identity, as no variable correlates simply with gender or social category. The major generalization in Belten High seems to be that girls are putting these phonological resources to greater use than the boys, as the greater social polarization between jock and burnout girls emerges in a greater linguistic polarization as well. This view of gender and variation can lead to a generalization, but not a generalization that would yield a consistent male–female difference across the board that would allow statements such as "women are linguistically more conservative than men." Rather, the generalization is likely to have more to do with women's greater use of symbolic resources to establish member-ship and status. And since the communities of practice in which women are seeking status vary widely, the particular linguistic nature of these symbolic resources will vary widely as well.

NOTES

1   For a more thorough discussion of these and other variables in the same community, see Eckert (forthcoming).
2   The variable rule program, in this case Goldvarb, a multiple regression package for the analysis of linguistic variation, is described in Rousseau and Sankoff (1978). The numbers shown in the tables and figure are probabilities of the occurrence of vernacular variants, within the context of an overall probability of occurrence in the population as a whole. These numbers should be regarded as indications of relations among the speaker groups represented, rather than as absolute values of occurrence.
3   These figures are based on 50 occurrences of each variable per speaker, extracted from free-flowing tape-recorded speech. For details of the methods used in data collection and analysis in this study, see Eckert (forthcoming).

REFERENCES

Bourdieu, Pierre and Boltanski, Luc (1975) 'Le fétichisme de la langue'. *Actes de la recherche en sciences sociales*, 4, 2–32.
Brown, Penelope (1980) 'How and why are women more polite: some evidence from a Mayan community', in S. McConnell-Ginet, R. A. Borker and N. Furman (eds) *Women and Language in Literature and Society*, pp. 111–36. New York: Praeger.
Deuchar, Margaret (1989) 'A pragmatic account of women's use of standard speech', in J. Coates and D. Cameron (eds) *Women in Their Speech Communities*, pp. 27–32. London and New York: Longman.
Eckert, Penelope (1989) *Jocks and Burnouts: Social Categories and Identity in the High School*. New York: Teachers College Press.
Eckert, Penelope (1990) 'Cooperative competition in adolescent girl talk'. *Discourse Processes*, 13, 92–122.
Eckert, Penelope (forthcoming) *Variation and Social Practice: The Linguistic Construction of Social Meaning in Belten High*. Oxford: Blackwell.
Eckert, Penelope and McConnell-Ginet, Sally (1995) 'Constructing meaning, constructing selves: snapshots of language, gender and class from Belten High', in K. Hall and M. Bucholtz (eds) *Gender Articulated: Language and the Socially Constructed Self*, pp. 469–508. New York: Routledge.
Labov, William (1966) *The Social Stratification of English in New York City*. Washington, DC: Center for Applied Linguistics.
Labov, William (1972) 'The social motivation of a sound change', in W. Labov (ed.) *Sociolinguistic Patterns*, pp. 1–42. Philadelphia: University of Pennsylvania Press.
Labov, William (1991) 'The intersection of sex and social class in the course of linguistic change'. *Language Variation and Change*, 2, 2, 205–51.
Macaulay, Ronald K. S. (1977) *Language, Social Class and Education: A Glasgow Study*. Edinburgh: University of Edinburgh Press.
Milroy, Lesley (1980) *Language and Social Networks*. Oxford: Blackwell.
Rousseau, Pascale and Sankoff, David (1978) 'Advances in variable rule methodology', in D. Sankoff (ed.) *Linguistic Variation: Models and Methods*, pp. 57–70. New York: Academic Press.

Sankoff, D., Cedergren, H., Kemp, W., Thibault, P. and Vincent, D. (1989) 'Montreal French: language, class, and ideology', in W. Fasold and D. Schiffrin (eds) *Language Change and Variation*, pp. 107–18. Amsterdam: John Benjamins.

Sankoff, David and Laberge, Suzanne (1978) 'The linguistic market and the statistical explanation of variability', in D. Sankoff (ed.) *Linguistic Variation: Models and Methods*, pp. 239–50. New York: Academic Press.

Trudgill, Peter (1972) 'Sex, covert prestige and linguistic change in the urban British English of Norwich'. *Language in Society*, 1, 179–95.

Trudgill, Peter (1974) *The Social Differentiation of English in Norwich*. Cambridge: Cambridge University Press.

Wolfram, Walt (1969) *A Sociolinguistic Description of Detroit Negro Speech*. Washington, DC: Center for Applied Linguistics.

Woolard, K. (1985) 'Language variation and cultural hegemony'. *American Ethnologist*, 12, 738–48.

Part II
Gender Differences in Conversational Practice

This section is devoted to research which explores the way in which women and men characteristically draw on different strategies in conversational interaction. Such research moves away from the traditional linguistic preoccupation with phonetics/phonology and syntax/morphology to an investigation of linguistic strategies such as paying compliments, hedging, apologizing, or swearing, to mention just a few. Our knowledge as members of a speech community of how to pay a compliment or how to apologize is part of our communicative competence (Hymes 1972): we learn which linguistic forms are conventionally used to 'do' a compliment or an apology, and in what social circumstances it is appropriate to use them. The research evidence suggests that women and men develop differentiated communicative competence: in other words, women's and men's behaviour in conversation suggests that they have a different understanding of how a compliment or an apology is done. Such differences have led some researchers to talk of different female and male 'styles' in conversation. (A key work presenting such an argument is that by Maltz and Borker, included in Part VII, p. 417.)

The four papers in this section represent only a small fraction of the work carried out in recent years by researchers interested in gender differences in conversational style (for an overview, see Coates 1993). The first paper – by Penelope Brown – focuses on politeness and its linguistic realizations, drawing on the model of politeness developed by Brown and Levinson (1987). According to this model, politeness consists in respecting the face needs of others, that is, in showing consideration for other people's feelings. People have two kinds of face needs that have to be attended to in interaction: the need not to be imposed on (known as *negative face*); and the need to be liked and admired (known as *positive face*). Penelope Brown studied the language of women and men in a Mayan community in Mexico, and in her paper, 'How and Why Are Women More Polite', she tests the hypothesis that women are more polite than men, that is, more sensitive to the face needs of others. She focuses her research on a class of particles in Tzeltal (the language spoken in this community) which modify the force of the speech act. They either strengthen the force of what is said, so can roughly be translated as *I emphatically/sincerely/really . . . assert/ request/promise*, or they weaken the force of what is said, as in *I tentatively/maybe/ perhaps . . . assert/request/promise*. Her analysis reveals that the usage of women and men in this community differs systematically. She argues that this differential usage stems in part from women's awareness that, as speakers with lower status than men, what they say might be face-threatening.

The second paper in this section focuses on compliments. Janet Holmes's paper, 'Complimenting – A Positive Politeness Strategy', also draws on Brown and Levinson's model of politeness to argue that compliments are prime examples of speech acts which pay attention to the positive face needs of others. Her analysis of compliment usage in New Zealand reveals that female speakers both give and receive significantly more compliments than male speakers. This confirms research carried out in the USA and elsewhere. Holmes argues that it may be the case that women perceive compliments as positive politeness strategies while men are more ambivalent about the meaning of compliments and sometimes interpret them as face-threatening acts. Like Brown, Holmes suggests that the differential usage of women and men can be linked to women's subordinate social status.

The third paper is Marjorie Goodwin's 'Cooperation and Competition Across Girls' Play Activities'. Goodwin focuses on a single type of speech sequence, the directive, in a range of different situations (a directive is a speech act that tries to get someone to do something). This paper draws on her long-term research into the talk of black children playing on a Philadelphia street. Goodwin looks at the way the children organize their play activities, in particular, at the way they get each other to do things. She observed that, when they were engaged in a specific task activity (making slingshots), the boys preferred to use aggravated directives such as direct commands, while the girls, by contrast, preferred more mitigated forms such as *let's*. Goodwin argues that the linguistic forms used reflect (and in turn reproduce) the social organization of the group. The boys' group was hierarchically organized, with leaders using very strong directive forms to establish control, while the girls' group was non-hierarchical, with all girls participating in decision-making on an equal basis. But Goodwin is concerned to show that this is far from the whole picture: the second half of the paper examines directive usage when the girls play house. When the girls act out family relationships such as parent–child or older sibling–younger sibling, they use directives and directive-responses which accomplish asymmetry. In other words, Goodwin demonstrates that the girls have a repertoire which includes both cooperative and competitive ways of talking.

The final paper in this section, Susan Gal's 'Peasant Men Can't Get Wives', looks at a very different aspect of communicative competence, our competence in switching between different languages. Because the most powerful societies in the world are currently dominated by elite groups who are monolingual, it is sometimes forgotten that multilingualism is a common feature of societies all over the world. Where members of a speech community use two or more languages, then these languages will tend to become specialized in certain domains. Gal investigated linguistic usage in a bilingual community in eastern Austria, a community which until 1921 was part of Hungary. In this community, a shift is occurring from German–Hungarian bilingualism to German monolingualism. Hungarian was the national language until 1921, and therefore had high prestige as the language of intellectuals and of the upper classes. German, by contrast, was associated with merchants, bureaucrats, and people from other villages. Now, however, Hungarian is increasingly associated with peasant status, while knowledge of German is an economic necessity for anyone wanting employment of any kind apart from on the land. Gal's survey of linguistic usage pinpoints the fact that the youngest women in the community use less Hungarian and more German than any other group. Gal argues that the young women's rejection of Hungarian is a rejection of peasant life.

All these papers show the role language plays in our construction of ourselves as *gendered beings*. It has been understood for a long time that language and identity are crucially intertwined (see, for example, Bruner 1990; Edwards 1985; Gumperz 1982), but it is only recently, with the insights afforded by poststructuralism, that researchers in language and gender have begun to explore the way that language practices accomplish gender. The young women observed by Gal made strategic choices about which language to use in terms of *who they wanted to be*: they did not want to be peasant wives like their mothers and grandmothers. All of us make language choices all the time which index our identity (or rather, identities, since none of us is monolithic) (see Ochs 1992 for further discussion of the idea of gender and indexicality). It is through paying compliments, giving directives, swearing, being polite in particular ways in particular speech communities, that we constitute ourselves as women or men in these speech communities.

REFERENCES

Brown, Penelope and Levinson, Stephen (1987) *Politeness*. Cambridge: Cambridge University Press.

Bruner, Jerome (1990) 'Autobiography as self', pp. 33–66 of J. Bruner, *Acts of Meaning*. Cambridge, MA: Harvard University Press.

Coates, Jennifer (1993) 'Gender differences in communicative competence', pp. 106–40 in J. Coates, *Women, Men and Language*. London: Longman.

Edwards, John (1985) *Language, Society and Identity*. Oxford: Blackwell.

Gumperz, John (ed.) (1982) *Language and Social Identity*. Cambridge: Cambridge University Press.

Hymes, Dell (1972) 'On communicative competence', pp. 269–93 in J. B. Pride and J. Holmes (eds) *Sociolinguistics*. Harmondsworth: Penguin.

Maltz, Daniel and Borker, Ruth (1982) 'A cultural approach to male–female miscommunication', pp. 417 of this Reader (originally published in J. Gumperz (ed.) *Language and Social Identity*. Cambridge: Cambridge University Press).

Ochs, Elinor (1992) 'Indexing gender', pp. 335–58 in A. Duranti and C. Goodwin (eds) *Rethinking Context: Language as an Interactive Phenomenon*. Cambridge: Cambridge University Press.

RECOMMENDED FURTHER READING

Goodwin, Marjorie Harness (1990) *He-Said-She-Said: Talk as Social Organisation Among Black Children*. Bloomington, IN: Indiana University Press.
Hall, Kira and Bucholtz, Mary (eds) (1995) *Gender Articulated*. London: Routledge.
Holmes, Janet (1995) *Women, Men and Politeness*. London: Longman.

7

How and Why Are Women More Polite: Some Evidence from a Mayan Community

Penelope Brown

Introduction

Two separate lines of linguistic inquiry have yielded results which suggest that women are "more polite" than men. On the one hand we have the observations by sociolinguists like William Labov and Peter Trudgill (Labov 1972; Trudgill 1975, revised version reprinted in this volume, p. 21), which claim that women typically "hypercorrect," that (in terms of particular phonological variables sensitive to social status and level of formality) women speak more formally, using a higher proportion of standard ("prestige") forms than men do in comparable situations. The explanation Trudgill proffers for this phenomenon is that, since women tend to gain their status through how they *appear* (rather than through what they *do* – job or income), they try to secure their social status (and social connotations of refinement and sophistication) through signals of status in their speech (Trudgill 1975: 91–2). By contrast, the tendency of men to actually *lower* the status level of their speech is seen as evidence that men have a "covert norm" of prestige that runs contrary to that assigning prestige to the standard forms.

To this claim that women generally speak in a more formal style than men, we may add an apparently related claim to be found in the work of Robin Lakoff. In *Language and Woman's Place*, Lakoff describes traits which she suggests are characteristic of "women's language" and which crosscut the grammar, occurring in the lexicon, in syntax, in phonology and prosodics; they build up to a "style" in which women express themselves hesitantly, tentatively, weakly, trivializingly, "politely." Asking why women speak in this style, Lakoff answers in terms of a psychological analysis of the nature of women's secondary status, that is, her sense of inferiority: women feel unsure of themselves (and hence are thus treated by others) because they have been taught to express themselves in "women's language," which abounds in markers of uncertainty.[1] This insecurity, it could be further argued, accounts as well for their propensity to use more standard forms in speaking.

Now intuitively it seems reasonable to predict that women in general will speak more formally and more politely, since women are culturally relegated to a secondary status relative to men and since a higher level of politeness is expected from inferiors to superiors. We might even predict that the internalization of inferior status would lead to a conventionalization of more polite forms in women's speech so that their speech would be more polite than men's even when addressed to equals or to inferiors. If we turn from English to Japanese, a language spoken in a culture where women's subordinate status is more overtly institutionalized, we do indeed find evidence that women are more polite in many situations (Martin 1964: 407–15; Miller 1967; Uyeno 1971; Jorden 1974).

However, in opposition to such a sweeping generalization we find that in the Malagasy village studied by Elinor Keenan, women are considered to be *less* polite than men – that in fact women regularly and habitually violate the norms that both men and women say should govern speaking: norms favouring non-confrontation and indirectness in speech (Keenan 1974). There is no suggestion that women are higher status than men in this Malagasy community; on the contrary, the way in which men obey the norms is seen by members of the society as support for and evidence of their superiority to women.

So the relationship between the status of women and the politeness or formality of their speech is by no means as simple and straightforward as has been assumed. The bulk of recent research on language and sex has focused on documenting differences between the speech of men and women in some respect for some sample, usually accompanied by the suggestion that the differences in language usage are attributable to social differences in the position of women and men in the society. What is notably lacking, however, is a way of analysing language usage so that the features differentiating the speech of men and women can be related in a precisely specifiable way to the social-structural pressures and constraints on their behaviour.

Specifically, I have three basic complaints about the work on women's speech to date:

1   Linguistic features said to differentiate women's and men's speech have been treated as a collection of random linguistic facts. But the elements that make up any one of these putative "feminine" styles are not just an odd collection; they make an internally coherent picture, they "go together" naturally. I suggest that this is because when women speak, they are following certain strategies, intending to do certain kinds of things, such as create rapport with the addressee, or flatter the addressee that her/ his opinion is worth soliciting, or assure the addressee that no imposition is intended.

2   The sociological concepts utilized in studies of women's speech have been equally random and arbitrary. Women are seen as following certain "rules" or "norms" of linguistic behaviour laid down by society, such as "Be polite" or "Speak correctly," with no sense of the rational choices that lie behind such rules.

3 There is no explicit connection drawn between the linguistic facts (traits of women's speech) and the sociological facts (the secondary position of women in society) in analyses to date.

This study, then, is in part a reaction against the behaviouristic poverty of much sociolinguistic analysis, the view of people as truncated *homunculi sociologici* who do what they do because of the social slot in which they find themselves. What is missing from accounts of women's speech is an account of the choices being made and the reasons for the choices.

If we bring humans as rational actors into the picture, we come up with a set of connections between language usage and social categories which makes sense of the data. *Social networks* (the kinds of people with whom one interacts regularly) give the individuals involved in them certain *social motivations* (the goals and desires that motivate their actions), which in turn suggest certain *communicative strategies* as means to achieve those goals, and these in turn suggest certain *linguistic choices* which will effectively implement those communicative strategies. The linguistic choices then are seen to be not random with respect to the communicative strategies, and the coherence which relates the features of a style (such as a "feminine style") is explained. With such a model we can relate strategic use of language styles to sex roles and social relationships in a particular society, thereby connecting the linguistic facts with the socio-political system within which they occur.

To illustrate the power of a strategic analysis in explicating the contention that women are "more polite," I will examine the class of social motivations related to the preservation of face, to the general desire that members of a speech community attribute to one another, the desire that one's face be respected. If we assume that all (normal adult) interactants have face wants, then a number of strategies for satisfying these wants may be derived. Taken in reverse, an examination of samples of speech can reveal what politeness strategies are being followed by the speakers, and an account can then be given of what the speakers are trying to do. A formal model of politeness along these lines has been developed in detail by myself and Stephen Levinson. That model delineates the universal assumptions underlying polite usage in all languages, defining politeness as rational, strategic, face-oriented behaviour and predicting the kinds of linguistic strategies which will be employed in particular circumstances. In this study the model is informally presented and applied to the analysis of the differences between women's and men's speech in Tenejapa, a community of Mayan Indians in Chiapas, Mexico. Finally, I suggest some implications of this approach for cross-linguistic studies of women's speech, and some hypotheses about in what senses and under what social conditions we do indeed find that women are more polite.[2]

A Theory of Politeness

What politeness essentially consists in is a special way of treating people, saying and doing things in such a way as to take into account the other person's feelings. On the whole that means that what one says politely will be less straightforward or more complicated than what one would say if one wasn't taking the other's feelings into account.

Two aspects of people's feelings seem to be involved. One arises when whatever one is about to say may be unwelcome: the addressee may not want to hear that bit of news, or to be reminded of that fact, or be asked to cooperate in that endeavour. A request, for example, or anything that requires a definite response directly imposes on the addressee. One way of being polite in such situations is to apologize for the imposition and to make it easy for the addressee to refuse to comply. So we try to give the most interactional leeway possible, and this, in one sense, is what it is to be polite.

Our long-term relations with people can also be important in taking their feelings into account. To maintain an ongoing relationship with others, one greets them on meeting them in the street, inquires about their health and their family, expresses interest in their current goings-on and appreciation of the things they do and like and want.

These two ways of showing consideration for people's feelings can be related to a single notion: that of FACE. Two aspects of people's feelings enter into face: desires to not be imposed upon (negative face), and desires to be liked, admired, ratified, related to positively (positive face). Both can be subsumed in the one notion of face because it seems that both are involved in the folk notion of "face loss." If I walk past my neighbour on the street and pointedly fail to greet her, I offend her face; and if I barge into her house and demand to borrow her lawnmower with no hesitation or apology for intrusion (for example, "Give me your lawnmower; I want it") I equally offend her face. So blatantly and without apologies *imposing on* and blatantly and without apologies *ignoring* the people with whom one has social relationships are two basic ways of offending their faces.

Three factors seem to be involved in deciding whether or not to take the trouble to be polite:

1   One tends to be more polite to people who are socially superior to oneself, or socially important: one's boss, the vicar, the doctor, the president.

2   One also tends to be more polite to people one doesn't know, people who are somehow socially distant: strangers, persons from very different walks of life. In the first situation politeness tends to go one way upwards (the superior is not so polite to an inferior), while in the second situation politeness tends to be symmetrically exchanged by both parties.

3   A third factor is that kinds of acts in a society come ranked as more or less imposing, and hence more or less face-threatening, and the more face-threatening, the more polite one is likely to be.

These three factors appear to be the main determinants of the overall level of politeness a speaker will use.

Now given that politeness is about respecting the other's face, the way to incorporate politeness into the structure of one's utterance is to ensure that in the very act of threatening face, one disarms the threat by showing that one does indeed care about the other's face. *Positive politeness* aims to disarm threats to positive face. Essentially approach-based, it treats the addressee as a member of an in-group, a friend, a person whose desires and personality traits are known and liked, suggesting that no negative evaluation of the addressee's face is meant despite any potentially face-threatening acts the speaker may be performing. Especially clear cases of positive politeness include expressions of interest in the addressee ("What magnificent roses you have, Mrs. Jones, where did you get them?"); exaggerated expressions of approval ("That's the most fabulous dress, Henrietta!"); use of in-group identity markers (slang, code-switching into the "we" code, in-group address forms and endearments, as in "Give me a hand with this, pal"); the seeking of agreement and avoidance of disagreement (using safe topics, such as the weather, and stressing similarity of point of view); joking; claiming reflexivity of goals (that I want what you want and you want what I want); claiming reciprocity (you help me and I'll help you); and the giving of gifts, in the form of goods, sympathy, understanding, and cooperation.

Strategies of *negative politeness*, on the other hand, are essentially avoidance-based, and consist in assurances that the speaker recognizes and respects the addressee's negative face and will not (or will only minimally) interfere with his or her freedom of action. The classic negative politeness strategies are characterized by self-effacement, formality, restraint, where potential threats to face are redressed with apologies for interfering or transgressing ("I'm terribly sorry to bother you, but . . ."); with hedges on the force of the speech act (using expressions like: *maybe, perhaps, possibly, if you please*) and questioning rather than asserting ("Could you do X for me?"); with impersonalizing mechanisms (for example, passives) that distance the act from both speaker and addressee; and with other softening mechanisms that give the addressee an "out" so that a compliant response is not coerced.

Evidence of such strategies in people's speech allows us to infer, given the appropriate supporting context, that they are attending to one another's face wants, they are "being polite." Presumably this is quantifiable: the more face-saving strategies in evidence, the more polite.

Such strategies in speech take time and effort. As such, they contrast with segments of speech where no face redress appears at all – where the speaker is expressing him/herself in the most direct, clear, unambiguous and concise way possible, following H. P. Grice's Maxims of Conversation (Grice 1975) (for example, saying: "Give me five dollars now," meaning exactly that). Such *bald on record* expression involves a gain in clarity and efficiency, but runs whatever risk attends ignoring the addressee's face.

Since two of the three factors influencing level of politeness have to do with the social relationship between the interlocutors, and since relationships (except among lovers, and so on) tend to be relatively stable, particular stable relationships of politeness will reflect particular relationships. So strategies are tied to relationships, and politeness level is relative to the expected level for that relationship. [. . .]

Given then a range of politeness level over a wide range of kinds of acts, we can infer degrees of social closeness and degrees of relative power in relationships. Thus, politeness strategies are a complicated but highly sensitive index in speech of kinds of social relationships. It is for this reason that they provide a useful tool for analysing the differences between the speech styles of men and women.

Under what conditions and in what situations do women actually use more polite expressions than men do in comparable situations? And why? If women are more polite than men, our theory suggests that women are either, (1) generally speaking to superiors, (2) generally speaking to socially distant persons, or (3) involved in more face-threatening acts, or have a higher assessment than men have of what counts as impositions. We may then look to the minutiae of utterances in context to distinguish the facts of women's speech from the images and stereotypes that seem to be the basis of many claims that women are "more polite." Let us now apply this approach to data from Tenejapa, to see what insights about the differences between men's and women's speech emerge.

The Tenejapan Case

Men and women in Tenejapa: an impressionistic overview

Tenejapa is a Tzeltal (Mayan) municipio situated in the central highlands of Chiapas, Mexico, some 20 miles by precipitous dirt road from the town of San Cristóbal de las Casas. Following the ancient Mayan pattern, the Indians live in scattered hamlets and subsist largely by milpa agriculture. As a single corporate entity, Tenejapa has its own native civil-religious hierarchy, and Tenejapans have their own characteristic dialect of Tzeltal, their own Indian dress, and a strong sense of identity as Tenejapans, distinguishing them from the 16 other corporate communities of Tzeltal-speaking Indians and from the surrounding Tzotzil-speaking communities.

An outsider entering this community notices immediately the marked separation of the spheres of activity of women and men. Indeed, the sex-role division appears to be the most salient distinction between kinds of people in this relatively homogeneous egalitarian society. (Age is the other salient basis for differentiation, and hierarchy based on age is firmly institutionalized in ritual. But it does not have such a clear-cut effect on everyday interaction (except adult–child interaction) as sex does.) Women's activities center in the home, focusing on cooking, food preparation, child-rearing, and weaving; men's work takes place primarily outside the home, in the fields, in the market, or in Tenejapa Center. Furthermore, antagonism between the sexes is institutionalized in a number of customs: men commonly beat their wives, marriage by capture is not uncommon (and is the terror of unmarried girls), and even courtship traditionally is initiated with a hostile act: the boy pelts the girl with orange peels, and she (in public) responds by pelting him with stones. On the symbolic level, women and men are seen as entirely different kinds of beings: men are "hot" like the sun, the sky, the day, while women are "cold" like the moon, the earth, the night.

The quality of interaction of women is likewise noticeably differentiated from that of men. Women appear to be highly deferent to men, but are extremely warm and supportive to other women. Thus, women are highly deferential and self-effacing in public; they walk behind the men on the trails, stepping aside to let men pass them if the men come up behind; they speak in a high pitch falsetto voice with kinesic humbling (hunched-over shoulders, avoidance of eye contact); in short, they give avoidance-type respect in the presence of men. By contrast when talking to women in the security of their homes, or even in public when in encounters with women not in the center of the public gaze, women are highly supportive and empathetic, stressing their closeness with many prosodic modifications and rapport-emphasizing expressions. In short, they emphasize commonality and appreciation of each other's personality.

Men, on the other hand, treat people in general in a much more matter-of-fact and businesslike manner. Their trail greetings are often short, even brusque, and their speech habitually lacks many of the elaborate mechanisms for stressing deference as well as for stressing solidarity that abound in women's speech.

From an impressionistic point of view, then, women's speech and demeanour appear to be elaborated for the extremes of both positive and negative politeness; men's speech and demeanour tend to be baldly on record to a much greater extent. The few notable exceptions to this general pattern have significant implications for the meaning of the general rule. The negative politeness pattern for women is modified somewhat by age – women become more assertive, less deferential, when they pass child-rearing age, when they become, as it were, socially sexless. The behaviour of men is modified in two situations: when drunk, exaggerated positive politeness expression appears, with joking, back-slapping, and repeated assurances of solidarity. And in ritual contexts, when addressing the gods and saints, men's speech takes on many of the vocal and prosodic features that characterize women in daily interaction: exaggerated rhythmicity, falsetto, high trailing-off pitch contours (cf. Stross 1977). But apart from these exceptions, we may take the initial impressionistic generalization as a working hypothesis: that relative to men's, women's speech is highly elaborated for both positive and negative politeness. Now how can we test such a hypothesis? How can we find an index of positive politeness and of negative politeness with which to measure the differences between men's and women's speech?

Being polite in Tzeltal

Tzeltal has a built-in apparatus which is highly sensitive to nuances of social relations between speaker and hearer. There is a syntactically definable class of particles in Tzeltal which operate as adverbs on the highest performative verb, modifying the force of a speech act by expressing something about the speaker's attitude toward the act being performed (or toward the addressee). There are some 20 of these particles, and although the usage conditions for each one differ somewhat, what they basically do for any speech act is say, in effect, either "I maybe, perhaps, tentatively, in some respects, assert/request/promise/declare/, and so on" or "I emphatically, sincerely, really assert/request/promise/declare, and so on." So they may be classified crudely as strengtheners or weakeners of the force with which the speaker performs the speech act.

Some examples should clarify how the particles operate (the Tzeltal transcription is roughly phonemic, where <x> corresponds to the sound spelled <sh> in English, <j> corresponds to <h>, and <'> indicates a glottal stop between vowels or glottalization of the preceding consonant):

Strengtheners – rhetorical assurances of sincerity or emphatic opinion:
   (1)   we'an me *ts'in ch'i.*
         Do eat, *then*! (polite emphatic offer of a meal)

   (2)   *melel* te jo'one, ma jk'an.
         Truly, as for me, I don't want it. (stresses the speaker's sincerity)

Weakeners – performative hedges:
   (3)   tal *me* kilat jway*uk.*
         I've come *if I may* to see you for a night *or so.* (hedged request)

   (4)   mach'a mene ts'i *bi?*
         Who is that one, *do you suppose?* (avoids presuming that the addressee knows the answer)

Although the meanings conveyed by these particles in context are extremely subtle and complex, in combination with intonation and prosodic patterns that themselves either emphasize or weaken, it is usually possible in particular cases to identify whether they are acting as speech act strengtheners or weakeners.

Now the point to stress here is that any particles or words or expressions in any language that do this kind of thing, that is, that modify the performative force of speech acts, are prime candidates for formulating polite utterances. This is because speech acts are intrinsically potent things, because they presuppose various things about the addressee (for example, that he/she doesn't know the truth of what is being asserted, or that he/she is able to carry out the order, or that he/she is willing to perform the act requested, and so on). Therefore, to hedge these acts is in general to be negatively polite, and to emphasize them (in many cases) is to be positively polite. (Of course, the validity of such a generalization depends on the semantics of the sentence in question. If a speaker emphasizes a speech act of criticizing or insulting the addressee, it is hardly positively polite.)

It seems clear that the Tzeltal particles provide rich resources for performing strategies of positive politeness (which requires emphasizing one's appreciation of, approval of, similarity with, the addressee) and of negative politeness (which requires hedging of one's encroachment on the addressee's territory, or softening the force with which one does face-threatening speech acts, or giving the addressee an "out" in interpreting what speech act is being done). So it might be reasonable to expect that a simple count of particle usage would provide a rough index of the extent of face redress being employed in speech. On the basis of our above hypothesis about the differences between men's and women's speech in Tenejapa, we might predict that:

1 Women use more strengthening particles when speaking to women (more than to men, and more than men speaking to men);
2 Women use more weakening particles when speaking to men (more than to women, and more than men use to men); and
3 Women speaking to women use more particles, overall, than men to men.

If we compare the speech of male and female dyads, matched so as to neutralize status differences, familiarity (social distance) differences, and differences in the culturally rated face-threateningness of the material being discussed (the three factors which our theory claims form the basis for determining politeness levels), insofar as natural conversation data allow such matching, it turns out that some such crude correlations do appear, differentiating the speech of women and men. But they appear only when the particle counts are corrected for the subtleties of the semantics, which vary depending upon a number of factors. For example, the topic under discussion is a crucial variable, for both men and women use many more hedging particles when talking about something for which they do not have firsthand knowledge; similarly, they use many more emphatic particles when giving value judgments about what they think or feel. But when such factors are minimized by choosing passages with (roughly) comparable topic valency, gross counts of particle usage do show interesting sex differences.

The results for a few samples are summarized in table 1 (for further details, see Brown 1979: ch. 4). To begin with the counts of particle usage in same-sex dyads, it appears that women do use more particles. That is, their speech is more elaborated than men's speech is for both positive-politeness emphasizing and negative-politeness hedging, as far as the use of particles is concerned, for on the

Table 1 Summary table of particle usage (average number of particles for 100 speech acts)

	Strengtheners	*Weakeners*	*Total particles*
Women to women	25.2	34.1	59.3
Women to men	35.7	24.4	60.2
Men to men	14.4	18.1	32.6
Men to women	24.1	33.1	57.2
Totals regardless of sex of addressee:			
Female speakers			
(n = 10)	28.3	31.2	59.5
Male speakers			
(n = 6)	19.2	25.6	44.9

Source: Original data.

order of half again to twice as many particles, both weakeners and strengtheners, appear in the female conversations. So our hypotheses about the speech of women to women as opposed to that of men to men appear to be supported by these passages, although of course we would need larger samples to ascertain statistical significance. The hypotheses for cross-sex dyads, however, are not confirmed in my counts. There appear to be no clear-cut differences between men and women in terms of the number of particles they use when speaking to one another. That is, I have not found as predicted that women use more strengthening particles to women than to men, nor that women use more weakening particles to men than to women. Indeed, in both these cases the data actually reverse the order expected. Women use more strengtheners to men than to women, and women use more weakeners to women than to men, although I hesitate to draw any broad conclusions from this very small sample. This result is at least partly due to the fact that natural conversation yields little of comparable semantics in the speech of cross-sex dyads in my data, so the comparability of samples is highly questionable.

However, the gross differences between women and men in same-sex dyads are very large, and even when sex of addressee is ignored and particle usage of women is compared with that of men (see table 1, lower section), female speakers came out as using considerably more particles than male speakers. We may conclude, then, that despite the semantic/pragmatic difficulties in counting particles, they do appear to offer a possible quantitative index to politeness strategies, albeit a very crude one.

More revealing differences between the speech of men and women appear when we examine qualitative differences in their particle usage. To get a real understanding of the sex differences in verbal strategies, we must look at the characteristic feminine and masculine usages to which the particles are put. For women, irony, rhetorical questions, and negative assertions used to convey the opposite (positive) assertion, are characteristic usages. For example:

(5)   *mak* yu' *wan* ma ja'uk ya'wil!
      Lit: *Perhaps* because *maybe* it's not so, *as it were, you see.*
      Implicating: Isn't that just how it is!

(6)   ja' yu'un ma ya *nix* xlaj jtak'intik yu'une, yakubeli.
      Lit: It's because our money *just* doesn't get used up because of drunkenness.
      Implicating: It *does* get used up!

(7)   yu' *bal* jo'on ay ba ya jta tak'in?
      Lit: Because as for me, *is there* anywhere I'll come up with money?
      Implicating: Of course not!

(8)   bi yu'un *nix* ay *xa'*na' sts'isel ek a?
      Lit: Just *why would* you know how to sew?
      Implicating: Of course you wouldn't.

Ironies and ironic rhetorical questions are used to stress feelings and attitudes; by asserting the opposite of what one feels or thinks, one stresses the shared assumptions about such feelings between speaker and addressee, the shared views that make such ironies interpretable. In this way they are positive-politeness strategies, emphasizing in-group feelings and attitudes. As reflected in my data, women spend more time talking about feelings and attitudes toward events than do men, hence the ironies.

Another positively polite feature of particle usage among women is the extensive use of the diminutive *ala* as a marker of small talk. This particle, usually glossed as 'a little', appears repeatedly in conversations between women where little or no new information is being conveyed, but the purpose of speaking is to stress their shared interests and feelings. The following passage, for example, comes from a conversation between an elderly woman and her visiting married daughter:

(9) DA: ay binti ya k*ala* pas xane, xon yu'un, nail to joy ta koral k*ala* mut.
            There is something else I'll *a-little* do, I said to myself, first I'll gather together my-*little* chickens in an enclosure.
      MO: Ia wan a'joy ta koral a'w*ala* mut.
            You perhaps put your-*little* chickens into an enclosure!
      DA: Ia. ja'in ya slo'laben k*ala* k'ale.
            I did. It's because they eat my-*little* cornfield up for me (if I don't confine them).
      MO: ya slo' ta me ya x'*ala* ch'iixe.
            They eat (it) if it *a-little* grows up (big enough).
      DA: *ala* lawaltikix!
            It's *a-little* grown already!

The subject to which the diminutivizing *ala* is applied moves from what Da is going to do, to her chickens, to her cornfield, to the size to which the corn grows: the function of *ala* here is to stress the emotional bond between Mo and Da in engaging in this conversation, not to literally describe Da's actions, corn, chickens, and so on. This emphasizing usage of *ala* is a trait of women's speech; men consider it to be feminine and "soppy," although men certainly use the particle for other reasons, for example, to minimize an imposition, as in a negatively polite request:

(10)   ya jk'an k*ala* k'inal, ya jpas k*ala* na.
       I want my-*little* bit of land, to make my-*little* house (there).
       (as when a son asks his father for his share of land)

or to minimize the implications of what one is doing:

(11)   ya x'*ala* yakubon jo'tikike.
       We are ⎰ sort of ⎱ getting drunk.
              ⎱ a little bit ⎰
              ⎰ merely ⎱

I even have one example on tape where a man proliferates the use of *ala* in one utterance in a way apparently similar to the women's usage:

(12)   ma 'yuk, ya nax jk'an, wokol k'opta, ay sts'isben y*ala* jun k*ala* ch'in kerem, ay laj jatsem y*ala* jun.
    It's nothing, I just want to please ask if she would sew up for me the *little* book of my *little* small boy, his *little* book is ripped, he says.

But as the gloss indicates, the *ala*s here are functioning as negative politeness, to minimize what is actually an unusually humiliating request – since the man is asking his sister to do what his wife should have done, thereby revealing a serious domestic breach. So the *ala*s are making a plea for sympathy, perhaps, but their main function here is to minimize an awkward request, and they certainly are not oriented to stressing shared attitudes and values as the *ala*s in (9) are doing.

On the negative-politeness side, women also have some characteristic usages. Thus it appears that while both men and women use hedging particles in cases of genuine doubt, only women use them even in utterances where there is no doubt, where in fact only the speaker herself can know the truth of the proposition, for example, hedging on one's own feelings:

(13)   ya nix jmel ko'tantik yu'un ts'in *mak*.
    I just really am sad then because of it, *perhaps*.
(14)   chajp nix me ko'tan ta melel yu'un ts'i *bi*.
    My heart is just really terrible (that is, miserable) because of it then, *isn't it*.

Here the hedges in combination with emphatic expression of the speaker's feelings serve purely negative-politeness functions; the woman appears to think it an imposition to express her feelings strongly to the addressee – or rather, she appears to feel it is necessary to act as if she were thus hesitant. As a form of understatement these hedges can even make the assertion more exclamatory, by implying the necessity to suppress the full expression of one's outrage. For example:

(15)   *puersa* k'exlal ts'in *mak*!
    She's *really* embarrassed then *maybe*!
    (Compare English: She's really a bit upset!)

As for the men, they too have characteristically sex-typed usages of the particles. One of the most noticeable occurs with the particle *melel*, which is a sincerity emphasizer usually glossed as "truly" or "really." This particle abounds in male public speaking or any male speaking with the aim of political persuasion. For example:

(16)   *melel* ja'lek tey nax ya x'ainon jo'tik, *melel* muk'ul paraje yilel ta ba'ayon jo'tik.
    Really, it's good if we just stay there, *really*, ours is a big village.

(17)   ma me xtun ta me ya'wak'ik tey a te sna maestro tey a, *melel* ma me xtun.
    It's no good if you put the teacher's house there, *really* it's no good.

In a heated attempt at persuasion, *melel* and other sincerity emphasizers can occur in virtually every sentence for several minutes of discourse. Another markedly male feature of such public speaking is the liberal interpolation of Spanish words into the stream of speech. Men tend to publicly flaunt their knowledge of Spanish; women, in contrast, tend to hide their knowledge and pretend to understand Spanish less well than in fact is the case. In male public speaking one also hears three Spanish-derived words used like the Tzeltal emphatic particles: to stress the strength of the speaker's commitment to what he is saying. These are *meru*, *puru*, and *bun*:

(18)   *meru melel* ya kil!
       That's *really* true, (as) I see it!

(19)   *melel* lom bol te promotor, *puru* bats'ilk'op ya yak' ta nopel, *puru* lom bolik.
       The teacher is *really* stupid, he teaches nothing but Tzeltal, he's *really* (that is, purely, completely) stupid.

(20)   lom spas k'op, *bun* lom xchukawan, te maestro.
       He fights very much, *boy does he ever* jail people a lot, that teacher.

This kind of particle-like use of Spanish-derived expressions appears to be restricted to male speech.

Speech and style in Tzeltal

I hope to have demonstrated that the speech of men and women in Tzeltal differs in systematic ways. First of all, it differs in terms of how many particles members of each sex tend to use, thus establishing frequency of speech-act modifiers as a promising index of the complex verbal strategies that speakers are employing. We may conclude that such quantitative comparisons are useful as a rough guide to what is going on at the strategic level, although they will not replace the painstaking comparison of individual strategies employed in speech. Theoretically it should be possible to quantify underlying intentions such as strategies and count them up, but a methodology that would allow us to do that in any rigorous way is still in its infancy (see Brown and Levinson 1987). While one could count up Tzeltal ironies, it would be much more difficult to isolate all the instances of positive-politeness strategies in a passage, quantify their relative strength of face redress, add them up, and compare the speech of women and men on this basis. If we were to attempt such an enterprise for Tzeltal, we would need an inventory of the kinds of politeness strategies (in addition to the use of particles to modify performative force) available in the Tzeltal repertoire.

An inventory of the conventionalized linguistic resources for positive politeness, available potentially to both women and men, would include the following: the emphatic particles (as illustrated above, and including a number of others); exaggerated empathetic intonation and prosodic patterns; negative questions ("Won't you eat now?") as offers which presuppose an affirmative reply; repeats and other ways of stressing interest and agreement; irony and rhetorical questions as ways of stressing shared point of view; use of directly quoted conversation; diminutives and in-group address forms; expressions like "you know" (*ya'wa'y*) and "you see" (*ya'wil*) which claim shared knowledge; joking (which also presupposes shared knowledge and values); and the Tzeltal inclusive-*we* used to mean "I" or "you," pretending that the speech act is for the common weal.

Linguistic realizations of negative-politeness strategies in Tzeltal include performative hedges; indirect speech acts; pessimistic formulation of requests and offers ("You wouldn't have any chickens to sell"); minimization of impositions ("a little," "for a moment," "just," "merely," "only"); deference (including ritually falsetto high pitch and other forms of symbolic self-minimization); and depersonalizing and deresponsibilizing mechanisms which imply that the speaker is not taking responsibility for the force of this particular speech act.

Although members of both sexes have access to these resources, the usage of men and women differs systematically both in terms of which strategies they choose to use and how much effort they put into face redress, whether positive or negative. The results of comparing male and female use of these strategies (nonquantitatively, so far) supports the two claims I have made on the basis of simple particle counts: (a) that women use the extremes of positive and of negative politeness, while men speak much more matter-of-factly, and (b) that women have characteristically feminine strategies of positive politeness and negative politeness so that what might be called "feminine styles" can be isolated. Similarly, there are usages characteristic of men, especially sexy joking (*ixta k'op*) and the preaching/declaiming style discussed above, which define kinds of typical "masculine style."

In labeling these systematic patterns of language usage "styles," however, a clarification is in order. "Style" is frequently used to label surface-structural features of language with no reference to why particular stylistic features go together or what is the reason for using them, rather than others, in a given instance. I am claiming rather that there is a coherence among the features of positive politeness, and among those of negative politeness, at the strategic level. The features of positive politeness all contribute to the aim of a positively polite conversational style: to stress in-group knowledge, shared attitudes and values, appreciation of the addressee, and so on; and the features of negative politeness contribute to the aim of distancing, non-imposing, that defines negative politeness. It is the employment of strategies that generate surface-structural features that can be called "style". If linguistic form differs in two styles it is because language is being used for different ends. This argument has significant implications for sociolinguistic theory, for the claim is that only by probing below the surface and identifying the strategies that actors are pursuing when they speak can we see how the linguistic minutiae of utterances are related to the plans of human actors. And only thus can we claim that there is a deep, intrinsic relationship between language usage and social facts.

Ethos and social context

We may conclude that women are, overall, more polite than men in Tenejapan society. That is, the general quality of interaction between women, their interactional ethos, is more polite than that for the men, as measured by the particles and other strategies in usage. It remains to integrate these linguistic facts with the social context that gives rise to them, in order to explain the basis for the patterns that are observable.

This result contradicts our initial hypothesis, that women are positively polite to women and negatively polite to men. Rather, the data suggest that women are overall more sensitive to possibly face-threatening material in their speech, and hence use negative politeness to women as well as men, and are more sensitive to positive face wants and hence use positive politeness to men as well as women. [. . .] Recalling that according to our theory there are three reasons for increasing face redress in speech, it appears that women are speaking as if the social power of addressee and social distance between interlocutors are higher overall than they are for men, and therefore their overall politeness level is higher. In comparison, men are speaking in a relatively familiar manner, treating each other as though power and social distance were both very low. The social weighting of seriousness of impositions, based on the potential face-threateningness of acts, varies to account for the variations in politeness level in members of each sex's speech over time, severely for women, mildly for men. Thus I am suggesting that women are more sensitive from moment to moment to the potential face-threateningness of what they are saying and modify their speech accordingly.

Ethnographic support for this interpretation comes from three salient facts of Tenejapan life. The first is that women are vulnerable to men in this society where wives, sisters, and daughters are likely to be beaten if there are threats to their reputation, and women are vulnerable to women as possible sources for slights on their reputations. Secondly, in speech to women, a higher level of politeness may be due to the fact that residence is generally patrilocal, so that women marry into their husband's family's household. For this reason there is likely to be a somewhat greater social distance between the women than between the men of a household. Thirdly, women treat some kinds of speech acts more cautiously than men; the vulnerability of women means that more acts, as well as certain particular acts (such as talking to an unrelated male at all), are defined as face-threatening. This also motivates the particular strategies that women choose, most obviously the ubiquitous expression denying knowledge or responsibility: *maxkil* ("I don't know"), which is used conventionally as a self-protective device.

As for men, it may simply be the case that they have a higher evaluation of wants that conflict with face wants – for example, those supporting a goal of communicative efficiency which conflicts with the elaboration of face-redressive strategies. One other possible factor is a process akin to Gregory Bateson's "schismogenesis" (Bateson 1958): it is possible that men are stressing their brusqueness as a sign of tough masculinity, and women their polite graciousness as a display of feminine (contrasting to masculine) values. This parallels Trudgill's suggestion that middle-class men in England use linguistic forms typical of working-class usage as a way of stressing their masculinity, whereas women tend to hypercorrect, using forms typical of persons of a higher social class (Trudgill 1975).

The negative politeness between women is a surprising result in the light of our initial predictions, and implies that there is not a dichotomizing of the social world into men vs. women, with the former receiving negative politeness and the latter positive politeness, but that overall women are paying more attention to face redress than men are. This would parallel the suggestions of Peter Trudgill for British English, and of Roger Shuy for American English, that women show greater sensitivity to the socially diagnostic features of their language, so that they use a higher percentage of valued (standard) forms (Trudgill 1975; Shuy 1974). Women, in this view, maintain a degree of "normativeness" over men in English. Tenejapan women, then, appear to be like English women in this respect. (While comparisons of phonological standardness and use of polite strategies are not necessarily one-to-one, they seem to be both aiming at a common goal of social approval.)

We still need some explanation of cross-sex relations in Tenejapa. Although certain social forces make women vulnerable, there are several reasons why women are not totally powerless in the society. Women make a considerable economic contribution to the household; they help with work in the fields and are solely responsible for food preparation, raising of small domestic animals, child-rearing, and weaving. In Tenejapa it is frequently said by young women that they "don't want to marry." They fear separation from their natal families, husbands' physical power over wives, and the embarrassment or shame of illness and physical deterioration due to childbirth. In fact there seems to be no opprobrium attached to unmarried women (*tektom antsetik*); there were six such adult women in the hamlct in which I worked, living with parents or siblings. Men, on the other hand, all want to be married, for they cannot get along without a woman to cook for them. This may be one reason for the relative courtesy with which men treat women in this society.

A second important fact is that Tenejapan culture interactionally downplays differences in status and power. Fear of envy and witchcraft provides a powerful motive for minimizing differentials in wealth and status. Political positions (cargos) are rotated annually or triannually; men are coerced into taking them on and the ritual accoutrements of a cargo are very expensive, so that anyone with accumulated wealth is more than likely to be forced into spending it on a cargo position. There is an ideology of complementarity in sex roles: the overseeing gods are called *me'tiktatik* ("mother-father"), and cargos all involve a complementary female role requiring ritual food preparation and prayers. So women are seen as indispensable to the order of things, not simply in their reproductive function but in maintaining and guarding the society in a role parallel to that of men. The egalitarian ethos and downplaying of wealth and power differentials mean that women (indeed, all adult members of the household) generally take a major role in decision making at the domestic level.

While these facts mitigate the status differences between the two sexes, that there remains a power/status difference between men and women is indisputable. Physically – men beat women, women do not beat husbands or fathers or brothers. Interactionally – husbands routinely give wives direct bald on record imperatives: "Cook that meal," for example. However, I never heard a woman give her husband a direct order of that sort. In public, women given men (especially unrelated males) marked interactional deference; the reverse is not the case. Politically – men hold the positions that are prestigious and publicly visible, and it is men who make the decisions affecting the community as a whole. Women's role in decision making, while very important domestically, is from a society's-eye view more or less invisible.

Conclusions

What then can we learn about women from looking at language? [. . .] In recent years sexism in language has been enthusiastically examined and well documented [. . .]. But the area that has been most disappointing has been the attempt to show how the ways in which women choose to express themselves reveal truths about their social relationships and their social status in the society. I have argued here that a prerequisite to such an inquiry is an adequate theory of the relationship between language usage and social relationships, and I have offered the present sketch of a strategic analysis of language usage to suggest a means to pursuing relatively subtle indications of the position of women in society. The approach has several advantages which should be stressed.

The analysis of communicative strategies provides an intervening variable allowing us to relate language and society in a direct and motivated way, rather than simply to correlate them. The ethos of women, in this view, is tied to culture and social structure via strategies for behaviour. By linking behaviour to social structure we are thereby enabled to ask these questions: why do women talk the way they do in this society, and what social-structural pressures and constraints are moulding their behaviour?

Another important feature of analysis in terms of communicative strategies is that it allows us to work from the point of view of the speakers themselves. Through looking at the strategies women are pursuing in their speech, we can get a woman's-eye view of her networks of relationships, who she esteems, who she looks down on, and who she feels intimate with. This is a distinct step forward from the prevailing methodology in sociolinguistics, which provides correlations between linguistic and social facts which may have no reality for the speakers themselves.

Furthermore, the link between behaviour and social structure also provides a basis for predictions about when and where and under what conditions women's speech will take on certain characteristics – of positive as opposed to negative politeness, or of high overall politeness in both domains as opposed to low levels overall, for example. It allows us to predict universals in linguistic usage based on universals in the position of women cross-culturally; to the extent that women occupy similar social-structural loci with similar social-structural constraints on behaviour, women will behave similarly at the strategic level. Thus we would not expect linguistic similarities between West African women or high-caste Indian women and Tenejapan women, the former having apparently much more structural power. But we can predict similarities between language usage of Tenejapan women and other peasant women in egalitarian small-scale societies with similar social-structural features. I suggest two hypotheses which could fruitfully be tested in further cross-cultural research:

1   Deference (and, in general, negative politeness) prevails if and where people are in a position of vulnerability or inferiority in a society. Hence women in an inferior, less powerful position than men will be likely to use more negative politeness. However if women are so far inferior as to have no face at all (like children, or beggars, or slaves, who in many societies are treated as having no face), the particular strategies of negative politeness they use will be different than in societies where women are accorded some social esteem.

2   Positive politeness prevails if and when social networks involve multiplex relationships, that is, members have many-sided relationships with each person they interact with regularly, so that each relationship involves the whole person, or a large part of his/her person (Bott 1957). In many societies like Tenejapa, where men dominate the public sphere of life and women stick largely to the domestic sphere, it seems likely that female relationships will be relatively multi-stranded, male ones relatively single-stranded (Rosaldo 1974). And where these conditions prevail, positive politeness should be strongly elaborated in women's speech.

NOTES

1   Critiques of this work have been both theoretical and empirical; see for example Dubois and Crouch 1975; Brown 1976; Smith 1979.
2   The analysis presented here is based on 15 months' fieldwork in Tenejapa, supported by National Science Foundation and National Institute of Mental Health grants. The data base for the linguistic analysis consists of tape-recorded natural conversations which were transcribed in the field with extensive annotations as to meanings and context provided by informants. The formal model is presented in Brown and Levinson 1987. See also Brown 1993, 1995 for further analysis of politeness in the speech of Tenejapan women and men.

REFERENCES

Bateson, G. (1958) *Naven*. Stanford, CA: Stanford University Press.
Bott, R. (1957) *Family and Social Network*. New York: Free Press.
Brown, P. (1976) 'Women and politeness: a new perspective on language and society'. *Reviews in Anthropology*, 3, 240–9.
Brown, P. (1979) 'Language, Interaction and Sex Roles in a Mayan Community: A Study of Politeness and the Position of Women'. Unpublished PhD dissertation, University of California, Berkeley.
Brown, P. (1993) 'Gender, politeness and confrontation in Tenejapa', pp. 144–62 in D. Tannen (ed.) *Gender and Conversational Interaction*. Oxford: Oxford University Press.

Brown, P. (1995) 'Politeness strategies and the attribution of intentions', pp. 153–74 in E. Goody (ed.) *Social Intelligence and Interaction*. Cambridge: Cambridge University Press.

Brown, P. and Levinson, S. (1987) *Politeness*. Cambridge: Cambridge University Press.

Dubois, B. and Crouch, I. (1975) 'The question of tags in women's speech: they don't really use more of them, do they?' *Language and Society*, 4, 289–94.

Grice, H. P. (1975) 'Logic and conversation', pp. 41–58 in P. Cole and J. Morgan (eds) *Syntax and Semantics, vol. 3*. New York: Academic Press.

Jorden, E. H. (1974) 'Language – female and feminine', pp. 57–71 in B. Hoffer (ed.) *Proceedings of a US–Japan Sociolinguistics Meeting*. San Antonio: Trinity University.

Keenan, E. O. (1974) 'Norm-makers, norm breakers: uses of speech by men and women in a Malagasy community', pp. 125–43 in R. Bauman and J. Sherzer (eds) *Explorations in the Ethnography of Speaking*. Cambridge: Cambridge University Press.

Labov, W. (1972) *Sociolinguistic Patterns*. Philadelphia: University of Pennsylvania Press.

Lakoff, R. (1989) *Language and Woman's Place*. New York: Harper & Row.

Martin, S. (1964) 'Speech levels in Japan and Korea', pp. 407–15 in D. Hymes (ed.) *Language in Culture and Society*. New York: Harper & Row.

Miller, R. (1967) *The Japanese Language*. Chicago: Chicago University Press.

Rosaldo, M. (1974) 'Women, culture and society: a theoretical overview', pp. 17–42 in M. Rosaldo and L. Lamphere (eds) *Women, Culture and Society*. Stanford, CA: Stanford University Press.

Shuy, R. (1974) *Sociological Research at the Center for Applied Linguistics: The Correlation of Language and Sex. Georgetown Monographs in Language and Linguistics*. Washington, DC: Georgetown University Press.

Smith, P. M. (1979) 'Sex markers in speech', pp. 271–85 in U. Scherer and H. Giles (eds) *Social Markers in Speech*. Cambridge: Cambridge University Press.

Stross, B. (1977) 'Tzeltal conceptions of power', pp. 271–85 in R. D. Fogelson and R. N. Adams (eds) *The Anthropology of Power*. New York: Academic Press.

Trudgill, P. (1974) *Sociolinguistics*. London: Penguin.

Trudgill, P. (1975) 'Sex and covert prestige, and linguistic change in the urban British English of Norwich', in B. Thorne and N. Henley (eds) *Language and Sex: Difference and Dominance*. Rowley, MA: Newbury House.

Uyeno, T. Y. (1971) 'A Study of Japanese Modality: A Performative Analysis of Sentence Particles'. PhD dissertation, University of Michigan.

8

Complimenting – A Positive Politeness Strategy

Janet Holmes

Do women and men differ in the way they use particular speech acts to express politeness? How would one measure any differences? Should the relative frequency with which women and men use compliments, greetings, or expressions of gratitude be considered, for instance? The form of a directive (e.g. *Shut up!* versus *Let's have a bit of hush now*) is very obviously relevant in assessing how polite it is in any particular situation (Leech 1983; Brown and Levinson 1987). What can we deduce about female and male patterns of politeness by examining who uses particular speech acts to whom? In this paper I will focus on compliments to show how analysing particular speech acts can provide interesting suggestions about gender differences in politeness behaviour.

Paying Compliments

Example 1
Two colleagues meeting in Pat's office to discuss a report.
CHRIS: Hi Pat. Sorry I'm late. The boss wanted to set up a time for a meeting just as I was leaving.
PAT: That's OK Chris. You're looking good. Is that a new suit?
CHRIS: Mm. It's nice isn't it. I got it in Auckland last month. Have you had a break since I last saw you?
PAT: No, work work work I'm afraid. Never mind. Have you got a copy of the report with you?

Positive politeness can be expressed in many ways but paying a compliment is one of the most obvious. A favourable comment on the addressee's appearance, as illustrated in example 1, is a very common way of paying a compliment as we shall see. Compliments are prime examples of speech acts which notice and attend to the hearer's 'interests, wants, needs, goods', the first positive politeness strategy identified and discussed by Brown and Levinson (1987: 102).

What is a compliment?

But what is a compliment? There are a number of positively polite speech acts in the exchange between Pat and Chris – greetings, friendly address terms, expressions of concern and compliments. I would want to count *you're looking good* and *is that a new suit* as examples of compliments. The first is a direct compliment, while the fact that the second counts as a compliment is inferable from the discourse context and the fact that things which are new are generally highly valued in western society (see Manes 1983). When collecting and analysing examples of a particular speech act, it is important to have a clear definition in order to decide what counts and what does not. This is how I have defined a compliment:

> A compliment is a speech act which explicitly or implicitly attributes credit to someone other than the speaker, usually the person addressed, for some 'good' (possession, characteristic, skill, etc.) which is positively valued by the speaker and the hearer. (Holmes 1986: 485)

As the utterance *is that a new suit* illustrates, a compliment may be indirect, requiring some inferencing based on a knowledge of the cultural values of the community. There are other ways in which a compliment may be indirect too. Compliments usually focus on something directly attributable to the person addressed (e.g. an article of clothing), but examples 2 and 3 demonstrate that this is not always the case.

Examples 2 and 3
(2) *Rhonda is visiting an old schoolfriend, Carol, and comments on one of Carol's children.*
RHONDA: What a polite child!
CAROL: Thank you. We do our best.

(3) *Ray is the conductor of the choir.*
MATT: The choir was wonderful. You must be really pleased.
RAY: Yes, they were good weren't they.

The complimenters' utterances in these examples may look superficially like rather general positive evaluations, but their function as compliments which indirectly attribute credit to the addressee for good parenting in (2), and good conducting in (3), is unambiguous in context.

Why give a compliment?

Compliments are usually intended to make others feel good (see Wierzbicka 1987: 201). The primary function of a compliment is most obviously affective and social, rather than referential or informative. They are generally described as positively affective speech acts serving to increase or consolidate the solidarity between the speaker and addressee (see Wolfson 1981, 1983; Holmes 1986; Herbert 1989; Lewandowska-Tomaszczyk 1989). Compliments are social lubricants which 'create or maintain rapport' (Wolfson 1983: 86), as illustrated in all the examples above, as well as in example 4.

Example 4
Two women, good friends, meeting in the lift at their workplace.
SAL: Hi how are you? You're looking just terrific.
MEG: Thanks. I'm pretty good. How are things with you? That's a snazzy scarf you're wearing.

Compliments are clearly positive politeness devices which express goodwill and solidarity between the speaker and the addressee. But they may serve other functions too. Do compliments have any element of referential meaning, for instance? While the primary function of compliments is most obviously affective, they also convey some information in the form of the particular 'good' the speaker selects for comment. They provide a positive critical evaluation of a selected aspect of the addressee's behaviour or appearance, or whatever, which in some contexts may carry some communicative weight. Johnson and Roen (1992), for instance, argue that the compliments they analysed in written peer reviews simultaneously conveyed both affective (or interpersonal) meaning and referential (or ideational) meaning in that a particular aspect of the review was chosen for positive attention. It is possible that some compliments are intended and perceived as conveying a stronger referential message than others. Very clearly, the relationship between the complimenter and recipient is crucial in accurately interpreting the potential functions of a compliment.

In some contexts, compliments may function as praise and encouragement. In an analysis of over a thousand American compliments, Herbert (1990: 221) suggests some compliments serve as expressions of praise and admiration rather than offers of solidarity. This seems likely to reflect the relationship between the participants. Praise is often directed downwards from superordinate to subordinate. So the teacher's compliment about a student's work in example 5 would generally be regarded as praise.

Example 5
TEACHER: This is excellent Jeannie. You've really done a nice job.

Tannen seems to be referring to this function of compliments when she identifies compliments as potentially patronising.

> Giving praise . . . is . . . inherently asymmetrical. It . . . frames the speaker as one-up, in a position to judge someone else's performance. (Tannen 1990: 69)

It is possible, then, that in some relationships compliments will be unwelcome because they are experienced as ways in which the speaker is asserting superiority. Compliments directed upwards from subordinate to superordinates, on the other hand, are often labelled 'flattery'. In analysing differences in the way women and men use and interpret compliments, it will clearly be important to consider compliments between status unequals, exploring the possible alternative interpretations which they may be given.

Compliments may have a darker side then. For some recipients, in some contexts, an apparent compliment may be experienced negatively, or as face-threatening. They may be patronising or offensively flattering. They may also, of course, be sarcastic. When the content of a compliment is perceived as too distant from reality, it will be heard as a sarcastic or ironic put-down. I was in no doubt of the sarcastic intent of my brother's comment 'You play so well' as I was plonking away at the piano, hitting far more wrong than right notes. Focusing on a different perspective, Brown and Levinson suggest (1987: 66) that a compliment can be regarded as a face-threatening act to the extent that it implies the complimenter envies the addressee in some way, or would like something belonging to the addressee. This is perhaps clearest in cultures where an expression of admiration for an object imposes an obligation on the addressee to offer it to the complimenter, as in example 6.

Example 6
Pakeha woman to Samoan friend whom she is visiting.
SUE: What an unusual necklace. It's beautiful.
ETI: Please take it.

In this particular instance, Sue was very embarrassed at being offered as a gift the object she had admired. But Eti's response was perfectly predictable by anyone familiar with Samoan cultural norms with respect to complimenting behaviour. In other cultures and social groups too, compliments may be considered somewhat face-threatening in that they imply at least an element of envy and desire to have what the addressee possesses, whether an object or a desirable trait or skill (see Brown and Levinson 1987: 247). And in 'debt-sensitive cultures' (1987: 247), the recipient of a compliment may be regarded as incurring a heavy debt. In such cultures, then, the function of a compliment cannot be regarded as simply and unarguably positively polite.

Even if intended as an expression of solidarity, a compliment might be experienced as face-threatening if it is interpreted as assuming unwarranted intimacy. Lewandowska-Tomaszczyk (1989: 75) comments that in her Polish and British compliment data, compliments between people who did not know each other well caused embarrassment. Compliments presuppose a certain familiarity with the addressee, she suggests. This is likely to be true of certain types of compliments in many cultures. Compliments on very personal topics, for instance, are appropriate only from intimates, as in example 7.

Example 7
Young woman to her mother who is in hospital after a bad car accident.
Oh mum you've got your false teeth – they look great

The mother had been waiting for some time to be fitted with false teeth to replace those knocked out or broken in the car accident. There are not many situations in which such a compliment could be paid without causing embarrassment.

At the darkest end of the spectrum are utterances which have been called 'stranger compliments' or 'street remarks' (Kissling and Kramarae 1991; Kissling 1991).

Example 8
Man on building site to young woman passing by.
Wow what legs. What are you doing with them tonight sweetie?

These serve a very different interpersonal function from compliments between friends and acquaintances. Though some women interpret them positively as expressions of appreciation, others regard them as examples of verbal harassment. It seems likely that both the speaker's intentions and the hearer's interpretations of these speech acts are extremely variable, and require detailed analysis in context. Though I have mentioned them here for completeness, the discussion below is not based on data which included 'stranger compliments'.

Different analysts have thus identified a number of different functions of compliments in different contexts:

1   to express solidarity;
2   to express positive evaluation, admiration, appreciation or praise;
3   to express envy or desire for hearer's possessions;
4   as verbal harassment.

These functions are not necessarily mutually exclusive, but the relationship between the participants is crucial in interpreting the primary function of a particular compliment: analysis in context is essential. Distributional data can also be suggestive, however, as we shall see in the next section which describes the way compliments are used between New Zealand women and men, and discusses what this suggests about their function as politeness devices.

Who Pays Most Compliments?

Shall I compare thee to a summer's day?

The following analysis of the distribution of compliments between New Zealand women and men is based on a corpus of 484 naturally occurring compliments and compliment responses. The data was collected using an ethnographic approach (Holmes 1986), a method which derives from anthropology, and which has been advocated by Hymes over many years (1962, 1972, 1974), and very successfully adopted by researchers such as Nessa Wolfson (e.g. 1983, 1988). This approach combines some of the advantages of qualitative research with the generalisability gained from

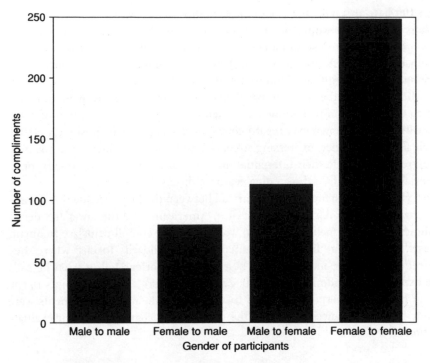

Figure 1 Compliments and gender of participants

quantitative analysis. Compliments and their responses are noted down, together with relevant features of the participants, their relationship, and the context in which the compliment occurred. Using a number of people as data collectors, it was possible to gather a large number of compliments from a wide variety of contexts. Most, however, were produced by adult Pakeha New Zealanders, and it is therefore the compliment norms of this group which are being described.

The New Zealand compliments collected in this way revealed a very clear pattern. Women gave and received significantly more compliments than men did, as figure 1 illustrates.

Women gave 68 per cent of all the compliments recorded and received 74 per cent of them. By contrast, compliments between males were relatively rare (only 9 per cent), and, even taking account of females' compliments to males, men received overall considerably fewer compliments than women (only 26 per cent). On this evidence, complimenting appears to be a speech behaviour occurring much more frequently in interactions involving women than men.[1]

Other researchers report similar patterns. Compliments are used more frequently by women than by men, and women are complimented more often than men in two different American studies (Wolfson 1983; Herbert 1990), and in research on compliments between Polish speakers (Lewandowska-Tomaszczyk 1989). This same pattern also turned up in a rather different context – that of written peer reviews (Johnson and Roen 1992). In this more information-orientated context which involved writing rather than speech, one would not have predicted gender contrasts. But even in writing women tended to use more compliments (or 'positive evaluative terms' to quote Johnson and Roen's precise measure) than men, though the differences were not quite statistically significant (Johnson and Roen 1992: 38).

These differences in the distribution of compliments between women and men have led to the suggestion that women and men may perceive the function of compliments differently. Women may regard compliments as primarily positively affective speech acts, for instance, expressing solidarity and positive politeness, while men may give greater weight to their referential meaning, as evaluative judgements, or to the potentially negative face-threatening features discussed above.

Herbert (1990), for instance, draws a parallel between the lower frequency of compliments given by South Africans compared to Americans, and the lower frequency of compliments between men compared to women. Where compliments are frequent, he suggests, they are more likely to be functioning as solidarity tokens; where they are less frequent they are more likely to be referentially orientated or what he calls 'genuine expressions of admiration' (1990: 221). In support of this, he points to the fact that in his data the responses elicited by the rarer male–male compliments were more likely to be acceptances, reflecting the recipients' recognition of their evaluative function.

Example 9
Mick and Brent are neighbours. They meet at Brent's gate as he arrives home.
MICK: New car?
BRENT: Yeah.
MICK: Looks as if it will move.
BRENT: Yeah it goes well I must say.

Female compliments, however, were more likely to elicit alternative responses, such as shifting or reducing the force of the compliment.

Example 10
Friends arriving at youth club.
HELEN: What a neat outfit!
GERRY: It's actually quite old.

Responses which shift or reduce the compliment's force reflect the function of such compliments as tokens of solidarity, he suggests, since they indicate the recipient's desire to restore the social balance between speakers. There were no such gender differences in compliment responses in the New Zealand corpus, so this explanation cannot account for the less frequent use of compliments by New Zealand men.

It is possible, however, that men may more readily perceive compliments as face-threatening acts than women do. They may feel embarrassed or obligated by these unsolicited tokens of solidarity. The male threshold for what counts as an appropriate relationship to warrant mutual complimenting may differ from the female. Wolfson's 'bulge' theory (Wolfson 1988) suggested that certain linguistic behaviours, such as compliments, occurred more frequently between friends than between strangers or intimates. The bulge represented the higher frequency of such polite speech acts to friends and acquaintances. But the 'bulge' or the range of relationships within which compliments are acceptable politeness tokens may be much narrower for men than women. Female and male norms may differ. While one cannot be sure of the reasons for the imbalance in the distribution of compliments in women's and men's speech, it is widely agreed that women appear to use compliments mainly as a means of expressing rapport, while they do not appear to function so unambiguously for men.

This interpretation would be consistent with research which suggested that women's linguistic behaviour can often be broadly characterised as facilitative, affiliative, and cooperative, rather than competitive or control-orientated. In much of the research comparing patterns of male and female interaction, women's contributions have been described as 'other-orientated'. If women regard compliments as a means of expressing rapport and solidarity, the finding that they give more compliments than men is consistent with this orientation. Conversely, if men regard compliments as face-threatening or controlling devices, at least in some contexts, this could account for the male patterns observed.

In studies of compliments elsewhere, women also received more compliments than men (Wolfson 1984; Holmes 1988; Herbert 1990; Johnson and Roen 1992). Compliments between women are most frequent in all the studies, but it is noteworthy that men compliment women more often than they compliment other men. One explanation for this might be that women's positive attitude to compliments is recognised by both women and men in these speech communities. Perhaps people pay more compliments to women because they know women value them.

Alternatively, one might focus on why people do not compliment men as often as they do women. It appears to be much more acceptable and socially appropriate to compliment a woman than a man. One possible explanation based on an analysis of the power relations in society points to women's subordinate social position. Because compliments express social approval one might expect more of them to be addressed 'downwards' as socialising devices, or directed to the socially insecure to build their confidence. Nessa Wolfson (1984: 243) takes this view:

> women because of their role in the social order, are seen as appropriate recipients of all manner of social judgements in the form of compliments . . . the way a woman is spoken to is, no matter what her status, a subtle and powerful way of perpetuating her subordinate role in society.

In other words, she suggests, compliments addressed to women have the same function as praise given to children, that is they serve as encouragement to continue with the approved behaviour. They could be regarded as patronising socialisation devices. Interestingly, even in classrooms it seems that females receive more praise or positive evaluations than males (e.g. de Bie 1987). It is possible that one of the reasons people do not compliment males so often as females is an awareness of men's ambivalence about compliments and of the possibility that men may regard some compliments as face-threatening acts, as embarrassing and discomfiting, or experience them as patronising strategies which put the speaker 'one-up'. If this is the case, then it is not surprising that the fewest compliments occur between men.

The way compliments are distributed suggests, then, that women and men may use and interpret them differently. While women appear to use them as positive politeness devices, and generally perceive them as ways of establishing and maintaining relationships, men may view them much more ambiguously as potentially face-threatening acts, or as having a more referential evaluative message which can serve a socialising function. In the next section an examination of the syntactic patterns of compliments will throw a little further light on these speculations.

How Do Women and Men Pay Compliments?

Examples 11–15
(11)   You're looking nice today.

(12)   What great kids!

(13)   That's a beautiful skirt.

(14)   I really love those curtains.

(15)   Good goal.

Compliments are remarkably formulaic speech acts. Most draw on a very small number of lexical items and a very narrow range of syntactic patterns. Five or six adjectives, such as *good, nice, great, beautiful,* and *pretty* occurred in about two-thirds of the New Zealand compliments analysed. Wolfson noted the same pattern in her American corpus of nearly 700 compliments (1984: 236). And syntactic patterns prove similarly unoriginal. One of just four different syntactic patterns occurred in 78 per cent of all the compliments in the New Zealand corpus (Holmes 1986). Similarly, three alternative syntactic patterns accounted for 85 per cent of the compliments in the American corpus (Manes and Wolfson 1981). Compliments may be polite but they are rarely creative speech acts.

Nor are there many gender differences in this aspect of politeness behaviour. Most of the syntactic patterns and lexical items occurring in compliments seem to be fairly equally used by women and men, as table 1 demonstrates.

There are, however, two patterns which differ between women and men in an interesting way in the New Zealand corpus. Women used the rhetorical pattern *What (a) (ADJ) NP!* (e.g. *What lovely children!*) significantly more often than men. Men, by contrast, used the minimal pattern *(INT) ADJ (NP)* (e.g. *Great shoes*) significantly more often than women. The former is a syntactically marked formula, involving exclamatory word order and intonation; the latter, by contrast, reduces the syntactic pattern to its minimum elements. In other words, a rhetorical pattern such

Table 1 Syntactic patterns of compliments and speaker gender

Syntactic formula*	Female %	Male %
1 NP BE (LOOKING) (INT) ADJ e.g. *That coat is really great*	42.1	40.0
2 I (INT) LIKE NP e.g. I *simply love that skirt*	17.8	13.1
3 PRO BE (a) (INT) ADJ NP e.g. *That's a very nice coat*	11.4	15.6
4 What (a) (ADJ) NP! e.g. *What lovely children!*	7.8	1.3
5 (INT) ADJ NP e.g. *Really cool ear-rings*	5.1	11.8
6 Isn't NP ADJ! e.g. *Isn't this food wonderful!*	1.5	0.6
Subtotals	85.7	82.4
7 All other syntactic formulae	14.3	17.6
Totals	100.0	100.0

Note: * Following Manes and Wolfson (1981) copula BE represents any copula verb; LIKE represents any verb of liking: e.g. *love, enjoy, admire*; ADJ represents any semantically positive adjective; and INT represents any boosting intensifier: e.g. *really, very*.

as *What a splendid hat!* can be regarded as emphatic and as increasing the force of the speech act. (D'Amico–Reisner (1983: 111–12) makes the same point about rhetorical questions as expressions of disapproval.) Using a rhetorical pattern for a compliment stresses its addressee- or interaction-orientated characteristics.

But the minimal pattern represented by *nice bike*, which was used more by men, tends to reduce the force of the compliment; it could be regarded as attenuating or hedging the compliment's impact. Interestingly, too, there were no examples of the more rhetorical pattern (*what lovely children!*) in the male–male interactions observed. So there seems good reason to associate this pattern with female complimenting behaviour.

Examples 16–18

(16) I love those socks. Where did you get them?

(17) I like those glasses.

(18) *Referring to a paper written by the addressee.*
I really liked the ending. It was very convincing.

Studies of compliments by other researchers provide support for this suggestion that women's compliments tend to be expressed with linguistically stronger forms than men's. Having analysed over one thousand American compliments, Herbert (1990: 206) reported that only women used the stronger form *I love X* (compared to *I like X*), and they used it most often to other women. In written peer reviews, Johnson and Roen (1992) noted that women used significantly more intensifiers (such as *really*, *very*, *particularly*) than men did, and, as in Herbert's data, they intensified their compliments most when writing to other women.

These observations provide further support for the point that it is important in analysing hedging and boosting behaviour to examine the particular types of speech acts which are being boosted, and, in particular, to note whether the speech act is intended and perceived as affectively positive or negative. It is possible to strengthen or alternatively to reduce the force of a positively affective speech act such as a compliment in a variety of ways. By their selections among a narrow range of syntactic formulae and lexical items, men more often choose to attenuate the force of their compliments, while women tend to increase their compliments' force. This supports the suggestion that women expect addressees to interpret compliments as expressions of solidarity rather than as face-threatening speech acts. By contrast, men's tendency to attenuate compliments supports the proposal that men perhaps perceive compliments as less unambiguously positive in effect. In other words, the differences which have been noted in the distribution of syntactic and lexical patterns between women and men is consistent with the view that women tend to regard compliments as primarily positively affective acts while men may feel more ambivalent about using them.

Examples 19 and 20
(19)   You're looking stunning.

(20)   I especially liked the way you used lots of examples.

In general, it is also true that women use more personalised compliment forms than men, while men prefer impersonal forms. There is some evidence for this in the New Zealand data, as table 1 illustrates, but it is even more apparent in Herbert's (1990) American corpus, and Johnson and Roen's (1992) written peer reviews. Well over half (60 per cent) of the compliments offered by men in Herbert's corpus were impersonal forms, for example, compared to only a fifth of those used by women. By contrast women used many more forms with a personal focus (Herbert includes both *you* and *I* as personalised forms). Almost 83 per cent of female–female interactions used personalised forms compared to only 32 per cent of male–male compliments (Herbert 1990: 205). The peer reviews analysed by Johnson and Roen revealed a similar pattern. The women used more personal involvement strategies, especially to other women (1992: 44).

This evidence echoes the patterns noted in research on verbal interaction, which suggested that women tend to prefer personalised and expressive forms as opposed to impersonalised forms (see Kalcik 1975; Swacker 1979; Aries 1982), and supports a view of women's style as more interpersonal, affective and interaction-orientated compared to the impersonal, instrumental and content-orientated style more typical of male interaction (e.g. Piliavin and Martin 1978; Baird and Bradley 1979; Preisler 1986; Aries 1976, 1987; Schick Case 1988; Tannen 1990). So, where the linguistic features of women's compliments differ from men's, the differences tend to support the proposition that women regard compliments as other-orientated positive politeness strategies which they assume will be welcome to addressees, whereas for men, and especially between men, their function may not be so clear-cut.

What Do Women and Men Compliment Each Other About?

Examples 21–24

(21)   *Appearance compliment.*
       I like your outfit Beth. I think I could wear that.

(22)   *Ability/performance compliment.*
       Wow you played well today Davy.

(23)   *Possessions compliment.*
       Is that your flash red sports car?

(24)   *Personality/friendliness.*
       I'm very lucky to have such a good friend.

Women and men tend to give compliments about different things. To be heard as a compliment an utterance must refer to something which is positively valued by the participants and attributed to the addressee. This would seem to permit an infinite range of possible topics for compliments, but in fact the vast majority of compliments refer to just a few broad topics: appearance, ability or performance, possessions, and some aspect of personality or friendliness (Manes 1983; Holmes 1986). In fact, compliments on some aspect of the addressee's appearance or ability accounted for 81 per cent of the New Zealand data.

Within these general patterns, there is a clearly observable tendency for women to be complimented on their appearance more often than men. Over half (57 per cent) of all the compliments women received in the New Zealand data related to aspects of their appearance. And women give compliments on appearance more than men do, so that 61 per cent of all the compliments between women related to appearance compared to only 36 per cent of the compliments between males, as figure 2 demonstrates. Men, by contrast, appear to prefer to compliment other men, but not women, on possessions.

Provided it is not sarcastic, a compliment on someone's appearance such as *you're looking wonderful* is difficult to interpret as anything other than a positively polite utterance. An appearance compliment is clearly an expression of solidarity, a positively affective speech act. The predominance of this type of compliment in women's interactions is consistent with the view that women use compliments primarily for

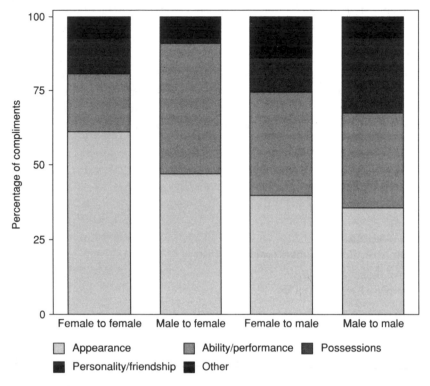

Figure 2   Compliment topic and gender of participants

their positively polite function. Compliments on possessions, on the other hand, are much more vulnerable to interpretation as face-threatening acts since, as illustrated in example 6 above, there is the possibility that the complimenter will be heard as expressing desire for or envy of the object referred to. To this extent, men's greater use of these compliments reinforces the suggestion that they are more likely to perceive and experience compliments as potential face-threatening acts. In other words, if possession-orientated compliments are experienced as more face-threatening than others – which seems feasible since they focus on things which are in theory transferable from complimenter to recipient – then men certainly use more potentially face-threatening compliments than women.

Compliments on appearance seem to cause some men embarrassment.

Example 25
Middle-aged male to elderly male at a concert.
MALE 1:   I haven't seen you since the Festival.
MALE 2:   We haven't been here much since the Festival.
MALE 1:   You've got a new tie in the meantime.
MALE 2:   It's a very old one actually.
MALE 1:   It's quite splendid anyway.
MALE 2:   (*Looks extremely embarrassed.*) No no. What have you been up to anyway?

The recipient's response to the first somewhat indirect compliment is a disclaimer, while his response to the second overt compliment is acute embarrassment followed by a rejection. Wolfson comments (1983: 93) that appearance compliments are remarkably rare between American males. It seems that in America compliments on appearance may be experienced by males as very big face-threatening acts. And while New Zealand men do give and receive compliments on their appearance, there are a number of examples where compliments on their appearance clearly caused surprise.

Example 26
Two colleagues meet at coffee machine at work.
BILL: You're looking very smart today.
TOM: (*Looking very embarrassed.*) I'm meeting Mary and her mother for lunch.

Appearance compliments are clearly not the common currency of politeness between men that they are between women.

A number of men have commented that at least one of the reasons for the scarcity of appearance compliments between men is fear of the possible imputation of homosexuality.

> To compliment another man on his hair, his clothes, or his body is an *extremely* face threatening thing to do, both for speaker and hearer. It has to be very carefully done in order not to send the wrong signals. (Britain, personal communication)

In support of this David Britain provided the following example.

Example 27
Male flatmate, Alex, to Dave, referring to the latter's new haircut.
Jesus Christ tell me who did that and I'll go and beat him up for you!
Laughter. Then
No it's OK.
Finally, a week later.
That's a good haircut.

In this case, it took a week for Alex to get round to saying he liked Dave's haircut, that is to pay a clearly identifiable compliment on his appearance to another male.

Figure 2 also shows that nearly half (44 per cent of all) the compliments given by males to females were compliments on abilities, skills or performance. Women do not compliment men or other women so often on this topic. This raises the question of whether a compliment can act as a power play. As mentioned above, praise is often directed downwards. A compliment could be experienced as patronising if the recipient felt it was given as encouragement rather than as a token of solidarity. Compliments on skills and abilities are particularly vulnerable to being interpreted in this way.

Example 28
Husband to wife about her painting of a wall.
You've made a pretty good job of that.

One has the feeling that the husband is a little surprised his wife has done so well and is patting her on the head approvingly. The tendency for men to compliment women on their skills and abilities may reflect women's subordinate social status in the society as a whole, as well as, perhaps, a male tendency to perceive compliments as means of conveying referential or evaluative, as well as affective, messages. The next section will illustrate that the way compliments are used to those of different status provides further support for such an interpretation.

Can a Compliment Be a Power Play?

People pay most compliments to their equals. As Wolfson puts it, 'the overwhelming majority of all compliments are given to people of the same age and status as the speaker' (1983: 91). New Zealanders' compliments followed this pattern (see also Knapp et al. 1984; Herbert 1990). Almost 80 per cent of the corpus consisted of compliments between status equals. Compliments typically occur in informal interactions between friends.

The distribution of the small proportion of compliments that occurred between people of different status is interesting, however, because it throws further light on the question of the functions of compliments for women and men.

If it is true, as Wolfson suggests, that the fact that women receive more compliments than men reflects their subordinate status in the society as a whole, then one would also expect more compliments to subordinates than to superiors, regardless of gender. Wolfson's American data evidently confirmed this expectation. She comments that 'the great majority of compliments which occur in interaction between status unequals are given by the person in the higher position' (1983: 91).

Example 29
Manager to her secretary.
You are such a treasure Carol. What would I do without you!

Another American study, which was based on self-report data rather than observation, reports the same pattern (Knapp et al. 1984). Most compliments occurred between status equals, but when there was a status imbalance, higher status participants complimented more often than lower status ones. In other words, people seem generally less willing to compliment someone of higher rather than lower status. Neither of these studies examined the interaction of gender and status, however.

In the New Zealand data, as mentioned, the great majority of compliments occurred between status equals. There were no significant differences in the numbers addressed to those of higher rather than lower status. But, interestingly, it was

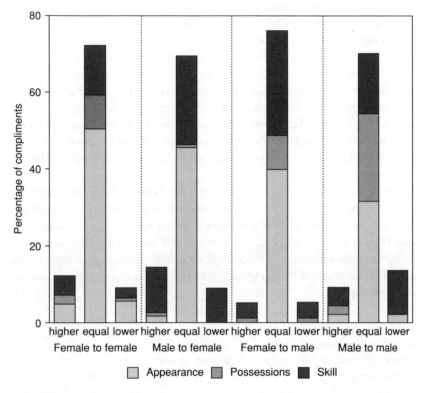

Figure 3   Compliments by relative status and gender of participants and topic

found that higher status females were twice as likely to receive compliments as higher status men.

Example 30
Secretary to boss.
That's a lovely dress.

If high status generally reduces the likelihood that one will receive compliments, then this data indicates it reduces it less with women than with men. This is true whether the complimenter is male or female, as can be seen in figure 3. In fact, despite the general pattern that women pay more compliments than men, males are even more likely to compliment women of higher status than women are.

Example 31
Male caretaker to woman executive as she leaves work.
You're a hard working woman Mrs Thomas. I hope they pay you well.

This is further support for the view that it is more acceptable to compliment high status women than high status men.

Perhaps higher status women are perceived as more receptive to compliments (especially from men) than their male counterparts, because in the society as a whole women are generally regarded as socially subordinate, and less powerful and influential than men. This may legitimate behaviour that might otherwise be considered presumptuous. Tannen's (1990: 69) suggestion that giving praise 'frames the speaker as one-up' is again relevant here. Higher status males may be perceived as high risk addressees by both genders. But female gender apparently overrides high status in determining how risky a compliment is perceived as being. Alternatively, perhaps women are seen as more approachable because they value solidarity more highly than status, and tend to reduce rather than emphasise status differences (Troemel-Ploetz 1992).

This interpretation of the patterns is consistent with the suggestion that men are more likely to experience a compliment as a face-threatening act whereas women are more likely to perceive compliments as positively affective speech acts, regardless of relative status. If true, this would be likely to encourage complimenters to address compliments upwards to women, and discourage compliments to higher status men where the risk of offence would be too great. Note the male's discouraging reaction in the following example.

Example 32
Young woman to Minister's personal secretary at a reception.
WOMAN: What an interesting job you have. You must be very bright.
MAN: I just do my job.

The young woman was lively and friendly. The tone of the man's reply made it clear he thought her presumptuous. Complimenting a higher status male is obviously a risky business. There is further support for this interpretation when we look at differences in the way women and men use compliments on appearance, in particular. As figures 2 and 3 illustrate, appearance was the most common topic of compliments in this corpus, as in others. Figure 3 shows that appearance was also by far the most frequent topic of compliments between equals (30–50 per cent of all compliments). But status differences reduced the likelihood of appearance compliments quite dramatically, especially in cross-sex relationships. Fewer than 2 per cent of the compliments analysed were appearance compliments between cross-sex pairs of different status – a clear indication of the link between appearance compliments and solidarity-based relationships.

On the other hand, appearance compliments are the most obvious examples of compliments which are likely to be interpreted or experienced differently by women and men, as discussed above, and illustrated in the following example.

Example 33
Office receptionist to high status male whom she knew only slightly.
RECEPTIONIST: That's a nice suit.
MALE: Mr Avery's expecting me I think.

The man ignores the compliment completely. The receptionist was almost certainly being positively polite and intended her compliment as a solidarity signal. But an appearance compliment is vulnerable to being interpreted as presumptuous when addressed by a subordinate to a superior of either gender. If men also tend to regard compliments as potential face-threatening acts and find compliments on their appearance particularly discomfiting, the negative effect will be even greater.

The patterns revealed by the distribution of compliments in this corpus suggest, then, that women and men may use and interpret compliments differently. While women seem to use compliments to establish, maintain and strengthen relationships, they are much less clearly positive politeness devices for men, where they need to be used with care – especially to other men – since they can be face-threatening. The fact that men pay more compliments to women than they do to men may indicate that men are aware of the value of compliments in women's eyes – a solidarity-based explanation. Alternatively, this pattern may reflect the fact that men perceive compliments as appropriate encouragement or evaluative feedback to subordinates. In other words, male compliments to women may reflect the different social power positions of women and men.

[. . .]

Conclusion

In concluding this paper it is worth emphasising the range of functions any utterance may perform. The detailed analysis of compliments illustrated well that the 'same' utterance may simultaneously convey a range of meanings. The 'same' utterance may also be used and interpreted differently by different social groups, including women and men. Just as a gift expresses solidarity and appreciation in some cultures, but is a form of one-upping a rival in others (Tannen 1990: 295–6), so at least some compliments may be accepted as tokens of solidarity by women but experienced as an embarrassment by men. The same is likely to be true of other potential positive politeness devices. They are likely to be used and interpreted very differently in different contexts and cultures.

On the basis of a number of different aspects of the distribution of compliments in the New Zealand corpus, I have suggested that women tend to perceive and use compliments as positively affective speech acts and expressions of solidarity, whereas the responses of men may be more ambivalent. It seems possible that in some situations, at least, and with some types of compliment in particular, men may be more likely to interpret compliments as face-threatening acts. The pattern I have suggested provides an intriguing mirror-image of Kuiper's (1991, reprinted in this volume, p. 285) analysis of the way insults which would certainly be experienced as face-threatening acts by women, appear to perform a solidarity-maintaining function for at least some men. Kuiper describes the verbal interaction of members of a rugby team in the locker room before a match. The team members insult and abuse each other, using terms of address such as 'wanker', 'fuck-face' and the more overtly sexist 'fucking old woman', and 'girl's blouse'. For this group 'sexual humiliation is used as a means of creating group solidarity through the loss of face the individuals who belong to the group suffer' (1991: 200). (See also Labov 1972 on ritual insults among Black gang members and Dundes et al. 1972 on Turkish boys' verbal duelling.) Insults function for these men as expressions of solidarity, whereas the data in this chapter has suggested women prefer compliments for this function.

It also seems possible that the way men use compliments to women, in particular, may reflect the subordinate status of women in the society generally. Like endearments, compliments gain their force from the context of the relationship in which they are used. When used non-reciprocally by superiors to subordinates, these may underline patterns of societal power which place women in a clearly subordinate position to men. When used between equals and friends, on the other hand, and especially female equals and friends, a compliment could be considered a quintessential example of a positive politeness strategy.

NOTE

1   As noted in Holmes (1988), the predominance of females among the data collectors was a potential source of bias. The figures nevertheless suggest that even with equal numbers of female and male data collectors, compliments between females will be more frequent than compliments between males, though the imbalance would not be so dramatic.

REFERENCES

Aries, E. J. (1976) 'Interaction patterns and themes of male, female and mixed groups'. *Small Group Behaviour*, 7, 1, 7–18.
Aries, E. J. (1982) 'Verbal and non-verbal behaviour in single-sex and mixed-sex groups: are traditional sex roles changing?' *Psychological Reports*, 51, 127–34.
Aries, E. J. (1987) 'Gender and communication', pp. 149–76 in P. Shaver and C. Hendrick (eds) *Sex and Gender*. Newbury Park, CA: Sage.
Baird, J. E. and Bradley, P. H. (1979) 'Styles of management and communication: a comparative study of men and women'. *Communication Monographs*, 46, 101–11.
Brown, P. and Levinson, S. (1987) *Politeness: Some Universals in Language Use*. Cambridge: Cambridge University Press.
D'Amico-Reisner, L. (1983) 'An analysis of the surface structure of disapproval exchanges', pp. 103–15 in N. Wolfson and E. Judd (eds) *Sociolinguistics and Language Acquisition*. Rowley, MA: Newbury House.
De Bie, M. L. W. (1987) 'Classroom interaction: survival of the fittest', pp. 76–88 in D. Brouwer and D. de Haan (eds) *Women's Language, Socialisation and Self-Image*. Dordrecht: Foris.
Dundes, A., Leach, J. W. and Özkök, B. (1972) 'The strategy of Turkish boys' verbal dueling rhymes', pp. 130–60 in J. J. Gumperz and D. Hymes (eds) *Directions in Sociolinguistics*. New York: Holt, Rinehart & Winston.

Herbert, R. K. (1989) 'The ethnography of English compliments and compliment responses: a contrastive sketch', pp. 3–35 in W. Olesky (ed.) *Contrastive Pragmatics*. Amsterdam: John Benjamins.

Herbert, R. K. (1990) 'Sex-based differences in compliment behaviour'. *Language in Society*, 19, 201–24.

Holmes, J. (1986) 'Compliments and compliment responses in New Zealand English'. *Anthropological Linguistics*, 28, 4, 485–508.

Holmes, J. (1988) 'Paying compliments: a sex-preferred positive politeness strategy'. *Journal of Pragmatics*, 12, 3, 445–65.

Hymes, D. (1962) 'The ethnography of speaking', pp. 15–53 in T. Gladwin and W. Sturtevant (eds) *Anthropology and Human Behaviour*. Washington, DC: Anthropological Society of Washington.

Hymes, D. (1972) 'On communicative competence', pp. 269–93 in J. B. Pride and J. Holmes (eds) *Sociolinguistics*. Harmondsworth: Penguin.

Hymes, D. (1974) 'Ways of speaking', pp. 433–51 in R. Bauman and J. Sherzer (eds) *Explorations in the Ethnography of Speaking*. Cambridge: Cambridge University Press.

Johnson, D. M. and Roen, D. H. (1992) 'Complimenting and involvement in peer reviews: gender variation'. *Language in Society*, 21, 1, 27–57.

Kalcik, S. (1975) ' "... like Ann's gynaecologist or the time I was almost raped" – personal narratives in women's rap groups'. *Journal of American Folklore*, 88, 3–11.

Kissling, E. A. (1991) 'Street harassment: the language of sexual terrorism'. *Discourse and Society*, 2, 4, 451–60.

Kissling, E. A. and Kramarae, C. (1991) ' "Stranger compliments": the interpretation of street remarks'. *Women's Studies in Communication*, Spring, 77–95.

Knapp, M. L., Hopper, R. and Bell, R. (1984) 'Compliments: a descriptive taxonomy'. *Journal of Communications*, 34, 4, 12–31.

Kuiper, K. (1991) 'Sporting formulae in New Zealand English: two models of male solidarity', pp. 200–9 in J. Cheshire (ed.) *English Around the World: Sociolinguistic Perspectives*. Cambridge: Cambridge University Press.

Labov, W. (1972) 'Rules for ritual insults', pp. 265–314 in T. Kochman (ed.) *Rappin' and Stylin' Out*. Chicago: University of Illinois Press.

Leech, G. N. (1983) *Principles of Pragmatics*. London: Longman.

Lewandowska-Tomaszczyk, B. (1989) 'Praising and complimenting', pp. 73–100 in W. Olesky (ed.) *Contrastive Pragmatics*. Amsterdam: John Benjamins.

Manes, J. (1983) 'Compliments: a mirror of cultural values', pp. 96–102 in N. Wolfson and E. Judd (eds) *Sociolinguistics and Language Acquisition*. Rowley, MA: Newbury House.

Manes, J. and Wolfson, N. (1981) 'The compliment formula', pp. 115–32 in F. Coulmas (ed.) *Conversational Routine*. The Hague: Mouton.

Piliavin, J. A. and Martin, R. R. (1978) 'The effects of the sex composition of groups on style of social interaction'. *Sex Roles*, 4, 281–96.

Preisler, B. (1986) *Linguistic Sex Roles in Conversation*. Berlin: Mouton de Gruyter.

Schick Case, S. (1988) 'Cultural differences, not deficiencies: an analysis of managerial women's language', pp. 41–63 in S. Rose and L. Larwood (eds) *Women's Careers: Pathways and Pitfalls*. New York: Praeger.

Swacker, M. (1979) 'Women's verbal behaviour at learned and professional conferences', pp. 155–60 in B. Dubois and I. Crouch (eds) *The Sociology of the Languages of American Women*. San Antonio, TX: Trinity University.

Tannen, D. (1990) *You Just Don't Understand: Women and Men in Conversation*. New York: William Morrow.

Troemel-Ploetz, S. (1992) 'The construction of conversational equality by women', pp. 581–9 in K. Hall, M. Bucholtz and B. Moonwomon (eds) *Locating Power. Proceedings of the Second Berkeley Women and Language Conference* (4 and 5 April 1992), vol 2. Berkeley, CA: Berkeley Women and Language Group, University of California.

Wierzbicka, A. (1987) *English Speech Acts Verbs: A Semantic Dictionary*. New York: Academic Press.

Wolfson, N. (1981) 'Compliments in cross-cultural perspective'. *TESOL Quarterly*, 15, 2, 117–24.

Wolfson, N. (1983) 'An empirically based analysis of complimenting in American English', pp. 82–95 in N. Wolfson and E. Judd (eds) *Sociolinguistics and Language Acquisition*. Rowley, MA: Newbury House.

Wolfson, N. (1984) ' "Pretty is as pretty does": a speech act view of sex roles'. *Applied Linguistics*, 5, 3, 236–44.

Wolfson, N. (1988) 'The bulge: a theory of speech behaviour and social distance', pp. 21–38 in J. Fine (ed.) *Second Language Discourse: A Textbook of Current Research*. Norwood, NJ: Ablex.

9

Cooperation and Competition Across Girls' Play Activities

Marjorie Harness Goodwin

In an attempt to characterize women as speaking "in a different voice," recent research on female interaction patterns has tended to examine those features of female communication which are clearly different from those of males to the exclusion of those which females and males share in common. For example, cooperative aspects of female language usage have been examined (e.g., Brown, 1980, reprinted in this volume, p. 81; Maltz & Borker, 1982, reprinted in this volume, p. 417), while ways in which disagreement may be expressed have been largely ignored. Investigations of girls' play have also neglected to analyze the full range of female interactional competencies. According to Piaget (1965: p. 77), Lever (1976: p. 482), and Gilligan (1982: pp. 9–20) the lack of complex rule structure and forms of direct competitiveness in girls' games (as for example are found in marbles (Piaget, 1965) or team sports (Lever, 1976)) limits their opportunities for practicing negotiational skills. [...]

Detailed ethnographic study of girls in play situations (Goodwin, 1985; Hughes, in press) presents a different view of girls' competencies. In my studies of urban black girls I found that, with respect to boys, while some of girls' activities are conducted with what appears to be minimal disagreement or competition (Goodwin, 1980b), others provide for extensive negotiation (Goodwin, 1980a; Goodwin, 1985; Goodwin & Goodwin, 1987). The forms of social organization which girls select to carry out their play vary across different types of play activities. In order to investigate such variation, this paper focuses on a single type of speech sequence, yet the primary one through which children achieve organization in domains of play: sequences of "directives" or speech actions that try to get another to do something (Austin, 1962), and their responses. Directives will be examined within two play contexts – activities in which children are accomplishing a task and pretend play – as well as within cross-sex and caretaking situations. In this way it will be possible to examine how girls' directives and social organization take different forms across various activities.

For comparative purposes I will first summarize findings regarding how boys conduct themselves in a specific task activity, making slingshots and organizing a

slingshot fight.[1] The types of hierarchical differences they establish between participants while performing a task permeate all aspects of their peer activities (comparing
one another, arguing, storytelling, etc.). Next I will analyze how girls interact as they
undertake a comparable task activity – making rings from the rims of glass bottles.
In contrast to the boys, when girls organize tasks they select a more egalitarian form
of social structure, avoiding the creation of distinctions between participants. Such
a form of organization is consistent with the way in which they normally conduct
their daily interactions with one another. When the full repertoire of female interaction patterns is investigated it can be seen that girls exhibit ways of formulating
and sequencing their talk which display both cooperative and competitive forms. For
example, in the activities of repairing utterances or disagreeing with one another
girls use argumentative speech forms shared by the boys (Goodwin, 1983; Goodwin
& Goodwin, 1987). Girls do not, however, customarily use bald commands, insults
and threats – actions which are commonplace among the boys. Such actions are
reserved for situations in which girls sanction the behavior of one of their members.
Nonetheless the forms of accounts girls use in directive sequences express concerns
that are distinctive from those used by the boys. Across different domains, girls
exhibit a range of ways of executing decisions about courses of action and evolve
distinctive forms of social organization.

Fieldwork and Background for the Study

The present study is based on fieldwork among a group of children in a black
working class neighborhood of West Philadelphia whom I encountered during a
walk around my neighborhood. I observed them for a year and a half as they played
on the street, focussing on how the children used language within interaction to
organize their everyday activities. The children (whom I will call the Maple Street
group) ranged in age from four through 14 and spent much of the time in four same
age/sex groups (older and younger girls and older and younger boys). Here I will be
concerned principally with children in the older age group, from 10–13. As they
played on the street after school, on weekends and during the summer months I
audiotaped their conversation. In gathering data I did not focus on particular types
of events that I had previously decided were theoretically important (for example
stories or rhymes) but instead tried to observe and record as much of what the
children did as possible, no matter how mundane it might seem. Moreover I tried to
avoid influencing what the children were doing. The methods I used to gather data
about the children were thus quite different from those characteristically used in
psychological and sociological studies of children's behavior; in such studies efforts
are typically made to systematically collect particular types of information deemed to
be theoretically important in a carefully controlled fashion. Rather than being based
on a laboratory model, the methodology I used was ethnographic, and designed to
capture as accurately as possible the structure of events in the children's world as
they unfolded in the ordinary settings where they habitually occurred. Therefore I

did not have to rely on what subjects or interviewees might tell a researcher and could observe the conduct of children in a range of situations.

Alternative Forms of Directives

The ways in which speakers format their directives and sequence turns to them provide for a range of possible types of social arrangements between participants. Some directive/response sequences display an orientation towards a differentiation between participants, and result in asymmetrical forms of relationships. Others, by way of contrast, display an orientation towards seeking to minimize distinctions between participants and result in more egalitarian or symmetrical arrangements of social relationships. Within different clusters there may also be a division of labor with respect to the delivery of certain types of moves. This has consequences for the type of social organization a group evolves.

Directives have been discussed as forms of "social control acts" ("moves in which there is a clear intention to influence the activities of the partner" (Ervin-Tripp, 1982: p. 29)) and "persuasive talk" (Cook-Gumperz, 1981). One way in which directives may be formatted is in a very straightforward or "aggravated" (Labov & Fanshel, 1977: pp. 84–86) way, as imperatives (i.e., "Do X!"). Alternatively, directives may take more softened or "mitigated" (Labov & Fanshel 1977: pp. 84–86) forms, as requests ("Could you please do X?").
[. . .]

The Organization of a Task Among Boys

Making slingshots from wire coat hangers is a pastime which could be organized in a variety of different ways. The slingshot is an individual instrument, and, in theory, play with it could be construed as an individual activity in which all participants fend for themselves, the only preparation being that each have a slingshot and an adequate supply of "slings." Among the boys of Maple Street, however, the activity of making and using slingshots became organized into a competition between two separate "sides" or teams (not unlike those in football or basketball) with a hierarchical organization of participants on each team.[2] The slingshot fight itself was preceded by an extended preparation period during which, not only were weapons and slings made, but the organization of the group was also negotiated. All of the elements in this process, such as the allocation of necessary tools, the spatial organization of participants, where the preparation would occur, who would provide materials, who had rights to resources, when the activity was to move from stage to stage, what battle strategy would consist of, etc., became the focus for status negotiations between participants.

The formatting of leaders' directives and accounts in a boys' task activity

One key resource that was used in negotiation among the boys about their relative status was alternative formats for asking or ordering someone else to do something. A typical way that one party attempted to display or establish his position with respect to another party was by making directives in the form of explicit commands to that party rather than as hints, suggestions, or indirect requests. In organizing the slingshot session the team leaders, Michael and Huey, constructed their directives using the imperative form ("Do X!"). In the terminology developed by Labov and Fanshel (1977: pp. 84–86) they thus choose relatively "aggravated" or explicit directive forms. The following data are transcribed according to the system developed by Jefferson and described in Sacks, Schegloff, and Jefferson (1974: pp. 731–733). A simplified version of this transcription system appears in Transcription Conventions 1 (p. xviii).

(1) MICHAEL: *All* right. Gimme some rubber bands.
     CHOPPER: ((*Giving rubber bands to Michael*)) Oh.

(2) HUEY: Go downstairs. I don't care *what* you say you aren't – you ain't no good so
                go down*stairs*.
     BRUCE: ((*Moves down the steps*))

(3)   ((*Regarding coat hanger wire*))
     MICHAEL: Give it to me man. Where's yours at. Throw that piece of shit out.
     CHOPPER: ((*Gives Michael his cut-off piece of hanger*))

The turn containing the imperative arguing for the speaker's relative control vis-à-vis the recipient may be accompanied by various types of "semantic aggravators" (Becker, 1982: p. 8) i.e., threats, phrases demanding immediate action, etc., which display the speaker's view of the recipient's subordinate status. As is shown in examples 2 and 3, negative descriptions of the other (e.g., "you ain't no good") or of his objects (e.g., referring to one of Chopper's slings as "shit") may accompany the imperative to further denigrate the recipient's character. In response to these sequences, recipients comply with the requests. Of course other types of next responses, such as counters, are possible next moves, as in lines 2, 4, and 7 of the following:

(4)   ((*Michael asks for pliers*))
     1 MICHAEL: Gimme the thing.
     2 POOCHIE:→   Wait a minute. I gotta chop it.
     3 MICHAEL: Come on.
     4 POOCHIE:→   I gotta chop it.
     5 MICHAEL: Come on Poochie. You gonna be with
     6   them? Give it to me. I'll show you.
     7 POOCHIE:→   I already had it before you.
     8 MICHAEL: So? I brought them out here. They
     9   mine. So I use em when I feel like it.

In this sequence Michael responds to counters with actions which argue for his ultimate control of the situation. For example in line 5 through his question "You gonna be with them?" Michael counters Poochie by threatening to make Poochie be on another team. In lines 8–9 Michael refutes the relevance of Poochie's counter by arguing that he has ultimate jurisdiction concerning the allocation of resources. In other instances when players counter Michael or Huey's imperatives, the leaders display their authority by reminding subordinates that they can also make them leave their property (i.e., "Get off my steps." or "I'll tell you to get out of *here* if I *want* you to.").

The imperative forms of the leaders' actions differ from the ways in which other players formulate actions to Michael and Huey. Requests for information such as "Can I have some hangers?" or "Can me and Robert play if Robert be on Huey's team?" are used in actions to team leaders. In contrast to the actions which Michael and Huey use towards their teammates, requests for information display deference towards the addressee and permit options in the way in which the recipient should respond. When answering such mitigated types of directives, those assuming leadership positions do not comply with the proposed actions, as in examples 1–3, but instead provide arbitrary definitions of the situation (example 5), return imperatives (example 6), and flat refusals (example 7):

(5) BRUCE: Can me and Robert play if Robert be on Huey's team?
     MICHAEL: IT'S ALREADY TOO *M*ANY OF US.

(6)   ((*Tokay takes a hanger*))
     TOKAY: Can I have some hangers?
     MICHAEL: Put that thing *b*ack!

(7) ROBBY: Michael could I be on your side?
     MICHAEL: *Heck* no!

A form of asymmetry is established through the alternative ways in which directives and their responses are formatted. While Michael delivers aggravated actions getting compliance in return, his teammates issue mitigated directives receiving counters as next moves.

Michael's actions are not only direct and aggravated but also arbitrary. To see the import of this it is important to note that not all direct imperatives constitute degrading actions to a recipient. Thus in many cases the situation of the moment itself warrants the use of directive formats that in other circumstances would be seen as aggravated. For example in the midst of a game of jump rope girls yell "Watch out!" as a car comes, or "Go ahead Nettie!" to urge a player to take her turn. Similarly, imperatives may be appropriate in work settings where differences in rank call for the subordination of one party to the other (Ervin-Tripp, 1976: p. 29). However, the directives Michael issues display no obvious reason why certain tasks need to be performed "right now" except for his own whims. The use of "need statements" (Ervin-Tripp, 1976: p. 29), "desire statements" (Ervin-Tripp, 1982: p. 30) or "explicit statements" (Ervin-Tripp, 1982: p. 35) has been argued (Garvey, 1975: pp. 52, 60; Ervin-Tripp, 1976: p. 29) to constitute among the most aggravated ways of formulating a directive. For example:

(8)   MICHAEL: PL:IERS. I WANT THE PLIERS! Man y'all gonna have to get y'all *own* wire cutters if *this* the way y'all gonna be.
       NATE: Okay. Okay.

(9)

→   MICHAEL: Everybody. Now I don't need all y'all down here in this little space. Get back *up* there. Get *up* there. Now! Get back up there please.

In brief, through the way in which Michael constructs his directives he proposes his superior status with respect to others, and others' inferior positioning vis-à-vis him. He uses actions which imply that he independently can define for others how the task should proceed and how their actions can be interpreted. In response others assuming an inferior position with respect to him often provide compliance through either a nonvocal carrying out of the requested action (as occurred in examples 1–3) and/or signals of vocal agreement (as in examples 1 and 8).

Instructing others

There is one aspect of Michael's performance as team leader – instructing his subordinates – in which the use of aggravated social control acts appears less arbitrary. The job of teaching teammates how to make slings makes use of a participation framework common to other teaching situations. Instructing implies an asymmetrical relationship of participants, with the teacher providing actions such as getting the attention of the subordinates, giving them information, and criticizing them (Cazden, et al., 1979: p. 210). Assertions, such as "See this how we gonna do ours." in example 10 below may stand for speech acts with directive force. Frequently, as in the next two examples, an account for why the stated course of action should be pursued is provided: either that the leader's way is a superior way of executing the task, as in example 10, or simply that the leader has a particular plan for how the activity should take place (example 12):

(10)   MICHAEL: See this how we gonna do ours. It's a lot better and faster. Bend that side and then we bend this side too.

(11)   MICHAEL: Look I wanna show you how to do it so when you get the things you gonna know how to do it.

(12)   MICHAEL: I know what we gonna do. Poochie, a- after I cut these up all y'all- all y'all gonna cut these things off and Poochie gonna bend them and I cut em. And I just chop em. And then y'all pick em up. And they be ours.

Michael, as leader of his group, not only prescribes the working procedures and division of labor for sling making; in addition he dictates team strategy:

(13) 1 MICHAEL: Now. Re*mem*ber what I sai:d. And
    2   don't try to shoot till
    3 TOKAY: Like- like they in sight?
    4 MICHAEL: That's *right*.
    5 TOKAY: What if they ain't.
    6 MICHAEL: But if they- if they hidin in some
    7   bushes, don't you shoot. = You let them
    8   waste theirs. Count for the man how
    9   many he waste. Then after he waste as
   10   many as you got you let him shoot his.
   11   But then you let him waste some more.

As is clearly illustrated by this example, Michael's role as leader of the peer group is ratified through the types of actions, such as Tokay's requests for information (lines 3 and 5), which are initiated towards him. Because Michael is felt to be in control of knowledge regarding the craft, his opinion and assistance is summoned repetitively:

(14)   ((*Michael illustrates bending and cutting coat hangers*))
     MICHAEL: You bend it over like that and when- when you finish I'll show you how to just do these.
→   TOKAY: After it break, stomp down?
     MICHAEL: Just clap em.

(15)   MICHAEL: After I cut these up
→   POOCHIE: Who turn is it.
     CHOPPER: Mine. Mine. *Uh* uh. Ain't it my turn Michael,
     MICHAEL: ((*nods yes*))
     CHOPPER: See?

[. . .]

As proprietors of the house where play occurs both Michael and Huey can exert considerable leverage in getting boys to do what they want them to do, in that they can threaten them with having to leave the premises:
[. . .]

(16)   ((*Michael moves into Poochie's space*))
     POOCHIE: Get outa here.
→   MICHAEL: Hell it's my house.
     POOCHIE: You always gettin in the way. You talkin about we can't even come up there.
     HUEY: That's *right*. It's mine *too*.
     POOCHIE: So.
→   MICHAEL: I'll tell you to get out of *here* if I *want* you to.
     HUEY: Yep.

Thus, despite the fact that participants other than those acting as team leaders may initiate instruction sequences or counter the instructions from them, there is an asymmetry with respect to whose instructions are treated as binding. Considerable power resides in the party who sponsors a task activity at his home, and this may account for the differential success with which his proposals are eventually heeded.

Summary of observations on how boys construct task activities

Within the boys' group a pattern of asymmetry in the formatting and usage of directives and their responses develops in the interaction between players, creating the positions of leaders and followers. Michael and Huey, who assume the position of leaders for this activity, issue bald imperatives to others and characteristically get compliance. These commands concern every aspect of the slingshot making, including access to resources, site for play, procedure for manufacturing "slings," future battle strategy, etc. Many of their imperatives contain insult terms or implicit comparisons which place the recipient in a degraded position with respect to the speaker; accounts that accompany Michael and Huey's directives propose that the activity should be performed because of their personal definition of the situation or needs of the moment, rather than any requirements of the current activity. Michael assumes the position of instructor vis-à-vis the others, and the other boys ratify this claim. A division of labor develops with respect to the distribution of various types of actions. Boys other than Michael and Huey do not initiate new phases of the activity through giving bald imperatives; instead they use more mitigated forms, requests for information. Michael's position in the group is displayed and validated in a number of different ways: through issuing direct commands while receiving indirect requests and through contradicting proposals and requests of others, while expecting and getting compliance to his own.

The Organization of Girls' Task Activity

In this section I will analyze how girls go about organizing a task activity which is comparable to that of the boys, making rings from glass bottle rims. In making the rings, girls carefully scrape bottle rims over metal manhole covers or other rough surfaces so that the rims break evenly, leaving as few jagged edges as possible. The jobs faced by girls in making their objects do not substantially differ from those faced by boys; they involve procuring and allocating resources and establishing techniques for the objects' manufacture. Thus, in making rings the girls must decide where they will get the bottles necessary to make the rings, how many bottles are needed, who should break the bottles, how precisely the rims of bottles should be broken over metal manhole covers, how used bottles should be disposed of, and how the rings should be decorated.

The formatting of directives and accounts in girls' task activity

With the exception of the domain of pretend play, hierarchical forms of organization are uncommon in girls' play. In accomplishing a task activity girls participate jointly in decision-making with minimal negotiation of status. This process is both reflected in and achieved through the selection of syntactic formats for the production of directives as well as forms of accounts which are quite different from those selected by the boys. The following provide examples of the types of directives typically found among the girls:

(17)   ((*Girls are searching for bottles from which to make rings*))
      TERRI: Well let's go- let's go around the corner- Let's let's go around the corner where whatchacallem.

(18)   ((*Girls are looking for bottles*))
      TERRI: Let's go. There may be some more on Sixty Ninth Street.
      SHARON: Come on. Let's turn back y'all so we can safe keep em. Come on. Let's go get some.

(19)   ((*Girls are looking for bottles*))
      SHARON: Let's go around Subs and Suds.
      PAM: Let's ask her "Do you have any bottles."

Whereas boys' directives typically constitute commands that an action should be undertaken at the time the imperative is issued, girls' directives are constructed as suggestions for action in the future. Syntactically the forms utilized by the boys generally differentiate speaker and hearer. One party is either ordering another to do something, or alternatively, requesting action from some other party. By way of contrast the verb used by the girls, "*let's*" (generally used only by the boys when shifting a major phase of the activity underway),[3] includes both speaker and hearer as potential agents of the action to be performed,[4] thus mitigating the appearance of control. *Let's* signals a proposal rather than either a command or a request and as such shows neither special deference towards the other party (as a request does) nor claims about special rights of control over the other (as a command does). Thus, through the way in which they format their directives, the girls make visible an undifferentiated, "egalitarian" relationship between speaker and addressee(s), that differs quite markedly from the asymmetrical, hierarchical relationship displayed in boys' directives.

The structure of directives used to organize making rings is not different from the types of actions which are used to direct other girls' activities which involve a joint task, as can be seen in the examples below in which participants undertake playing jacks (example 20), jumping rope to a particular rhyme called "one two three footsies" (example 21) and hunting for turtles (example 22).

(20) DARLENE: Let's play some more jacks.

(21) PAM: Let's play "one two three footsies." First!

(22)   ((*Searching for turtles*))
      PAM: Let's look around. See what we can find.

In alternation to the use of "*let's*" the auxiliary verb "*gonna*" with a plural subject and the modal verbs "*can*" or "*could*" can also be used to format an action as a mitigated directive form (Blum-Kulka & Olshtain, 1984: p. 203), proposing a suggestion or a joint plan as in the following which occur in the midst of making glass rings:

(23) SHARON: We gonna paint em and stuff.

(24) PAM: We could go around lookin for more bottles.

(25)   ((*Discussing keeping the ring making secret from boys*))
      TERRI: We can *l*imp back so nobody know where we *g*ettin them from.

In some cases the overt tentativeness of the modal is further intensified through the use of terms such as *maybe*:

(26) TERRI: Maybe we can slice *them* like that.

Directives which include verbs such as *gotta* (which place more demands on recipient than modal verbs) may also contain an account providing explicit reasons for why an action should be undertaken. Characteristically, such accounts consider the benefits which would accrue to all members of the group:

(27) SHARON: Pam you know what we could do, (0.5) We gotta *cl*ean em first, We gotta
            *cl*ean em.
      PAM: Huh,
      SHARON: We gotta *cl*ean em first, / / You know,
      PAM: I know.
        → [[Cuz they got germs.
      SHARON: Wash em and stuff cuz just in case they
        →   got germs on em.
            [[And then you clean em,
      PAM: I got some paints.
               (3.5)
      SHARON: Clean em, and then we *cl*ean em and we gotta be careful with em before we
            get the glass cutters. You know we gotta
        →   be careful with em cuz it cuts easy.

In circumstances of urgency, e.g., when the safety of a group member is at stake,[5] imperatives constitute the appropriate and even expected form (Brown & Levinson, 1978: pp. 100–101). Characteristically, when imperatives are used by girls they are accompanied by accounts which take into consideration the situation of the addressee, such as her safety:

(28)   ((*Regarding Pam's finger cut while making glass rings*))
      SHARON: Pam don't you lick your own blood.
        →   That way it gonna go right back there through your body.

(29)   ((*Terri and Sharon attempt to put mercurochrome on Pam's cut finger*))
      TERRI: Take it out now Pam.

PAM:	No I'm not.	
TERRI:	Get- it ain't gonna hurt you girl. You	
→	got- and you want to get your hand	
	infected and they take- they take the hand taken off?	

Thus despite the relative infrequency of imperatives used in organizing girls' task activities, there are nevertheless circumstances which occur when imperatives constitute the most appropriate form of directive. The type of account which girls offer to support their imperatives during task activities contrast markedly with the accounts accompanying boys' commands. Rather than arguing that an action should be performed because of one party's personal desires, girls' imperatives deal with the requirements of the current activity.

Instructing others

When girls use imperatives during instruction they may qualify their talk in ways which are sensitive to both the form of their social organization and other aspects of context. In the next example girls actively negotiate who has the right to address others with imperatives while demonstrating how to break the glass rim of the bottles; it is not assumed that any one party has exclusive rights to instruct another. When Pam takes over the job of teaching in lines 11–18 she uses a range of para-linguistic cues to frame her talk (Goffman, 1974), or contextualize it in a particular way (Gumperz, 1982). Thus she speaks with singsong intonation, caricaturing a teacher (lines 14–18) and colors her talk with laughter.

(30)	1	PAM:	Get that one. Here! Yeah give it to
	2		her.
	3		(2.0)
	4	SHARON:	This won't know the difference.
	5	PAM:	Get outa the street.
	6		(0.8)
	7		See you gotta do it real hard.
	8	SHARON:	Gimme this. I wanna do it. You're
	9		cracked. I wanna show you how to do
	10		it. I know how to do it *Pam!*
	11	PAM:	*I* know. I ju- So you won't have to
	12		break it. Like y'know. Do it like ((*as she demonstrates scraping it against a metal manhole cover at the correct angle for getting a smooth bottle rim*))
	13	SHARON:	Yeah.
	14	PAM:	⌈ ((*singsong instructing voice*)) But when
	15		⎮ you get at the end you do it hard so
	16		⎮ the thing would break off right, eh heh
	17		⎮ heh! ((*laughing at style of teaching*))
	18		⌊ Harder!
	19	SHARON:	Do it *harder*.
	20	PAM:	Eh heh heh! / / Oh:.

The negotiation which takes place here has features of what developmental psychologists Stone and Selman (1982: pp. 169–179) describe as a considerably advanced form of "social negotiation strategy." They note that in the "collaboration" stage of negotiation children make use of various paralinguistic expressions to "communicate multiple, often ironic, meanings" (Stone & Selman, 1982: p. 175), employing "a contrast between the form they use and the form generally used in peer interaction." Here, while instructing others, Pam gives them orders in lines 1–2, 5, and 7; Sharon in lines 8–10 counters that she wants to do it herself and does not need any instruction from Pam. Such active objection to letting another issue orders is congruent with the ways that the girls in other contexts actively monitor each other for actions that could be seen as claiming that one girl is setting herself above the others. When Pam takes up the instructor role again in lines 14–18 she modifies the intonation of her voice; by adopting a singsong lilt she mocks the way she is delivering her instructions to the group. Through this caricaturing of the talk of an instructor Pam distances (Goffman, 1961: pp. 120–132) herself from the teaching role she is currently enacting, thereby making herself a more equal partner in the play.

This sequence of instructing thus differs from comparable ones among the boys (examples 10–13). Michael took his instructor role quite seriously, with little deviation from a strict interpretation of his notion of himself as someone superior to the others present. Interaction from other parties supported the image of Michael as more knowledgeable than others (see example 13) and portrayed their current social relationships as asymmetrical. By way of contrast, Sharon's objections to Pam's teaching challenge the position of superordination Pam has adopted. Pam begins modifying her role as instructor when Sharon objects, and eventually even laughs at her own speaking style. The negotiation in this sequence thus resembles the symmetrical features of roles observable in other phases of task activities, with girls extending to one another equivalent types of actions and avoiding the appearance of hierarchy.

Achieving symmetry in interaction within girls' directive sequences

It was noted earlier that asymmetry among the boys was displayed not only in the formatting of particular directives, but also in the differential usage of both directives and responses to them. In the boys' group generally only the party acting as leader issued the directives prescribing actions for others, and he responded to others' directives with refutations. In the girls' group, however, proposals for certain courses of action can be made by many different participants, and the girls generally agree to the suggestions of others. For example:

(31) SHARON: You can get people to cut this though.
      PAM: Yep.

(32) TERRI: Hey y'all. Let's use these first and then come back and get the rest cuz it's too *many* of em.
      SHARON: That *right*.

> TERRI: We can *l*imp back so nobody know where we *g*ettin them from.
> (0.8)
> SHARON: That's right.
> TERRI: And w- and wash our hands. And wash your hands when you get *f*inish now.
> SHARON: If the boys try to follow us we don't know. Okay?
> TERRI: Yep.

Thus in terms of both how directives are constructed, and the way in which others respond to them, the girls' system of directive use displays similarity and equality rather than differentiation among group members.

[...]

Although girls do not characteristically respond to directives in ways which show one party superior to another, they do counter one another's proposals for action. Argumentation is as common an activity in the girls' group as it is among boys or in mixed-sex groups (Goodwin & Goodwin, 1987). The following is an example of a directive/counter sequence in the midst of a task activity:

(33)   ((*On reaching a city creek while turtle hunting*))
> 1   PAM: Y'all gonna walk in it?
> 2   NETTIE: *Walk* in it, You know where that
> 3   water come from? The toilet.
> 4   PAM: So, I'm a walk in it in my dirty feet.
> 5   I'm a walk in it and I don't care if it
> 6   do come.=You would / / easy wash your
> 7   feet.
> 8   NETTIE: ((*to ethnographer*)) Gonna walk us
> 9   across? Yeah I'll show y'all where you
> 10   can come.

In this example negotiations occur with regard to directives. The directive initially posed by Pam in line 1 ("Y'all gonna walk in it?") is countered by Nettie (line 2). Pam then opposes Nettie's counter to her (line 4). Subsequently, in the midst of Pam's turn (line 6) Nettie interrupts to reinstate Pam's initial request and issue a second directive regarding where to step in the creek. Upon completion of this fragment, each of the major parties to the conversation has both given a directive and countered the other's action. The form of the argumentation, however, has not attempted to affirm the relative superiority of one party with respect to the other. The directives in lines 1 and 8 are requests for information and in line 6 the directive is framed as a proposal using a modal verb. Moreover the counters do not flatly refuse prior actions; instead they provide first (lines 2–3) an argument against the appropriateness of the suggested action and second (line 4) an argument against the consequentiality of the suggested action. The directive/counter sequences promote a symmetrical rather than an asymmetrical social situation in that counters to proposals are themselves considered counterable, and a proposal initiated by one party may be reinstated subsequently by another.

Summary of findings about differences in the organization of task activities among girls and boys

Though boys and girls make use of a common system of directives for the coordination of behavior in task activities, they construct these actions in quite different ways. By selecting alternative directive forms and responses and by creating differing divisions of labor with respect to who can issue particular forms, they build different forms of social organization. Boys' directives are formatted as imperatives from superordinate to subordinate, or requests, generally upward in rank. The usage of alternative asymmetrical forms for the directive, such as the request and the command, is differentially distributed among members of the boys' group; however, among the girls all have access to similar types of actions. Girls characteristically phrase their directives as proposals for future activity and frequently mitigate even these proposals with a term such as *maybe*. They tend to leave the time at which the action being proposed should be performed somewhat open, while a boy in a position of leadership states that he wants an action completed *right now*. Syntactically the directives of the boys differentiate speaker from hearer. Among the girls, however, the party issuing the directive is usually included as one of the agents in the action to be performed. From the point of view of cognitive psychologists who study "social perspective taking" ("an individual's capacity to coordinate psychological perspectives of self and other" (Stone & Selman, 1982: p. 164)) and "social negotiation strategies" (Stone & Selman, 1982) it can be argued that girls' directives *display* taking into consideration the other's point of view to a far greater extent than boys' directives do.[6] Thus the details of how participants select to build a turn either requesting another to do something or responding to talk make relevant two contrasting modes of interaction; hierarchical or more egalitarian social organization may be proposed through the syntactic structures which are chosen. Though within task activities a symmetrical form of social organization is established by the girls in their same-sex group, in other circumstances, girls can select more aggravated forms and construct quite different forms of social organization.

Directive Use in Playing House

Girls on Maple Street distinguish between various types of directives and degrees of mitigation, as is apparent from the ways in which they talk about alternative polite and impolite forms:

(34)   ((*Concerning a 4-year-old girl, Delin*))
   NETTIE: Delin wanted to come in the house. I said "You say 'ex*cuse* me.' = *Not* '*mo:*ve.' "

(35)   ((*Pam describing how she confronted another girl*))
   PAM: I s'd *I* said "You c'd *roll* your eyes all you *want* to. Cuz I'm *t*ellin you. (0.5) *T*ellin- I'm not *ask*in you." And I ain't say no plea:se *ei*ther.

A major circumstance in which girls make use of aggravated directives is when taking care of younger children and enacting such roles in their favorite pastime, playing house. For example when girls give directives to younger children in their charge, they frequently use aggravated forms or imperatives which resemble those their mothers use in disciplining them.[7] Directives may be accompanied by accounts which can explicitly describe a benefit (such as safety) for the recipient of the imperative as in example 37:

(36)   SHARON: Stay out of the street now man. Come on punk. Hurry up Glen.

(37)   ((*Sharon cautions Delin to stand away from girls making glass rings*))
       SHARON: Delin you get back cuz I don't want nothin fallin in your eyes or in your face. Get back. Get back.

(38)   ((*Delin puts down the hood of her jacket on a windy day*))
       TERRI: *Don't* put that down. Put that back *up*! It's sup*posed* to be that way.

Such types of actions constitute the models for communication which takes place when older children play house with younger children.

Here a specific episode of playing house will be investigated. In order to provide a point of reference for observations made about interaction occurring within this session of pretend play, a diagram of dramatized kinship relationships will be provided. Deniece and Sharon, who enact "sisters" who are "mothers," establish two separate households at the onset of this session.[8] As this diagram shows, Aisha (age 10) is a childless sister of Deniece (10) and Sharon (12). At the onset of play Pam (12), Brenda (8), and Terri (age 12, who frequently acts as parental child[9] taking care of younger sibling Brenda) are the children of Deniece. However during the session Terri negotiates a position as sister of Deniece, Sharon and Aisha. Priscilla (7) and Shahida (5) are Sharon's children.

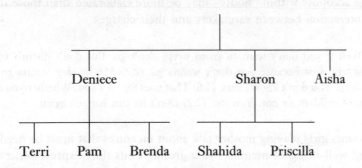

The structure of directives and accounts in house

When playing house girls enacting the role of mother address their "children" with directives that are very similar in structure to those that mothers or caretakers use. Such patterning is consistent with other research on role playing among children's groups (Andersen, 1978: p. 89; Corsaro, 1985: p. 82; Ervin-Tripp, 1982: p. 36; Garvey, 1974, 1977; Mitchell-Kernan & Kernan, 1977: pp. 201–207; Sachs, 1987) which has demonstrated that directives constitute the principal means through which children realize positions of dominance and submission between characters such as those in the mother/child relationship. "Mothers" typically deliver imperatives to their "children":

(39)   DENIECE: Hurry up and go to bed!

(40)   SHARON: BRING THOSE CARDS BACK, BRING THAT BOOK IN THE HOUSE AND C:OME HOME! Don't *climb* over that way. You climb over the *right* way.

(41)   SHARON: PRISCILLA, BRENDA, SHAHIDA, GET IN THE CAR! Get in the car. Shahida and Brenda, and all y'all get in the car.=Where Priscilla at. GET IN THE CAR. YOU GOIN OVER *MY* HOUSE. GO ON OVER AND GET- UH- WHERE'S PRISCILLA AT.

In addition to the job of enacting the roles of characters relative to one another, a principal task for participants is determining what scene is being enacted and making visible that scene. Directives not only constitute the principal ways in which roles in house are dramatized; they also provide the means through which the stage is set and the plot line is developed, as scene-changing guides are embedded in them and reference is made to nonpresent objects and spaces as well as future undertakings.

Accounts which accompany mothers' directives (such as "IT'S TIME TO GO *IN*.=YOU GOTTA GO TO *SCHOOL* TOMORROW!") supply warrants for the imperatives, culturally appropriate reasons for why activities should be done in specific ways. They thus provide the primary ways that participants playing house develop domestic roles and introduce new information into the ongoing action. Consequently the accounts within "house" may be more elaborated than those that occur in actual interaction between caretakers and their charges:

(42)   DENIECE: Well if you don't want to go to sleep, don't go. But don't disturb your sisters. Just because *you* don't wanna go. (2.8) Maybe *they* wanna go to sleep. You don't know:: that. (3.6) That goes for *all* a you. Whether you not my- children or not. You *too*. (2.2) *Don't* let this happen again.

In providing accounts girls playing mother talk about measures that must be heeded for the safety and well-being of members of a group. Thus they express concerns which are similar to those in accounts during girls' task activities.

The positions of those in control in house (as with the boys' slingshot episode) are maintained not simply through the issuing of directives which maintain a particular format. They are also manifested through the *receipt* of various forms of action from others. The actions enacted by smaller children are largely requests for permission, actions which imply an asymmetry of role relationships:[10]

(43)   BRENDA: Mommy can um Aisha play with our baby brother?

(44)   SHAHIDA: Can I hold your book?

(45)   BRENDA: Mommy may *we* go out and play,

When speaking outside an enacted role concerning details of the drama, requests for information are also used to address girls who manage the activity:

(46)   PAM: How old am *I*,

With respect to the roles of mother and children there is thus a form of asymmetry built into the structure of behavior which closely models that in caretaker/child interaction as well as that in leader/follower interaction among the boys during task activities.

Although Maple Street girls playing the roles of subordinates in "house" display deference through their requests for information they do not always display deference through their *responses* to imperatives, as has been reported for other groups (i.e., Corsaro, 1985: p. 83). Excuses rather than agreements are often provided – for example in line 4 of example 47; a counter accusation occurs in line 7.

(47)   1   BRENDA: Maanaa. I want some *pea*nuts.
      2   TERRI: Well you ain't *g*ettin none.
      3   DENIECE: Hurry up and go to bed!
      4   BRENDA: →   ((*whining*)) I was *j*ust eating a *p*eanut.
      5   DENIECE: GO TO *BED*! YOU SUPPOSED- YOU SUPPOSED
      6   TO GET YOURS IN THE MORNINGTIME.
      7   BRENDA: →   ((*whining*)) Well *Y*ou eating them all
      8   *u*:p.
      9   DENIECE: Do you want me to tell her to go- uhm
   10   make you go to bed?

[. . .]

In example 47 mother Deniece persists over several turns in her strategies to attempt to get her child Brenda to comply with directives. Mothers' imperatives are repetitively answered by children's counters as children negotiate their roles with respect to their caretakers.

[. . .]

By framing directives as requests for information, girls playing younger children display their subordination vis-à-vis girls playing mother. However, girls playing children do not assume passive roles in "house." Instead considerable negotiation occurs among girls playing subordinate roles, in both their responses to girls playing roles of mother and among themselves.

Asymmetry in roles in playing house

Symmetrical types of exchanges take place within house in interactions in which siblings exchange equivalent argumentative forms and "mothers" exchange stories about their "children." By comparison with task activities, however, there is a minimum of egalitarianism in decision making. In so far as those acting as children play subordinate roles there is asymmetry built into the activity itself. In addition girls who play the role of mother act in the capacity of stage manager. As overseers of the unfolding drama, both Deniece and Sharon monitor the actions of participants, commenting on them in utterances such as "Hey Brenda you supposed to be sleep." or "Priscilla you can't hear them." For example, in the following Deniece and Sharon, as commenters on Brenda's actions, describe for her appropriate behavior as a child (line 1) and warn her of her precarious tenure in the play through a negative categorization of her behavior ("not even *play*ing right") (lines 4–5), commands (lines 6 and 8) and an account "THAT'S WHY NOBODY WANT YOU FOR A CHILD." (lines 6–7):

(48) 1   DENIECE: HEY BRENDA YOU OUGHTTA / / be sleep!
     2   TERRI: I can't even get her in the bed.
     3   DENIECE: I know.
     4   DENIECE: SHE'S NOT / / EVEN PLAYIN RIGHT. SHE
     5   NOT EVEN *PLAY*IN RIGHT.
     6   SHARON: BRENDA PLAY RIGHT. THAT'S WHY NOBODY
     7   WANT YOU FOR A CHILD.
     8   DENIECE: GET IN THERE AND GO TO SLEEP!

Girls in the position of "mother" can thus dictate for others dimensions of play *outside* the frame of play as well as within it. They not only can control who has rights to play what roles but also who can be members of the group. In example 48, important with respect to issues of social organization is the fact that while Deniece's actions towards Brenda are produced as complaints using third-person references, Sharon (line 6) delivers an imperative directly to Brenda. As the party who takes control of duties of principal stage manager, Sharon assumes the right to issue commands to players, even those not her own children.

Asymmetry is extended to other aspects of the activity as well. For example, while one might expect a certain equality among two girls who play mother, only one of them characteristically makes decisions for the group. In the present case Sharon assumes the right to change frame through "pretend" directives and in general it is she who plays the role of stage manager:

(49) SHARON: Hey y'all. = Pretend it's a- like- it's about twelve o'clock. = okay?
     DENIECE: It's twelve o'clock in the afternoon so y'all should settle down.
     SHARON: Don't be too late.
     TERRI: I'll fix their lunch!

(50) SHARON: Come on. = Pretend it's two o'clock in the morning.
     DENIECE: OH: I'm goin to *bed*.

(51) SHARON: Pretend it's gettin night time. =
     TERRI: *Good* night child*ren*!

Responses to pretend directives are not randomly distributed among participants. While many girls are present, generally the person responding to a request to pretend is another girl situated in an equivalent role. In these examples Deniece, a household head, and Terri, an older child performing caretaking responsibilities, are the ones who reply to Sharon's overt proposals for shifts in activity. Their talk elaborates the relevance of the directives for current and future activities. While not all initiations of frame shifts are begun by girls in the "mother" role, those who pass final judgment on proffered frame switches do overwhelmingly occupy that position. Thus asymmetrical role relationships are played out during "house."

Positions of subordination and superordination between Deniece and Sharon are further evident in forms of interactions between them. Deniece repetitively displays deference to Sharon. In the following, for example, Deniece relays a request made by someone in her household to Sharon rather than responding to it herself:

(52) TERRI: Okay. Pretend it's just about seven o'clock in the morning.
DENIECE: → What time is it Sharon, (1.8) What time is it Sharon. (0.6) *Sh*aron what
        time is it.
SHARON: Seven o *clock.*
DENIECE: In the morning.

Meanwhile Sharon asserts her position as above that of Deniece in a variety of ways, for example by issuing imperatives to her:

(53) SHARON: Where Deniece go. You better get your children in the *house.*

(54) SHARON: Hey- you should beat your children cuz- You let her do her hair when she
        supposed to be in bed.

Repetitively Sharon's definition of the situation is asserted above Deniece's. In the following, after Sharon states that she has to fix dinner (lines 1–2), Deniece (line 3) offers an alternative plan of action using a modal verb: "*They* could eat dinner with us,". This suggestion is flatly opposed in a next turn by Sharon (lines 4–5), and subsequently the group follows up on Sharon's plan.

(55) 1 SHARON: Don't sit over here or stand over here
    2   cuz I gotta fix dinner.
    3 DENIECE: *They* could eat dinner with *us,*
    4 SHARON: No *uh* uh I'm fixin- I brought all this
    5   food out here and they gonna eat over here.

Not only do girls establish hierarchical arrangements among members of their groups. In addition they form coalitions against particular girls. Among the Maple Street girls, as occurs among other girls' groups (i.e., Eder & Hallinan, 1978; Lever, 1976; Thorne & Luria, 1986), negotiating who is to be included within the most valued roles is an important feature of social organization. Within task activities girls were positioned in equivalent identities. Greater social differentiation is possible while playing house as the division into families and households provides for the playing of alternative roles. The position of sibling to the party playing principal decision maker is the most coveted position. In the particular session of playing house being examined, Sharon's best friend Aisha had no difficulty acquiring the identity of sibling sister. However considerable negotiation took place regarding Terri's identity in a similar slot. In the following the girls conspire to exclude Terri from the position of sister to Sharon:

```
(56)   1   TERRI:     I'm not your daughter.=all right? Um,
       2              I'm- I'm her sister.
       3   DENIECE:   N:OO! / / You-
       4   SHARON:    YOU CAN'T BE STAYIN WITH ME!
       5   TERRI:     I know.=I'm staying with her! But I
       6                 ⌈can-
       7   DENIECE:   ⌊YOU- Uh uh! You- you my daughter.
       8   TERRI:     Mm mm.
       9   DENIECE:   Uh huh, / / Until Pam get back.
      10   TERRI:     Pam your daughter.
      11   DENIECE:    ⌈I know.=I-
      12   SHARON:    ⌊WELL HOW CAN YOU BE HER SISTER,
      13   DENIECE:   UH HUH BECAUSE WE S:/ /ISTERS, HOW CAN
      14              YOU BE HER SISTER.
      15   SHARON:    NOW HOW CAN YOU BE MY SISTER,
      16   DENIECE:   How can you be my / / sister.
      17   AISHA:     That's r- that's right.
      18                  (0.8)
      19   AISHA:     We all three sisters.
      20   SHARON:    I know.
      21   AISHA:     Well how come you don't wanna be
      22                 ⌈her daughter.
      23   BRENDA:    ⌊THERE SHARON, AISHA / / AND
      24   TERRI:     I'm another sister.
      25   BRENDA:     ⌈There Sharon and Aisha is her-
      26   SHARON:    ⌊N:O.
      27   BRENDA:    Is your- and / / she-
      28   SHARON:    WELL YOU STAY HERE WITH HER.
```

The dispute about Terri's position in playing house begins in lines 1–2, where Terri proposes that she enact the role of Deniece's sister rather than her daughter. This proposal is first objected to by Deniece (line 3) with "N:OO!" and then by Sharon (line 4): "YOU CAN'T BE STAYIN WITH ME!" Deniece counters Terri again in line 7, arguing that Terri is her "daughter," rather than sister. The dispute becomes more intense when Sharon (lines 12, 15, 20), Deniece (lines 9, 13–14, 16), and Aisha (lines 17, 19) argue that they are the only ones who can be sisters in playing house. The argument nears closure when Terri (line 24) states "I'm another sister." Subsequently Sharon (line 28) concedes that she can be a sister under the condition that she live with Deniece. In this way Sharon terminates the dispute while distancing herself from Terri. Thus in the midst of dramatic play, as in other of their interactions (Goodwin, 1982), girls take considerable care to delineate their friendship alliances. Though an issue which is highly charged is debated, the girls continue playing together for nearly an hour after this dispute.

Conclusion

Various researchers (Lever, 1976; Gilligan, 1982: p. 242) have proposed that the structure of games itself influences the form of social organization that children evolve. As the argument goes, because girls do not participate in complex games (team sports having a large number of players, high degrees of interdependence of players, role differentiation, rule specificity, and competitiveness), with respect to males females are considered less able to develop the negotiational skills which prepare one for "successful performance in a wide range of work settings in large, formal organizations" (Lever, 1974: pp. 240–241).

As can be seen from the data on playing house within a fairly unstructured form of play (that is, a form of play with relatively few explicit rules), an incipient hierarchy emerges. As within any focused gathering or activity requiring the close coordination of participants in differentiated roles, decisions regarding how the play is to proceed must be made from moment to moment; this allows for the emergence of the role of manager of the activity. Though both girls playing mother as well as the girl who is "parental child" may give directives to children in the play frame, one girl in particular controls the staging of the activity. She makes frequent use of imperatives in her talk, and in general uses explicit speech forms to oversee aspects of the activity. Concurrently those in positions subordinate to principal character (as both characters in the drama and actors in the dramatic play) display their positions of subordination vis-à-vis those in a position of authority, thereby constructing a complementarity of roles. Within dramatic play girls further create a differentiation of participants through the ways in which they criticize certain girls or exclude them from valued positions. Alliances of girls against particular individuals are played out in a fashion which resembles alliance formation in a gossip event called "he-said-she-said" (Goodwin, 1980a). Supportive evidence for girls' competence in developing elaborated forms of social organization while playing games comes from Hughes' (1983, in press) studies of white middle class girls; within a nonteam game such as "foursquare," girls evolve quite sophisticated forms of social organization which entail contests between incipient teams.

The form of social organization which evolves in the midst of pretend play differs from that which characterizes girls' task activities. Girls, in contrast to boys, interpret task activities as needing relatively little control. In coordinating the actions of participants, events are treated as involving parallel rather than tightly interdigitated events, which are typical of a game such as jump rope or house. Girls make use of actions which include the speaker as well as others within the scope of the action and suggest rather than demand courses of next action. In addition, making decisions regarding what happens next is rotated among group members. When imperatives are used in this frame they are in some way modified from the bald forms which occur among the boys, either through accounts which specify safety of the individual involved, or benefits for the entire group. During the giving of instructions, imperatives are further modified through the shading of laughter and mimicry which surrounds them.

Thus girls exhibit a range of different types of social organization in the organization of their activities. Many studies of gender differences tend, as Thorne (1986: p. 168) argues, to promote the notion of "separate worlds" of males and females – "to abstract gender from social context, to assume males and females are qualitatively and permanently different." Here I have attempted to show that some features of girls' activities resemble the ways in which boys hierarchically structure their play. However, while girls in a stage manager position direct play in ways similar to the ways that boys in a leadership position make decisions for the group, the accounts they provide to support their imperatives speak to female rather than male concerns.

The findings reported here would thus seem to counter many of the prevalent notions about girls' social organization. Typically girls are seen as avoiding direct competition and spending little time on "negotiational involvements" (Lever, 1976; Sutton-Smith, 1979; Gilligan, 1982); such a view supports the view of females as powerless speakers. As I have argued here, within the "house" frame, girls devote considerable attention to negotiating features of their play, making use of language which expresses disagreement in an aggravated fashion. Moreover, such negotiation takes place without the disruption of the ongoing activity or a breach in social relationships, as is frequently argued to occur among girls (Lever, 1976: p. 482; Gilligan, 1982: pp. 9–10). The form of differentiated social organization within a comparatively large cluster that girls evolve within playing house defies the often cited typifications of girls as interacting within small groups or friendship pairs (Waldrop & Halverson, 1975; Eder & Hallinan, 1978; Maltz & Borker, 1982). The fact that girls' social organization varies substantially across different domains makes it imperative that studies of girls' play or interaction be grounded in detailed analysis of specific contexts of use.

NOTES

An earlier version of this paper was presented at the American Folklore Society 1986 Annual Meeting and at the Indiana University Sociolinguistics Seminar. I am indebted to Charles Goodwin, Barrie Thorne and Linda Hughes for helpful and insightful comments on an earlier version of this analysis.

1   For more detailed analysis of how the boys organized their slingshot fight see Goodwin (1980b) and Goodwin & Goodwin (1990).
2   The organization of boys' activities into "teams" has been extensively commented upon by a number of researchers, most notably Lever (1974, 1976). Among the Maple Street

boys, even the making of go carts evolved into play divided into two highly competitive "pit crews," each with its own professional secrets regarding the manufacture of the carts.

3   Among the boys, "let's" is used when a boy proposes to move to a new stage of an activity in utterances such as "Let's play some football Poochie. Two against two." or "Mic*hael*! Let's get a game." "Let's" was used two times during the boys' slingshot making session reported on here. Michael requested (a) that boys move around to the back of the house to make slings ("Let's go around back and make some slings") and (b) that boys move from a stairwell to a cement backyard area ("All right. It's too crowded in here. Let's go somewhere.").

4   According to Blum-Kulka & Olshtain (1984: p. 203), such a "point of view" provides a more mitigated form of directive.

5   Grant (1984: p. 108) in her study of peer interaction in a desegregated school found that "black girls were above the mean in care-giving in four classrooms."

6   This is not meant to imply that boys are *in fact* less able to deal with the perspective of the other than girls are.

7   Studies comparing child-rearing practices of black parents with those of Euro-American (Bartz & Levin, 1978; Baumrind, 1972) and Chicano parents (Bartz & Levin, 1978) report "a pattern of increased strictness, high control, and high support (nurturance) among African-American parents" (McLoyd, Ray, & Etter-Lewis, 1985: p. 40). The white middle class mothers studied by Bellinger & Gleason (1982) deliver directives which appear far more mitigated than those I found in black mother–child interaction.

8   The importance of female sibling ties among black families has been discussed by Aschenbrenner (1975), Ladner (1971), McAdoo (1983), and Stack (1974). McLoyd, Ray, & Etter-Lewis (1985: p. 41) and Pitcher & Schultz (1983) report that among pre-school children there is little development of the father/husband role during pretend play.

9   Commenting upon the role of parental child within black families, McLoyd, Ray, & Etter-Lewis (1985: p. 40) state "Older children often assume caretaking responsibilities for younger children (Aschenbrenner, 1975; Lewis, 1975; Young, 1970) and, as a consequence, may acquire advanced role-taking skills."

10 Corsaro (1985: p. 83) also found that requests for permission were most frequently used by children playing younger children to "mothers" and constituted a way of displaying subordination. McLoyd, Ray, & Etter-Lewis (1985: p. 37) found that "children" used more direct forms with each other than with their "mothers." Gordon and Ervin-Tripp (1984: p. 308) argue that "true permission requests imply that the addressee has control over the speaker and that the speaker's wishes are subject to the hearer's approval."

REFERENCES

Andersen, E. S. (1978). Learning to speak with style: A study of the sociolinguistic skills of children. Unpublished Ph.D. Dissertation, Department of Linguistics, Stanford University.

Aschenbrenner, J. (1975). *Lifelines: Black Families in Chicago*. New York: Holt, Rinehart and Winston.

Austin, J. L. (1962). *How to Do Things with Words*. Oxford: Oxford University Press.

Bartz, K. W., & Levin, E. S. (1978). Childrearing by black parents: A description and comparison to anglo and chicano parents. *Journal of Marriage and the Family*, *40*, 709–719.

Baumrind, D. (1972). An exploratory study of socialization effects on black children: Some black–white comparisons. *Child Development, 43*, 261–267.

Becker, J. (1982). Children's strategic use of requests to mark and manipulate social status. In S. Kuczaj II (Ed.), *Language Development v. 2: Language, Thought and Culture* (pp. 1–35). Hillsdale, N.J.: Lawrence Erlbaum Associates.

Becker, J. A. (1984). Implications of ethology for the study of pragmatic development. In S. Kuczaj II (Ed.), *Discourse Development: Progress in Cognitive Development Research* (pp. 1–17). New York: Springer-Verlag.

Bellinger, D. C., & Gleason, J. B. (1982). Sex differences in parental directives to young children. *Sex Roles, 8*, 1123–1139.

Blum-Kulka, S., & Olshtain, E. (1984). Requests and apologies: A cross-cultural study of speech act realization patterns (CCSARP). *Applied Linguistics, 5*, 196–213.

Brown, P. (1980). How and why are women more polite: Some evidence from a Mayan community. In S. McConnell-Ginet, R. Borker, & N. Furman (Eds.), *Women and Language in Literature and Society* (pp. 111–149). New York: Praeger.

Brown, P., & Levinson, S. C. (1978). Universals of language usage: Politeness phenomena. In E. N. Goody (Ed.), *Questions and Politeness. Strategies in Social Interaction* (pp. 56–289). Cambridge: Cambridge University Press.

Cazden, C., Cox, M., Dickerson, D., Steinberg, Z., & Stone, C. (1979). "You all gonna hafta listen": Peer teaching in a primary classroom. In W. Collins (Ed.), *Minnesota Symposia on Child Psychology* (Vol. 12, pp. 183–231). Hillsdale, N.J.: Lawrence Erlbaum Associates.

Chance, M. R. A., & Jolly, C. J. (1970). *Social Groups of Monkeys, Apes and Men*. London: Jonathan Cape.

Cook-Gumperz, J. (1981). Persuasive talk – the social organization of children's talk. In J. L. Green & C. Wallat (Eds.), *Ethnography and Language in Educational Settings* (pp. 25–50). Norwood, N.J.: Ablex.

Cook-Gumperz, J., & Corsaro, W. (1979). Social–ecological constraints on children's communicative strategies. *Sociology, 11*, 411–434.

Corsaro, W. A. (1985). *Friendship and Peer Culture in the Early Years*. Norwood, N.J.: Ablex.

Eder, D., & Hallinan, M. T. (1978). Sex differences in children's friendships. *American Sociological Review, 43*, 237–250.

Ervin-Tripp, S. (1976). "Is Sybil there?": The structure of some American English directives. *Language in Society, 5*, 25–67.

Ervin-Tripp, S. (1982). Structures of control. In L. C. Wilkinson (Ed.), *Communicating in the Classroom* (pp. 27–47). New York: Academic Press.

Garvey, C. (1974). Some properties of social play. *Merrill-Palmer Quarterly, 20*, 163–180.

Garvey, C. (1975). Requests and responses in children's speech. *Journal of Child Language, 2*, 41–63.

Garvey, C. (1977). *Play*. Cambridge, MA: Harvard University Press.

Gilligan, C. (1982). *In a Different Voice: Psychological Theory and Women's Development*. Cambridge, MA: Harvard University Press.

Goffman, E. (1961). *Encounters: Two Studies in the Sociology of Interaction*. Indianapolis: Bobbs-Merrill.

Goffman, E. (1974). *Frame Analysis: An Essay on the Organization of Experience*. New York: Harper and Row.

Goodwin, M. H. (1980a). 'He-Said-She-Said': Formal cultural procedures for the construction of a gossip dispute activity. *American Ethnologist, 7*, 674–695.

Goodwin, M. H. (1980b). Directive/response speech sequences in girls' and boys' task activities. In S. McConnell-Ginet, R. Borker, & N. Furman (Eds.), *Women and Language in Literature and Society* (pp. 157–173). New York: Praeger.

Goodwin, M. H. (1982). 'Instigating': Storytelling as social process. *American Ethnologist*, 9, 799–819.

Goodwin, M. H. (1983). Aggravated correction and disagreement in children's conversations. *Journal of Pragmatics*, 7, 657–677.

Goodwin, M. H. (1985). The serious side of jump rope: Conversational practices and social organization in the frame of play. *Journal of American Folklore*, 98, 315–330.

Goodwin, M. H., & Goodwin, C. (1987). Children's arguing. In S. Philips, S. Steele, & C. Tanz (Eds.), *Language, Gender, and Sex in Comparative Perspective* (pp. 200–248). Cambridge: Cambridge University Press.

Goodwin, C., & Goodwin, M. H. (1990). Interstitial argument. In A. Grimshaw (Ed.), *Conflict Talk* (pp. 85–117). Cambridge: Cambridge University Press.

Gordon, D., & Ervin-Tripp, S. (1984). The structure of children's requests. In R. L. Schiefelbusch & J. Pickar (Eds.), *The Acquisition of Communicative Competence* (pp. 295–321). Baltimore: University Park Press.

Grant, L. (1984). Black females' "place" in desegregated classrooms. *Sociology of Education*, 57, 98–111.

Gumperz, J. J. (1982). *Discourse Strategies*. New York: Cambridge University Press.

Hughes, L. A. (1983). Beyond the rules of the game: Girls' gaming at a friends' school. Unpublished Ph.D. dissertation, University of Pennsylvania, Graduate School of Education.

Hughes, L. A. (in press). The study of children's gaming. In B. Sutton-Smith, J. Mechling, & T. Johnson (Eds.), *A Handbook of Children's Folklore*. Washington, DC: Smithsonian Institution Press.

Labov, W., & Fanshel, D. (1977). *Therapeutic Discourse: Psychotherapy as Conversation*. New York: Academic Press.

Ladner, J. A. (1971). *Tommorrow's Tommorrow: The Black Woman*. New York: Anchor Books.

Lever, J. R. (1974). Games children play: Sex differences and the development of role skills. Unpublished Ph.D. Dissertation, Department of Sociology, Yale University.

Lever, J. (1976). Sex differences in the games children play. *Social Problems*, 23, 478–487.

Lewis, D. (1975). The black family: Socialization and sex roles. *Phylon*, 36, 221–237.

Maltz, D. N., & Borker, R. A. (1982). A cultural approach to male–female miscommunication. In J. Gumperz (Ed.), *Language and Social Identity* (pp. 196–216). Cambridge: Cambridge University Press.

McAdoo, H. P. (1983). *Extended Family Support of Single Black Mothers*. Columbia, MD: Columbia Research Systems.

McLoyd, V. C., Ray, S. A., & Etter-Lewis, G. (1985). Being and becoming: The interface of language and family role knowledge in the pretend play of young African American girls. In L. Galda & A. D. Pellegrini (Eds.), *Play, Language, and Stories: The Development of Children's Literate Behavior* (pp. 29–43). Norwood. N.J.: Ablex.

Mitchell-Kernan, C., & Kernan, K. T. (1977). Pragmatics of directive choice among children. In S. Ervin-Tripp & C. Mitchell-Kernan (Eds.), *Child Discourse* (pp. 189–208). New York: Academic Press.

Piaget, J. (1965). *The Moral Judgment of the Child* (1932). New York: Free Press.

Pitcher, E., & Schultz, L. (1983). *Boys and Girls at Play: The Development of Sex Roles*. New York: Praeger.

Sachs, J. (1987). Preschool boys' and girls' language use in pretend play. In S. Philips, S. Steele, & C. Tanz (Eds.), *Language, Gender and Sex in Comparative Perspective*. Cambridge: Cambridge University Press.

Sacks, H., Schegloff, E. A., & Jefferson, G. (1974). A simplest systematics for the organization of turn-taking for conversation. *Language, 50*, 696–735.

Stack, C. (1974). *All Our Kin: Strategies for Survival in a Black Community*. New York: Harper and Row.

Stone, C. R., & Selman, R. L. (1982). A structural approach to research on the development of interpersonal behavior among grade school children. In K. H. Rubin & H. S. Ross (Eds.), *Peer Relationships and Social Skills in Childhood* (pp. 163–183). New York: Springer-Verlag.

Sutton-Smith, B. (1979). *Play and Learning*. New York: Gardner Press.

Thorne, B. (1986). Girls and boys together – but mostly apart: Gender arrangements in elementary school. In W. W. Hartup & Z. Rubin (Eds.), *Relationships and Development* (pp. 167–184). Hillsdale, N.J.: Erlbaum.

Thorne, B., & Luria, Z. (1986). Sexuality and gender in children's daily worlds. *Social Problems, 33*, 176–190.

Vaughn, B. E., & Waters, E. (1980). Social organization among preschool peers. In D. R. Omark, F. F. Strayer, & D. G. Freedman (Eds), *Dominance Relations: An Ethological View of Human Conflict and Social Interaction* (pp. 359–379). New York: Garland STPM Press.

Waldrop, M. F., & Halverson, C. F. (1975). Intensive and extensive peer behavior: Longitudinal and cross-sectional analyses. *Child Development, 46*, 19–26.

Wood, B., & Gardner, R. (1980). How children "get their way": Directives in communication. *Communication Education, 29*, 264–272.

Young, V. H. (1970). Family and childhood in a southern Negro community. *American Anthropologist, 72*, 269–288.

10

Peasant Men Can't Get Wives: Language Change and Sex Roles in a Bilingual Community

Susan Gal

Introduction

Differences between men's and women's speech are no longer thought to be characteristic only of 'exotic' languages and need no longer be categorical differences in
order to be noticed by linguists (cf. Bodine 1975). In accordance with the sociolinguistic assumption that speech differences reflect the social distinctions deemed
important by the community of speakers, sexual differentiation of speech is expected
to occur whenever a social division exists between the roles of men and women – that
is, universally. Further, recent work has shown that linguistic differences between
men and women can appear at various levels of grammar, as well as in patterns of
conversational interaction.

   However, the effects of such sex differences on linguistic *change* have so far been
noted only with respect to phonology, where it has been demonstrated that, along
with other social correlates of synchronic linguistic diversity such as class and ethnicity, '. . . the sexual differentiation of speech often plays a major role in the mechanism of linguistic evolution' (Labov 1972: 303). The substantive aim of this paper
is to describe the way in which the women of a Hungarian–German bilingual town
in Austria have contributed to a change in patterns of language choice. The entire
community is gradually and systematically changing from stable bilingualism to the
use of only one language in all interactions. Sex-linked differences in language choice
have influenced the overall community-wide process of change.

   In the language usage patterns to be described here, young women are more
advanced or further along in the direction of the linguistic change than older people
and young men. This is one of the patterns which has been noted in correlational
studies of phonological change in urban areas. Most such studies report that women
use the newer, advanced forms more frequently than men. Newly introduced forms
used mostly by women are sometimes prestigious (Trudgill 1972, revised version

reprinted in this volume, p. 21) and sometimes not (Fasold 1968). In many cases women, as compared to men of the same social class, use more of the new non-prestigious forms in casual speech, while moving further towards prestige models in formal speech. In other cases women do not lead in the course of linguistic change (reported in Labov 1972).

Although such findings are well documented, adequate explanations of them have not been offered. General statements about the linguistic innovativeness or conservatism of women will not account for the data. Neither Trudgill's (1972) suggestion that women are 'linguistically insecure', nor Labov's (1972) allusion to norms of linguistic appropriateness which allow women a wider expressive range than men, can convincingly explain why women are linguistically innovative in some communities and not in others (Nichols 1976, reprinted in this volume, p. 55). Women's role in language change has rarely been linked to the social position of women in the communities studied and to the related question of what women want to express about themselves in speech. In the present study, men's and women's ways of speaking are viewed as the results of strategic and socially meaningful linguistic choices which systematically link language change to social change: linguistic innovation is a function of speakers' differential involvement in, and evaluation of, social change.

Specifically, in the linguistic repertoire of the bilingual community to be described here, one of the languages has come to symbolize a newly available social status. Young women's language choices can be understood as part of their expression of preference for this newer social identity. The young women of the community are more willing to participate in social change and in the linguistic change which symbolizes it because they are less committed than the men to the traditionally male-dominated system of subsistence agriculture and because they have more to gain than men in embracing the newly available statuses of worker and worker's wife. In order to make this argument in detail several words of background are necessary, first about the community and second about its linguistic repertoire.

The Community

Oberwart (Felsőőr) is a town located in the province of Burgenland in eastern Austria. It has belonged to Austria only since 1921 when as part of the post-World War I peace agreements the province was detached from Hungary. The town itself has been a speech island since the 1500s when most of the original Hungarian-speaking population of the region was decimated by the Turkish wars and was replaced by German-speaking (and in some areas Croatian-speaking) settlers. In Oberwart, which was the largest of the five remaining Hungarian-speaking communities, bilingualism in German and Hungarian became common.

During the last thirty years Oberwart has grown from a village of 600 to a town of over 5,000 people because, as the county seat and new commercial center, it has attracted migrants. These new settlers have all been monolingual German speakers, mainly people from neighboring villages, who have been trained in commerce or administration. The bilingual community today constitutes about a fourth of the town's population.

The indigenous bilinguals who will be the focus of this discussion have until recently engaged in subsistence peasant agriculture. Since World War II, however, most of the agriculturalists have become industrial workers or worker-peasants. By 1972 only about one third of the bilingual population was employed exclusively in peasant agriculture.

In short, Oberwart is an example of the familiar post-war process of urbanization and industrialization of the countryside often reported in the literature on the transformation of peasant Europe (e.g. Franklin 1969).

The Linguistic Repertoire

Bilingual communities provide a particularly salient case of the linguistic heterogeneity which characterizes all communities. In Oberwart the linguistic alternatives available to speakers include not only two easily distinguishable languages but also dialectal differences within each language. These 'dialects' are not homogeneous, invariant structures, but rather are best characterized as sets of covarying linguistic variables which have their own appropriate social uses and connotations (cf. Gumperz 1964; Ervin-Tripp 1972). It is possible for bilingual Oberwarters to move along a continuum from more standard to more local speech in either of their languages (cf. Gal 1976: III).

Of the many functions that code choice has been shown to serve in interaction (Hymes 1967) this paper focuses on just one and on how it is involved in change. As Blom & Gumperz (1972) have argued, alternate codes within a linguistic repertoire are usually each associated with sub-groups in the community and with certain activities. It has been pointed out that a speaker's choice of code in a particular situation is part of that speaker's linguistic presentation of self. The speaker makes the choice as part of a verbal strategy to identify herself or himself with the social categories and activities the code symbolizes. The choice, then, allows the speaker to express solidarity with that category or group of people. It will be argued here that because codes (in this case languages) are associated with social statuses and activities, changes in language choice can be used by speakers to symbolize changes in their own social status or in their attitudes towards the activities the languages symbolize.

The Meanings of Codes

Although bilingual Oberwarters use both standard and local varieties of German as well as of Hungarian, and although the choice between local and standard features in either language carries meaning in conversation, here we will be concerned only with the symbolically more important alternation between German of any sort (G) and Hungarian of any sort (H).

Today in Oberwart H symbolizes peasant status and is deprecated because peasant status itself is no longer respected. Peasant is used here for a native cultural category that includes all local agriculturalists and carries a negative connotation, at least for young people. Young bilingual workers often say, in Hungarian, that only the old peasants speak Hungarian. There is no contradiction here. The young workers know that they themselves sometimes speak Hungarian and they can report on their language choices accurately. The saying refers not to actual practice but to the association of the Hungarian language with peasant status. All old peasants do speak Hungarian and speak it in more situations than anyone else.

The preferred status for young people is worker, not peasant. The world of work is a totally German-speaking world, and the language itself has come to represent the worker. The peasant parents of young workers often say about their children 'Ü má egisz nímët' (He/she is totally German already).[1] This is not a reference to citizenship, nor to linguistic abilities. Oberwarters consider themselves Austrians, not Germans, and even young people are considered bilingual, often using Hungarian in interactions with elders. The phrase indicates the strong symbolic relationship between the young people's status as workers and the language which they use at work.

German also represents the money and prestige available to those who are employed, but not available to peasants. German therefore carries more prestige than Hungarian. The children of a monolingual German speaker and a bilingual speaker never learn Hungarian, regardless of which parent is bilingual. In addition, while in previous generations the ability simply to speak both German and Hungarian was the goal of Oberwarters, today there is a premium not just on speaking German, but on speaking it without any interference from Hungarian. Parents often boast that in their children's German speech 'Nëm vág bele e madzsar' (The Hungarian doesn't cut into it). That is, passing as a monolingual German speaker is now the aim of young bilingual Oberwarters.

Such general statements about symbolic associations between languages, social statuses and the evaluations of those statuses do not in themselves predict language choice in particular situations. For instance, although H is negatively evaluated by young people it is nevertheless used by them in a number of interactions where, for various reasons, they choose to present themselves as peasants. Besides the values associated with languages, the three factors which must be known in order to predict choices and to describe the changes in these choices are the speaker's age and sex and the nature of the social network in which that speaker habitually interacts.

How Do Language Choice Patterns Change?

In any interaction between bilingual Oberwarters a choice must be made between G and H. While in most situations one or the other language is chosen, there are some interactions in which both appear to be equally appropriate. In such interactions it is impossible to predict which language will be used by which speaker and both are often used within one short exchange. Gumperz (1976) has called this conversational code-switching. When both languages may appropriately be used Oberwarters say

Table 1　Language choice pattern of women

Informant	Age	Social situations (identity of participant)										
		1	2	3	4	5	6	7	8	9	10	11
A	14	H	GH		G	G	G			G		G
B	15	H	GH		G	G	G			G		G
C	25	H	GH	GH	GH	G	G	G	G	G		G
D	27	H	H		GH	G	G			G		G
E	17	H	H		H	GH	G			G		G
F	39	H	H		H	GH	GH			G		G
G	23	H	H		H	GH	H		GH	G		G
H	40	H	H		H	GH		GH	G	G		G
I	52	H	H	H	GH	H		GH	G	G	G	G
J	40	H	H	H	H	H	H	GH	GH	GH		G
K	35	H	H	H	H	H	H	H	GH	H		G
L	61	H	H		H	H	H	H	GH	H		G
M	50	H	H	H	H	H	H	H	H	H		G
N	60	H	H	H	H	H	H	H	H	H	GH	G
O	54	H	H		H	H	H	H	H	H	GH	H
P	63	H	H	H	H	H	H	H	H	H	GH	H
Q	64	H	H	H	H	H	H	H	H	H	H	H
R	59	H	H	H	H	H	H	H	H	H	H	H

No. of informants = 18　　　　　　　　　　Scalability = 95.4%

1 = to god
2 = grandparents and their generation
3 = bilingual clients in black market
4 = parents and their generation
5 = friends and age-mate neighbors
6 = brothers and sisters

7 = spouse
8 = children and their generation
9 = bilingual government officials
10 = grandchildren and their generation
11 = doctors

G – German, H – Hungarian, GH – both German and Hungarian.

they are speaking 'ehodzsan dzsün' (as it comes). A description of language choice in such situations must include such variation and in this sense is comparable to the rule conflicts described for syntactic change by Bickerton (1973).

In predicting an individual's choice between the three possibilities – G, H or both – the habitual role-relationship between participants in the interaction proved to be the most important factor. Other aspects of the situation such as locale, purpose or occasion were largely irrelevant. Therefore, specification of the identity of the inter-locutor was sufficient to define the social situation for the purposes of the present analysis.

We can think of informants as being ranked along a vertical axis and social situations being arranged along a horizontal axis, as in tables 1 and 2. Note that all

Table 2   Language choice pattern of men

Informant	Age	Social situations (identity of participant)										
		1	2	3	4	5	6	7	8	9	10	11
A	17	H	GH		G	G	G			G		G
B	25	H	H		GH	G	G			G		G
C	42		H		GH	G	G	G	G	G		G
D	20	H	H	H	H	GH	G	G	G	G		G
E	22	H	H		H	GH	GH			G		G
F	62	H	H	H	H	H	H	GH	GH	GH	G	G
G	63	H	H		H	H	H	H		GH		G
H	64	H	H	H	H	H	H	H	GH	GH		G
I	43	H	H		H	H	H	H	G	H		G
J	41	H	H	H	H	H	H	H	GH	H		H
K	54	H	H		H	H	H	H	H	H		G
L	61	H	H		H	H	H	H	H	G	GH	G
M	74	H	H		H	H	H	H	H	H	GH	H
N	58	G	H		H	H	H	H	H	H	H	H

No. of informants = 14   Scalability = 95.2%

1 = to god   7 = spouse
2 = grandparents and their generation   8 = children and their generation
3 = bilingual clients in black market   9 = bilingual government officials
4 = parents and their generation   10 = grandchildren and their generation
5 = friends and age-mate neighbors   11 = doctors
6 = brothers and sisters

G – German, H – Hungarian, GH – both German and Hungarian.

speakers listed in these tables are bilingual. The information is drawn from a language usage questionnaire which was constructed on the basis of native categories of interlocutors and linguistic resources. Similar scales based on systematic observation of language choice were also constructed. There was a high degree of agreement between observed usage and the questionnaire results (average agreement for men 86%, for women 90%). That is, the questionnaire results were corroborated by direct observation of language choice.

The language choices of a particular informant in all situations are indicated in the rows of tables 1 and 2 and the choices of all informants in a particular situation are indicated in the columns. The choices of Oberwarters, arranged in this way, form a nearly perfect implicational scale. Note that for all speakers there is at least one situation in which they use only H. For almost all speakers there are some situations in which they use both G and H and some in which they use only G.

[. . .]

It is worth considering the factors that determine the place of a speaker on the scale. Two factors determine the degree to which a person uses H as opposed to G: the person's age and her or his social network. Because historical evidence (cf. Imre 1973; Kovács 1942: 73–6) shows that present-day age differences are not due to age-grading of language choice, we can take age (apparent time) as a surrogate for repeated sampling over real time (cf. Labov 1972 for details of this strategy).

Social network is defined here as all the people (contacts) an individual spoke to in the course of a unit of time. The average amount of time for all informants was seven days. Each of these network contacts was assigned to one of two categories: (a) those who lived in households which owned either pigs or cows, (b) those who lived in households which owned neither pigs nor cows. Oberwarters themselves define those who own cows and pigs as peasants. The peasantness of a person's network, expressed as the percentage of contacts who fit into category (a) is, in effect, a measure of that person's social involvement with the category of persons with which the use of H is associated.

The more peasants the individual has in her or his social network the greater the number of social situations in which that individual uses H. In fact, in most cases a *person's own status*, whether peasant, worker or some gradation in between, *was not as accurate a predictor of his or her choices as the status of the person's social contacts.* These results lend support to the notion that social networks are instrumental in constraining speakers' linguistic presentation of self (Gumperz 1964; Labov 1973).

The three-way relationship between language choices, age, and peasantness of social network can be demonstrated by ranking informants on each of the measures and then correlating the rankings with each other.

[. . .]

On the basis of the rank correlations the following brief outline of the synchronic pattern of language choice can be drawn. For the sample as a whole, the more peasants in one's social network the more likely it is that one will use H in a large number of situations. The older one is the more likely it is that one will use H in a large number of situations. Young people who interact only with workers use the least H, older people who interact mostly with peasants use the most H. Older people who associate mostly with workers are closest in their language choices to people much younger than themselves, while very young people who associate mostly with peasants use more H than others their own age.

Because historical evidence rules out the possibility of age-grading and because the sample allows one to disentangle the effects of time and that of networks, it is possible to hypothesize the following process of change. Changes in language choices occur situation by situation. The rule for one situation is always first categorical for the old form (H), then variable (GH), before it is categorical for the new form (G). As speakers' networks become less and less peasant they use H in fewer and fewer situations. And, in a parallel but separate process, as time passes new generations use H in fewer and fewer situations regardless of the content of their social networks.

Differences Between Men and Women

The implicational scales describing choices seem to indicate no differences between men and women. Both men and women show the same kinds of implicational relationships in the same ordered list of situations. However, the rank correlations of language choice, age and peasantness of network present a more complicated picture. Here the issue is whether age and social networks are equally well correlated with language choice for men and women. In fact they are not: for men the correlation between social network and language choice is about the same as the correlation between age and language choice (0.78 and 0.69 respectively). For women age alone is more closely correlated with language choice (0.93) than is the social network measure (0.74). This difference between men and women is significant at the 0.05 level.

In short there is a difference between men and women in the way each is going through the process of change in language choice. If we distinguish three twenty-year generations, separate the men from the women and those with very peasant networks from those with nonpeasant networks, it is possible to illustrate the process at work. Informants' networks ranged from 13% peasant contacts to 94% peasant contacts. This continuum was divided into two parts. All those scoring at or above the median were put in the peasant network category in figure 1, all those scoring below the median were in the nonpeasant network category.

Figure 1 illustrates the fact that for men there is a very regular pattern in the correlations. From the oldest to the youngest generation use of G increases, but for each generation this increase is greatest for those whose social networks include a majority of nonpeasants. Among the men the youngest group as a whole uses less H than any of the others. But those young men with heavily peasant networks do use more H. Regardless of the negative evaluations, for these young men expression of peasant identity is still preferred for many situations.

For women the process is different. First we find that in the oldest generation this sample includes not one person with a nonpeasant network. This is not a sampling error but reflects the limited range of activities, and therefore of social contacts, open to women before World War II. In the middle generation the women's pattern matches that of men exactly. Many women of the generation reaching maturity during and after World War II left the peasant home, if only temporarily, to work in inns, factories and shops. Often they remained in contact with those they befriended. As with the men, those who have heavily peasant networks use more H than those who do not.

The youngest generation of women differs both from the older women and from the men. First, these youngest women use more G and less H than anyone else in the community, including the youngest men. In addition, for these women, *peasantness of social network makes no difference in language choice*. Young women with peasant networks use Hungarian as rarely as young women with nonpeasant networks. Recall that for all the men, including the youngest, peasantness of network did make a difference since it was associated with more use of H.

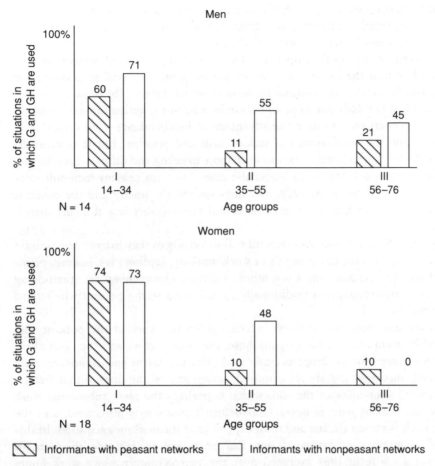

Figure 1 Percentage of G and GH language choices of informants with peasant and nonpeasant social networks in three age groups

To understand these differences it is necessary to go back to the activities from which the languages derive their meanings and evaluations. For the most recent generation of women, peasant life is a much less attractive choice than it is for men. Now that other opportunities are open to these young women, they reject peasant life as a viable alternative. It will be argued here that their language choices are part of this rejection.

There are some young men who, despite a general preference for industrial and commercial employment, want to take over family farms. Some of these young men have the newly developing attitude that farming can be an occupation, a 'Beruf', like any other. These are men whose families own enough land to make agriculture if not as lucrative as wage work at least a satisfactory livelihood. In contrast, young women, since World War II, have not been willing to take over the family farm when this opportunity is offered to them. More importantly, they specifically state that they do not want to marry peasant men. The life of a peasant wife is seen by Oberwart young women as particularly demeaning and difficult when compared to the other choices which have recently become available to them.

Let us compare the choices open to Oberwart young men and women as they see them. For men the life possibilities are (a) to be an industrial or construction worker (usually a commuter coming home only on weekends), (b) to be a peasant-worker, holding two full-time jobs, and (c) to be a full-time agriculturalist. This last is felt by Oberwart men to have the advantage of independence – no orders from strangers – and the disadvantage of lack of cash and prestige. But it is generally agreed that while agricultural work was once more grueling and difficult than factory and construction work, this is no longer the case. Although peasant men still work longer hours than those in industry, machines such as the tractor and the combine make men's farm work highly mechanized and considerably less difficult than it once was.

For women the life possibilities depend mainly on whom they marry. The peasant wife typically spends the day doing farm work: milking, feeding pigs, hoeing, planting and harvesting potatoes and a few other rootcrops. Her evenings are spent doing housework. Industriousness is traditionally considered a young peasant wife's most valuable quality.

There are machines now available which lighten the work of the peasant wife considerably, including the washing machine, the electric stove and the silo (which eliminates the need for rootcrops as cattle feed). But in peasant households the male labor saving machines are always acquired before any of the ones which lighten women's work. For instance the silo, which is perhaps the most substantial work saver for the peasant wife, is never built before a combine is purchased, and the combine itself is among the last and most expensive of the machines acquired. In this Oberwart exemplifies the pattern all over Europe, where, for instance, the German small peasant's wife in 1964 averaged over the year seventeen more work hours per week than her husband (Franklin 1969: 37–44). In addition, although peasant life in Oberwart is less male-dominated than, for instance, in the Balkans (compare Denich 1974 with Fél & Hofer 1969: 113–44), nevertheless for the peasant wife the independence which is said to compensate the peasant man for his work is not freely available. In fact, being a young peasant wife often means living under the authority of a mother-in-law who supervises the kitchen and women's farm work generally.

In marked contrast, marriage to a worker involves only household tasks and upkeep of a kitchen garden. Wives of workers are sometimes employed as maids or salespersons, but mostly they hold part-time jobs or are not employed at all. Because of the increased access to money, because agricultural equipment is not needed and because some of the women themselves contribute part of the money, electric stoves and washing machines are among the first appliances bought by working married couples, thereby further lightening the wife's work load. Peasant wives work far more than peasant men. Peasant men work more hours than worker men. Workers' wives, especially if not employed, often work fewer hours than their husbands.

Table 3   Endogamous marriages of all bilingual Oberwarters and bilingual male peasant Oberwarters

	% Endogamous marriages of all marriages	% Endogamous marriages of male peasants
1911–40	71%	87%
1941–60	65	54
1961–72	32	0

Source: Marriage Register, City of Oberwart.

This contrast is not lost on young Oberwart women. When discussing life choices they especially dwell on the dirtyness and heaviness of peasant work. Rejection of the use of local Hungarian, the symbol of peasant status, can be seen as part of the rejection, by young women, of peasant status and life generally. They do not want to be peasants; they do not present themselves as peasants in speech.

Mothers of marriageable daughters specifically advise them against marriage to peasants. Oberwarters agree that 'Paraszt legin nëm kap nüöt' (Peasant lads can't get women). For instance, in reference to a particular young couple an old man remarked: 'Az e Trüumfba jár, az fog neki tehen szart lapáni? Abbu má paraszt nëm lesz, az má zicher!' (She works at the [local bra factory], *she*'s going to shovel cow manure for him? She'll never be a peasant, that's for sure.) Although the young men themselves are usually also reluctant to become peasants, for those who nevertheless choose family agriculture as their livelihood, the anti-peasant attitudes of the community's young women present a problem.

If in recent years Oberwart young women have not wanted to marry peasant men, and if they have acted on this preference, then Oberwart peasant men must have found wives elsewhere. The town's marriage records should provide evidence for the difference in attitudes between young men and young women.

The general trend in Oberwart in the post-war years has been away from the traditional village endogamy and towards exogamy. For instance, table 3 shows that between 1911 and 1940 71% of the marriages of bilinguals in Oberwart were endogamous. Between 1961 and 1972 only 32% were. But for the bilingual peasant men of Oberwart the figures are different. As table 3 indicates, between 1911 and 1940 a larger percentage of peasant men married endogamously than all bilingual Oberwarters (87%). Between 1941 and 1960, however, this was reversed. Finally, by 1961–72, when 32% of all bilingual Oberwarters married endogamously, not one peasant man married endogamously. Those peasant men who did marry during those years found wives in the neighboring small German monolingual villages where being a peasant wife has not been negatively valued. In short, the marriage records provide evidence that young Oberwart women's stated attitudes towards peasant men have been translated into action. The effect of this is discussed below.

Conclusion

There are two ways, one direct and one indirect, in which the attitudes and choices of young bilingual women are changing the language usage pattern in this community. Directly, the young women, even those with heavily peasant networks refuse, in most situations, to present themselves as peasants by using H. This contrasts with the language choices of older women and has the general effect that more German is used in more interactions in the community. It also contrasts with the choices of young men, who use Hungarian in more interactions than the young women and who are constrained by the peasantness of their social networks so that those with heavily peasant networks choose local Hungarian in more interactions than those with non-peasant networks.

Indirectly, young women's marriage preferences are also having a linguistic effect. They refuse to marry local peasant men, preferring workers instead. As a result, exactly that small group of young men most likely to be using Hungarian in many situations, that is the ones engaged in peasant agriculture, are the ones who have married German monolingual women with the greatest frequency in the last decade or so. Because the children of marriages between monolingual German speakers and bilingual Hungarian–German speakers in Oberwart rarely if ever learn Hungarian, in an indirect way the present generation of young women is limiting the language possibilities of the next generation.

In exploring the reasons for the difference between young men's and young women's language choices, evidence was presented showing that in their stated attitudes and their marriage choices the women evaluate peasant life more negatively than the men and reject the social identity of peasant wife. The women of Oberwart feel they have more to gain than men by embracing the new opportunities of industrial employment. Also, considering the male-dominated nature of East European peasant communities generally and the lives of Oberwart women in particular, women have less to lose in rejecting the traditional peasant roles and values.

This paper has argued that women's language choices and their linguistic innovativeness in this community are the linguistic expressions of women's greater participation in social change. The linguistic pattern is best understood by considering the social meanings of the available languages and the strategic choices and evaluations which men and women make concerning the ways of life symbolized by those languages.

NOTES

The data reported here were gathered during 1974 as part of dissertation fieldwork supported by a N.I.M.H. Anthropology Traineeship at the University of California, Berkeley. My thanks to Paul Kay, John Gumperz and E. A. Hammel for their many suggestions. An earlier version of this paper was presented at the symposium on 'Language and Sex Roles' at the 74th Annual Meeting of the AAA, December 1975.

1   The orthography is a modified version of Imre (1971) and of the Hungarian dialect atlas.

REFERENCES

Bickerton, D. (1973). The nature of a creole continuum. *Language* 44, 640–69.

Blom, J. P. & Gumperz, J. J (1972) Social meaning in linguistic structures: Code-switching in Norway. In J. J. Gumperz & D. Hymes (eds), *Directions in sociolinguistics*. New York: Holt, Rinehart & Winston.

Bodine, A. (1975). Sex differentiation in language. In B. Thorne & N. Henley (eds), *Language and sex: Difference and dominance*. Rowley, Massachusetts: Newbury House.

Denich, B. (1974). Sex and power in the Balkans. In M. S. Rosaldo & L. Lamphere (eds) *Women, culture and society*. Stanford: Stanford University Press.

Ervin-Tripp, S. (1972). On sociolinguistic rules: Alternation and co-occurrence. In J. J. Gumperz & D. Hymes (eds), *Directions in sociolinguistics*. New York: Holt, Rinehart & Winston.

Fasold, R. (1968). A sociolinguistic study of the pronunciation of three vowels in Detroit speech. Washington, D. C.: Center for Applied Linguistics. Mimeo.

Fél, E. and Hofer, T. (1969). *Proper peasants*. Chicago: Aldine.

Franklin, S. H. (1969). *The European peasantry*. London: Methuen.

Gal, S. (1976). *Language change and its social determinants in a bilingual community*. Ann Arbor, Michigan: University Microfilms.

Gumperz, J. J. (1964). Linguistic and social interaction in two communities. *American Anthropologist* 66 (6). Part II. 137–54.

——(1970). Verbal strategies in multilingual communication. Language Behavior Research Laboratory Working Paper # 36, Berkeley: University of California.

——(1976). The sociolinguistic significance of conversational code-switching. Ms.

Hymes, D. (1967). Models of the interaction of language and social setting. *Journal of Social Issues* 23 (2), 8–28.

Imre, S. (1971). A felsőőri nyelvjárás (The Oberwart dialect). *Nyelvtudományi Értekezések* 72. Budapest.

——(1973). Az ausztriai (burgenlandi) magyar szorványok (The Hungarian minority group in Austria). In *Népi Kultura – Népi Társadalom* (Folk Culture – Folk Society). Budapest: Akadémiai Kiadó.

Kovács, M. (1942). A felsőőri magyar népsziget (The Hungarian folk-island of Oberwart). Budapest: Sylvester-Nyomda.

Labov, W. (1972). *Sociolinguistic patterns*. Philadelphia: University of Pennsylvania Press.

——(1973). The linguistic consequence of being a lame. *LinS* 2, 81–115.

Nichols, P. (1976). Black women in the rural south: Conservative and innovative. Paper presented to the conference on the Sociology of the Languages of American Women. Las Cruces, New Mexico.

Trudgill, P. (1972). Sex, covert prestige and linguistic change in the urban British English of Norwich. *LinS* 1, 179–95.

Part III

Conversational Dominance in Mixed Talk

The last section focused on gender differences in conversational practice. In this section, we shall concentrate on the way certain conversational strategies can be used to achieve dominance in talk. 'Conversational dominance' is the phrase used to refer to strategies which enable speakers to dominate their partners in talk. Research focusing on mixed talk in a variety of social contexts has revealed asymmetrical patterns, with men's greater usage of certain strategies being associated with male dominance in conversation.

Interruptions are perhaps the most unambiguous linguistic strategy which achieves dominance, since to interrupt someone is to deprive them – or at least to attempt to deprive them – of the right to speak. The classic paper on gender differences in interruptions is that of Zimmerman and West (1975). Zimmerman and West drew on the model of turn-taking established by Sacks, Schegloff and Jefferson (1974) to refine the distinction between overlaps (brief, non-threatening instances of simultaneous speech) and interruptions (major incursions into another speaker's turn at talk). The first paper in this section is a later paper by the same writers, Candace West and Don Zimmerman. This paper – 'Women's Place in Everyday Talk' – recapitulates their earlier research project and compares the patterns they found there with patterns found in parent–child interaction. Their earlier finding – that male speakers regularly interrupt female speakers in mixed pairs, even though interruptions are rare in male–male and female–female pairs – is compared with the finding that adults regularly interrupt children. West and Zimmerman claim that women in contemporary American society, like children, have restricted rights to speak, and that interruptions are used both to exhibit and to accomplish socially sanctioned relations of dominance and submission.

Interruptions are not the only linguistic strategy implicated in conversational dominance. The next paper in this section, Victoria DeFrancisco's 'The Sounds of Silence: How Men Silence Women in Marital Relations', focuses on non-cooperation in interaction. DeFrancisco got seven married couples to record themselves at home for a week or more, using the method developed by Pamela Fishman (1980). She subsequently interviewed each of the participants on their own and asked them to comment on extracts from their recorded conversations. She found that, although the women talked more than the men, and introduced more topics, this was not associated with dominance. In fact, the women were less successful than the men in getting their topics accepted. The men used various non-cooperative strategies to control conversation: no response, interruption, inadequate or delayed response, and silence. DeFrancisco concludes that men have the power to establish the norms of everyday conversation in the home, and that women have to adapt to these norms.

While DeFrancisco's research restricts itself to the domestic environment, the other two papers in this section look at patterns of dominance in language used in the public sphere. Joan Swann, in her paper 'Talk Control', examines linguistic and paralinguistic behaviour in the school classroom. She analyses her data in terms of a range of variables: amount of talk, chipping in, teachers' gaze. Her paper problematizes various issues, in particular the notion that dominance can be achieved by male speakers without the complicity of women. She shows how, in the classroom situation, female teachers and girl pupils collude with boys to construct male dominance. Her insights into the construction of dominance and control suggest that change will be difficult to achieve.

The last paper in this section – Susan Herring, Deborah Johnson and Tamra DiBenedetto's 'Participation in Electronic Discourse in a "Feminist" Field' – brings us right up to date, with an analysis of interactive behaviour on the Internet. It focuses primarily on amount of talk as a measure of dominance. Susan Herring had observed (Herring 1992) that participation on the e-mail discussion list known as Linguist (subscribed to by professional linguists world-wide) was highly asymmetrical, with male participants contributing 80 per cent of the total discussion. Herring, Johnson and DiBenedetto therefore undertook an investigation of a smaller, more woman-friendly list, to see if a less adversarial environment would facilitate more symmetrical patterns of participation. In fact, women still only contributed 30 per cent of the discussion. But during the five weeks of discussion chosen for analysis, there were two days when women's contributions exceeded men's. The resulting disruption, with men claiming they were being 'silenced' and threatening to 'unsubscribe' from the network, suggests that there is an underlying cultural assumption that women and men do not have equal rights to speak.

The papers in this section present a consistent picture of male–female relations, with men dominating talk in a range of environments. Not all conversations involving both women and men display the patterns illustrated in the four papers in this section: in some mixed groups, in some settings, participants converse as equals for at least some of the time (see Edelsky 1981; Tannen 1984). However, the main finding of sociolinguistic research into mixed talk is that women and men do not have equal rights to the conversational floor. We shall return to this issue in Part VI, 'Theoretical Debates: Gender or Power?' (p. 373).

REFERENCES

Edelsky, Carole (1981) 'Who's got the floor?' *Language in Society*, 10, 3, 383–421 (reprinted in Deborah Tannen (ed.) (1993) *Gender and Conversational Interaction*, Oxford: Oxford University Press).

Fishman, Pamela (1980) 'Conversational insecurity', pp. 127–32 in Howard Giles, Peter Robinson and Philip Smith (eds) *Language: Social Psychological Perspectives*. Oxford: Pergamon Press.

Herring, Susan (1992) 'Gender and Participation in Computer-Mediated Linguistic Discourse'. Washington, DC: ERIC Clearinghouse on Languages and Linguistics. Document no. ED345552.

Sacks, Harvey, Schegloff, Emanuel A. and Jefferson, Gail (1974) 'A simplest systematics for the organization of turn-taking for conversation'. *Language*, 50, 696–735.

Tannen, Deborah (1984) *Conversational Style: Analysing Talk Among Friends*. Norwood, NJ: Ablex.

Zimmerman, Don and West, Candace (1975) 'Sex roles, interruptions and silences in conversation', pp. 105–29 in Barrie Thorne and Nancy Henley (eds) *Language and Sex: Difference and Dominance*. Rowley, MA: Newbury House.

RECOMMENDED FURTHER READING

Fishman, Pamela (1983) 'Interaction: the work women do', pp. 89–102 in Barrie Thorne, Cheris Kramarae and Nancy Henley (eds) *Language, Gender and Society*. Rowley, MA: Newbury House.

Fitzpatrick, Mary Anne (1988) *Between Husbands and Wives: Communication in Marriage*. London: Sage.

Henley, Nancy and Kramarae, Cheris (1991) 'Gender, power and miscommunication', pp. 18–43 in N. Coupland, H. Giles and J. W. Wiemann (eds) *'Miscommunication' and Problematic Talk*. London: Sage.

Sattel, J. W. (1983) 'Men, inexpressiveness and power', pp. 118–24 in Barrie Thorne, Cheris Kramarae and Nancy Henley (eds) *Language, Gender and Society*. Rowley, MA: Newbury House.

11

Women's Place in Everyday Talk: Reflections on Parent–Child Interaction

Candace West and Don H. Zimmerman

Introduction

It is sometimes said that children should be seen and not heard and that they should speak only when spoken to. To be sure, situations abound in which children are seen and most definitely heard without prior invitation to talk from adults. Nevertheless, these maxims do tell us that children have restricted rights to speak resulting in special problems in gaining adults' attention and engaging them in conversation. For example, Sacks (1966) has observed that children frequently use the form "D'ya know what?" when initiating talk with an adult. The answer to this particular question is ordinarily another question of the form "What?" and the adult so responding finds that he/she has given the child opportunity to begin an utterance to which a listener attends – at least for the moment.

Fishman (1975) observed that in fifty-two hours of tape-recorded conversation collected from three couples the women employed the "D'ya know what?" opening twice as frequently as men. Overall, the women asked almost three times as many questions as the men. The implication is, of course, that the greater reliance on such question forms by women stems from *their* limited rights as co-conversationalists with men.

The difficulties children encounter in verbal interaction with adults follow perhaps from their presumed lack of social competence. A child is a social actor whose opinion may not be taken seriously and whose verbal and non-verbal behavior is subject to open scrutiny, blunt correction, and inattention. It is thus potentially illuminating when parallels between the interaction of adults and children and men and women are observed.

Goffman (1976) characterizes the relation of middle-class parents to their children in face-to-face situations as one of benign control. The child is granted various privileges and the license to be a child, i.e., merely to play at or practice coping with the manifold demands of the social occasion. Goffman (1976: 72–73) notes that "there is an obvious price that the child must pay for being saved from seriousness," a price that includes suffering parents' intervention in his/her activities, being discussed in the presence of others as if absent, and having his/her "time and territory . . . seen as expendable" due to the higher priority assigned to adult needs. This sort of relation in face-to-face interaction can characterize other encounters between subordinate and superordinate parties:

> It turns out . . . that in our society whenever a male has dealings with a female or a subordinate male (especially a younger one), some mitigation of potential distance and hostility is quite likely to be induced by application of the parent–child complex. Which implies that, ritually speaking, females are equivalent to subordinate males and both are equivalent to children. (Goffman, 1976: 73)

Perhaps this ritual equivalence of women and children includes as a common condition the risk that their turns at talk will be subject to interruption and hence control by a superordinate.

In this paper, we compare the results of our previous study of interruptions in same-sex and cross-sex conversations (Zimmerman and West, 1975) with similar data from parent–child verbal interaction and find striking similarities between the pattern of interruptions in male–female interchanges and those observed in the adult –child transactions. We use the occasion of this comparison to consider the function of interruptions in verbal exchanges, particularly in conversations between parties of unequal status. Since interruptions are a type of transition between speakers, our point of departure in this as well as the previous paper is the model of turn-taking in conversation advanced by Harvey Sacks, Emanuel Schegloff and Gail Jefferson (1974) which provides a systematic approach to speaker alternation in naturally occurring conversation.

The Turn-Taking Model

Sacks, *et al.* (1974) suggest that speech exchange systems in general are arranged to ensure that (1) one party speaks at a time and (2) speaker change recurs. These features organize casual conversation, formal debate, and high ceremony. Conversation is distinguished from debate and ceremony by variable distribution of turns, turn length, and turn content.

A turn consists of not merely the temporal duration of an utterance but of the right and obligation to speak allocated to a particular speaker. Turns are constructed out of what Sacks, *et al.* (1974) call "unit-types" which can consist of words, phrases, clauses, or sentences.[1] Unit-types are projective, that is they provide sufficient information prior to their completion to allow the hearer to anticipate an upcoming transition place.

Sacks, *et al.* (1974) represent the mechanism for speaker transition as an ordered set of rules speakers use to achieve a normatively constrained order of conversational interaction. For each possible transition place, these rules provide, in order of priority: that (1) current speaker may select the next speaker, e.g., by using a term of address, and if not choosing to do so, that (2) a next speaker may self-select, and if not, that (3) the current speaker may continue. The exercise of any of these three options recycles the rule-set to the first option. The operation of the rule-set accounts for a number of regularly occurring features of observed conversations – including the alternation of speakers in a variable order with brief (if any) gaps or overlaps between turns, as well as variable length of turns. That is, the model provides for the systematic initiation, continuation and alternation of turns in everyday conversation.[2] Our concern here is with the phenomenon of simultaneous speech, i.e., the occurrence and distribution of overlap among categories of speakers.

Elsewhere (Zimmerman and West, 1975: 114) we have defined overlap as a brief stretch of simultaneous speech initiated by a "next" speaker just before the current speaker arrives at a possible transition place, often in a situation where the current speaker has elongated the final syllable of his/her utterance (cf. Sacks, *et al.*, 1974: 706–708; Jefferson and Schegloff, 1975: 3):[3]

(T14:213–214) B2: Um so where's your shoror-sorORity
house. Is it on campus or off: :?
B1:   [No] it's
off=all thuh sororities and fraternities
are off campus.

The significance of overlap occurring in such an environment follows from the fact that speakers apparently "target" the starting of their stream of speech just at completion by the current speaker (Jefferson and Schegloff, 1975). When successfully managed, the next speaker "latches" his/her utterance to the utterance of the preceding speaker as in the following:

(Jefferson and Schegloff, 1975: 3)
EARL: How's everything *look*.=
BUD: =Oh looks pretty *goo*:d,

Jefferson and Schegloff (1975: 3) also observe that the addition of tag-questions or conjunctions to a possibly complete utterance furnishes another locus for overlap:

(Sacks, *et al.*, 1974: 703, n. 12)
BERT: Uh *you* been down here before ⌈havenche⌉
FRED: ⌊Yeh.   ⌋

(T14:59–60) B1: I don't like it at all ⌈but- ⌉
B2:   ⌊You d⌋ on't

An interruption, in contrast, involves a "deeper" intrusion into the internal structure of the speaker's utterance, i.e., prior to a possible transition place:

(T1:114–115)   A1:   It really sur ⌈prised me becuz- ⌉
                 A2:   ⌊It's jus' so smo :g⌋ gy . . .

Thus, what we call "overlaps" (Sacks, *et al.* use the term to refer to all instances of simultaneous speech) are events occurring in the immediate vicinity of a possible transition place and can be seen as generated by the ordinary workings of the turn-taking system (cf. Sacks, *et al.*, 1974: 706–708). Interruptions, however, do not appear to have a systemic basis in the turn-taking model as such, i.e., they are not products of the turn-constructional and turn-allocation procedures that make up the model. Moreover, there is nothing in the model to suggest that patterned asymmetries should occur between particular categories of speakers. Quite to the contrary, the model is posited to hold for all speakers and all conversations (cf. Sacks, *et al.*, 1974: 700) and represents a mechanism for the systematic allocation of turns across two or more speakers while minimizing gap and overlap.[4]

Viewed strictly in terms of the turn-taking model, then, the deep incursion into the turn-space of a current speaker constitutes a violation of turn-taking rules.[5] Interruptions accomplish a number of communicative acts, among them the exhibition of dominance and exercise of control in face-to-face interaction.

Findings

Our preliminary findings (Zimmerman and West, 1975) suggested marked asymmetries in overlaps, interruptions, and silences between, same-sex and cross-sex conversational pairs. These interactional episodes were (like the parent–child segments introduced below) selected from longer stretches of talk by excerpting all topically coherent segments exhibiting (a) two or more noticeable silences between speaker turns or (b) two or more instances of simultaneous speech, without regard for who overlapped whom. That is, they were selected precisely because of the presence of gaps and overlaps. Three fourths of the exchanges between eleven adult male–female, ten adult male–male, and ten adult female–female parties were recorded in coffee shops, drug stores, and other public places in a university community; the remainder in private dwellings (cf. Zimmerman and West, 1975: 111–112).

The same-sex transcripts displayed silences in nearly equal distributions between partners. And while overlaps occurred with greater frequency than interruptions, both were distributed symmetrically between male–male and female–female speakers. In all, there were seven interruptions in the same-sex conversations coming from three transcripts: in two of these there were three interruptions, and in one of them, a single interruption. These were divided as equally as possible between the two parties in each conversation: 2 vs. 1, 2 vs. 1, and 1 vs. 0. By comparison, cross-sex conversations displayed gross asymmetries. Interruptions were far more likely to occur than overlaps, and both types of simultaneity were much more frequently initiated by males than females. For example, forty-six out of forty-eight, or 96%, of the interruptions were by males to females.[6] Females, on the other hand, showed a greater tendency toward silence, particularly subsequent to interruption by males. These patterned asymmetries – most striking in the case of interruption – led us to conclude tentatively that these females' rights to complete a turn were apparently abridged by males with impunity, i.e., without complaint from females.[7]

Recall Goffman's (1976: 73) observation that children – in interaction with adults – are accorded treatment characteristically extended to "non-persons," i.e., their status as co-participants in conversation is contingent on adult forbearance, and their "time and territory may be seen as expendable." If we regard conversational turn-space as the "time and territory" of a speaker, then the tendency of males to interrupt females implies that women's turn at talk is – at least some of the time – expendable and that women can be treated conversationally as "non-persons." With these considerations in mind, we present our parent–child transcripts.

Five interactions between parents and children were recorded in a physician's office, either in the open waiting room, or in the examination room before the doctor–patient interaction began.[8] Each author inspected the transcripts of these exchanges to locate instances of simultaneous speech. In the five parent–child exchanges, we found seventeen instances of simultaneity, of which fourteen were interruptions. Of the fourteen, twelve or 86%, were by the adult. The remaining two interruptions were by the same child to an adult (trying to get her attention).

Hence the striking asymmetry between males and females in the initiation of interruptions is reproduced in the transcripts of parent–child conversation. However, in contrast to the broader range of situations where the adult conversations were recorded, the parent–child segments are two-party conversations drawn from a single setting. But one might argue that interactions between children and their parents in other, more relaxed situations might have a markedly different character.[9] The pertinent point, in any event, is whether or not interruptions occur *when* the issue of who is to control the interaction is salient. Hence, the conversational exchanges recorded in the physician's office, while insufficient in themselves to establish the point, do suggest that interruptions are employed by the dominant party, the adult, to effect control in the exchange.[10] Let us consider some of the ways interruptions may function to achieve control and to display dominance in both parent–child and male–female conversations.

Discussion

Taking the similarities in the patterns of interruptions between adults and children and males and females to mean that females have an analogous status to children in certain conversational situations implies that the female has restricted rights to speak and may be ignored or interrupted at will. However, we suggest that the exercise of power by the male (or, for that matter, the parent) is systematic rather than capricious, and is thus subject to constraint. That is, wholesale trampling of speaker rights, even in the case of children, is not culturally approved, and those speakers who indiscriminately interrupt or otherwise misuse their conversational partner are subject to characterization as rude, domineering, or authoritarian. We believe interruptions are a tool used to fashion socially appropriate interactional *displays* which both exhibit and accomplish proper relationships between parties to the interaction.

Parent–child interaction

A common-sense observation about physicians' offices is: many (if not most) young children are apprehensive about what will happen to them there. Moreover, parents are likely to feel some anxiety about the behavior of their children in that setting: control over the child is necessary to insure cooperation in the medical examination, to suppress protest or other expressions of reluctance to participate, and to prevent uninvited handling of equipment in the examining room (cf. Goffman, 1976). We can thus expect interactions of the following sort:

```
CHILD:    But I don't wanna shot! ((sobs)) you said (x)
          said you said ⌈I      ⌉
PARENT:              ⌊Look⌋ just be quiet and take that
          sock off or you'll get more than just a shot!
```

Or:

```
CHILD:    If I got one wi⌈th a  ⌉
PARENT:              ⌊Leave⌋ that alone Kurt
(1.8)
CHILD:    Huh?
PARENT:   Don't touch that roller
```

The rule-set described earlier is a system of rules governing the construction of speaker turns and the transitions between them. Observance of these rules results in the distribution of opportunities to speak among participants and hence, the allocation of a segment of time to the speaker. The time slot under control of a speaker is potentially (a) a time when the speaker may engage in activities other than speaking, e.g. handling some object, and (b) a time when the speaker's utterance itself may unfold as a definite *action*, e.g. as a complaint or insult. The turn-taking system assigns the current turn-holder the right to that interval, to reach at least a first possible transition place (Sacks, *et al.*, 1974: 706) and the listenership of those present and party to the talk ratifies that right. Given that many utterances project not only their ending but their sense as well (cf. Jefferson, 1973: 54–60), to listen (or to be witness to some unfolding behavior), is an *act* in its own right according at least provisional approval or acquiescence to the action heard (or witnessed), and acknowledging the right of the speaker to be speaking. What is said and *listened to* combine to permit inferences about the character and relationship of the speaker and hearer.

Thus, in the case of the parent–child interactions discussed above, adult forbearance of the child's protest or failure promptly to disrobe could be seen as tolerance of – if not acquiescence to – the child's "unruly" behavior. If the child is simultaneously engaged in taking a turn at talk *and* some problematic non-verbal behavior, or if *what* the child is using the turn to do (e.g., to protest) is problematic, then the parent's presumed obligation to correct or control the child's behavior may take precedence over the child's already uncertain right to complete a turn. Moreover, the parent's intrusion into the child's turn *exhibits* the adult's control over the situation and the child, displaying it to the parent, the child, and to any others witnessing the interaction. The parent's failure to act in problematic situations also shows a lack of control or the child's dominance. Insofar as the parent–child relationship is *essentially* asymmetrical by our cultural standards, those occurrences warranting adult intervention may warrant interruption of the child's turn at talk as well.

Woman's place

The similarity between parent–child and male–female conversational patterns in our data has been noted. The suggested parallel is clear: men interrupt women in situations where women's verbal or non-verbal behavior is somehow problematic, as in the following:

FEMALE: Both really (#) it just strikes me as too
1984ish y'know to sow your seed or whatever
(#) an' then have it develop miles away not
caring i ⌈f   ⌉
MALE: ⌊Now: :⌋ it may be something uh quite
different (#) you can't make judgments like
that without all the facts being at your
disposal

Or:

FEMALE: I guess I'll do a paper on the economy business
he laid out last week if ⌈I can   ⌉
MALE: ⌊You're⌋ kidding!
That'd be a *terrible* topic.

And:

FEMALE: So uh you really can't bitch when you've got
all those on the same day (4.2) but I uh *asked*
my physics professor if I couldn't chan ⌈ge that⌉
MALE: ⌊Don't ⌋ touch that
(1.2)
FEMALE: What?

(#)

MALE: I've got everything jus' how I want it in that
notebook (#) you'll screw it up leafin' *through*
it like that.[11]

Our reflections here touch on three matters. First, we take the view that the use of interruptions by males is a *display* of dominance or control to the female (and to any witnesses), just as the parent's interruption communicates an aspect of parental control to the child and to others present. Second, the use of interruptions is *in fact* a control device since the incursion (particularly if repeated) disorganizes the local construction of a topic, as in the following:

FEMALE: How's your paper coming?=
MALE: Alright I guess (#) I haven't done much in
the past two weeks
(1.8)
FEMALE: Yeah::: know how that ⎡can ⎤
MALE: ⎣Hey⎦ ya' got an extra cigarette?
(#)
FEMALE: Oh uh sure ((hands him the pack))
like *my* ⎡pa ⎤
MALE: ⎣How⎦ 'bout a match?
(1.2)

FEMALE: Ere ya go uh like *my* ⎡pa   ⎤
MALE: ⎣Thanks⎦
(1.8)
FEMALE: Sure (#) I was gonna tell you ⎡my ⎤
MALE: ⎣Hey⎦ I'd really like
ta' talk but I gotta run (#) see ya
(3.2)
FEMALE: Yeah

Third, and perhaps most important, the occurrence of asymmetrical interruption signals the presence of issues pertinent to the activation of dominating behavior by the male. That is, just as the physician's examining room is a setting likely to engender adult concerns for control of the child (and hence, interruption of the child's utterance, among other things) so too may various occasions, *and the talk within them* trigger male displays of dominance and female displays of submission. Thus, the presence of male-initiated simultaneity – particularly interruptions – provides a clue where to search in interactional materials to find the particulars accounting for the occurrence of situationally induced attempts at dominance, in part through the suspension or violation of the rule-set.[12] Those "situational inducements", viewed from within the matrix of our present culture, constitute the warrant for interruption of the female by the male.

Concluding Remarks

These are preliminary findings, based on suggestive but far from definitive results. We report them here to show their potential significance for the study of gender behavior. The notion that language and speech communicate the cultural significance of gender is reflected by the growing literature in this area (cf. Key, 1975; Lakoff, 1975; and Thorne and Henley, 1975). Earlier research has utilized verbal interaction as an index of power in familial interaction (Farina and Holzberg, 1968; Hadley and Jacob, 1973; and Mishler and Waxler, 1968).

However, the use of features of conversational interaction as measures of power, dominance and the like has produced inconclusive – and sometimes contradictory – findings (cf. Shaw and Sadler, 1969) in the absence of an explicit model of conversational interaction *per se*. The work of Sacks, Schegloff, and Jefferson (1974) provides a theoretical basis for analyzing the very organization of such social interaction. We have tried to sketch the outlines of an approach to the study of male–female interaction utilizing this model.

NOTES

This is a revised version of a paper presented at the American Sociological Association Annual Meetings, August 25–30, 1975, San Francisco, California. We wish to acknowledge the many helpful comments and suggestions of Thomas P. Wilson and Michelle Patterson. We owe Gail Jefferson more than we could ever acknowledge.

1 The criteria for determining a unit-type are only partially syntactic. For example, the status of a word as a unit-type is a sequential and hence, social-organizational issue, as in saying "Yes" in answer to another's question.

2 The model is further characterized as *locally managed*, i.e., it operates to effect transitions between adjacent turns, the focus being upon the next turn and next transition. The turn-taking system is also said to be *party administered* and *interactionally managed*, i.e., under the control of speakers and employed on a turn-by-turn basis by conversationalists each exercising options contingent upon, and undertaken with the awareness of, the options available to the other.

3 The transcribing conventions used for our data are presented in Transcription Conventions 1, p. xviii.

4 The model is proposed as a context-free mechanism that is at the same time finely context-sensitive. "Context-free" here means that it operates independently of such features of actual conversations as topics, settings, number of parties, and social identities. Given this independence, the mechanism can accommodate the changing circumstances of talk posed by variation in topic, setting, number of speakers and their identities; that is, its context-sensitivity permits it to generate the particulars of unique conversations. The model is thus posited to pertain to "any speakers" and "any conversation" (cf. Sacks, *et al.*, 1974: 699–701, especially n. 10 p. 700 for a brief consideration of the issues raised by this claim). Such a proposal of course runs counter to the basic sociological notions of social and cultural variability. Can different ethnic groups, social classes, or

even males and females within such categories be assumed to use the same mechanisms for effecting turn transition? Here we simply assume that white, middle-class university students – male and female alike – are oriented to turn-taking in the fashion Sacks, *et al.* (1974) assert, thus permitting us to focus on the communicative and interactional implications of violations of turn-taking rules. The issue of the generalizability of the model across other social and cultural categories we leave to further inquiry.

5   The turn-by-turn organization of talk means that both the relevance and coherence of talk are locally managed by participants at any particular point in conversation (e.g. given a subsequent occurrence, what may have begun as topic X may be transformed into topic Y). Clearly, not all instances of simultaneous speech are disruptive. Jefferson (1973), for example, comments on the precision placement of a characteristic class of events which overlap a present speaker's utterance in such a way as to indicate both active listenership and independent knowledge of what the overlapped utterance is saying. Such displays occur *prior* to completion of a unit-type (i.e. by our schema, at points of interruption). Our point here is that beginning to speak prior to a possible transition place can be a communicative act with sequential consequences for conversation (cf. Jefferson and Schegloff, 1975).

6   Ten of the eleven cross-sex interactions exhibited interruptions, ranging from a low of two to a high of thirteen and averaging 4.2 per transcript. In every conversation, the male interrupted the female more frequently than vice versa.

7   The collection of conversations analyzed here and in Zimmerman and West (1975) does not constitute a probability sample of conversationalists or conversations. Hence, simple projections from findings based on this collection to conversationalists or conversations at large cannot be justified by the usual logic of statistical inference. Thus, the present research is intended to illustrate the utility of Sacks' *et al.* (1974) model as a means of locating significant problems in the area of language and interaction and as a point of departure for further study.

8   The children in these exchanges ranged from four to eight years of age. Parties to conversation include two mother–son pairs, two mother–daughter pairs, and one father–daughter pair.

9   For example, multi-party conversations in the home might be situations in which children have greater needs to compete for the attention of adults than in the case of two-party exchanges in public. Hence, these "competitive" situations would be more likely to produce instances of interruption of adults by children. We have seen some indications to this effect, in other transcripts of exchanges in this same setting (i.e. the physician's office). However for purposes of comparability with our adult conversations, we are interested only in two-party exchanges here.

10   We should note that more systematic study is called for to control for setting itself. Our current research utilizes variations on a standardized experimental setting in which dyads of equivalent ages and educational backgrounds – but differing sex compositions – interact.

11   This last excerpt is an exchange embedded in a longer sequence marked by pronounced "retarded minimal responses" i.e., silences prior to issuing a brief acknowledgement of prior speaker's utterance, e.g., "unhuh."

12   Clearly, to test a hypothesis that particular types of situations induce male displays of dominance and female displays of submission would require that we define such situations independently of the occurrence of interruption.

REFERENCES

Farina, Amerigo, and Jules D. Holzberg (1968) "Interaction patterns of parents and hospital-ized sons diagnosed as schizophrenic or non-schizophrenic." *Journal of Abnormal Psychology* 73: 114–118.

Fishman, Pamela (1975) "Interaction: The work women do." Paper presented at the American Sociological Association Annual Meetings, San Francisco, California, August 25–30, 1975.

Goffman, Erving (1976) "Gender advertisements." *Studies in the Anthropology of Visual Communication* 3: 65–154.

Hadley, Trevor and Theodore Jacob (1973) "Relationship among measures of family power." *Journal of Personality and Social Psychology* 27: 6–12.

Jefferson, Gail (1973) "A case of precision timing in ordinary conversation: Overlapped tag-positioned address terms in closing sequences." *Semiotica* IX: 47–96.

Jefferson, Gail and Emanuel Schegloff (1975) "Sketch: Some orderly aspects of overlap in natural conversation." Unpublished Manuscript.

Key, Mary Ritchie (1975) *Male/Female Language*. Metuchen, New Jersey: Scarecrow Press.

Lakoff, Robin (1975) *Language and Woman's Place*. New York: Harper & Row.

Mishler, Elliot G. and Nancy E. Waxler (1968) *Interaction in Families: An Experimental Study of Family Process and Schizophrenia*. New York: Wiley.

Sacks, Harvey (1966) Unpublished Lectures, University of California, Los Angeles.

Sacks, Harvey, Emanuel Schegloff and Gail Jefferson (1974) "A simplest systematics for the organization of turn-taking for conversation." *Language* 50: 696–735.

Shaw, Marvin E. and Orin W. Sadler (1965) "Interaction patterns in heterosexual dyads varying in degree of intimacy." *The Journal of Social Psychology* 66: 345–351.

Thorne, Barrie and Nancy Henley (1975) *Language and Sex: Difference and Dominance*. Rowley, Massachusetts: Newbury House.

Zimmerman, Don H. and Candace West (1975) "Sex roles, interruptions and silences in conversation." Pp. 105–129 in Barrie Thorne and Nancy Henley (eds.), *Language and Sex: Difference and Dominance*. Rowley, Massachusetts: Newbury House.

12

The Sounds of Silence: How Men Silence Women in Marital Relations

Victoria Leto DeFrancisco

I want him to tell me what he's thinking, what he's feeling. . . . About a month ago I said, 'Hal talk to me, just don't sit there like a bump on a log. Talk to me . . .'. He'll, when we're arguing mostly, I'll say, 'just explain to me now, what are you saying, what is it?' And he won't. He takes it as an insult I guess that I don't understand what he's saying and he won't explain. . . . (A 21-year-old Hispanic woman describes communication with her husband.)

Part of the impetus for this research project was my personal dissatisfaction in conversing with some men; a dissatisfaction similar to that expressed above by a woman in the present study. This project was also influenced by the growing body of research on gender and conversation. Many earlier studies have seemed to accept gender differences as a given and have failed to consider social or relational contexts (see critiques by Rakow, 1986; Spitzack and Carter, 1989; Thorne et al., 1983). Instead, the research which seemed most insightful and challenging to me was that which attempted to link larger social hierarchies to the less assuming, day-to-day interactions between women and men (e.g. Davis, 1988; Fishman, 1983; Henley, 1977; Hite, 1987; Rubin, 1976, 1983; Sattel, 1983; Spender, 1980; West and Zimmerman, 1983). Nancy Henley (1977) called this the study of micropolitics, meaning that larger social inequalities can be observed in the microcosm of our personal relations where these inequalities are created, maintained and even justified.

An example of such research is Pamela Fishman's more naturalistic examination of ongoing interactions in white heterosexual couples' homes. She examined a number of conversational devices used to build conversation or to detour it and found that for the three couples studied, the women worked harder to initiate and maintain conversation than the men, but were less successful in their efforts. Her conclusion was that women do the 'shitwork' of conversation. This controversial thesis made an important connection between other domestic duties traditionally ascribed to women, and the work of conversational development and relational maintenance.

However, like much communication research on conversation, Fishman's work still omitted an important source of information: the individual speaker's views. I chose to extend Fishman's methods of studying conversational development in ongoing interactions by adding private interviews. The primary purpose of the interviews was to discover the individuals' communication preferences in reviewing specific interactions with their spouses.[1] When I combined these methods I found several intricate means by which these women have been silenced, not only by the non-responsive men in their lives, but also by the social science methods commonly employed in such communication research.

Participants and Methods Description

There were seven couples in the study. I accepted only those who worked outside the academy. Couples were paid US$20 for participation. The couples lived in two medium-sized midwestern cities. Their ages ranged from 21 to 63. They had lived together for between 2 and 35 years and this was the first marriage for all persons involved. Three of the couples had children living at home. All the participants described their marital relationships as being generally satisfying and stable, and their descriptions of relational and domestic duties suggested they follow fairly traditional gender-role behaviors (Fitzpatrick, 1988; Maltz and Borker, 1982, reprinted in this volume, p. 417). One woman described herself as Hispanic, the others were Anglo-Americans.

I chose to study ongoing interactions where individual attempts to initiate conversation could be noted over time. To do so, a tape recorder with an omnidirectional microphone was set up in the central living area of each couple's home for a week to 10 days, which produced an average of 12 hours of recording. The participants were asked to run the recorder whenever both partners were present for an extended period of time and to go on about their regular household activities. They had the right to erase recordings or turn off the machine at any time, but only two brief comments were reportedly erased. The participants said they became comfortable with the taping and that the conversations were representative of their daily interactions, although I realize some degree of artificiality may be inevitable.

After the taping I conducted a private interview with each person. The individual listened to two or three different episodes, totaling approximately 30 minutes. The participant was asked to stop the recorder to note anything she or he liked or disliked about the episode. To help clarify this task I first asked the person to brainstorm some examples of what likes and dislikes might be, and I stressed that I was not looking for any one type of information. Interviews were conducted within one week of the tape recordings and lasted an average of 90 minutes.

The episodes participants reviewed, plus an additional 30 minutes of interaction per couple, were transcribed using an adaptation of Jefferson's system (see Transcription Conventions 1, p. xviii). I worked with the transcripts, the actual recordings and participants' comments to compile relative frequencies on the following conversational components identified as problematic in previous gender research: talk time (Fitzpatrick and Dindia, 1986; Martin and Craig, 1983; Spender, 1980);

question-asking (Fishman, 1978a, 1983); topic initiations (Fishman, 1978b; Tannen, 1984; West and Garcia, 1988); topic success/failure (Fishman, 1978a, 1978b, 1983); and turn-taking violations, including interruptions (Dindia, 1987; Kennedy and Camden, 1983; Roger, 1989) and turns at talk which seem minimal, delayed or complete failures to respond (labeled the no-response – Fishman, 1978a, 1983; West and Zimmerman, 1983).

Criteria for Identifying Conversational Components

I began with the assumption most gender and conversation research has been based upon Sacks et al.'s (1974) model of turn-taking. Underlying tenets of this model are that a turn at talk is seen as a right and an obligation to speak. Generally one person speaks at a time, and speaker turns recur. Conversational partners are said to be conscious of their speaker/listener roles, as turns at talk tend to occur with few or no silences between. Thus behavioral failures to follow these norms may be considered uncooperative, inattentive and turn-taking violations. I included in my analyses of turn-taking violations those which seemed delayed (1–3 seconds average); minimal (monosyllabic turns at talk, 'mhm', 'yeah', not to be confused with active-listening cues); complete failure to take one's turn at talk, the 'no-response' violation (Fishman, 1983, 1978a); and interruptive (the listener begins to speak at a point that is unlikely to be a completion point in the current speakers' utterance).[2]

While Sacks and his colleagues' (1974) model served as a guideline for identifying these violations, I soon realized, as others have noted (Murray, 1985), that the tenets of their model were not universal. Consequently, identifications were also based on information gleaned from the tapes and the interviewees' reactions (Murray, 1985). Topic changes were identified by criteria adapted from previous research (Fishman, 1978b; Tannen, 1984) and from contextual information. A number of indicators were used to distinguish successful and unsuccessful topics. These included responses which directly shut off an attempted topic; topics which received a higher frequency of interruptions, minimal, delayed or no-response violations from the other speaker; and indicators that the original speaker knew her or his topic was in trouble, such as increases in verbalized pauses (Fishman, 1978b: 14). Talk time was measured with a hand-held stopwatch and total word count.

Results

After learning first-hand how complex and interpretive the work of identifying conversational components is, the reader is cautioned against making any conclusive judgments based on the numbers reported below. While the risks of quantifying gender differences across individuals, couples, and contexts are apparent, I conducted these frequency counts in an effort to provide preliminary parallels with previous studies of gender and conversation. Thus the following should be viewed as suggestive and not exhaustive. Furthermore, the patterns of behaviour and other ethnographic information are what is important, not the individual results.

There are two general findings which lead to the conclusion that the men were relatively silent and that their behaviors silenced the women. First, the no-response was the most common turn-taking violation, particularly for the men. Second, results from the components of conversation combined with the ethnographic information strongly suggest that the women in this project worked harder to maintain interaction than the men, but were less successful in their attempts. Together these findings reveal the multiple ways in which these women have been silenced.

No-responses accounted for 45 percent of the total 540 violations; interruptions were the second most common violation, but only accounted for 24 percent. Among the total violations, the women were responsible for 36 percent and the men were responsible for 64 percent. The men were responsible for more turn-taking violations across all categories studied (no-response, 32 percent women, 68 percent men; interruption, 46 percent women, 54 percent men; delayed response, 30 percent women, 70 percent men; and minimal response, 40 percent women, 60 percent men).

The higher percentage of no-response violation was not expected given the previous focus in gender research on the interruption as a central dominance behavior (e.g. Dindia, 1987; Kennedy and Camden, 1983; Roger, 1989; West and Zimmerman, 1983). However, in general, these conversations were not interactive enough to necessitate interruption. The television ran the entire recording time in two couples' homes, and when simultaneous talk did occur, the participants did not always perceive it as a turn-taking violation. They heard it as a sign of their partner's enthusiasm toward the conversation. Among the fourteen participants, interruptions were rarely listed as a complaint about their partners. The problem, particularly for the women in this study, seemed to be more basic – getting a response at all.

The second point which led me to conclude that the men generally silenced the women is that, similar to Fishman's earlier work (1978a, 1978b, 1983), there were several indicators which suggested communication was more important for the women, that they worked harder at it than the men, and yet were less successful. The women talked more (139 minutes total, 63 percent; men spoke 83 minutes, 37 percent), yet seemed to have far less turn-taking violations (197, 36 percent to 343, 64 percent); and they raised more topics (236, 63 percent to 140, 37 percent), yet succeeded less often than the men in getting these developed into conversations (156, 66 percent succeeded compared to 106, 76 percent).

Certainly there may be other explanations for these results. First, talking more could have been a dominance behavior. However, when a person dominates by doing most of the talking, the person will also tend to interrupt more (Spender, 1980) and be more likely to have her or his topics succeed, neither of which occurred here. Second, merely raising a topic is not necessarily a positive effort toward conversation since some things may be better left unsaid. However, in the topic analysis, I found women and men were both as likely to raise all categories of topics except one – personal emotions or concerns. Since there were only five instances of this topic initiation on all the tapes (all raised unsuccessfully by the women), it seems reasonable to suggest that topic selection was generally not the problem. Furthermore, regardless of the topics' positive or negative nature, when one person seems to do most of the decision-making regarding which topics are successful and which are not, that decision-making may be a form of control and silencing.

The following is an example of the variety of strategies one man used to detour his partner's topic and her response efforts.

1   MARY: I went to Diana's ((food store)) today, for lunch, got a salad you know? (.)
2   BUD: Ahha.
3   MARY: = Ran into your mom.
4   BUD: = Ran into who? (1)
5   MARY: Your mom. (1) She didn't even know who l was. (2)
6   BUD: Ahhh. (1)
7   MARY: She was at the, she was at the meat case and, and I was looking at, you know I was gettin my salad, and I come around and she was at the meat case and then she took off, and then (2)
8   BUD: {Be right back ((goes outside)) Ouch, my elbow! (45) ((door bangs, he returns)) (7) Emm (2)
9   MARY: So I followed her all the way up through the store (1) and she was ((word))
10 BUD: {well, you have to remember my mom, my mom has tunnel vision, too, I mean she don see nothin but straight ahead.

                              *   *   *

11 MARY: I've got this all figured out. (3) I talked to Doyle today? (4) And, (4) you know explained to him the fact that you know, come April I'll probably have to (1) ahm (.)
12 BUD: {Excuse me, open the back door, I'm gonna give this to (the dogs). (8) ((He returns.))
13 MARY: I'll probably have to terminate my appointment.

During our interview Bud said he did not feel like talking at the time of the conversation and that he had 'heard it all before'. His lack of attentiveness was apparent: he went outside twice during her stories (lines 8, 12); he seemed to diffuse her punch-line for the first story (line 10); he seldom provided any apparent participative listening cues (lines 2, 6); and he seemed to exhibit no-response violations (e.g. lines 11, 12, 13). In the total 12.5-minute conversation, he had 18 turn-taking violations, she had 9. She raised 7 topics, 5 of which were successful; he raised 4, all successfully. Together these suggest she was working harder at the conversation, but with less success than Bud.

All the women expressed concern about getting their husband's attention and mentioned the extra efforts they made to try to do so. One woman, Sandy, said: 'He doesn't talk to me! If it were up to him, we wouldn't talk.' She described various attention-getting strategies: she quizzed him if she suspected he had not been listening; she used guilt and jealousy strategies, and she purposefully raised topics he enjoyed.

In contrast to the women's efforts to encourage talk, they noted in the taped interactions a variety of what they termed 'patronizing', 'put-down' and 'teachy' behaviors by their husbands. Paternalistic statements are said to limit another's behavior through what are presented as well-meant intentions (Davis, 1988: 23). In the taped interactions the men's patronizing comments seemed to detour the women's efforts to develop conversation. In a more blatant case, when Sharon asked Jerry's opinion about responding to a newspaper advertisement he warned, 'Be careful you don't get into somethin you can't get out of. Like don't give em your credit card number', to which she replied, 'I know. I'm not stupid.' In another case, Sue labeled her husband's behavior as 'teachy', because of the way he explained tennis or technical processes related to their joint careers in television production. On the tapes, her husband Robert slowed his speech and used more careful articulation, similar to the way adults sometimes try to teach children. Less blatant cases of condescending behaviors which silenced the women may be the several instances of husbands who cautioned their wives to quit worrying about a topic the wives had tried to discuss. 'Why worry about something until it happens?', Curt said.

A final type of patronizing behavior is what two women called 'faked listening', pretending to listen by offering only token acknowledgments. Sharon said when Jerry got bored with her topic he would change it by 'getting mushy', meaning he would make a romantic or sexual comment. She knew the next thing he said would have nothing to do with the topic she had raised. The effect of these various patronizing behaviors seemed to be to trivialize the women's concerns and make further discussion of a topic irrelevant.

There was also other evidence that talk was more important to the women than the men. I received eighteen responses to my solicitations for participants; women initiated the contact in all but one case. Of these, six chose not to participate (five were ineligible), because they said their husbands were not comfortable with the project. Of those who completed the project, four men (Curt, Hal, Ted and Warren) said they agreed to do so because their wives had been feeling lonely and they thought getting to talk with another woman (rather than increasing an awareness of their own communication inadequacies) might make their wives feel better.

I am not trying to suggest that the men in this study failed to value talk at all, or that the stereotypical 'silent male' is a universal phenomenon. However, the men consistently preferred 'not talking' and/or 'light conversation' in their continual vigilance for conflict avoidance. According to previous research, conflict-avoidance strategies are techniques people use to deal with unwelcome requests from others (Belk et al., 1988: 165). Both the women and men voiced desires to avoid conflict, but the strategies they preferred for doing so were different. The women chose to voice objections, seek compromises and talk out a problem. These are behaviors consistent with what previous researchers have labeled 'collaborative' conflict-avoidance strategies (Belk et al., 1988). The men chose what previous researchers have labeled 'unilateral conflict avoidance' (Belk et al., 1988), as exemplified by their desires to withdraw, for their wives to be less emotional, to have more efficient conflict resolutions, and to generally avoid sensitive topics of discussion.

The men's stated preference for conflict avoidance seemed consistent with their greater use of no-response violations because the conflict avoider is generally thought to be apathetic and disinterested (Fitzpatrick, 1988; Folger and Poole, 1984). It is plausible that a person who unilaterally avoids conflict may do so, as these men did: by avoiding sensitive topics; using more no-response violations as opposed to interruptions; talking less; and using patronizing behaviors to control conversation. The women's preferences for collaborative conflict avoidance seemed consistent with the greater amount of work they did to generate communication with their husbands.

The problem, then, is that these different preferences for how to avoid conflict may themselves come into conflict. And, while no one piece of evidence reported here would be highly meaningful alone, together the information demonstrates that when these needs did compete, the men seemed to be able to put forth less effort and still obtain their wishes more often than the women. As a result, the men seemed to have more control in defining the day-to-day reality of these couples' communication styles, and the women did more of the adapting.

Thus, through the variety of research methods employed, we can see connections between speaker preferences, components of conversation, and the consequences for relational and social control. Although this was a preliminary effort to understand how gender inequalities may be created and maintained on a daily basis, the methods do offer directions for future work. Analyses of isolated conversational components are not enough if we want to understand how relational and social realities are developed through interaction. Anita Pomerantz (1989) suggested that researchers need to bridge the gap between the more technical analyses of conversation and that which is socially relevant for the speakers. While such translational links are susceptible to misrepresentations (Jefferson, 1989), failure to make such attempts seems elitist and does little to inform people's lives. This concern is particularly important for feminists, since the violations of one's communication expectations and preferences in intimate relations may actually be covert dominance strategies. Research methods which fail to make such political links serve to further camouflage women's realities and maintain the silence.

NOTES

A special thanks to Marsha Houston, Cheris Kramarae and Richard West for suggestions on earlier drafts of this paper.

1   The term communication preferences as used here refers to individuals' likes and dislikes in communication with their spouse, not the structure-based preferences Schegloff (1988) discussed.
2   In the transcripts, the symbol [is used at the beginning of an utterance to show overlap, that is, to show where a speaker began her/his turn within two or less syllables of the other speaker's ending. The symbol { is used to show where a speaker interrupted the other's turn by beginning to speak when it was not a transition-relevance place (a point beyond the two syllable rule of thumb).

REFERENCES

Belk, Sharyn S., Garcia-Falconi, Renan, Hernandez-Sanchez, Julita Elemi and Snell, William E. (1988) 'Avoidance Strategy Use in the Intimate Relationships of Women and Men from Mexico and the United States', *Psychology of Women Quarterly* 12: 165–74.

Davis, Kathryn (1988) 'Paternalism under the Microscope', in A. D. Todd and S. Fisher (eds) *Gender and Discourse: The Power of Talk*, pp. 19–54. Norwood, NJ: Ablex.

Dindia, Kathryn (1987) 'The Effects of Sex of Subject and Sex of Partner on Interruptions', *Human Communication Research* 13: 345–71.

Fishman, Pamela (1978a) 'Interaction: The Work Women Do', *Social Problems* 25: 397–406.

Fishman, Pamela (1978b) 'What Do Couples Talk about When They're Alone?', in D. Butturff and E. Epstein (eds) *Women's Language and Style*, pp. 11–12. Akron, OH: University of Akron.

Fishman, Pamela (1983) 'Interaction: The Work Women Do', in Barrie Thorne, Cheris Kramarae and Nancy Henley (eds) *Language, Gender and Society*, pp. 89–102. Rowley, MA: Newbury House.

Fitzpatrick, Mary Anne (1988) *Between Husbands and Wives: Communication in Marriage*. Newbury Park, CA: Sage.

Fitzpatrick, Mary Anne and Dindia, Kathryn (1986) 'Couples and Other Strangers: Talk Time in Spouse–Stranger Interaction', *Communication Research* 13: 625–52.

Folger, Joseph P. and Poole, M. Scott (1984) *Working through Conflict: A Communication Perspective*. Glenview, IL: Scott, Foresman & Co.

Henley, Nancy (1977) *Body Politics*. Englewood Cliffs, NJ: Prentice-Hall.

Hite, Shere (1987) *Women and Love: A Cultural Revolution in Progress*. New York: Alfred A. Knopf, Inc.

Jefferson, Gail (1989) 'Letter to the Editor', *Western Journal of Speech Communication* 53: 427–9.

Kennedy, C. W. and Camden, C. L. (1983) 'A New Look at Interruptions', *Western Journal of Speech Communication* 47: 45–58.

Maltz, Daniel and Borker, Ruth (1982) 'A Cultural Approach to Male–Female Miscommunication', in John Gumperz (ed.) *Language and Social Identity*. pp. 196–216. Cambridge: Cambridge University Press.

Martin, J. N. and Craig, R. T. (1983) 'Selected Linguistic Sex Differences during Initial Social Interactions of Same-sex and Mixed-sex Student Dyads', *Western Journal of Speech Communication* 47: 16–28.

Murray, Stephen (1985) 'Toward a Model of Members' Methods for Recognizing Interruptions', *Language in Society* 14: 31–40.

Pomerantz, Anita M. (1989) 'Epilogue', *Western Journal of Speech Communication* 53: 242–6.

Rakow, Lana (1986) 'Rethinking Gender Research in Communication', *Journal of Communication* 36: 11–26.

Roger, Derek (1989) 'Experimental Studies of Dyadic Turn-taking Behavior', in Derek Roger and Peter Bull (eds) *Conversation: An Interdisciplinary Perspective*, pp. 75–95. Clevedon: Multilingual Matters.

Rubin, Lillian (1976) *Worlds of Pain: Life in the Working-class Family*. New York: Basic Books.

Rubin, Lillian (1983) *Intimate Strangers*. New York: Harper & Row.

Sacks, Harvey, Schegloff, Emanuel, and Jefferson, Gail (1974) 'A Simplest Systematics for the Organization of Turn-taking for Conversation', *Language* 50: 696–735.

Sattel, J. W. (1983) 'Men, Inexpressiveness, and Power', in Barrie Thorne, Cheris Kramarae and Nancy Henley (eds) *Language, Gender and Society*, pp. 118–24. Rowley, MA: Newbury House.

Schegloff, E. A. (1988) 'On an Actual Virtual Servo-mechanism for Guessing Bad News: A Single Case Conjecture', *Social Problems* 35: 442–57.

Spender, Dale (1980) *Man Made Language*. London: Routledge & Kegan Paul.

Spitzack, Carole and Carter, Kathryn (1989) 'Research on Women's Communication: The Politics of Theory and Method', in Kathryn Carter and Carole Spitzack (eds) *Doing Research on Women's Communication: Perspectives on Theory and Method*, pp. 11–39. Norwood, NJ: Ablex.

Tannen, Deborah (1984) *Conversational Style: Analyzing Talk among Friends*. Norwood, NJ: Ablex Publishing.

Thorne, Barrie, Kramarae, Cheris and Henley, Nancy (1983) 'Language, Gender and Society: Opening a Second Decade of Research', in Barry Thorne, Cheris Kramarae and Nancy Henley (eds) *Language, Gender and Society*, pp. 7–24. Rowley, MA: Newbury House.

West, Candace and Garcia, Angela (1988) 'Conversational Shift Work: A Study of Topical Transitions between Women and Men', *Social Problems* 35: 551–75.

West, Candace and Zimmerman, Donald (1983) 'Small Insults: A Study of Interruptions in Cross-sex Conversations between Unacquainted Persons', in Barrie Thorne, Cheris Kramarae and Nancy Henley (eds) *Language, Gender and Society*, pp. 103–17. Rowley, MA: Newbury House.

13

Talk Control: An Illustration from the Classroom of Problems in Analysing Male Dominance of Conversation

Joan Swann

Women and Men Talking

The stereotype of the over-talkative woman stands out in stark contrast to most research studies of interactions between women and men, which argue that, by and large, it is men who tend to dominate the talk.
[. . .]
However the notion of male 'dominance' itself is rather problematical. While many studies have shown that men's interests tend to be better served than women's in mixed-sex conversation (as, for instance, in Fishman's 1978 study, where topics initiated by men are more often followed up and pursued), it is likely that both women and men contribute to this state of affairs. In other words, the use of terms such as 'dominate' and 'control' should not suggest that men need linguistically to bludgeon women into submission. Where it is seen as normal that men talk more, etc. they may do so with the complicity of women. [. . .]

Classroom Talk: An Illustration

Classroom talk is an interesting area of study partly because many educationists argue that talk itself is an important vehicle for learning:

> The way into ideas, the way of making ideas truly one's own, is to be able to think them through, and the best way to do this for most people is to talk them through. Thus talking is not merely a way of conveying existing ideas to others; it is also a way by which we explore ideas, clarify them, and make them our own. Talking things over allows the sorting of ideas, and gives rapid and extensive practice towards the handling of ideas. (Marland 1977: 129)

The classroom is also one place in which children learn social roles. An influential argument is that socially appropriate behaviour (including gender-appropriate behaviour) is learnt in part (though not by any means exclusively) through classroom talk.

Studies of classroom life have found many ways, linguistic and nonlinguistic, in which girls and boys are treated differently. For instance, pupils are often segregated by gender as an aid to classroom administration, or told to do things as boys or as girls as a form of motivation (girls may be told to leave first very quietly, boys to sing as nicely as the girls); pupils are often told that certain topics are 'boys'' topics or will 'mainly appeal to the girls'; topics are often chosen specifically with a view to maintaining boys' interests; boys insist on, and are given, greater attention by the teacher; in practical subjects such as science boys tend to hog the resources; boys are more disruptive; and boys, in various ways, dominate classroom talk. (See Byrne 1978; Deem 1978; and Delamont 1980, for a general discussion of these and other findings; Whyte 1986, for a report on science teaching; and Clarricoates 1983, for a discussion of classroom interaction.)

Talk may, therefore, be seen to play its part alongside much more general patterns of difference and discrimination. Studies that focus on characteristics of mixed-sex classroom talk produce results that are similar in many respects to general studies of talk between women and men. For instance, in an American study of over 100 classes Sadker and Sadker (1985) found that boys spoke on average three times as much as girls, that boys were eight times more likely than girls to call out answers, and that teachers accepted such answers from boys but reprimanded girls for calling out. French and French (1984) suggest that particular strategies may enable talkative boys to gain more than their fair share of classroom talk. In a study of (British) primary classrooms they found that simply making an unusual response to a teacher's question could gain a pupil extra speaking turns – and those who made such responses were more often boys.

Most studies of classroom talk focus on the role of the teacher as much as on different pupils. One characteristic of classroom talk (that distinguishes it from talk in many other contexts) is that this is often mediated (if not directly controlled) by the teacher. If boys are to dominate, therefore, they must do so with the teacher's assistance or at least tacit acceptance. The argument that teachers pay boys more attention and, in other ways, encourage them to talk more has led some people consciously to attempt to redress the balance. Such evidence as is available, however, suggests that old habits are hard to break. Spender (1982) claims that it is virtually impossible to divide one's attention equally between girls and boys. Whyte (1986) is less pessimistic. Observations of science lessons by researchers involved in the Manchester-based Girls Into Science and Technology project revealed that teachers were able to devote an equal amount of attention to girls and boys, and therefore to encourage more equal participation from pupils. This was only achieved with some effort, however. Whyte reports a head of science who, having managed to create an atmosphere in which girls and boys contributed more or less equally to discussion, remarked that he had felt as though he were devoting 90 per cent of his attention to the girls (1986: 196).

While the fact of male dominance of classroom talk makes this similar to mixed-sex talk in other contexts, it's worth noting that not all of the same indicators of conversational dominance are present.

[. . .]

If boys are to attempt to dominate classroom talk (relative to girls), such dominance must fit with the context and with the behaviour of other participants – in this case chiefly the teacher, who is meant to be in control, overall, of what is going on.

I want to discuss some of these issues further in relation to an exploratory study of classroom talk that I carried out with a colleague, and which is described in greater detail elsewhere (see Swann and Graddol 1988).

An Exploratory Study of Classroom Talk

Given imbalances that had been found in earlier work between girls' and boys' participation in classroom talk the intention in this study was to examine in detail:

1   the mechanisms of turn allocation and turn exchange that support male dominance of classroom talk;
2   the roles played by different participants (girls, boys and the class teacher) in the achievement of such interactional dominance.

To do this, we made a close examination of video-recordings of two twenty-minute sequences of small-group teaching with primary school children. The sequences were recorded in two different schools: one, which I shall refer to as the 'pendulum' sequence, was recorded in the East Midlands; the other, the 'mining' sequence, was recorded in the north-east of England. In the 'pendulum' sequence there were six children (three girls and three boys) aged between 10 and 11 years, and a female teacher. The children were reporting back on experiments they had carried out with pendulums, and discussing their findings. The 'mining' sequence involved eight children (four girls and four boys) aged from 9 to 10 and a female teacher. These children were having a follow-up discussion after having seen a television programme on coal-mining (the school was situated in a mining area). In both cases the discussion was 'set up' to the extent that it was being recorded for research purposes. However, the work the children were engaged in was part of their normal classwork at the time.

Because the sequences were video-recorded we could observe teachers' and pupils' nonverbal behaviour as well as their talk (I shall return to this point below). We could also note any activities, etc. that accompanied the talk and that might contribute to the overall interpretation of what was going on. For instance, in the 'pendulum' sequence the seating arrangements were such that the teacher could more easily face the boys. In the 'mining' sequence the teacher was standing but turned more often towards the boys. In the 'pendulum' sequence a girl was helped by the teacher to adjust a slide on an overhead projector. Boys were not helped, but a boy was asked to focus the projector, and also to handle other equipment. In the 'mining' sequence the seating arrangements were such that the boys could more easily see a model pit that was used for part of the lesson. A boy was also asked to put on some miner's equipment. On any one occasion such factors may, of course, be coincidental, but it is interesting that they were similar to aspects of classroom organization recorded in the other general studies mentioned above (p. 186).

Having transcribed each video-recorded sequence we made various measures of the amount of talk contributed by each pupil. The number of turns and the number of words for each pupil are given in table 1.

Table 1   Contribution to classroom talk from girl and boy pupils in 'pendulum' and 'mining' sequences

Pupils	*Amount spoken*		
	Total words spoken	*Total spoken turns*	*Average words per turn*
'Pendulum' sequence			
Sarah	79	17	4.6
Laura	20	5	4.0
Donna	37	5	7.4
Unidentified girls	18	9	2.0
Total girls	154	36	4.3
Matthew	133	23	5.8
Trevor	83	20	4.1
Peter	55	10	5.5
Unidentified boys	48	20	2.5
Total boys	319	73	4.4
'Mining' sequence			
Kate	127	9	14.1
Lorraine	13	7	1.8
Anne	23	8	2.9
Emma	8	4	2.0
Unidentified girls	—	—	—
Total girls	171	28	6.1
Mark	47	9	5.2
Ian	80	23	3.5
John	35	5	7.0
Darren	101	15	6.7
Unidentified boys	3	2	1.5
Total boys	266	54	4.9

On average, boys contributed more in each sequence, both in terms of the number of turns taken and the number of words uttered. There were, however, intra-group differences: there were quieter boys and more talkative girls – including one particularly talkative girl in the 'mining' sequence. Clearly we could not make any generalizations on the basis of word- and turn-counts from such small samples: as with the aspects of classroom activities and organization mentioned above our results at this point simply confirmed that the distribution of talk in our groups was similar to that recorded in work carried out in other classrooms and with larger samples of pupils (such as French & French 1984, and Sadker & Sadker 1985).

When we came to examine more closely the interactional mechanisms by which boys obtained more turns than girls, we found differences between the two sequences. I shall describe briefly the findings from each sequence in turn.

The 'pendulum' sequence

This sequence was one in which pupils apparently had a great deal of freedom to contribute. However, there were differences between how girls and boys began an interchange with the teacher. When selecting pupils to speak by name the teacher chose girls rather more often than boys (11 occasions for girls and eight for boys). It was most common, however, for pupils simply to chip in to answer questions, without raising their hands or being selected by name. Boys were at a clear advantage here, chipping in or volunteering responses on 41 occasions, as opposed to girls' 13.

It seemed, then, as if boys were able to use the relatively unconstrained atmosphere to dominate the talk. However, certain aspects of the teacher's behaviour may also have favoured the boys. An example of this is the teacher's gaze behaviour, which we were able to analyse for part of the sequence. For the portion of the videotape in which the teacher was clearly in view and in which we could measure her gaze towards the pupils, we found that she looked towards the boys for 60 per cent of the time and towards the girls for 40 per cent of the time. The following brief extract provides an illustration of the distribution of the teacher's gaze and shows how this may encourage the boys to participate more. The extract comes about half way into the sequence, when pupils have finished reporting on their experiments and are engaged with the teacher in a more general discussion of their results.

Questions are numbered in sequence.[1]
...... = teacher's gaze towards the girls
----- = teacher's gaze towards the boys
      (Where gaze is not marked this is because the teacher is looking elsewhere – for
      instance, at the overhead projector.)

         ....
TEACHER: If you have a pendulum (.) which we established last

         ....------   ---------.....
      week was a weight a mass (.) suspended from a string

or whatever (.) and watch I'm holding it with my hand

so it's at rest at the moment (.) what is it that makes

the pendulum swing in a downward direction for

instance till it gets to there? [1] ⌈(.) just watch it

MATTHEW: ⌊gravity

TEACHER: What is it Matthew? [2]

MATTHEW: Gravity

⌠TEACHER: ⌈Yes (.)⌉ now we mentioned gravity when we were
⌡BOY: ⌊((xxx))⌋

TEACHER: actually doing the experiments but we didn't discuss it

too much (.) OK so it's gravity then that pulls it

down (.) what causes it to go up again at the other

side? [3]

⌠BOY: ⌈Force the force⌉

⌡BOY: ⌊The string Miss⌋ it gets up speed going down.

⌠TEACHER: It gets up speed going ⌈down (.) does⌉ anyone know the
⌡BOY: ⌊(force)(xxx) ⌋

TEACHER: word for it when you get up speed? [4] (.) as in a car

when you press the pedal? [5]

⌠BOY: ⌈accelerate ⌉
⌡BOY: ⌊momentum⌋

⌠TEACHER: You get momentum (.) ⌈Matthew (.)⌉ it accelerates
⌡MATTHEW: ⌊(xxx)   ⌋

TEACHER: going down doesn't it and it's the (.) energy the force

that it builds up that takes it up the other side (.)

watch (.) and see if it's the same (.) right (.) OK (.)

em (.) anything else you notice about that? [6] (.) so

it's gravity what about the moon? [7] (.) that's a bit

tricky isn't it? [8] (.) is ⌈ there grav ⌉ ity on the

BOYS: ⌊ (xxx) ⌋

⌈ TEACHER: moon? = [9]

⌊ BOYS: = No no it would float

TEACHER: There isn't gravity on the moon? [10] (.)

SEVERAL: No

MATTHEW: There is a certain amount

⌈ TEACHER: A certain amount Matthew? = [11]

⎨ MATTHEW: = ⌈ (xxx) ⌉

⌊ BOY: ⌊ Seven ⌋ times less

TEACHER: You reckon it's seven? [12]

BOY: Times less than on earth

TEACHER: Yes (.) well it's a it's a difficult figure to arrive at but

it is between six and seven

The transcript shows, first of all, that the teacher is looking much more often towards the boys. The teacher is also more often looking towards the boys at critical points, when a question requires to be answered. (Of the 12 questions, eight are directed towards the boys and four towards the girls.)

Of the four girls' questions, two (numbers 4 and 6) occur after a last-minute switch of gaze from the boys to the girls. Another (number 8), although we coded it as a question to give it the benefit of the doubt, seems to function more as an aside, or a comment on the activity, than as an attempt to elicit information.

Although in the 'pendulum' sequence, then, the boys seemed able to contribute more to the discussion by simply 'chipping in', our analysis of the teacher's gaze behaviour during a portion of the interaction suggests she may be distributing her attention selectively between the pupils and thus favouring the boys. It is also worth noting from the transcript that boys' speech often overlaps the teacher's. General 'muttering' from the boys occurs at various points during the interaction and may have the function of attracting, or maintaining the teacher's attention.

The 'mining' sequence

The teacher in this sequence had a different teaching style. The interaction was lively but kept more directly under the teacher's control: pupils rarely called out an answer – normally they raised their hands and were selected to speak. The following interchange is an example of the commonest way pupils obtained a speaking turn. Gaze is marked as in the 'pendulum' transcript. The superscript shows the order of hand-raising.

Interchange between teacher and Kate:

Notes

TEACHER: How did they know that those   Teacher looking at boys but can see girls. As

              (KJMEA)   K's hand goes up, teacher turns to look at
                                     girls. By the time boys' hands are raised,
        men were alive? (.) yes   teacher has already begun to turn to girls.
                                 By the time E's hand rises, teacher's gaze is
KATE: Miss they were knocking   already directed towards K.

TEACHER: They were knocking

(K = Kate; J = John; M = Mark; E = Emma; A = Anne)

Here the teacher looks towards the boys then switches to the girls. Kate is selected to answer, and hers was the first hand raised. The teacher seemed to have a strategy of occasionally selecting a quiet child whose hand was not raised and encouraging them to answer (Lorraine and Emma obtained all their speaking turns this way, and Anne half of hers). On the whole, though, when she was in a position to see it, the teacher responded to the first or most decisively raised hand (Kate, and the boys, obtained most of their speaking turns this way). The teacher was in fact

extraordinarily sensitive to the first hand raised. Presumably she was responding intuitively to this (and no doubt to additional nonverbal cues) as hands were
raised very rapidly and, in analysing the sequence, we had to play the video frame
by frame to determine the order of hand-raising. Although the teacher appeared
quite directive, therefore, this gave the pupils considerable scope: they could ensure
they were selected to speak more often if they were confident enough to raise their
hands first.

As with the 'pendulum' sequence there seemed to be an interaction here between
the behaviour of different participants that guaranteed the boys (on average) more
speaking turns:

First, more confident pupils (who tended more often to be boys) simply raised
their hands first and more decisively, thereby attracting the teacher's attention.

Second, we were able to analyse the teacher's gaze behaviour for the whole of the
'mining' sequence. This analysis showed that, as with the 'pendulum' sequence, the
teacher's gaze was more often directed towards the boys (for 65 per cent of the time
as opposed to 35 per cent of the time towards the girls). This occurred during general exposition as well as during more interactive parts of the sequence. Furthermore,
when the teacher began to formulate a question with her gaze towards the boys she
tended to maintain this gaze direction (unless a girl's hand was raised before a boy's
and attracted her attention). However, on those (fewer) occasions in which the
teacher began a question with her gaze directed towards the girls she tended to
switch towards the boys half-way through the question, or to switch back and
forth between girls and boys. This overall pattern of gaze behaviour may give boys
generally more positive feedback and encourage them to respond to questions when
they came.

Third, all the girls (and not just Kate) did frequently raise their hands during this
sequence. Even Emma, the quietest pupil, often had her hand in the air. As in the
example given above, however, Emma normally raised her hand just after the teacher's
gaze had been directed towards the pupil she intended to select to speak. Such girls'
hand-raising strategies, then, contribute to their relatively poor level of participation
just as much as many boys' strategies enable them to contribute more.

Male Dominance Reconsidered

Many points arising from a consideration of classroom talk, and from the exploratory
analysis of teacher and small-group interaction that I have just described, can illu-
minate some of the issues raised at the beginning of this paper in relation to gender
differences in conversation.

[. . .]

The exploratory study (in common with other studies of classroom talk) raises
problems for the notion of female and male styles, first because differences between
girls and boys are not categorical: boys may take more turns on average, but there are
quiet boys (and more talkative girls). Second, while those who dominate classroom

talk (in this case largely by talking more often) do tend to be boys, different interactional mechanisms are used in each context. In the relatively informal atmosphere of the 'pendulum' discussion, boys chip in much more often than girls. In the 'mining' sequence talk seems to be more overtly under the teacher's control and pupils (of either sex) rarely chip in: boys are selected to talk more often by the teacher, but this seems to be related to their ability to raise their hands more decisively and fractionally earlier than girls. It appears then that certain 'interactional resources' are available that might allow a speaker to have more say in a discussion, but that the resources available differ in different contexts. Rather than there being a particular set of 'controlling tactics', would-be dominant speakers would need to select features as appropriate to a context (taking account of the roles played by participants, the activities in which they are engaged, etc.).

It can be argued that a complete analysis of inequalities in talk would need to take account, not only of a range of linguistic factors, but also of nonverbal components of an interaction. It's worth pointing out here that many studies of talk have relied on audio-recordings and transcripts and so cannot take account of nonverbal features, nor (reliably) of any accompanying activities. Studies of gender and classroom life, or classroom interaction (carried out perhaps more often by sociologists or educationists than by linguists or conversation analysts) have often seen talk as playing a part *along with other factors* in establishing and maintaining inequalities between girls and boys. It might be useful now to have more detailed studies showing the interplay between these different factors. This would mean expanding the metaphorical box of 'interactional resources' to include nonverbal features that interact with talk and may fulfil similar functions. In the 'mining' sequence, for instance, hand-raising strategies were crucial in obtaining (or not obtaining) speaking rights. Gaze was an important interactional mechanism in both sequences (though we were not able to analyse its use by pupils). Other features such as posture and gesture no doubt played their part, though they did not form part of our analysis. Finally, other accompaniments to the talk such as seating arrangements and the positioning and use of equipment may have contributed to the overall achievement of 'male dominance', though more work is needed to see how, on any one occasion, such factors interact with talk. There is, of course, a methodological problem here, in that, while it would seem useful to have a more complete record of what is going on in any sequence of talk, two or three video cameras would be needed even to cope with a small group discussion (let alone a whole class). Any observation may affect what is going on but the introduction of so much hardware would probably be unacceptably intrusive. In our exploratory study we lost some (no doubt) valuable information in the interests of remaining rather less intrusive.

Finally, there are problems with the notion of male 'dominance' itself. The studies of classroom talk that I have discussed suggested that to speak of boys 'dominating' classroom talk, while a useful shorthand, may risk oversimplifying things. It seems more plausible to argue that there is an interaction between the behaviour of all participants: for instance, the greater attention paid by teachers towards boys may encourage boys' fuller participation, which in turn encourages greater attention from the teacher, and so on. It is likely that everyone is an accomplice in the tendency by boys to contribute more to classroom talk – girls too by, arguably, using the resources available in the interaction to contribute less.

The points made above have theoretical implications, and also practical implications for anyone wishing to analyse gender differences in talk. Studies of classroom talk are, however, also important in relation to (educational) policies on gender. For instance, if a whole variety of linguistic and nonlinguistic features can be used to achieve or support 'male dominance', how successful are local solutions (such as changes in teachers' classroom management strategies) likely to be?

Furthermore, if inequalities in talk between girls and boys are regarded as normal by all parties, they are likely to be resistant to change. If girls are encouraged to become more assertive, and to adopt conversational tactics more commonly associated with boys, will such behaviour be tolerated by others or regarded as deviant?

NOTES

This article relies for part of its discussion on an analysis of classroom talk that I carried out with an Open University colleague, David Graddol.

The 'Pendulum' extract comes from data originally collected by Derek Edwards, Neil Mercer and Janet Maybin for their ESRC-funded project 'The Development of Joint Understanding in the Classroom' (ESRC No. C00232236). I am very grateful to Derek, Neil and Janet, and to the East Midlands school where the 'Pendulum' extract was recorded, for allowing access to these data. The 'Mining' extract comes from material collected at Escomb school, County Durham. Again, I am grateful to the staff and pupils for allowing one of their lessons to be video-recorded. (In both cases, I have changed the children's names to protect their identity, and the teachers are not referred to by name.)

1   Questions are marked with a ?. Utterances so marked were assessed by us to be functioning as questions, sometimes because of their syntactic form, but at other times for other reasons; we relied on cues such as intonation, but our interpretation relied on intuition. It is in fact difficult, on any occasion, to itemize the cues that are being attended to and that lead to an utterance being interpreted as a question.

REFERENCES

Byrne, E. M. (1978) *Women and Education*. London: Tavistock Publications.

Clarricoates, K. (1983) 'Classroom interaction', in J. Whyld (ed.) *Sexism in the Secondary Curriculum*. New York: Harper & Row.

Deem, R. (1978) *Women and Schooling*. London: Routledge & Kegan Paul.

Delamont, S. (1980) *Sex Roles and the School*. London: Methuen.

Fishman, P. M. (1978) 'What do couples talk about when they're alone?', in D. Butturff and E. L. Epstein (eds) *Women's Language and Style*. Akron, OH: University of Akron, Department of English.

French, J. and French, P. (1984) 'Gender imbalance in the primary classroom: an interactional account'. *Educational Research*, 26, 2, 127–36.

Marland, M. (1977) *Language Across the Curriculum*. London: Heinemann.

Sadker, M. and Sadker, D. (1985) 'Sexism in the schoolroom of the 80s'. *Psychology Today*, March 1985, 54–7.

Spender, D. (1982) *Invisible Women: The Schooling Scandal*. London: Writers and Readers Publishing Cooperative Society.

Swann, J. and Graddol, D. (1988) 'Gender inequalities in classroom talk'. *English in Education*, 22, 1, 48–65.

Whyte, J. (1986) *Girls into Science and Technology: The Story of a Project*. London: Routledge & Kegan Paul.

14

Participation in Electronic Discourse in a "Feminist" Field

Susan C. Herring, Deborah A. Johnson and Tamra DiBenedetto

Introduction

Studies of gender differences in amount of talk have shown that men consistently talk more than women in public settings. Talk in such settings – which include conferences, seminars, formal and informal meetings, and television discussions – draws attention to the speaker in ways that are potentially status-enhancing (Holmes 1992). Moreover, sheer amount of talk may garner speakers credit they do not deserve, as when subjects in a study conducted by Rieken attributed insightful solutions to those who had talked the most during the discussion, even when the solutions had in fact been proposed by other participants (reported in Wallwork 1978). In short, amount of talk is related to status, power, and influence in the public domain.

In recent decades, a new forum for public discourse has emerged: the Internet. The possibility of communicating via computer networks has led to the formation of multi-participant electronic discussion groups (known variously as lists, conferences or newsgroups, depending on the technology involved), in which individuals scattered in diverse locations around the world can participate in discussions on topics of common interest by sending electronic mail (e-mail) messages to a common site, where they are posted for others to read and respond to. Participation is typically open to all interested parties, and some groups are exceedingly active, generating hundreds of messages per week.

Enthusiasts of the new electronic medium claim that it exercises a democratizing influence on communication. Citing studies conducted in educational settings, Kahn and Brookshire (1991: 245) conclude that individuals communicating via computer "tend to participate more equally in discussions, and discussion is likely to be more democratic in the absence of nonverbal status cues". Users also wax enthusiastic. As one male member of a discussion list recently wrote to another:

> One of the greatest strengths of e-mail is its ability to break down socio-economic, racial, and other traditional barriers to the sharing and production of knowledge. You, for example, have no way of knowing if I am a janitor or a university president or an illegal alien – we can simply communicate on the basis of our ideas, not on any preconceived notions of what should be expected (or not expected) from one another.

The electronic medium is claimed to break down gender barriers as well. Graddol and Swann (1989: 175) observe that "the introduction of [computer conferencing] . . . [leads] to a change in the traditional pattern of contributions from female and male participants". A number of characteristics of the medium mitigate the likelihood of gender asymmetries: sex non-specific electronic return addresses,[1] the absence of physical (including intonational) cues signaling relative dominance or submission, and the fact that interruption and overlap are effectively precluded – a participant may choose to delete messages, but each message selected appears on his or her screen in its entirety, in the order in which it was received.[2]

Despite this optimistic early prognosis, what little research has directly investigated the relationship between gender and participation in electronic discourse calls into question the claim that computers exercise an equalizing effect. In a study of the participation patterns of professional linguists on the Linguist electronic discussion list, Herring (1992) found that female linguists contributed significantly less overall than male linguists – 20% and 80%, respectively. Moreover, when surveyed, both men and women reported feeling put off by the bombastic and adversarial postings of a small minority of male contributors who effectively dominated the discussions. Herring concluded that women refrain from participating on Linguist due in part to their aversion to the adversarial tone of such discussions.

In the present study, we report on an investigation of participation on a smaller list serving an academic field – composition and rhetoric – in which feminism currently enjoys considerable influence.[3] This list, Megabyte University (hereafter MBU), is considered by its members to be especially "friendly" and "supportive" relative to other lists. We hypothesized that in a non-adversarial computer-mediated environment, women would be more likely to participate equally in discussions, as predicted by the claims cited above. However, this hypothesis was not supported: while the overall tone of the list was indeed less adversarial, women still contributed only 30% of the messages as compared to 70% contributed by men. Even more revealing patterns emerge when participation is considered on a day-by-day and topic-by-topic basis. In discussion of a feminist topic, the contributions of women at one point exceeded those of the men for two consecutive days. The subsequent disruptions that took place, including male accusations of being "silenced" in the discussion and threats from several men to unsubscribe from the list, provide support for the view that women and men do not have equal rights to speak in public; by contributing more, even temporarily, and on a feminist (and female-introduced) topic, women in the group violated the unspoken convention that control of public discourse belongs rightfully to men.

The "Men's Literature" Discussion

Our investigation focuses on a particularly lively discussion that took place on MBU between November 7 and December 16, 1991. It began as a request by one of the subscribers for reading suggestions for a university course he planned to offer on "men's literature". The "men's literature" question soon revealed itself to be controversial, with participants becoming polarized along gender lines regarding the legitimacy of offering such a course.[4] Some women feared that the course might be used to perpetrate male hegemony, e.g., by co-opting resources that might otherwise be used for women's literature courses. The men, in turn, argued that women on the list were trying to deny them the right to talk about how gender shapes their identity. In addition to being concerned with gender issues, the "men's literature" discussion contains meta-commentary on gender and "silencing" in the discussion itself.

Participation by Gender

The first and most obvious indication of gender-based inequality comes from the figures for participation in the "men's literature" discussion as a whole. These figures are summarized in table 1.

Table 1 Participation in the "men's literature" discussion

	Female	Male
Number of contributors	18 (30.5%)	41 (69.5%)
Number of contributions	87 (36%)	155 (64%)
Average words per contribution	162	211.5
Total words contributed	14,114 (30%)	32,774 (70%)

As table 1 shows, men contributed significantly more than women to the discussion overall. 69.5% of the participants were men, who in turn were responsible for contributing 70% of the total words and 64% of the total messages.[5] Moreover, the average message length for men was 211.5 words, as compared with 162 words for women. Rather than demonstrating a new, democratic form of discourse, these figures support "the traditional pattern of contributions from male and female participants" alluded to by Graddol and Swann, whereby men dominate (i.e., in face-to-face conversation) by taking longer and more frequent turns.

A rather more complex picture emerges if we consider a day-by-day breakdown of the number of messages contributed by participants of each sex to the "men's literature" discussion, as shown in figure 1.[6]

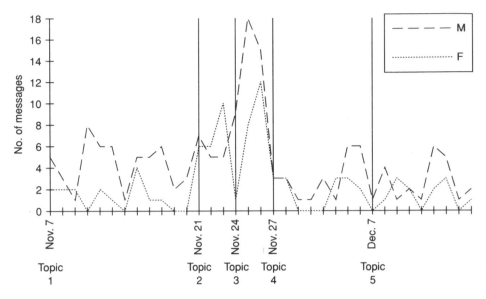

Figure 1   Number of messages by day

Figure 1 shows that males (M) contributed more than females (F) nearly every day on which the discussion took place. However, the number of contributions by both sexes rose dramatically in the period between November 21 and November 27, and during a two-day span (November 22–23), the contributions of women exceeded those of the men. Immediately thereafter, participation in the discussion soared to a peak of intensity (November 24–27), dropping off and stabilizing after Thanksgiving, which was celebrated on November 28 that year.

What accounts for this variability in participation? Explanations begin to suggest themselves when we take into account what MBU-ers were talking about at any given time. The vertical lines in figure 1 indicate transitional points at which new topics of discussion were taken up by the group. Five such topics arose in the course of the discussion as a whole:

> Topic 1:   Men's literature course (M)
> Topic 2:   Silencing of women in the discussion (F)
> Topic 3:   Threats of three members to unsubscribe, and reactions to this (M)
> Topic 4:   Male hegemony in English departments (F)
> Topic 5:   Statistics posted by one of the members (similar to those in table 1) showing male and female participation in the discussion to date (M)

Topics 1, 3, and 5 were introduced by males; Topics 2 and 4 were introduced by females. Participation by gender and topic is shown in figure 2.

As figure 2 shows, men contributed the greatest number of messages on Topics 1 and 3, both introduced by men, and the least on Topic 2, which was introduced by

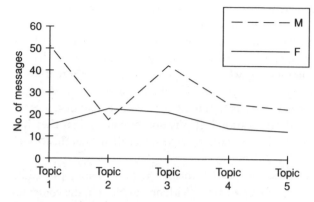

Figure 2 Number of messages by topic

women. Women, on the other hand, contributed the most on Topic 2. Indeed, this is the only period in the discussion when the usual pattern of men posting more messages than women is reversed. We suggest that this reversal – the fact that women were participating more, and on a female-introduced topic – made men uncomfortable to the point of threatening to unsubscribe, and that it was ultimately responsible for male perceptions of having been "silenced" and of women having dominated the discussion.

It might seem strange that when men participated significantly more than women in the five-week discussion overall, two days in which women happened to contribute more would be perceived as a threat. Several factors may have contributed to producing this effect. First, the number of women's contributions took a leap on November 21 relative to what had come before, as can be seen from figure 1. Second, female participants continued to contribute actively the next day and the next, exceeding the contributions of men for two days straight, a situation without precedent in the discussion thus far. Finally, Spender (1979) found that male academics perceive women as dominating in public when they contribute as little as 30% of the talk. What would men then feel if women contributed more than half, as they did in this case?[7] It is likely that from the perspective of the men in the group, the women's increased participation was not only unexpected, it also appeared to be more than it actually was.

In support of this view, note that during Topic 2 men posted no fewer messages in absolute terms than they had previously. Yet on November 23, a male contributor (the one who posted the original request for texts on "men's literature") wrote and, addressing two of the more vocal women in the group by name, complained, "You may not feel very powerful outside this net or this discourse community, but here on the inside you've come very close to shutting all of us men up and down". The perception that men had been shut up (or down) is clearly contradicted by the fact of their participation – this man's message alone is 1098 words, the longest in the entire discussion, and four other lengthy messages were contributed by men on the same day as well – yet it is consistent with Spender's observation that women need not truly dominate in order to be perceived as doing so.

What happened next is also revealing. The evening of November 23, and the morning of November 24, three men (none of whom had participated in the discussion thus far) posted public messages in which they announced their intention to unsubscribe from the list.[8] The reasons given were that the discussion, having begun as a well-intentioned request for help in selecting texts for a course, had degenerated into "insults", "vituperation", and "vilification". It was not, of course, that they had any problem with discussing gender issues; rather, what upset them was the "tone" of the debate.

However, if one examines the messages posted during the immediately preceding days, one finds little evidence of a vituperative tone. With one exception, the contributions of the women appear to be aimed primarily at furthering communication: they raise questions about the interaction at hand (specifically, the lack of male response to female concern about the proposed course), explain their own views, and encourage others to respond in kind.[9] The only message indisputably negative in tone was posted by the man who proposed the men's literature course in the first place. In it, he accuses women on the list of "posting without thinking [their contributions] through carefully first", of leveling "charges" [rather than questions] at the men, and in general, of "bashing", "guilt-tripping", and "bullying" men who didn't toe a strict feminist line. A man who overtly sided with the female participants also comes under attack: he is accused of betraying his brothers out of feminist-induced guilt.

If the only vituperation comes from the man whose cause they allegedly support, why then did the three men threaten to leave the list? The real reason did not escape the notice of participants on MBU at the time: it was a "boy"cott, a "power play" intended to silence those women who persisted in speaking uncomfortable truths about the gender/power dynamics on the list. It is no coincidence that threats of withdrawal occurred on and immediately following a day when the majority of messages were posted by women.

Ironically, however, the boycott had the reverse of its intended effect – it shamed the other men on the list into cooperating, at least temporarily, with the women's attempts to change the topic of discussion to one of feminist concern: the issue of male hegemony within the field of English. The period labelled "Topic 3" in figures 1 and 2 above was thus a turning point in the gender dynamics of the discussion, a turning point, as we demonstrate below, that is reflected on various levels of the discourse.

A Temporary Reversal of Control

Responses

The first evidence of a temporary reversal of influence in the discussion comes from a consideration of how – and how often – participants of each sex were responded to.

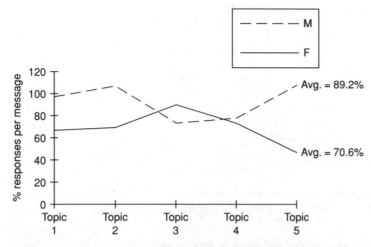

Figure 3 Responses received in relation to messages posted

Male participants received more responses than female participants overall: 89.2% of male postings in the "men's literature" discussion received explicit responses, as compared with only 70.6% of female postings. This disparity led one female participant to observe:

> I am fascinated that my thoughtful . . . response on the "men's lit" thread was met with silence . . . while an anonymous man . . . with a silly little 3-liner gets fascinated and committed responses. . . . When threads initiated by women die from lack of response that's silencing; when women do not respond on threads initiated by men for reasons to do with fear (and the fear may be fear of verbal or other reprisal, ridicule, whatever) . . . – that's silencing.

Lack of response to postings questioning the proposed "men's literature" course prompted another frustrated woman to write, "Are you (in general) listening to what's being communicated?", and a third to conclude a message by "shouting" in capital letters: "IS THERE ANYBODY OUT THERE?"

Figure 3 charts the percentage of response (100% = 1 response per message posted) received by females and males according to topic.[10]

As figure 3 shows, men were responded to more than women at all times during the discussion, except during Topic 3, the period immediately following the threats by several men to leave the list. The reversal of the usual pattern of response during Topic 3 appears to be a reaction to the reversal in participation during Topic 2 (see figure 2 above), and reinforces the notion that amount of talk is power: by contributing more, women earned a higher rate of response to their messages.

Also of interest is the matter of who responds to whom. The most frequent direction of response is men to men (33.4%), followed by women to men (21.3%), men to women (15.8%), and finally women to women (11.2%). (The remaining responses (18.3%) were addressed to the group as a whole.) Both men and women thus

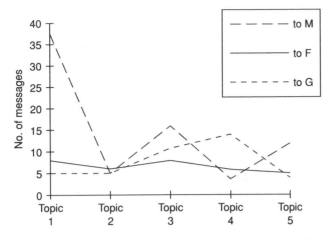

Figure 4   Responses to males, females, and group by topic (men only)

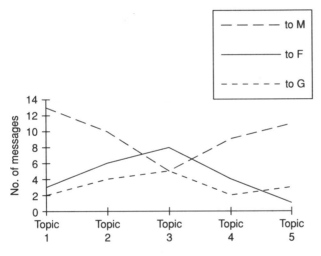

Figure 5   Responses to males, females, and group by topic (women only)

respond more to men, an indication of the more powerful status of men in the group overall. The number of responses directed to participants of each sex is shown for men in figure 4, and for women in figure 5.

Men on MBU are consistent in responding most to men on topics introduced by men, as shown in figure 4. Their rate of response to postings by women is consistently low throughout. Note that in acknowledging the women's topic of hegemony – Topic 4 – men avoided responding directly to women (to do so would be to concede power) by addressing most of their postings to the group (G) as a whole.

Women show a different pattern. As figure 5 indicates, women respond most to men throughout, except during Topic 3, when the pattern of response is temporarily reversed.

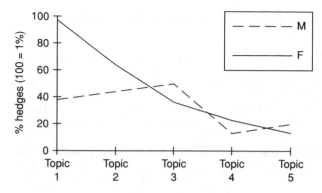

Figure 6   Percentage of words that are hedges

It might appear from figure 5 that women responded most to other women about the threats of men to leave the list (Topic 3). In fact, however, many women at this point are virtually ignoring Topic 3 and pursuing the topic of hegemony (Topic 4) among themselves instead. This is further evidence that the control of the discourse has shifted; the women, after struggling throughout the earlier part of the discussion to make themselves heard, and having succeeded in gaining the floor on the topic of silencing (Topic 2), are finally empowered to talk about what they want, and they do so among themselves. The increases in both women's responses to women during the time period identified as Topic 3, and men's responses to the group during Topic 4, can be seen as reactions to women having gained control of the conversational floor.

Hedges

Yet another revealing piece of evidence comes from the use of hedges. Hedges – qualifiers such as *sort of, a little,* and *somewhat,* the modals *may* and *might,* and expressions such as *perhaps, conceivably,* and *it seems* – have been observed to occur more frequently in the speech of women especially in situations where women are relatively powerless (Lakoff 1975; O'Barr and Atkins 1980, reprinted in this volume, p. 377). In the "men's literature" discussion, women use more hedges than men overall.[11] However, while women's use of hedges *decreases* steadily throughout the discussion, men's use of hedges *increases* as the discussion builds in intensity, dropping off after the worst of the conflict has passed. This is charted in figure 6.

Men hedge most during the period identified as Topic 3, thus exhibiting features of powerless language at a time when women are relatively more empowered in the discourse. This results in another temporary reversal of the overall pattern.

Survey results

Finally, the hypothesis that power relations underwent a reversal in the discussion is supported by the results of a survey we created and disseminated on MBU two

Table 2   Survey results for question (1): Who won the "men's literature" debate?

	Pro	*Con*	*Neither*	*Other*
Female	10.0%	30.0%	*40.0%*	20.0%
Male	11.1%	*50.0%*	33.3%	5.6%
Both	10.7%	42.9%	35.7%	10.7%

months after the "men's literature" discussion had ended. The survey included the following two questions:

(1) In the course of the debate, two basic positions were expressed: a "pro" position, which essentially supported the offering of courses on men's literature, and a "con" position opposed to or concerned by the offering of courses of this type. If you had to choose, which side would you say was ultimately more successful in persuading the group as a whole to its point of view?

(2) How satisfied were you personally with the outcome of the debate?

Twenty-eight people responded to the survey (M = 18; F = 10) either privately or by posting their responses publicly to the list.[12] Their responses to question (1) are summarized in table 2. While the greatest percentage (40%) of women responded that neither side had been more persuasive, the majority of men (50%) indicated that the "con" (i.e., female) position had prevailed. These responses are especially revealing in that the original question could be interpreted as biased towards a "pro" response: the person who suggested the "men's literature" course did, in fact, go on to teach it, and survey respondents were aware of this fact. Why did more men than women say that the "women's side" had won the debate? Clearly, they perceived the women to have been more powerful than the women perceived themselves to have been, or than the external circumstances warranted.

Not coincidentally, male survey respondents also indicated a lower level of satisfaction than females with the outcome of the debate (question 2). On a scale where 2 = very satisfied, 0 = indifferent, and −2 = very dissatisfied, the men's responses averaged −.06 (indifferent to somewhat dissatisfied), while the women's averaged .6 (somewhat satisfied). Additional comments made by survey respondents on the tone of the debate provide further evidence of differing levels of satisfaction. Female respondents tended to comment that they found the discussion 'interesting", "provocative", "gratifying", and "impressive", although several also expressed weariness at having to fight the "same old battles". The comments of the male respondents, in contrast, range from "initially shocked", to a "no-win" discussion, "whining", "yelling and screaming", and (from the man who posted the original "men's literature" request) "a bad-tempered festival of condemnation and defense". Such comments are consistent with Spender's (1980) observation that women who express feminist views, no matter how rationally and calmly, tend to be perceived as hostile and emotional by men.

Ironically, these attitude differences emerge despite the fact that subscribers to MBU – male and female alike – overwhelmingly consider themselves to be feminists. In response to a question on the survey asking: "Do you consider yourself to be a feminist, and if so, how strongly?", 100% of respondents of both sexes indicated that they were either strong feminists or supporters of feminist principles.

Conclusions

We have presented data to show that despite considerable external evidence to the contrary (amount of participation, rate of response, real-world outcome of the debate), men perceived women as having dominated the "men's literature" discussion. This perceptual reversal of dominance can be traced to a two-day period during which women contributed more messages than men. Immediately following this period, men threatened to leave the list, began hedging more, and ultimately abandoned a male-introduced topic to talk about a female-introduced topic instead (although without responding directly to the women involved). Moreover, when surveyed later, men were more inclined to state that the women's side of the argument had "won", and to express dissatisfaction with the discussion overall.

The feminist overtones of the women's contributions, along with the fact that they were critical of a topic introduced and supported by men, no doubt contributed to the discomfort experienced by the men in the group. Yet the implied accusations that the women were "vituperative" and "unreasonable" are not supported by our analysis, nor indeed is such a characterization consistent with the women's supposedly greater rhetorical effectiveness in persuading others to their point of view, as male survey respondents claimed. In fact, we suggest that women on the list were neither vituperative, nor especially persuasive – what won them the floor was their persistence in participating, and male (over)reactions to that persistence.

These findings have implications for participation in electronic discourse more generally. It is significant that after their brief period of more-or-less equal participation, women on MBU retreated back to a lower level of participation, such that their contributions to the discussion overall did not exceed 30%. Moreover, in discussions on MBU in the four months following the "men's literature" discussion, women's contributions averaged slightly less than 20%, even on topics of broad general interest.[13] The 20% figure is also consistent with earlier findings (Herring 1992) for women's participation on the Linguist list. If it is true that women, including successful, well-educated, academic women, are accorded less than equal speaking rights in mixed-sex public discourse on the Internet, then it appears that the amount they are expected to speak, all other factors being equal, is between 20–30%.

The 20–30% figure is supported by evidence from a variety of other public discourse types, both spoken and written. In an academic seminar, Spender (1979) found that 30% was the upper limit before men felt that women were contributing more than their share. In publishing, women writers average only 20% of those published; despite the fact that more women than men buy books, male publishers consider that to publish more women authors would be "risky" (Spender 1989). Finally, in two recent surveys of American television commercials, students in sociolinguistics courses taught by the first author of this article found that although women are frequently depicted, they have significant speaking roles in only 28% of the commercials aired. This last observation is particularly interesting, given the normalized appeal of commercial television: it suggests that society at large recognizes as normal a less than equal amount of talk by women. In a society where such an expectation is conventionalized and even exploited for commercial ends, it is small wonder that the electronic medium does not – cannot – by itself make for equal communication between the sexes.

Nevertheless, increased feminist awareness may help. The fact that MBU women spoke up, persisted in speaking up even when ignored, and appealed successfully to other women in the group for support can be attributed to widespread feminist consciousness within the field of composition/rhetoric. Further, the political reality of feminism in the field constrained the males in the group (according to self-report) to hedge their objections and ultimately to concede the floor – at least temporarily – to the women. Of course, these results did not come about without effort (as one woman later put it, "a small war was necessary on MBU for a bit of consciousness raising"), and female participants' communicative efforts were met with resistance as soon as they appeared to be taking up more than their rightful "share" of the discussion.

Women may never gain the right to equal participation, however, unless we assume that the right is ours already, and act accordingly. Given the growing importance of computer-mediated communication in the current information age, electronic discussion groups might well be a good place to start.

NOTES

This is a slightly revised version of an article by the same title published in 1992 in *Locating Power: Proceedings of the Second Berkeley Women and Language Conference* (Berkeley, CA: Berkeley Women and Language Group). An expanded analysis of male reactions to women's participation in the "men's literature" discussion can be found in Herring, Johnson and DiBenedetto (1995).

1   Gender non-specific return addresses (such as those containing sender's last name only, or a more or less random sequence of letters and numbers) were apparently used in the communication observed by Graddol and Swann, which took place at the Open University in the United Kingdom. In the lists reported on in this paper, however, the sex of participants is generally known, either because their first name is part of their return address, or because they sign their messages, or because their address is otherwise known within the community.

2   Messages on lists and computer conferences are typically posted to an intermediary machine, or listserver, before being distributed to subscribers. Some lists have a moderator who exercises a degree of editorial control over the content (and less commonly, the order) of messages; generally, however, messages are distributed on a strict "first come, first served" basis.

3 For example, at the 1992 College Composition and Communication Conference (CCCC) in Cincinnati, the number of sessions on "gender and feminist theory" ranked third out of 27 topics. The only two topics that had more sessions were devoted to practical teaching issues.

4 One man supported the feminist position throughout, and several others supported parts of it during the later portions of the discussion; overall, however, most men favored the idea of a men's literature course, and all participating women expressed concerns about such a course.

5 The subscription figures for MBU are 42% female and 58% male (out of a total of 178 subscribers), based on a count of names from which gender can reliably be determined. The majority of subscribers are teachers and graduate students in English departments at United States universities.

6 The intervals between dates in Topics 1, 4, and 5 are fewer than the number of calendar days, as we have included in figure 1 only those days on which messages related to "men's literature" were contributed.

7 At the height of the "reversal", on November 23, women contributed 66.6% of the day's messages. However, since the women's messages were shorter, men still contributed more words on that day.

8 One man did in fact unsubscribe; the other two were persuaded to remain on the list.

9 The one exception is a contribution in which the writer presents her feminist views dogmatically, rather than cooperatively; this message accuses one of the male participants of "intellectualizing".

10 *Responses* were counted as only those messages which explicitly acknowledge an earlier posting. Excluded were messages pertaining to the topic under discussion but addressed to the group as a whole, as well as first postings on a new topic.

11 Hedges constitute .48% of the words contributed by women, and .36% of the words contributed by men.

12 Of these, 18 ($M = 13$; $F = 5$) had participated in the original discussion.

13 For example, in a discussion of the usefulness of composition theory in teaching writing, contributions by women accounted for only 16.9% of the 142 message total.

References

Graddol, David & Joan Swann (1989) *Gender Voices*. Oxford: Basil Blackwell.

Herring, Susan (1992) Gender and participation in computer-mediated linguistic discourse. Washington, D.C.: ERIC Clearinghouse on Languages and Linguistics. Document no. ED345552.

Herring, Susan, Deborah Johnson, & Tamra DiBenedetto (1995) 'This discussion is going too far!' Male resistance to female participation on the Internet. In K. Hall & M. Bucholtz (eds.), *Gender Articulated: Language and the Socially Constructed Self*. New York: Routledge, 67–96.

Holmes, Janet (1992) Women's talk in public contexts. *Discourse and Society* 3.2; 131–50.

Kahn, Arnold & Robert Brookshire (1991) Using a computer bulletin board in a social psychology course. *Teaching of Psychology* 18.4; 245–9.

Lakoff, Robin (1975) *Language and Woman's Place*. New York: Harper & Row.

O'Barr, William & Bowman K. Atkins (1980) 'Women's language' or 'powerless language'? In Sally McConnell-Ginet, Ruth Borker & Nelly Furman (eds.), *Women and Language in Literature and Society*. New York: Praeger, 93–110.

Spender, Dale (1979) Language and sex differences. In *Osnabrücker Beiträge zur Sprach-theorie: Sprache und Geschlect II*; 38–59.

——(1980) *Man Made Language*. London: Pandora Press.

——(1989) *The Writing or the Sex (or why you don't have to read women's writing to know it's no good)*. The Athene Series. New York: Pergamon.

Wallwork, Jean (1978) *Language and People*. London: Heinemann Educational Books.

Part IV
Same-Sex Talk

By contrast with the previous section, which focused on interaction involving both women and men, this section deals with women's and men's talk in same-sex groups. This is an important and still developing area of language and gender research: it allows researchers to look at women's and men's linguistic usage outside a dominance framework. In other words, it allows women's talk to be examined outside a framework of oppression or powerlessness, and it allows men's conversational strategies to be assessed in terms other than dominance. (These issues will be discussed again in Part VII, 'Theoretical Debates: Difference or Dominance?')

It was the publication of Robin Lakoff's classic paper 'Language and Woman's Place' in 1974 that marked the beginning of a new, less androcentric, phase in sociolinguistic research. The topic of all-female talk, however, was not explicitly addressed until Deborah Jones's paper 'Gossip: Notes on Women's Oral Culture' was published in 1980. Since then, a great deal of research has been carried out on same-sex talk, though nearly all of it has had a comparative focus. For example, Deborah Tannen (1990) compared the talk of same-sex pairs of friends at different ages; Jenny Cheshire (see paper in Part I) compared the language used by adolescent single-sex groups in adventure playgrounds in Reading, England; and Marjorie Goodwin (see paper in Part II) compared the language used by pre-adolescent single-sex peer groups in a Philadelphia street. All these papers focus on children or adolescents, and all investigate both female and male speakers. It is still rare to find research being carried out which has as its aim the description of women's conversational practices for their own sake.

The first paper in this section, 'The Talk of Women Friends', by Fern Johnson and Elizabeth Aries, is written from an ethnographic rather than a linguistic perspective. I've included it because of the light it sheds on women's cultural practices, on the way talk functions for women who are friends. The authors carried out a series of research projects on talk and friendship using a range of methodologies. They got large numbers of young men and women to fill in questionnaires about their friendships, including details such as what they did with friends and what they talked about (see Johnson and Aries 1983; Aries and Johnson 1983). They also interviewed individual women about their friendships, and the results were written up in the paper included here. This paper makes the point very strongly that, for women, talk has a key role in friendship. While this is only one study, carried out in the early 1980s in one particular locality in the USA, more recent research suggests that these results are widely generalizable, as is the contrast that Johnson and Aries point up between male and female friendship patterns.

The second paper in this section, 'Gossip Revisited: Language in All-Female Groups', was written in response to Jones's innovative piece on all-female talk, with the aim of moving the debate on. I wanted to provide detailed linguistic evidence in support of her claims about women's oral culture. The paper presents a qualitative analysis of a 45-minute conversation between five women friends. I argue that women's friendly talk has as its chief goal the establishment and maintenance of good social relations. This has consequences for the way talk is structured: friendly talk, or talk-as-play, is very different from talk-as-serious-business. In the paper, the following features of all-female talk are selected for analysis: topic development; minimal responses; simultaneous speech; epistemic modality (or hedging); and tag questions. The paper ends with the claim that women's friendly talk is cooperative in the strong sense that speakers collaborate in the construction of talk, and that the voice of the group has priority over the voice of the individual.

This paper was originally published in 1989, but subsequent research (especially Coates 1996) has confirmed that the features analysed here are typical of all-female talk in informal contexts. Jane Pilkington's paper, ' "Don't try and make out that I'm nice!" The Different Strategies Women and Men Use when Gossiping', is a good example. Pilkington examines the talk of four groups of speakers, two all-female and two all-male, in Wellington, New Zealand. She shows how important overlapping turns, co-constructed talk and positive feedback are in women's friendly talk. By contrast, the all-male talk she recorded is characterized by silences, lack of verbal feedback, monologues, and the direct expression of disagreement, something women seem to avoid in talk. She concludes that the goal of friendly talk for both women and men is solidarity, but that women and men adopt very different strategies to achieve this.

The section finishes with two papers focusing exclusively on male speakers. The best-known example of sociolinguistic research into all-male talk is probably Labov's (1972) study of the language of black adolescent peer groups in Harlem, but the unmarked character of maleness is demonstrated by the title of Labov's book: *Language in the Inner City*. Presumably because of the semantic conflation of being-a-male and being-a-human-being, research focusing specifically on male speakers *qua* male speakers – particularly in informal settings – is still relatively rare. This is beginning to change, however, with the growth of Men's Studies, and with a general sense that current forms of masculinity are in crisis (see, for example, the 1996 BBC television series, *Trouble with Men*). The first collection of papers focusing on language and masculinity was published in 1997 (Johnson and Meinhof 1997).

The men whose talk is investigated in the two papers included here are friends in that they have chosen to spend leisure time together. In this sense they are comparable to the women friends investigated by Aries and Johnson, and by Coates. Deborah Cameron, in her paper 'Performing Gender Identity', analyses the conversation of a group of male students to show how gender is performed through talk, drawing on Butler's (1990) notion of performativity. The group was recorded while they watched sport on television (one of their commonest shared activities). One of the ways that these men perform gender in their talk is through their comments on the basketball game they are watching. Cameron suggests that 'sports talk' is a typically masculine conversational genre (see Johnson and Finlay 1997 for discussion of the way adult males use sportstalk as a form of gossip). Besides sport, these friends talk about women and about alcohol, topics stereotypically associated with all-male conversation. But they also gossip about non-present others: they discuss in great detail certain males of their acquaintance, accusing them of being gay. Overall, the talk is solidary: the five friends are bonded by their shared denigration of the supposedly gay outsiders. Cameron argues that for men in a context such as this, demonstrating that they are not gay is as important as demonstrating that they are not women. In other words, they perform not just masculinity, but heterosexual masculinity. Interestingly, Cameron shows how the talk of these men involves several features normally associated with 'cooperative' women's talk – hedges, overlapping speech, latching. But it also displays more competitive features – two speakers dominate the talk, and speakers vie for the floor. She argues that cooperation and competition as styles of talking cannot be simplistically attributed to one gender or the other. In fact, one of her aims in this paper is to deconstruct the opposition cooperative/competitive.

The final paper in this section – Koenraad Kuiper's 'Sporting Formulae in New Zealand English: Two Models of Male Solidarity' – demonstrates very clearly that men cooperate closely in certain interaction rituals, even though some of these rituals are highly competitive. Kuiper looks at men interacting in the public sphere, doing sport together. As many researchers have pointed out, shared activities are central to male friendship but not to female friendship. Kuiper examines the linguistic strategies used by two different groups of men to create solidarity. The first group met twice a week to play volley-ball; the second group were members of a rugby team. Kuiper demonstrates that, while the first group have evolved a set of linguistic routines to save face, the second, like Pilkington's male groups, draw on a strategy of explicit sexual humiliation, and thus of loss of face. Kuiper names this face-threatening tactic 'the dark side' of politeness phenomena, and asks whether dark-side strategies are solely the preserve of male speakers.

The face-threatening strategies described by Kuiper for New Zealand males have been found in a range of societies in the talk of male speakers, for example among black adolescents in New York (Labov 1972), boys in south London (Hewitt 1997), adult males in Barcelona (Pujolar 1997). In so far as such strategies are designed to create solidarity, they fit well with Wolfson's (1988) 'bulge' model, which predicts that speakers will be more polite to acquaintances and casual friends than to people at the two extremes of a social distance continuum: strangers (people we don't know at all) and intimates (people we know very well indeed). Yet we still have to explain why such strategies are associated with male and not with female speakers. Cameron's paper is a useful reminder that all-male gatherings are problematic for men, who need constantly to perform being not-gay as well as being not-a-woman. For many men, then, connection with others is accomplished in part through ludic antagonisms, in contrast to the mirroring self-disclosure more typical of women friends.

REFERENCES

Aries, Elizabeth and Johnson, Fern (1983) 'Close friendship in adulthood: conversational conduct between same-sex friends'. *Sex Roles*, 9, 12, 183–96.
Butler, Judith (1990) *Gender Trouble: Feminism and the Subversion of Identity*. London: Routledge.
Coates, Jennifer (1996) *Women Talk: Conversation Between Women Friends*. Oxford: Blackwell.
Hewitt, Roger (1997) ' "Box-out" and "taxing" ', pp. 27–46 in Sally Johnson and Ulrike Hanna Meinhof (eds) *Language and Masculinity*. Oxford: Blackwell.
Johnson, Fern and Aries, Elizabeth (1983) 'Conversational patterns among same-sex pairs of late-adolescent close friends'. *Journal of Genetic Psychology*, 142, 225–38.
Johnson, Sally and Finlay, Frank (1997) 'Do men gossip? An analysis of football talk on television', pp. 130–43 in Sally Johnson and Ulrike Hanna Meinhof (eds) *Language and Masculinity*. Oxford: Blackwell.
Johnson, Sally and Meinhof, Ulrike Hanna (eds) (1997) *Language and Masculinity*. Oxford: Blackwell.
Jones, Deborah (1980) 'Gossip: notes on women's oral culture', pp. 193–8 in Cheris Kramarae (ed.) *The Voices and Words of Women and Men*. Oxford: Pergamon Press (reprinted in Deborah Cameron (ed.) *The Feminist Critique of Language* (1992), London: Routledge).
Labov, William (1972) *Language in the Inner City*. Oxford: Blackwell.
Lakoff, Robin (1975) *Language and Woman's Place*. New York: Harper & Row.
Pujolar i Cos, Joan (1997) 'Masculinities in a multilingual setting', pp. 80–106 in Sally Johnson and Ulrike Hanna Meinhof (eds) *Language and Masculinity*. Oxford: Blackwell.
Tannen, Deborah (1990) 'Gender differences in topical coherence: creating involvement in best friends' talk'. *Discourse Processes*, 13, 1, 73–90.
Wolfson, Nessa (1988) 'The bulge: a theory of speech behaviour and social distance', pp. 21–38 in J. Fine (ed.) *Second Language Discourse: A Textbook of Current Research*. Norwood, NJ: Ablex.

RECOMMENDED FURTHER READING

Coates, Jennifer (1996) *Women Talk: Conversation Between Women Friends*. Oxford: Blackwell.
Goodwin, Marjorie (1990) *He-Said-She-Said: Talk as Social Organisation Among Black Children*. Bloomington, IN: Indiana University Press.
Johnson, Sally and Meinhof, Ulrike Hanna (eds) (1997) *Language and Masculinity*. Oxford: Blackwell.
Seidler, Victor (1989) *Rediscovering Masculinity: Reason, Language and Sexuality*. London: Routledge.

15

The Talk of Women Friends

Fern L. Johnson and Elizabeth J. Aries

Writing about the talk of women friends is an act infused with contemporary import. From at least three vantage points, the topic emerges from an historical context of both inattention and selected attention.

First, there is the issue of friendship itself. Friendship is certainly not a contemporary invention, yet friendship as a significant and important part of the continuing fabric of personal existence has received nowhere near the attention given to other relationships, notably kinship, marriage, work and neighbourhood relationships. [. . .]

Second, there is the issue of *female* friendship. Just as friendship has taken a back seat to other relationships, female friendship has historically taken a back seat to male friendship. Looking back on the literature, Bell (1981) finds that history records the great friendships of men. This is no surprise since men are valued above women in most societies and since men have done most of the historiography. It is also the case that males in most societies enjoy greater mobility and social contact outside of the kinship system, and therefore have greater opportunities for forming friendships independent of kinship ties (DuBois 1974). Seiden and Bart (1975) aptly describe the attention paid to female friendship as follows: 'Significant female friendships are either not portrayed at all, are interpreted as lesbian, or considerably depreciated in importance' (p. 194). The slighting of female friendship is part, then, of the more general slighting and devaluation of those activities of women that go beyond their traditional connections to men and family.

Much of what we are about when we address any issue pertaining to female friendship is rectifying the pervasive stereotypes and preconceptions about the differential capabilities of men and women for friendships. [. . .]

Treating female friendships seriously and treating them as they exist, rather than as they are presumed to exist, is an important part of the contemporary movement to reclaim and recount women's lives. The friendships that women have with one another serve important functions for their participants, and the value of these relationships deserves careful attention.

Finally, the issue of studying the *talk* of female friends shapes the focus of this paper and defines what we believe may be the most significant component of female friendship. Featuring talk takes on importance both within the context of studying friendship and within the context of studying women. [. . .]

We believe that talk has been neglected in the research literature because it is viewed as mundane, is difficult to study, and is not the basis of friendships among men. Within the context of studying women's friendships, talk may also have been neglected because of the more general devaluation of *women's talk*. Certainly scholars of both speech communication and sociolinguistics take talk (or speech) as central to their studies, but the substance of women's talk rarely, until recently, appears as a legitimate focus for investigation, e.g. Kramarae (1981); Lakoff (1975); Spender (1980). Folk wisdom has long denigrated women's talk as 'idle chatter,' 'yackedy yack,' 'hen cackling,' 'gabbing,' and 'gossip.' Such folk wisdom pejoratively places women in the position of having nothing better to do with their time than talk and of having nothing important to talk about. Kramer's (1977) study of perceptions of male and female speech among high school and college students confirmed this folk wisdom: her respondents thought that 'gossip,' 'talk a lot,' 'talk about trivial topics,' and 'gibberish' were much more characteristic of female than male speakers.

We are focusing on the talk of women friends not simply because talk is a variable that has received little attention but because our research demonstrates that talk is the substance of women's friendship. By highlighting and featuring talk as the *central feature* of women's friendship, we are attempting to contribute to the more general trend of feminist scholars to reconceptualize women's experience in terms that grow from and validly capture their experience. A large part of this task requires exposing the double standard that operates to defame an activity when performed by women while inflating a similar activity when performed by men. In her discussion of woman talk, Spender (1980) views the double standard as serving patriarchal order: '*No matter what women may say* it fosters the conviction that you cannot trust the words of a woman and that it is permissible to *dismiss* anything she might say' (p. 107, first emphasis added).

The focus of this paper is on providing a clearer understanding of the nature of female friendship and, in particular, the function of talk in this relationship. We will begin by looking at the differences in friendship patterns that are attributable to sex and gender roles. We will then take a closer look at female friendship through qualitative interview data that we have collected. [. . .]

Sex Differences in Friendship Patterns

Female friendships are frequently described in contrast to male friendships. 'There is no social factor,' writes Bell (1981), 'more important than that of sex in leading to friendship variations' (p. 55). Females engage in more intimate, one-to-one relationships involving mutual exploration, understanding and security, while males form friendships in groups, showing less concern for the relational aspects of friendship and putting more stress on activities (Douvan and Adelson 1966; Lowenthal *et al.* 1976; Wright and Crawford 1971).

One of the most salient dimensions of this difference is what men and women talk about, with their same-sex friends. Females are more self-disclosing to same-sex friends (Jourard 1971; Mulcahy 1973), and in particular about intimate topics (Morgan 1976). In adulthood, close female friends converse more frequently than close male friends about personal and family problems, intimate relationships, doubts and fears, daily activities, and hobbies and shared activities; male friends, on the other hand, discuss sports more frequently than female friends (Aries and Johnson 1983). Adult women also report greater depth of discussion with their female friends about personal problems, family activities, and reminiscences about the past; men report greater depth in conversations with same-sex close friends about the topics of work and sports (Aries and Johnson 1983).

The major contrast, then, between male friendships and female friendships appears to grow from different orientations toward close relationships. Male friendships involve more communication about matters peripheral to the self; they engage more in sociability than in intimacy (Pleck 1975). Female friendships encompass personal identities, intimacy, and the immediacy of daily life.

The Interview Study

As part of a larger research program on same-sex close friendships (Aries and Johnson 1983; Johnson and Aries 1983), we conducted a depth interview study with a small sample of men and women from a New England city. This was an exploratory study employing the richness of idiographic response to provide a general description of the close friendship relationship. We report here on the interviews with women.

Procedures and sample

We arrived at a sample of 20 adult females through a procedure that would ensure socio-economic heterogeneity among participants. We began by randomly selecting 40 female names from the street list of the city we had targeted, stratifying the sample by areas within the city. Each woman in the sample was sent a letter describing the study and was phoned several days later to determine her willingness to participate. Half accepted our invitation, and half declined. While the sample is not random, it is representative of a diverse group of women.

The final sample of 20 included white women only. They ranged in age from 27 to 58 years, with a mean age of 39 years. All but one completed high school; five had finished college; and three had done graduate work. Seventy-five per cent of the women had engaged at some time in full- or part-time work outside the home as nurses, teachers, secretaries, dressmakers, home economists, telephone operators, etc. In terms of marital status, fifteen were currently married, two were widowed, one was divorced, and two were single. All but three had children. For those who were or had been married, the husband's occupational category ranged from blue-collar to professional, e.g. factory worker, firefighter, lawyer. Because the sample was small, it was not possible to examine the effects of demographic variables on the nature of close friendship relationships.

We interviewed all participants in their homes at their convenience. The interviews were audio recorded and ranged in length from 45 to 90 minutes. During the interview, each woman first was asked some general questions about the role of friendship in her life, and then was asked a number of questions about one relationship with a woman she defined as a close friend. Questions covered the history of the friendship, types of interaction between the two friends, functions of the friendship, and feelings about the friendship.

Qualitative analysis of the interviews

We found considerable diversity in the nature of the close friendships that the women described. For some women, the close friend was a person known for only a year or two; for others, the relationship had been ongoing for 20 to 30 years. Half reported that their closest friend had always lived nearby, but four reported their closest friend to be a person currently living hundreds or thousands of miles away. Seventy-five per cent said they carried out their relationships through daily or weekly visits and phone conversations, while a few, e.g. a 41-year-old teacher and mother of five, said that phone calls were very frequent, with visits occurring only monthly or less often. For those friends living far apart, lengthy letters and/or phone conversations provided the connection.

We also found some common characteristics to the friendships. First, all but one of the women reported substantial dyadic contact with the close friend, although six women said that they also spent time with their friends in a group setting. Second, when asked 'Where do you usually see each other?' the women over and over gave the same answer: at each other's homes. Even those women whose best friend was a co-worker spent time together with her outside of work in each other's homes. Here they often enjoyed a cup of coffee or tea and some conversation: viz. 'We never did anything together. We just sat around and talked. We sit and eat and talk and drink tea.' Third, half engaged in activities together such as sewing, knitting, baking, canning, crafts, and in one case, research. When the friends saw each other outside of their homes, they shopped, went out to eat or have a drink, and sometimes took their children to a park or for a walk. Finally, we found that for more than half of the women, there was an ongoing exchange of favours and services between friends. A few women depended upon their friends for transportation, for weekly trips to the grocery store, or simply for time away from home. Others exchanged household items, cooking utensils, dishes, tools, recipes, sewing patterns, and clothes. Friends were there for each other to help out with babysitting and household chores, especially in times of sickness or trouble.

What emerges from these reports is the centrality of talk in all their contacts. Situations in which women meet are occasions for conversation:

'It doesn't matter if the kids are running through the house or the phone is ringing. We sit down and pick up with our conversation.'

The women we interviewed isolate talk as the most important aspect of the relationship. When asked 'What is the most important thing you feel you get out of the relationship?' almost identical words were spoken:

'Someone to talk to.'
'Just knowing I've got somebody I can talk to about anything.'
'Just the fact that we can talk.'
'You need somebody you can talk to.'

When one woman described her visits to her closest friend who had moved away, she reported:

'We would get up in the morning and talk for several hours. Then P. would go off. We'd stay up half of the night talking more.'

Women also gave the same answers again and again to the question 'What do you talk about?'

'We talk about anything and everything.'
'We talk about everything from A to Z. We talk about the kids a lot, cooking, furniture, or if she has a problem or I have a problem.'
'We talk about a lot of personal things that you wouldn't discuss with just anybody.'

Women talk about the significant relationships in their lives: their children, their husbands, their families of origin, and their inlaws. They talk of their relationships with co-workers, with other friends, and with each other. They discuss their work and daily lives and activities. They engage in 'very personal talk', sharing their deepest feelings, problems, concerns, things they often can discuss with no one else. While some women report that they discuss politics, civic affairs, religion, or books and articles they've been reading, these topics are discussed with less frequency and are usually spoken of as less important to the fabric of the friendship.

Several themes emerge from these descriptions of talk between female friends. First, friends listen to one another and do so in a noncritical fashion:

'If I had a problem or I was upset, she would listen to me and talk and not try to tell me, "Well, you should ought to do this, or you should ought to do that". She's willing to accept me the way I am . . . She's willing to listen when I need someone to listen. Day or night, it doesn't make any difference.'
'We don't cut each other down. We just accept what's going on, and I feel this is different from relatives who always want you to be a certain way.'

The willingness of a close friend to listen noncritically appears to be the key to a second theme in the descriptions of talk. Almost all of the women spoke of the support they got from their close friends:

'There have been some family problems, and I've needed a lot of encouragement, and she gives me that encouragement. She makes me feel really good about being myself.'
'I've gone through a time in the past few years when I've found that I needed a lot of support that I haven't gotten from the marriage situation, and my friends have been able to provide the support that I needed as a person.'
'She's somebody you can depend on, someone you can turn to when you need any help at all in any way.'
'I just always know that she's there.'
'If I've got a problem and I want someone to talk to, I'd go to her . . . If I've got any problems, she's going to feel sorry for me or make me feel better.'

As a result of the kind of talk these women report, the close friends enhance each other's feelings of self-worth. Although expressed in many different ways, this theme characterized almost every interview. These comments are typical:

'If I had to capture the friendship overall, she makes me feel good about myself. I mean, she's the kind of person who I think values friendship and does lots of little things to tell you that. Whenever she knows that I'm not feeling well, she calls. She calls if something important is going on in my life, you know, she wants to wish me well or check up on me, so that she's very careful about those kinds of things.'
'I get a sense of self-worth because there's somebody out there who I like and who feels the same way about me.'
'She lets me like myself. She lets me value myself.'

As one woman put it, a close friend 'makes you feel like a worthwhile human being – that you are capable of loving and sharing'.

These conversations give life and validity to aspects of the self that cannot be shared with other people. In this way, the conversations between close friends establish what we see as a theme of exclusiveness:

'I can discuss things with her – whatever – that I don't with other people . . . things that involve something personal.'
'She makes me get in touch with myself again.'
'You can't survive without friends. Everything is inside, so you have to let it out. If S. weren't there, I'd be lost.'
'I feel when I'm with her, I'm totally honest. I can say whatever I want to. Sometimes I feel there are very few times in my life when I really can do that.'

As a particular part of this theme of exclusiveness, half of the married women noted that the type of communication they engage in with their close friend is not something they can experience with their husbands. Husbands have a difficult time listening to or understanding what is being said, or responding appropriately. As one woman put it:

'You can't talk to your husband. My husband keeps things inside. He doesn't tell me what's on his mind or what bothers him. You have to really get after him. When I get close to someone, I'm there body, soul, and mind, all the way, and him . . . he

isn't like this. You can't talk to your husband the way you can to your best girlfriend.
I wish I could.'

Husbands, too, often make it difficult for women friends to talk with one another.
One woman commented that husbands are 'always telling you to stop gossiping'.
This simply provides further confirmation that what appears senseless or mindless
to men is of considerable importance to women. Chesler (1972) writes that female dialogue 'on its most ordinary level . . . affords women a measure of emotional reality
and a kind of comfort that they cannot find with men' (p. 268).

A final theme (and one that certainly grows from the others) captures the importance of the close friend in the process of self-discovery and personal growth. The
specifics are far-ranging, but the theme was uniform:

> 'She's made me realize that if I had to be independent, I could hack it. She's told me
> that and made me really aware of what I am . . . E. really taught me a lot – to really
> have more self-confidence.'
> 'My relationship with P. has helped me get over being overly sensitive and to develop
> my own sense of humour about myself.'
> 'B. helped bring me out of my shell to a certain degree. She gave me much more
> confidence in myself than I had ever had before she and I met.'
> 'She encouraged me to go and study and do what you want to do. You've got to better
> yourself.'

Another woman whose friend had recently moved to another part of the country
discussed her letter writing in these terms:

> 'Right now I'm involved in school business, and, you see, I went through a whole thing
> and decided I really do have more potential in my life than to be just a secretary, so I'm
> trying to find some direction, where I'm going. She really helps me with that, so I write
> a lot about what I'm thinking and how things are going.'

In sum, we find consistent evidence in our interview data that talk – either as the
raison d'être for being together or as an outcome of other activities – creates for
female friends an elaborate and on-going mosaic of noncritical listening, mutual support, enhancement of self-worth, relationship exclusiveness, and personal growth and
self-discovery. Through extensive talk about the most routine of daily activities to
the most private of personal problems and crises, women friends establish connections with one another that function significantly in their lives.

Our description of women's close friendships is, of course, a portrayal of what is
typical. Not everyone follows the pattern: one of our interviewees who expressed
affection for her close friend also admitted that she did not care to share intimacies
with anyone but her husband; another woman was sceptical of the likelihood that she
and her friend would remain close because they shared little of what was important in
their lives. The first case probably shows an individual departure from what is typical,
while the second case may be more related to the constraints of a specific situation
or time of life.

Conclusions

We see the continued study of all aspects of women's friendships as important to building a conscious awareness for women about women's experiences. Close friendships among women persist despite their social diminution. Women's talk, which cements friendships, also persists despite its social diminution. This persistence certainly tells us something about the value that women derive from the closeness they build with other women. We are reminded here of Jones's (1980) serious treatment of 'gossip' as an important component of the oral culture of women. She turns the tables on the social construal of gossip as mere trifling, idle, and groundless rumour by viewing it as well structured, highly functional, and an important vehicle for transmitting female values and concerns. The same turning of the tables is now well under way regarding women's friendship. Rather than viewing these relationships as vacuous fillers of time that are rife with idle chatter, we are now redefining this closeness as a primary social relationship holding unique values for women that are elsewhere unattainable.

Like any research, ours raises more issues than it settles. We mention some of the major ones here.

First, there are limitations to the conclusions that can be drawn from an interview study with a small sample of women. Self-selection may have played a part in the sample characteristics such that those women most predisposed to the importance of female friendship agreed to participate. In addition, the study relies on accounts by women about the centrality of talk in their friendships rather than on direct behavioral observation. Ideally, the character of women's friendships is best captured through a variety of research approaches. Expanding the interview format used in the present research to include both members of the friendship pair would provide insights about both co-perceptions and relationship types. Field studies too would be helpful in providing valid data about female friendships, but it is unlikely that field studies could penetrate the intimate, dyadic quality of interaction shared between friends. The point, simply, is that any method imposes constraints on the type of data gathered. Diverse methods will ultimately enrich our understanding of the properties of female friendship.

Second, there is the issue of cross-cultural comparisons. To what extent do the women we interviewed and the women studied by other researchers speak to the experience of female friends in other cultures? Obviously we have no adequate answer. There is, however, one important structural dimension to suggest at least some cross-cultural similarity. Since most societies substantially differentiate male and female roles, subordinating the latter to the former, women across a broad range of societies may bond together for similar functional reasons. As so cogently stated by Bernikow (1980):

> Women friends help each other to remain perpendicular in the face of cultures that attempt to knock them over with the hurricane forces of ideology about what a woman should be or pull the ground out from under them by denying the validity of their

experience, denigrating their frame of reference, reinforcing female masochism, self-doubt, passivity, and suicide. (p. 144)

So although the specific ways in which women friends in different cultures interact will probably vary depending on world view and values, e.g. differences in the value of talk, we suspect that there may be a strong resemblance in the functions and outcomes of close female bonds from culture to culture. We hope that future anthropological work will address this issue and that friendship will receive attention even in societies where it is largely embedded in kinship.

The related issue of sub-cultural comparison also needs further study. With the exception of social class, the empirical research on women's friendship bypasses systematic investigations of sub-cultural patterns. Race, affectional preference, and ethnicity, for example, may shape female relationships in important ways, and we need to pay much closer attention to these factors.

Finally, there are political issues and questions that arise about the bonds established among women through friendship. On one level, the themes we found in our respondents' descriptions of their talk with female friends (noncritical listening, supportiveness, enhancement of self-worth, exclusiveness, and self-discovery and growth) reflect a humaneness that is admirable. But on another level, these themes reveal a response against global deficiencies in the larger social world that women confront on a daily basis. Women accomplish in the privacy of friendship what is publicly denied to them. Their friendships may well provide a strength-giving buffer between themselves and the persistent social denial of female integrity. If female friendship functions this way, whether consciously or unconsciously, it has tremendous subversive value; it subverts the devaluation of women by allowing them to develop a self-defined identity. Gerda Lerner (1979), for example, has asserted that women's close and essential ties have historically been to men rather than women, making women collaborators in their own subordination. Female ties are a powerful force in opposition to this pattern. We suspect that many men may understand this – at least on some level – and that this understanding accounts in part for male attempts to trivialize women's friendships and to trivialize or scorn the female proclivity for talk with other females. The threat that female friendship poses for men is the possibility that it can disrupt the asymmetry between male and female and ultimately lead females to reject male–female pairing as the pinnacle of human relationships.

These speculations lead logically to questions about the impact of female liberation on female friendship. The character of close female friendship obviously owes much to women's historic social position. The quintessence of these friendships is deeply rooted in sex-segregation and its division of male and female spheres. Where sex-segregation occurs, women come together as friends quite naturally. Women who devote most of their time to family nurturance and homemaking usually find it both convenient and desirable to seek relationships with women in similar positions; they find in these relationships many bases for sharing and many opportunities for mutual support and comfort. Similarly, women in the work force who hold positions that are sex-typical will find their most natural alliances with women in like positions – secretaries with secretaries, nurses with nurses, etc.

As women move out of sex-typical roles, particularly in the work place, there are several potential obstacles to their relationships with other women. Some women find themselves almost exclusively in the company of men; their jobs afford few opportunities to meet and form friendships with women, and in some cases may set them against women either by forcing them to compete with one another or by structurally placing them in superior–subordinate relationships. Professional women, especially those with families, often find themselves consumed by the overwhelming demands of both work and domestic life; they have little time left over for either keeping up with old friends or developing new ones.

Do these obstacles militate against the bonds of female friendship? Or do women continue despite these obstacles to establish close bonds with other women? Answers to these questions depend in large part on whether women continue to embrace female values or whether they abandon them. Our informal evidence (and we hope that it is not idiosyncratic) suggests that even in situations where women have little time and opportunity for friendship with other women, they still place high priority on these relationships. For married women, the contacts may occur in the couples context – much like the pattern observed by Babchuck (1965). Or they might grow quite independently through other relationship networks. For single women and for women who are single parents, the contacts can be diverse, ranging from strong similarity of position to great difference in personal situation. For lesbian women, the search is for others with whom to build a community that fosters the values they cherish.

Whatever the pattern, there are many women who are struggling to maintain and to build new ties with women friends. That struggle often entails transcending the pressures of the work situation itself, the simultaneous pressures of work and domestic demands, and the all too frequent pressures on women to relinquish their women-centred activities as a way of achieving professional accomplishment. One very positive force in helping women in their continuing struggle to be with one another is the growing recognition of the value of sisterhood. No matter how intensely or mildly political the sentiment, sensing the commonalities and attachments of women helps focus more specific values about female friendship.

REFERENCES

Aries, Elizabeth J. and Fern L. Johnson (1983) Close friendship in adulthood: conversational conduct between same-sex friends. *Sex Roles* 9 (12): 1, 183–196.
Babchuck, Nicholas (1965) Primary friends and kin: a study of the associations of middle class couples. *Social Forces* 43: 483–493.
Bell, Robert R. (1981) *Worlds of Friendship*. Sage, Beverly Hills.
Bernikow, Louise (1980) *Among Women*. Crown, New York.
Chesler, Phyllis (1972) *Women and Madness*. Avon, New York.

Douvan, Elizabeth A. M. and Joseph Adelson (1966) *The Adolescent Experience*. John Wiley, New York.

DuBois, Cora (1974) The gratuitous act: an introduction to the comparative study of friendship patterns. In Elliott Leyton (ed.) *The Compact: Selected Dimensions of Friendship*, pp. 15–32. University of Toronto Press, Toronto.

Johnson, Fern L. and Elizabeth J. Aries (1983) Conversational patterns among same-sex pairs of late adolescent close friends. *J. Genet. Psychology* 142: 225–238.

Jones, Deborah (1980) Gossip: notes on women's oral culture. *Women's Studies Int Q.* 3: 193–198.

Jourard, Sydney (1971) *Disclosure: An Experimental Analysis of the Transparent Self*. John Wiley, New York.

Kramarae, Cheris (1981) *Women and Men Speaking*. Newbury House, Rowley, Mass.

Kramer, Cheris (1977) Perceptions of female and male speech. *Language and Speech* 20: 151–161.

Lakoff, Robin (1975) *Language and Woman's Place*. Harper & Row, New York.

Lerner, Gerda (1979) *The Majority Finds Its Past: Placing Women in History*. Oxford University Press, Oxford.

Lowenthal, Marjorie F., Majda Thurnher, David Chiriboga, and associates (1976) *Four Stages of Life*. Jossey-Bass, San Francisco.

Morgan, Brian S. (1976) Intimacy of self-disclosure topics and sex differences in self-disclosure. *Sex Roles* 2: 161–166.

Mulcahy, Gloria A. (1973) Sex differences in patterns of self-disclosure among adolescents: a developmental perspective. *J. Youth Adolescence* 2: 343–356.

Pleck, Joseph H. (1975) Man to man: is brotherhood possible? In Nona Glazer-Malbin (ed.) *Old Family/New Family*, pp. 229–244. Van Nostrand, New York.

Seiden, Anne M. and Pauline B. Bart (1975) Woman to woman: is sisterhood powerful? In Nona Glazer-Malbin (ed.) *Old Family/New Family*, pp. 189–228. Van Nostrand, New York.

Spender, Dale (1980) *Man Made Language*. Routledge & Kegan Paul, London.

Wright, Paul H. and Andrea C. Crawford (1971) Argument and friendship: a close look and some second thoughts. *Representative Res. Social Psychol.* 2: 52–69.

16

Gossip Revisited: Language in All-Female Groups

Jennifer Coates

Introduction

During the last ten years, interest in, and knowledge of, the relationship between language and gender has grown enormously. But attention has focussed on gender *differences*: sociolinguistic research has aimed to quantify differences in women's and men's usage of certain linguistic forms. The linguistic forms examined range from phonological or syntactic variables to interactive forms such as interruptions, directives and questions. Where the latter are concerned, a majority of researchers have drawn their data from mixed interaction (that is, interaction involving both male and female speakers); research has rarely focussed on women in single-sex groups. As a result, we know little about the characteristics of all-female discourse. Worse, we accept generalisations about 'the way women talk' which derive from women's behaviour in *mixed* groups, groups where the differential use of linguistic features such as interruptions, directives or questions is part of the social process which maintains gender divisions.

Deborah Jones's paper, 'Gossip: notes on women's oral culture' (1980), was a landmark. While Jones was not the first to focus on all-woman interaction (cf. Abrahams 1975; Kalcik 1975; Aries 1976; Jenkins & Kramer 1978), she was the first to locate her analysis firmly in the sociolinguistic field. Jones glosses 'female oral culture' as 'language use in women's natural groups' (using 'natural' to refer to groupings which in our *culture* are construed as 'natural'). Her paper offers a description of such language use in terms of the relations between setting, participants, topic, form and function, following Ervin-Tripp (1964). The strength of Jones's paper is that it puts women talking to women firmly centre-stage; its weakness stems from the lack of empirical data. Her common-sense description of the setting, participants and topics typical of all-woman talk provides a clear set of norms to be tested in further research. Her statement that 'Little is known about any distinctive formal features of women's language in all-female groups' is a challenge to linguists which this paper will take up.

Since the publication of Jones's paper, some linguists have developed the notion, originally used in inter-ethnic communication studies, that linguistic differences might be the result in part of subcultural differences rather than simply a reflection of dominant–subordinate relationships. Work adopting this model has explored mis-communication between the sexes (e.g. Maltz & Borker 1982, reprinted in this volume, p. 417; Tannen 1982, 1987). Such work makes the assumption, either implicitly or explicitly, that the conversational strategies which lead to miscommunication in mixed groups are acquired and developed in single-sex groups. But this assumption is unverified. The evidence presented in the few studies available (Kalcik 1975; Aries 1976; Goodwin 1980; Wodak 1981) is hardly conclusive (but does suggest that such conversational strategies may not be restricted to white middle-class women). We still know very little about the norms of spoken interaction in single-sex groups.

While they lack detail, the papers listed above all draw on a notion of **co-operativeness** to characterise all-female interaction. Early work on women's language had labelled it as 'tentative' or 'powerless'. More recently, and in reaction to this, there has been a move to value women's language more positively, using terms such as 'co-operative'. This is laudable; but in order to avoid the creation of new linguistic myths, it is important that such claims are substantiated by linguistic evidence.

In this paper, I want to analyse in detail part of a corpus of conversation between women friends. The corpus is small (135 minutes of running text), and the approach used is qualitative rather than quantitative.[1] I want firstly to see whether the evidence supports Jones's general claims, secondly to establish what formal features are typical of all-woman discourse, and thirdly to explore the notion of co-operativeness.

The Data

I recorded a group of women friends over a period of nine months during 1983–4. These women were an established group who met once a fortnight at each other's houses in the evening to talk. I had belonged to this group since 1975, when it began to meet, and I recorded my friends surreptitiously each time it was my turn to have the group to my house during the period in question. All participants were informed subsequently that recordings had been made, and they agreed to this material being used for research purposes.[2] I shall discuss this data in relation to Jones's five headings, dealing briefly with setting, participants and topic, and at greater length with formal features and functions.

Setting

Jones follows Ervin-Tripp (1964) in using the term **setting** to cover both time and place. She identifies the private domain as the **place** for women's talk, and names the home, the hairdresser's, the supermarket as typical locations. Her identification of the private sphere as the setting for women's subculture seems to me to deserve more emphasis than she gives it. The division between public and private as we now understand it was established at the beginning of the nineteenth century (see Hall (1985) for an account of the historical background). As the division became more highly demarcated, patterns of gender division also changed: 'men were firmly placed in the newly defined public world of business, commerce and politics; women were placed in the private world of home and family' (Hall 1985: 12). This split was to have significant sociolinguistic consequences.

Jones describes the setting of gossip in terms of **time** as brief and fragmented: 'Time to gossip is usually snatched from work time' (1980: 194). The claim that snatched episodes are an intrinsic feature of gossip seems debatable, and depends too heavily on seeing women as mothers with small children. Old women, for example, sit on park benches or in social clubs, chatting for extended periods; adolescent girls often congregate on neutral territory (not home or school) and have considerable spare time in which to talk, especially if they are playing truant from school (see Cheshire 1982). Even mothers with small children meet in settings where the quality of the talking cannot be defined as 'snatched' – outside the school gate at the end of the day; waiting in the clinic to weigh the baby; at the mother and toddler group. According to Milroy, in traditional working-class communities such as Belfast, 'speakers valued various kinds of conversational arts very highly. *Many hours were spent simply chatting*' (my italics) (Milroy 1980: 100). Of course, some interaction between women which we would want to label as typical women's talk is brief, but it seems that length of time is not a salient feature of gossip.

The setting for the conversations I recorded was the living room of my home in Birkenhead, Merseyside. People sat on sofas or on the floor around the gas fire, drinking wine. Sessions lasted three hours or more, starting at about 9.0 in the evening. Food was served about half way through the evening; this was usually bread and cheese, but sometimes something more elaborate such as home-made soup or pizza.

Participants

'Gossip is essentially talk between women in our common role *as* women' (Jones 1980: 195). Jones argues that gossip arises from women's perception of themselves as a group with a great deal of experience in common. The members of the women's group I recorded are white, middle class, aged in their late 30s and early 40s. The group was formed (in 1975) at a time when all members had children still at school, and some had babies (who attended in carry cots). The group's *raison d'être* shifted gradually over the years: it initially provided a support network for mothers with young children; it now encourages these same women in their struggle to establish a career in their middle age. Urwin (1985) has commented on the importance for young mothers of friendships with other women. The need for contact with other women at various stages of one's life, not just as young mothers, is certainly borne out by the Birkenhead group which has now existed for 12 years.

Topic

Jones claims that the topics discussed by women are crucially related to their roles as wives, girlfriends and mothers. This claim seems to me to be over-strong, and again to overemphasise the place of motherhood in women's lives. The conversations that I recorded cover a wide range of topics, from discussions of television pro- grammes, to mothers' funerals and child abuse. However, as I have commented in an earlier paper (Coates 1987), it seems to be typical of all-women groups that they discuss people and feelings, while men are more likely to discuss things. This find- ing fits Jones's general claim that 'the wider theme of gossip is always personal experience' (1980: 195).

Functions

Unlike Jones, I shall discuss the functions of gossip before I discuss its formal features, since I want to argue that the linguistic forms which characterise women's interaction can be explained in terms of the functions they serve. Jones's section on functions is weak: she merely catalogues four different types of gossip. I want to use the term **function** in relation to the **goals** of all-woman interaction. All-woman conversation, like most informal interaction between equals, has as its chief goal the maintenance of good social relationships.

Grice's conversational maxims (Grice 1975) assume that referential meaning is all- important, and that speakers' only aim is to exchange information. The falsity of this assumption has been demonstrated by Lakoff (1973) and discussed by many other linguists subsequently (e.g. Brown 1977; Leech 1983; Tannen 1984). The distinction between public and private spheres, discussed above, leads to a distinction between public and private discourse. In public discourse, the exchange of information is an important goal. Male speakers in our culture are socialised into public discourse, while female speakers are socialised into private discourse (cf. Gilligan 1982; Smith 1985; Wells 1979). Until recently, the androcentric view that information-focussed discourse should be the object of linguistic analysis was not challenged. In private discourse, the exchange of information is not the chief goal. I hope to show in the central section of this paper that the formal features which are typical of women's language in all-female groups can be explained by direct reference to the functions of such interaction, that is the establishment and maintenance of social relationships, the reaffirming and strengthening of friendship.

Formal Features

I shall examine in detail four aspects of the interactional pattern found in the all- female conversation I recorded. I shall look at topic development, at minimal re- sponses, at simultaneous speech, and finally at epistemic modality. I have chosen to concentrate on these aspects of women's talk because they have been picked out by other writers as markers of co-operative style.

Topic development

It has become a truism in accounts of women's discourse that women develop topics progressively in conversation (see Maltz & Borker 1982: 213). Yet, as far as I know, this claim has not been supported by empirical evidence. The claim is multifaceted: women are said to build on each other's contributions, preferring continuity to discontinuity, and topic shift is supposed to occur gradually (rather than abruptly, as in all-male conversation). Consequently, the discussion of a single topic can last for some time (up to half an hour according to Aries 1976: 13).

In order to examine the nature of topic development in all-female conversation, I shall analyse one episode in detail from one of my recordings. This passage is about mothers' funerals and lasts just under $4\frac{1}{2}$ minutes. There are five participants. The structure of the funeral extract is as follows:

1   A introduces topic;
2   B tells anecdote on same theme;
3   C tells another anecdote on same theme, leading into;
4   general discussion;
5   D summarises;
6   A has last word.

In musical terms, (1), (2) and (3) form the exposition, (4) is the development, (5) the recapitulation, and (6) the coda. The development section is by far the longest (2 minutes 47 seconds). This pattern of topic development is typical of the material I have transcribed (see Coates 1987, where I analyse the development of a different topic).

The telling of anecdotes is a common way of introducing a new topic in conversation; sometimes one anecdote is sufficient, sometimes more than one occurs. What characterises these introductory sections, and sets them off from the central development section, is that they are **monologues**: the telling of a story gives the speaker unusual rights to speak. Example 1 below is a transcript of A's introductory anecdote. (A key for the transcription notation used is given in Transcription Conventions 2, p. xx.)

Example 1

. . . .

A: this bloke I met today who's doing . he- he's doing some postgraduate research at- at Stirling/ . anyway I asked him- he- he wanted to talk to me about a professional matter/ and I . I said- . I was asking him his sort of background/ and he said that he'd done philosophy/ . so I was just interested with little snippets of philosophy that came my way you see/ and he said one of the things that he was interested in was taboo/ . the

nature of taboo/ . and he said that- . a- and he gave this example that um . if you didn't
go to your mother's funeral . because you'd got something else to do/ . it would be very

```
A:   much frowned ⌈upon/ um     even though what you had to do could
B:               ⎜         =mhm/
D:               ⌊oh god =
```

```
A:   easily be more important/ and after all she was dead= .      and
C:                                                     =mhm/
```

A: wouldn't know you weren't going kind of thing/

Note that A's fellow participants say nothing until the very end of her narrative.
They accord her the right to establish a new topic – something she doesn't do until
the end of her turn – and it is only when this point is reached that other participants
volunteer supportive noises. No one attempts to make a substantive contribution
until it is clear that A has finished her turn.

Once A has finished – and the group has accepted the new topic – B tells a
personal anecdote which illustrates A's general theme of whether it is taboo to miss
your mother's funeral. B's anecdote is reproduced below.

Example 2

```
B:   oh we – it's so odd you see because we had this
?:   ((xxx))
```

```
2    A:                               = mhm=
     B:   conversation at dinner tonight=      =because Steve
```

B: MacFadden's mother died at the weekend+ and she

4   B: 1- . well she lived in Brisbane/ ((they were

```
B:   at Brisbane/)) ⌈so he's going over there/ Australia/
E:                  ⌊what – Australia?
```

```
6    B:   so he's going to the ⌈funeral/    it's obviously
     D:                        ⌊oh my god/
```

```
B:   gonna cost him a f⌈ortune/ . and John said
E:                     ⌊fortune/ <WHISPERS> ((s'about
```

```
8    B:   –                    ((he was)) just astonished/
     E:   four hundred pounds/))
```

B: I said . well I wouldn't go Steve/ . and the- and the

- -

10 B: whol- as you say it was just taboo/ I mean as far
      C: mhm/

- -

      B: as Steve was concerned I mean that was ⌈just
      C: mhm/
      D: ⌊you just

- -

12 B: no/ and I s- and my response I
      D: can't say that/
      ?:   no/

- -

      B: must 'oh John' – but sorry ((xxx))/ ⌈it's so
      ?:   ((xxx))
      C: ⌊I didn't

- -

14 B: odd that you should-
      C: go over for my father/ . . . .

- -

While B's right to hold the floor is never challenged, the other participants are far more active than they were during A's narrative. They support her with well placed minimal responses (staves 2, 6, 10, 11, 12), they complete her utterances either at the same time as her ('fortune', stave 7) or by briefly taking over from her ('you just can't say that', staves 11–12), they ask for clarification ('what – Australia?', stave 5). None of these contributions constitutes an attempt to take the floor from B – they are signals of active listenership.

B's final comment is unfinished as C starts at a point which she interprets as the end of B's turn (though co-participants were clear what B intended to say, namely, that it was a coincidence that A should bring up this subject when she herself had been discussing it that evening in relation to her neighbour). Clearly, the members of the group now feel they have established what topic is under discussion. Thus, C is granted the normal monologue rights when she begins *her* personal anecdote, but as soon as she reaches her first punch line, other speakers intervene and the discussion section begins.

Discussion sections, where speakers evaluate the topic, are multiparty in nature. Often several speakers speak at once, and speaker turns tend to be brief. Example 3 below gives C's anecdote and the opening of the general discussion.

Example 3

- -

      C: ⌈I didn't go over for my father/ I asked my mother
      B: ⌊it's so odd that you should-

- -

2 C: if she wanted me/ I mean . I- I immediately said

- -

      C: 'Do you want me to come over?'/ – and she said

- -

··

4   C: 'Well no I can't really see the point/ he's dead

··

C: isn't he?/ <LAUGHS>   . and .   ⌈and she
A: mhm/
B: well that's right/ ⌊that's

··

C: said no/ I mean   ((xxx))   ⌈no point in
6   B: what John was saying/ . that they- |
E: ⌊you've got

··

C: coming/   so-
A: ⌈yeah/
E: terribly forward-looking parents you ⌊see/ it

··

8   C:
E: depends on the attitude of- . mean is- is his

··

C: ⌈I don't
B: %I don't know/% |
E: father still alive?   ⌊because

··

10   C: think- I don't think they had a funeral either/
E: that would have a very big bearing on it/

··

C:
D: if they were religious I mean/ yes/ ⌈it would all
E: ⌊yeah/

··

C: yeah I don't think they had a funeral/ .
12   D: depend/   ⌈if there were life
E: yeah/ . I mean ⌊if there was- if there

··

C: they had a memorial service/
D: after death/   ⌈then they'd KNOW
E: was-   ⌊if they- if-

··

C:
14   D: that you hadn't come/
E: that's right/ ((xx))

··

Discussion sections are complex. At one level, individual speakers are dealing with their own feelings about the topic under discussion. In the funeral episode, C keeps returning to the theme of missing her father's funeral, expanding on the reasons for this, and hypothesising that she would go now. A says that she would be upset if her brothers and sister failed to come to her mother's funeral (and since her sister, like C's father, lives in the United States, A is implicitly challenging the assumption that the Atlantic is an insuperable barrier). E, whose parents live in Sheffield, asserts that she would definitely go to their funerals and that it is unthinkable that she wouldn't. These speakers are in effect asking for support from the group, even though their positions are to some extent mutually exclusive; they need to air their feelings in order to deal with them.

At another level, speakers are debating more general points: is it the purpose of funerals to comfort surviving relatives? or are they a public statement about one's feelings for one's dead mother? How important is distance in the decision about whether or not to attend a funeral? The general and personal are intertwined; crucially, speakers work together to sort out what they feel.

From an analytical point of view, the taken-for-granted view of conversation (originating in Sacks, Schegloff & Jefferson 1974) as interaction where one speaker speaks at a time is of little use when dealing with such material. As Example 3 illustrates, more than one speaker speaks at a time: C continues her account of not attending her father's funeral, while B ties this in with her anecdote and E adds a comment about C's parents, responding both to C ('you' in stave 6 refers to C) and to B ('is his father still alive?', staves 8 and 9, is addressed to B – 'his' refers to B's neighbour Steve). E's comment ('that would have a very big bearing on it' at stave 10) coincides with C providing further information to fit E's description of her parents as 'forward-looking'. The link between having or not having a funeral service and religious belief is picked up, slightly tongue-in-cheek, by D; E joins in with D, while C continues to refine her account.

The discussion section is long and there isn't space to give it in full nor to analyse it in detail here: specific aspects relating to minimal responses, simultaneous speech and epistemic modality will be picked up in the following three sections. Example 4 gives the end of the discussion, with D's summary and A's final comment.

Example 4

....

C: I probably I mean it would have also would have

....

2 C: been if- . I'd go now/ – Daniel was sort of

....

A: ⌈mhmmhm/
C: . 18 months old/ ⌊and it would have been rather

....

A: ⌈yes/   ⌈yes/
4 C: ⌊difficult and ⌊this kind of thing=
D: =that's right/

....

C: um   I think I
D: I suppose there's two things/ there's-

....

6 C: would go now/ because probably because I would want

....

. . . .

```
   C:   to go=        =cos it would be be very easy to go=
   D:                                                    =yeah=
   E:            =mhm=
```
. . . .
```
       A:   =yeah =
8      C:            =it would have been- -- I don't⌈know/ --
       D:                                          ⌊there's TWO
```
. . . .
```
       C:                              ⌈anyway ((xx perfectly all-
       D:   things aren't there/ ⌊there's the- the other people
```
. . . .
```
       C:   right xx))
10
       D:   like your mother or father who's left/ and- or- or
```
. . . .
```
       D:   siblings/ and there's also how how you feel at that
```
. . . .
```
       A:                                  mhm/
       B:                                          yeah/
12     C:                                  mhm/
       D:   time about . the easiness of going/
       E:                                  mhm/
```
. . . .
```
       A:                  ⌈well to go to Australia seems a bit
       D:   I mean I would ⌊I-
```
. . . .
```
14   A: over the top/
```
. . . .

It seems that the group jointly senses that this topic has been satisfactorily dealt with: C receives lots of support in her final statement that she *would* go now since circumstances have changed. Note that D has to make two attempts to provide a summary, starting once before C has finished. C's last turn gets two *yeah*s in sequence (staves 7 and 8). D's summary, like A's initial anecdote, is notable for *lack* of interruption: only when she has completed it do the others respond, all four co-participants indicating, in a perfectly timed sequence of *mhm* and *yeah*, their acceptance of what D has said. A, who initiated the topic, then has the last word.

This brief account of the development of one topic in a conversation between women friends provides an example of the way that women develop topics progressively. These women work together to produce the funeral episode, both by recognising opening and closing moves (i.e. granting one speaker the right to initiate a topic through the telling of an anecdote, or to summarise at the end), and by jointly negotiating an understanding of the problem in question (is it taboo to miss your mother's funeral?). This latter part of joint production involves both the right to speak and the duty to listen and support. The five speakers deal with their own and each other's feelings and experiences, juggling speaker and listener roles with great skill. There is no sense in which it is possible to sum up the funeral topic by saying

'A talked about taboo and funerals' or 'C talked about not going to her father's funeral'. The funeral episode is jointly produced by all speakers.

Aries' claim that topics can last up to half an hour is not apparently borne out by this example (which lasts 4 minutes 29 seconds), but this may depend on the definition of 'topic'. Certainly, topic shift is normally gradual rather than abrupt as the following example demonstrates (Example 5 follows on from Example 4).

Example 5

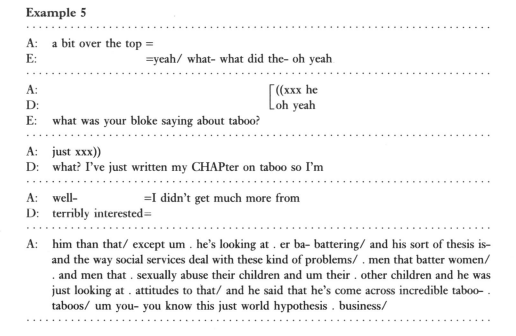

```
........................................................................
A:   a bit over the top =
E:                        =yeah/ what- what did the- oh yeah
........................................................................
A:                                          ⌈((xxx he
D:                                          ⌊oh yeah
E:   what was your bloke saying about taboo?
........................................................................
A:   just xxx))
D:   what? I've just written my CHAPter on taboo so I'm
........................................................................
A:   well-              =I didn't get much more from
D:   terribly interested=
........................................................................
A:   him than that/ except um . he's looking at . er ba- battering/ and his sort of thesis is-
     and the way social services deal with these kind of problems/ . men that batter women/
     . and men that . sexually abuse their children and um their . other children and he was
     just looking at . attitudes to that/ and he said that he's come across incredible taboo- .
     taboos/ um you- you know this just world hypothesis . business/
........................................................................
```

Note how E's question refers back to A's original anecdote (see Example 1), thus providing a very cohesive link.

In fact, this kind of gradual topic shift continues for many topics:

funerals
↓
child abuse
↓
wives' loyalty to husbands
↓
Yorkshire Ripper
↓
fear of men

These five topics are smoothly linked and overall they last for 15 minutes 54 seconds. Perhaps Aries' figure more appropriately refers to coherent sequences of topics such as the above. At all events, my data suggest that women do build progressively on each other's contributions, that topics are developed jointly, and that shifts between topics are gradual rather than abrupt.[3]

Minimal responses

Research on the use of minimal responses is unanimous in showing that women use them more than men (Strodtbeck & Mann 1956; Hirschmann 1974; Zimmerman & West 1975; Fishman 1980). This research is, however, mainly concerned with **mixed** interaction; the finding that women use minimal responses more frequently, and with greater linguistic sensitivity, in such contexts is said to demonstrate yet again the fact that women do the 'interactional shitwork' (to use Fishman's 1977 term).

It shouldn't be automatically assumed that the use of these forms denotes power-lessness, however. The same form functions in different ways in different contexts (see Cameron, McAlinden & O'Leary, 1989). Certainly it is clear from my data that the use of minimal responses also characterises linguistic interaction between women who are friends and equals.

Minimal responses are used in two different ways in the women's conversations I recorded. In the interaction-focussed discussion sections, they are used to support the speaker and to indicate the listener's active attention. The opening of Example 4 (the end of the funeral discussion section) illustrates this. While C talks, first A (staves 3 and 4), then E (stave 7), then D and A one after the other (staves 7 and 8) add their minimal responses. These responses are well placed: they are mostly timed to come at the end of an information unit (e.g. a tone group or clause), yet so well anticipated is this point that the speaker's flow is not interrupted. (Both Zimmerman & West and Fishman have shown how the *delayed* minimal response is used by male speakers to indicate lack of interest and/or attention.) These minimal responses signal the listeners' active participation in the conversation; that is, they are another aspect of the way text is *jointly* produced.

In the narrative or more information-focussed sections of the conversation, minimal responses seem to have another meaning. They are used far less frequently, and when they occur they signal agreement among participants that a particular stage of conversation has been reached. For example, when a speaker introduces a new topic, as in Example 1, it is only at the very end that other speakers indicate that they are attending. At this point it seems that D, B and C are indicating to A that they have taken the point of her anecdote, and that they accept it as a topic.

In Example 4, D's summary is followed by minimal responses from all the other participants (stave 12). Clearly the women feel the need to indicate their active agreement with D's summing-up. In both these examples, it is not just the presence of minimal responses at the end, but also their absence during the course of an anecdote or summary, which demonstrates the sensitivity of participants to the norms of interaction: speakers recognise different types of talk and use minimal responses appropriately.

So while it is true to say that the use of minimal responses characterises women's speech in both mixed and single-sex conversation, it would be wrong to claim that you have only to say *mhm* or *yeah* every few seconds to talk like a woman. On the contrary, women's use of minimal responses demonstrates their sensitivity to interactional processes; they use them where they are appropriate. In mixed conversations, the use of minimal responses by women will only become 'weak' where women's skill as listeners is exploited by male speakers. In all-female groups, it seems that the use of these linguistic forms is further evidence of women's active participation in the joint production of text.

Simultaneous speech

The Sacks, Schegloff and Jefferson (1974) model of turn-taking in conversation views simultaneous speech by two or more co-conversationalists as an aberration. Their model assumes a norm of one speaker speaking at a time. The evidence of my data is that, on the contrary, for much of the time (typically in discussion sections) more than one speaker speaks at a time. The same phenomenon has been observed by Edelsky (1981) and Tannen (1984), both of whom analysed mixed conversation. Edelsky's analysis of five staff meetings reveals what she describes as two types of 'floor': F1, where one speaker dominates, and F2, where several speakers speak at once to jointly produce text. Tannen's analysis of a Thanksgiving dinner involving six speakers (two women, four men) describes two kinds of talk, one more information-focussed, the other more interaction-focussed: the latter involves more than one speaker speaking at the same time.

It is certainly not the case in the conversations I have recorded that where more than one speaker speaks this normally represents an attempt to infringe the current speaker's right to a turn. I have analysed all instances of simultaneous speech which occur during the funeral episode; only a minority can be described in this way (see table 1).

Table 1 Simultaneous speech in the funeral episode (4 mins 29 secs)

Type I.	Two speakers self-select at the same time, one stops	3
Type II.	Speaker B self-selects at TRP, A carries on, B stops	3
Type III.	Speaker B self-selects at TRP, A tails off	3
Type IV.	Speaker B completes A's utterance	5
Type V.	Speaker B asks question or comments while A is speaking	7
Type VI.	Speaker B comments, A stops speaking	2
Type VII.	Two speakers speak at the same time	7
		30

(TRP = Transition Relevance Place, i.e. the end of a 'unit type' such as a phrase or clause. See Sacks, Schegloff and Jefferson 1974.)

Type I, where more than one speaker starts at the same time, is trivial: where next speaker self-selects, such infelicities are inevitable. Types II and III are more serious:

they are illustrated in Examples 6 and 7 below. In Example 6, E's interruption fails and B completes her own utterance: in Example 7, B stops talking and C claims the floor.

Example 6

. . . .

```
B:   I mean ⌈it's not as if I'm particularly religious/
E:         ⌊but if-                              yeah/ but if
```

. . . .

E: you've got a fa- if there's a spouse then perhaps they would

. . . .

E: want you to go/

. . . .

Example 7

. . . .

```
B:   but sorry ((xxx))/ ⌈it's so odd that you should-
?:            ((xxx))   ⌊
C:                      ⌊I didn't go over for my father/
```

. . . .

C: I asked my mother if she wanted me/ . . . .

. . . .

Even with these two examples, the term 'interruption' seems inappropriate. In Example 6, speaker E is guilty of what Tannen calls the 'overlap-as-enthusiasm' strategy: she is not so much trying to stop B from talking as jumping in too soon because of her enthusiasm to participate. She realises her mistake and comes in again once B has finished. (Another example of this phenomenon can be seen in Example 5 where D's enthusiasm delays the start of A's turn.) In Example 7, C assumes that B has finished, and in fact B is one of those speakers, like D (see Example 4, stave 13) who typically tail off rather than finishing their turns crisply. It could be argued that B and D's personal style results from their expectation that others know what they mean (so they don't need to say it in full), and that they invite overlap by their habit of ending their turns with utterances which peter out, both syntactically and prosodically. An example of such tailing-off is given below:

Example 8

. . . .

E: but if there's no spouse I mean <u>and there's very few</u>

. . . .

```
B:                                        mhm/
E:   relatives left it doesn't really seem much of a- <LAUGHING>
```

. . . .

In Example 8, E's contribution is not overlapped: this example therefore illustrates more starkly how such tailing-off turns are not 'unfinished', in the sense that E has made her contribution and her co-participants know what she means. (To get the full quality of this utterance, it is of course necessary to hear the tape.)

Type IV simultaneous speech is closely related to the above: if a speaker tails off, then it is open to other participants to complete the utterance. Speaker B's habit of not completing her turn often results in others (usually E) doing it for her:

Example 9

```
..........................................................................
B:   I just thought/ if the car breaks down on the way home
..........................................................................
B:   I mean I'll die of fear/ <LAUGHS> I'll never get out/
..........................................................................
B:   I'll just-
E:              just sit here and die/
..........................................................................
```

In this case there is no overlap, but often speakers' completion of each other's utterances results in simultaneous speech:

Example 10

```
..........................................................................
B:   I mean that was ⌈just-                =no/
D:                   ⌊you just can't say that=
..........................................................................
```

Note that B acknowledges D's contribution and in fact continues speaking: D's overlap in no way constitutes an attempt to get the floor.

Such completion-overlaps can involve more than two speakers:

Example 11

```
..........................................................................
A:   i- it'll become a s- public statement about=
E:                                   =the family/
..........................................................................
A:   er          ⌈((xx))                 yeah/
D:      yeah/    ⌊and that YOU're close/
E:   ((to do with)) ⌊you/
..........................................................................
```

Again, as in Example 10, the current speaker (A) acknowledges the others' contributions before continuing.

Type V is a very common type of simultaneous speech: it involves one of the co-participants asking the speaker a question, or commenting on what the speaker is saying, during the speaker's turn. One could describe this phenomenon as a relation of the minimal response: the questions or comments function as a sign of active listenership, and do not threaten the current speaker's turn. Speakers in fact acknowledge such questions/comments while continuing to hold the floor. Examples 12 and 13 illustrate the question, where listeners seek clarification.

Example 12

B: well she lived in Brisbane/ ((they were at Brisbane/))

B: ⌈so he's going over there/ Australia/ so he's going
E: ⌊what – Australia?

B: to the funeral/

Example 13

A: and I imagine that my two far-flung sibs will
E:

A: actually make the journey/ ⌈I'm just- . I'm ((almost-))
E: ⌊what . to your parents?

A: ⌈yes/ I'm sure they will/ but it'll be because
E: ⌊to- to your mother's?

A: i- it'll become a s- public statement about=
E: =the family/

In Example 12, B tucks 'Australia' into her exposition to satisfy E, while A, in 13, interrupts herself to say 'yes' to E before continuing her statement about her sister and brother.

Comments occur more frequently than questions and normally don't threaten a speaker's turn:

Example 14

A: I'm absolutely sure they'll come/ but I mean in fact it

A: won't make any odds/ but I think I . would be .

A: ⌈. hur- hurt and angry if they hadn't/
E: ⌊it'll be nicer for you/

In this example, E's comment goes unacknowledged, but speakers often do respond to listener comments:

Example 15
. . . .
A:
E: if there's a spouse then perhaps they WOULD want
. . . .
A: yeah for their comfort/ for them=
E: you to go/   you know/ but if- but if   =that's
. . . .
E: right/ comfort for them/ but if . . .
. . . .

Here E acknowledges A's comment before continuing.

Occasionally comments of this kind coincide with the current speaker stopping speaking (Type VI). In the following example, C finishes making her point during E's comment about her parents, and it is E who then takes the floor. C's *so* is ambiguous: it could be a bid for a longer turn (which fails), or it could be a tailing-off noise.

Example 16

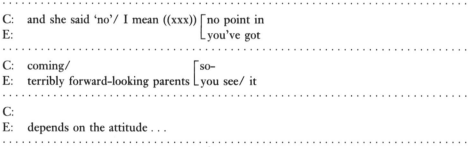

This example is complicated by the fact that B is also talking at the same time (see Example 3, staves 5–9 for the full version). However such an example is categorised, what is important is that E's contribution here is constructive: she is embellishing C's turn, putting C's mother's behaviour in context.

The final type of simultaneous speech, Type VII, involves two or more speakers speaking at once; for this type it is not possible to say one speaker has the floor and the other is merely interjecting a comment. There are seven examples of this during the funeral episode (i.e. nearly a quarter of all examples of simultaneous speech). The obvious analogy is again a musical one: the speakers contribute simultaneously to the same theme, like several instruments playing contrapuntally (the notion of contrapuntal talk is also invoked in Reisman 1974). Examples 17 and 18 below illustrate this type:

Example 17

```
C:                                              ⌈I don't
B:                         %I don't know/%      |
E:    is his father still alive?                ⌊because
```

```
C:    think- I don't think they had a funeral either/
E:    that would have a very big bearing on it/
```

Example 18

```
A:    I mean I've o- I've op- for many year⌈s ((have wondered))
E:                                         ⌊cos that's what
```

```
A:    about my own mother's funeral/
E:    funerals are for/ it's for the relatives/
```

Without providing an audio-tape, it is hard to describe the quality of such passages: crucially, there is no sense of competition, or of vying for turns. Speakers do not become aggrieved when others join in. The feel of the conversation is that all the participants are familiar with each other and with the way the interaction is constructed. It is very much a joint effort, with individual speakers concerned to contribute to a jointly negotiated whole.

A final more extended example, containing four instances of simultaneous speech, will serve to give the flavour of the conversation as a whole.

Example 19

```
C:    I mean I think it really depends on the ATTitude of the
```

```
B:                          ⌈yeah/
C:    surVIvors who are     ⌊THERE/. if- if they want the person
```

```
A:            I don't think it depends on that Cathy/
C:    to ⌈go/    . then the person should go/
E:      ⌊mhm/
```

```
A:    I think it depends on ⌈um-
E:                          ⌊oh I do/ if one of mine died/
```

```
E:    and . er I mean – my- . if it were- whichever one
```

```
E:    it were the other one would expect me to go/ –
```

. . . .

```
D:                                        ⌈mhm/
E:    they'd be ABSolutely STAggered if I didn't/ – ⌊especially
```

. . . .

```
C:                                             =no I mean if
D:                                     ⌈Sheffield= <LAUGHS>
E:    as it's only . <LAUGHS> two hours a ⌊way/
```

. . . .

```
C:    my mother had wanted me to come/ if she'd said 'oh yes
```

. . . .

```
A:        mhm/                                yeah/
C:    please'/    ⌈or 'of course' or- or something/     then
E:             ⌊you would've gone/
```

. . . .

```
A:                                    yeah/
C:    I would've- . of course I would've gone/
```

. . . .

At the beginning of Example 19, A's conflicting point of view overlaps with C's talking (note that C completes her utterance) and E's support for C overlaps with A, who tails off. That an interpretation of this as conflict is false is shown by A's support (given in minimal responses) for C's restatement of her point of view at the end. The contrapuntal nature of such text is exemplified by D's contribution 'Sheffield', which glosses E's 'it's only two hours away', and by E's anticipation of C's words which leads her to butt in with 'you would've gone' before C herself says it.

As someone who was a participant in this discourse, there is no doubt in my mind that the term 'interruption' is hardly ever appropriate as a description of instances of simultaneous speech which occur in gossip. In public domains, where the norm is that one speaker speaks at a time, and where the goal of participants is to grab speakership, then interruption is a strategy for gaining the floor. In private conversation between equals, on the other hand, where the chief goal of interaction is the maintenance of good social relationships, then the participation of more than one speaker is iconic of joint activity: the goal is not to take the floor *from* another speaker, but to participate in conversation *with* other speakers. The examples of simultaneous speech given here illustrate the way in which women speakers work together to produce shared meanings.[4]

Epistemic modality

Epistemic modal forms are defined semantically as those linguistic forms which are used to indicate the speaker's confidence or lack of confidence in the truth of the proposition expressed in the utterance. If someone says *Perhaps she missed the train*, the use of the word *perhaps* indicates lack of confidence in the proposition 'she missed the train'. Lexical items such as *perhaps, I think, sort of, probably*, as well as certain prosodic and paralinguistic features, are used in English to express epistemic modality.

Table 2   Sex differences in the use of epistemic modal forms

	Women	*Men*
I mean	77	20
well	65	45
just	57	48
I think	36	12
sort of	35	10

Such forms, however, are used by speakers not just to indicate their lack of commitment to the truth of propositions, but also to hedge assertions in order to protect both their own and addressees' face (for a full account of the role of epistemic modality in spoken discourse, see Coates 1987). It is my impression (based on an admittedly small corpus of data) that women in single-sex groups exploit these forms more than men. Table 2 gives the totals for the most commonly used forms in two parallel texts, each lasting about 40 minutes.[5]

Utterances such as those in Examples 20 and 21 below are typical of the discussion sections of the all-women conversations recorded (epistemic modal forms in italics).

Example 20
[funeral discussion]
I mean I think it *really* depends on the ATTitude of the survivors who are THERE/

Example 21
[speaker describes old friend she'd recently bumped into]
she looks very *sort of* um – *kind of* matronly *really*/

It is my contention (see Coates 1987: 129) that women exploit the polypragmatic nature of epistemic modal forms. They use them to mitigate the force of an utterance in order to respect addressees' face needs. Thus, the italicised forms in Example 21 hedge the assertion *she looks matronly* not because the speaker doubts its truth but because she does not want to offend her addressees by assuming their agreement (describing a friend in unflattering terms is controversial). Such forms also protect the speaker's face: the speaker in Example 21 can retreat from the proposition expressed there if it turns out to be unacceptable. Where sensitive topics are discussed (as in Examples 20 and 21), epistemic modal forms are used frequently. This seems to provide an explanation for women's greater use of such forms (see table 2). The women's conversations I have analysed involve topics related to people and feelings (see, for example, the topic sequence given above, page 236); in the parallel all-male conversation I have analysed, the men talk about *things* – home beer-making, hi-fi systems, etc. Presumably such topics do not trigger the use of epistemic modal forms because they are not so face-threatening.

Women also use these forms to facilitate open discussion (and, as I've said, epistemic modal forms are mostly found in the discussion sections of conversation). An underlying rule of conversation between equals, where the exchange of information is not a priority, is 'Don't come into open disagreement with other participants' (see Leech 1983: 132). Examples 20 and 21 are contributions to discussion which state a point of view but allow for other points of view. More positively, epistemic modal forms can be used to invite others to speak, a function often fulfilled by the tag question.

As Perkins (1983: 111) says: 'since questions qualify the truth of a proposition by making it relative to the speaker's uncertainty, they may be regarded as expressing epistemic modality'. An analysis of the tag questions used in the conversations I have recorded shows that the vast majority are addressee-oriented rather than speaker-oriented (cf. Holmes, 1984; Cameron, McAlinden & O'Leary, 1989). In one of the conversations (about 40 minutes of taped material) there are 23 tag questions, yet of these only four are used to elicit information (i.e. only four are speaker-oriented), as in Example 22:

Example 22
you don't know what colour their bluè is dó you (Note the rising intonation contour on the tag.)

Addressee-oriented tags can be used either to soften the force of a negatively affective utterance, or to facilitate interaction. Of the 19 addressee-oriented tags in the conversation, only one functions as a softener; the rest are all facilitative. Facilitative tags are given this name precisely because they are used to facilitate the participation of others; they invite them into the discourse. The following examples illustrate this (tags are italicised):

Example 23
. . . .
E: but I mean so much research is male-dominated/ I mean it just .
. . . .
A: =mhm/
E: it's staggering *isn't it=*
. . . .

Example 24
. . . .
D: it was dreadful *wasn't it=*
E: =appalling Caroline/ absolutely
. . . .
E: appalling/
. . . .

What is surprising about the tag questions in my data is that, while I would argue that they are facilitative, they are mostly not found in contexts like Examples 23 and

24, that is, where the tag results in another speaker taking a turn. Instead, they occur in mid-utterance, and the speaker seems to expect no verbal response (or at most a minimal response). Examples 25 and 26 illustrate this type:

Example 25

I think the most difficult thing is is that when you love someone you you half the time you forget their faults (yes) *don't you* and still maybe love them but I mean . . .

Example 26

. . . .

A: and they had they had a very accurate picture of him
D:
. . . .

A: *didn't they?* they roughly knew his age=
D: =at one point
. . . .

A: =yeah=
D: they knew about his gap teeth too *didn't they=*
. . . .

A:
D: =then they got rid of that/
. . . .

A further example is given in Example 4 (page 234), where D's summary at the end of the funeral discussion begins *there's twò things àren't there.* Of the 18 facilitative tags, nine occur in mid-utterance, like these; another three come at the end of a speaker's turn but elicit no overt response – for example, during the funeral discussion, E comments on the theme of missing a funeral *it's just not gòing isn't it.* Most of the other facilitative tags appear as comments by active listeners (Type V simultaneous speech) as in Example 27:

Example 27

. . . .

D: cos I'm fed up of travelling to conferences/ ⌈but I'm
B: ⌊oh it's so
. . . .

D: giving a paper/
B: typical *isn't it?*
. . . .

All these examples involve falling intonation, and all expect the answer *yes* (like *nonne* in Latin).

The women conversationalists seem to use these tags to check the taken-for-grantedness of what is being said. Paralinguistic cues, and sometimes minimal responses, signal to the speaker that what she is saying has the support of the group. [. . .]

I want to argue that these tags are not only addressee-oriented, in the normal sense of 'facilitative', but that they also function, sometimes simultaneously, to mark the speaker's monitoring of the progress of the conversation. This may involve the establishment and development of new topics. The following example is taken from the point in the conversation where the topic shifts from child abuse to wives' loyalty to husbands.

Example 28

. . . .

A:		=mhm/	‖	*[end of*
B:		=mhm/ . mhm/	‖	*child abuse*
C:	and your husband has become a monster=		‖	*topic]*

. . . .

C:		mhm/
E:	I mean it's like that woman that turned in- was it Pri- Prime?	

. . . .

E: [. . .] one of those . spy cases/ it was his wife/ *wasn't it?*

. . . .

A:		=yeah/
D:		=oh yes/
E:	who turned him in=	

. . . .

E's tag question here serves to get agreement from the group to pursue a new aspect of the topic; it functions as a *check* on the co-operative progress of the discourse.

Co-operativeness

In some senses, co-operativeness is a taken-for-granted feature of conversation: Grice, in his well known analysis of conversational norms (Grice 1975), used the term 'co-operative' to underscore the obvious but often overlooked fact that conversations can only occur because two or more participants tacitly agree to co-operate in talk. The notion of co-operativeness that has become established in the literature on women's language, however (see, for example, Kalcik 1975; Aries 1976; Goodwin 1980; Maltz & Borker 1982), is less general: co-operativeness in this sense refers to a particular *type* of conversation, conversation where speakers work together to produce shared meanings. Set against this notion of co-operativeness is the notion of competitiveness; competitiveness is used to describe the adversarial style of conversation where speakers vie for turns and where participants are more likely to contradict each other than to build on each other's contributions. (Whether competitiveness in this sense is typical of all-male discourse is a folklinguistic myth which has still to be tested.)

At the heart of co-operativeness is a view of speakers collaborating in the production of text: the group takes precedence over the individual. How far does my data support the idea that women's language is co-operative in this more specific sense? Do the formal features described in the previous section function as collaborative devices?

At one level, we have seen that topics develop slowly and accretively because participants build on each other's contributions and jointly arrive at a consensus. At a more delicate level, both minimal responses and epistemic modal forms function as enabling devices. Participants use minimal responses to signal their active listenership and support for the current speaker; they use them too to mark their recognition of the different stages of conversational development. Epistemic modal forms are used to respect the face needs of all participants, to negotiate sensitive topics, and to encourage the participation of others; the chief effect of using epistemic modal forms is that the speaker does not take a hard line. Where a group rather than an individual overview is the aim of discussion, then linguistic forms which mitigate the force of individual contributions are a valuable resource. Finally, simultaneous speech occurs in such discourse in various forms, and is rarely a sign of conversational malfunctioning. On the contrary, in much of the material I have collected, the norm of one-speaker-at-a-time clearly does not apply. Co-conversationalists ask questions or make comments which, like minimal responses, are signals of active listenership, but which more substantially help to produce joint text. Simultaneous speech also occurs when speakers complete each other's utterances: this seems to be a clear example of the primacy of text rather than speaker. Finally, simultaneous speech occurs most commonly because speakers prefer, in discussion, the affirmation of collaborative talk to the giving of the floor to one speaker. Participants in conversation can absorb more than one message at a time; simultaneous speech doesn't threaten comprehension. On the contrary, it allows for a more multilayered development of themes.

Topic development, minimal responses, epistemic modal forms and simultaneous speech are formal features of very different kinds. Yet where minimal responses and epistemic modal forms are used frequently and with sensitivity, where simultaneous speech is contrapuntal and doesn't mark conversational breakdown, and where topics develop slowly and progressively, all can be seen to function to promote co-operative talk. It seems that in conversations between women friends in an informal context, the notion of co-operativeness is not a myth.

Conclusions

In this chapter I have tried to refine Jones's description of gossip, in particular by analysing some of the formal features which characterise all-female discourse. A comprehensive account of the formal features typical of gossip remains to be carried out. But it is possible on the basis of the four features analysed here to conclude that women's talk *can* be described as co-operative. This, however, brings us up against the conflicting findings of those working on women's language in the context of *mixed* interaction. Women's use of minimal responses, tag questions, and hedging devices in general (epistemic modal forms) has been interpreted as a sign of weakness, of women's subordinate position to men (see, for example, Lakoff 1975; Fishman 1977, 1980). Moreover, research on interruption and overlap in mixed and single-sex pairs has shown that men use interruptions to dominate conversation in mixed interaction, but that simultaneous speech of any kind is rare in single-sex conversation (Zimmerman & West 1975; West & Zimmerman 1983).

Firstly, it is clearly not the case that any one linguistic form has one single function irrespective of contextual factors; linguists are now aware that linguistic forms are potentially multifunctional (see Cameron, McAlinder & O'Leary, 1989, for a full discussion of this point). Secondly, as I argued above, the forms that characterise all-female discourse need to be understood in the framework of the goals they serve. Since it is the aim of such talk to create and maintain good social relationships, then forms which promote such ends will be preferred. I have tried to show that women's frequent use of minimal responses and epistemic modal forms, their way of developing topics progressively, and their preference for all-together-now rather than one-at-a-time discussion, all serve the function of asserting joint activity and of consolidating friendship. Women's talk at one level deals with the experiences common to women: individuals work to come to terms with that experience, and participants in conversation actively support one another in that endeavour. At another level, the *way* women negotiate talk symbolises that mutual support and co-operation: conversationalists understand that they have rights as speakers and also duties as listeners; the joint working out of a group point of view takes precedence over individual assertions.

This discussion of underlying goals should help to explain the differences between language use in same-sex and mixed interaction. It is undoubtedly the case, all other things being equal, that when women interact with other women they interact with equals, while when they interact with men they are relating to members of the dominant group. This means that analysis of mixed interaction has to be conducted in a framework which acknowledges dominance and oppression as relevant categories. Giving a minimal response to an equal in conversation, for example, is very different from giving a minimal response to a superior. Where the main goal of relaxed informal conversation between equals is the maintenance of good (equal) social relationships, one of the goals of mixed interaction is inevitably the maintenance of gender divisions, of male–female inequality.

Furthermore, it is now agreed that sociocultural presuppositions are a key factor in explaining how speakers make sense of conversation (Gumperz 1982). Since it is arguable that women and men in our culture do not share these sociocultural presuppositions, then another difference between same-sex and mixed interaction will be that the latter will exhibit communication problems similar to those found in inter-ethnic conversation.

For both these reasons, it is very important that we do not conflate the 'women's language' said to be typical of mixed interaction with the 'women's language' which characterises all-female discourse. The two need to be analysed separately. However, growing awareness of the norms of all-female discourse may help us to reassess our interpretation of the linguistic forms used by women in mixed interaction.

Jones's original paper marked the beginning of an important shift in focus in work on language and gender differences. It drew attention not just to women's language *per se*, but to the *strengths* of such discourse. This positive approach has provided an important counterbalance to the more negative tone of researchers who see women's language as weak and tentative. Much remains to be done in the study of women and language: the majority of studies so far have concentrated on white educated women in the United States and Britain. We still know very little about variation in women's language relating to age or class or ethnic group. The notion of co-operativeness needs to be tested against all these parameters. Jones's argument is that, despite differences of age or class or ethnicity, women form a speech community. In so far as human interaction is constitutive of social reality, and in so far as interaction with other women plays an important role in our dealing with our experiences as women, then the study of interaction in all-woman groups is, as Jones says, 'a key to the female subculture'.

Notes

1 I describe, and give a justification of, this approach in greater detail in Coates (1987).
2 I would like to place on record my gratitude to my friends for their tolerance and support.
3 Abrupt shifts do occur, when the emphasis switches from interaction-focussed to more information-focussed episodes. Such shifts, however, form a minority of cases.
4 See Coates 1996 (ch. 6) and 1997 for further development of these ideas.
5 The two texts used were one of my own, and one from the Survey of English Usage (University College, London). The speakers in both were white, middle-class, well educated, aged in their 30s and early 40s. Both texts were recorded in the evening in the homes of linguists who had invited their friends over for a drink. Five women are involved in the first text; three men in the other. (My thanks to Professor Greenbaum for allowing me to use SEU material.)

References

Abrahams, R. (1975) 'Negotiating respect: patterns of presentation among black women', in C. R. Farrar (ed.) *Women in Folklore*. Austin: University of Texas Press.

Aries, E. (1976) 'Interaction patterns and themes of male, female and mixed groups'. *Small Group Behaviour*, 7, 1, 7–18.

Brown, G. (1977) *Listening to Spoken English*. London: Longman.

Cameron, D., McAlinden, F. and O'Leary, K. (1989) 'Lakoff in context: the social and linguistic functions of tag questions', in J. Coates and D. Cameron (eds) *Women in Their Speech Communities*. Harlow: Longman.

Cheshire, J. (1982) *Variation in an English Dialect*. Cambridge: Cambridge University Press.

Coates, J. (1987) 'Epistemic modality and spoken discourse'. *Transactions of the Philological Society*, 110–31.

Coates, J. (1996) *Women Talk: Conversation Between Women Friends*. Oxford: Blackwell.

Coates, J. (1997) 'The construction of a collaborative floor in women's friendly talk', in T. Givón (ed.) *Conversation: Cognitive, Communicative and Social Perspectives*. New York: John Benjamins.

Edelsky, C. (1981) 'Who's got the floor?' *Language in Society*, 10, 383–421.

Ervin-Tripp, S. (1964) 'An analysis of the interaction of language, topic and listener'. *American Anthropologist*, 66, 6 (part 2), 86–102.

Fishman, P. M. (1977) 'Interactional shitwork'. *Heresies*, 2, 99–101.

Fishman, P. M. (1980) 'Conversational insecurity', in H. Giles, W. P. Robinson and P. Smith (eds) *Language: Social Psychological Perspectives*. Oxford: Pergamon.

Gilligan, C. (1982) *In a Different Voice*. Cambridge, MA: Harvard University Press.

Goodwin, M. H. (1980) 'Directive–response speech sequences in girls' and boys' task activities', pp. 157–73 in S. McConnell-Ginet, R. Borker and N. Furman (eds) *Women and Language in Literature and Society*. New York: Praeger.

Grice, H. P. (1975) 'Logic and conversation', pp. 41–58 in P. Cole and J. L. Morgan (eds) *Syntax and Semantics, vol. 3: Speech Acts*. New York: Academic Press.

Gumperz, J. (1982) *Discourse Strategies*. Cambridge: Cambridge University Press.

Hall, C. (1985) 'Private persons versus public someones: class, gender and politics in England, 1780–1850', pp. 10–33 in C. Steedman, C. Urwin and V. Walkerdine (eds) *Language, Gender and Childhood*. London: Routledge & Kegan Paul.

Hirschmann, L. (1974) 'Analysis of Supportive and Assertive Behaviour in Conversations.' Paper presented to the Linguistic Society of America, July 1974 (see abstract in B. Thorne and N. Henley (eds) (1975) *Language and Sex: Difference and Dominance*. Rowley, MA: Newbury House).

Holmes, J. (1984) 'Hedging your bets and sitting on the fence: some evidence for hedges as support structures'. *Te Reo*, 27, 47–62.

Jenkins, L. and Kramer, C. (1978) 'Small group process: learning from women'. *Women's Studies International Quarterly*, 1, 67–84.

Jones, D. (1980) 'Gossip: notes on women's oral culture', pp. 193–8 in C. Kramarae (ed.) *The Voices and Words of Women and Men*. Oxford: Pergamon Press.

Kalcik, S. (1975) '"... like Ann's gynaecologist or the time I was almost raped": personal narratives in women's rap groups'. *Journal of American Folklore*, 88, 3–11.

Lakoff, R. (1973) 'The logic of politeness'. *Papers from the Ninth Regional Meeting of the Chicago Linguistics Society*, 292–305.

Lakoff, R. (1975) *Language and Women's Place*. New York: Harper & Row.

Leech, G. (1983) *Principles of Pragmatics*. London: Longman.

Maltz, D. N. and Borker, R. A. (1982) 'A cultural approach to male–female miscommunication', in J. Gumperz (ed.) *Language and Social Identity*. Cambridge: Cambridge University Press.

Milroy, L. (1980) *Language and Social Networks*. Oxford: Blackwell.

Perkins, M. (1983) *Modal Expressions in English*. London: Frances Pinter.

Reisman, K. (1974) 'Contrapuntal conversation in an Antiguan village', in R. Bauman and J. Sherzer (eds) *Explorations in the Ethnography of Speaking*. Cambridge: Cambridge University Press.

Sacks, H., Schegloff, E. and Jefferson, G. (1974) 'A simplest systematics for the organization of turn-taking for conversation'. *Language*, 50, 696–735.

Smith, P. (1985) *Language, the Sexes and Society*. Oxford: Blackwell.

Strodtbeck, F. and Mann, R. (1956) 'Sex role differentiation in jury deliberations'. *Sociometry*, 19, 3–11.

Tannen, D. (1982) 'Ethnic style in male–female conversation', in J. Gumperz (ed.) *Language and Social Identity*. Cambridge: Cambridge University Press.

Tannen, D. (1984) *Conversational Style: Analyzing Talk among Friends*. Norwood, NJ: Ablex.

Tannen, D. (1987) *That's Not What I Meant*. London: Dent.

Urwin, C. (1985) 'Constructing motherhood: the persuasion of normal development', in C. Steedman, C. Urwin and V. Walkerdine (eds) *Language, Gender and Childhood*. London: Routledge & Kegan Paul.

Wells, G. (1979) 'Variation in child language', in V. Lee (ed.) *Language Development*. London: Croom Helm.

West, C. and Zimmerman, D. (1983) 'Small insults: a study of interruptions in cross-sex conversations between unacquainted persons', in B. Thorne, C. Kramarae and N. Henley (eds) *Language, Gender and Society*. Rowley, MA: Newbury House.

Wodak, R. (1981) 'Women relate; men report: sex differences in language behaviour in a therapeutic group'. *Journal of Pragmatics*, 5, 261–85.

Zimmerman, D. and West, C. (1975) 'Sex roles, interruptions and silences in conversation', in B. Thorne and N. Henley (eds) *Language and Sex: Difference and Dominance*. Rowley, MA: Newbury House.

17

'Don't try and make out that I'm nice!' The Different Strategies Women and Men Use when Gossiping

Jane Pilkington

Introduction

In this paper, I shall attempt to define and describe some of the features of gossip. On the basis of data collected in single-sex groups, differences in the gossip of women and men will be identified and discussed. Although the aims of the women's and the men's gossip appeared to be similar, in that both expressed solidarity and group membership, the strategies adopted to achieve these aims were quite different. While the women tended to use positive politeness strategies (Brown and Levinson 1978), the men appeared to operate within the context of the Mateship Culture (James and Saville-Smith 1989), and used ways of interacting which were far more aggressive.

[. . .]

Function of Gossip

The basic function of gossip can be seen as signifying group membership. To be fully part of a group you must be able to understand and participate in the gossip of that group (Gluckman 1963: 309).

Gossip within groups can play a conservative role in maintaining morals and unity. Competing groups within the community can also be controlled by gossip, or gossip may serve to mark the community as distinct from a larger group. In order to avoid being gossiped about members of the community must live their lives within the moral code of the community.

In a group under threat such as the Makah Indians (Gluckman 1963: 311 citing Colson 1953), the distinctive Makah traditions are kept alive through gossip. As each person seeks to claim a greater status within the community by claiming to be more Makah than other members of the community, others must retaliate by being able to refute that person's claim while building up a claim of their own. Through this constant gossiping the knowledge of the history and traditions of a distinctive minority are kept alive.

This also illustrates the fact that gossip has a levelling function. Anyone gaining too much power or overstepping their role leaves themselves open to be gossiped about. Gossip may also enable gossipers to covertly assert their status. By assessing the behaviour of others, a gossiper can demonstrate their own position in relation to the person they are gossiping about.

Gossip can enable groups to have differences of opinion while at the same time presenting a united front to outsiders. Since gossip is carried out within a community and in such a way that outsiders may not be able to recognize some of the vicious barbs, outsiders may see a united group while animosities are worked out behind the scenes.

Gossip is also entertaining. Gluckman (1963: 313) states that gossip is enjoyed by people in close social relationships with one another. It is a form of entertainment open only to group members. It is a considerable faux-pas for an outsider to gossip about a group member while insiders are free to gossip about their friends and enemies without censure. Outsiders will not be able to derive the same enjoyment from gossip as group members due to the strategies of indirectness already mentioned.

Attitudes

It is interesting to note that in spite of the enjoyment that groups derive from gossip and the positive light in which all the above writers approach the style, gossip is generally downgraded or condemned by any community. Gossip is largely seen as worthless and has low social prestige; Jones (1975: 10) comments that it tends to be restricted to low prestige settings.

Jones (1980: 195) also points out that men see women's gossip as a threat and try to discourage it. Perhaps the cohesive power that gossip has in small groups makes the powerful groups of society nervous. The general belief that gossip is trivial is perhaps derived from the intimacy that characterizes gossip. In any society it is the large scale events that are seen as important. Gossip as an intimate style occurring in informal settings is seen as small scale and receives little attention.

From these observations, it is possible to define gossip as characterized by the following features:

1 Gossip is focused on the personal rather than global, private rather than public.
2 Gossip is widely regarded as trivial yet is valued by individuals.
3 Gossip is entertaining and enjoyable.
4 Gossip occurs in a sympathetic environment, among friends and intimates not strangers.

5   There is probably an upper limit on the size of a group involved in gossip; the lower limit is two.

6   The smaller and closer the group the more personal and probing the gossip will be.

7   Gossip is ephemeral and has limited interest outside the participating group.

[. . .]

Method

I recorded two different all-female groups and two all-male groups. The female groups consisted of (i) the women whom I was flatting with and our friends, (ii) the women I worked with in a bakery.

My women in my flat and the friends visiting when I taped were all known to one another except for Fr and Ls who had not met previously, but were both known by all the other participants and had heard of each other previously. All participants were university students from similar socio–economic backgrounds aged between 20 and 25 years.

The women I worked with were aged 34–43. Again all the participants knew one another but, apart from me, the socio–economic background of the members of this group was somewhat lower than that of the first group.

Taping all-male groups was more difficult since there was a particularly problem-atic version of the observer's paradox to overcome: if I was present the group was no longer an all-male group, yet if I wasn't present who would do the taping? My solution was to ask the group of men that I worked with at the bakery if I could tape them. I told them when I was beginning taping and then I left the room. I left the tape running for most of one day and for a shorter period on a second day. I hoped this would result in the participants gradually forgetting its presence as well as my role as a future female overhearer. This strategy was very successful. Wariness of the tape recorder gradually diminished over the two days.

On the first day there were four participants present aged between 20 and 25 years. On the second occasion there were five participants present aged between 20 and 39. All the participants knew each other and had all left school after either the sixth or seventh form and had a similar socio–economic background.

The differences between the data collected from the two groups of women (one at home and one at work) turned out to be slight. The different ages and educational background of the participants, and the different environments in which the data were recorded, did not seem to result in any great differences in the gossip style. On the whole the women seemed to talk about similar things and use similar strategies. The strategies that I attribute to women in my analysis of the data are thus strategies that were used by both groups of women.

The taping produced about 250 minutes of data from the female groups, and 210 minutes of usable data from the male group. From this, using the list of criteria outlined above, I selected small sections of gossip.

Results

The female groups: cooperative talk

One very clear feature of the interaction of the female groups was the large degree of positively oriented involvement that the different speakers had in each conversation. Instead of finding that one speaker spoke for a time while the others listened, and then another person spoke while everybody else listened, I found that while one speaker might be taking the central talk role, the other participants were continuously contributing. It was rare for a speaker to talk alone for more than about 30–35 words.

The more interesting and exciting the participants found the conversation, the more often they would contribute, and the more feedback they would provide. Often laughter was more frequent and more general, and the volume and speed at which the speakers spoke increased. In such episodes, the length of turn of each participant was extremely short. This can be seen in Example 1 from the home setting where three of the participants are discussing a character in *Days of Our Lives*, a TV programme with which they were much absorbed.

(In the transcribed conversations the following symbols are used to join sections of simultaneous speech or latched speech: ⌈ ⌊. Capitals are used to indicate strong stress.)

Example 1

MAY:	⌈
SAL:	⌊ who's this?
PAM:	⌊
SAL:	reprobate! oh it's ⌈
MAY:	⌊friend of Sean's
PAM:	(sing song) Kimberly's client.
SAL:	oh yuk!
MAY:	what what what!
PAM:	one of Kimberly's clients
MAY:	what does she do?
PAM:	she's a whore
MAY:	is she?
PAM:	yes!
MAY:	Kimberly?
PAM:	shocking eh
MAY:	do they know
PAM:	no nobody knows

SAL: ⌈really?
MAY: ⌊really?
SAL: that old reprobate, look and a friend of the father's too ohhhh!
MAY: wild! is she still being a whore now?
PAM: Linda forced her back into it
MAY: oh my Gooood

Most of the turns are no more than three words long with the longest turn only 11 words long. The speech was very rapid and there were no pauses between participants' turns.

Example 2 is taken from the interaction in the work group at a similar point of extreme interest for the participants. The women are talking about a series of road accidents that happened on the motorway nearby that morning.

Example 2

LIZ: I thought you'd be stuck in that thing Jen, there was just a
      big crash at the end of Tawa
JEN: yes yes ⌈I know
LIZ: ⌊that's why I came a bit earlier
JEN: um well actually there must have been a crash just aft-
      there was a prang up which I went through
LIZ: yeah they said it was (. . .)
JEN: really well
SAL: Liz had visions of ⌈you in there! (laughing)
LIZ: ⌊yes well (laughing)
JEN: that'll be why they rang up from John's work
SAL: did they?
LIZ: yeah yes
JEN: just as I was leaving they were ringing up for ⌈John but I said
SAL: ⌊oh
JEN: that he left just after seven o'clock
SAL: oh right so they would have all heaved a sigh of relief!

While the turns are not as short as in Example 1, there are still many different turns in a short space of time with little pausing between each turn.

Short turns with minimal pauses between are one indication of involvement. Another feature of the women's involvement in each other's talk was the amount of encouraging feedback they provided to each other, and the ways in which they extended each other's topics. In Example 3, the two participants, who are watching *Days of Our Lives*, are not showing a great amount of interest in the issue of Marlene's age. The turns are longer, the pauses between turns are longer, and there is little feedback. However, once the topic of *Our House* comes up, the time between turns drops and the amount of feedback increases.

Example 3

PAT: how old's Marlene?
Pause of several seconds

SAL: um . . . she must be in her 30's, she's been married to Don
Pause of several seconds
SAL: if not in her 40's because in that *Our House* um . . . she's the mother
of teenage kids ⌈and she
PAT: ⌊oh yeah that's an awful program isn't it
SAL: mmmm
PAT: it's got that dick who's in the Cocoon film
SAL: oh god he's insufferable!
PAT: and he's so fucking wise ⌈and so so FUCKING American
SAL: ⌊yeah
SAL: and everybody else is always WRONG
PAT: yes and he's always right . . .

This example shows that female speakers not only contribute feedback to their interlocuters, but also actively contribute to the development of their interlocuter's topic. When Pat replies to Sal's comment 'Oh god he's insufferable' she begins with 'and' in effect conjoining her comment to Sal's earlier comment. When Sal follows up Pat's comment she too uses 'and' to begin her utterance, conjoining it to Pat's preceding comment. Both Pat and Sal are using the same American accents in these conjoined turns, another indication that they are both telling the same story and see themselves as sharing the same role. Example 4 provides a further illustration of these strategies for signalling positive involvement and support for other speakers.

Example 4
SAL: perhaps next time I see B I'll PUMP him for information . . .
⌈so B tell me
MAY: ⌊ the goss
SAL: ⌈I know it's about six years old but
MAY: ⌊ (*laugh*) but I'd forgotten it

May indicates her agreement with Sal's comments by finishing them for her or by carrying on with them. Sal makes the opportunity available to her the first time by trailing off. May provides an end to Sal's utterance and Sal continues her utterance but breaks it when she reaches the conjunction 'but', allowing May to continue the utterance for her. This example could plausibly have been spoken by one speaker only. This sharing of turns is clearly done with the approval of both participants. May having finished one of Sal's utterances then pauses and allows Sal to continue. Sal then creates another opportunity for May to join in which May laughingly takes. The two are both enjoying the contributions of the other, they are sharing the right to speak rather than competing for it. There is no sense that Sal is being 'interrupted'. Rather the discourse is very clearly a joint production.

Another interesting cooperative interactive strategy is illustrated in Example 5, a joint story-telling by May and Sal. They are telling Pam the story of Liz and Neil's latest fight from the previous episode of *Days of Our Lives*. May contributes to Sal's narrative by adding excited 'oh's at various points which serve to underline and enforce the entertainment value of this story.

Example 5

SAL: yeah he kicked Carlo out and said he had to get out in five seconds or he was [May: ohh!] going to KILL him [May: ohhh!] and he said that if um Liz wanted to bonk him she'd have to go to a CHEAP [May: ohhh!] HOTEL LIKE ALL THE REST OF THE WHORES!

MAY: ohhh ohhh ohhh!   (*general laughter*)

As already mentioned the amount of feedback that the women give one another increases in proportion to the amount of enjoyment they are deriving from this point of the conversation. As the enjoyment and interest increases, the feedback increases. This feedback is often in the form of minimal responses although lengthier responses will often also be used. These responses often seem to be used by the listeners as a prompt to the speakers as if to say 'yes please carry on'. In Example 6, for instance, Sal introduces a new topic and identifies the subject of the gossip as Roz's mother. She then locates the gossip in terms of when the event took place. If May had not remembered the time or the person that Sal was referring to, I think she would have put a question in at this point such as 'who?' or 'when was this?' By making a positive minimal response she effectively indicates that she has nothing to say here, and that the story can continue. Sal having received the prompt then goes on to reveal the complicating action without seeing any need to give any further background.

Example 6

SAL: like Roz's mother, one of the times that oh that time I went to Himitangi
       ⌈ with the family   and she was going on like . . .
MAY: ⌊   yeah

[. . .]

Minimal responses are not the only feedback that participants use to encourage the speaker to continue. Sometimes the other participants will use questions about what the speaker was talking about to get them to continue with their narrative. The speaker will also use these questions as a guide to what the other participants are interested in hearing. In Example 7, Pam has questioned the other participants about a previous episode of *Days of Our Lives*. Sal has been describing the scene Pam had asked about, but stops the narrative when May joins in. The narrative, however, does not continue so Pam asks another question to prompt the continuation of the narrative.

Example 7

SAL: yeah like they were sort of you know lying there on top of one another it
       was oh quite crude ⌈ oh
MAY: ⌊ so we presume
SAL: yeah we kind of presume
PAM: yeuk
SAL: but yeah
PAM: so has he moved out?
SAL: yeah he kicked Carlo out he said . . .

Echoing or repeating each other's comments was another strategy that the women used as a means of showing agreement. In Example 8, May is retelling a story that was told to her by a woman she knows.

Example 8

MAY: . . . and they used to go to this youth group and all be all over each other in 1920 or whenever

PAM: ⌈eugh

SAL: ⌊eugh

MAY: and then um . . . er . . . then one day she was sick so the boyfriend took it upon himself to ask her cousin out eughh

PAM: ⌈eughh

SAL: ⌊eughh

Sal and Pam make *yuk*-type noises (represented as *eugh(h)*) when May mentions the young couple's physical relationship. When May continues the story she makes a similar noise when another physical relationship is implied. Pam and Sal follow this noise with similar noises of their own thus indicating agreement with May's reaction and even the reaction of the woman whom the story is about.

A more articulate example of repetition with expansion of the previous speaker's point can be seen in Example 9 when Sal and Liz are discussing the fate of a character in a film they saw.

Example 9

LIZ: well I'm amazed he survived I thought he'd have died

SAL: yes died of blood loss or ⌈something like that

LIZ: ⌊yes it's a wonder he didn't haemorrhage

Liz expresses surprise that the character didn't die. Sal develops this by agreeing, and stating what she thought that the character would have died of. Liz follows this comment by expressing surprise that the character did not die in the way that Sal had guessed he might.

Even when they disagree, the women do so in an indirect way consistent with their cooperative and generally supportive approach to interaction. A speaker would question the previous speaker's utterance, for instance, without explicitly stating that they disagreed with the statement. Example 10 illustrates this strategy. Sal, May and Pam are talking about the number of fur coats currently seen on *Days of Our Lives*. May says that Marlene was wearing one in the previous episode.

Example 10

SAL: oh was Marlene wearing one?

PAM: oh my God!

Sal's question indicates surprise, but invites May to elaborate. Pam supports Sal's question by also expressing surprise at the idea of Marlene wearing a fur coat. Sal and Pam have thus indirectly expressed their disbelief at May's statement but have not stated that they disagree with May. May takes up the invitation to elaborate and describes the coat, finishing her description with a rising intonation which may function as an invitation to Sal and Pam to comment further, while also perhaps indicating tentativeness. All three speakers, then, have tried to play down the disagreement.

From these examples it can be seen that in general the women are cooperatively involved in the enterprise of joint talk. They take short turns with little pausing. They also support one another with their responses. They provide positive minimal feedback, and they ask questions to indicate that they are interested in and are understanding what the speaker is saying. Often several speakers will echo a point or an expression used by a previous speaker. Sometimes the women complete each other's turns, or collaborate to produce a joint text by adding to what the previous speaker has just said, effectively indicating agreement with the previous utterance. As presented in print some of these responses and supportive turns may appear to be interruptions, but it is quite clear from the recording that the function of the latched and overlapping turns is quite the opposite of disruptive.

The strongest feeling I got from these data was a feeling of cooperation and sharing. The women were talking to one another sharing opinions and views and providing one another with encouragement.

The male groups: uncooperative talk?

The male talk was very different from the female talk in a variety of ways. Perhaps the most noticeable feature of the recordings of the male groups were the long silences. Silences during the women's recordings were fairly short. The males by contrast seemed to spend a great deal more of the time that they spent together *not* talking. Several minutes could elapse before someone would say something. At first I thought this might relate to the work environment but the recording of the women in exactly the same work environment did not have such lengthy silences.

There were also much longer pauses between turns, even when it seemed to me that the speaker expected or even invited a response by using tags or questioning intonation. The response was often slow in coming and sometimes it never came. Example 11 illustrates this pattern. Ben is discussing his wife's relative sporting strengths.

Example 11
BEN: I think she has a certificate for swimming a mile . . . that's a bloody long swim isn't it?
Pause of about 5–10 seconds
BEN: she has a life saving certificate . . .

Ben invites Sam to join the conversation by using a tag question. Sam however makes no comment so Ben continues. Ben did not seem to think that there was anything unusual about Sam's lack of response. There was no evidence that the men found lack of response or feedback from the other men unusual or upsetting. This is further illustrated in Example 12. Jim has been singing a song that was used in a television commercial that was screened several years ago.

Example 12
JIM: remember that Wales ad!
Pause of about 5–10 seconds
JIM: (laughing) obviously nobody does.

Jim asks if anyone remembers that commercial. Nobody replies. Jim eventually laughingly comments on this but he seems to find the lack of response amusing rather than annoying.

I think that a similar lack of response in female gossip would indicate extreme lack of interest. The silence in Example 12, for instance, would not have been allowed to continue for so long in the female groups. One of the participants would have given some form of feedback, even if only to say that she didn't remember or to ask which commercial was being talked about. Jim however takes silence as a response in itself. It is only when he makes the assertion that nobody remembers that any response is made, and then there is still a pause of about 5 seconds before it comes.

The men seemed to be far more willing to continue talking without verbal feedback than the women were. As mentioned above, the women seldom spoke for a long period without receiving any verbal response, and would often pause and only continue when some feedback was given as a prompt. The men by contrast could carry on long monologues with very long pauses between utterances. At one point, for instance, Ben spends about 5 minutes talking about fishing in fits and starts with very long pauses between each utterance. None of the other males make any comment on this at all. The monologue continues until one of the other males asks a question related to fishing but not directly related to the previous utterance.

A less extreme version of this use of monologues can be seen in Example 13 when Jim continues to talk about the old television commercial and then begins to talk about another old commercial without receiving any feedback from any of the other males.

Example 13
JIM: ... that kid walks into the bank with the piggy bank under his arm looking real mean ... (*pause of about 5 seconds*) ... we used to all come home from school singing that song ... dad wasn't too pleased eh ... (*pause of about 10 seconds*) ... then that zip-zap National Bank visa ad came on and we all started singing that ... (*pause of less than 5 seconds*) dad was all real happy about that

Another feature that characterized my male data that was not present in my female data was the occurrence of frequent, direct, and repeated expression of disagreement or hostility. The men often openly disagreed with one another. They seemed to have several different strategies for doing this. Example 14 illustrates one such strategy. Ben has been talking about the intelligence of fish.

Example 14

BEN: . . . and ah they're very smart
DAN: well then how come they keep getting caught all the time?
SAM: maybe that's why they ⌈(. . .)
BEN: ⌊they don't Dan. you've got to be
really clever to pull one you know

Dan challenges Ben's point of view by questioning it. He asks how fish can be seen as intelligent if they are always getting caught. Ben responds to this by disagreeing with the challenge, thus defending his beliefs and attacking the truth of Dan's argument. There are two different strategies for disagreement in this example: firstly questioning the other's proposition and secondly negating the other's proposition.

Another strategy the males used for disagreeing was to make a statement that conflicted with the previous speaker's statement. In Example 15, Sam and Jim are talking about the problems they have been having with one of the machines.

Example 15

SAM: I came in Saturday and turned it on and it started to run very hot
JIM: Ben turned it on

Sam and Ben cannot have both turned on the same machine so Jim disagrees with Sam's account of events. He doesn't openly challenge Sam's statement, however, he simply makes a statement that is in conflict with one of Sam's statements.

Another very common strategy that males used for expressing disagreement was criticism. This criticism was often strong enough to be considered abusive. By either criticizing the person who had made an earlier comment, or criticizing some aspect of the comment, the men could express their opposing viewpoint. In Example 16, Ray and Dan have been discussing different lexical items used in Australia and New Zealand. Dan has mentioned *Esky*. Ray claims that everyone uses the word *Esky*. He then asks Dan what word he uses.

Example 16

RAY: what do you call an Esky?
DAN: chilly bin
RAY: huh another one another fuckhead.

Here Ray makes a criticism and then increases its force. He uses *huh* indicating by the tone of voice that he thinks that those who don't use the word *Esky* are deficient, and then makes the criticism stronger by using the word *fuckhead*.

Similarly in Example 17, Sam and Ray have made an issue out of whether apples are kept in cases or crates. What follows is a burst of quite vicious-sounding abuse which the participants do not seem to take personally as the conversation then quite suddenly changes from mutual abuse to another topic.

Example 17

RAY: crate!

SAM: case!

RAY: what?

SAM: they come in cases Ray not crates

RAY: oh same thing if you must be picky over every one thing.

SAM: just shut your fucking head Ray!

RAY: don't tell me to fuck off fuck (. . .)

SAM: I'll come over and shut yo

JIM: (*Laughingly using a thick sounding voice*) yeah I'll have a crate of apples thanks

RAY: no fuck off Jim

JIM: (A dozen . . .)

DAN: (*amused*) shitpicker!

RAY: (*laughing to another person not participating in this exchange*) I'm sorry I yelled at . . . what's yer name?

In the free-for-all abuse session illustrated in this example Sam criticizes Ray, Ray criticizes Sam, Jim criticizes Ray and Dan criticizes Jim. Yet no one seems to take the criticisms too seriously. There were several smaller such exchanges in my data; yet these people all continued after such abuse to work alongside each other and to talk with each other without any evidence of hard feelings. Indeed the participants in these sessions seem to be quite enjoying themselves and the exchanges. Jim is laughing when he criticizes Ray, and Dan sounds amused rather than angry. The fact that Ray suddenly changes topic and addressee and begins to laugh indicates that he isn't taking the abuse as a genuine threat.

It is interesting to note how direct and specific the male criticism was. Critical comments were addressed to others by name. The men made quite explicit who they were referring to. This appeared to me to increase the force of the criticism and make it more of a threat. A critical comment cannot possibly be interpreted as a general criticism when it has been addressed to one person.

The sudden change of topic that occurs in Example 17 is not unusual in my data. The topics that the men discuss do not seem to be linked as clearly as the topics that the women discuss. In Example 17, Ray suddenly switches from attacking and being attacked by one group and laughingly apologizes to another person whom he had shouted at several minutes beforehand. Such sudden changes of topic seem to make the interaction of the men have less of a flowing quality to it. Example 18 provides another example. Ben has been conducting a near monologue about various aspects of fishing for around 5 minutes. Finally Dan responds to Ben with a fish-related topic but Ray then cuts through all this with a question about beer.

Example 18

DAN: we used to feed them to the cat but the cat used to choke all these bones

RAY: have you tried that (. . .) lager?

Beer is a new topic which has not been mentioned previously. All talk of things fishy then totally ceased; the topic change is sudden and total.

This jerkiness seemed to be characteristic of the male data. There would be long periods of silence followed by spells of speech. The speech itself was often disjointed, due to pausing by the speakers and lack of response by the listeners, and the topic could change with no warning and seemingly for no reason. The tendency that the males had to take issue with one another meant that arguments would suddenly occur and then just as suddenly cease when the participants moved on to the next topic.

The male talk contrasts with the female talk then in a variety of ways. Males do not provide minimal feedback and often do not respond in any way to others' comments. They disagree very directly and bluntly with others' statements. They abuse each other and criticize each other very directly. And they appear to feel no need to provide topic support or to develop others' topics. They appear to switch topic abruptly and without regard for the previous speaker's topic.

Discussion

The examples have illustrated a variety of ways in which female and male talk differs. The women generally seemed to treat gossip as a cooperative venture. They prompted one another and gave positive feedback. Their turns echoed and linked to previous turns in interesting ways. I found examples of mimicking of accents and repetition of ideas from the previous turn. The women deliberately provided each other with opportunities to join in and take a turn at speaking. When they disagreed with each other they did so indirectly.

The men by contrast spent a lot of their time talking without receiving any feedback, or even without anyone seeming to take any notice of them. When they did interact verbally the interaction was often apparently very negative and unsupportive involving disagreement, criticism and abuse.

The women's talk appears to be observing generally recognized principles of politeness. The women use a high number of the positive politeness strategies identified by Brown and Levinson (1978) as strategies which emphasize group membership and solidarity. The following strategies could all be identified in the recordings of the women's talk:

1   Noticing H (e.g. commenting on each other's knitting and asking about H's children).
2   Exaggerate (e.g. the women would give positive feedback even when the topic under discussion was of no particular interest to them; all the group would laugh even though not all of them necessarily agreed that the topic was amusing).
3   Use of in group identity markers (e.g. the *Days of Our Lives'* audience all referred to the programme as *Days* to one another, and collectively referred to a couple on the programme as 'Ho and Bope').
4   Seek agreement (they selected topics that had often been discussed before and were known to be enjoyable to all; Jen and Sal would scandalize about S's son; Liz and Sal would scandalize about S).

5 Avoid disagreement (e.g. Jen and S wait until Sal has left the room before discussing Db who is quite friendly with Sal).

6 Assert common ground (e.g. frequent reference to events that all particip- ants have some knowledge of).

7 Include both S and H in activity (e.g. comments such as 'we're going well this morning').

8 Joke (e.g. Pat planning to buy a house with her overdraft; Jen and Sal planning to borrow some priceless antiques from a neighbour since she has so many).

9 Give gifts to H (e.g. the *Days of Our Lives* audience filling one another in on episodes that they have missed; admiring comments about the speed at which a jersey has been knitted).

The men by contrast not only fail to use these positively polite strategies, they often explicitly contradict them. They tend to emphasise disagreement rather than agree- ment and this is a feature of men's speech which has been noted in other contexts as well (see, for example, Holmes 1989).

Women then seem to put more effort into cultivating a satisfying interaction along the lines of conventional politeness strategies. The men, by contrast, seem to feel no qualms about meeting a challenge with a counter challenge. They are quite willing to let the challenges develop into open hostility, and in fact appear to enjoy expressing hostility towards one another. They frequently abuse one another. It seems possible then that while women use positive politeness strategies to express solidarity, the men use abuse as a means of signalling solidarity. The men often made comments that indicated that they looked upon this abusive behaviour as a positive thing and polite behaviour as something negative. Jim says to Ray at one point 'Don't try and make out that I'm nice'; he then goes on to comment 'I like complete bastards'. Not only does he claim that being nice is something to be ashamed of, but he also claims that being a dishonourable sort of a male is a positive attribute in his eyes. Jim is speaking jokingly when he makes these comments, but they do seem to indicate that the men do not feel that abusive behaviour is necessarily anti-social behaviour. The men appear to identify with such behaviour and see it as appropriate masculine behaviour. The women's groups are a total contrast in this respect. Disagreement is avoided and agreement is built upon.

Why should this be the case? Why should one group use one set of norms while the other uses an opposing set of norms? Within each group there seems to be a strong awareness of their group's respective norms. The women wait to be prompted and expect constant feedback, while the men are happy to talk without feedback and are quite aware that the abuse is not meant to be taken as a genuine threat. The women's behaviour follows the rules for polite interaction described by Brown and Levinson (1978). From this perspective, then, it is the men's behaviour which requires explanation.

An answer can perhaps be found by considering the 'male mateship culture' as described by Bev James and Kay Saville-Smith (1989). Using their description

(James and Saville-Smith 1989: 49), the men can be seen as behaving in a way that will impress masculine associates with their own fearlessness in flouting social norms. The men insult one another to demonstrate their own bravery, but if they are insulted in return they risk humiliation. The risk that they are taking in insulting one another is a risk that James and Saville-Smith argue is central to many male leisure time activities.

James and Saville-Smith cite a passage from Mataira (1987) in which Mataira notes that men in a small North Island East Coast rugby club use ritualized violence in the game 'argy-bargy' where group members knock one another to the ground to signal their allegiance to their mateship group. I think that the verbal sparring that goes on between the males in my data is a verbal form of this same game. By knocking one another down with words the men are signalling their solidarity and their mateship. I would add from my knowledge of this group that the verbal sparring sometimes becomes physical and this seems to be enjoyed by the particip-ants as much as their verbal arguments.

Conclusion

From the data that I have gathered I have argued that men and women in same-sex interaction behave very differently when they gossip. Both these groups however seem to have the same goals for their interaction. Speakers in both wish to demon-strate their membership of the group and the solidarity that they feel with the other members. The women do this by employing well recognized positive politeness strategies. However, the men in my sample, by these standards, appear to be behav-ing in an anti-social and impolite way. It seems likely they are using different norms.

The men's norms are those of a masculine mateship culture which requires dis-plays of masculine fearlessness and power. These displays commonly manifest them-selves in the form of abuse and challenges. The men did not spend all their time openly challenging and abusing one another, but even when their interaction was more peaceful, it was not cooperative in the same way as the women's interaction. The men showed their support for other speakers by failing to prevent them from speaking, rather than by encouraging them to speak.

Members of each group were well aware of their own group's norms, but I am not so sure that they were aware of the norms of the other group. At first when I listened to the male data I found the challenges, abuse and lack of support rather alien. The men that I taped commented to me that they felt that the way women talked behind each other's backs was equally alien to them. We both felt that our own sex group's norms were the more friendly and more acceptable norms. These differing models of supportive interaction then could be one source of miscommunication between the sexes (see Tannen 1990). Men may not actually be ignoring women when they speak, but simply failing to give them the feedback that they expect in a supportive environment. Women may not be 'two faced' when they agree with an interlocuter, only to criticize them when they are no longer present. They are simply maximizing the common ground between them and their interlocuter, while at the same time expressing their own feelings.

The conventional linguistic models of verbal politeness do not account for the competitive and less supportive aspects of male gossip. What is going on on the surface of these interactions seems to be totally at variance with the behaviour that established models describe. These men are not seen by one another as behaving in an unfriendly manner. They are conforming to what they expect of each other. Their behaviour is interpreted as supportive and appropriate. In accounting for the line between acceptable challenges and abuse and true aggression, it seems possible that a new approach will be needed.

In this project I have considered gossip only in single-sex groups. It would be interesting to consider the features of the two groups' styles in mixed interactions. Are the norms of one sex used more than the others? Or is an altogether new set of norms established? Michael King comments that he was taught that men were to be more polite when in the company of women than with men (1988: 138). Now that men and women share a wider range of environments, this double standard may no longer be applicable.

REFERENCES

Brown, Penelope and Stephen Levinson (1978) Universals in language usage: politeness phenomena. In Esther Goody (ed.) *Questions and Politeness. Strategies in Social Interaction.* Cambridge: Cambridge University Press. 56–289.

Gluckman, Max (1963) Gossip and scandal. *Current Anthropology* 4: 307–316.

Holmes, Janet (1989) Stirring up the dust: the importance of sex as a variable in the ESL classroom. *Proceedings of the ATESOL 6th Summer School, Sydney.* Vol. 1: 4–39.

James, Bev and Kay Saville-Smith (1989) *Gender Culture and Power.* Auckland: Oxford University Press.

Jones, Deborah (1975) Gossip: A Perspective on Women's Speech and Writings. Unpublished essay paper contributing to MA Hons in English: Department of English, Victoria University of Wellington.

Jones, Deborah (1980) Gossip: notes on women's oral culture. In Cheris Kramarae (ed.) *The Voices and Words of Women and Men.* Oxford: Pergamon. 193–198.

King, Michael (1988) Contradictions. In Michael King (ed.) *One of the Boys? Changing Views of Masculinity in New Zealand.* Auckland: Heinemann. 135–155.

Mataira, P. (1987) *A Study of Alcohol Consumption on Maraes and of Contemporary Drinking Patterns in Ruatoria.* M.Phil. Thesis. Department of Sociology, Massey University, Palmerston North.

Tannen, Deborah (1990) *You Just Don't Understand. Women and Men in Conversation.* New York: William Morrow.

18

Performing Gender Identity: Young Men's Talk and the Construction of Heterosexual Masculinity

Deborah Cameron

Introduction

In 1990, a 21-year-old student in a language and gender class I was teaching at a college in the southern USA tape-recorded a sequence of casual conversation among five men; himself and four friends. This young man, whom I will call 'Danny',[1] had decided to investigate whether the informal talk of male friends would bear out generalizations about 'men's talk' that are often encountered in discussions of gender differences in conversational style – for example that it is competitive, hierarchically organized, centres on 'impersonal' topics and the exchange of information, and foregrounds speech genres such as joking, trading insults and sports statistics.

Danny reported that the stereotype of all-male interaction was borne out by the data he recorded. He gave his paper the title 'Wine, women, and sports'. Yet although I could agree that the data did contain the stereotypical features he reported, the more I looked at it, the more I saw other things in it too. Danny's analysis was not inaccurate, his conclusions were not unwarranted, but his description of the data was (in both senses) *partial*: it was shaped by expectations that caused some things to leap out of the record as 'significant', while other things went unremarked.

I am interested in the possibility that Danny's selective reading of his data was not just the understandable error of an inexperienced analyst. Analysis is never done without preconceptions, we can never be absolutely non-selective in our observations, and where the object of observation and analysis has to do with gender it is extraordinarily difficult to subdue certain expectations.

One might speculate, for example, on why the vignettes of 'typical' masculine and feminine behaviour presented in popular books like Deborah Tannen's *You Just Don't Understand* (1990) are so often apprehended as immediately *recognizable*.[2] Is it because we have actually witnessed these scenarios occurring in real life, or is it because we can so readily supply the cultural script that makes them meaningful and 'typical'? One argument for the latter possibility is that if you *reverse* the genders in Tannen's anecdotes, it is still possible to supply a script which makes sense of the alleged gender difference. For example, Tannen remarks on men's reluctance to ask for directions while driving, and attributes it to men's greater concern for status (asking for help suggests helplessness). But if, as an experiment, you tell people it is women rather than men who are more reluctant to ask for directions, they will have no difficulty coming up with a different and equally plausible explanation – for instance that the reluctance reflects a typically feminine desire to avoid imposing on others, or perhaps a well-founded fear of stopping to talk to strangers.[3]

What this suggests is that the behaviour of men and women, whatever its substance may happen to be in any specific instance, is invariably read through a more general discourse on gender difference itself. That discourse is subsequently invoked to *explain* the pattern of gender differentiation in people's behaviour; whereas it might be more enlightening to say the discourse *constructs* the differentiation, makes it visible *as* differentiation.[4]

I want to propose that conversationalists themselves often do the same thing I have just suggested analysts do. Analysts construct stories about other people's behaviour, with a view to making it exemplify certain patterns of gender difference; conversationalists construct stories about themselves and others, with a view to performing certain kinds of gender identity.

Identity and Performativity

In 1990, the philosopher Judith Butler published an influential book called *Gender Trouble: Feminism and the Subversion of Identity*. Butler's essay is a postmodernist reconceptualization of gender, and it makes use of a concept familiar to linguists and discourse analysts from speech-act theory: *performativity*. For Butler, gender is *performative* – in her suggestive phrase, 'constituting the identity it is purported to be'. Just as J. L. Austin (1961) maintained that illocutions like 'I promise' do not describe a pre-existing state of affairs but actually bring one into being, so Butler claims that 'feminine' and 'masculine' are not what we are, nor traits we *have*, but effects we produce by way of particular things we *do*: 'Gender is the repeated stylization of the body, a set of repeated acts within a rigid regulatory frame which congeal over time to produce the appearance of substance, of a "natural" kind of being' (p. 33).

This extends the traditional feminist account whereby gender is socially constructed rather than 'natural', famously expressed in Simone de Beauvoir's dictum that 'one is not born, but rather becomes a woman'. Butler is saying that 'becoming a woman' (or a man) is not something you accomplish once and for all at an early stage of life. Gender has constantly to be reaffirmed and publicly displayed by repeatedly performing particular acts in accordance with the cultural norms (themselves historically and socially constructed, and consequently variable) which define 'masculinity' and 'femininity'.

This 'performative' model sheds an interesting light on the phenomenon of gendered *speech*. Speech too is a 'repeated stylization of the body'; the 'masculine' and 'feminine' styles of talking identified by researchers might be thought of as the 'congealed' result of repeated acts by social actors who are striving to constitute themselves as 'proper' men and women. Whereas sociolinguistics traditionally assumes that people talk the way they do because of who they (already) are, the postmodernist approach suggests that people are who they are because of (among other things) the way they talk. This shifts the focus away from a simple cataloguing of differences between men and women to a subtler and more complex inquiry into how people use linguistic resources to produce gender differentiation. It also obliges us to attend to the 'rigid regulatory frame' within which people must make their choices – the norms that define what kinds of language are possible, intelligible and appropriate resources for performing masculinity or femininity.

A further advantage of this approach is that it acknowledges the instability and variability of gender identities, and therefore of the behaviour in which those identities are performed. While Judith Butler rightly insists that gender is regulated and policed by rather rigid social norms, she does not reduce men and women to automata, programmed by their early socialization to repeat forever the appropriate gendered behaviour, but treats them as conscious agents who may – albeit often at some social cost – engage in acts of transgression, subversion and resistance. As active producers rather than passive reproducers of gendered behaviour, men and women may use their awareness of the gendered meanings that attach to particular ways of speaking and acting to produce a variety of effects. This is important, because few, if any, analysts of data on men's and women's speech would maintain that the differences are as clear-cut and invariant as one might gather from such oft-cited dichotomies as 'competitive/cooperative' and 'report talk/rapport talk'. People *do* perform gender differently in different contexts, and do sometimes behave in ways we would normally associate with the 'other' gender. The conversation to which we now turn is a notable case in point.

The Conversation: Wine, Women, Sports . . . and Other Men

The five men who took part in the conversation, and to whom I will give the pseudonyms Al, Bryan, Carl, Danny and Ed, were demographically a homogeneous group: white, middle-class American suburbanites aged 21, who attended the same university and belonged to the same social network on campus. This particular conversation occurred in the context of one of their commonest shared leisure activities: watching sports at home on television.[5]

Throughout the period covered by the tape-recording there is a basketball game on screen, and participants regularly make reference to what is going on in the game. Sometimes these references are just brief interpolated comments, which do not disrupt the flow of ongoing talk on some other topic; sometimes they lead to extended discussion. At all times, however, it is a legitimate conversational move to comment on the basketball game. The student who collected the data drew attention to the status of sport as a resource for talk available to North American men of all classes and racial/ethnic groups, to strangers as well as friends, suggesting that 'sports talk' is a typically 'masculine' conversational genre in the US, something all culturally competent males know how to do.

But 'sports talk' is by no means the only kind of talk being done. The men also recount the events of their day – what classes they had and how these went; they discuss mundane details of their domestic arrangements, such as who is going to pick up groceries; there is a debate about the merits of a certain kind of wine; there are a couple of longer narratives, notably one about an incident when two men sharing a room each invited a girlfriend back without their roommate's knowledge – and discovered this at the most embarrassing moment possible. Danny's title 'Wine, women, and sports' is accurate insofar as all these subjects are discussed at some length.

When one examines the data, however, it becomes clear there is one very significant omission in Danny's title. Apart from basketball, the single most prominent theme in the recorded conversation, as measured by the amount of time devoted to it, is 'gossip': discussion of several persons not present but known to the participants, with a strong focus on critically examining these individuals' appearance, dress, social behaviour and sexual mores. Like the conversationalists themselves, the individuals under discussion are all men. Unlike the conversationalists, however, the individuals under discussion are identified as 'gay'.

The topic of 'gays' is raised by Ed, only a few seconds into the tape-recorded conversation (6):[6]

ED: Mugsy Bogues (.) my name is Lloyd Gompers I am a homosexual (.) you know what the (.) I saw the new Remnant I should have grabbed you know the title? Like the head thing?

'Mugsy Bogues' (the name of a basketball player) is an acknowledgement of the previous turn, which concerned the on-screen game. Ed's next comment appears off-topic, but he immediately supplies a rationale for it, explaining that he 'saw the new Remnant' – *The Remnant* being a deliberately provocative right-wing campus newspaper whose main story that week had been an attack on the 'Gay Ball', a dance sponsored by the college's Gay Society.

The next few turns are devoted to establishing a shared view of the Gay Ball and of homosexuality generally. Three of the men, Al, Bryan and Ed, are actively involved in this exchange. A typical sequence is the following (14–16):

AL: gays=
ED: =gays w[hy? that's what it should read [gays why?
BRYAN: [gays]   [I know]

What is being established as 'shared' here is a view of gays as alien (that is, the group defines itself as heterosexual and puzzled by homosexuality: 'gays, why?'), and also to some extent comical. Danny comments at one point, 'it's hilarious', and Ed caps the sequence discussing the Gay Ball (23–5) with the witticism:

. . . .

ED: the question is who wears the boutonnière and who wears the corsage, flip for it? or do they both just wear flowers coz they're fruits

. . . .

It is at this point that Danny introduces the theme that will dominate the conversation for some time: gossip about individual men who are said to be gay. Referring to the only other man in his language and gender class, Danny begins (27):

. . . .

DANNY: My boy Ronnie was uh speaking up on the male perspective today (.) way too much

. . . .

The section following this contribution is structured around a series of references to other 'gay' individuals known to the participants as classmates. Bryan mentions 'the most effeminate guy I've ever met' (29) and 'that really gay guy in our Age of Revolution class' (34). Ed remarks that 'you have never seen more homos than we have in our class. Homos, dykes, homos, dykes, everybody is a homo or a dyke' (64). He then focuses on a 'fat, queer, goofy guy . . . [who's] as gay as night' [*sic*] (78–80), and on a 'blond hair, snide little queer weird shit' (98), who is further described as a 'butt pirate'. Some of these references, but not all, initiate an extended discussion of the individual concerned. The content of these discussions will bear closer examination.

'The antithesis of man'

One of the things I initially found most puzzling about the whole 'gays' sequence was that the group's criteria for categorizing people as gay appeared to have little to do with those people's known or suspected sexual preferences or practices. The terms 'butt pirate' and 'butt cutter' were used, but surprisingly seldom; it was unclear to me that the individuals referred to really were homosexual, and in the one case where I actually knew the subject of discussion, I seriously doubted it.

Most puzzling is an exchange between Bryan and Ed about the class where 'everybody is a homo or a dyke', in which they complain that 'four homos' are continually 'hitting on' (making sexual overtures to) one of the women, described as 'the ugliest-ass bitch in the history of the world' (82–9). One might have thought that a defining feature of a 'homo' would be his lack of interest in 'hitting on' women. Yet no one seems aware of any problem or contradiction in this exchange.

I think this is because the deviance indicated for this group by the term 'gay' is not so much *sexual* deviance as *gender* deviance. Being 'gay' means failing to measure up to the group's standards of masculinity or femininity. This is why it makes sense to call someone '*really* gay': unlike same- versus other-sex preference, conformity to gender norms can be a matter of degree. It is also why hitting on an 'ugly-ass bitch' can be classed as 'homosexual' behaviour – proper masculinity requires that the object of public sexual interest be not just female, but minimally attractive.

Applied by the group to men, 'gay' refers in particular to insufficiently masculine appearance, clothing and speech. To illustrate this I will reproduce a longer sequence of conversation about the 'really gay guy in our Age of Revolution class', which ends with Ed declaring: 'he's the antithesis of man'.

· ·

BRYAN: uh you know that really gay guy in our Age of
Revolution class who sits in front of us? he wore
shorts again, by the way, it's like 42 degrees out he
wore shorts again [laughter] [Ed: That guy] it's like
a speedo, he wears a speedo to class (.) he's got
incredibly skinny legs [Ed: it's worse] you know=
ED: =you know
like those shorts women volleyball players wear? it's
like those (.) it's l[ike

· ·

BRYAN: [you know what's even more ridicu[lous? when
ED: [French cut spandex]

· ·

BRYAN: you wear those shorts and like a parka on . . .
(5 lines omitted)

· ·

BRYAN: he's either got some condition that he's got to
like have his legs exposed at all times or else he's
got really good legs=
ED: =he's probably he'[s like
CARL: [he really likes

· ·

BRYAN: =he
ED: =he's like at home combing his leg hairs=
CARL: his legs=

· ·

BRYAN: he doesn't have any leg hair though=   [*yes* and oh
ED: =he *real* [*ly* likes

· ·

ED: his legs=
AL: =very long very white and very skinny

· ·

BRYAN: those ridiculous Reeboks that are always (indeciph)
and goofy white socks always striped=   [tube socks
ED: =that's [right

· ·

ED: he's the antithesis of man

· ·

In order to demonstrate that certain individuals are 'the antithesis of man', the group engages in a kind of conversation that might well strike us as the antithesis of 'men's talk'. It is unlike the 'wine, women, and sports' stereotype of men's talk – indeed, rather closer to the stereotype of 'women's talk' – in various ways, some obvious, and some less so.

The obvious ways in which this sequence resembles conventional notions of 'women's talk' concern its purpose and subject-matter. This is talk about people, not things, and 'rapport talk' rather than 'report talk' – the main point is clearly not to exchange information. It is 'gossip', and serves one of the most common purposes of gossip, namely affirming the solidarity of an in-group by constructing absent others as an out-group, whose behaviour is minutely examined and found wanting.

The specific subjects on which the talk dwells are conventionally 'feminine' ones: clothing and bodily appearance. The men are caught up in a contradiction: their criticism of the 'gays' centres on their unmanly interest in displaying their bodies, and the inappropriate garments they choose for this purpose (bathing costumes worn to class, shorts worn in cold weather with parkas which render the effect ludicrous, clothing which resembles the outfits of 'women volleyball players'). The implication is that real men just pull on their jeans and leave it at that. But in order to pursue this line of criticism, the conversationalists themselves must show an acute awareness of such 'unmanly' concerns as styles and materials ('French cut spandex', 'tube socks'), what kind of clothes go together, and which men have 'good legs'. They are impelled, paradoxically, to talk about men's bodies as a way of demonstrating their own total lack of sexual interest in those bodies.

The less obvious ways in which this conversation departs from stereotypical notions of 'men's talk' concern its *formal* features. Analyses of men's and women's speech style are commonly organized around a series of global oppositions, e.g. men's talk is 'competitive', whereas women's is 'cooperative'; men talk to gain 'status', whereas women talk to forge 'intimacy' and 'connection'; men do 'report talk' and women 'rapport talk'. Analysts working with these oppositions typically identify certain formal or organizational features of talk as markers of 'competition' and 'co-operation' etc. The analyst then examines which kinds of features predominate in a set of conversational data, and how they are being used.

In the following discussion, I too will make use of the conventional oppositions as tools for describing data, but I will be trying to build up an argument that their use is problematic. The problem is not merely that the men in my data fail to fit their gender stereotype perfectly. More importantly, I think it is often the stereotype itself that underpins analytic judgements that a certain form is cooperative rather than competitive, or that people are seeking status rather than connection in their talk. As I observed about Deborah Tannen's vignettes, many instances of behaviour will support either interpretation, or both; we use the speaker's gender, and our beliefs about what sort of behaviour makes sense for members of that gender, to rule some interpretations in and others out.

Cooperation

Various scholars, notably Jennifer Coates (1989, reprinted in this volume, p. 226), have remarked on the 'cooperative' nature of informal talk among female friends, drawing attention to a number of linguistic features which are prominent in data on all-female groups. Some of these, like hedging and the use of epistemic modals, are signs of attention to others' face, aimed at minimizing conflict and securing agreement. Others, such as latching of turns, simultaneous speech where this is not interpreted by participants as a violation of turn-taking rights (cf. Edelsky, 1981), and the repetition or recycling of lexical items and phrases across turns, are signals that a conversation is a 'joint production': that participants are building on one another's contributions so that ideas are felt to be group property rather than the property of a single speaker.

On these criteria, the conversation here must be judged as highly cooperative. For example, in the extract reproduced above, a strikingly large number of turns (around half) begin with 'you know' and/or contain the marker 'like' ('you know like those shorts women volleyball players wear?'). The functions of these items (especially 'like') in younger Americans' English are complex and multiple,[7] and may include the cooperative, mitigating/face-protecting functions that Coates and Janet Holmes (1984) associate with hedging. Even where they are not clearly hedges, however, in this interaction they function in ways that relate to the building of group involvement and consensus. They often seem to mark information as 'given' within the group's discourse (that is, 'you know', 'like', 'X' presupposes that the addressee is indeed familiar with X); 'you know' has the kind of hearer-oriented affective function (taking others into account or inviting their agreement) which Holmes attributes to certain tag-questions; while 'like' in addition seems to function for these speakers as a marker of high involvement. It appears most frequently at moments when the interactants are, by other criteria such as intonation, pitch, loudness, speech rate, incidence of simultaneous speech, and of 'strong' or taboo language, noticeably excited, such as the following (82–9):

. . . .

ED: he's I mean he's **like** a real artsy fartsy fag he's **like** (indeciph) he's so gay he's got
         this **like** really high voice and wire rim glasses and he sits next to the ugliest-ass
         bitch in the history of the world

. . . .

ED: [and
BRYAN: [and they're all hitting on her too, **like** four

. . . .

ED: [I know it's **like** four homos hitting on her
BRYAN: guys [hitting on her

. . . .

It is also noticeable throughout the long extract reproduced earlier how much latching and simultaneous speech there is, as compared to other forms of turn transition involving either short or long pauses and gaps, or interruptions which silence the interruptee. Latching – turn transition without pause or overlap – is often taken as a mark of cooperation because in order to latch a turn so precisely onto the preceding turn, the speaker has to attend closely to others' contributions.

The last part of the reproduced extract, discussing the 'really gay' guy's legs, is an excellent example of jointly produced discourse, as the speakers cooperate to build a detailed picture of the legs and what is worn on them, a picture which overall could not be attributed to any single speaker. This sequence contains many instances of latching, repetition of one speaker's words by another speaker (Ed recycles Carl's whole turn, 'he really likes his legs', with added emphasis), and it also contains something that is relatively rare in the conversation as a whole, repeated tokens of hearer support like 'yes' and 'that's right'.[8]

There are, then, points of resemblance worth remarking on between these men's talk and similar talk among women as reported by previous studies. The question does arise, however, whether this male conversation has the other important hall-mark of women's gossip, namely an egalitarian or non-hierarchical organization of the floor.

Competition

In purely quantitative terms, this conversation cannot be said to be egalitarian. The extracts reproduced so far are representative of the whole insofar as they show Ed and Bryan as the dominant speakers, while Al and Carl contribute fewer and shorter turns (Danny is variable; there are sequences where he contributes very little, but when he talks he often contributes turns as long as Ed's and Bryan's, and he also initiates topics). Evidence thus exists to support an argument that there is a hier-archy in this conversation, and there is competition, particularly between the two dominant speakers, Bryan and Ed (and to a lesser extent Ed and Danny). Let us pursue this by looking more closely at Ed's behaviour.

Ed introduces the topic of homosexuality, and initially attempts to keep 'owner-ship' of it. He cuts off Danny's first remark on the subject with a reference to *The Remnant*: 'what was the article? cause you know they bashed them they were like'. At this point Danny interrupts: it is clearly an interruption because in this context the preferred interpretation of 'like' is quotative (see note 7) – Ed is about to repeat what the gay-bashing article in *The Remnant* said. In addition to interrupting so that Ed falls silent, Danny contradicts Ed, saying 'they didn't actually (.) cut into them big'. A little later on during the discussion of the Gay Ball, Ed makes use of a common competitive strategy, the joke or witty remark which 'caps' other contributions (the 'flowers and fruits' joke at 23–5, quoted above). This, however, elicits no laughter, no matching jokes and indeed no take-up of any kind. It is followed by a pause and a change of direction if not of subject, as Danny begins the gossip that will dominate talk for several minutes.

This immediately elicits a matching contribution from Bryan. As he and Danny talk, Ed makes two unsuccessful attempts to regain the floor. One, where he utters the prefatory remark 'I'm gonna be very honest' (20), is simply ignored. His second strategy is to ask (about the person Bryan and Danny are discussing) 'what's this guy's last name?' (30). First Bryan asks him to repeat the question, then Danny replies 'I don't know what the hell it is' (32).

A similar pattern is seen in the long extract reproduced above, where Ed makes two attempts to interrupt Bryan's first turn ('That guy' and 'it's worse'), neither of which succeeds. He gets the floor eventually by using the 'you know, like' strategy. And from that point, Ed does orient more to the norms of joint production; he overlaps others to produce simultaneous speech but does not interrupt; he produces more latched turns, recyclings and support tokens.

So far I have been arguing that even if the speakers, or some of them, compete, they are basically engaged in a collaborative and solidary enterprise (reinforcing the bonds within the group by denigrating people outside it), an activity in which all speakers participate, even if some are more active than others. Therefore I have drawn attention to the presence of 'cooperative' features, and have argued that more extreme forms of hierarchical and competitive behaviour are not rewarded by the group. I could, indeed, have argued that by the end, Ed and Bryan are not so much 'competing' – after all, their contributions are not antagonistic to one another but tend to reinforce one another – as engaging in a version of the 'joint production of discourse'.

Yet the data might also support a different analysis in which Ed and Bryan are simply *using* the collaborative enterprise of putting down gay men as an occasion to engage in verbal duelling where points are scored – against fellow group members rather than against the absent gay men – by dominating the floor and coming up with more and more extravagant put-downs. In this alternative analysis, Ed does not so much modify his behaviour as 'lose' his duel with Bryan. 'Joint production' or 'verbal duelling' – how do we decide?

Deconstructing oppositions

One response to the problem of competing interpretations raised above might be that the opposition I have been working with – 'competitive' versus 'cooperative' behaviour – is inherently problematic, particularly if one is taken to exclude the other. Conversation can and usually does contain both cooperative and competitive elements: one could argue (along with Grice, 1975) that talk must by definition involve a certain minimum of cooperation, and also that there will usually be some degree of competition among speakers, if not for the floor itself then for the attention or the approval of others (see also Hewitt, 1997).

The global competitive/cooperative opposition also encourages the lumping together under one heading or the other of things that could in principle be distinguished. 'Cooperation' might refer to agreement on the aims of talk, respect for other speakers' rights or support for their contributions; but there is not always perfect co-occurrence among these aspects, and the presence of any one of them need not rule out a 'competitive' element. Participants in a conversation or other speech event may compete with each other and at the same time be pursuing a shared project or common agenda (as in ritual insult sessions); they may be in severe disagreement but punctiliously observant of one another's speaking rights (as in a formal debate, say); they may be overtly supportive, and at the same time covertly hoping to score points for their supportiveness.

This last point is strangely overlooked in some discussions of women's talk. Women who pay solicitous attention to one another's face are often said to be seeking connection or good social relations *rather than* status; yet one could surely argue that attending to others' face and attending to one's own are not mutually exclusive here. The 'egalitarian' norms of female friendship groups are, like all norms, to some degree coercive: the rewards and punishments precisely concern one's status within the group (among women, however, this status is called 'popularity' rather than 'dominance'). A woman may gain status by displaying the correct degree of concern for others, and lose status by displaying too little concern for others and too much for herself. Arguably, it is gender-stereotyping that causes us to miss or minimize the status-seeking element in women friends' talk, and the connection-making dimension of men's.

How to do Gender with Language

I hope it will be clear by now that my intention in analysing male gossip is not to suggest that the young men involved have adopted a 'feminine' conversational style. On the contrary, the main theoretical point I want to make concerns the folly of making any such claim. To characterize the conversation I have been considering as 'feminine' on the basis that it bears a significant resemblance to conversations among women friends would be to miss the most important point about it, that it is not only *about* masculinity, it is a sustained performance *of* masculinity. What is important in gendering talk is the 'performative gender work' the talk is doing; its role in constituting people as gendered subjects.

To put matters in these terms is not to deny that there may be an empirically observable association between a certain genre or style of speech and speakers of a particular gender. In practice this is undeniable. But we do need to ask: in virtue of what does the association hold? Can we give an account that will not be vitiated by cases where it does *not* hold? For it seems to me that conversations like the one I have analysed leave, say, Deborah Tannen's contention that men do not do 'women's talk', because they simply *do not know how*, looking lame and unconvincing. If men rarely engage in a certain kind of talk, an explanation is called for; but if they do engage in it even very occasionally, an explanation in terms of pure ignorance will not do.

I suggest the following explanation. Men and women do not live on different planets, but are members of cultures in which a large amount of discourse about gender is constantly circulating. They do not only learn, and then mechanically reproduce, ways of speaking 'appropriate' to their own sex; they learn a much broader set of gendered meanings that attach in rather complex ways to differ-ent ways of speaking, and they produce their own behaviour in the light of those meanings.

This behaviour will vary. Even the individual who is most unambiguously com-mitted to traditional notions of gender has a range of possible gender identities to draw on. Performing masculinity or femininity 'appropriately' cannot mean giving exactly the same performance regardless of the circumstances. It may involve differ-ent strategies in mixed and single-sex company, in private and in public settings, in the various social positions (parent, lover, professional, friend) that someone might regularly occupy in the course of everyday life.

Since gender is a relational term, and the minimal requirement for 'being a man' is 'not being a woman', we may find that in many circumstances, men are under pressure to constitute themselves as masculine linguistically by avoiding forms of talk whose primary association is with women/femininity. But this is not invariant, which begs the question: under what circumstances does the contrast with women lose its salience as a constraint on men's behaviour? When can men do so-called 'feminine' talk without threatening their constitution as men? Are there cases when it might actually be to their advantage to do this?

When and Why do Men Gossip?

Many researchers have reported that both sexes engage in gossip, since its social functions (like affirming group solidarity and serving as an unofficial conduit for information) are of universal relevance, but its cultural meaning (for us) is undeni-ably 'feminine'. Therefore we might expect to find most men avoiding it, or disguis-ing it as something else, especially in mixed settings where they are concerned to mark their difference from women (see Johnson and Finlay, 1997). In the conver-sation discussed above, however, there are no women for the men to differentiate themselves from; whereas *there is* the perceived danger that so often accompanies Western male homosociality: homosexuality. Under these circumstances perhaps it becomes acceptable to transgress one gender norm ('men don't gossip, gossip is for girls') in order to affirm what in this context is a more important norm ('men in all-male groups must unambiguously display their heterosexual orientation').

In these speakers' understanding of gender, gay men, like women, provide a con-trast group against whom masculinity can be defined. This principle of contrast seems to set limits on the permissibility of gossip for these young men. Although they dis-cuss other men besides the 'gays' – professional basketball players – they could not be said to gossip about them. They talk about the players' skills and their records, not their appearance, personal lives or sexual activities. Since the men admire the basketball players, identifying *with* them rather than *against* them, such talk would border dangerously on what for them is obviously taboo: desire for other men.

Ironically, it seems likely that the despised gay men are the *only* men about whom these male friends can legitimately talk among themselves in such intimate terms without compromising the heterosexual masculinity they are so anxious to display – though in a different context, say with their girlfriends, they might be able to discuss the basketball players differently. The presence of a woman, especially a heterosexual partner, displaces the dread spectre of homosexuality, and makes other kinds of talk possible; though by the same token her presence might make certain kinds of talk that take place among men *im*possible. What counts as acceptable talk for men is a complex matter in which all kinds of contextual variables play a part.

In this context – a private conversation among male friends – it could be argued that to gossip, either about your sexual exploits with women or about the repulsiveness of gay men (these speakers do both), is not just one way, but the most appropriate way to display heterosexual masculinity. In another context (in public, or with a larger and less close-knit group of men), the same objective might well be pursued through explicitly agonistic strategies, such as yelling abuse at women or gays in the street, or exchanging sexist and homophobic jokes. *Both* strategies could be said to do performative gender work: in terms of what they do for the speakers involved, one is not more 'masculine' than the other, they simply belong to different settings in which heterosexual masculinity may (or must) be put on display.

Conclusion

I hope that my discussion of the conversation I have analysed makes the point that it is unhelpful for linguists to continue to use models of gendered speech which imply that masculinity and femininity are monolithic constructs, automatically giving rise to predictable (and utterly different) patterns of verbal interaction. At the same time, I hope it might make us think twice about the sort of analysis that implicitly seeks the meaning (and sometimes the *value*) of an interaction among men or women primarily in the style, rather than the substance, of what is said. For although, as I noted earlier in relation to Judith Butler's work, it is possible for men and women to performatively subvert or resist the prevailing codes of gender, there can surely be no convincing argument that this is what Danny and his friends are doing. Their conversation is animated by entirely traditional anxieties about being seen at all times as red-blooded heterosexual males: not women and not queers. Their skill as performers does not alter the fact that what they perform is the same old gendered script.

NOTES

1   Because the student concerned is one of the speakers in the conversation I analyse, and the nature of the conversation makes it desirable to conceal participants' identities (indeed, this was one of the conditions on which the data were collected and subsequently passed on to me), I will not give his real name here, but I want to acknowledge his generosity in making his recording and transcript available to me, and to thank him for a number of insights I gained by discussing the data with him as well as by reading his

paper. I am also grateful to the other young men who participated. All their names, and the names of other people they mention, have been changed, and all pseudonyms used are (I hope) entirely fictitious.

2   I base this assessment of reader response on my own research with readers of Tannen's book (see Cameron, 1995, ch. 5), on non-scholarly reviews of the book, and on reader studies of popular self-help generally (e.g. Lichterman, 1992; Simonds, 1992).

3   I am indebted to Penelope Eckert for describing this 'thought experiment', which she has used in her own teaching (though the specific details of the example are not an exact rendition of Eckert's observations).

4   The German linguist Karsta Frank (1992) has provocatively argued that so-called gender differences in speech-style arise *exclusively* in reception: women and men are heard differently, as opposed to speaking differently. I do not entirely accept Frank's very strong position on this point, but I do think she has drawn attention to a phenomenon of some importance.

5   I mention that this was 'at home' because in the United States it is also common for men, individually or in groups, to watch televised sports in public places such as bars and even laundromats; but this particular conversation would probably not have happened in a public setting with others present. It appears to be a recurrent feature of male friends' talk that the men are engaged in some other activity as well as talking. The Swedish researcher Kerstin Nordenstam, who has an impressive corpus comprising data from twelve different single-sex friendship groups, has found that the men are far less likely than the women to treat conversation as the exclusive or primary purpose of a social gathering. Many of the women's groups recorded for Nordenstam were 'sewing circles' – a traditional kind of informal social organization for women in Sweden – but they frequently did not sew, and defined their aim simply as 'having fun'; whereas the men's groups might meet under no particular rubric, but they still tended to organize their talk around an activity such as playing cards or games. (Thanks to Kerstin Nordenstam for this information.)

6   Numbers in parenthesis refer to the lines in the original transcript. Transcription conventions are given in Transcription Conventions 2, p. xx.

7   For example, *like* has a 'quotative' function among younger US speakers, as in 'and she's like [= she said], stop bugging me, and I'm like, what do you mean stop bugging you?'. This and other uses of the item have become popularly stereotyped as markers of membership in the so-called 'slacker' generation.

8   It is a rather consistent research finding that men use such minimal responses significantly less often than women, and in this respect the present data conform to expectations – there are very few minimal responses of any kind. I would argue, however, that active listenership, involvement and support are not *absent* in the talk of this group; they are marked by other means such as high levels of latching/simultaneous speech, lexical recycling and the use of *like*.

REFERENCES

Austin, J. L. (1961) *How to Do Things with Words*. Oxford: Clarendon Press.
Butler, Judith (1990) *Gender Trouble: Feminism and the Subversion of Identity*. New York: Routledge.
Cameron, Deborah (1995) *Verbal Hygiene*. London: Routledge.

Coates, Jennifer (1989) 'Gossip revisited', pp. 94–121 in J. Coates and D. Cameron (eds) *Women in Their Speech Communities*. London: Longman.

Edelsky, Carole (1981) 'Who's got the floor?' *Language in Society*, 10, 3, 383–422.

Frank, Karsta (1992) *Sprachgewalt*. Tubingen: Max Niemeyer Verlag.

Grice, H. P. (1975) 'Logic and conversation', pp. 41–58 in P. Cole and J. Morgan (eds) *Syntax and Semantics*, vol. 3: *Speech Acts*. New York: Academic Press.

Hewitt, Roger (1997) ' "Box-out" and "taxing" ', pp. 27–46 in Sally Johnson and Ulrike Hanna Meinhof (eds) *Language and Masculinity*. Oxford: Blackwell.

Holmes, Janet (1984) 'Hedging your bets and sitting on the fence: some evidence for hedges as support structures'. *Te Reo*, 27, 47–62.

Johnson, Sally and Finlay, Frank (1997) 'Do men gossip? An analysis of football talk on television', pp. 130–43 in Sally Johnson and Ulrike Hanna Meinhof (eds) *Language and Masculinity*. Oxford: Blackwell.

Lichterman, Paul (1992) 'Self-help reading as a thin culture'. *Media, Culture and Society*, 14, 421–47.

Simonds, Wendy (1992) *Women and Self-Help Culture: Reading between the Lines*. New Brunswick, NJ: Rutgers University Press.

Tannen, Deborah (1990) *You Just Don't Understand: Women and Men in Conversation*. New York: Ballantine Books.

19

Sporting Formulae
in New Zealand English:
Two Models of Male Solidarity

Koenraad Kuiper

Introduction

This is a study of two ways in which adult males in New Zealand become members of groups. It is, in other words, a study in solidarity. The models which will be put forward both achieve the same ends: induction into a group through the acquisition of certain routines, specifically certain linguistic routines. These routines are most clearly seen in the acquisition and use of a set of routine formulae (Coulmas 1979, 1982) which exemplify the strategies the two groups use to make men members of their groups. The two strategies are quite different. In one group, formulae are used to save face; specifically, the face of players in a recreational volleyball squad. In the other group, sexual humiliation is used as a means of creating group solidarity through the loss of face the individuals who belong to the group suffer.

Preliminary Remarks

If I use the New Zealand English formula *Gidday* with a wink and a characteristic quick southeast to northwest movement of the head, the conditions of use for such a greeting are relatively specific; it is an informal greeting to one with whom one is not intimate. It is not middle class but characteristically working class, and/or rural. It is often used when no response is expected.

While learning the linguistic aspects of such a formula can be regarded as a part of language acquisition, learning conditions of use is a function of acculturation:

> patterns of message construction, or 'ways of putting things', . . . are part of the very stuff that social relationships are made of (or, as some would prefer, crucial parts of the expression of social relationships). (Brown and Levinson 1978: 60)

In previous work (Kuiper and Haggo 1984) it has been shown that being an auctioneer involves mastering a set of specialised formulae used only for auctioning and, for each formula, mastering its conditions of use. It is clear from the speech of auctioneers that the acquisition of these formulae is almost sufficient to make one who has acquired them a member of a group whose identity is a partial function of such knowledge. To generalise, vocabulary acquisition is a function of socialisation and the particular sub-vocabularies which one acquires as a native are no exception.

As a consequence, group membership can be identified by particular kinds of vocabulary acquisition. But it is possible to take a further step in the case of some groups. There are groups which do not need to share a common vocabulary to be a group. For example, sports teams share a common goal of playing a particular game together for a particular purpose which may, for example, be recreational or competitive. Yet many sports teams develop a common vocabulary which is only tangentially related to the game the team is playing. Some formulae will be common to all those playing the particular game, or playing that game in a particular place or for a particular club. Other formulae may be unique to a particular team. Such formulae can serve primarily to create group solidarity. How they do that is the question posed in the present study.

Face Saving as a Strategy for Solidarity: Recreational Volleyball Formulae

The group which provides the model for the first pattern meets twice a week for recreational volleyball. Its members are all male employees of a large organisation and they come from all over the organisation. Few of them meet each other regularly in the normal course of events; in fact, many members of the group meet only through their membership of the group which plays recreational volleyball.

When the group meets to play there are no set teams, since attendance fluctuates. The official rules of the game are regarded as a guideline only for what is done. There is a set of common law rules which includes a number of the official rules and the absence of others as well as additional conventions developed over the years. As a result, overly legalistic members of the group tend either to adapt or to leave in frustration. The game is played for a set period rather than to win and frequently players do not know or care what the score is.

As well as playing volleyball, members of the group frequently talk and shout to and at each other during play. This verbal interaction is partly oral-formulaic in that the group knows a number of formulae which are used on a regular basis in the game. The inventory of formulae is not large and it is not the only way that the members of the group address each other. It is, however, an interesting indication of the dynamics of the group.

The formulae used in recreational volleyball are related to particular episodes in the game as it is played.

Start of game formula:

1. Our serve.

This is a formula very frequently used to start the game after the warm up.

Serving formulae:
There is a set of formulae used before a serve. Many of these are used only by particular individuals but they are recognised as belonging to the group.

2. They drop quickly.
3. Watch the spin on these.

These two formulae are spoken by the server and addressed to the receiving team to warn them of the quality of the coming serve.

4. Once today.

This formula is addressed to the server by a member of the receiving team and is an invitation to the server to serve into the net or out of bounds.

Formulae used between the gaining of a point and the next serve being taken:

5. It's like taking candy off a baby.

This formula is said by a member of the team which has just scored an easy point.

6. Always a winner.

This formula is used by the winner of a point when that point has been won by the unorthodox method of punching the ball over the net and the opposing team having failed to return it. It is also used ironically when the same tactic results in the ball going under or into the net or out of bounds. In such a case it is almost always used by someone in the team opposing the user of the punch tactic.

7. He's worth two to the opposition any day.

This formula is used with reference to one player only and is used by someone in the team opposing that in which this particular player plays. It is used when the particular player has made an error costing a point or a service turn.

8. Two points for that one.

This formula is used by a player when someone in his team has scored a point which is regarded as having been done particularly well.

9.   The old one, two, three.

This formula is used by a member of a team which has scored a point as a result of touching the ball on its side of the net the normal three times.

10.   The old sucker shot.

This formula is used by a member of a team when that team has just scored a point through a ball being directed into the net at close range by a member of the opposing team.

11.   Justice!

This formula is used when a team considers, after winning a point, that the previous point won by the opposing team was unfairly won (for example, if it was won as a result of someone insisting that the rules of the game should be invoked).

12.   Play the setups.

This formula is used by a member of a team when a player in that team who should know and be able to do better does not set the ball up for the other players in the team. Note that this is always a general exhortation and it is never said when a player is new to the group or relatively less able at volleyball.

13.   Where was the block on that one?

Used by a member of a team which has just lost a point to a particularly hard spike. Used ironically, since conventional blocking as used in actual volleyball is a rare occurrence in recreational volleyball particularly when the spike looks to be a hard one.

Scoring formula:

14.   14–3.

This formula is used, usually by the serving team, after a point has been scored, when the score has not been kept track of, or merely as a jocular way of confusing the opposition. (The winning point in a match is usually fifteen. The formula thus indicates that the team which has just won a point is only one point away from winning the game.)

There are other formulae which might be similarly analysed for their role in discourse. However, what is interesting about the above cases is the question of why they are used at all. They are clearly a response to situations in the game, but they serve no function in the game as game. The rules of volleyball explicitly forbid excessive calling on the court. Their use therefore has to be explained on grounds other than their role in the game. Their role can be explained in terms of the theory of politeness developed by Brown and Levinson (1978, 1987) who suggest that politeness is a way of saving face: either saving the speaker's face or the hearer's face. Face 'is the public self image that everyone wants to claim for himself, consisting of two related aspects:

(a) negative face . . . the freedom of action and freedom from imposition
(b) positive face: the positive consistent self image or 'personality' (crucially including the desire that this self image be appreciated and approved of) claimed by interactants'. (Brown and Levinson 1978: 66)

Let us call a face-threatening act which threatens positive face 'humiliating' and one which threatens negative face 'coercive'. Politeness strategies thus mitigate humiliating or coercive acts.

In social volleyball there are ample opportunities for the loss of positive face, that is, for humiliation. The players are not terribly proficient and therefore there are frequent errors. Since it is a game where a score is kept (even if in a perfunctory way), an error may result in a loss of positive face for the team, namely in defeat. Furthermore, the players are drawn from the whole of the organisational hierarchy and thus someone higher in the hierarchy may lose face in the eyes of people lower down, whereas people lower down may have their position on the hierarchy reinforced if they make playing errors of which their organisational superiors are aware. However, the purpose of the game is recreational and therefore some way has to be found for there to be no loss of face. Most of the formulae outlined above have this function if their relationship to the discourse is reanalysed in terms of politeness strategies.

The serving formulae tell the receiver (and everyone else) that the serves to come (which everyone knows to be suitably innocuous) may for the purposes of politeness be perceived as particularly dangerous. Thus, if a receiver fails to deal adequately with the serve there is no loss of face in that for the receiver. If the receiver does not fail, so much the more credit. The formula *on the line* which is said in the face of the evidence says to the player who has just served the ball out, that as far as the members of the player's team are concerned the serve was good, without it making any practical difference. The point is always conceded. Thus, the player who has served out saves face through the politeness strategy which is inherent in the use of the formula. The formula *justice!* might be used on the next exchange to show the server again that the serve was good in the eyes of team members, without there being faulty perception of the actual facts.

The formula *14–3* which is used after winning a point tells everyone that the score is of so little relevance that there is no loss of face in losing the game. (It also functions as a morale booster for one's own team, of course.) Even the formula *He's worth two to the opposition any day* can be regarded as a politeness formula since, although it expresses an element of censure against a particular player, it does so in terms which suggest that the player is of worth even if it is to the opposition team which uses this formulae. The fact that the censure does not come from the members of the censured player's own team allows a measure of face saving. Thus most of these formulae receive a functional explanation as face-saving politeness formulae.

What effect does the use of these formulae have? Clearly it has the potential to create group solidarity. Just simply learning the formulae of a small group can have this result, but in the case of these formulae it is even more likely, since players who are members of the group know, when they know the group's formulae, that the group has and uses the resources of a set of politeness formulae which will allow any player, regardless of status, to save face in potentially face-threatening situations. This makes belonging to the group agreeable. It is clear that a group whose members use such politeness strategies as the dominant mode of verbal interaction can be termed civilised.

Face-threatening Rituals of Sexual Humiliation as a Strategy for Solidarity: Rugby Football Locker Room Formulae of Address

The contrasting situation is based on the verbal interaction of members of a rugby team before and after a game or practice. The formulae here do not have specific links with episodes in the game. Instead they function in the banter that seems to pervade locker rooms. The examples which will be used here are modes of address, greetings and vocative formulae. The following are not the only modes of address, but they have been selected to illustrate a particular and dominant strategy:

15. ..., cock.
16. Morning girls.
17. ..., you fucking old woman.
18. ..., you fucking ugly girl.
19. If I left it any longer, cunts, you'd say I was fucking around.
20. You're late, cunt.
21. ..., you wanker.
22. ..., you bastard.
23. ... didn't catch the name; girl's blouse, was it?
24. ... fuck-face.
25. ... get a fucking great dog right up you.
26. ... you great penis.
27. Fuck off, wanker.

One dominant and characteristic function of these formulae is sexual humiliation; that is, these vocatives threaten the hearer's (and sometimes the speaker's) positive face in the sexual domain. This can be shown by an analysis of their ritual value. For example, a number of the formulae use as a form of address the word *wanker*.

Literally the word *wanker* in New Zealand English denotes a male who masturbates. But it is also used as a general term of abuse among New Zealand males. Masturbation is popularly regarded as a sign of sexual inadequacy. Therefore a wanker is one who is sexually inadequate. *Cunt*, like *wanker*, is also a popular form of abuse among these males. It denigrates a man's masculinity by apparently suggesting that he is a part of the female sexual anatomy. The phrase *get a great dog right up you* again denigrates male sexuality by suggesting that the one addressed will be subjected to anal intercourse by a large dog. Even the forms of address *cock* and *you great penis* are demeaning, since they suggest that the man being addressed is no more than a sexual organ. Since, in New Zealand society, the public exhibition of a penis is illegal, equating a man with a penis is to say that he himself is a proscribed form of sexual exhibition and thus a sexual embarrassment. Forms of address which equate men with women and girls hint at effeminacy and thus, it can be argued, at sexual inadequacy and impotence.

But why sexually humiliate one's team mates in the intimate surroundings of the locker room? Clearly, if the locker room is a place where one's sexuality is called into question in an arbitrary fashion, then the team all know the formulae of sexual humiliation and every member of the team knows that he can both use these formulae and be the object of their use. This, then, is a factor creating solidarity partly because mutual knowledge of a restricted vocabulary is involved but also because that vocabulary is coercive. It ensures that everyone who knows this vocabulary, that is all the members of the team, can, both in the privacy of the locker room and, potentially, outside it, damage any team member's face since, in New Zealand society, sexual humiliation is one of the most damaging actions social beings inflict on each other. Thus solidarity is created through fear of sexual humiliation: actual humiliation in private and potential humiliation in public. The way to avoid it is clear to team members; it is not to make mistakes, such as showing fear, in the game. This is, of course, always and only temporary since there are always further games.

We have here a clear case which runs counter to Brown and Levinson's assertion (1978: 65) that 'it will in general be to the mutual interest of two MPs (Model Persons) to maintain each other's face'. It may be that the men involved in the above strategy are not model persons. More likely they participate in a social group which does not value face within the group and instead uses potentially and actually face-threatening acts as a coercive strategy to maintain solidarity and discipline in a group which is involved in physically dangerous activity.[1] We can call this side of politeness phenomena 'the dark side'. The rituals of sexual humiliation thus promote solidarity by making all the men in a group which uses such rituals active and passive participants (perpetrators and bystanders) in a positive and negative face-threatening strategy. Far from such rituals being deviant, as Brown and Levinson suggest, they seem instead to be a different but equally significant human interactional strategy. That such rituals are threatening to positive face is clear. If others outside the group know that one is thought by one's male friends to be involved in bestial anal intercourse, one is unlikely to be thought well of. But such rituals are also coercive; that is, threatening to negative face. This is because their object is to make men conform to group requirements and thus they impede 'the freedom of action and freedom from imposition' (Brown and Levinson 1978: 66).

Note too that the solidarity ritual of sexual humiliation has a significant double bind consequence outside of the membership of the team, since it suggests that heterosexual activity cannot help in making one accepted as a man among men. This is because women or their sexual organs are seen in the rituals of sexual humiliation as contemptible, and thus heterosexual activity with them is portrayed as just as contemptible as with a dog – since *getting a great dog up you* and *cunt* are functionally equivalent as supposedly jocular terms of address. Rugby football itself thus becomes the only acceptable norm for sexual activity. Initially this seems absurd. It is not.

> The tone of men's house culture is sadistic, power oriented, and latently homosexual, frequently narcissistic in its energy and motives. (Millett 1977: 50)

Phillips (1984) supports this view by showing how the same ethos is to be found in New Zealand myths about the nature of New Zealand soldiers and rugby players round the turn of the twentieth century.

> It was claimed that rugby, like Cadets, provided moral discipline. The chairman of the Southern Rugby Club in 1904 argued that the success of the club team was in itself 'evidence of a clean life'. Cleanliness, of course, meant in particular sexual repression . . . (Phillips 1984: 99)

Thus, rugby and war become sublimated sexual activity and a man's partners in this activity are his mates. And they are partners, at least in part, because of their mutual knowledge of the destructive potential of the strategies of sexual humiliation.

Conclusion

The analysis of the two sets of sporting formulae tells us a number of things. First, it supports the following suggestive comment:

> Idioms . . . set up shared frames for perception, culturally transmitted boundaries with which individuals tacitly recognise or ignore patterns of phenomena. (Herdt 1981: 197)

Second (and in conflict with some radical feminist ideology), it suggests that while some New Zealand men may not always be model persons in the terms of Brown and Levinson (1978), others are, at least some of the time. The two contrasting rituals of face-saving and face-threatening which these men use create two contrasting kinds of solidarity, the first of which I have termed civilised.

Third, it has shown that there is a dark side to politeness, a side where humiliation and coercion are the object of language use. It remains to be seen whether such dark-side strategies are solely the preserve of men.

NOTES

The research reported in this paper was supported by research grants from the New Zealand University Grants Committee and the University of Canterbury. An earlier and longer version of this paper was read at the 8th Commonwealth Conference in Laufen, West Germany. I am grateful to the following for helpful comments on earlier drafts of this paper: Paddy Austin, Robyn Carston, Gareth Cordery, Michele Dominy, Geoff Fougere, Colin Goodrich, Elizabeth Gordon, Janet Holmes, Rosemary and David Novitz.

1   I am not suggesting that this strategy is the only one which can be used in physically dangerous circumstances. It does, however, appear to be a common one among men.

REFERENCES

Brown, P. and Levinson, S. (1978) Universals in language usage: politeness phenomena. In Goody, E. (ed.), *Questions and Politeness: Strategies in Social Interaction*. Cambridge: Cambridge University Press.

——(1987) Revised and extended version published as *Politeness: Some Universals in Language Usage*. Cambridge: Cambridge University Press.

Coulmas, Florian (1979) On the sociolinguistic relevance of routine formulae. *Journal of Pragmatics* 3: 239–66.

——1982. *Conversational Routine*. The Hague: Mouton.

Herdt, Gilbert, H. (1981) *Guardians of the Flutes*. New York: McGraw Hill.

Kuiper, Koenraad and Haggo, Douglas, C. (1984) Livestock auctions, oral poetry and ordinary language. *Language in Society* 13: 205–34.

Millett, Kate (1977) *Sexual Politics*. London: Virago.

Phillips, J. O. C. (1984) Rugby, war and the mythology of the New Zealand male. *The New Zealand Journal of History* 18: 83–103.

Part V

Women's Talk
in the Public Domain

This section will focus on language use in the public domain. The public domain is a male-dominated domain, and the discourse patterns of male speakers have become the established norm in public life. Historically, the split between public and private is associated with industrialization. In Britain, for example, it was established in the early nineteenth century, and involved a new demarcation of gender roles: 'men were firmly placed in the newly defined public world of business, commerce and politics; women were placed in the private world of home and family' (Hall 1985: 12).

Now, in the late twentieth century, as a consequence of Equal Opportunities legislation, women are entering the public domain – as lawyers, doctors, Members of Parliament, for example – with growing expectations in terms of career progression. And as women start to enter the professions in greater numbers, the long struggle to give them equal access to professions and to careers is giving way to a struggle over whether women have to adapt to androcentric working practices. In linguistic terms, this means that women are expected to adopt the more adversarial, information-focused style characteristic of all-male talk, and typical of talk in the public domain. But women who successfully adapt to characteristically male linguistic norms run the risk of being perceived as aggressive and confrontational, as unfeminine – in other words, there is a clash between what is expected of a woman and what is expected of a person with high status in the public sphere.

This clash is the topic of the first paper in this section, 'Female Speakers of Japanese in Transition'. Katsue Reynolds claims that there is conflict in Japan between the contemporary ideology that women and men are equal, and the pressure on women to speak in a way that is *onna-rasiku*. *Onna-rasiku* language expresses an older female identity, one which is more in line with the Confucian doctrine of 'men superior, women inferior'. Reynolds shows that, in Japanese, some rules for gender-marking are categorical, and that, overall, women have a much more restricted stylistic range available to them than men have. This asymmetry is in conflict with the communicative requirements of the late twentieth century where women are taking on new roles in the public sphere and need to talk to men as equals. 'In order to be accepted as a "good" woman, a female speaker of Japanese must choose to talk nonassertively, indirectly, politely, deferentially: but in order to function as a supervisor, administrator, teacher, lawyer, doctor, etc. or as a colleague or associate, she must be able to talk with assurance' (p. 302). This sort of conflict exists world-wide, but the Japanese situation is more extreme than most. Reynolds reports current perceptions of women in public life (many of whom deny that they have experienced any problems relating to language) and describes the linguistic strategies they are (often unconsciously) adopting to resolve the conflicting demands on them. These strategies seem to consist predominantly of 'defeminizing' their language, that is, choosing variants towards the middle of an imaginary masculine–feminine spectrum, and avoiding variants associated with the feminine end of the spectrum.

The defeminization of interactional patterns is the focus of the second paper in this section, Bonnie McElhinny's 'I don't smile much anymore'. McElhinny analyses the linguistic behaviour of women police officers in the Pittsburgh police. The police force is a workplace which has traditionally been defined as all-male and masculine, and McElhinny argues that such a workplace is itself gendered and that this affects how people are able to behave. She shows how women police officers have learned to adopt the strategies typically employed by male police officers, which damp down the personal and the emotional. Her telling analysis of two specific incidents of domestic violence where the police were called in, one involving a male police officer and one a female police officer, illustrates the way in which police officers stick to a prescribed agenda of questions and fail to respond to the emotion of the woman who has asked for police help. She argues that gender differences in language are not found when both women and men work in a workplace with established masculine practices.

There is, however, evidence to suggest that in some workplaces women are resisting the androcentric discourse norms of the public sphere and are employing their own more cooperative speech style in the working environment. The next two papers in this section illustrate this phenomenon (see also Atkinson, in press; Fisher 1991; Graddol and Swann 1989). Candace West's paper, 'Not just doctors' orders', focuses on doctor–patient talk. West analysed directive–response speech sequences between doctor and patient, and discovered that women and men doctors issued directives in very different ways. While male doctors preferred to use imperative forms, or statements in which they told patients what they 'needed' to do, or what they 'had' to do, female doctors preferred to use more mitigated forms. Moreover, women doctors were more likely than men to use directive forms which elicited a compliant response from the patient. West shows how women doctors' use of more mitigated directive forms had the effect of minimizing status distinctions between themselves and their patients. The more egalitarian relationships they established with their patients emphasized doctors' obligations as well as patients' rights. The evidence from this study is that such an approach has better outcomes for patients than more traditional approaches which emphasize asymmetry in doctor–patient relationships.

The last paper in the section – Marie Wilson Nelson's 'Women's Ways: Interactive Patterns in Predominantly Female Research Teams' – again focuses on the successful use of collaborative interactive strategies by women professionals. Nelson observed and recorded the interactive patterns of five successive teacher-research teams, working in a university writing centre in Washington, DC. These teams were made up of graduate Teaching Assistants (TAs), who were mostly female. Nelson's research shows how the women successfully used the interactive patterns familiar to them, while the occasional male TAs adapted to these interactive patterns and were positive about the experience. Transcripts of team discussion sessions confirm the claim that the interactions are based on an ethic of reciprocity, and are cooperative rather than competitive. They show what Miller (1978) calls 'productive conflict', that is, conflict which is beneficial to all participants, as opposed to conflict which results in one winner and many losers. Nelson discusses the problems women face in trying to maintain their collaborative style in more competitive environments, but argues that we must try to overcome these problems since the interactive patterns into which women are socialized 'offer substantial benefits to academic and professional teams' (p. 357).

These four papers do not give a unified message. They demonstrate that, in professional contexts where women have some autonomy, then women's interactional patterns can be used to good effect. In these contexts, it appears that gender and status don't come into conflict. But in many workplaces, women have to adapt to traditional – androcentric – working practices, and here the conflict between gender and status is highly problematic for women. It remains to be seen whether this conflict is a temporary phenomenon, arising during a period of social transition from an all-male to a mixed workforce, or whether it will prove to be an enduring problem for women in the public sphere.

REFERENCES

Atkinson, Karen (in press) *Elderly Talk*. London: Longman.
Fisher, Sue (1991) 'A discourse of the social: medical talk/power talk/oppositional talk?' *Discourse and Society*, 2, 2, 157–82.
Graddol, David and Swann, Joan (1989) 'Linguistic intervention', ch. 7 of *Gender Voices*. Oxford: Blackwell.
Hall, Catherine (1985) 'Private persons versus public someones: class, gender and politics in England, 1780–1850', pp. 10–33 in Carolyn Steedman, Cathy Urwin and Valerie Walkerdine (eds) *Language, Gender and Childhood*. London: Routledge.
Miller, Jean Baker (1978) *Towards a New Psychology of Women*. Harmondsworth: Penguin.

RECOMMENDED FURTHER READING

Coates, Jennifer (1995) 'Language, gender and career', in Sara Mills (ed.) *Language and Gender: Interdisciplinary Perspectives*. London: Longman.
Holmes, Janet (1992) 'Women's talk in public contexts', *Discourse and Society*, 3, 2, 131–50.
McElhinny, Bonnie (forthcoming) *Policing Gender: The Work Language Does*.
West, Candace (1984) *Routine Complications: Troubles with Talk Between Doctors and Patients*. Bloomington, IN: Indiana University Press.

20

Female Speakers of Japanese in Transition

Katsue Akiba Reynolds

Introduction

The Confucian doctrine of "men superior, women inferior" (*Dan-Son Jo-Hi*), an indispensable element in the hierarchical structure of Japanese society, began to give way when women were guaranteed equal status in the new Constitution soon after the end of World War II. At that time, women began to assert their existence in various public fields. However, the average person's image of women has not changed significantly, and the notion that women should behave *onna-rasiku* "as expected of women" is still predominant.
[. . .]
   When one inspects the ways in which Japanese women talk at a variety of social levels, a complex interaction between social change and language change emerges, and changes in women's speech become visible. There is no doubt that social changes during the post-war era have had an incalculable impact on women's perceptions of reality, giving rise to "status conflict" (Pharr 1984) in various areas of social life. Language use is one such area: the female/male speech dichotomy stands in obvious contradiction to the new social order based on egalitarian ideology. As shown in Reynolds (1985), language use reflects Japanese society of the past, in which women were viewed as the inferior, weaker sex and were expected to talk accordingly. Women may perceive themselves as equals of men but women's language calls up the older image of women.
[. . .]

Historical Background

During the feudal era, which lasted up to 1868, Japan maintained its internal integrity under one of the most extreme forms of hierarchical society. The *samurai* "warrior" class held control and people were required to adhere strictly to behavioral norms.

The slightest deviation from the norms could provoke the most severe punishment – decapitation. The introduction of the ideology of democracy into the Japanese political system at the time of the Meiji Restoration in 1868 led to the outlawing of such extreme feudal practices, but interactional expectations based on social ranking, an outgrowth of two hundred years of feudalistic practices, have persisted as a cultural characteristic. Even after the radical changes in social institutions after the war, the expectations remain at almost all levels of interaction among the Japanese. Thus, Nakane (1970) analyzes contemporary Japanese society as a hierarchical society governed by the "vertical" principle of human interaction. Because of intransigent adherence to this principle, many social scientists, including Nakane, maintain that the changes in political/social institutions have not reached down to the foundation of the culture. To many researchers Japan still appears to be a hierarchically organized, harmonious society with a high degree of internal integrity.

Recently, this view has been explicitly challenged by Krauss, Rohlen and Steinhoff (1984). They present examples of intergroup conflicts in Japan during the post-war period, and convincingly argue that the hierarchy/harmony model of Japanese society, which does not take such conflicts into consideration, is not adequate, being unable to account for the source, development, and outcome of various social phenomena. [. . .]

Japanese Female Speech

It was only two or three generations ago that women were all but prevented from entering the public arena: they occupied their respective positions within family structures as wives, mothers or mothers-in-law and had contact with the world outside the family only through male relations, or as substitutes. In Reynolds (1985), I attempted to show that most linguistic rules applying only if the speaker is female have the effect of reducing assertion, or expressing formality or politeness (hearer orientation), which indicates that the social foundation of female speech is a sex-segregated hierarchical society in which women are viewed as inferior. [. . .]

I do not mean to imply by my analysis of Japanese female speech that the normative rules for female speakers are always strictly adhered to. On the contrary, this study takes note of the fact that many women deviate from the norm in many situations. But certain features of female speech can still be extensively observed among the majority of Japanese women, and some rules are even obligatory if the speaker is female. For example, as a woman I am not allowed to say to anybody, even to my younger sibling, *Tot-te-kure* "Get (it) for me" using Informal-Benefactive-Imperative. I have to say instead *Tot-te*, applying the imperative deletion rule. I am not allowed to say *It-ta ka?* "Did you go?". I must suppress the interrogative marker *ka* and say *It-ta* (/), shifting the rising intonation to the tense marker. Some rules for gender-marking in Japanese are categorical, while in English rules are variable. However, this does not mean that the distinction between female speech and male speech is always clear-cut. Furthermore, there are several stylistic variants of female and male speech signifying different degrees of femininity or masculinity. Roughly speaking, the division between female and male speech is schematized as in the diagram below, V_1 being the most masculine – assertive/forceful variants – and Vn its opposite extreme.

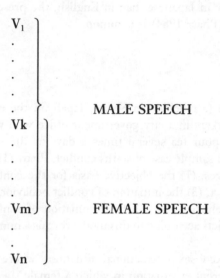

That is, women are supposed to choose a style closer to the least assertive end, which men are supposed to avoid. Also, it seems that the risk of stepping into the overlapping area (Vk–m) is greater for females than for males. A woman using a style in this area may be considered impolite in more situations than a man talking in the same way. If we limit ourselves to informal speech (i.e., excluding from our consideration formal and written styles, which exhibit different patterns of distribution), the option for a style is much narrower in the case of a female speaker.

This asymmetric linguistic division may not have created serious problems in a sex-segregated society, where the wife, a woman in the only legitimate female category, occupied "the lowest rung on the entire social ladder, subordinated within the feudal hierarchy and within the family hierarchy as well" (Pharr 1984: 224). There was no need for women to talk assertively/forcefully/authoritatively since they were defined as subordinate to others. With the legal and economic changes after the war, however, the barriers between women and men were removed in most social and educational institutions: women are no longer confined to the home but are taking up various social/public roles which used to belong to men. Inevitably, mixed sex interactions have significantly increased, causing remarkable changes in the way people relate. Mixed sex interaction in which women and men can talk almost as equals is no longer taken as exceptional. There are many situations in which a woman talks as a superior to her male subordinates. It is mostly in such emerging patterns of interaction that speakers (especially, female speakers) face the conflict between traditional patterns and the need to meet the communicative requirements arising from their new roles. In order to be accepted as a "good" woman, a female speaker of Japanese must choose to talk nonassertively, indirectly, politely, deferentially: but in order to function as a supervisor, administrator, teacher, lawyer, doctor, etc. or as a colleague or associate, she must be able to talk with assurance. Given the constraint that a woman should talk *onna-rasiku* "as expected of women" regardless of her role, which is far more mandatory in Japanese than in English, the presence of an "objective condition for conflict" (Pharr 1984) is common.

Women and Status Conflict

In analyzing the "tea-pourers" rebellion (a rebellion in Kyoto, Japan, in the early 1960's by a group of female clerical workers in a city government office who were protesting against having to make and pour tea several times a day for the male members of their respective sections) as a sample case of status conflict, Pharr (1984) argues that conflict develops in five stages: (1) the objective basis for the conflict, (2) the subjective awareness of the conflict, (3) the initiation of conflict behavior, (4) the escalation/deescalation of conflict behavior and (5) the termination of conflict. Examination of female/male speech conflicts according to this model reveals a number of important facts.[1]

There are at least two types of mixed sex interactional situations where the objective conditions for conflict are inherent: a situation in which a female speaker is superior in social status to a male speaker and a situation in which both sexes are supposed to have equal status.

A woman in a superior position – a position defined as such by the male-established hierarchy – is expected to signify her authoritative power in her language, but female speech does not provide a means to this end. Formal speech may be interpreted as the speaker's means of keeping a distance from the addressee, or it may be taken as a manifestation of the speaker's genuine humility – a virtue – only if it comes from someone who has an option of a more overtly assertive/intimidating style, i.e., a male speaker. But formal speech is a sign of deference, an expected quality of the powerless, when it is used by a speaker who is constrained to using a nonassertive style, i.e. by a female speaker.

In mixed sex conversations where there is no vertical relationship among the participants, linguistic equality will be maintained only if both female and male members talk in formal speech, keeping a distance from each other. The odds are in favor of male speakers in any competition in informal speech.

Actions such as tea-pouring are intentional and the actors are well aware of what they are doing, so the fact that the duty is a burden imposed only on female workers is apparent to everybody. The question of what can be done to make the situation more fair can be discussed openly. But decisions as to what linguistic style to use must often, on the other hand, be made subconsciously by individuals. It is characteristic of linguistic conflict that subjects are seldom aware of it. Initially, interviews with women who are in social positions that require assertive talk – women who administer predominantly male groups or mixed sex groups with large percentages of male members, women critics, women in the media, women teachers and women politicians – suggest that they have never experienced any difficulties due to their language use. Yet later in the same interviews these women admit that their language does not have the same authoritative force as that of their male counterparts, that they must be aware of their language so they will not offend others, or be considered improper as women. However, there is evidence that women are attempting, subconsciously, to resolve the conflict, mostly by defeminizing their speech within limits, using variants in the Vk–m area in the diagram shown earlier. They even use some variants closer to V_1 than Vk when sentences are not explicitly directed towards the addressee: e.g., *Sooda naa* (/) instead of *Soo (desu) nee* (/), both of which are reflexive questions – questions directed towards the speaker him/herself; or the use of *sikasi*, the conjunction "however/but" commonly used in male speech/public discourse, instead of *desukere-do*, *kere-do*, *kedo*, *demo*, conjunctions with the same semantic function as *sikasi* but more commonly used in female speech/conversational discourse. I hear these expressions when women talk to me, a female stranger: this suggests that they are used more extensively in communication in work situations, especially when conflict is intense. One incident might be seen as an escalation of conflict behavior. A woman principal's thundering *Bakayaroo!* "Stupid!" silenced a group of faculty members. (*Yaroo* is a vulgarism referring to men: the word does not belong to the female vocabulary.) She said, "We must sometimes show who is the boss," when the incident, which must have been spread among the teachers and other principals in the community, was brought up by another woman principal. Variants at the V_1 level were employed by several angry women among about 200 observers of a Diet session discussing a bill to legislate equal employment opportunities for men and women (Notes, July 24, '84, no taperecording permitted).

A social conflict like the one concerning tea-pouring duties is externally observable and the existence of conflict is apparent. The conflict of male/female linguistic style under discussion, however, takes place mostly within individuals: subjects may not have full awareness of the existence of the objective conditions for conflict and may not consciously initiate conflict behavior. An individual who initiates conflict behavior under such conditions might easily yield to the pressure of society and be persuaded that it is she who is wrong, that it is her behavior that must be corrected. The role of society in this process is crucial, especially in Japan, where the desire for harmony is so deep-rooted in the culture that deviating from the cultural norm – destroying the harmony – is almost suicidal. The government proposal to put into law the principle of equal employment opportunity for men and women in response to the egalitarian ideology of the International Decade for Women was met with strong opposition by proponents of a "cultural ecology" theory.

Michiko Hasegawa, a female philosophy teacher, states, "The pattern of men's and women's roles is an important element of the system of each culture. It is analogous to religion or language, and if one attempts to change it recklessly, one might destroy the whole system of the culture" (Hasegawa 1984: 83). She argues that the Law, if it is ratified, would undermine the well-balanced system of Japanese traditions. To think of removing the male/female speech dichotomy is absurd to her, and to many others. It is understandable that individual female speakers' attempts to rebel against traditional female speech patterns do not escalate beyond a very limited domain. Conflicts either remain unresolved or end in failure.

Linguistic Dilemmas: The Example of Women Teachers

One group of women who are particularly vulnerable to the linguistic dilemma are female teachers in junior high schools,[2] as well as teachers teaching older age groups in elementary schools. They must handle boys and girls (the average class of a Japanese school has more than 40 students) who demand that the teacher be attentive and friendly to them while at the same time displaying a defensive and resistant attitude themselves. Displays of both solidarity and authority are necessary for a teacher to be successful in a Japanese junior high school: it is informal male speech that can satisfy these two requirements simultaneously. Let us look at an example of a male teacher's discourse in class.[3]

T: . . . Please present a lot of your opinions or impressions. First, the boy. About the boy . . . You probably remember what you have written down yesterday. Well, what have you thought about the boy? *I want you to present it, OK?* (*Kore o dasi te-morai-tai na.*)
P (Male): . . .
T: Yes, that's right. That's correct . . . What I wanted you to write about . . . among the subjects that you had strong feelings about, there are probably a lot besides it, aren't there? Well . . . to confirm those points with each other. *Well how about you A, first?* (*Ee, mazu saisyo ni A doo da.*)
P (Male): . . .
T: Yes. *You felt thrilled at what the boy was doing, is it?* (*Syoonen ga yat-te-iru koto ni suriru o kanzi -ta, da na.*)

The italic parts are in an informal male speech style and those which are not marked are either formal or are in a written language style, which is very common in lecturing. Note that this male teacher teaching Tolstoy in Japanese translation to seventh graders regularly switches the code from formal to informal at the point where he attempts to elicit responses from students. Female informal speech, which has long been limited to private discourse among women, does not work in the same way as male informal speech in the public environment. For a woman teacher to be successful under the present circumstances, she has no choice but to use defeminized patterns to strengthen solidarity with her students without losing authority.

However, a teacher is evaluated not only by students but also by parents and the principal, who are critical if female teachers' behavior deviates from traditional standards. All the female principals that I interviewed criticized female teachers' language one way or another, although most of them admit that female teachers cannot be like "normal" women. One of the principals revealed that she had called in a young female teacher to admonish her about her language. The principal said that since that time the teacher in question seemed to be improving her language.

In the discussion on female speech held during a three-day seminar on women's studies at the National Women's Education Center (*Kokuritu Huzin Kyooiku Kaikan*)[4] a participant expressed concern about her daughter's language, which she thought was too rough for a girl, "perhaps, because of her (female) teacher's influence." Several younger participants who could still identify themselves with students rather than mothers responded that when they were students they always favored female teachers who talked a little bit like male teachers over those who talked too formally. It is the conflict inherent in being a female teacher that has been brought into focus by these two opposing views, the view of the mothers and the view of students as recalled by younger participants at the seminar.

The social expectation that women, regardless of their roles, should talk *onna-rasiku* is so strong that women teachers themselves often view defeminization negatively. A 26-year-old female teacher responds to a newspaper reporter. "I tend to speak rough language with an imperative tone in spite of my efforts not to, perhaps, because I am a teacher. I always think regretfully that this is not good for me" (the *Asahi*, July 18, 1984), and she adds that she, ambivalent about language use, won't be able to meet the demands of the career. It is interesting that the reporter (female or male?) admiringly describes the teacher as sitting *onna-rasiku* on the floor with her hands arranged in front of her folded knees in a poised manner. It seems to be only a matter of time before this teacher will terminate the conflict by returning to the traditional woman's place – home. Sensing society's disapproval of her language, this female teacher is punishing herself while the same society (represented by the reporter) lauds her for her femininity.

Female principals are in positions where they can control the female speech conflict to a certain extent. Unlike teachers, principals do not come into direct contact with students, and they can handle most interactions in formal language. Furthermore, even if they use rough language like [*Bakayaroo!*] they are relatively free from others' criticism since they are at the top rank within a school system. Difficulties that women principals experience are more subtle. First, a woman principal must demonstrate that she does not display linguistic traits which are believed to be typical of women: especially, she must avoid giving an impression in her talk that she is indecisive, indirect or picky. At the same time she cannot be as authoritative as a male counterpart would be. One of the women principals interviewed who seemed to be quite successful in establishing a good rapport with the teachers confided that she was careful not to be too informal with the teachers so that the male headmaster,[5] who is in between herself and the teachers, would not be crowded out (Recorded, July 18, 1983). A male headmaster talks to the principal deferentially according to the traditional principle of vertical relationships and at the same time he attempts to maintain his face as the superior *vis-à-vis* the teachers. Thus, the principal must allow enough distance between the teachers and herself to make room for the headmaster. She said, "I am formal and short with teachers in my office, but I try to make up for it by saying one or two words in a personal/casual manner to convey to them that I remember their cooperation and support when I see them around." Second, a woman principal has to deal with difficulties in her communication with male principals. A woman principal who talks to male principals too informally does not have a good reputation among male principals – the majority. Male principals' informal talk of course creates no difficulty. "We should not be carried away and address male principals with *-san* – a suffix very roughly corresponding to *Mr.* in English – just because male principals do so among themselves. We should address them with the title *Sensei* 'Master/Teacher' or *Kootyoo Sensei* 'Mr. Principal' or with family name and title (e.g., *Yamada Sensei* and *Yamada Kootyoo*) as we are expected."

It has been noted that the use of *boku* "I" (Male) by junior high school girls has recently become quite common in Tokyo. Girls who were interviewed in a TV program explain that they cannot compete with boys in classes, in games or in fights with *watasi* "I" (Female), reports Jugaku (1979). What we see here is a case of conflict behavior consciously initiated by a large group of female speakers who are fully aware of the disadvantage of female speech in school situations where they are expected to compete with boys for good grades and choose to ignore traditions openly. The use of *boku* and other expressions in the male speech domain by young female speakers has escalated to a larger area and to older groups of speakers.[6] However, since they know that *boku*-language is not acceptable in the society outside schools, they use *watasi*-language in talking to "members of the society."[7] In other words, as school girls they are bilinguals who have two distinct codes, *boku*-language and *watasi*-language. They select a code according to the situation.

In spite of the surface defiance of the trend, however, *boku*-language may not have as much subversive force as it appears. The avowedly rebellious behavior on the part of teenage girls rouses curiosity but never the anger that would be invoked if females with full membership in society stepped over the gender boundary in a less self-conscious and less forthright manner. This is because *boku*-language can be dismissed as a passing phase – it does in fact taper off by the time the students leave school – while defeminization/masculinization by adult female members is a serious threat to the established norms of society.

Conclusions

The female/male language dichotomy in Japanese is not a mere differentiation of the two sexes but it reflects the structure of a society where women were defined as the inferior sex. Jugaku (1979) points out that the structure of the Japanese language has a far greater effect on the way Japanese women live than one may expect. The examples of conflict processes that we have seen show that female speech plays a crucial role in keeping Japanese women in traditional roles. Attempts to remove the boundary between the male/female speech division inevitably end in failure, as a result of self-restraint on the part of female speakers who foresee social punishment. It appears that the way women are supposed to talk has changed little; the norm functions as a conservative force.

To predict from this, however, that female speech has not changed and will not change may be wrong. Even though individual processes of conflict may terminate in failure, "the effects of the conflict feed back into the objective conditions that potentially will give rise to further conflicts" (Pharr 1984: 219). One individual's conflict behavior can have an impact on a wide range of female speakers who come into contact with it, who may initiate conflict behaviors and influence in turn other women. As long as there are objective conditions for female language conflict, conflict behaviors will recur in various social segments and will spread with increasingly greater speed. Even if all conflict behaviors are suppressed, the ripple effect of conflict may eventually generate the energy necessary to undermine the traditional division of the language, into assertive styles for men and nonassertive/polite styles for women. It is certain, to say the least, that the female/male speech dichotomy will not remain as it is at present, just as the traditional role division based on sex has been fluctuating widely in various aspects of social life.

[. . .]

If equality between men and women enhances linguistic equality, and if linguistic equality entails equal access for all the speakers of a language to all the resources of the language, it is a logical conclusion that the female/male speech dichotomy must be removed. Although the observations that I have presented here may very well be proof that the change towards linguistic equality is already under way, there is no guarantee that the change will proceed without interruption or digression. It is in fact quite likely that the present form of dichotomy will simply shift to another – perhaps less obvious – form of dichotomy. Inoue (1984) concludes her essay on the image of women presented through the mass media saying that, in place of the traditional role division of domestic work for women and career work for men, a new system of dividing men's and women's roles may be developing: for example, a system in which administrative positions are assigned to men and secretarial positions to women, cooking to entertain the guests is men's work and cleaning up afterward women's.[8] If Inoue's analysis is correct, language may follow the same pattern of change: even if the obvious dichotomy between female and male speech disappears, the overall dominance of male speakers over female speakers may survive in a different form. I would like to suggest therefore that it is an important task for researchers of gender in relation to language to observe and analyze various phenomena related to the sex dichotomy, especially conflict phenomena, and to work against changes that create a new male/female language dichotomy rather than leading to linguistic equality.

NOTES

1   Georganne Weller, Director of Center for Interpretation and Translation. University of Hawaii, has brought to my attention that the sociolinguistic studies using aspects/variants of conflict theory have increased during the past decade. E.g., Chapter IV, "The Conflict Paradigm," of Christina Bratt Paulson's *Bilingual Education: Theories and Issues* (Newbury House, 1980).

2   According to *Nihon Kyooiku Nenkan* (The Almanac of Japanese Education) 1985, the percentages of female teachers in Japanese schools are as follows (as of May 1, 1984): elementary schools, 56.0%; junior high schools, 33%; senior high schools, 18.1%. Female teachers in junior high schools are still a minority. Furthermore, the subjects that female teachers teach are often, though not always, limited: most of them teach home economics, gymnastics for girls, Japanese, or perhaps music.

3   The sample was taken from the transcribed material published in *"Rokuonki"* in *Gengo Seikatu* 172, 1966.

4   This seminar of women's studies is held for three days every summer with over 200 participants who include teachers at various levels, women working in government offices and in other professions, students and housewives, and is subsidized by the Ministry of Education. The discussion in question was held in the evening of the second day of the 1984 seminar.

5   There seems to be an unwritten rule that a female headmaster is never assigned to a school with a female principal.

6   Jugaku (1979) made a study of *boku* used by school girls in Osaka and discovered that *boku* is used quite often by high school girls in Osaka, too, although the use is accompanied by a joking playful tone. Several people have pointed out to me that *boku* is easier to use in woman-to-woman communication than in mixed sex communication. It seems that in the process of expansion of *boku* from high school girls to college girls the sociolinguistic significance of *boku*-language used by girls has undergone a slight change.

7   At the commencement ceremony, Japanese students are congratulated by guest speakers for "becoming members of society," that is, students are not regarded as members of society in Japan.

8   *The Asahi* (July 25, 1985) reports a tendency for male employees to be placed in the main office while female employees of the same company are placed in branch offices.

REFERENCES

Hasegawa, M. (1984) "Danzyo koyoo byoodoo hoo wa bunka no seitaikei o hakai suru. [The law of equal employment opportunity will destroy the ecological system of the culture]." *Tyuuoo Kooron* 5, 78–87.

Inoue, T. (1984) "Masukomi to zyosei no gendai. [Today's women and mass media]". *Onna no Imeezi* [Image of Woman], ed. Zyoseigaku Kenkyuukai, 316–29. Tokyo: Keisoo-syoboo.

Jugaku, A. (1979) *Nihongo to Onna* [Japanese and Women]. Tokyo: Iwanami-syoten.

Krauss, E. S., T. P. Rohlen and P. G. Steinhoff, eds. (1984) *Conflict in Japan*. Honolulu: University of Hawaii Press.

Nakane, C. (1970) *Japanese Society*. Berkeley: University of California Press.

Pharr, S. J. (1984) "Status conflict: The rebellion of the tea pourers." *Conflict in Japan*, eds. E. S. Krauss, T. P. Rohlen and P. G. Steinhoff, 214–40. Honolulu: University of Hawaii Press.

Reynolds, Katsue Akiba (1984) "Evidence for masculinity constraint: Fillers in Japanese." Paper presented at the annual meeting of the Linguistic Society of America, Baltimore.

——(1985) "Female speakers of Japanese." *Feminist Issues* 5, Fall, 13–46.

21

"I don't smile much anymore": Affect, Gender, and the Discourse of Pittsburgh Police Officers

Bonnie S. McElhinny

Gender and the Workplace

One of the implicit assumptions evident in much sociolinguistic research on gender is that gender is an attribute of a person, but institutions are also often gendered in ways that delimit who can properly participate in them and/or how such participation can take place (see Gal 1991; Keller 1990; Scott 1988; Sherzer 1987). Workplaces are gendered both by the numerical predominance of one sex within them and by the cultural interpretations of given types of work which, in conjunction with cultural norms and interpretations of gender, dictate who is understood as best suited for different sorts of employment (so that, as Reskin and Roos (1990) illustrate, women are preferred as food servers in the United States because they are believed to be neater and to smile more). In the United States, work considered appropriate for women has traditionally been an extension of their work as mothers and wives, such as teaching, nursing, sewing, and cleaning. More recently this has included work like bank management, public relations, and systems analysis, for which women's reputed skill at interpersonal relationships and interpersonal communication is said to suit them (Reskin & Roos 1990: 50−1). The passage of the 1964 Civil Rights Act and the 1972 Equal Opportunity Act, however, has slowly opened up workplaces which previously excluded women and minorities (S. Martin 1980: 11). Tracing the results of these hirings is important for understanding how women learn to integrate themselves successfully into previously all-male and masculine workplaces and how the workplaces adapt to this integration. Of particular interest to sociolinguists is how women adapt to styles and kinds of interaction not normally understood as feminine.

In this paper, I describe linguistic interactions within a workplace that has traditionally been defined as all-male and masculine − the police force - but which has recruited large numbers of women in the last fifteen years through a variety of affirmative-action measures. In 1975 a court injunction was issued to the city of

Pittsburgh requiring each incoming police recruit class to be 25% black females, 25% white females, 25% black males, and 25% white males. Large movements of women into male-dominated workplaces are rare (historical examples include clerical workers, telegraph operators, bank tellers, and waitresses), and such movements are usually rapidly followed by the complete reversal of the gender-typing of the workplace (Reskin & Roos 1990: 12–15). In Pittsburgh the quota-hiring system has led to a slow, steady increase of women and African Americans, so that now women and African Americans each compose approximately 25% of the force (no separate figures are available to indicate what percentage of women are white and what percentage of women are black, nor are the categories of black and white broken down into male and female) – a larger percentage of female police officers than in any other major American city outside of Detroit (U.S. Department of Justice 1987a, 1987b).[1] This workplace thus provides a unique opportunity to consider whether gender differences in language exist between men and women when both participate in a community with masculine practices. In this paper, I begin by describing why police work has traditionally been considered men's work. I then develop a brief ethnographic fragment which concentrates on one attribute of this gendering: the non-projection of emotion. This cultural description will provide crucial context for the interpretation of two linguistic interactions: a female and male police officer each taking a report from an apparent victim of domestic assault. I close with a brief review of implications for the study of language and gender and for gender theory more generally.

The Gendering of Police Work

Policing has traditionally been viewed as men's work and, despite increasing numbers of women, is still so viewed by many citizens and by police officers, even by female police officers who consider themselves and other females very good at their work. The explanation for this goes beyond the historical and present numerical predominance of men in the job. Men's work is stereotypically associated with the outdoors, with strength, and with highly technical skills that involve mechanical or scientific knowledge. It is heavy, dirty, and dangerous and requires creativity, intelligence, responsibility, authority, and power. Women's work is stereotypically indoor, lighter, cleaner, safer, repetitive; it calls for dexterity rather than skill, has domestic associations, is tied to a certain work station, and often requires physical attractiveness and charm (Bradley 1989: 9). Some of these characteristics are more important than others in determining the gender of a workplace and in determining how masculine or feminine a workplace is. Blue-collar jobs are generally considered more masculine than white-collar ones, and blue-collar jobs which require strength are considered more masculine than others. Susan Martin has suggested:

> . . . for blue-collar men whose jobs often do not provide high incomes or great social prestige, other aspects of the work, including certain 'manly' features, take on enormous importance as a means through which they confirm their sex-role identity. Work that

entails responsibility, control, use of a skill, initiative and which permits the use of strength and/or physical agility characteristic of males is highly valued not only for its own sake but for its symbolic significance. Similarly working in an 'all-male' environment reinforces the notion that they are doing 'men's work' and is a highly prized fringe benefit of a job. (1980: 89)

In public representations and in police officers' minds, police work is defined by the situations in which police officers are required to exert physical force to keep the peace – separating combatants in a bar fight or a girlfriend and boyfriend in a domestic dispute, or wrestling a criminal into handcuffs. Male officers who do not believe women should be on the job often cite women's inability to handle these situations. Female officers, while recognizing differences in physical ability, argue that on serious calls one rarely needs to act without backup and can cooperate with other officers to bring the situation under control. Female police officers also tend to distinguish between physical strength, which they agree they do not have, and institutional force, which they decidedly agree they do have. As one officer put it, "It's never just a fight between a man and a woman – it's a fight between a man and a *police officer*." Female police officers also note that there are some frightened, weak, do-nothing men on the job, a reply which suggests that women should not be regarded as a group, but rather as individuals, and which thus contests hegemonic interpretations of gender. The dark-blue uniform required for the job is also more masculine than feminine; it has a stripe down the seam on the outside of each leg, back pockets with top buttons, sharp pointed collars (rather than large round or squared ones), and ties and tie pins (rather than scarves or decorative pins). The gun belt is wide, heavy leather and carries the radio, nightstick, blackjack, and revolver or semi-automatic.[2] Bullet-proof vests square off body outlines, and hair has to be either short or pulled up above the collar. Most female police officers have been addressed as *sir*.

Also part of the gendering of police work are the emotional displays required by it. Police officers must often act tough, suspicious, distant, and uninvolved. I turn now to a closer investigation of this aspect of the work.

Gender and Affect at Work

The projection of emotion is a type of often uncompensated work shaped by the requirements of work structures within which individuals find themselves. Kanter (1977) shows how the patrimonial relationship that exists between boss and secretary requires and rewards the projection of emotion in the latter. The display of positive affect is one of the chief privileges of secretaries (who are not more concretely rewarded with large salaries, benefit packages, or promotional opportunities), one of their chief sources of power (as Kanter argues, "Whether or not [secretaries], as women, were intrinsically any more 'emotional' than men, they learned to display their emotions as a very useful way to get what they wanted", 1977: 66), and one of their chief tasks (secretaries are expected to see to the comfort of bosses and guests, remember anniversaries and birthdays, take note of daily changes in dress, hair, and mood in those around them, and create a welcoming office environment). It is also one of secretaries' few avenues to professional advancement, since loyalty to and care for a particular boss can lead to promotion when that boss is promoted. In corporate workplaces there is a *division of emotional labor* in which the secretary comes to "feel for" the boss by caring for him and by doing his feeling for him (see Kanter 1977 for elaboration of this argument).

Hochschild (1983) shows how airlines train flight attendants in the projection of warmth, care, and cheerfulness, emotional traits which they then market to airline customers in commercials and advertisements which strive to establish that airplane cabins are as welcoming, comfortable, cozy, and safe as one's own living room. Hochschild notes that over a third of all jobs are those involving emotional labor, especially service jobs, but while they form only one quarter of the jobs men do, they form over one half of those women do. When men are required to perform emotional labor, it is often the projection of negative emotion, such as threatening those who haven't paid corporate bills, as bill collectors do, or "acting crazier than they do," as police officers do.

An Economy of Affect: Emotional Requirements of Policing

The emotion work that policing exacts is quite different from that of typically feminine jobs. One young female rookie, formerly a teacher, describes how she adapted to workplace interactional norms:[3]

(1) (Do you think women who come on this job start to act in masculine ways?) umhm. un-huh. (Like what are some of the things you see?) Your language. I know mine, mine changes a lot from. *When I'm at work I I always feel like I have to be so (.) so like gruff you know.* (umhm) And normally I'm not like that. I'm usually kinda bitchy (Hhh) but I'm not like real (un-huh). Sometimes I try to be like such a hard ass. I *I don't smile as much.* I'm not saying that men, you know [that] that's a masculine trait (right). I think you um (.) you have to pick up maybe not necessarily fighting but techniques to subdue people or just hold them or whatever (un-huh) and I don't think that's naturally feminine either you know (un-huh). I think it's mostly language. You know (.) My mine's atrocious sometimes. I've toned it down a lot. *When I first started you know cause I worked with a lot of guys (umhm) it seemed like, they didn't may not even have swore but I felt like I had to almost like be tough or something around them you know (umhm). And that was my way of being tough.* (Is it like mostly profanity, or do you do it like with tone of voice or something?) Little bit of both. um Like I said I've toned down my profanity a lot. I just kinda use it to describe things now, like I don't call people names and stuff (un-huh-hh). But I don't know. Sometimes I try to like talk to people. Like I said about how black women were able to kinda command respect from people in the projects, I try to like pick up some of their their slang, either their slang or their tone something. Then I like I listen to myself sometimes. I'm like God I sound like you know (hhh) I sound like a

HILL person [a person who lives in a largely black, largely poor area of Pittsburgh, known for having a large number of housing projects in a small area]. *And then I think I should just be able to be me. I shouldn't have to be everybody else.*

This police officer feels that her occupational persona is a mask: *I should just be able to be me – I shouldn't have to be everybody else.* This sort of alienation from the emotional labor required by a job was also widespread among the flight attendants interviewed by Hochschild: the ways that they were required to act had little to do with how they themselves felt. This woman's experience demonstrates that her occupational persona is shaped both by her interactions with the public and her perception of the expectations of other police officers. The result is that she smiles less, is gruffer and tougher, and that much of this behavior is done with language. When I asked her why smiling mattered she said that when people smile, they drop their guard. Letting down her guard means that someone can challenge, test, or hurt her.

Many officers believe that some sense of reserve or emotional distance is the only way to survive on the job; otherwise, it is too stressful. One female police officer who had been on the job for twelve years was describing the drinking problems among officers and the frequency of divorce and suicide. She described her reaction to seeing her first serious accident and her way of coping with this and other traumatic scenes:

(2)   So my first dead body, which was one that was a girl that was very young, nineteen. She met this guy in this bar with her girlfriend, you could see her blouse had been moved and her bra was pulled up, and they had empty beer cans. Apparently there were two girls, because the second girl (uh) jumped out and she didn't get hurt at all. He speeded it up, when they realized what he was gonna do (umhm) the first girl jumps out of the Bronco and she's telling her friend, Jump! Jump! Well he pulls her back in and he speeds up and she's finally able to get out and she jumps and she hits her head on the on the uh on the railing. Split it open like a melon. (um) Just like if you took a watermelon and threw it down and it perforates, that's what her face head was. Rest of her body was like a broken little doll. And I had never seen there was all this blood. The lieutenant called me, he said okay okay kid this is your first (.) time for a dead body I want you to take a look at this. Think you can handle it? And I see this body covered up. And I see ALL this, this pool of blood came all the way down and made a huge pool at the end of the street. So much blood. And I said I don't know if I can handle it or not boss, I never seen one before. Said okay, said if you think you're gonna throw up, turn around and don't throw up on my shoes. I remember him saying that. DON'T THROW UP ON MY SHOES! So he pulls back the sheet and I look at this and I was SO: FASCINATED. I couldn't get over it. I couldn't stop looking at her. I walked around and looked and her eyeball was hanging out. I mean everything was all – I was TOTALLY fascinated and he said THAT'S ENOUGH. He said ARE YOU GETTING SICK? I said NO:! He said SOMETHING'S WRONG WITH YOU KID – he said YOU SEEN ENOUGH. He put the sheet back on her. After I went and got in the car and I sat there my stomach started to eew, heave-ho, started to heave a little bit, but I wouldn't let on. *That is when I looked and decided that was not a person.* That was a – they were no longer people if they were dead to me. I didn't get involv- think of them as people. I didn't think about her as having a family, as having a full life, you know, anything. *If I did it would kill me. So I didn't I never, I don't get emotionally involved. In*

anything. I just think – they're like clients. I don't get emotionally involved. And I don't have nightmares. I know guys that have nightmares. That's because you take it PER-SONALLY. You see the baby with the cigarette burns and you get all emotional. You can't do that. *You always have to be impartial. You can never allow your opinion – you can't you can't be opinionated. You are an impartial person.* So that's just the way I do it. And it works for me. I don't have to drink myself to sleep at night.

The expenditure of emotion on others, especially sympathy or empathy, is here understood as support lost for oneself and one's family. Emotion is a limited commodity and using it means losing it. Being impartial is also being professional, as doctors, lawyers, and coroners are with their clients.

In addition to dealing with traumatic incidents, officers often find themselves in situations in which seemingly innocuous calls suddenly turn into life-threatening ones. One officer described being called to pick up a nonviolent shoplifter who was quietly sitting in a security office. The officer was talking to the security guards when the shoplifter, hearing that she was going to jail, suddenly pulled a knife out of an open desk drawer and lunged. Another officer was called to take a criminal-mischief report for some broken windows and discovered when she arrived on the scene that the windows had been shot out, and furthermore, that the gunman was in a crowd she had walked past on her way into the apartment. One officer who had arrested a drug dealer received a seemingly innocuous call to check an abandoned house. The man he had arrested had arranged a rug over a large hole in the second story, and the officer fell through. Police officers learn to be suspicious of even the most seemingly straightforward accounts and situations (Rubinstein 1973). Depending on the situation, this suspicion may manifest itself as emotional guardedness or anger.

The result of such experiences is the development of an occupationally conditioned *habitus*, which I will call an *economy of affect*. Habitus is the notion developed by Bourdieu to describe how experience structures interactional behavior, or in his own words, "a system of lasting transposable dispositions which, integrating past experiences, functions at every moment as a matrix of perceptions, appreciations and actions" (1977: 82–3). It is "history turned nature," interactional experiences incorporated into memory to form the common sense with which people's expectations about and reactions to subsequent incidents are shaped.

[. . .]

My revision of Bourdieu's notion of habitus is twofold: I focus more centrally on the role of the labor market in shaping adults' speech styles, and I consider occupationally conditioned norms for the appropriate expression of affect. The traumatic, dangerous, and hostile interactions which police officers regularly experience produce an *economy of affect*. By *economy* I mean to suggest the extent to which this style is shaped by officers' particular involvement in the labor market – not only that they are economical (in the sense of thrifty) in their expenditure of (especially positive) affect with citizens, but also that they understand the expenditure of positive affect in terms of a closed economy (a significant expenditure of sympathy or grief on others means that less is available for themselves). Police officers do express positive affect on the job, but they choose the situations in which they do so carefully, as if they were on a limited budget. They will often invest emotion where a payoff seems most likely: with children or with an individual clearly asking for help/recommendations. Some officers choose particular sorts of cases – crack addicts who are mothers, for example, or particular individuals such as a slightly retarded homeless woman – as the focus of their sympathy and attention. But most emphasize that they cannot serve as social workers and also do the job they are asked by their superiors and the public to do.[4] Because the set of experiences the police have had are quite different from that of most other citizens, there are often marked differences between a complainant's perception of the sort of reaction her/his predicament merits and that which the police officer's experiences have trained her or him to believe is appropriate or wise. Since the situations in which most complainants meet police officers are characterized for the former by high emotional intensity (fear, anger, grief), the businesslike way that officers set about taking their reports is likely to strike complainants as cold or heartless. The possibility for miscommunication is immanent in Western interpretations of *unemotional* as either calm and rational or withdrawn and alienated (Lutz 1986: 289–90; 1990). That which police officers interpret as the first, citizens may interpret as the second.[5]

Learning Not to Smile

Although psychological tests of police officers are devised to screen out candidates who are perceived as overly timid or overly aggressive, police officers are not selected for their ability to distance themselves emotionally from people. This ability is developed within interactions required by the job. The young female officer quoted above in excerpt 1 describes an incident in which she believes she may have smiled too much:

(3)   Like the other week I had to take a report from [she names a company]. And uh one of their supervisors had gotten punched by an ex-employee. (umhm) I go down there, it it was about seven or eight in the evening, it wasn't real late or real early. I just went down there, I guess I was like real nonchalant, you know (umhm). I took the report and the information and stuff and I said well I'll get a warrant for the guy, as soon as I pick him up I'll let you know. He um he apparently got the impression that I didn't want to handle the case, and he called a friend and they called the plainclothesmen and told them to take the case. Cause I'm like what do they want me to do, you know. *I was real you know I think I smiled down there and I was very friendly. Maybe they didn't WANT that. Maybe they wanted somebody who was a little more serious. We tend not to take things as seriously as the person who's making the report sees it. Well you take we take assault reports all the time. It's not a big deal. But it was a big deal for for this man I guess and for the boss and all that (.) I guess you just have to give the public whatever they want.*

The lesson the rookie learned in this interaction was that to behave in ways which deviate from how the public believes officers should act is to risk being perceived as unprofessional or incompetent. For officers, reports may be routine, but they cannot treat them as such. Disinterestedness can mask boredom and pass for seriousness or authoritativeness. That an economy of affect may be demanded by the public, given their understanding of the role of police, is embedded in the officer's last comment: *You just have to give the public whatever they want.*

The ways that public reactions shape police behavior were also made clear in the recent removal of one veteran officer from his regular beat. The beat is infamous for the large crowd of heroin addicts, dealers, and prostitutes that it attracts at all times of day, in all kinds of weather. This officer, a fundamentalist Christian, regularly requested the beat and spent much of his time trying to wheedle, preach, or bully the street's denizens into treatment programs, school, or jobs. He was acknowledged by other officers to have established a rapport with the people on the street. A reverend of a nearby church demanded his removal, arguing that he was "too friendly with the junkies" and that he should have been clearing them off the streets each day, not talking to them. The commander of the station responded, as most commanders do to such requests, and the veteran was replaced by a rookie who makes an arrest or two every day on some minor charge (often possession of drug paraphernalia). Many experienced officers believe that the antagonism this new officer has awakened on the street will create problems for him and other police officers. In this case, a police officer was reprimanded for not being tough enough.

Police officers learn to act like "tough cops" who limit their conversation to the formalities of the investigation because increased interaction offers further opportunities for excuses, arguments, complaints, or worse (Rubinstein 1973: 264). If they cannot minimize the amount of interaction or contact, they can engage as little as possible – with terse comments, body positioned half-turned away, or lack of eye contact. Goffman (1971) notes that such behaviors are typical on buses or in elevators where passengers must come into close physical contact. Passengers carefully focus on scenery outside a bus window or on the floor indicator so as to preserve their own personal space and to prevent (further) intrusion on others (1971: 30–2). Similar reactions are evident on the part of police when it is emotional rather than physical crowding which is at issue. Reducing the amount of interaction affords others some personal space in what is often an intrusively intimate, if necessary, interaction with a stranger.[6] Urban dwellers required to engage in unpleasant interactions with strangers often assume an unfriendly countenance and a brusque manner (Milgram 1988). Police officers are required to enter into many interactions that other city dwellers avoid, and their interactional style seems to be an accentuation of that of other city dwellers rather than one that is qualitatively different.

I'm Not a Person, I'm a Police Officer: Facelessness in Face-to-Face Interaction

I turn now to a detailed consideration of two calls that officers I was accompanying on patrol responded to, both of which were described by the radio dispatcher as "violent domestic." By the time the police arrived on the scene the actors had fled and the police officers took assault reports. I attended the first call with an African American woman who had been on the force for twelve years, the second with an African American man who had been on for about a year. I chose these two incidents because their similarity makes a comparison of the two officers' behavior possible. Often calls are so different that comparison is impossible. I was not able to tape the first call, but was able to take detailed field notes while the officer herself was taking notes for the report. The second call was taped with a Sony TCD5M. The first call takes place in an affluent, largely white area of the city; the second takes place in one of the city's largely black housing projects.

Call #1

When the complainant saw the police car pulling up she came out of the house with blood dripping from her mouth down her chin. When the officer saw her, she simply said, "Oh." Once we went into the house the woman started telling her story. It was difficult at first to sort out what had happened. "The father of my daughter's son, he just got out of jail for threatening someone with a gun, he lives out there in a stolen car with stolen plates, his mother won't let him live there, but his father keeps getting him out, her daughter lives with her with the baby, I told him not to come back, I came out, he came towards me, I pushed, he punched me in the mouth." The woman repeated this story over and over. Gradually it became clear that her daughter's boyfriend had punched her when she asked him not to return to her house. The officer said very little aside from getting the woman's address, date of birth, and other information necessary for the incident report. The woman said over and over, "I don't know if I can have her [her daughter] back. I know nothing's gonna come of this. I don't know what to do. I don't know if she'll come back." The officer replied to none of this for the first fifteen minutes of the call, so that at one point the complainant even said in some frustration, "You don't say much." Not until all the necessary information had been obtained and the officer had moved to the door did she offer some advice: "Next time he comes back, call 911 – that's an emergency. Call him in for trespassing, to prevent all this pushing, verbal confrontation. We'll be right here." The woman replied, "I don't know if she'll come back." The officer responded, "I've got a daughter too – she'll come back. How old is [daughter's name]." "19." "She'll do what she has to do." Woman: "I don't know if she'll be back." Officer: "She'll be back." As we were leaving, the daughter returned to the house and emphatically declared that her boyfriend did not punch her mother, that her grandmother had been trying to punch her, but had hit her mother instead. Once we were back in the car the officer said rather bemusedly, "Grandma might have done it – she never did come out of the kitchen." She added, "See what I mean. I was on the mother's side, but you just don't know."

This episode characterizes several aspects of police–citizen interaction on report-taking calls. The officer is concentrating on obtaining the information needed for the incident report. She doesn't react with horror or sympathy, as other interactants might (and do).[7] In this case, the woman's remark that the police officer doesn't "say much" is a mitigated complaint that she doesn't say enough. Often, however, as the police officer is leaving, she or he will offer some advice or make a personal comment. These personal comments aren't always integrated into the rest of the interaction – they constitute a marked frame break (see Goffman 1977; Tannen 1984: 23–7). Here the officer has already put away her notes for the incident report and moved from where she had been standing throughout the call to the doorsill, so that she is literally speaking from a different, liminal point of view when she offers her advice and says, "I have a daughter too."[8] The police officer's final, more personal comments, while removing some of the impersonality of the encounter, also, in their sharp separation from the interaction dictated by institutional requirements, serve to highlight the distinction between the two, between her reaction as a police officer and her reaction as a person.

Finally, we should note that the officer's need to suspend judgment, or remain impartial, means that she never ratifies the account of the complainant. She produces no back-channellers like *umhm* or *right* which could be interpreted either as "I'm listening" or "I agree." The return of the daughter at the end of the call with her own story reinforces the officer's belief that this is the appropriate strategy. In the incident report she includes both the mother's and the daughter's versions of what went on. A training tape which officers were shown on how to testify in a courtroom repeatedly emphasized that officers should be professionally impartial: present the facts, the narrator said, not your conclusions and not your opinions. You're a fact-finder, not a judge. These instructions should be seen less as directives for police behavior than as a distillation of officers' experiences of what works (compare excerpt 2 above) which is then encoded in their training.

Call #2

As the officer and I walked into the apartment building, a man saluted us, "Hi, how you doin'?" The police officer responded, continued upstairs, and immediately discovered that this man was the one who had assaulted the caller. Had this been a more dangerous situation, the officer would have unknowingly come face to face with someone desperate to escape. Experiences like these train officers to be wary of all people around the scene of even the most innocuous call. The assaulted woman proceeded to tell her story. The domestic dispute apparently took place after the woman, who had found out that she had contracted venereal disease, tried to talk to her longtime partner about it. She asked if he had been fooling around and asked him to seek treatment. He responded by punching her.

For me, as participant and observer, the most striking aspect of the subsequent exchange between the police officer and the woman was again the near-complete absence of responses, including back-channellers, to the complainant's ongoing description of the incident, her description of her feeling of betrayal, and especially to her direct, repeated questions as to whether she was right to feel this way (see excerpts 4, 5, 8, and 9). I was reluctant to respond, in part because I wanted to see how the officer would respond and in part because I didn't want to be perceived by the officer as interfering. Clearly the woman expected some response: more than once she waited for one through a long pause, or insistently repeated her question, sometimes eliciting a response from me (usually a barely audible back-channeller like *umhm* or *yes* produced after a noticeable delay, as in excerpts 6 through 9), sometimes not.

(4) COMPLAINANT: This is the point don't, if somebody care about you, DON'T HURT the people who care about you. (10.0) Okay I know. xx I have nobody now. (9.0)

(5) COMPLAINANT: I'm so good to him he never want for ANY thing and I'm gonna really – You understand? (5.0) I want something out of life. I thought I had it.

(6) COMPLAINANT: You know we just having I was sitting right there, he was sitting there and we just if you CARE about somebody, don't you think you can talk to them about situations? (2.0) (Bonnie: umhm)

(7) COMPLAINANT: When he knocked me down on the bed and stuff I don't even know how it happened. (.) I just can't believe it. (.) I just don't want my son over here. He'll tear him up. (2.0) It's (.) I just thought I had it MADE. (.) Ever love anybody? (Bonnie: [barely audible] umhm)

(8) COMPLAINANT: I mean that's what hurts, when you try to be honest with somebody, and they just gonna punch you in the face. You see this. You see it! (.) (Bonnie: umhm (.) I see it) (6.0)

(9) COMPLAINANT: I can't say that he's transmitting shit out there. I know what I caught. I know that I don't DEAL. (4.0) And it hurts. I was only trying to talk to him about that. "Oh you drunk bitch. You wanna talk shit." It's not fair. If I didn't care about him, you think I would TALK to him about it? (2.0) You think I would? (Bonnie: [barely audible] hm.)

During the interval when the police officer was taking the report (the first twenty minutes or so of the call), he produced no responses to the woman's questions. All his comments were guided by the script of the incident report. Sometimes this script led to interruptions of the woman's ongoing account, as in (10).

(10) COMPLAINANT: I mean I just wanted, I mean you go to the health depart-
POLICE OFFICER [interrupts]: Spell your name for me.

In other instances, his response to her questions and remarks, while not actually interrupting her in midclause, still constituted an interruption because he failed to respond to a question or abruptly changed the topic (Murray 1985: 33–5), as in (11) and (12):

(11) COMPLAINANT: You know and all of a sudden he said old drunken bitch. I said what're you talking about. I said (.) we're together, we gotta help each other. You know?
POLICE OFFICER: What's your date of birth?

(12) COMPLAINANT: I said something's going ON here. I said I'm gonna tell you what I'm
                      gonna do for you. I'm gonna xxx. (.) xxx. I cannot – me, have disease
                      [incredulously]. Now wouldn't you be honest if you got something for
                      somebody (Bonnie: (.) umhm) and not be shooting drugs? I don't shoot
                      drugs! I don't play it! I don't have it in my house! (6.0) And I hurt.
      POLICE OFFICER: What color was his pants?

These interruptions might be perceived as inattentiveness to the complainant's ongoing account. At one point it did become clear that the officer hadn't heard all that
she had said. He asked what her relationship was with the actor at the point at which
the report form dictates that question, though she had already told him. In at least
one case, however, the officer's interruption was an attempt to accord the woman
some privacy by preventing her from sharing personal and perhaps painful intimate
details that he might not need to know for his report:

(13) COMPLAINANT: The point is, I tell you what this started from, xx he's been messing
                      with other women and –
      POLICE OFFICER [interrupts]:   Okay, just have a seat there.

That the officer also, in another role, would believe a response to the woman's
questions would be appropriate, even necessary, was evident again in the frame
break at the end of the call. Although throughout the call he had been seated across
the room from the woman, head bent to his writing, at the end of the call he gathered
his papers together, stood up, came over to her side of the room, told her he did
indeed understand, and asked if she would be okay for the rest of the evening
(14–15). This response can also be understood as a very belated production of a
preferred second to the woman's repeated questions about whether he understood
her pain.

(14) COMPLAINANT: Can you understand how that makes me feel?
      POLICE OFFICER: I understand. I understand perfectly how you feel.
      COMPLAINANT: If you can't talk to somebody that you care about, about transmitting
                      disease, then what is it.
      POLICE OFFICER: I understand exactly what you're saying. xx he had no reason to hit
                      you either. Nope, I understand exactly what you're saying. You guys
                      are grown, you should be able to sit down and talk-

(15) POLICE OFFICER: Sure you're okay now, don't need anything?
      COMPLAINANT: No no I'm all right.

This increased intimacy allows the woman to ask how he would react in a similar
situation – to treat him, that is, as a man rather than a police officer:

(16) COMPLAINANT: You know, if I was your woman, and you was messing around (Police
                      officer: I don't do) would you want me to tell you?

POLICE OFFICER: No. [silent laughter]

COMPLAINANT: (3.0) No seriously.

POLICE OFFICER: The reason why I'm laughing is because see I don't do that and I don't beat on women. I mean I you know it's it's not funny but I don't do that.

COMPLAINANT: It hurts. (.)

POLICE OFFICER: I understand.

COMPLAINANT: You take someone into your heart like that, you know, I was in my glory. You know, that hurts. I'm hurting. (pause)

POLICE OFFICER: Well if he's downstairs I'm taking him with me.

The officer's immediate response was to try to recreate emotional distance between himself and the complainant with quick laughter, a quick apology, and an insistence that he doesn't act like that. This is the only point where his speech contained any false starts. He quickly returned to his professional role by emphasizing the action he would take if he found the man lurking downstairs.

It is important to add that this officer when talking to me earlier had strongly emphasized that two things that really bothered him were men who beat women and adults who abused children. Although every officer talks about how difficult it is to see hurt, lost, and abandoned children, many of them have become impatient with domestic-violence calls, either because victims won't show up at the hearing once officers make the arrest or they do show up but won't press charges, or because the police are called in frequently and, in their view, unneccessarily. This officer, perhaps because he is a rookie, doesn't yet feel this way. Furthermore, he is perceived by other officers as caring and perceptive. "He listens," they say of him. Similarly, others said of the female police officer above, "She's good people." It isn't, then, any marked lack of compassion that produced these interactions. Police officers, male and female, will say, "When I'm in uniform, I'm not a woman/man – I'm a police officer." They mean to emphasize their lack of sexuality, but also that they have set aside personal lives, personal opinions, and personalities while they are on the job.

The linguistic devices used to remove traces of opinion and personality in written language – passive voice, substitution of *one* for *I*, etc. – have been widely studied (Biber & Finegan 1989; Chafe & Tannen 1987). Biber and Finegan (1989) call texts like newscasts, newspapers, professional letters, and official documents which are characterized by the absence of markers of affect and evidentiality "faceless" texts.[9] In popular usage, this sort of language is called *bureaucratese*. By and large, different linguistic resources are available in face-to-face interaction than in writing to prevent interaction from becoming too personal and to create impersonality. Some of these are the discourse-management techniques we have seen above: long silences, nonresponsiveness, interruptions, frame breaks, and nonproduction of preferred seconds in adjacency-pair sequences. Because both male and female officers have the same experiences and the same tasks, and because they interpret these tasks and experiences similarly, they report to the same linguistic style while taking reports – a sort of bureaucratese, or facelessness, in face-to-face interaction.[10]

Objectivity, Masculinity, and Changing Workplaces

In many institutional settings (confessional booths, psychotherapy sessions, class-rooms, bureaucratic interviews and job interviews, as well as in police reports) listeners expose themselves to an interlocutor who has the power to judge and act upon the account (see Foucault 1978: 61–3; Gal 1991: 175; Gumperz 1982; Sattel 1983). The ability to remain silent and require justification of behavior is a prerogat-ive of the powerful. Inexpressivity can be used to make behavior appear to be the result of unemotional rationality in order to forestall challenges and questions.

That women who move into powerful and masculine institutions sometimes adopt the interactional behavior characteristic of these institutions might disappoint some feminists. But it seems clear that who we think can do certain jobs changes more rapidly than expectations about how those jobs should be done. The process by which women enter a masculine workplace necessarily includes some adoption, as well as adaptation, of institutional norms. The interesting question is not whether women adapt, but how. I have focused here on an interactional style that male and female police officers share, in part because I want to represent their work environ-ment as they understand it, and one of the important ideologies which structure this workplace is that "it's us versus them" and "we all wear the blue." I also, however, focus on these similarities between the interactional styles of female and male police officers as a response to the extant literature on language and gender, which often begins by asking what the differences between men's and women's language are, and which, in its focus on women versus men, threatens to reify social differences in ways not so very different from sex-based essentialist theories. I argue here for a more flexible definition of gender and its effects on language use, one that accords speakers more agency to develop a speaking style based upon their occupational choices, personal histories, sexuality, lifestyles, and more. Eckert and McConnell-Ginet (1992; see also this volume, p. 484) have also recently urged scholars of language and gender to consider the complex array of interests and meanings that are attached to interaction within a given community of practice. Close attention to local meanings attached to interaction will produce a more dynamic view of gender and power relations because it can recognize the resources for challenges and change which are already available and used within every community. Although resistances to and reinterpretations of hegemonic interpretations of gender may be particularly evident in some settings – women doing "men's" work, or lesbians' and gay men's choices about how to project their own gender identities – they exist in every community.[11]

Because masculinity is not referentially (or directly) marked by behaviors and attitudes but is indexically linked to them (in mediated non-exclusive probabilistic ways; see Ochs 1991), female police officers can interpret behaviors that are normatively or frequently understood as masculine (like noninvolvement or emotional distance) as simply "the way we need to act to do our job" in a professional way. In addition to exploiting this indexicality of gender, female police officers are also redefining mas-culinity and femininity. Female officers attach less importance to appearance than do traditional versions of femininity (see Brownmiller 1984). Attention to appearance may even be understood as excessive attention to appearance, as when police officers, both male and female, dismiss some women ("those women with the long polished fingernails") as being unable to work the job. These women are dismissed as overly feminine. The redefinitions of masculinity and femininity that female police officers undertake (including their understanding of affect and objectivity) make it possible for them to think of police work as not incompatible with their own felt gender identities. In the end, such redefinitions could free women and men from the tyranny of the everlasting binary associations we find in our culture between masculine/objective/rational/strong/cultural and feminine/subjective/emotional/weak/natural. The implicit recognition of the historicity and indexicality of the link between masculinity and objectivity evident in female police officers' interpretations of their own behavior shows that indexicality can be exploited in ways that foster the integration of women into workplaces from which they were previously barred.

NOTES

I gratefully acknowledge the financial and institutional support given to this project by the National Science Foundation, the Wenner-Gren Foundation for Anthropological Research, the Stanford Humanities Center, the Mellon Foundation, and the Women's Studies Program at the University of Pittsburgh. Commanders Freeman, McComb, Patterson, and Wind graciously allowed me to patrol with officers under their command and thus made this project possible. The generous cooperation of the officers themselves made it worthwhile. Earlier versions of this paper have benefited from the questions and comments of participants in the Stanford Sociolinguistics Rap Session, the University of Pittsburgh Women's Studies Lunch Series, and the Swarthmore Linguistics and Psychology Department Colloquia. Pam Saunders provided bibliographic assistance.

1   I alternate between using *black* and *African American* here and elsewhere. Pittsburgh police officers of African American heritage almost universally refer to themselves as *black*, and citizens are also generally described by black and white officers as *black* or *white*. *African American*, however, has increasingly become the accepted term in academic references and other liberal sociopolitical contexts. This variation reflects linguistic and attitudinal change in progress.

2   Although carrying and using a gun is typed as a masculine activity in the West, a poster which female officers have up in one station (between the door to the cellblock and the door to their locker room) works to disrupt this. It has a picture of a frazzled-looking black cat with the text, "I have PMS . . . and a gun. Any questions?" Someone has written "Fuck no" in pencil on the bottom of the poster. Though this statement plays into recent cultural interpretations of women with PMS as irrational and out of control (see E. Martin 1987), it also uses that stereotype to argue that women, too, can be threatening and forceful. Because one of the skills officers acknowledge as important is being able to "act crazier than they do," this is also a successful bid to be perceived as competent workers.

3   In all transcriptions, comments in parentheses are my questions or reactions. (.) indicates a pause of one second. Longer pauses are timed, so that (10.0) indicates a ten-second

pause. A series of x's represent unintelligible speech. Hhh represents laughter. A colon (*so: funny*) represents a prolonged vowel. Capital letters represent increased volume (*I said DON'T DO THAT*). Italics in the transcriptions are my emphasis, not the speaker's.

4   Curiously, anger does not participate in the economy of affect in the same way that sympathy/empathy does. Anger is performed – "You just have to act crazier than they do" – in ways that are assumed to leave the inner person untouched. It is not a limited resource, but a dramatic mask. I will explore this in a later paper. Because the sociocultural study of affect is so recent, it isn't clear whether other Americans share police officers' understanding of positive affect as a limited resource. Several officers that I have patrolled with do refuse this understanding of how the production and use of emotion works. One is an officer with a college degree in the social sciences who, having grown up in a ghetto herself, believes that the criminal-justice system treats poor citizens inequitably, and she wants to try to change negative public perceptions of police officers. She works hard to be patient with citizens (even saying "I'm *more* patient than I used to be" – a marked contrast with other officers' beliefs about how they have changed), but she admits that this work takes its toll at home. She is less patient with her boyfriend, often needs time alone to recuperate from the job, and is concerned that their relationship is endangered. Here, the economy of affect is still closed, though the opinion about where the expenditure should take place is work rather than family and self. Another exception is a born-again Christian whose actions are governed by a metaphor of "The Lord shall replenish my cup." He is clearly still spending emotion, but he believes that he can tap into a limitless source of patient love. Emotion is still a commodity for him, but a limitless one.

5   Linguistic analyses which suggest that interactional differences between two groups within a single culture are analogous to cross-cultural interaction are often (rightly) critiqued for ignoring relations of power between the subcultural groups. One needs to ask whose interactional norms prevail when interpretations disagree (see Eckert & McConnell-Ginet (1992) for a thoughtful review of the strengths and weaknesses of the dual-culture approach; see also this volume, p. 484). The question of power is clearly a relevant one in police–citizen interaction. A cautionary note, however – as our knowledge grows about how conversational interaction proceeds, many different sorts of interaction have been subsumed under the dual-culture approach: men and women (Tannen 1990; Maltz & Borker 1982, reprinted in this volume, p. 417). New York Jews and Californians (Tannen 1984), and native-born and foreign-born British workers (Gumperz 1982). The question of power (whose interpretation prevails) has been raised for most of these. Nonetheless, the sorts of power wielded by police officers in interaction is only sanctioned to a limited extent by the society at large while that wielded by men is reinforced repeatedly in most societal institutions. The power of New York Jews interacting with other Americans is a source of their denigration in the wider culture. The texture of each of these sorts of interactions and the workings of power and different *kinds* of power in each requires considerable attention.

6   All police reports require officers to obtain information on complainant's age, address, employment, etc. One officer told me she had decided to stop asking about employment because it was none of her business. Other officers say the same about age, especially the age of women. One officer would, when he got to that part of the form, cup his hand around his mouth and drop his voice to a whisper as if asking for secret information. The woman would usually laugh and then tell him. In asking men about their marital status he would say, "Married or smart" (sometimes eliciting a laugh and sometimes not).

Officers are also sometimes uncomfortable with asking for information on missing persons – including information on scars hidden by clothing and on circumcision.

7 In many cases medics and police officers are asked to respond together to scenes that involve both crime and injury. The difference between their reactions to victims is telling. Medics bustle around with a steady stream of questions and reassurances, administering medical assistance. Officers stand back, moving forward to obtain information as necessary and when possible. When I asked one officer why one accident victim who had just emerged seemingly unhurt from an overturned vehicle was being placed on a blackboard with a neck brace by medics, he shrugged, "That's them, they're always fluttering around." Medics' role is feminized when compared with the police officers: their ministrations are perceived as overly solicitous.

8 Occasionally a complainant will explicitly ask for these personal comments. One woman, pregnant and recently beaten up by her boyfriend, had refused to allow a female police officer to take a report. Instead she asked the officer what she should do. The officer at first demurred, saying she didn't offer advice, but the woman persisted: "Take off your uniform, just for a minute – what would you do?" The officer finally replied, "No one hits me. I get paid to get hit – that's all." Again this incident reveals that personal comments are not perceived as coming from the police officer but from the person inside the uniform.

9 That Finegan and Biber's "faceless stance" category also includes such widely different genres as mystery fiction, humor, biographies, and face-to-face conversations indicates that some considerable refinement of the category is necessary before it can be adequately described, let alone explained. Though broadly based quantitative studies like theirs are useful for indicating genres where the production of negative or positive affect are more prevalent, the explanation of why affect, or a particular sort of affect, does or does not occur in a particular genre can only be derived from a thick description (see Geertz 1973; Eckert & McConnell-Ginet 1992) of the social situations in which it occurs and the uses to which it is put.

10 The extent to which men or women might tend to economize more on affect is, of course, a relevant question here, but one that is extremely difficult to answer. The situations experienced by the different officers are so varied that it is difficult to make the appropriate comparisons.

11 The recent interest in feminist circles in the study of gender ambiguity and crossover gendering (see Butler 1990; Devor 1989; Epstein & Straub 1991; Garber 1991) marks a new era in feminist thought, which is characterized by a movement away from earlier feminist attempts to celebrate woman and establish what she is towards an attempt to explore the malleability of gender. The rapidly growing field of lesbian and gay studies, in addition to raising its own questions about constructions of heterosexism, homophobia, and sexual identity, also raises important questions about the flexibility of gender identity.

REFERENCES

Biber, Douglas, & Edward Finegan (1989). Styles of stance in English: Lexical and grammatical marking of evidentiality and affect. *Text* 9(1): 93–124. Special issue on the pragmatics of affect, Elinor Ochs (ed.).

Bourdieu, Pierre (1977). *Outline of a theory of practice.* Cambridge: Cambridge University Press.

Bradley, Harriet (1989). *Men's work, women's work: A sociological history of the sexual division of labour in employment*. Minneapolis: University of Minnesota Press.

Brownmiller, Susan (1984). *Femininity*. New York: Fawcett.

Butler, Judith (1990). *Gender trouble: Feminism and the subversion of identity*. New York: Routledge.

Chafe, Wallace, & Deborah Tannen (1987). The relationship between spoken and written language. *Annual Review of Anthropology* 16: 383–407.

Devor, Holly (1989). *Gender blending: Confronting the limits of duality*. Bloomington: Indiana University Press.

Eckert, Penelope, & Sally McConnell-Ginet (1992). Think practically and look locally: Language and gender as community-based practice. *Annual Review of Anthropology*. 21: 461–90.

Epstein, Julia, & Kristina Straub (eds.) (1991). *Body guards: The cultural politics of gender ambiguity*. New York: Routledge.

Foucault, Michel (1978). *The history of sexuality*. Vol. 1. New York: Pantheon.

Gal, Susan (1991). Between speech and silence: The problematics of research on language and gender. In Micaela di Leonardo (ed.), *Gender at the crossroads of knowledge: Feminist anthropology in the postmodern era*. Berkeley: University of California Press, 175–203.

Garber, Marjorie (1991). *Vested interests*. New York: Routledge.

Geertz, Clifford (1973). Thick description: Toward an interpretive theory of culture. In *The interpretation of cultures*. New York: Basic Books, 3–32.

Goffman, Erving (1971). *Relations in public*. New York: Harper & Row.

——(1977). *Frame analysis*. New York: Harper & Row.

Gumperz, John (ed.) (1982). *Language and social identity*. Cambridge: Cambridge University Press.

Hochschild, Arlie Russell (1983). *The managed heart: Commercialization of human feeling*. Berkeley: University of California Press.

Kanter, Rosabeth Moss (1977). *Men and women of the corporation*. New York: Basic Books.

Keller, Evelyn Fox (1990). Gender and science. In Joyce McCarl Nielsen (ed.). *Feminist research methods: Exemplary reading in the social sciences*. San Francisco: Westview Press, 41–57.

Lutz, Catherine (1986). Emotion, thought and estrangement: Emotion as a cultural category. *Cultural Anthropology* 1(3): 287–309.

——(1990). Engendered emotion: Gender, power and the rhetoric of emotional control in American discourse. In Lila Abu-Lughod & Catherine Lutz (eds.), *Language and the politics of emotion*. Cambridge: Cambridge University Press, 69–91.

Maltz, Daniel N., & Ruth A. Borker (1982). A cultural approach to male–female miscommunication. In John Gumperz (ed.), 196–216.

Martin, Emily (1987). *The woman in the body: A cultural analysis of reproduction*. Boston: Beacon Press.

Martin, Susan (1980). *Breaking and entering: Policewomen on patrol*. Berkeley: University of California Press.

Milgram, Stanley (1988). The urban experience: A psychological analysis of urban life. In George Gmelch & Walter Zenner (eds.), *Readings in urban anthropology*. Prospect Heights, IL: Waveland, 53–62.

Murray, Stephen (1985). Toward a model of members' methods for recognizing interruptions. *Language in Society* 14(1): 31–40.

Ochs, Elinor (1991). Indexing gender. In Alessandro Duranti & Charles Goodwin (eds.), *Rethinking context*. Cambridge: Cambridge University Press.

Reskin, Barbara, & Patricia Roos (1990). *Job queues, gender queues: Explaining women's inroads into male occupations*. Philadelphia: Temple University Press.

Rubinstein, Jonathan (1973). *City police*. New York: Farrar, Strauss, & Giroux.

Sattel, Jack (1983). Men, inexpressiveness, and power. In Barrie Thorne, Cheris Kramarae, & Nancy Henley (eds.), *Language, gender, and society*. Rowley, MA: Newbury House, 118–24.

Scott, Joan (1988). *Gender and the politics of history*. New York: Columbia University Press.

Sherzer, Joel (1987). A diversity of voices: Men's and women's speech in ethnographic perspective. In Susan Philips, Susan Steele, & Christine Tanz (eds.), *Language, gender, and sex in comparative perspective*. Cambridge: Cambridge University Press, 95–120.

Tannen, Deborah (1984). *Conversational style: Analyzing talk among friends*. Norwood, NJ: Ablex.

——(1990). *You just don't understand: Women and men in conversation*. New York: William Morrow.

U.S. Department of Justice (1987a). *Profile of state and local law enforcement agencies*. Washington: Office of Justice Programs, Bureau of Justice Statistics.

——(1987b). *Police departments in large cities*. Washington: Office of Justice Programs, Bureau of Justice Statistics.

22

'Not just doctors' orders': Directive–Response Sequences in Patients' Visits to Women and Men Physicians

Candace West

Introduction

> *Doctors' Orders*. This phrase, used to describe a physician's recommendations to a patient, implies that the patient has no choice but to do whatever told. (Shapiro, 1978: 170)

One of the most prevalent complaints in the literature on physician–patient communication concerns patients' failures to do as they are told (e.g. Becker and Maiman, 1975; Davis, 1966, 1968; DiMatteo and DiNicola, 1982; Francis et al., 1969; Kirscht and Rosenstock, 1977; Steele et al., 1985). Estimates suggest that 20–80 percent of patients do not follow their physicians' directives (DiMatteo and DiNicola, 1982; Sackett and Snow, 1979) and that, on average, one patient out of two does not do so (Ley, 1983). To the extent that physicians issue their directives in the interests of patients' health, one can understand why patients' failures to follow them would be deeply disturbing.

Despite this concern, the formulation of physicians' directives to patients has not been pursued as an object of investigation. As Frankel and Beckman (1989b) point out, the problem of non-adherence has traditionally been seen as a function of patients' lack of education or motivation, or as a function of physicians' failures to persuade patients of treatment benefits:

> Until very recently, little if any attention was paid to the sequences of interaction that transpire whenever a practitioner and patient meet face to face, and the possibility that non-adherence might be linked to the dynamics of speech exchange. (Frankel and Beckman, 1989b: 63)

As a result, we know very little about *how* physicians formulate their directives to patients or how patients respond to them.

And yet, a growing number of studies suggest that the dynamics of speech exchange are central to our understanding of physician–patient relations. For example, Maynard (in press) reports that patients' responses to bad diagnostic news are heavily dependent on the context of discourse in which physicians deliver it. Steele et al. (1985) find that patients' adherence is directly related to the form and specificity of physicians' questions. Moreover, Frankel and Beckman (1989a) observe that more than 90 percent of patients' formal complaints about their medical care focus on ways that health professionals communicate with them. Findings such as these indicate that the forms of talk that are employed between physicians and patients may well have practical consequences for patient care (cf. West and Frankel, 1991).

In this paper, I am concerned with how physicians formulate their directives to patients and how patients respond to them. Following Goodwin (1980; 1988, reprinted in this volume, p. 121; 1990), I view directive–response speech sequences as a means of establishing social order between parties to talk. Hence, my analysis focuses on the various social arrangements physicians propose through their directives and the responses these elicit from patients. My study of encounters between patients and family physicians suggests that women and men physicians use very different forms to issue their directives and that these forms yield different patient responses. In discussing my findings, I consider their relationship to the issue of patient adherence more generally and to the quality of patients' relations with women and men physicians.

On Giving Directives

As Goodwin (1980: 157) notes, *directives* are 'speech acts that try to get another to do something'. As she also notes, alternative means of formulating directives – and responses to them – provide for a variety of social arrangements between parties to talk (Goodwin, 1990: 74). For example, the use of *aggravated* forms, such as orders and demands, implies that a speaker can legitimately impose on another by stating their requirements baldly (Labov and Fanshel, 1977: 63, 84–5). By contrast, the use of *mitigated* forms, such as pleas and suggestions, allows a speaker to avoid offending another by putting forth their wishes in downgraded ways (Labov and Fanshel, 1977: 63, 84–5).

In her ground-breaking work on the subject, Ervin-Tripp (1976) found that directive forms vary with the rank and familiarity of speakers and hearers.[1] Her study of observed directives across a broad range of settings (including homes, hospitals, adult education classrooms, offices and a Marine Corps recruiting station) showed that their distribution followed a rough stratification system – according to the explicitness of the directive and 'the relative power of speaker and addressee in conventional usage' (Ervin-Tripp, 1976: 29):

Need statements, such as 'I need a match'.
Imperatives, such as 'Gimme a match' and elliptical forms like 'a match'.

Imbedded imperatives, such as 'Could you gimme a match?' In these cases, agent, action, object and often beneficiary are as explicit as in direct imperatives, though they are embedded in a frame with other syntactic and semantic properties.

Permission directives, such as 'May I have a match?' Bringing about the condition stated requires an action by the hearer other than merely granting permission.

Question directives, like 'Gotta match?' which do not specify the desired act.

Hints, such as 'The matches are all gone'.

Her findings indicate that the use of alternative directive forms varies considerably across settings and situations and, hence, that variation is not merely a function of politeness. Perhaps more important, they demonstrate that the interpretation of a directive *as* a directive is dependent on its context: 'if the form is inappropriate to the context, it may not be heard as a directive at all' (Ervin-Tripp, 1976: 59).

To be sure, 'context' often serves as a proxy for a broad range of factors in the study of interaction, including the setting, the nature of the situation, the task at hand (if any) and the identities of the participants involved (Ervin-Tripp, 1976: 59; Goffman, 1964: 134; Goodwin, 1990: 88; Hymes, 1964: 10). The distribution of different directive forms across diverse settings and situations raises important questions about how these factors are related to one another (Goodwin, 1990: 87–8). It also raises questions about the turn-by-turn organization of conversation in which speech actions achieve a particular meaning or delineated range of meanings in a situated context (West and Zimmerman, 1987: 511). Goodwin's (1980, 1988, 1990) research addresses these issues in fine detail by focusing on *how* alternative directive forms are fitted to the specific setting, situation and conversation in which they occur.

Her data consist of audiotapes and transcripts of conversations among Black working-class girls and boys (ages 9–14) at play in an urban neighborhood. She recorded these conversations over an eighteen-month period while observing the children's organization of their play groups. Goodwin's systematic analyses of these materials found that girls and boys used distinctive directive forms to coordinate their activities in dramatically different ways.

[. . .]

Her findings show that both girls and boys employ directives to organize their task activities, but they do so very differently. Whereas boys use imperative forms to address subordinates (and requests, to those superordinate to them), girls use the same mitigated forms reciprocally with one another. Goodwin (1990: 147) concludes that *'boys' directives display distinctions between participants and stress individual rights [while] girls' directives stress the connectedness of girls to each other and their caretaking concerns'*. Through these means, boys and girls establish contrasting forms of social organization.

Goodwin's work affords a systematic approach to the study of directives and responses – an approach grounded in the detailed empirical examination of tape-recorded conversations. Below, I employ this approach in my examination of encounters between physicians and patients; but first I describe my methods of data collection and analysis.

Methods

Data for this analysis consist of 21 encounters between physicians and patients that were videotaped in a family practice clinic in the southern United States. The physicians in these encounters are residents in family medicine, a medical specialty that demands three years of additional training beyond medical school. Most are in their late twenties and early thirties.[2] Seventeen of the encounters involve physicians who are white men and four involve white women.

Patients in these encounters range in age from 16 to 82 years. Their backgrounds are diverse, including those of unemployed carpenter, construction worker, domestic and professional. Of the 20 patients involved (one was seen by two different physicians in the course of his visit), five are white men; six, white women; five, Black women; and four, Black men.

The encounters themselves are actual patient visits to family physicians, so they are not standardized according to length, presenting complaint, or duration of relationship between physician and patient. The clinic at which they were recorded has used videotaping for over a decade as part of the ongoing training of residents. With their signed consent, patients are taped while visiting their physicians via ceiling microphones and unobtrusive cameras placed in the corners of examining rooms. In the analysis which follows, I employ pseudonyms to ensure the confidentiality of the physician–patient relationship.

To transcribe the tapes, I used a set of conventions developed by Gail Jefferson (see Transcription Conventions 1, p. xviii). The aim of these conventions is to capture as close to a verbatim version of interaction as is possible – to record what was said and how it was said in fine detail. In all, the 21 videotaped encounters yielded 532 pages of transcript.

Elsewhere (West, 1983, 1984a, 1984b (reprinted in this volume, p. 396), 1984c), I have used these data for other research purposes, such as the analysis of turn-taking, question–answer sequencing and repair between physicians and patients; and, in fact, the findings reported here did not emerge from any initial plan to study 'doctors' orders'. But in the course of a related research project, I observed such striking differences in the ways that men and women physicians formulated their directives to patients that it prompted a comprehensive examination of those directives in their own right.

I began my analysis by examining the transcripts to locate all instances of physicians' directives, that is 'speech acts that try to get another to do something'. I then examined the sequential contexts of these directives to further determine: (1) the speech environments in which they occurred, and (2) the responses – if any – they elicited from patients. Using this strategy, I encountered one problem that could not be resolved with the data at hand: it was virtually impossible to assess patients' responses to physicians' directives in the course of physical examinations. For example, when a physician told a patient to 'relax', 'loosen up' or 'tighten that muscle', I was often unable to determine what – if any – response this elicited, from examination of the videotape and transcript. And insofar as many of the directives issued during physical examinations had to do with patients' internal states, responses to them may not even have been detectable by the physicians involved. For this reason, I excluded directive–response sequences that occurred during physical examinations from the analysis which follows. With this exception, I inspected all the directive–response sequences that occurred in these data to assess how physicians formulated their directives and how patients responded to them. Because men and women physicians issued their directives in dramatically different ways, I present my findings separately for each.

Directives of Men Physicians

Imperatives

Among the men physicians in these encounters, directives to patients typically took the form of imperatives. For example, 49 of the 156 directives they issued (or 31 percent) were formulated as explicit commands:

(1) (Dyad 01:749+)
PATIENT: So if I fe- fee:l this coming on, an' I'm sidding up in a pla:ne, 'r
            I'm out somewhere in a *ca:r*, .h 'n I c ⌈an't lie dow-   ⌉
PHYSICIAN: ⌊LIE:: DOW:N!⌋

(2) (Dyad 02:114+)
PATIENT: I'm *try*in' tuh (.2) *sid* o::n this tailbone duh try an' ged it
            bedder an' ev'ry chance I could ⌈I try duh   ⌉
PHYSICIAN: ⌊(Oh:: don' even)⌋ try:::, if it
            *hur*ts when yuh *sid* on it, stay off of it.

(3) (Dyad 05:258+)
PHYSICIAN: Go ahead an' *get* thi:s, (.) ((hands patient the x-ray order)) an'
            then ⌈co:me ba: ⌉ck
PATIENT: ⌊hh-hh-hh ((audible sigh))⌋
PHYSICIAN: an:d um give it tuh the nurse here ut th' station.

(4) (Dyad 14:474)
PHYSICIAN: Jus' take one of ea:ch foah times a da:y.

(5) (Dyad 16:484+)
PHYSICIAN: Oka:y, ((while writing)) jus' rub it all over yer fa:ce in a light
            thin fi:lm, *twice::* a da:y.

Above, for example, physicians employed imperatives to command patients with respect to future courses of action: 'LIE DOWN!' (if you feel this coming on), 'stay off of it' (if it hurts when you sit on it), and 'rub it all over yer face' (twice a day). But they also used imperatives to command patients regarding immediate courses of action:

(6) (Dyad 08:216)
PHYSICIAN: TAKE OFF YER SHOES AN' SO::CKS.

(7) (Dyad 17:387)
PHYSICIAN: Take yer trousers o:ff.

(8) (Dyad 18:094+)
PHYSICIAN: .hh *Pull off* a *shirt* ((taps patient on the knee)) fo:r me.

(9) (Dyad 10:252)
PHYSICIAN: °Si:t for me right there:.

In these cases, physicians' directives required return actions from patients then and there.

One command characteristic of all these commands is the authority they imply on the part of the speaker. As Goodwin (1980) observes, the formulation of a directive in imperative form makes implicit claims about the speaker's right to be issuing such a directive in the first place. In excerpts 1–5, physicians' formulations propose the legitimacy of their right to command patients with respect to their physical activities ('LIE DOWN!', 'stay off of it') and treatment ('get this' (X-ray), 'Take one of each foah times a day'). And in excerpts 6–9, physicians' directives assert their authority to command patients to disrobe ('TAKE OFF YER SHOES AN' SOCKS', 'Pull off a shirt for me') and to move ('Sit for me right there'). What they thereby propose is an asymmetrical alignment between physician and patient, in which the patient 'has no choice but to do whatever told' (Shapiro, 1978: 170).

Need statements

Another way in which men physicians issued directives to patients was by stating those patients' requirements. For example, physicians frequently told patients what they 'needed to' or 'ought to' do:

(10) (Dyad 14:803+)
PHYSICIAN: I think yuh need duh *try:* duh ged ou:t, even if yuh- .h y'know, *si:t* an' watch
o:ther people *da:nce* 'r whatever.

(11) (Dyad 18:208+)
PHYSICIAN: It dozen *hurt* tuh keep movin' *arou::n*', but cha *nee:d* duh put the *hea:t* o:n it.
(.6) An':: (.) yuh nee:d tuh get the *as:prun* into yuh tuh sorda make it *to:l*er'ble.

(12) (Dyad 18:261+)
PHYSICIAN: We:ll, .hh *I'll* write chew a *thy::ung* ((meaning an excuse from work)) cuz I
think you oughtta . . .hh I think you oughtta knock tha::t o:ff fer awhy:ule-hhh.
((now writing))

Physicians also told patients what they 'had to' or 'had got to' do:

(13) (Dyad 02:393)
PHYSICIAN: So yuh gotta be *ril care:*ful no:w (.) you been (.8) .h BE:IN' CARE:FUL
'BOUT CUTTIN' YER TOE:NAILS?

(14)   (Dyad 05:481)
PHYSICIAN: YOU AN' ⌈DOCKTUR⌉ MOR:SE will hafta con:s ⌈ult o:n⌉ tha:t
PATIENT: ⌊Ye:ss.   ⌋   ⌊°OKay⌋

(15)   (Dyad 02:708)
PHYSICIAN: An' you haf tuh sign the above: on thi:s

(16)   (Dyad 07:682)
PHYSICIAN: ⌊Lissen, I KNOW:! Un-un, It's your problem!
             You gotta⌋ dihci:de!

Ervin-Tripp (1976) describes 'need statements' as some of the most aggravated of
directive forms, noting that they routinely occur between superiors and subordinates. However, in her data, such directives focused on the requirements of speakers
themselves:

(Ervin-Tripp, 1976: 29)
(Physician to technician):
I'll need a routine culture and a specimen.
(Doctor to hospital nurse):
I'll need a 19 gauge needle, IV tubing, and a preptic swab.

In the data at hand, physicians' 'need statements' did not refer to their own requirements, but to those of the patient.

The only exceptions to this rule were directives that employed 'we' in statements
of pseudo-mutual requirements:

(17)   (Dyad 13:016+)
PHYSICIAN: As I *sai::d*, I don' think that- ((rifling through a drawer)) (.4) we should use:
             the: (1.4) that you: should use: (1.4) an Eye Yew Dee anymore. (3.6) Whi:ch-
             (.) mea:::ns:::s (.6) that wih haf tuh dihcide on another method a birth control
             for yuh.

Above, for example, the physician first uses 'we' to refer to the-ones-who-should-be-
using-an-intrauterine-device, but he quickly replaces this with 'you'. So, when he
subsequently uses 'wih' to refer to the-ones-who-have-to-decide, the object of his
decision-making belies the collaborative syntax he employs – here, 'we' have to
decide for 'you' (not us). In this context, 'we' who-should-not-use-an-IUD-anymore
is the patient, but 'we' who-need-to-decide-on-another-method-of-birth-control is
the physician himself.

The next excerpt shows a similar statement of pseudo-mutual requirements:

(18)   (Dyad 20:234+)
PHYSICIAN: So yuh might wanna take some li:ddle no:tes. h Yer gunna ha:f tuh .hh yer
             gunna take some rihsponsuhbi:lidy fer this ((taps foot)) cuz we're gonna 'aftuh
             ((points his right index finger at her)) *figg*er ou:t whethe:r .hh we need duh do
             some *tes::ts* er no:t.

Here, again, the physician invokes the prospect of joint decision-making by his use of 'we' with reference to the-ones-who-are-going-to-have-to-figure-out-whether-to-do-some-tests. However, this pseudo-mutual statement appears in the same stretch of talk in which the physician tells the patient that *she's* going to take some responsibility for this, and as he formulates what 'we're' going to have to do, *he points his finger directly at the patient*. Hence, like other statements of patients' requirements (e.g. excerpts 10–17), these directives propose the physicians' authority to assess patients' needs and determine what is best for them. What they propose simultaneously is a hierarchical relationship between physician and patient.

Want statements

Still another means of issuing directives to patients was the physician's statement of his own preferences for patient action. Typically, such statements were formatted with reference to what the physician 'wanted' or 'didn't want' the patient to do:

(19) (Dyad 05:323+)
PHYSICIAN: Uh:m, if *you*:: in th' MEAN::time start havin' FE::Ver er shakin'=CHI:lls (.) .h any problems like tha:t, .h then ah wa:n' uh- then I wa:n' cha duh git back with who'sever on ca::ll

(20) (Dyad 09:109)
PHYSICIAN: I *do:* wan' cha tuh go ahead an' *get* that Li:ght Salt.

(21) (Dyad 20:220+)
PHYSICIAN: Whud I: wan' cha duh *do:* fer me: is I wan' cha duh keep a *goo:d* record of *whe:n* yuh have that pai:n. How *o:ff*un yuh have it? (1.2) *Whe:n* it occu:rs? (.2) .h an' whu:t cher *do:*ing whe:n yuh *ha:ve* it.

But sometimes physicians' statements of preference were modulated by what they 'would like' patients to do:

(22) (Dyad 08:183+)
PHYSICIAN: AH'D *AL:*SO LIKE FER YUH TUH TAKE OFF YER SHOES AN SOCKS UN- AH: ((drawing curtain to 'create' an examining/dressing room)) TROU:SERS

(23) (Dyad 09:684+)
PHYSICIAN: Lemme *tell* yuh whud I- .h lemme tell yuh whud ah'd *like* yuh duh do: now, ah'd like yuh to::: (.) *see* whut arrangemun's yuh wanna make.

And, occasionally, they were further downgraded by their formulation as physicians' own desires:

(24) (Dyad 05:296+)
PHYSICIAN: So::. (.4) tch whud ah'd *li:ke* tuh do: (.) is
⌈go ahead   ⌉ an' put cha on some asprun.
PATIENT: ⌊hh-hh-hh ((sigh))⌋

(25)   (Dyad 05:423+)
PHYSICIAN: A:n Uh'd like duh see yuh ba:ck on Thurs:day

Above, for example, the physician involved in both excerpts states what *he* would like to do (i.e. put the patient on some aspirin and see her back on Thursday). However, fulfillment of his wishes will in both cases require specific actions on the part of the patient: namely, that she *take* the aspirin and that she return to *be* seen on the appointed day. Thus, his statements function like other statements of physician preference (excerpts 19–23): that is, as directives for patient action.

As others have observed, statements that refer to the speakers' wishes are among the most aggravated of directive forms (Goodwin, 1980: 160), proposing that speakers' preferences imply an obligation on the part of their addressees (Ervin-Tripp, 1976: 29).

Quasi-question directives

Closely related to statements of preferences and needs were physicians' directives that employed 'Why don't you . . .' to preface stipulations for patient action:

(26)   (Dyad 09:266+)
PHYSICIAN: Why don' yuh ((patient rises)) take (.) .h in that case, bo:th yer shirt a::n' yer undershirt off.

(27)   (Dyad 16:365+)
PHYSICIAN: Why don' chew *co::me i:n* (.2) in: (.) I guess that ah'm gonna hafta make that in two: weeks

(28)   (Dyad 17:378+)
PHYSICIAN: *Oka:y*, wull, why don't cha jump up on the table. ((doctor leans forward to push himself out of the chair. As he does so, patient does too.)) (.6) An' ah'll take a loo:k ad it.

As Ervin-Tripp (1976: 29) notes, the objects of such directives are put forth as baldly as in imperatives (e.g. 'take both yer shirt an' yer undershirt off', 'come in in two weeks', and 'jump up on the table'). And despite their interrogative forms, these directives are rarely advanced with the rising intonation that characterizes questions. Indeed, physicians formulated them in ways that demanded actions – rather than answers – in return. Thus, these directives also implied an asymmetrical alignment between parties to talk, highlighting the distinction between speakers and their addressees.

Permission provisions

Yet another form of aggravated directive I observed in these data was the giving of permission for a particular course of patient action. In this case, physicians' syntax proposed a strong contrast between themselves and the patients they addressed:

(29)   (Dyad 02:249+)

PHYSICIAN: I think that's-that's alright from time-duh-time. .h I would ex::*peck* thut-
prob:ably::::: within: the next *wee:k* or so, hh you won' need it anymore.

(30)   (Dyad 09:126)

PHYSICIAN: ⌊Ah'm not s⌋ a:yin' yuh never cun ⌊ha::ve⌋ these th ⌊i:ngs, it's just⌋ as a ru::le, that
shouldn'b ⌊e a dai:ly .hh⌋

(31)   (Dyad 13:116+)

PHYSICIAN: Yih cun start on the three-month supply:, an' yih cun re:fill that three ti:mes,
over the course of a ye:ar.

(32)   (Dyad 17:725+)

PHYSICIAN: (I'm) jus' gonna ((pulls the curtain open)) get '*t's all*- open for yuh- jus' hold
o:n fer a sekkin'=.h you cun put cher trou:zers o::n. (.4) In the *mean*time.

Above, for example, 'you can' and 'that's alright' specify what the patient is permitted to do, while 'I think' and 'I'm not sayin'' specify the physician's authority to
be granting permission. Among these physicians, the identity of the authority giving
permission ('I', the physician) was often omitted (as in the cases of excerpts 31 and
32), thus granting authority by fiat.

Of course, Ervin-Tripp (1976) also discusses 'permission directives', noting that
they tend to occur between parties who differ in rank. But there (1976: 37–8), she is
dealing with directives that *request* permission from addressees (e.g. 'Can I have my
records back?', 'May I have the salt?'); here, I am dealing with directives that *grant*
it. In this sense, the forms of directives we identify are mirror images of one another:
both propose a hierarchical relationship between speakers and their addressees, but
'permission directives' imply the speakers' subordination ('Can I have X?') while
'permission provisions' assert their superiority ('You can have X').

Directive by example

Another distinctive way that men physicians 'tried to get patients to do things' was
by stating what they themselves would do:

(33)   (Dyad 05:519+)

PHYSICIAN: ⌊Ah⌋ would do that. ⌊Ah'd drink⌋ *plen*'y a flu:ids,= ah'd take that as:prun
ruh*lig*:ously (.) .h an' if yuh need duh stay ho:me=stay home.

(34)   (Dyad 10:862+)

PHYSICIAN: An' ah'd take one: a tho:se *four* times a da:y, an' if *ne:*cessary, .h yuh cun take
two: at bedti:me. (.2) .h An': (.) whut *ah:* would do: is tuh *sta::y* on that fer
about- .h ten da:ys 'r two wee:ks?

(35)   (Dyad 18:275+)

PHYSICIAN: Wu:ll, if tuhda::y's Mo::nday, hh (1.2) ah'd prob'ly lay off till about *Thurs*:day.

In these cases, the status of physicians' directives *as* directives is hardly unclear. Like
Ervin-Tripp's (1976: 29) need and want statements, these assertions specify what the

patient is to do as explicitly as any imperative ('drink plen'y a fluids', 'take that asprun ruhligously', 'stay on that fer about ten days 'r two weeks', and 'lay off (of work) till Thursday'). But here, the form of the directive ('I would do X') implies that the patient should engage in a particular course of action simply because the physician would do so. Ironically, then, this 'indirect' directive is perhaps the most aggravated of them all: not only does it exaggerate the distinction between speaker and addressee, but its form proposes that the speaker's inclinations should serve as a model for others' behaviors.

Imbedded imperatives

To this point, I have focused on the most aggravated forms of directives because these constituted the vast majority (81 percent) of the directives men physicians used. However, there were occasions on which they employed less aggravated directives, such as imbedded imperatives:

(36) (Dyad 02:695)
PHYSICIAN: Could ju give that tuh th' bizness office on yer way ou:t?

(37) (Dyad 09:103+)
PHYSICIAN: We:ll the *mo*st I cun ask yuh duh do
            i:s ⌈tuh cut dow:n   ⌉
PATIENT: ⌊Cut down, uh-huh⌋

(38) (Dyad 20:143)
PHYSICIAN: Can you: put cher fing:er on the place where yuh uj:'ly have the pa:in?

Above, the imbedding of 'can' and 'could' into otherwise explicit commands ('give that to the business office', 'cut down', and 'put cher finger on the place') downgrade the imperatives to requests – rather than demands – for patient action. The use of 'ask' in excerpt 37 and questioning intonation in excerpts 36 and 38 further modulate these directives as requests.

But as others have pointed out, such directives still explicate the agent and object of action (Ervin-Tripp, 1976: 33), and they still emphasize the distinction between the speaker who poses the request and the addressee who is asked to fulfill it (Goodwin, 1980: 160). Thus, they too propose an asymmetrical relationship between parties to talk.

False collaboratives

A final form of directive I identified in the talk of men physicians was the 'false collaborative' – a directive that is formatted as a proposal for joint action, yet actually proposes action to be undertaken by a single individual. For example, on first inspection, the excerpts just below would appear to present suggestions for collaborative activity between speakers and their addressees:

(39)   (Dyad 10:708+)

PHYSICIAN: Oka:y ((doctor walks around to the rear of the patient)) Let's slip this back off, an' get chur blouse back o:n ((doctor carefully unties the patient's gown; he removes one sleeve from her arm, and then removes the other))

(40)   (Dyad 12:309+)

PHYSICIAN: 'Bout uh: let's have yuh come back in about- .hh *two:* weeks.

Here, physicians employ the 'Let's do X' format that Goodwin (1980, 1990) identifies as a means of proposing joint plans of action between speakers and hearers. But in these excerpts, actions specified by the directives are *not* ones that both parties can or do engage in: in excerpt 39, it is the physician who removes the patient's gown; and in excerpt 40, it is the patient who must return in two weeks. In these contexts, 'let's' implies a form of pseudo-participation in joint action (Ervin-Tripp, 1976: 48), one that parodies, rather than enacts, a true proposal. Simultaneously, it exaggerates status differences between physician and patient by highlighting (almost satirically) the distinction between them.

In short, men physicians employed directives that functioned as comparisons, emphasizing the distinctions between their patients and themselves (Goodwin, 1990: 74). Through imperatives, imbedded imperatives and statements of their needs and wants, they made implicit claims regarding their authority to impose their demands on patients and patients' obligations to fulfill them. Moreover, physicians' 'permission provisions' and 'directives by example' afforded a stark contrast between those who have rights to issue 'doctors' orders' and those with obligations to follow them. Even physicians' use of less aggravated forms – imbedded imperatives and false collaboratives – stressed the difference between the speakers who posed the directives and the addressees who were expected to comply with them. Through these means, men physicians proposed an asymmetrical relationship between their patients and themselves – one that stressed patients' obligations in contrast to physicians' rights.

Directives of Women Physicians

By contrast with men, women physicians issued their directives in decidedly mitigated forms. Through such means, they minimized distinctions between themselves and their patients and proposed symmetrical physician–patient relationships.

Proposals for joint action

For example, women physicians often formulated their directives as proposals for joint action. One way of advancing these proposals was the 'Let's do X' format Goodwin (1980, 1990) describes:

(41)   (Dyad 04:370)

PHYSICIAN: .h Let's talk about ⌈cher press:ure fer a minnit 'r two.⌉
PATIENT: ⌊.h-.h-.h-ch-hhhhew! °Okay.   ⌋
                                   ((sounding congested))

(42)   (Dyad 11:569+)
PHYSICIAN: OKa:y! Wull *let's* make that our *pla:n,*

(43)   (Dyad 04:499+)
PHYSICIAN: *So:::* Let's stay on- uh::: what we're doin' right no:w. Okay?

(44)   (Dyad 11:813)
PHYSICIAN: .h Let's get a fa:sting sugar nex' time too: (.2) OKa:y?

Above, physicians use 'Let's' to include themselves and their patients as partners in the actions they propose: talking (about the patient's blood pressure), making a plan for future treatment, staying on their present plan, and getting a 'fasting sugar' on the occasion of the patient's next visit. Unlike the false collaboratives discussed earlier, these directives formulate activities that *both* parties will play a part in, be it having a conversation or planning a course of treatment. Even getting a 'fasting sugar' will in this case require the coordination of two people: the patient, who must refrain from eating prior to taking this blood test, and the physician, who must schedule the test and interpret its results.[3]

Another way of proposing joint actions was formulating them as characterizations of what 'we' can or could do:

(45)   (Dyad 11:484+)
PHYSICIAN: O:kay. hh (2.2) .h We:ll, I thi:nk- (.8) ah'll go: (.2) with tha:t (.2) along wi:th you, an' th- I think y'know, if we cun (.2) contro:l it, in fa:ct, if yuh've- been f- (.2) quite a bi::t- uh:m (.2) off yer di:et, .h (1.0) E:n ah'm not even su:re I should u:h a' suggest yuh go u:p to (.4) .h seven hunnerd an' fi:fty. (1.6) Can yuh help me with tha:t?

(46)   (Dyad 19:682+)
PHYSICIAN: OKay, so: whadda yuh thi:nk,=maybe wih'd jus' take the top of yer- yer dress o:ff?

Here, for example, 'we cun' and 'wih'd jus'' emphasize the tentative character of what physicians and patients might undertake.

Women physicians also employed 'wc' in formulations of what they and their patients 'ought to' or 'had to' do:

(47)   (Dyad 11:495+)
PHYSICIAN: Maybe whut we ought a do: is- is *sta:y* with (.2) .h the *do:se* of di(avameez) yer o:n.

(48)   (Dyad 04:393+)
PHYSICIAN: We *both* hafta take rihspon ⌊sabil⌋ ity, ⌊ri:ght?⌋

Albeit 'ought to' and 'have to' are commonly used in aggravated directives, here, their coupling with 'we' includes both the physician and the patient in the actions they propose (staying with the present dose and taking responsibility). Thus, such formulations do not construct demands, as they might if only the addressees were subjects of actions they specified (Goodwin, 1980: 167). Rather, they build proposals for joint action between speakers and addressees. Through such formulations, women physicians made implicit claims to symmetrical relationships with their patients – ones in which they '*both* had to take responsibility'.

Singular suggestions

Of course, all 'doctors' orders' cannot involve physicians as co-partners in the actions they propose. Some tasks, such as those that will be required after leaving the physician's office, can only be performed by patients. In the case of such tasks, women physicians used 'you' to formulate their directives to patients but they typically imbedded these in 'can' and 'could' modal verbs:

(49) (Dyad 04:226+)

PHYSICIAN: One thing yuh could d ⌊o::⌋ . . . .h= is tuh ea:t, say, the *meat firs'*. Yuh know:, but if yuh have a *sal*:ud tuh eat, t' sa:ve that till *af*ter yuh eat the meat. (.) Cuz the sal:ud's suhpose' tuh be co:ld. .hh Somethin- like tha:t (.) °OKa:y?

(50) (Dyad 04:243+)

PHYSICIAN: An:d u:h- (.) an' then maybe yuh can stay away from the dihsserts an' stay away from the- .h foo:d in buhtwee:n meals. All the snacking, °that kinda thing.

(51) (Dyad 19:342+)

PHYSICIAN: We:ll, you could *try*: taking .h two: ev'ry four *hou::rs* if yuh needed to: . . . you could take that many an' *see:* an' that's- .h it's a *ver:y strong* medicine fer arthri [:tus.]

Like the imbedded imperatives discussed earlier, these directives identify actions to be performed in explicit terms (i.e. 'eat the meat firs'', 'stay away from the dihsserts', and 'take that many an' see'). But here, imbedded imperatives are downgraded to the status of mere suggestions through the inversion of subjects and verbs: not 'could you eat the meat first' but 'you could . . . eat the meat firs''; not 'can you stay away from the desserts' but 'you can stay away from the dihsserts'; and not 'could you take that many' but 'you could take that many'. The resulting directives advance proposals – rather than requests – for action, thereby de-emphasizing distinctions between speakers and addressees.

To be sure, the directives issued in excerpts 49–51 were further mitigated by the local contexts in which they occurred. Eating the meat first is put forth as just 'one thing' among many the patient in excerpt 49 could do; staying away from desserts is an action the patient in excerpt 50 'maybe' can take; and taking two every four hours is something the patient in excerpt 51 'can try . . . an' see'. Such modulations were typical of women physicians, who rarely issued their directives baldly. For example, they often used 'maybe' to underscore the suggestive nature of their directives:

(52)   (Dyad 11:619+)

PHYSICIAN: It's good duh look,=an' loo:k between yer toe:s,=make sure they're clea:n an'
dry:, maybe yuh wanna put pow:der on um . . . Depen'ing on how swe-heh-ty
yer feet get! (.2) .h But y'know, *check* 'um! Maybe: y'know, maybe: (.4) .h if yer
no:t feelun' (.2) the:n yuh might *see:* somp'um thet cha don' fee:l.

(53)   (Dyad 04:292+)

PHYSICIAN: *May*be yuh ne- yuh nee:d tuh *dis*ciplun yerself a liddle bi:t? .hh When yuh come
ho:me from work? .h sometimes I fi:ne thet when I ride my *bi:ke* home thet
that's a goo:d way of unwi:n ⌊ding⌋

Here, 'maybe' downgrades statements of patients' wants ('yuh wanna put powder
on um') and needs ('yuh need tuh disciplun yerself') to the status of propositions, thereby mitigating their impact. In the process, the physicians imply a non-
hierarchical alignment with their patients – one in which patients' wants and needs
are perhaps hypothesized, but left to be determined by patients themselves.

Permission directives

On occasion, women physicians even sought patients' permission to *be* directed
through the formats they employed. As Ervin-Tripp (1976: 37–8) observes, permission directives require some action by addressees beyond the granting of permission:

(54)   (Dyad 11:716+)

PHYSICIAN: Could I: u:m (.) um: (.6) Ra:ther thun having yuh wai:t tuhday, since I know:
yer takin' off wor:k, an' I need duh see another pa:tien', .h (.8) Could I have yer
pho:ne number? an' give yuh a ⌊ca:ll then⌋ When I get that ⌊report⌋ from hi:m?

(55)   (Dyad 03:270+)

PHYSICIAN: Okay:, lemme jus' say o:ne thing: at thi:s poin', an' that i:s (.6) .h no:t tuh be
dis*cou*raged by whut happened.

In excerpt 54, the physician asks the patient for her telephone number, in addition
to her consent to being called later on. In excerpt 55, the physician asks the patient
to *listen* to her forthcoming suggestion by formulating her request ('Lemme jus' say
one thing') as a 'preliminary' to the action being proposed (Schegloff, 1980). In these
cases, physicians avoided comparisons between their patients' status and their own
by highlighting patients' prerogatives to counter the proposals they advanced.

Inverse imperatives

As I have already noted, women physicians in these encounters made little use of
aggravated directive forms. Those they did use were often noteworthy not only for
their rarity but for the contexts in which they appeared:

(56)   (Dyad 04:061+)

PHYSICIAN: Yih wan' me tuh- tuh- give yih some guide:lines here? (1.0) *Tell* me whut chuh
ate: tuhday. Umka:y?

(57) (Dyad 19:033+)

PHYSICIAN: Cuz if you: duh*cide* you want it o:ff, you let me know. (.) *Okay?*

(58) (Dyad 19:522+)

PHYSICIAN: O:kay, .hh *So:* ((looking at the patient)) priddy much right *no:w*, .h you tell me
if I *go:t* this, you got duh- (.2) duh pro- .h you need duh get yer me:dicine filled?
. . . An' yih feel like yer pressure's okay, you are:n't having *head*ache:s, or
*prob*lums *see:*ing,

Above, physicians formatted their directives as explicit commands, but they did so
in contexts that implied patients should direct *them*: 'Yih wan' me to give you some
guidelines here?', 'If you duhcide you want it off', and 'You tell me if I've got this'.
Insofar as physicians thereby implied that patients were the ultimate authorities regarding the actions they specified, they affirmed their obligations to respect patients'
rights to make the final decisions in such matters.

In sum, women physicians employed directives that minimized status differences
between their patients and themselves and provided for more symmetrical arrangements of their relationships (cf. Goodwin, 1990: 74–5). Through proposals for joint
action, they made implicit claims regarding the collaborative character of the activities they suggested and patients' status as co-partners in decisions to implement these.
Their directives regarding patients' individual actions were modulated by 'can', 'could',
and 'maybe', stressing patients' prerogatives in planning such actions. Even their
aggravated directives emphasized patients' authority to direct *them*, affirming their
responsibilities to patients. Thus, women physicians proposed a more egalitarian relationship between their patients and themselves – one that emphasized physicians'
obligations as well as patients' rights.

Responses to Directives

As noted earlier, the data at hand consist of actual patient visits, so they are not
standardized by duration, presenting complaint or length of relationship between
physician and patient. Some physicians and patients had sustained a three-year
relationship at the time they were recorded, whereas others were meeting for the
first time. Some visits were routine follow-up checks on chronic conditions; others
entailed discoveries of new complaints. And although all visits were scheduled for at
least 30-minute time slots, some took considerably longer than 30 minutes; others
took less. For these reasons, the tasks involved in particular visits varied widely and
it is difficult to classify responses to directives via a standardized coding scheme.

Moreover, as Goodwin's work (1980, 1988, 1990) demonstrates, directive–response
speech sequences form adjacency pairs (Schegloff, 1972; Schegloff and Sacks, 1974),
whose meaning is established through the turn-by-turn organization of talk in situated
contexts. Some directives formulate future courses of action; others specify actions to
be taken then and there. Some directives require verbal responses from addressees;
others require no other response than performance of the action they propose.

Hence, the intelligibility of responses to directives *as* responses to directives cannot be determined apart from the contexts in which they occur.

Below, I provide a detailed examination of two directive–response sequences in which it is possible to compare responses to aggravated and mitigated directive forms. Following this comparison, I present overall rates of compliance with alternative directive forms among patients in this collection.

Aggravated vs. mitigated directives

A common site for directives in these data was where physicians needed to get patients to disrobe in preparation for physical examinations. In the excerpts just below, two physicians attempt to achieve this end with patients they are meeting for the first time. Excerpt 59 involves a man physician and a man patient; excerpt 60 involves a woman physician and woman patient.

(59)   (Dyad 17:385)
PHYSICIAN: You can dro:p yer trou:sers, fact, why don' cha jus' take 'um o:ff.
            (.6)
PATIENT: ((leans forward on the examining table, looking at the physician))
PHYSICIAN: Take yer trousers o:ff.
            (.6)
PATIENT: Eh::::::-hh
            (1.0)
PHYSICIAN: Oh:, *o::*kay, yuh wan' the cam'ra? ((physician reaches over and draws the curtain around the table so that the patient is hidden from the camera))
            (.8)
PATIENT: °Uh:::: eh:::::- °eh-huhh! (.4) Ah don' *wa:n*na drop my trousers, at's alright-heh!
            (.2)
PHYSICIAN: You don' *want* to:=
PATIENT: =No::

(60)   (Dyad 19:682+)
PHYSICIAN: Okay, so: whadda yuh thi:nk,=maybe wih'd jus' take the to:p of yer- yer dress o:ff?
            ⌈Would that be oka::y⌉ with ⌈you::?   ⌉
PATIENT: ⌊Uh, o::kay,   ⌋   ⌊fah:ne, go⌋ o:d,
            ye⌈:s.⌉
PHYSICIAN: ⌊O ⌋ *kay!*

In excerpt 59, the physician issues two aggravated directives in quick succession: first, a permission provision ('You can drop yer trousers') and then, an imbedded imperative ('why don' cha jus' take 'um off'). Following a brief pause (.6), during which the patient does not undertake the action he specifies, the physician reissues his directive as an explicit command ('Take yer trousers off').

As in the case of other adjacency pairs (e.g. questions and answers or summonses and replies), directives and responses form a conditionally relevant two–part sequence

(Schegloff, 1972; Schegloff and Sacks, 1974). In other words, given the occurrence of a directive, or 'first pair part', a response, or 'second pair part' is expected. And, given the occurrence of the first pair part, the absence of a second pair part is accountable – that is, it provides a warrant for repeating the first pair part or for some inference regarding the absence of the second (Schegloff, 1972: 77). In the case of excerpt 59, the patient's lack of response to the physician's initial directives provides grounds for his repetition (and, apparently, his starker formulation) of the directive in his next turn. It also provides the warrant – following the patient's further lack of response – for the physician's inference regarding the patient's reluctance to comply.

Finally, the patient issues a negative response to the physician's directive in aggravated form (he doesn't *want* to). And when the physician repeats the patient's response, thereby offering him the chance to repair it (cf. Schegloff et al., 1977), the patient instead states his refusal baldly ('no').

By contrast, the physician in excerpt 60 puts forth her directive as a proposal for joint action ('maybe wih'd jus' take the top of yer dress off?'). Before she can fully follow this up with a request for the patient's permission ('Would that be okay with you?'), the patient has already issued an affirmative response ('Okay'). Moreover, the patient provides further affirmative replies ('fahne', 'good', 'yes') as the physician's request unfolds.

The difference I want to focus on in these very rich excerpts is between the two approaches to formulating directives. In excerpt 59, the physician's aggravated forms imply that the patient has no choice but to comply with his demands; in excerpt 60, the physician's mitigated form implies that the patient can counter her proposal, should she choose to do so. In each excerpt, the physician's directive form is implicative for the formulation of the patient's response: an aggravated reply in excerpt 59, and a mitigated one, in 60.[4] And in excerpt 59, the aggravated reply is a negative response; in 60, the mitigated reply is an affirmative one.

Of course, neither response constitutes execution of the action specified by the physician's directives – namely, to disrobe. However, in the case of excerpt 60, what follows is compliance with the directive:

(60 cont'd)   (Dyad 19:693+)
PATIENT: It- uh:m ((beginning to pull the hem of her dress up)) (2.0) It 'o:n' zi:p y'know,
              .h I gaw' no zippuh (°thad it can come o:ff) °eh-hunh!
              (1.0)
              ((physician walks toward the patient, who is standing by her chair with her dress
              halfway up))
PHYSICIAN: ((leaning sideways to see the patient's back)) Yih godda zi:pper there yih wan'
              me duh help with?
              (.4)
PATIENT: Ain' got no sor:ta zip- ((as physician reaches over to help)) tuh come dow::n?
              (.)
PHYSICIAN: Oh::::, the zipper's *sew* ⌈*n* u:::p! Oh::! You go:dit taken   ⌉
PATIENT: ⌊Yay::us! .engh-hengh-hengh-hengh⌋

PHYSICIAN: *car:e* of! ⌈huh: heh-heh!⌉
PATIENT: ⌊Yeah-heh-heh⌋ heh!=
PHYSICIAN: = .h heh °Ah:kay! ((turning to walk back toward the examining table as the patient proceeds to undress))

But in the case of excerpt 59, what follow are further negotiations regarding the patient's refusal to comply. For example:

(59 cont'd)   (Dyad 17:406+)
PHYSICIAN: This kine a personal to: yuh?
              (.2)
PATIENT: *Ye::ah*! (.4) °Um-hmm.
              (1.0)
PHYSICIAN: Anything yuh'd like tuh *as:k* me about? 'r (uh:)=
PATIENT: =°*No::::::*(.) °engh-hh!
PHYSICIAN: Cuz I ain' gonna- .h y'know, I: *ain*' gonna mess
              arou::n' y'know. I ⌈jes' wanna take a loo:k   ⌉
PATIENT: ⌊No::::! °engh-hunh! hengh!⌋ at
PHYSICIAN: cher knee::s
              (.4)
PATIENT: °*Oh:::::*. (.6) No:, (ah'd love tuh have yuh check 'em,) buh=not=right=there,
              that's why I don' like tuh go duh the dock:tuh that much. (.4) Cuz uh::::: (1.2)
              Nu:hh:::hh (1.2) I let yih check any o:thuh things, but no:t down he::ah. Drop
              my pa::n's?=*no::::::siree:::*!

Finally, following this series of unsuccessful attempts, the physician switches to a mitigated approach:

(59 cont'd)   (Dyad 17:421+)
PHYSICIAN: Would juh like- (.2) .h it's- *see:*, it's RI:LLY HAR:D, ay:e-=y'know: that's yer
              ri:ght,=it's *ri:lly hard* duh get a good look at cher *knee:s* .h without gettin' yer
              pa::n's undone so far (1.0) .hh Now, if yuh'd *li::ke* me to:, I could get a *shee::t*.
              (.8) Tuh put over yuh, an' *then* yuh could drop yer pa:nts. (.2) An' you could
              stay covered up aroun' yer wai:st. (.6) *Oka:y*?=
PATIENT: =°Ye:ah, wull m ⌈ay:be, buh uh⌉
PHYSICIAN: ⌊CUZ I: JUS'⌋ don't thi:nk I could
              pu:ll these pa::nts up far en ⌈ough to-⌉
PATIENT: ⌊°Okay. ⌋
              (.2)
PHYSICIAN: .h Cun yuh try: 'n do tha:t?
              (.2)
PATIENT: Yeah, I:'ll try a do: it.

And here, the patient finally issues an affirmative response: initially qualified ('wull maybe'), then mitigated ('°Okay'), and ultimately – following the physician's reiteration – in explicit terms ('I'll try a do it').

Ironically, despite the success he has just experienced with a mitigated approach, this physician closes the interchange by reverting to an aggravated directive:

(59 cont'd.)   (Dyad 17:440+)
PHYSICIAN: I:'ll tell yuh wha:t. Ah:'ll close a drapes hh (1.0) ((walking over to the curtain pull)) Here (.6) ((sound of curtains being closed fully around the examining table)) hh 'N I wan' chew: (1.0) ((more curtain noises)) tuh drop yer trou:sers, .h jus' lay: them back *dow:n* there on that *be:d.*

In effect, his reversion reasserts his authority to command the patient in the first instance.

The point of this detailed comparison has been to show that patients' responses to 'doctors' orders' are highly sensitive to the ways in which those orders are advanced. From this vantage point, an affirmative response is not merely the product of one individual (i.e. the patient), but the outcome of highly intricate negotiations between speakers and their addressees (cf. Frankel and Beckman, 1989b).

Patients' compliance with physicians' directives

With the data at hand, it is impossible to determine long-term patient adherence to medical advice. Videotapes and transcripts of patient visits simply do not permit access to what happens after physicians and patients part company. So, while physicians issue many instructions for future action, these data permit me to assess patients' responses to those instructions only then and there.

However, as in the case of the excerpts just presented, there is much to be learned from the detailed examination of physicians' formulations of their directives – and patients' responses to those directives – in the situated contexts in which they occur. For example, I can identify cases of compliance with physicians' directives where patients undertake actions specified by those directives in adjacent turns:

(61)   (Dyad 15:542+)
PHYSICIAN: °Ah wancha duh *gi:t* back *u:p* heah foah me pleez. hhh
PATIENT: ((walks over to and sits down on the examining table))

I can also identify cases in which patients' responses to physicians' directives assert their willingness to comply in the future, either by explicit statements:

(62)   (Dyad 18:336+)
PHYSICIAN: Now, don' jus' la::y *arou::n'* without that *hea::t* on it, cuz 'at rilly- hh (.6) Ah cain' tell yuh how it duz:: it, but (.) it wi::ll (1.2) you'll gedda fee:lin: *bed*der *quick*er. h
             (.2)
PATIENT: Ah: won't. hh

Or, by affirmation:

(63)   (Dyad 11:642+)

PHYSICIAN: *Those* 'r some a the things thut (.4) *ma::y* be a problum layder o::n, but right
now: (.2) I don' see thut they *are::*. (1.2) But. °Let me know: if any of 'um are:,
an' we'll work tuhge:ther on thum.=

PATIENT: =°Alright.

By contrast, I can identify non–compliance with physicians' directives where
patients refuse or fail to undertake actions that are specified in next turns (as in
excerpt 59, presented earlier). I can also identify cases of non–compliance where
patients' responses display their lack of agreement with physicians' directives:

(64)   (Dyad 09:631+)

PHYSICIAN: *Why* don' yuh do thi::s, why don' yuh *call* them, an:d u:h. (.) See whut they
sa:y. An' after tha:t, you call back here, an'- an' talk duh Norma, an' leddum
know whut they *sai:d*, an' then ah'll get back to yuh:. (.4) .h An' we cun arrange
whudever's necessary fo:r
yu ⌈h::, so: ⌉
PATIENT: ⌊Wull=I=wan⌋ na check on it
muh:ney-wise fi:rs'.

(65)   (Dyad 14:803+)

PHYSICIAN: I think yuh need duh *try:* duh ged ou:t, even if yuh- .h y'know, *si:t* an' watch
o:ther people *da:nce* 'r whatever
(.4)

PATIENT: (°M: that's-) Wull, that's- *tha:t's* the trouble with not bein' able duh dri:ve,
y'know? yer dih*pe:n*dun' on othuh people.

In excerpts 64 and 65, for example, neither patient explicitly refuses to comply with
their physician's directive. But insofar as physicians' directives constitute their assessments of what patients should do, and insofar as agreement with assessments is strongly
preferred in next turns at talk (Pomerantz, 1984), these patients' *lack* of agreement
with physicians' directives ('Wull, I wanna check on it muhney-wise firs'; and 'Wull,
that's the trouble with not bein' able duh drive') can be seen as something other than
willingness to comply with 'doctors' orders'.

Finally, I can also identify non–compliance with physicians' directives where
patients fail to respond to those directives:

(66)   (Dyad 13:116+)

PHYSICIAN: Yuh cun start on the three month supply:, an' yih cun re:fill that three ti:mes,
over the course of a ye:ar.
(13.8)
((patient is silent as the physician makes notes in her medical record))

PHYSICIAN: If yih *should* have any problum with (.) pai:n an' swelling in yer lay:gs 'r any
difficuldy brea:thing, (.8) .h yuh let me know right away. Okay?
(26.4)
((patient is still silent as the physician continues to write))

Above, the patient issues neither verbal nor nonverbal responses to the directives her physician has issued. Given that the occurrence of a directive warrants the occurrence of a response (Schegloff, 1972; Schegloff and Sacks, 1974), the *absence* of a response can be seen as an 'official' absence, and hence as non-compliance with the directive.

Among patients in this collection, rates of compliance varied with the forms of physicians' directives. For example, men physicians' imperatives (e.g. 'LIE DOWN!') elicited compliant responses in 47 percent of the total (49) cases in which they were used – in short, less than half the time. Their statements of preference (e.g. 'Ah don' wan' cha duh take both') were more successful, yielding compliance in 59 percent of the total (22) cases. However, their statements of patients' needs ('What cha need tuh do is . . .'), permission provisions ('you can refill these three times') and directives by example ('Ah'd take two ev'ry four hours') fared much worse, eliciting compliance in only 38 percent of the (16) need statements; 36 percent of the (11) permission provisions; and 29 percent of the (7) directives by example. The directives of men physicians that were most successful in eliciting compliant responses were those that took less aggravated forms. False collaboratives ('Let's slip this back off') yielded compliance in 65 percent of the total (23) cases, and physician requests ('Can you put cher finger on the place?') achieved their objectives in 4 out of 5 (or 80 percent) of the cases in which they were used. As a rule, *the more aggravated the directive, the less likely it was to elicit a compliant response.*

Among women physicians, this rule also held, albeit since the vast majority of their directives took a mitigated form, there was less variation among the responses they received. For example, proposals for joint action (e.g. 'Let's make that our plan') elicited compliant responses in 67 percent of the (9) cases in which they were used. Singular suggestions for patient action ('you could try taking two ev'ry four hours') fared even better, yielding compliance in 75 percent of the total (8) cases. Perhaps most remarkable were their inverse imperatives ('You tell me if I got this'): these produced compliant responses in 8 out of 9 – or 88 percent – of the cases in which they appeared. By contrast, of the 4 cases in which women employed quasi-question directives ('Why don' chew put these away'), only one was successful in achieving its specified aim.[5]

Thus, for women physicians too, the more aggravated the directive, the less likely it was to elicit a compliant response. The difference is that women physicians *used* aggravated imperatives less often than men did. And, their overall rate of compliant responses was 67 percent – in comparison to 50 percent for men.[6]

Conclusions

'Doctors' orders' are often satirized in the admonition 'Take two aspirin and call me in the morning'. Quite apart from the banality of this directive (employed under a seemingly infinite set of circumstances), we can note that it takes the form of an imperative – an explicit command from the physician to the patient. As I have already pointed out, the formulation of a directive in this aggravated form emphasizes the distinction between the speaker and the addressee and asserts the speaker's authority to be issuing commands in the first place (Goodwin, 1980).

Among physicians in this collection, men used aggravated forms that emphasized differences between their patients and themselves, and proposed hierarchical physician–patient relationships. Women physicians employed mitigated directives, which minimized status differences between physician and patient and stressed their connectedness to one another (cf. Goodwin, 1990: 147). These alternative formulations were consequential for patients' responses: not only were aggravated forms less likely to elicit compliant responses, but women physicians elicited such responses more often than men did.

Since my data were not generated by random sampling techniques, and since there were only four women physicians in this collection, it would be inappropriate to generalize from my results to women and men physicians at large. But should these findings hold in larger systematic samples of physicians, they might prove useful in explaining why patients are more satisfied with women physicians (Linn et al., 1984) and less likely to sue them for malpractice (Holder, 1979).

To be sure, compliance with physicians' directives is not the same thing as long-term adherence to medical advice. Further research is needed to determine precisely how patients' responses to physicians' directives relate to their adherence to medical advice over time. However, in light of Carter and his colleagues' finding that patients' indicated willingness to follow medical advice is the best predictor of their actual adherence (Carter et al., 1986), my results offer a promising new direction for future work on this problem.

Finally, it would be difficult to close this paper without commenting on the significance of my findings for our understanding of the relationship between language and gender. For example, what should we make of the fact that the distribution of aggravated and mitigated directives among these white middle-class physicians is so similar to their distribution among Black working-class boys and girls (Goodwin, 1980, 1988, 1990)? The lesson to be learned here is not that the 'essential natures' of women and men determine their interactional styles – including their tendencies toward politeness (Brown, 1976); 'indirect' language (Lakoff, 1975); and 'conversational insecurity' (Fishman, 1980). After all, women physicians *can* use aggravated directives on occasions of conflict with patients (see notes 5 and 6), and girl children *do* use aggravated forms to order their younger siblings around (Goodwin, 1980, 1990). The lesson, I think, is that the mundane activities of social life – be they making slingshots or getting patients to disrobe – provide the interactional resources for 'doing gender' (West and Zimmerman, 1987), that is, exhibiting, dramatizing or celebrating our 'essential natures' as women or men in accountable ways.

NOTES

For their helpful comments on an earlier draft, I thank Richard Frankel, Marjorie Goodwin, Barbara Sharf, Gilly West and James West.

1   Other factors associated with variation in directive forms were 'territorial location, difficulty of task, whether or not a duty is normally expected [and] whether or not non-compliance is likely' (Ervin-Tripp, 1976: 25).

2   Two physicians in this collection are in their late thirties and are not residents. One is an alumnus of the training program who still sees patients at the clinic after completing his residency. The other is a faculty member who trains residents. In the analyses that follow, I find no differences between their directives to patients and those of the residents.

3   The patient involved in excerpt 44 is a diabetic whose blood sugar level was somewhat higher than usual on the occasion of this visit. Some people with diabetes can test their urine at home and follow their sugar levels themselves. But as this patient told her physician earlier in the encounter, 'th' sugar dudun' show up in my ur:ine . . . Dat's why ah alweez haf tuh dipen' on the bloo:d' (Dyad 11:501–5).

4   Here, 'okay' can be seen as a mitigated response in that it affirms but does not explicitly state the patient's willingness to comply with the physician's directive (in contrast to 'let's do that', 'we could do that' or the 'yes' that follows it).

5   Of these relatively aggravated forms, three out of four appeared in the course of a single interchange in which a man patient repeatedly interrupted his physician to dispute the wisdom of her advice (West, 1984a: 66–9). In these instances, the physician's escalation to more aggravated directive forms followed the onset of the patient's intrusions, and may have served to assert her right to be issuing directives in the first place.

6   The overall rate of compliance with women physicians' directives would have been higher, save for the patient discussed in note 5. His lack of agreement with his physician's directives and lack of responses to her directives constituted 58 percent of the 12 cases of non-compliance I observed.

REFERENCES

Becker, M. H. and Maiman, L. A. (1975) 'Sociobehavioral Determinations of Compliance with Health and Medical Care Recommendations', *Medical Care* 13: 10–24.

Brown, P. (1976) 'Women and Politeness: a New Perspective on Language and Society', *Reviews in Anthropology* 3: 240–9.

Carter, W. B., Beach, L. R., Inui, T. S., Kirscht, J. P. and Prodzinsky, J. C. (1986) 'Developing and Testing a Decision Model for Predicting Influenza Vaccination Compliance', *Health Services Research* 20: 897–932.

Davis, M. (1966) 'Variations in Patients' Compliance with Doctors' Orders: Analysis of Congruence between Survey Responses and Results of Empirical Investigations', *Journal of Medical Education* 41: 1037–48.

Davis, M. (1968) 'Variations in Patients' Compliance with Doctors' Advice: an Empirical Analysis of Patterns of Communication', *American Journal of Public Health* 58: 274–88.

DiMatteo, M. R. and DiNicola, D. D. (1982) *Achieving Patient Compliance: The Psychology of the Medical Practitioner's Role.* New York: Pergamon.

Ervin-Tripp, S. (1976) 'Is Sybil There? The Structure of Some American English Directives', *Language in Society* 5: 25–66.

Fishman, Pamela (1980) 'Conversational Insecurity', in *Language: Social Psychological Perspectives*, pp. 127–32. New York: Pergamon.

Francis, V., Korsch, B. M. and Morris, M. J. (1969) 'Gaps in Doctor–Patient Communication: Patients' Response to Medical Advice', *New England Journal of Medicine* 280: 535–40.

Frankel, R. M. and Beckman, H. B. (1989a) 'Communication Aspects of Malpractice'. Paper presented at the Midwinter Meeting of the International Communication Association, Monterey, California (February).

Frankel, R. M. and Beckman, H. B. (1989b) 'Conversation and Compliance: An Application of Microinteractional Analysis in Medicine', in B. Dervin, L. Grossberg, B. Okeefe and E. Wartella (eds) *Paradigm Dialogs in Communication*, pp. 60–74. Beverly Hills: Sage.

Goffman, E. (1964) 'The Neglected Situation', *American Anthropologist* 66: 133–6.

Goodwin, M. H. (1980) 'Directive–Response Speech Sequences in Girls' and Boys' Task Activities', in S. McConnell-Ginet, R. Borker and N. Furman (eds) *Women and Language in Literature and Society*, pp. 157–73. New York: Praeger.

Goodwin, M. H. (1988) 'Cooperation and Competition across Girls' Play Activities', in A. D. Todd and S. Fisher (eds) *Gender and Discourse*, pp. 55–94. Volume 30 in the series, Advances in Discourse Processes, edited by R. O. Freedle. Norwood, NJ: Ablex.

Goodwin, M. H. (1990) *He-Said-She-Said: Talk as Social Organization among Black Children*. Bloomington, IN: Indiana University Press.

Holder, A. R. (1979) 'Women Physicians and Malpractice Suits', *Journal of the American Medical Women's Association* 34: 239–40.

Hymes, D. (1964) *Language and Culture in Society*. New York: Harper and Row.

Kirscht, J. and Rosenstock, I. (1977) 'Patient Adherence to Antihypertensive Medical Regimens', *Journal of Community Health* 3: 115–24.

Labov, W. and Fanshel, D. (1977) *Therapeutic Discourse: Psychotherapy as Conversation*. New York: Academic Press.

Lakoff, R. (1975) *Language and Woman's Place*. New York: Harper and Row.

Ley, P. (1983) 'Patients' Understanding and Recall in Clinical Communication Failure', in D. Pendleton and D. Hasler (eds) *Doctor-Patient Communication*, pp. 89–107. London: Academic Press.

Linn, L. S., Cope, D. W. and Leake, B. (1984) 'The Effect of Gender and Training of Residents on Satisfaction Ratings by Patients', *Journal of Medical Education* 59: 964–6.

Maynard, D. (in press) 'Bearing Bad News in Clinical Settings', in B. Dervin (ed.) *Progress in Communication Sciences*. Norwood, NJ: Ablex.

Pomerantz, A. (1984) 'Agreeing with Assessments: Some Features of Preferred/Dispreferred Turn Shapes', in J. M. Atkinson and J. Heritage (eds) *Structures of Social Action: Studies in Conversation Analysis*, pp. 57–101. Cambridge: Cambridge University Press.

Sackett, D. L. and Snow, J. C. (1979) 'The Magnitude of Compliance and Non-Compliance', in R. B. Haynes (ed.) *Compliance in Health Care*, pp. 11–22. Baltimore, MD: Johns Hopkins University Press.

Schegloff, E. A. (1972) 'Discourse as an Interactional Achievement: Some Uses of 'Uh huh' and Other Things that Come between Sentences', in D. Tannen (ed.) *Analyzing Discourse: Text and Talk*, pp. 71–93; Georgetown University Roundtable on Languages and Linguistics, March 1981. Washington, DC: Georgetown University Press.

Schegloff, E. A. (1980) 'Preliminaries to Preliminaries: "Can I Ask You a Question?"', *Sociological Inquiry* 50:104–52.

Schegloff, E. A., Jefferson, G. and Sacks, H. (1977) 'The Preference for Self-Correction in the Organization of Repair in Conversation', *Language* 53: 361–82.

Schegloff, E. A. and Sacks, H. (1974) 'Opening Up Closings', in R. Turner (ed.) *Ethnomethodology: Selected Readings*, pp. 233–64. Baltimore, MD: Penguin (originally published in *Semiotica* 8: 289–327, 1973).

Shapiro, M. (1978) *Getting Doctored: Critical Reflections on Becoming a Physician*. Kitchener, Ontario: Between the Lines.

Steele, D. J., Jackson, T. C. and Gutmann, M. C. (1985) ' "Have You Been Taking Your Pills?" The Compliance Monitoring Sequence in the Medical Interview', unpublished manuscript.

West, C. (1983) ' "Ask Me No Questions" . . . an Analysis of Queries and Replies in Physician–Patient Dialogues', in S. Fisher and A. D. Todd (eds) *The Social Organization of Doctor–Patient Communication*, pp. 75–106. Georgetown: Center for Applied Linguistics.

West, C. (1984a) *Routine Complications: Troubles with Talk Between Doctors and Patients*. Bloomington, IN: Indiana University Press.

West, C. (1984b) 'When the Doctor is a "Lady": Power, Status and Gender in Physician–Patient Encounters', *Symbolic Interaction* 7: 87–106.

West, C. (1984c) 'Medical Misfires: Mishearings, Misgivings and Misunderstandings in Physician–Patient Dialogues', *Discourse Processes* 7: 107–34.

West, C. and Frankel, R. M. (1991) 'Miscommunication in Medicine', in N. Coupland, H. Giles, and J. Wiemann (eds) *'Miscommunication' and Problematic Talk*. New York: Sage.

West, C. and Zimmerman, D. H. (1987) 'Conversation Analysis', in K. R. Scherer and P. Ekman (eds) *Handbook of Methods in Nonverbal Behavior Research*, pp. 506–41. Cambridge: Cambridge University Press.

23

Women's Ways: Interactive Patterns in Predominantly Female Research Teams

Marie Wilson Nelson

In recent years activities in which most women participate have expanded. In *The Second Stage* Betty Friedan (1981) cites women's progress toward fuller "participation, power, and voice in the mainstream, inside the party, the political process, the professions, the business world." But participation is merely the first stage of change, Friedan claims; for to realize both "the limits and the true potential of women's power" requires more of women than merely learning to act like men. Equal participation in society requires women to learn new ways of interacting; it also requires a reciprocal commitment from men. True equality requires no less, according to Friedan, than literally "changing the terms" by which society operates, a goal she believes will improve institutions for women and men.

In this study I describe interactions typical of five successive teacher-research teams who took part, between 1981 and 1985, in the qualitative program evaluation of a university writing center. The study was conducted in the Composition Tutorial Center (CTC) at George Mason University, a state school of 17,000 in the Virginia suburbs of Washington, DC. Selections from transcripts of Team I's final session illustrate interactive patterns familiar to females on all teams but unfamiliar to the males who occasionally joined these teams. Follow-up interviews with members of Teams IV and V confirmed Team I's conclusion that their team functioned differently from most academic and professional groups. They also confirm similarities between Team I and later teams.

This study found several groups of women changing the terms by which academic groups have often operated. It also shows the men who joined them adapting to the unfamiliar women's ways and finding personal, professional, and academic advantages in doing so. Its goal was not to compare male and female interactions definitively, however, but to describe interactive patterns recurring on these largely female teams, to show how those patterns differ from those of traditionally male-led groups, and to document those patterns' importance for the men and women who experienced them.

The Context in Which Teams Operated

The Composition Tutorial Center, housed in the English Department, was established in 1981 to offer small-group tutorial instruction to undergraduates having problems with university writing. There graduate teaching assistants (TAs) led mixed groups of four or five native and second-language (ESL) speakers in writing workshops meeting twice a week for a semester. My job as center director was to design and administer the program, train the TAs to teach writing, and supervise their work. The teaching assistants were selected on the basis of experience as writers, experience in teaching or applied linguistics, and non-elitist attitudes. Most knew little about the center approach when the training began, for it was based on recent discoveries about how language abilities develop and was grounded in writers' testimony about how they learn to write. As a result, the program contrasted with the writing instruction most TAs had experienced themselves.

Tutor training, therefore, had several components. For two weeks in August new TAs attended a daily seminar to prepare them to start teaching the small tutorial groups. Training continued weekly throughout fall semester in a three credit-hour graduate course, and the teams met spring semester in regularly scheduled staff meetings and in occasional in-service or research sessions. To help TAs learn to help their students grow confident and independent, the training included several strands: reading and discussing recent writing research and theory, writing extensively and examining their own writing processes, and conducting qualitative teacher-research to learn how their students actually wrote. The personal experience on which teams drew in analyzing writing processes and in brainstorming methods of teaching from which they themselves would have benefitted as writers contributed to the trust and cohesion that developed on these teams. So did the one rule I make clear in all my writing classes – that because writing often dries up in the face of harsh evaluation, responses to each other's work should be honest but supportively phrased to avoid making light of any writer or her work.

To encourage classroom interactions from which TAs could learn about learning, I modeled from the first day of class the kinds of interactive processes that would help them experience first-hand the rewards of collaborative work. I knew that if they had experienced the motivation collaboration brings (Kohn, 1986), they would be more likely to use it in their own teaching. I therefore modeled the kinds of oral and written responses to writing that research has shown encourage developing writers at all levels. I shared personally motivated as well as professional writing of my own to demonstrate that they could do many kinds of writing in my class. To illustrate the critical stance I hoped they would assume toward their teaching, I revealed problems I experienced and asked for their suggestions. Modeling the kinds of risk-taking from which teaching and writing improve, I examined inconsistencies between how I write and how I teach, told them when I tried new approaches, and asked for help with writing I was doing that term.

I also praised or otherwise focused classroom attention on the kinds of behaviors I expected of students. I praised well-thought-out experiments, even when they failed, reinforcing students for taking risks and illustrating that classroom failures help people learn from mistakes. I focused team attention on strengths in what students were doing by pointing out thoughtful responses they gave to each other, saving time for talk about "breakthroughs" that followed risks taken with writing or teaching, noting developing commitment and motivation in their "learning logs," asking for (and dealing with) constructive criticism. I also modeled the process of dealing with negative feelings that emerged to reveal how doing so could help students work through common resistances to studying writing. And lest TAs misunderstand why I taught the course this way, I explained that trust and closeness functioned *not* as teaching goals but as serendipitous by-products of successful collaboration and as powerful rewards that motivate students to work hard (Kohn, 1986).

Team Participants

Team membership varied yearly but typically included six to 10 first-year tutors (ranging from 22 to 50 years of age) and (in all but the first year) one or two interns or doctoral students who joined the team because they were interested in the research. The first team, for example, included five female TAs, a female professor (myself), and a 23-year-old male who adopted (and commented on) the women's interactive style. In only one case were there two males on a team, and in five years the total number of males was five.

The roles the male tutor and professor played deserve special mention as they were somewhat different from those of others on the teams. The male TA, Arthur,[1] said this group was different from others he had been in:

> I just love being in here with all you women. You make it such a nice place to work. You're so warm and supportive that I never feel stupid when I make a mistake. It's different in here from how I've seen people do things before. Most graduate students are so competitive.

Arthur's comment echoes the view of female teammates that this group was different from academic groups they'd been in before. As one woman said: "It's so nice and relaxing to work with *women* for a change!"

This comment was part of a lunchtime chat about the team's approach in which the women of Team I described

1 their collegiality ("how much we learned from each other");
2 the noncompetitive atmosphere ("it motivates me more");
3 support they gave each other ("emphasizing strengths as well as weaknesses");
4 their relatively co-equal status with the professor ("you include·us in decisions"); and

5   benefits of emotional openness on the team ("It was talking about the anxieties we all felt that made me realize I wasn't alone in having failures and doubts").

All of these traits have been found to be common in women's interactions by other recent research on gender-related behavior (Gilligan, 1982; Miller, 1976; Pearson, 1985).

My position of authority in the university hierarchy – that is, my dual teacher/ supervisor role – gave me disproportionate power on these teams though I tried to minimize authoritarian behavior. In general, therefore, talk and decisions were collaborative and collegial. To provide some background on my perceptions as participant-observer, let me also say it was my intent to treat teammates as colleagues and my hope that they would respond in kind. I'd chosen this approach in part because former students and friends had noted that they felt happier and more productive working in supportive, collaborative women's groups. Another motivation, however, was that such a group was professionally important to me. It was my first year at GMU, and my office was distant from those of others in my department. With the team of graduate students whom I would see daily, however, I hoped to create a supportive environment for myself and them by treating them as a group with whom to discuss professional issues, a group who might come to take an interest in my work, a group who might offer the support I needed to be most productive, a group from whose varied experience I might also learn.

Among traits sometimes disparaged as "soft" or "weak" or "feminine" were two I had found helpful in growth- and learning-oriented groups and which writing research and theory indicate facilitate writing development. One was maintaining a nonthreatening atmosphere to make possible the frankness and risk-taking characteristic of successful learners. The other was dealing with whatever feelings arose in response to interpersonal interactions or to the group task itself. I therefore wove these into the fabric of the teacher-research teams. Only vaguely aware of specific studies (Miller, 1976; Pearson, 1985) showing that my preferences were typical of women (though experience told me this was probably so), I was trying to create the environment in which my students and I could best learn. My success at achieving this goal outstripped my expectations, expanded my awareness of the rewards of collaborative work, and convinced me of a point I hope to make in this essay – that the interactive patterns into which I as a woman had been socialized offer substantial benefits to academic and professional teams.

On the assumption, then, that conditions that helped me learn might also help others, I tried to create for the TAs and to model for them as tutors the kind of supportive, collaborative groups in which I am most comfortable and productive. I knew from other women that the kinds of interactions I sought were widely perceived as more typical of female than of mixed groups. The sewing circle, for example, and the quilting bee, were often mentioned as examples of traditional women's groups having collaborative production and mutual support as their primary goals and a lateral rather than hierarchical pattern of organization. Even the name "sewing circle," like the name of my mother's church group, reflects a nonhierarchic, context-dependent, shifting, lateral structure in which skillful group members (with neither position nor rank assigned) help less proficient groupmates develop skills as the need arises.

Such behavior is not regularly associated with male-originated groups. In Masonic orders, for example, or on many athletic teams, the division of labor and responsibility is determined by rank in a hierarchy or by direct competition for defined positions or roles. In football, coaches plot strategy; quarterbacks direct the team; and experienced first-string players, who need game practice the least, play more often than others because competition produces the need to win. In baseball, weaker players may be cut from the roster and sent to practice in the "minors" rather than getting a chance to work with more skillful members of the team. But even for the survivors, who make the final cut, it is coaches (near the top of the hierarchy) rather than proficient teammates who are designated responsible for improving player skills.

Aware of these different tendencies of female- and male-led groups, I chose the interactive style with which I was most at home to create a supportive learning/ working atmosphere for the center staff and to improve my own chances of success.

Team Goals

Together – in the graduate course, in staff meetings, and in special research sessions – five successive teacher-research teams tested and refined a program to help basic and ESL writers master academic writing. Though these three types of meetings went by different names, interactions in all were similar; for pedagogical, administrative, and research issues were (as one tutor put it) "not distinct." Three goals for the program shaped interactions on all five teams:

1   To help beginning TAs improve their teaching by studying it for patterns of greater or lesser success.
2   To conduct a program evaluation through which the tutorial program could be progressively adapted to meet the needs of basic writers.
3   To examine similarities and differences in ESL and native writers so an approach based on native-language writing research and theory could be adapted as needed for non-native students (40%) who enrolled in the CTC.

The Data

Patterns of team discussion, analysis, and decision making grew evident when I examined several types of data: research reports and other writing done for the tutor-training courses; audio-tapes of classes, staff meetings, and research sessions; and interviews with male and female members of several teams.

The Findings

During fall semesters, Teams I through V exhibited similar patterns of interaction:

1 All groups demonstrated a problem-solving orientation, the goal of which was helping students learn.

2 Decision making tended to be collaborative and field-dependent, with administrative, instructional, and research-related decisions influencing each other and rooted in consensus rather than authority.

3 Despite constraints (like evaluation) imposed by the university hierarchy, teams tended to function collegially, as laterally organized groups, with information being generated by and flowing to and from all members.

4 Analyses were as much emergent as preplanned, were more collaborative than individual, and involved intuitive and holistic as well as linear patterns of reasoning.

5 Teammates tended to offer each other emotional support and constructive criticism, interact good-naturedly, deal openly with negative feelings, and avoid competitive behaviors that threatened what they called the "sanctuary" atmosphere.

6 Positive and negative evaluation were balanced and sequential, tactfully phrased (to protect self-esteem and prevent defensive reactions) and designed to nurture growth more than to eliminate the weak.

In the remainder of this essay excerpts from Team I's final session illustrate the six patterns which characterized team interactions. The excerpts are followed by confirmatory interviews with members of Team IV to show the extent to which these findings are supported by contrasting participant views.

Team I: Excerpts from a Typical Teacher-Research Session

The following excerpts illustrate the six patterns that typified interactions on research teams I through V. For example, [. . .] in the sequence that follows, the pattern of logic is associative and unfocused, inching toward consensus in a holistic, intuitive, nonlinear way:

LYNN: Maybe we need a statement of what the CTC does because some composition teachers call and say their students need help with assignments "because of grammar problems."

FRAN: Yeah. Students get mixed expectations because the composition teachers don't always understand what we're trying to do.

MARIE: Maybe we need to clarify our approach to part-time faculty and TAs who teach our students in Freshman English.

CAROLINE: When students have been told by teachers to get help on papers, and we don't address those papers, there's a lot of emotion, a panic. You can see it in their faces.

MARIE: Maybe a memo to writing teachers. . . .

LYNN: People may be offended if they teach differently from us.

FRANCIE: They may get angry, so you need to lay out developmentally just what it is we are trying to do and why!

MARIE: I want us all to agree if we're making a policy statement? Tell me what to say.

FRANCIE: Sure! We're a place that focuses on the process of writing. We believe writing is developmental, that many factors affect writing, not the least of which are affective. We find that attitudes are very important, and that building motivation takes time. Also, about multiple revisions . . . Say that writing isn't perfect the first time.

LYNN: To some literature specialists who don't know new ways of teaching writing, you will have to explain – maybe in a footnote.

MARIE: "Note: see me for meaning of this memo" [much laughter].

LYNN: How about, "I think that writing is developmental and that one draft does not a paper make."

FRANCIE: "And twenty lashes with a wet noodle if you tell students we correct papers."

MARIE: Perhaps I should reassure them that we do, in fact, work on grammar and mechanics – but through the writing itself.

CAROLINE: And say that we do that toward the *end* of the process.

MARIE: What about "We work on grammar whenever the papers have been revised to the point that they are ready to be edited"?

FRANCIE: Oh, beautiful!

MARIE: Alright. Thanks. That's what I needed to know.

The excerpt above shows how Team I dealt good-naturedly with feelings, how collaborative analysis and decision making gradually led to consensus, and how teaching methods, administrative policies, and empirical observation all interacted in complex ways.

The following critique my teammates gave of the training program shows the supportive but constructive stance we teammates took toward each other. How the program benefitted from our frankness can also be seen in our discovery of a valuable research tool – "the records" or "the casework" – which later teacher-research teams came to call "log-keeping." We discovered its value when Lynn revealed that she had stopped doing assignments for my course in order to pursue her study of students because she learned more from them. As the observational logs she kept increased her teaching success and added to the whole team's knowledge of how natives and non-natives write, I decided to assign observation logs to members of subsequent teams and those they produced (on some 90 tutorial groups) became the project's most valuable data source. Without the openness and freedom encouraged by the lack of competition and evaluation anxiety, however, we might never have discovered the full potential of teacher-research.

Despite my mantle of "authority" and the risks it implied for students, we teammates, Lynn and Francie included, worked together toward a common goal – building the best program we could to help basic writers develop. Notice in the sequence below how secure the TAs seem to feel: Even when Francie asks *in my presence* whether Lynn has done all the readings, Lynn assumes (correctly) that the question is not a trap and exposes her lack of compliance with assignments for the course. The risk Lynn takes is warranted only because she is right in assuming that both Francie's and my behavior are less evaluation- than learning-oriented. Though Francie is her competitor and I determine her grade, Lynn apparently trusts we are not trying to judge her negatively but are looking for new methods of helping students learn.

MARIE: I'd like advice on improving tutor training for next year.

LYNN: The most helpful thing I did in your course was writing every day about the students in my notebook – aside from what I wrote in their folders. I wrote pages and pages and pages: "Today Timothy came in, and he did this and he did that. *And this is what I think it means.*"
　　　It was *great!* I learned so much. It helped me learn how to teach. A wonderful help! [Voice subsiding again] It's a lot of work, however.

MARIE: Maybe I should try to give tutors some scheduled time to do that kind of writing. Maybe we could shift to four groups of five students instead of five groups of four.

LYNN: [excited] If they wrote about students all semester long, they could do case studies as part of the course. Oh, I think it's a *wonderful* idea!

FRANCIE: I do too, but you're going to have to let something else go because it would be more work than anyone could do. [To Lynn] Were you able to do all the readings?

LYNN: No! I didn't do all the reading because I was very involved in keeping all these records for the case studies. I thought they were more important.

FRANCIE: I'm not putting you on the spot, Marie, but something would have to give.

Lynn was not the only TA using writing to teach herself to teach. Through these discussions the functions writing served in tutor learning became clear, with exploratory and observational writing assuming important roles and influencing the assignments I would give the following year:

ARTHUR: [who had come in late]: One thing that would help is separating the reading [response] journal from the writing in which we study students. Some of it needs to be kept as records of the teaching, but the rest is to figure out what we think about what we read.

FRAN: Thinkwriting!

MARIE: Discovery writing.

ARTHUR: I read a lot in people's journals that was not good for records and stuff in the records that should have been in the private journals.

LYNN: I didn't put any personal reactions to students in the records because students have access to them.

MARIE: Maybe it would be better not to keep the records in students' writing folders from now on.

Such feedback, conflict resolution, and negotiated planning led to other changes in the research process and in the structure and emphasis of the following year's course:

KATE: I think it would take some pressure off by not talking about writing [the research] up. Instead just say, "This is to help you keep track of students' progress." That's what it really was for.

CAROLINE: I disagree. I don't think Marie should wait until the course is over to encourage TAs to publish. In my [other graduate] classes, I never felt like I knew quite what was going on in the field, but this class made me feel like I was contributing something new. Not talking about publication at first is great, but later saying, "Hey, you could publish this if you work on it a little" – that's a really important motivator. It was really important to me.

FRANCIE: Yeah. Toward the end of the semester you can point out ideas that just jump out at you because they're so good, and then encourage the tutors to publish.

CAROLINE: It might be quite a surprise to find that you could write it up for something. That makes sense to me – not trying to get things to happen too fast.

MARIE: I guess I did talk a lot about publishing, but you had such incredible evidence. I mean, I was learning more from reading your notes than from reading published research.

My early acceptance of these master's level students as colleagues in research (and their ability to fulfil that role for me) apparently produced anxiety for some, for none had any experience with educational research. Soon, however, they began to see themselves as I saw them – as professionals basing decisions on carefully collected and considered evidence:

LYNN: I didn't know why you thought our findings were so remarkable until Fran and I presented our stuff at the developmental writing conference, and I'm telling you [voice rising], we were the only people talking about anything like this! That's what finally convinced me it's publishable stuff.

MARIE: Several of you got published, and [nodding] you two got reprinted!

FRANCIE: If [next year's tutors] keep their casework up, they shouldn't have any trouble writing up their results.

Informed by this discussion, the team helped me revise the research report assignments for the following year. The goal was to improve my training of tutors, thereby improving instruction basic writers would receive:

MARIE: If four groups of five were scheduled instead of five groups of four . . . they'd have more time for the casework. You keep saying slightly larger groups work better anyway . . .

TUTORS: Yeah!
             That'd be good.

MARIE: Maybe I should have several short researchy papers due every once in a while – so they could pull findings together a little at a time.

TUTORS: Sure.
             Yeah. That's a good idea.

MARIE: What's reasonable to assign? If we made schedule changes, they'd have two [working] hours out of ten for the records, so the analysis and writing would be all they had to do for the course . . .

TUTORS: Yeah.
              Fine.

MARIE: Do you think I should ask them for three shorter papers? One at midterm, one a few weeks later, and one at final time? Then they could build on each other.

TUTORS: Sure.
              That sounds fine.

FRAN: I think you should split it in thirds. Then they can use the first two as drafts for the final one.

ARTHUR: Yeah, they might get something out of that.

MARIE: Okay, good idea! And on the drafts I could give suggestions on how to tighten and confirm the analysis.

These excerpts illustrate the six patterns that characterized research-team interactions. They also support other research which suggests that women's interactions tend to be rooted in emotional openness and reciprocity (Ferguson, 1984; Miller, 1976; Pearson, 1985), that women are more cooperative than competitive (Ferguson, 1984; Gilligan, 1982; Lever, 1976; Miller, 1976; Pearson, 1985; Sassen, 1980), that women generally prefer helping others to self-enhancement at others' expense (Ferguson, 1984; Miller, 1976; Sassen, 1980), that women are more reluctant than men to be judgmental (Gilligan, 1982), and that women engage productively in honest but respectful conflict (Ferguson, 1984; Miller, 1976; Pearson, 1985).

These transcripts show what Miller (1976) calls "productive conflict" – conflict which benefits all participants rather than producing a single winner. Team success is enhanced by the women's "affiliative" habits (Gilligan, 1982; Miller, 1976) which lead to honest but supportive criticism (Miller, 1976; Pearson, 1985) and help teammates deal with negative feelings in supportive but direct ways (Miller, 1976; Pearson, 1985). A carefully honored commitment to protecting each other's self-esteem creates an environment in which these teammates feel safe exposing weaknesses, ask unselfconsciously for help in order to improve their work, and give each other generous support, all traits Miller (1976) found typical of women involved with learning. Cooperation subordinates self-advancement to the good of the group (Ferguson, 1984; Gilligan, 1982; Kohn, 1986; Miller, 1976; Sassen, 1980). It also improves the help TAs give learners in their care (Miller, 1976).

Observations and tapes of the five teams also lend support to Gilligan's (1982) and Ferguson's (1984) findings that women tend toward inclusive, lateral networks of relationship rather than toward more typically male hierarchies of power. They show women sustaining these networks by nonaggressive verbal conflict–resolution (Ferguson, 1984; see also Amidjaja & Vinacke, 1965; Vinacke, 1959) rather than by adopting a competitive (and exclusive) win–lose principle (see also Uesugi & Vinacke, 1963). Gilligan concludes that women's interactions are motivated by a morality of responsibility rather than by a more typically male ethic of individual rights and that women value relationship and connectedness over individual achievement. The interactions of these five largely female teams lend support to her conclusion.

I am not alone in my view of how the five teams operated. Many other teammates came to similar conclusions. Most women openly welcomed what one called the "sanctuary" atmosphere, stating that it was rare in academia: One wrote SANCTU-ARY in bold letters on a sign and hung it on the center door, and several wrote letters and/or poems expressing gratitude for the supportive learning atmosphere of the class. Apparently only the women had experienced such interactions before, however, for several men expressed surprise at my "unfamiliar" approach. The next section of this paper presents a male perspective, and shows the kind of interactions that characterized later teams.

Team IV – From a Male Perspective

Arthur was but one of several males who participated on the teams; exactly three years later Benyam, a poet, joined Team IV. A bilingual Ethiopian of thirty, Benyam had lived in the United States or Europe since the age of six and had received an entirely English-language education. After settling in the United States during his early teens, Benyam completed high school and college before taking an M.A. in poetry writing from Brown University. He became interested in the CTC program and applied to tutor in it while working on a second master's in applied linguistics.

As one of five male team members during the five-year project, Benyam's multicultural/multilingual background and reflective bent brought many valuable insights to his team's analysis. Also, as a male who was unaware of my study of gender and communication, he offered an ideal perspective against which to check my preliminary analysis. When he wandered between semesters into the office where I was drafting this essay, I at once inquired about his perceptions of Team IV. I refrained for some time, however, from bringing up the gender issue. I didn't want to influence the comments Benyam made.

To my surprise, Benyam had thought deeply about the issues I'd been studying. Like Arthur, he saw his team as different from groups he'd known before – in "open-ness," "equality," the way "everybody was a leader," and "evaluation approach":

BENYAM: [The team] was different in that everything was out in the open and everybody was a leader. The participation was very equal because there was no fear of evaluation attached to responses we gave each other, including those we gave you. In fact, the equality started with your coming to our level.

Benyam said his teammates gradually grew confident, cooperative, and willing to take risks to achieve a common goal. And because such participation was voluntary, the team differed from another group in which an employer had tried unsuccessfully to mandate "equality" from above:

So we became equal, and sources for each other, and the goal was to produce some-thing of value based on everybody's input. Each had to be open to everybody else as well as contributing all we could individually. That's the cooperative environment we sought, which made us different from other groups. Once another employer insisted a group I was in participate as equals, but it didn't happen in practice.

Competition was missing, said Benyam, but the team "challenged" each other to be open and trusting, take risks and give support, and "help" each other feel "secure" enough to learn:

> I'm not talking about *competition* but about *challenges* to resistances we felt against being judged. In most groups fear of evaluation inhibits learning by making us hide our ignorance, and at first that happened in this group too. So the challenge was not competition but to learn to help someone feel comfortable revealing themselves so they could learn from experience – because that kind of activity entails admitting your ignorance.

Benyam saw his team as "emotional," "open," "emergent," and "anticipatory," a view consistent with my observations of teams.
[. . .]
Benyam saw other benefits in the openness: It led to learning that was lateral, holistic, and participatory:

> The group was a haven for expressiveness, but the purpose of expressing feelings was not only communication. Its other goal was presentation, or *modeling*, of how we learned. Our task was to observe what went on in others so we could learn how people think, feel, and especially learn. In that environment, people could expose their feelings, so others could observe and respond honestly without feeling they were attacking or being attacked by anyone. We felt secure. If someone expressed a feeling against us, we didn't take it personally but saw it as something to observe and learn from.

[. . .]
Benyam saw benefits in the more lateral, interactive organization that let students share control of learning, and he confirmed what I had noticed – that such sharing led to emergent learnings unlikely to occur through top-down teaching alone.

> Exposing myself this way felt safe, and there were long-term rewards that made me do it more. I learned things that worked for me beyond that particular group. I learned that I could learn *by myself*, for example. So it's different from an authoritarian environment where somebody else decides what I have to learn. In this group I learned that I can motivate myself. In other groups you're usually led, in very concrete ways, and revealing incidents that emerge, when welcome, are secondary to planned instruction. This group balanced planned content with incidental learning.

Benyam was describing the kind of atmosphere I had tried to create, and his words confirmed my analysis of how the teacher-research teams functioned. After seeing that his perceptions were close to mine, I asked if he thought differences between this group and others might be gender-related. Benyam said he'd suspected a connection from the start when he was first exposed to the unfamiliar interactive patterns:

Considering differences I've observed in how men and women behave, our group had a strongly "feminine"[2] way of interacting. And this is not the first time I've brushed up against this masculine/feminine question in my thinking about that group. It's something I thought about from the beginning when asking myself, "What is going on?" and "How is this group different from groups I've been in before?"

Benyam saw his team as "feminine" in content as well as in process:

So far I've talked only about our interactions, but the group was also "feminine" in the content we built – both from our experience and by studying our students. And the methods that uncovered this material were different from what I'd been used to. By that I mean the course content was produced *together*, from shared research or experience.

The "feminine" aspect also showed up in the supportive atmosphere.

Here's where the feminine shows up again: In our emphasis on an unthreatening environment, we focus on a feminine principle – a safe and supportive setting where risk-taking leads to learning. (Many people have drawn analogies between the feminine principle and a vessel or container, and our work fits that metaphor in its emphasis on the *environments* in which learning takes place.) But its feminine nature also shows up in the *content* of that learning because in part it's the drives and motivations of the people in the environment. By dealing with their feelings and personal motivations, we help each other find an internal driving force to learn.

Benyam's experience in a women's supportive, open-ended learning environment is consistent with Miller's (1976) contention that women may know how to nurture learning in ways that men do not because "change and growth are intimately part of women's lives in a way in which they are not for men" (p. 56). It is consistent with Nancy Chodorow's (1978) conclusion that many typically female traits develop from the traditional women's work of raising children. And it supports Gilligan's (1982) assertion that women's reluctance to judge others harshly is rooted in their commitment to inclusive networks of relationship rather than in a more typically male drive for individual achievement, particularly if achievement must be gained at others' expense. Benyam echoes female perspectives documented by Ferguson (1984), Miller (1976), Friedan (1981), and Pearson (1985), all of whom suggest that men can learn much from women's ways of interacting; for though he found them initially unfamiliar, Benyam saw "feminine" interactive strategies as valuable alternatives for men:

As the only male, I learned that it's not important whether you're a man or woman because the "feminine"/"masculine" aspects of learning are available to anyone. What's "feminine" or "masculine" is the way of interacting and the method of generating and transferring content and information.

Benyam's words support my analysis of how teams worked co-equally, for through his team experience and his research on the twenty-odd tutorial groups he had taught, he had became convinced that

1 students in a "feminine environment" take more responsibility for learning and
2 they therefore begin to feel "equal" to their teachers.

That my own data confirm this view can be seen in the case of Lynn, the TA who openly ignored assignments to do unassigned writing of her own because she saw learning (rather than pleasing a teacher for a grade) as the goal of the course. Benyam explained how nonhierarchic interactions fostered growing independence in learners:

> The sense of equality comes from letting me be responsible for my learning, for in doing so I become equal with the teacher. The teacher remains the teacher, so it's not quite true equality, but once I go inward and get in touch with my own motivation instead of looking to an authority to tell me what I should learn, equality and hierarchy *as issues* disappear. Then whether I'm technically *equal* or not becomes irrelevant, for equality is not an issue when I control my learning.
>
> So you see, there's also *unlearning* that must take place: Inequality is perceived to the extent that we bring a hierarchical perspective to relationships, but when that perspective changes, the equality/inequality issue vanishes.

In the nonhierarchical "security" of his "strongly feminine" group, Benyam "unlearned" past perceptions of inequality and freed himself to adopt emotionally risky "feminine" ways of interacting:

> An example of not feeling equal was the baggage I brought to our group as a male. Being foreign was also part of the baggage. Those were two of my insecurities. Being black was the third. But I overcame them in that safe atmosphere.
>
> For example, I responded emotionally to something a woman wrote about a piece I'd written. Part of it showed admiration for my writing, but she also took liberties, making false assumptions about my African background. That was the first time I ever gave someone freedom to be expressive even though she was wrong. It was the first time I was able to take a negative expression as it was *intended* instead of taking it personally.

In a protected environment Benyam grew aware of interactive alternatives he had never chosen before, and because he was feeling less unequal than he had in the past, he was able to take the kind of risk that leads to learning:

> What saved me from responding irrationally was that the supportive environment helped me get *above* my feelings and see that they were natural. I asked, "What can I do with this comment?" and realized I had a choice: I could judge her and say "No! You're wrong!" or respond supportively. So I decided to respond to her enthusiasm for my writing rather than to her erroneous projections about my past.

By deciding to comment first on strengths in his teammate's response to his writing instead of attacking her ignorance or insensitivity, Benyam shifted from negative to more balanced evaluation approaches which were more protective of his teammate's self-esteem. By taking a risk (exposing himself further, despite her insensitivity), he turned a potentially hostile exchange into a learning experience for himself, the woman concerned, and others in the group. What he learned was to shift the focus and sequence of his evaluative response to protect the supportive atmosphere necessary for her to continue the risk-taking and collaborate in extending the learning opportunity he'd begun.

MARIE: Are you saying this new kind of interacting became possible for you *because* of the supportive environment?

BENYAM: Yeah. In that nonjudgmental atmosphere I was able to separate my preoccupation with her errors from that which was genuine and positive in her self-expression. Actually, what I learned was to address these issues *in a different sequence*. First I looked for the overall positive intention of her response and *accepted* it. Then I responded to the negative. To address her errors, I had to expose myself again, but *because I did*, her error resulted in a double learning situation which applied to us both and effectively caused her error to vanish: It no longer existed except in memory and in my understanding of what happened in our exchange.

Taking risks in a protected environment, Benyam experienced the kinds of rewards many women say they regularly get from women's groups. These motivated him to continue learning unfamiliar patterns of interaction that he referred to nonjudgmentally as "feminine":

This is the kind of learning that the feminine environment made possible, that the feminine way of interacting allowed us to learn. And this was one of the first steps I took in changing my way of interacting.

[. . .]

"Women's Ways" – Are They Only *Women's* Ways?

I make no claim that only women interact in "women's ways," that those who do so do so consistently, or that men rarely do so at all. In my data, however, women's ways are distributed unevenly across genders, with women being more likely to know and use them than are men though several men in the sample picked them up easily.

To perpetuate themselves hierarchies must exclude the weak. Women's ways, by contrast, enhance an opposite result, for they create environments in which all can succeed. In universities like mine, therefore, incompatible interactive paradigms co-exist. One is highly aggressive, rewarding only winners, even when winning means someone else has to lose. The other paradigm de-emphasizes success at others' expense in favor of cooperating to enhance progress for all by rewarding collaboration and mutual support. As others have noted, competitive approaches threaten such cooperation and are not only less efficient, they tend to subvert the goals for which they are pursued (Kohn, 1986). In light of these findings, universities (and other institutions as well) might increase their effectiveness by studying women's ways.

Many critics find the current dominant interactive paradigm inadequate, and this study supports their calls for change by showing how hierarchies are limited and limiting vis-à-vis women's ways. Friedan (1981), for one, calls for change in "the old, unequal, polarized male and female sex roles." What's needed now, she asserts, is to "transcend" those terms, to "transform the structure" of the institution itself (p. 40).

Friedan is not alone in maintaining that abandoning gender-typical interactions will improve society. Reviewing research on gender and language, Pearson (1985) concludes that communication will improve when women and men achieve inter-active flexibility by developing less stereotyped repertoires of communicative skills. Miller (1976) goes further to assert that by treating women's concerns as trivial, "male-led society" may have placed itself in jeopardy, unwittingly delegating to those it keeps powerless "not humanity's 'lowest needs' but its 'highest necessities.' " As a result, says Miller, women offer society hope in the form of "emotionally connected cooperation and creativity," traits she believes "necessary for human life and growth" (pp. 25–26). Like Friedan and Pearson, Miller believes women's ways will improve institutions by providing a "new framework" that is "inevitably different" from male-led hierarchies (p. 27).

Others also see women playing active roles in change. Affirming the need for institutional restructuring and asserting that survival for all people depends on this, Georgia Sassen (1980) proposes a "new agenda" for women in organizations: "Affirming the structures and values they bring to the question of competition versus relationships and . . . reconstructing institutions according to what women know" (p. 22). Her perspective is echoed by Kathy Ferguson (1984) who calls for recognition and use of women's "subjugated knowledges" (p. 156). Rejecting the false separation between public and private life, for example, Ferguson details the contributions of emotion to rational thought. This study confirms that her assertions have important implications for learning communities.

Consistent with theorists' calls for change are assessments of popular values which signal growing readiness for change in society at large. Friedan (1981) found support for change among men as well as women, and research confirms the existence of a "significant subculture" which holds alternative values "generally accepted as positive" and consistent with a "female language style" (Pearson, 1985, p. 203). Kramer (1978) found communicative traits associated with women perceived by women and men alike as close to ideal speech. Apparently there is readiness among the public at large for securing the rewards of women's ways for all.

Kohn's (1986) book, *No Contest: The Case Against Competition*, describes scholarly echoes of that readiness. Synthesizing findings from studies in fields as diverse as linguistics, psychoanalysis, cultural anthropology, business, and biology, Kohn concludes that by contrast with competition, cooperation leads to greater learning, athletic achievement, productivity, enjoyment, efficiency, and psychological health.

Even in nature, the concept of survival of the fittest – often offered by advocates as evidence that competition is inevitable – occurs at the group, not the individual level, Kohn states. Like Miller, Kohn concludes from his study that the safety of society stands in jeopardy unless it abandons its competitive ways.

Though research refutes the myth that competition is rooted in human nature rather than in learned behavior, Kohn explains, hierarchies create economies of artificial scarcity that inevitably lead to structural (i.e., hierarchically-induced) competition. Eliminating competition is therefore necessary, he believes, to create an environment in which healthy, safe, and productive interactions can survive. In so saying Kohn echoes female theorists' calls for sweeping change in the terms by which institutions operate.

Addressing the practical issue of how such change might take place, Friedan (1981), Gilligan (1982), Miller (1976), Pearson (1985), Sassen (1980) and Ferguson (1984) make similar suggestions. In Ferguson's words, instead of accepting current "dominance/subordinance relations" in which "constellations of instrumental and expressive traits [are] allocated . . . by gender," we must view such traits "as complementary dimensions of all individuals, male and female." In other words, she continues, in a changed society, the "tensions between [instrumental and expressive traits] would be more effectively expressed as tensions within individuals rather than tensions between groups."

Against this backdrop of suggestions that we change institutional terms by offering men and women more flexible "repertoires of communicative skills," this study shows that such changes have begun to appear and that, in learning contexts, women's interactive approaches are both possible and worthwhile. By showing women and men adopting new interactive strategies, it records solutions emerging from conscious efforts at change. [. . .] As men in this study were willing and able to adopt the constellation of behaviors and attitudes one of the female students called "women's ways," it becomes inappropriate to see such interactions only as *women's* ways. For as Benyam concluded, people of both genders can choose how they interact once they become aware of the options available:

> I learned that it's not important whether you're a man or woman because the "feminine"/"masculine" aspects of learning are available to anyone.

Again, I make no claim that all women interact in "women's ways," that those who do so do so consistently, or that men rarely do so at all. Though women's ways are apparently distributed unevenly across genders, with women being more likely to know and use them than are men, interactions documented on these largely female teams show men also being empowered by the "sanctuary atmosphere" which replaced the competition with which the men said they were more familiar.

Apparently enough dissonance exists between competition and women's ways that the latter have difficulty surviving within hierarchies unless those in power sponsor them. To complicate matters, lack of experience has left women few strategies for protecting women's ways. This can be explained historically, for women have traditionally worked around the fringes of the hierarchy or (in this case) within one or two levels (Ferguson, 1984). Chances to use women's ways across levels have therefore been rare, and women are just beginning to share strategies they have developed for protecting noncompetitive ways in the face of aggressive ones. Containing competition without reverting to authoritarian approaches, for example, was absolutely critical to my work with the teacher-research teams, but my knowledge of how to do so grew slowly, and largely by trial and error, for I had no known role models for what I was trying to do.

Though I speak of sharing strategies for protecting women's ways from their more aggressive counterparts, I don't mean to suggest that women's ways should be integrated into hierarchies, for they are in direct conflict with several assumptions on which hierarchies are based. Some aspects of the dominant paradigm may not be inconsistent, however, and blending the strengths of each paradigm might lead to a useful synthesis. Successful extended interactions require attention to both task and group maintenance functions – to producing quality results and to maintenance, climate, and interpersonal skills. These have been the respective emphases of hierarchy and women's ways, and both are required for the conduct of humane and efficient activity. Fortunately, blending positive aspects of these paradigms may not be as large a task as it might at first appear, for though studies like this one dramatize problems caused by the paradigm clash, they also confirm the potential of collaborative problem-solving. In doing so they eliminate the need to rely on competitive strategies when negotiating the terms by which restructured institutions will operate, for ground rules exist for productive conflict in which no one group dominates at another's expense.

NOTES

1 All names except mine have been changed.
2 In editing transcripts, I have preserved speakers' diction wherever possible, even when there is a chance their intentions will be obscured by connotations of which they are apparently unaware. But it should be noted that many women (consciously or unconsciously) avoided referring to women's communicative patterns as "feminine," a term which has often been used in uncomplimentary ways. Instead they used terms such as "women's styles" and "women's ways" to refer to collaborative, supportive, nonhierarchical patterns of interaction. It is therefore the language of one of the women that the title of this essay reflects.

REFERENCES

Amidjaja, I. M., & Vinacke, W. E. (1965). Achievement, nurturance, and competition in male and female triads. *Journal of Personality and Social Psychology*, 2, 447–451.
Chodorow, N. (1978). *The reproduction of mothering*. Berkeley: University of California Press.
Ferguson, K. (1984). *The feminist case against bureaucracy*. Philadelphia: Temple University Press.

Friedan, B. (1981). *The second stage*. New York: Summit Books.

Gilligan, C. (1982). *In a different voice: Psychological theory and women's development*. Cambridge, MA: Harvard University Press.

Kanter, R. (1975). Women and the structure of organizations. In M. Millman (Ed.), *Another voice*. New York: Doubleday/Anchor, pp. 34–74.

Kohn, A. (1986). *No contest: The case against competition*. Boston: Houghton Mifflin.

Kramer, C. R. (1978). Men's and women's ratings of their own ideal speech. *Communication Quarterly*, 26, 2–11.

Lever, J. (1976). Sex differences in the games children play. *Social Problems*, 23, 478–487.

Miller, J. B. (1976). *Toward a new psychology of women*. Boston: Beacon Press.

Pearson, J. C. (1985). *Gender and communication*. Dubuque, IA: William C. Brown Publishers.

Sassen, G. (1980). Success anxiety in women: A constructivist interpretation of its sources and its significance. *Harvard Educational Review*, 50, 13–24.

Uesugi, T. K., & Vinacke, W. E. (1963). Strategy in a feminine game. *Sociometry*, 26, 75–88.

Vinacke, W. E. (1959). Sex roles in a three-person game. *Sociometry*, 22, 343–360.

Part VI

Theoretical Debates (1): Gender or Power?

This section will focus on the debate which questions whether the linguistic features said to be typical of women's speech are actually associated with lack of power. The paper which first raised this question – William O'Barr and Bowman Atkins' ' "Women's Language" or "Powerless Language"?' – is now dated in several ways, but I've included it because of its historical importance in the debate. O'Barr and Atkins studied language variation in American courtrooms and became interested in questions of gender through noticing that legal manuals give special advice on the behaviour of female witnesses. Using the linguistic features highlighted by Robin Lakoff (1975), they analysed the speech of a range of witnesses, both male and female, to see if their language use varied along gender lines. While they found some female witnesses who used language in a way which accorded with Lakoff's categories, they found others who did not: these were typically expert witnesses, women of high social status, who spoke confidently and assertively in court. Male witnesses varied in the same way, with less statusful individuals using language with more 'female' features. These findings led O'Barr and Atkins to claim that what Lakoff described as 'women's language' would be better termed 'powerless language', since these features are associated with speakers of low status, irrespective of gender. The fact that the female witnesses in their sample were more likely than men to use powerless language they explain in terms of social structure: American society allocates women to relatively powerless social positions.

There are several problems with O'Barr and Atkins' account. The first is its uncritical use of Lakoff's set of 'women's language' features, features which Lakoff arrived at through introspection and personal observation, not through empirical research. The second is its assumption that any linguistic form, such as a hedge or a tag question, can be matched, one-to-one, with a specific function. This means that their analysis assumes that a hedge such as *sort of*, for example, must express tentativeness. This view has been challenged (see Cameron et al. 1989), and many linguists have written about the multifunctional nature of such linguistic forms (see, for example, Coates 1987, 1996; Holmes 1984, 1995).

More fundamentally, O'Barr and Atkins make the assumption that the value placed on the set of linguistic forms they call WL (Women's Language) is independent of culture; in other words, they seem to believe that hedges, for example, are *intrinsically* weak or tentative. Feminist linguists in English-speaking countries have suggested that the low value placed on forms such as hedges might have less to do with hedges and more to do with their supposed association with female speakers. In other words, because female speakers have low status, linguistic forms said to be typical of women will acquire low status by association. As Janet Holmes (1986: 18) puts it: 'one (female) person's feeble hedging may well be perceived as another (male) person's perspicacious qualification'.

Strong support for this position is given by the next paper in this section, Patricia Wetzel's 'Are "Powerless" Communication Strategies the Japanese Norm?' Wetzel investigates the notion of 'powerless' language. She shows that the conversational patterns associated with women and powerlessness in the West are associated with male speakers and with power in Japan. This rather undermines the idea that such conversational patterns are intrinsically weak or powerless. Wetzel's discussion of this issue puts power centre-stage: she examines culture-specific features of power, and shows how it is only through an understanding of the power structures of a society that we can come to an understanding of the meaning of any given conversational strategy. It is salutory to learn that the array of conversational strategies viewed in the West as strong, assertive, powerful, macho, are considered immature and childish by Japanese speakers. This paper is a forceful reminder that linguistic forms themselves mean nothing: it is the cultural value placed on these forms that matters.

In the third paper in this section – 'When the Doctor is a "Lady"' – Candace West sets out to disentangle the independent variables of status and gender. Her paper is a report of an exploratory study of doctor–patient talk (the paper by West in the previous section – 'Not just doctors' orders' – explores the same material from a different angle). The doctor–patient relationship is essentially asymmetrical: doctors have institutional power in the context of the doctor's surgery; patients have little or no power. West carried out a detailed analysis of all the interruptions which occurred in these doctor–patient encounters, focusing on interruptions because they are a linguistic strategy which both demonstrates and accomplishes dominance (see West and Zimmerman's paper, p. 165). As anticipated, West found that doctors interrupted patients disproportionately, except where the doctor was female, when patients interrupted as much as or more than the doctors. West explains this apparent anomaly by arguing that gender outweighs social status in determining social (including linguistic) behaviour. In other words, while male doctors use interruptions as devices for exercising control over interaction, women doctors are interrupted by their patients, which undermines their authority. (These results are supported by the work of Woods 1989, who found that in the work setting, gender was more important than status in predicting linguistic behaviour, with female bosses regularly interrupted by male subordinates.)

This is a complex debate. It throws up many questions: what is the relationship between gender, power and status? Should we see gender and power as being in an either/or relationship (as O'Barr and Atkins assume), or as being in a both/and relationship (as West assumes)? In other words, is it more accurate to argue that gender and power are intertwined, so that when a man interrupts a woman (for example) he is not just doing gender, but also doing power? These three papers present a range of answers, not all compatible, and all products of their time. The debate continues, and in the late twentieth century more sophisticated ideas of power and gender, inspired in particular by the work of Foucault, are stimulating new questions and new answers.

REFERENCES

Cameron, Deborah, McAlinden, Fiona and O'Leary, Kathy (1989) 'Lakoff in context: the social and linguistic functions of tag questions', pp. 74–93 in Jennifer Coates and Deborah Cameron (eds) *Women in Their Speech Communities*. London: Longman.

Coates, Jennifer (1987) 'Epistemic modality and spoken discourse'. *Transactions of the Philological Society*, 110–31.

Coates, Jennifer (1996) *Women Talk: Conversation Between Women Friends*. Oxford: Blackwell.

Holmes, Janet (1984) 'Hedging your bets and sitting on the fence: some evidence for hedges as support structures'. *Te Reo*, 27, 47–62.

Holmes, Janet (1986) 'Functions of *you know* in women's and men's speech'. *Language in Society*, 15, 1, 1–21.

Holmes, Janet (1995) *Women, Men and Politeness*. London: Longman.

Lakoff, Robin (1975) *Language and Woman's Place*. New York: Harper & Row.

Woods, Nicola (1989) 'Talking shop: sex and status as determinants of floor apportionment in a work setting', pp. 141–57 in Jennifer Coates and Deborah Cameron (eds) *Women in Their Speech Communities*. London: Longman.

RECOMMENDED FURTHER READING

Cameron, Deborah, McAlinden, Fiona and O'Leary, Kathy (1989) 'Lakoff in context: the social and linguistic functions of tag questions', pp. 74–93 in Jennifer Coates and Deborah Cameron (eds) *Women in Their Speech Communities*. London: Longman.

Fairclough, Norman (1989) *Language and Power*. London: Longman.

Fairclough, Norman (1992) *Discourse and Social Change*. Cambridge: Polity Press.

Gal, Susan (1992) 'Language, gender and power: an anthropological view', pp. 153–61 in Kira Hall, Mary Bucholtz and Birch Moonwomon (eds) *Locating Power. Proceedings of the Second Berkeley Women and Language Conference*. University of California, Berkeley: BWLG.

Henley, Nancy and Kramarae, Cheris (1991) 'Gender, power and miscommunication', pp. 18–43 in N. Coupland, H. Giles and J. W. Wiemann (eds) *'Miscommunication' and Problematic Talk*. London: Sage.

Woods, Nicola (1989) 'Talking shop: sex and status as determinants of floor apportionment in a work setting', pp. 141–57 in Jennifer Coates and Deborah Cameron (eds) *Women in Their Speech Communities*. London: Longman.

24

"Women's Language" or "Powerless Language"?

William M. O'Barr and Bowman K. Atkins

Introduction

The understanding of language and sex in American culture has progressed far beyond Robin Lakoff's influential and provocative essays on "women's language" written only a few years ago (Lakoff 1975). The rapid development of knowledge in what had been so significantly an ignored and overlooked area owes much to both the development of sociolinguistic interest in general and to the woman's movement in particular. But as a recent review of anthropological studies about women pointed out, this interest has grown so quickly and studies proliferated so fast that there is frequently little or no cross-referencing of mutually supportive studies and equally little attempt to reconcile conflicting interpretations of women's roles (Quinn 1977). A similar critique of the literature on language and sex would no doubt reveal many of the same problems. But in one sense, these are not problems – they are marks of a rapidly developing field of inquiry, of vitality, and of saliency of the topic.

Our interest in language and sex was sharpened by Lakoff's essays. Indeed, her work was for us – as it was for many others – a jumping off point. But unlike some other studies, ours was not primarily an attempt to understand language and sex differences. Rather, the major goal of our recent research has been the study of language variation in a specific institutional context – the American trial courtroom – and sex-related differences were one of the kinds of variation which current sociolinguistic issues led us to consider. Our interest was further kindled by the discovery that trial practice manuals (how-to-do-it books by successful trial lawyers and law professors) often had special sections on how female witnesses behave differently from males and thus special kinds of treatment they require.

In this paper, we describe our study of how women (and men) talk in court. The research we report here is part of a 30-month study of language variation in trial courtrooms which has included both ethnographic and experimental components. It is the thesis of this study that so-called "women's language" is in large part a language of powerlessness, a condition that can apply to men as well as women. That a complex of such features should have been called "women's language" in the first place reflects the generally powerless position of many women in American society, a point recognized but not developed extensively by Lakoff (1975: 7–8). Careful examination in one institutional setting of the features which were identified as constituting "women's language" has shown clearly that such features are simply not patterned along sex lines. Moreover, the features do not, in a strict sense, constitute a *style* or *register* since there is not perfect co-variation.

This paper proceeds as follows: first, it examines the phenomenon of "women's language" in the institutional context of a court of law; second, it shows that the features of "women's language" are not restricted to women and therefore suggests renaming the concept "powerless" language due to its close association with persons having low social power and often relatively little previous experience in the courtroom setting; [. . .] and finally, it calls for a refinement of our studies to distinguish power-less language features from others which may in fact be found primarily in women's speech.

How to Handle Women in Court – Some Advice from Lawyers

One of the means which we used in our study of courtroom language to identify specific language variables for detailed study was information provided to us in interviews with practicing lawyers. More useful, however, were *trial practice manuals* – books written by experienced lawyers which attempt to discuss systematically suc-cessful methods and tactics for conducting trials. Typically, little effort is devoted to teaching and developing trial practice skills in the course of a legal education. Rather it is expected that they will be acquired through personal experimentation, through watching and modeling one's behavior after successful senior lawyers, and through reading the advice contained in such manuals. Those who write trial prac-tice manuals are experienced members of the legal profession who are reporting on both their own experiences and the generally accepted folklore within the profession. In all these situations, the basis for claims about what works or what does not tends to be the general success of those who give advice or serve as models – judged primarily by whether they win their cases most of the time.

One kind of advice which struck us in reading through several of these manuals was that pertaining to the special treatment which should be accorded women. The manuals which discuss special treatment for women tend to offer similar advice re-garding female witnesses. Readers are instructed to behave generally the same toward women as men, but to note that, in certain matters or situations, women require some special considerations. Some of this advice includes the following:

1. *Be especially courteous to women.* ("Even when jurors share the cross-examiner's reaction that the female witness on the stand is dishonest or otherwise undeserving individually, at least some of the jurors are likely to think it improper for the

attorney to decline to extend the courtesies customarily extended to women.") (Keeton 1973: 149.)

2. *Avoid making women cry.* ("Jurors, along with others, may be inclined to forgive and forget transgressions under the influence of sympathy provoked by the genuine tears of a female witness." "A crying woman does your case no good.") (Keeton 1973: 149; Bailey and Rothblatt 1971: 190.)

3. *Women behave differently from men and this can sometimes be used to advantage.* ("Women are contrary witnesses. They hate to say yes. . . . A woman's desire to avoid the obvious answer will lead her right into your real objective – contradicting the testimony of previous prosecution witnesses. Women, like children, are prone to exaggeration; they generally have poor memories as to previous fabrications and exaggerations. They also are stubborn. You will have difficulty trying to induce them to qualify their testimony. Rather, it might be easier to induce them to exaggerate and cause their testimony to appear incredible. An intelligent woman will very often be evasive. She will avoid making a direct answer to a damaging question. Keep after her until you get a direct answer – but always be the gentleman.") (Bailey and Rothblatt 1971: 190–1.)

These comments about women's behavior in court and their likely consequences in the trial process further raised our interest in studying the speech behavior of women in court. Having been told by Lakoff that women do speak differently from men, we interpreted these trial practice authors as saying that at least some of these differences can be consequential in the trial process. Thus, one of the kinds of variation which we sought to examine when we began to observe and tape record courtroom speech was patterns unique to either women or men. We did not know what we would find, so we started out by using Lakoff's discussion of "women's language" as a guide.

Briefly, what Lakoff had proposed was that women's speech varies from men's in several significant ways. Although she provides no firm listing of the major features of what she terms "women's language" (hereafter referred to in this paper as WL), we noted the following features, said to occur in high frequency among women, and used these as a baseline for our investigation of sex-related speech patterns in court.

1 *Hedges.* ("It's sort of hot in here."; "I'd kind of like to go."; "I guess . . ."; "It seems like . . ."; and so on.)

2 *(Super) polite forms.* ("I'd really appreciate it if . . ."; "Would you please open the door, if you don't mind?"; and so on.)

3 *Tag questions.* ("John is here, isn't he?" instead of "Is John here?"; and so on.)

4 *Speaking in italics.* (Intonational emphasis equivalent to underlining words in written language; emphatic *so* or *very* and so on.)

5 *Empty adjectives. (Divine; charming; cute; sweet; adorable; lovely*; and so on.)

6 *Hypercorrect grammar and pronunciation.* (Bookish grammar; more formal enunciation.)

7   *Lack of a sense of humor.* (Women said to be poor joke tellers and to frequently "miss the point" in jokes told by men.)

8   *Direct quotations.* (Use of direct quotations instead of paraphrases.)

9   *Special lexicon.* (In domains like colors where words like *magenta, chartreuse*, and so on are typically used only by women.)

10   *Question intonation in declarative contexts.* (For example, in response to the question, "When will dinner be ready?", an answer like "Around 6 o'clock?", as though seeking approval and asking whether that time will be okay.)

What We Found

During the summer of 1974, we recorded over 150 hours of trials in a North Carolina superior criminal court. Although almost all of the lawyers we observed were males, the sex distribution of witnesses was more nearly equal. On looking for the speech patterns described by Lakoff, we quickly discovered some women who spoke in the described manner. The only major discrepancies between Lakoff's description and our findings were in features which the specific context of the courtroom rendered inappropriate, for example, *tag questions* (because witnesses typically answer rather than ask questions) and *joking* (because there is little humor in a courtroom, we did not have occasion to observe the specifically female patterns of humor to which she referred).

In addition to our early finding that some women approximate the model described by Lakoff, we also were quick to note that there was considerable variation in the degree to which women exhibited these characteristics. Since our observations were limited to about ten weeks of trials during which we were able to observe a variety of cases in terms of offense (ranging from traffic cases, drug possession, robbery, manslaughter, to rape) and length (from a few hours to almost five days), we believe that our observations cover a reasonably good cross-section of the kinds of trials, and hence witnesses, handled by this type of court. Yet, ten weeks is not enough to produce a very large number of witnesses. Even a single witness may spend several hours testifying. In addition, the court spends much time selecting jurors, hearing summation remarks, giving jury instructions, and handling administrative matters. Thus, when looking at patterns of how different women talk in court, we are in a better position to deal with the range of variation we observed than to attempt any precise frequency counts of persons falling into various categories. Thus, we will concentrate our efforts here on describing the range and complement this with some non-statistical impressions regarding frequency.

Our observations show a continuum of use of the features described by Lakoff.[1] We were initially at a loss to explain why some women should speak more or less as Lakoff had described and why others should use only a few of these features. We will deal with our interpretation of these findings later, but first let us examine some points along the continuum from high to low.

A. Mrs. W.,[2] a witness in a case involving the death of her neighbor in an automobile accident, is an extreme example of a person speaking WL in her testimony. She used nearly every feature described by Lakoff and certainly all those which are appropriate in the courtroom context. Her speech contains a high frequency of *intensifiers* ("*very* close friends," "*quite* ill," and so on often with intonation emphasis); *hedges* (frequent use of "you know," "sort of like," "maybe just a little bit," "let's see," and so on); *empty adjectives* ("this *very* kind policeman"); and other similar features. The first example below is typical of her speech and shows the types of intensifiers and hedges she commonly uses.[3] (To understand what her speech *might* be like without these features, example (2) is a rewritten version of her answers with the WL features eliminated.)

(1) L. State whether or not, Mrs. W., you were acquainted with or knew the late Mrs. E. D.
    W. Quite well.
    L. What was the nature of your acquaintance with her?
    W. Well, we were, uh, very close friends. Uh, she was even sort of like a mother to me.

(2) L. State whether or not, Mrs. W., you were acquainted with or knew the late Mrs. E. D.
    W. Yes, I did.
    L. What was the nature of your acquaintance with her?
    W. We were close friends. She was like a mother to me.

Table 1 summarizes the frequency of several features attributed to WL by Lakoff. Calculated as a ratio of WL forms for each answer, this witness's speech contains 1.14 – among the highest incidences we observed.

B. The speech of Mrs. N, a witness in a case involving her father's arrest, shows fewer WL features. Her ratio of features for each answer drops to .84. Her testimony contains instances of both WL and a more assertive speech style. Frequently, her speech is punctuated with responses like: "He, see, he thought it was more-or-less me rather than the police officer." Yet it also contains many more straightforward and assertive passages than are found in A's speech. In example (3), for instance, Mrs. N is anything but passive. She turns questions back on the lawyer and even interrupts him. Example (4) illustrates the ambivalence of this speaker's style better. Note how she moves quickly to qualify – in WL – an otherwise assertive response.

(3) L. All right. I ask you if your husband hasn't beaten him up in the last week?
    W. Yes, and do you know why?
    L. Well, I . . .
    W. Another gun episode.
    L. Another gun episode?
    W. Yessiree.

(4) L. You've had a controversy going with him for a long time, haven't you?
    W. Ask why – I mean not because I'm just his daughter.

Table 1   Frequency distribution of Women's Language features[a] in the speech of six witnesses in a trial courtroom

	Women			Men		
	A	*B*	*C*	*D*	*E*	*F*
Intensifiers[b]	16	0	0	21	2	1
Hedges[c]	19	2	3	2	5	0
Hesitation Forms[d]	52	20	13	26	27	11
W asks L questions[e]	2	0	0	0	0	0
Gestures[f]	2	0	0	0	0	0
Polite Forms[g]	9	0	2	2	0	1
Sir[h]	2	0	6	32	13	11
Quotes[i]	1	5	0	0	0	0
Total (all powerless forms)	103	27	24	85	47	24
# of Answers in Interview	90	32	136	61	73	52
Ratio (# powerless forms for each answer)	1.14	0.84	0.18	1.39	0.64	0.46

Notes: [a]The particular features chosen for inclusion in this table were selected because of their saliency and frequency of occurrence. Not included here are features of WL which either do not occur in court or ones which we had difficulty operationalizing and coding. *Based on direct examinations only.* [b]Forms which increase or emphasize the force of assertion such as *very*, *definitely*, *very definitely*, *surely*, *such a*, and so on. [c]Forms which reduce the force of assertion allowing for exceptions or avoiding rigid commitments such as *sort of*, *a little*, *kind of*, and so on. [d]Pause fillers such as *uh*, *um*, *ah*, and "meaningless" particles such as *oh*, *well*, *let's see*, *now*, *so*, *you see*, and so on. [e]Use of question intonation in response to lawyer's questions, including rising intonation in normally declarative contexts (for example, "thirty?, thirty-five?") and questions asked by witness of lawyer like. "Which way do you go . . . ?". [f]Spoken indications of direction such as *over there*, and so on. [g]Include *please*, *thank you*, and so on. Use of *sir* counted separately due to its high frequency. [h]Assumed to be an indication of more polite speech. [i]Not typically allowed in court under restrictions on hearsay which restrict the situations under which a witness may tell what someone else said.

Source: Original data.

C.   The speech of Dr. H, a pathologist who testifies as an expert witness, exhibits fewer features of WL than either of the other two women. Her speech contains the lowest incidence of WL features among the female witnesses whose speech we analyzed. Dr. H's ratio of WL features is .18 for each answer. Her responses tend to be straightforward, with little hesitancy, few hedges, a noticeable lack of intensifiers, and so on. (See table 1.) Typical of her speech is example (5) in which she explains some of her findings in a pathological examination.

(5) L.   And had the heart not been functioning, in other words, had the heart been stopped, there would have been no blood to have come from that region?

    W.   It may leak down depending on the position of the body after death. But the presence of blood in the alveoli indicates that some active respiratory action had to take place.

What all of this shows is the fact that some women speak in the way Lakoff described, employing many features of WL, while others are far away on the continuum of possible and appropriate styles for the courtroom. Before discussing the reasons which may lie behind this variation in the language used by women in court, we first examine an equally interesting finding which emerged from our investigation of male speech in court.

We also found men who exhibit WL characteristics in their courtroom testimony. To illustrate this, we examine the speech of three male witnesses which varies along a continuum of high to low incidence of WL features.

   D.   Mr. W exhibits many but not all of Lakoff's WL features.[4] Some of those which he does employ, like intensifiers, for example, occur in especially high frequency – among the highest observed among all speakers, whether male or female. His ratio of WL features for each answer is 1.39, actually higher than individual A. Example (6), while an extreme instance of Mr. W's use of WL features, does illustrate the degree to which features attributed to women are in fact present in high frequency in the speech of some men.

(6) L.   And you saw, you observed what?

      W.   Well, after I heard – I can't really, I can't definitely state whether the brakes or the lights came first, but I rotated my head slightly to the right, and looked directly behind Mr. Z., and I saw reflections of lights, and uh, very, very, very instantaneously after that, I heard a very, very loud explosion – from my standpoint of view it would have been an implosion because everything was forced outward, like this, like a grenade thrown into a room. And, uh, it was, it was terrifically loud.

   E.   Mr. N, more toward the low frequency end of the continuum of male speakers, shows some WL features. His ratio of features for each answer is .64, comparable to individual B. Example (7) shows an instance of passages from the testimony of this speaker in which there are few WL features. Example (8), by comparison, shows the same hedging in a way characteristic of WL. His speech falls between the highest and lowest incidences of WL features we observed among males.

(7) L.   After you looked back and saw the back of the ambulance, what did you do?

      W.   After I realized that my patient and my attendant were thrown from the vehicle, uh, which I assumed, I radioed in for help to the dispatcher, tell her that we had been in an accident and, uh, my patient and attendant were thrown from the vehicle and I didn't know the extent of their injury at the time, to hurry up and send help.

(8) L.   Did you form any conclusion about what her problem was at the time you were there?

      W.   I felt that she had, uh, might have had a sort of heart attack.

   F.   Officer G, among the males lowest in WL features, virtually lacks all features tabulated in table 1 except for hesitancy and using *sir*. His ratio of WL forms for each answer is .46. Example (9) shows how this speaker handles the lack of certainty in a more authoritative manner than by beginning his answer with "I guess . . .". His no-nonsense, straightforward manner is illustrated well by example (10), in which a technical answer is given in a style comparable to that of individual C.

(9)　L.　Approximately how many times have you testified in court?

　　　W.　It would only have to be a guess, but it's three or four, five, six hundred times. Probably more.

(10)　L.　You say that you found blood of group O?

　　　W.　The blood in the vial, in the layman's term, is positive, Rh positive. Technically referred to as a capital r, sub o, little r.

Taken together these findings suggest that the so-called "women's language" is neither characteristic of all women nor limited only to women. A similar continuum of WL features (high to low) is found among speakers of both sexes. These findings suggest that the sex of a speaker is insufficient to explain incidence of WL features, and that we must look elsewhere for an explanation of this variation.

Once we had realized that WL features were distributed in such a manner, we began to examine the data for other factors which might be associated with a high or low incidence of the features in question. First, we noted that we were able to find *more* women toward the high end of the continuum. Next, we noted that all the women who were aberrant (that is, who used relatively few WL features) had something in common – an unusually high social status. Like Dr. H, they were typically well-educated, professional women of middle-class background. A corresponding pattern was noted among the aberrant men (that is, those high in WL features). Like Mr. W, they tended to be men who held either subordinate, lower-status jobs or were unemployed. Housewives were high in WL features while middle-class males were low in these features. In addition to social status in the society at large, another factor associated with low incidence of WL is previous courtroom experience. Both individuals C and F testify frequently in court as expert witnesses, that is, as witnesses who testify on the basis of their professional expertise. However, it should be noted that not all persons who speak with few WL features have had extensive courtroom experience. The point we wish to emphasize is that a powerful position may derive from either social standing in the larger society and/or status accorded by the court. We carefully observed these patterns and found them to hold generally.[5] For some individuals whom we had observed in the courtroom, we analyzed their speech in detail in order to tabulate the frequency of the WL features as shown in table 1. A little more about the background of the persons we have described will illustrate the sort of pattern we observed.

　　A　is a married woman, about 55 years old, who is a housewife.

　　B　is married, but younger, about 35 years old. From her testimony, there is no information that she works outside her home.

　　C　is a pathologist in a local hospital. She is 35–40 years old. There is no indication from content of her responses or from the way she was addressed (always *Dr.*) of her marital status. She has testified in court as a pathologist on many occasions.

D   is an ambulance attendant, rather inexperienced in his job, at which he has
    worked for less than 6 months. Age around 30. Marital status unknown.
E   is D's supervisor. He drives the ambulance, supervises emergency treat-
    ment and gives instructions to D. He has worked at his job longer than D
    and has had more experience. Age about 30–35; marital status unknown.
F   is an experienced member of the local police force. He has testified in
    court frequently. Age 35–40; marital status unknown.

"Women's Language" or "Powerless Language"?

In the previous section, we presented data which indicate that the variation in WL
features may be related more to social powerlessness than to sex. We have presented
both observational data and some statistics to show that this style is not simply or
even primarily a sex-related pattern. We did, however, find it related to sex in that
more women tend to be high in WL features while more men tend to be low in these
same features. The speech patterns of three men and three women were examined.
For each sex, the individuals varied from social statuses with relatively low power to
more power (for women: housewife to doctor; for men: subordinate job to one with
a high degree of independence of action). Experience may also be an important
factor, for those whom we observed speaking with few WL features seemed more
comfortable in the courtroom and with the content of their testimony. Associated
with increasing shifts in social power and experience were corresponding decreases in
frequency of WL features. These six cases were selected for detailed analysis because
they were representative of the sorts of women and men who served as witnesses in
the trials we observed in 1974. Based on this evidence, we would suggest that the
phenomenon described by Lakoff would be better termed *powerless language*, a term
which is more descriptive of the particular features involved, of the social status of
those who speak in this manner, and one which does not link it unnecessarily to the
sex of a speaker.

Further, we would suggest that the tendency for more women to speak powerless
language and for men to speak less of it is due, at least in part, to the greater
tendency of women to occupy relatively powerless social positions. What we have
observed is a reflection in their speech behavior of their social status. Similarly, for
men, a greater tendency to use the more powerful variant (which we will term
powerful language) may be linked to the fact that men much more often tend to
occupy relatively powerful positions in society.

[. . .]

Conclusion

In this study, we have attempted to argue that our data from studying male–female
language patterns in trial courtrooms suggest that Lakoff's concept of "woman's

language" is in need of modification. Our findings show that, in one particular context at least, not all women exhibit a high frequency of WL features and that some men do. We have argued that instead of being primarily sex-linked, a high incidence of some or all of these features appears to be more closely related to social position in the larger society and/or the specific context of the courtroom. Hence, we have suggested a re-naming of the phenomenon as "powerless language." What has previously been referred to as "women's language" is perhaps better thought of as a composite of features of powerless language (which can but need not be a characteristic of the speech of either women or men) and of some other features which may be more restricted to women's domains.

Thus, Lakoff's discussion of "women's language" confounds at least two different patterns of variation. Although our title suggests a dichotomy between "women's language" and "powerless language," these two patterns undoubtedly interact. It could well be that to speak like the powerless is not only typical of women because of the all-too-frequent powerless social position of many American women, but is also part of the cultural meaning of speaking "like a woman." Gender meanings draw on other social meanings; analyses that focus on sex in isolation from the social positions of women and men can thus tell us little about the meaning of "women's language" in society and culture.

[. . .]

NOTES

The research reported here was supported by a National Science Foundation Law and Social Science Program Grant (No. GS-42742), William M. O'Barr, principal investigator. The authors wish to thank especially these other members of the research team for their advice and assistance: John Conley, Marilyn Endriss, Bonnie Erickson, Bruce Johnson, Debbie Mercer, Michael Porter, Lawrence Rosen, William Schmidheiser, and Laurens Walker. In addition, the cooperation of the Durham County, North Carolina, Superior Court is gratefully acknowledged.

1   Actually each feature should be treated as a separate continuum since there is not perfect co-variation. For convenience, we discuss the variation as a single continuum of possibilities. However, it should be kept in mind that a high frequency of occurrence of one particular feature may not necessarily be associated with a high frequency of another.
2   Names have been changed and indicated by a letter only in order to preserve the anonymity of witnesses. However, the forms of address used in the court are retained.
3   These examples are taken from both the direct and cross examinations of the witnesses, although table 1 uses data only from direct examinations. Examples were chosen to point out clearly the differences in style. However, it must be noted that the cross examination is potentially a more powerless situation for the witness.
4   This speaker did not use some of the intonational features that we had noted among women having high frequencies of WL features in their speech.
5   We do not wish to make more of this pattern than our data are able to support, but we suggest that our grounds for these claims are at least as good as Lakoff's. Lakoff's basis

for her description of features constituting WL are her own speech, speech of her friends and acquaintances, and patterns of use in the mass media.

REFERENCES

Bailey, F. Lee and Rothblatt, Henry B. (1971) *Successful Techniques for Criminal Trials.* Rochester, NY: Lawyers Cooperative Publishing Co.
Keeton, Robert E. (1973) *Trial Tactics and Methods.* Boston: Little, Brown.
Lakoff, Robin (1975) *Language and Woman's Place.* New York: Harper & Row.
Quinn, Naomi (1977) 'Anthropological studies of women's status'. *Annual Review of Anthropology*, 6, 181–225.

25

Are "Powerless" Communication Strategies the Japanese Norm?

Patricia J. Wetzel

Introduction

This article examines strikingly parallel claims concerning Japanese communication strategies and female communication strategies in the West. Miscommunication between Japan and the West is found to resemble miscommunication between the sexes in the West, yet the similarities are superficial. Any investigation into (mis)communication across cultures must take into account the cultural fabric within which interaction takes place. The notion of power is taken to be central to these issues, and a closer examination of how the notion of power in the West contrasts with the notion of power in Japan is shown to be one key to understanding miscommunication between Japan and the West.
[. . .]

Female Communication – Japanese Communication

Differences between Japan and the United States are the subject of a great deal of discussion – perhaps nowhere as much as the U.S. business community, which finds itself at once challenged and baffled by Japanese behavior. Consider the following generalization from Christopher's popular 1983 book, *The Japanese mind:*

> In their conversations . . . Japanese religiously shun explicit, carefully reasoned statements in favor of indirect and ambiguous ones basically designed not to communicate ideas but to feel out the other person's mood and attitudes. As the Japanese see it, plain speaking has one overwhelming drawback: it tends to commit the speaker to a hard-and-fast position, and thus can easily provoke direct confrontation – which all Japanese dread. (Christopher 1983: 43)

Though by no means scholarly in its approach to language, Christopher's statement nonetheless reflects a strong awareness of how different Japanese communication patterns are from those of the West. Or are they? A breakdown of those features of communication which surface again and again in research on Japan show a remarkable similarity to features that have been said to mark female interaction patterns in the West. The following is a direct comparison of some of the more striking parallels between observed female interaction patterns in the West and Japanese interaction patterns:[1]

Women show a greater tendency to make use of positive minimal responses, especially "mm hmm" and are more likely to insert these throughout the interchange not at the end. (Maltz & Borker 1982: 197 [reprinted in this volume, p. 417], citing Hirschman [1973] and Fishman [1978]

If properly empathetic, Alter assures and reassures Ego of his receptivity, congeniality, or agreement by frequently nodding and exclaiming "I'm listening," "That is so," or "Yes." . . . The listener constantly breaks his silence to let the speaker know that he is listening with interest and agreement. (Lebra 1976: 39)

Women are more likely than men to make utterances that demand or encourage responses from their fellow speakers. (Maltz & Borker 1982: 197)

Japanese conversation is marked by the frequency with which Ego interjects his speech with the particle *ne* ("isn't it"), which sounds as if he is soliciting Alter's agreement. (Lebra 1976: 39)

Men make more direct declarations of fact or opinion than do women . . . they are more likely to challenge or dispute their partners' utterances. (Maltz & Borker 1982: 198, citing Fishman [1978] and Hirschman [1973])

[T]here is an extremely strong attitude of consideration toward others and concern about what they are thinking. The Japanese seem to be speaking so as not to collide with each other. (Mizutani 1981: 78)

[Features of women's speech] have been coded under the general category of "positive reactions" including solidarity, tension release, and agreeing. (Maltz & Borker 1982: 197, citing Strodbeck & Mann 1956)

While debate is accepted to a certain degree . . . if outsiders will be present, the Japanese think about ways to turn them into insiders rather than ways to carry on the debate in words and thereby achieve certain results. (Mizutani 1981: 71–72)

[W]omen are more likely to adopt a strategy of silent protest after they have been interrupted. (Maltz & Borker 1982: 197–98, citing Zimmerman & West [1975] and West & Zimmerman [1977, reprinted in this volume, p. 165])

Once conflict is generated, the victim A may express his frustration or anger to B, the source . . . by not communicating it . . . in a message of silence. (Lebra 1984: 43)

The general orientation among women is interactional, relational, participatory, and collaborative. (Treichler & Kramarae 1983: 120)

[E]mpathy (*omoiyari*) ranks high among the virtues considered indispensable for one to be really human, morally mature, and deserving of respect. *Omoiyari* refers to the ability and willingness to feel what others are feeling. (Lebra 1976: 38)

Girls frame their accusations as reports about offenses heard from an intermediary (Goodwin 1980a: 172). Rather than stating the offense directly . . . [the] accusation is phrased in terms of a report by some intermediate party. (Goodwin 1980b: 682)

The request or protest is made in the name of another, which is less offensive to a Japanese listener (Lebra 1984: 46). Ego meets Alter face-to-face but conveys his message as being that of someone else. Ego thus pretends to be a delegate or messenger for a third party. (Lebra 1976: 123).

[W]omen attempt to link their utterance to the one preceding it by building on the previous utterance . . . [a signal] of women's desire to create continuity in conversation, and Hirschman 1973 describes elaboration as a key dynamic of women's talk. (Maltz & Borker 1982: 210)

In conversation the speaker does not complete a sentence but leaves it open-ended in such a way that the listener will take it over before the former clearly expresses his will or opinion, thereby showing a concern for maintaining consensus. (Lebra 1976: 38–39).

Japanese–Western Miscommunication

Maltz and Borker predict miscommunication between men and women based on the fact that their culturally determined rules for interaction are different. Based on the preceding, we might extend this and predict miscommunication of a similar nature between Japanese and males in the West.

Consider the following advice, written by a male for a primarily male audience – Western business concerns considering business ventures in Japan:

> [T]he purpose of the business luncheon in Japan is not to discuss problems or work out solutions. Rather it is to enhance a sense of intimacy between business affiliates and to serve as a lubricant for present or future negotiations. If you are being invited to such a lunch, this may not mean that there are any business matters to be discussed, but perhaps that your prospective partner or client would simply like to check out your personality. (*Business Japanese II*: 138)

The same textbook on business strategies in Japan provides the following characterization of negotiation in Japan:

> It has been observed that [executives in the West] arrive at the negotiation table with an itemized list of all the goals they intend to achieve, and then expect to proceed at a brisk pace right down this list so as not to waste everyone's precious time (*Business Japanese*: 246). [S]uccessful presentations in Japan are not always direct or logical, nor do they revolve primarily around a product's merits. Instead, a Japanese sales presentation is often rambling, ambiguous, and full of "unrelated" information about the product's (or company's) ongoing contributions to society and mankind – what we in the West sometimes jokingly refer to as "hearts and flowers". (*Business Japanese II*: 28)

I suggest that the feminine imagery here ("hearts and flowers") is not accidental.

A recent flyer for a seminar on doing business with the Japanese poses a series of questions which, presumably, perenially baffle the Western business*man*.

> "Why can't we get down to business?" "Why can't we give each other a simple 'yes' or 'no'?" "Why does it take so long to work things out?" "Who's responsible for conflicts?" . . . This seminar will provide an understanding of the American and Japanese business*man*'s [emphasis mine] way of thinking and will present skills necessary to communicate effectively with each other for maximum business success. ("Maximizing your business effectiveness in Japan/America" offered by the Japan–America Society of Oregon, 1986)

All of this sounds remarkably similar to traditional male evaluations of female behavior, and the parallels with Maltz and Borker's predictions about male–female miscommunication are also striking.

It is tempting to conclude that Japanese tend to use language akin to women's language in the West. However, this would be a gross oversimplification of the facts and would ignore the cultural framework within which linguistic behavior takes place. Rather, the parallels between Western women's communication styles and Japanese communication styles is taken here to indicate that analysis of both is somehow lacking and that the terms in which we describe this behavior should be reexamined.

Is Japanese–Female Communication Powerless?

First of all, research indicates that in the West, at least, differences in communication style often correlate less with gender than with factors such as role and status. O'Barr and Atkins (1980, reprinted in this volume, p. 377) found in their courtroom testimony data, for example, that women who tend to exhibit few or no features of *women's language* (as defined by Lakoff [1975]) had something in common: They were typically well-educated, professional, middle-class women. Correspondingly, men who tended to use features of women's language were typically men who held subordinate, lower status jobs or were unemployed (103–4). O'Barr and Atkins conclude that "the tendency for women to speak powerless language and for men to speak less of it is due, at least in part, to the greater tendency of women to occupy relatively powerless social positions" (104). Hence, they suggest a renaming of the concept of women's language as *powerless language*. They also allow that the two patterns – women's language and powerless language – interact and that it is part of the cultural meaning of speaking "like a woman" to speak powerlessly.[2]

Can we conclude, then, that the Japanese communicate in a "powerless" mode? Or, turning the perspective around, should we instead ask what these powerless features convey within a Japanese communicative context?

In their discussions of those qualities which make a child *ningen-rashii*, or "human-like" according to the Japanese, White and Levine (1986) observe that within Japan, first of all, to be *ningen-rashii* means to be able to maintain harmony in human relationships (56). And high among qualities that Japanese value in child rearing is "*yutaka*, meaning 'empathetic', 'receptive', or 'open hearted' " (58). "Sensitivity and anticipation of the needs of others," they go on to say, "sound passive and *feminine* [emphasis mine] to Western ears, but appearances are deceptive, *yutaka* has a very positive, active connotation and suggests a mature vigor" (58).

Given what it means to be a mature adult and *ningen-rashii* in Japan, it stands to reason that "nonconfrontational modes [of communication] must be exhausted" before resorting to other strategies (Lebra 1984: 42). The Japanese value those patterns of communication that indicate sensitivity to the other: demonstrations or signals of empathy, solicitation of agreement, concern about what others are think-ing, silent protest as a strategy for signaling disagreement or displeasure, and use of intermediaries – strategies that we in the West associate with female, and thereby powerless, interaction.

Contrast this with the strategies that we in the West associate with powerful communication style: assertion of dominance, interrupting while others have the floor, challenging or disputing others' utterances, ignoring comments of others, making direct declarations of fact or opinion. All contrast with what it means to be a mature adult in a Japanese framework, and as such are much more likely to be viewed as immature or childish behavior.

What, then, are the communicative strategies by which individuals assert power in Japan? The relationship between communication style, or any behavior, and per-ceptions of power is undeniably complex. In the case where we wish to compare linguistic strategies in Japan and the West, however, examination of a notion as basic as *power* is indispensable.

Power: Japan Versus the West

One striking feature of claims regarding powerful versus powerless language is the way in which the notion of power itself is taken for granted. *Power* is a complex term and the subject of a great deal of debate as regards its nature and forms (see, e.g., Galbraith 1983; Janeway 1981; Korda 1975; and McClelland 1975). Within the wide range of research on language and the sexes, only Henley (1977) provides a working definition of power: "Power is thus based on the control of resources, and their defense" (19). She distinguishes power from other related terms such as *dominance* (like power, but with a connotation of more blatancy), *authority* (power that is somehow legitimized, such as through law or tradition), and *status* (social position) (19–20).

Galbraith (1983: 2) introduces his discussion of power by defining it as follows: "Power is: the possibility of imposing one's will upon other persons." Webster's *Third international unabridged dictionary* contains the following sub-entry (one of many) for power: "2. The possession of sway or controlling influence over others; authority; command; government; influence; ascendancy, whether personal, social, or political; also, occasionally, permission or liberty to act."

The striking feature of all these English descriptions of power is that they define power as a substantive phenomenon, as something possessed by the individual.[3] It is safe to say that, in the West, the individual is generally viewed as the locus of power (Hengeveld 1984: 10).

A search for an appropriate equivalent for English *power* in Japanese yields two possibilities: *kenryoku* and *tikara*.[4] *Kenryoku* may be defined generally as "power, authority, or influence" while *tikara* is defined as "strength, force, power, ability, or capacity" (*Shogakukan progressive Japanese–English dictionary*, 1986). Yet neither of these provides a way of describing powerful and powerless language in Japanese. The phrase *tikara ga aru/nai hanasikata* "powerful/less speech style" is misleading in that it describes moving or affective speech but not powerful/less speech style in the sense sought here. The phrase *kenryoku ga aru/nai hanasikata* "powerful/less speech style", rather than being misleading, conveys nothing in Japanese. (Hengeveld [1984: 1] briefly relates her own experience wrestling with this problem of talking about powerful and powerless speech in Japanese.) The reasons for this translation problem, in large part, have to do with the nature of power in Japan.

Hengeveld (1984) observes that power in Japan is less an attribute of the individual than of role and position. Japanese analyses of power (Maruyama 1964; Matsushita 1978; Matsuzawa 1978; Nakane 1970) reflect such a relational view of power and place emphasis on role interaction within the power structure or hierarchy and far less on the individual. Individuals may make use of the power inherent in the role or position that they occupy, but as Hengeveld observes, "*kenryoku* isn't 'held over someone' as 'power' is in English. Rather, it simply exists in a particular individual within a given sphere, and the severing of power from the [concomitant] network of obligations will result in an instant loss of *kenryoku*" (85–86). In short, to speak of an individual as possessing a powerful speech style is to view the individual as the locus of power, and this is not how Japanese perceive the phenomenon of power.

Conclusion

Parallels between descriptions of female interaction in the West and Japanese interaction are not coincidental. Much of Japanese behavior viewed from a Western perspective is reminiscent of what we consider to be feminine (and therefore powerless) interaction.

What this investigation suggests is that the cultural underpinnings of a unified set of linguistic behaviors in the West (such as those that connote power or powerlessness) may be radically different from what underlies similar behavior in Japan. In both our practical dealings with the Japanese and in our theoretical analysis of Japanese and Western linguistic behavior, we would do well to realize this.

Similarly, the search for powerful and powerless speech styles in Japanese that parallel this distinction in the West will prove misleading or meaningless if our assumptions about the nature of power do not allow for cultural variation. Our descriptions of Japanese linguistic behavior should take into account the differences that distinguish Japanese culture from our own, as should our descriptions of cross-ethnic (mis)communication.

NOTES

I would like to thank Elizabeth Hengeveld for her painstaking readings and lengthy discussions of earlier versions of this paper, and Mari Noda for her comments on the final analysis. Their help is evident throughout.

1   These observations reflect a variety of perspectives on female and Japanese interaction patterns, including anthropological and sociological research. There are, in fact, more data supporting the claims made regarding female communication strategies than there are supporting the claims made regarding Japanese communication strategies. Only recently has data-oriented sociolinguistic research on Japanese begun to appear in the literature (e.g., Shibamoto 1985). Nonetheless, the data that have appeared tend to support the observations cited above.

2   What is problematic about this analysis is the fact that it continues to implicitly promote "the assumption that white, heterosexual, male speech constitutes the norm for American speakers of English" (Hayes 1979: 28). It is this issue that Kramarae (1980) and others have begun to address by recognizing that, "By and large men have controlled the norms of use; and this control, in turn, has shaped the language system available for use by both sexes and has influenced the judgements made about the speech of women and men" (58). We might also ask whether men and women in the West, particularly in the United States, evaluate power differently. Gilligan (1982) addresses this issue in her analysis of women's moral development.

3   One exception to this is Janeway (1981), who looks very carefully at the relational nature of power. Is it coincidental that Janeway is female and tends to write from and affirm the female perspective?

4   The Chinese character for *tikara* is the same as the one used for *ryoku* in *kenryoku*.

REFERENCES

Business Japanese, vols. I and II. (1985). Tokyo: Nissan Motor Company.
Christopher, R. C. (1983). *The Japanese mind: The goliath explained.* New York: Linden Press/Simon & Schuster.
Fishman, P. M. (1978). Interaction: The work women do. *Social Problems* 25(4): 397–406.
Galbraith, J. K. (1983). *The anatomy of power.* Boston: Houghton Mifflin.
Gilligan, C. (1982). *In a different voice: Psychological theory and women's development.* Cambridge, Mass.: Harvard University Press.
Goodwin, M. (1980a). Directive–response speech sequences in girls' and boys' task activities. In S. McConnell-Ginet et al. (1980), 157–73.
——(1980b). He-said-she-said: Formal cultural procedures for the construction of a gossip dispute activity. *American Ethnologist* 7(4): 674–95.
Hayes, P. (1979). Lesbians, gay men, and their "languages." In J. W. Cheesbro (ed.), *Gayspeak: Gay male and lesbian communication.* New York: Pilgrim, 28–42.
Hengeveld, E. C. (1984). The lexicographic representation of power vocabulary in Japanese. Unpublished M.A. thesis, Cornell University, Ithaca, N.Y.
Henley, N. M. (1975). Power, sex, and nonverbal communication. In B. Thorne & N. Henley (1975), 184–203.
——(1977). *Body politics.* Englewood Cliffs, NJ: Prentice-Hall.

Hirschman, L. (1973). Female–male differences in conversational interaction. Paper presented at Linguistic Society of America, San Diego.

Janeway, E. (1981). *Powers of the weak.* New York: Morrow Quill.

Korda, M. (1975). *Power: How to get it, how to use it.* New York: Random House.

Koschman, J. V. (ed.) (1978). *Authority and the individual in Japan.* Tokyo: Tokyo University Press.

Kramarae, C. (1980). Proprietors of language. In S. McConnell-Ginet et al. (1980), 58–68.

Kraus, E. S., Rohlen, T. P., & Steinhoff, P. G. (eds.) (1984). *Conflict in Japan.* Honolulu: University of Hawaii Press.

Lakoff, R. (1975). *Language and woman's place.* New York: Harper & Row.

Lebra, T. S. (1976). *Japanese patterns of behavior.* Honolulu: University of Hawaii Press.

——(1984). Nonconfrontational strategies for management of interpersonal conflicts. In E. S. Kraus et al. (1984), 41–60.

Maltz, D. N., & Borker, R. A. (1982). A cultural approach to male–female miscommunication. In J. J. Gumperz (ed.), *Language and social identity.* Cambridge: Cambridge University Press, 196–216.

Maruyama, M. (1964). Some problems of political power [translation of *Sihai to hukuzyuu*, 1953, D. Sisson, trans]. In I. Morris (ed.), *Thought and behavior in modern Japanese politics.* London: Oxford University Press, 268–89.

Matsushita, K. (1978). Citizen participation in historical perspective. In J. V. Koschman (1978), 171–88.

Matsuzawa, H. (1978). "Theory" and "organization" in the Japanese communist party. In J. V. Koschman (1978), 108–27.

McClelland, D. C. (1975). *Power: The inner experience.* New York: Irvington.

McConnell-Ginet, S., Borker, R., & Furman, N. (eds.) (1980). *Women and language in literature and society.* New York: Praeger.

Mizutani, O. (1981). *Japanese: The spoken language in Japanese life.* Tokyo: The Japan Times.

Nakane, C. (1970). *Japanese society.* Berkeley: University of California Press.

O'Barr, W. M., & Atkins, B. K. (1980). "Women's language" or "powerless language"? In S. McConnell-Ginet et al. (1980), 93–110.

Shibamoto, J. (1985). *Japanese women's language.* Orlando, Fla: Academic.

Stevenson, H., Azuma, H., & Hakuta, K. (eds.) (1986). *Child development in Japan.* New York: W. H. Freeman.

Strodbeck, F. L., & Mann, R. D. (1956). Sex role differentiation in jury deliberations. *Sociometry* 19: 3–11.

Thorne, B., & Henley, N. (eds.) (1975). *Language and sex: Difference and dominance.* Rowley, Mass.: Newbury House.

Treichler, P. A., & Kramarae, C. (1983). Women's talk in the ivory tower. *Communication Quarterly* 31(2): 118–32.

West, C., & Zimmerman, D. H. (1977). Women's place in everyday talk: Reflections on parent–child interaction. *Social Problems* 24(5): 521–29.

White, M. I., & Levine, R. A. (1986). What is an *ii ko* (good child)? In H. Stevenson et al. (1986), 55–62.

Zimmerman, D. H., & West, C. (1975). Sex roles, interruptions, and silences in conversations. In B. Thorne & N. Henley (1975), 105–29.

26

When the Doctor is a "Lady": Power, Status and Gender in Physician–Patient Encounters

Candace West

Introduction

[. . .] Spoken interaction is widely recognized as a fundamental means of regulating social activities and organizing social relationships (e.g., Goffman, 1981; Hymes, 1974; Labov and Fanshel, 1977; Scherer and Giles, 1979.) For example, an extensive body of research indicates that men interrupt women much more often than the reverse, across a variety of situations (Argyle et al., 1968; Eakins and Eakins, 1976; McMillan et al., 1977; Natale et al., 1979; Octigan and Niederman, 1979; Willis and Williams, 1976.) A succession of studies by West and Zimmerman (Zimmerman and West, 1975; West and Zimmerman, 1977, reprinted in this volume, p. 165; West, 1979, 1982; West and Zimmerman, 1983) leads them to conclude that men's interruptions of women in cross-sex conversations constitute an exercise of power and dominance over their conversational partners.

To be sure, power is an important facet of many other social relationships, such as those between whites and Blacks, bosses and employees, and – of immediate interest – doctors and patients. Moreover, a great deal of our existing knowledge of sex differences in behavior confounds gender with status. Given a world in which men make more money, earn greater prestige, and exert more control over public affairs, it is hardly surprising to find women are less "dominant."[1] Yet the lesser dominance (or lesser power) of women in society cannot be attributed to their gender without considering their lesser opportunities in the marketplaces where commodities are distributed. Where women earn less, are accorded less prestige, and exert less control over affairs, we might reasonably expect to discover them in subordinate positions to men. What happens, though, when the conventional stratification of the sexes is reversed, e.g., when a doctor is a "lady"?[2]

Insofar as the physician–patient relationship is essentially asymmetrical by our cultural standards, it is here that we would expect to find highlighted the micropolitical dynamics of social interaction, through, among other things, a greater proportion of interruptions initiated by superordinate parties to talk. This paper reports results of an exploratory study of interruptions in encounters between physicians and patients during actual "visits to the doctor." My findings offer some empirical support for an asymmetrical view of the physician–patient relationship; male physicians interrupt patients far more often than the reverse, and they appear to use interruptions as a means of exerting control over patients. However, encounters between patients and female physicians display markedly different patterns: there, patients interrupt as much or more than physicians, and their interruptions seem to subvert the physicians' authority. Consideration of these results leads me to address such issues as the respective roles of power, status and gender in face-to-face interaction.

Methods

Data collection

Data for this analysis consist of 21 dyadic encounters between doctors and patients recorded in a family practice center in the southern United States. The doctors involved were residents in family practice, a specialty requiring three years of additional training beyond medical school.[3] Residents are typically in their late twenties to early thirties when completing their training at the Center. Seventeen of the encounters involve white male physicians, and four involve white females. (These four female physicians were among the first cohort – i.e., group of more than two women – ever to enter the program at the Center.)

Patients in these exchanges range in age from 16 to 82 years. They come from a variety of backgrounds, including those of professional, domestic, construction worker and unemployed carpenter. Of the 21 encounters, five involve Black female patients, six, white females, four, Black males, and six, white males.

All of these encounters were recorded during actual "visits to the doctor." Thus, they are not standardized by duration of interaction, purpose of visit, or length of relationship between physician and patient. The family practice center at which they were recorded has employed video taping for many years now, as part of the medical education of residents. With patients' signed consent, they are recorded with their doctors via ceiling microphones and unobtrusive cameras located in the corners of examining rooms. Hence, recordings were not made for purposes of this study but they were later transcribed for these purposes.[4]

[. . .]

Coding interruptions

West and Zimmerman's studies of interruptions in cross-sex interaction (e.g., 1977, 1983) base their definition of "interruption" on Sacks, Schegloff and Jefferson's (1974) model of turn-taking in talk. There, it is argued that speech exchange systems in general are arranged to ensure that (1) one party speaks at a time and (2) speaker change recurs. These features thus organize a variety of forms of speech exchange including casual conversation, interviewing, formal debate and high ceremony.

Sacks et al. (1974) suggest that a turn consists of the right and obligation to speak which is allocated to a particular speaker. Turns are built out of what they call "unit-types," consisting of possibly complete words, phrases, clauses or sentences, depending on their context. Unit-types are described as "projective" devices in that they allow enough information prior to their completion to allow a hearer to anticipate an upcoming transition place. The end of a possibly complete unit-type is the proper place for turn transition between speakers.[5]

West and Zimmerman (1977) employ these ideas to distinguish between two categories of simultaneous speech: overlaps (briefly, errors in transition timing) and interruptions (violations of speaker turns.) Overlaps are defined as stretches of simultaneity initiated by a "next" speaker just as a current speaker arrives at a possible turn-transition point (West and Zimmerman, 1977: 523). For example, these may occur where a current speaker stretches or drawls the final syllable of an utterance, or adds a tag-question to an otherwise possibly complete statement:

(Dyad 19: 305–307)[6]
PATIENT: I li:ve better and so I- they don' bo:ther
            me too mu:ch. ⌈y'know?⌉
PHYSICIAN: ⌊O::kay. ⌋

Here (as indicated by the brackets), the physician begins an "Okay" just at what would ordinarily be the proper end of the patient's utterance ("They don't bother me too much"). But the patient's addition of a tag-question ("Y'know?") results in their collision. Such an instance of simultaneous speech would be regarded as a possible error in transition timing (cf. West and Zimmerman, 1977) rather than as an indication that the physician is not listening. Certainly, one must listen very carefully in order to anticipate the upcoming completion of a current speaker's utterance and begin speaking precisely on cue with no intervening silence.[7]

Interruptions, in contrast, are defined as deeper incursions into the internal structure of a current speaker's utterance (West and Zimmerman, 1977: 523). Operationally, they are found more than a syllable away from a proper place for turn transition. Since the rules for turn-taking assign a current speaker the rights to a turnspace until a possible turn-transition point is reached, interruptions are seen as violations of current speakers' rights to be engaged in speaking. Just below, we see an example of their potential disruptiveness:

(Dyad 1: 945–954)
((Here, doctor and patient debate the effectiveness
of sleeping pills over extended intervals. The
doctor argues that the patient will be better off
without such medication: the patient argues that
her anxieties over a forthcoming trip will interfere

with her effectiveness on the job for which the trip
is to be taken.))

PHYSICIAN: . . . prob'ly settle dow:n gradjully, a little
bit, once yuh get used to it. =

PATIENT: = The- press:: ⌈ure's gonna–   ⌉
PHYSICIAN: ⌊Well if it doe::sn',⌋

Seco*bar:*bital's not gonna help.
(.2)

PATIENT: We:ll,
(.2)

PHYSICIAN: It's gonna make things worse.

Here, the physician's intrusion ("Well, if it doesn't, Secobarbital's not gonna help")
occurs at a point at which the patient is nowhere near completion of her utterance
– and the patient drops out, leaving her utterance hanging incomplete. As noted in
the preface to this excerpt, the physician and patient had been arguing about whether
or not he ought to prescribe sleeping pills for her. One might imagine that the
physician's impatience with the argument might have induced his cutting off the
patient's protests, especially since the patient was asking for renewals of sixteen
other medications (including Valium and Serax) prior to making her trip. The point
here is that the way in which the physician imposes his opinion over the patient's is
through interruption of her turn at talk – technically, violation of her right to speak.

Later, I will address the content of such incursions in some detail. But next, I turn
to general distributions of interruptions between physicians and patients in my
collection.

Findings

First, I located all instances of simultaneous speech in the 532 pages of transcribed
encounters. Using the criteria specified above, instances of interruption (i.e., deep
incursions more than a syllable away from possible turn-transition places) were
separated from other types of simultaneity. Then I examined the initiations of
interruptions by physician and patient in each dyad in the collection.[8]

Inspecting table 1, we see that a total of 188 instances of interruption occurred. Of
these, physicians initiated 67% (126) and patients initiated 33% (62). Thus, in the
aggregate, doctors interrupted patients far more often than the reverse. Moreover, in
the two encounters that contained more interruptions by patients than physicians
(those to which the footnotes are appended), the patient is hard of hearing in one
case, and mentally retarded in the other. With the exception of these encounters,
doctors interrupted patients more in every dyad in this collection.

However, this collection is comprised only of encounters between patients and male
physicians. When we turn to the distributions of interruptions between patients and
female physicians, we can see that the asymmetries depicted in table 1 are exactly
reversed (see table 2). Whereas male physicians (as a group) initiated 67% of all

Table 1   Interruptions in encounters between patients and male physicians

	Physician Interruptions	Patient Interruptions
Black male patient, 26 years	100% (7)	— (0)
Black female patient, 20 years	100% (1)	— (0)
White male patient, 16 years	100% (1)	— (0)
White female patient, 17 years	100% (1)	— (0)
Black female patient, 16 years	91% (10)	9 (1)
White female patient, 58 years	80% (4)	20 (1)
Black female patient, 31 years	77% (20)	23 (6)
White female patient, 36 years	73% (11)	27 (4)
White female patient, 53 years	71% (29)	29 (12)
White female patient, 32 years	67% (10)	33 (5)
Black male patient, 36 years	67% (4)	33 (2)
White male patient, 16 years	67% (2)	33 (1)
White male patient, 31 years	60% (3)	40 (2)
White male patient, 36 years	58% (7)	42 (5)
Black male patient, 17 years	56% (5)	44 (4)
White female patient, 82 years*	37% (7)	63 (12)
White male patient, 56 years**	36% (4)	64 (7)
TOTAL	67% (126)	33% (62)

Notes: * This patient is hard of hearing.   ** This patient is mentally retarded.

Table 2   Interruptions in encounters between patients and female physicians

	Physician Interruptions	Patient Interruptions
Black female patient, 52 years	50% (7)	50 (7)
Black female patient, 67 years	40% (6)	60 (9)
Black male patient, 58 years	28% (5)	72 (13)
White male patient, 38 years	8% (1)	92 (11)
TOTAL	32% (19)	68% (40)

interruptions relative to their patients' 33%, female physicians (as a group) initiated only 32% of interruptions relative to their patients' 68%. Moreover, patients in encounters with female physicians interrupted as much or more than their physicians in each dyad in this collection.

While the collection of encounters involving women physicians only contains four dyads, it is at least worth noting that the two encounters that display nearly symmetrical relations between the parties involved (the first two listed in table 2) are same-sex interactions between female doctors and female patients. These symmetries are all the more noteworthy when one considers the differences in race and age between them (the patients in both dyads are Black and the physicians are white; the patients are both much older than their physicians). Zimmerman and West's (1975) earlier research on same-sex interactions between white females conversing in public places also indicates that casual conversations between females tend to display symmetrical distributions of interruptions.

Obviously, the variety of race, age and gender combinations in a sample of this size precludes extensive extrapolation regarding the composite effects of these factors. There is, for example, only one white male patient engaged in interaction with a white female physician; and, there is only one sixty-seven year old patient engaged in talk with a physician of half her years. Still, the consistency of patterns of interruption displayed in tables 1 and 2 offer evidence of an asymmetrical relationship between doctors and patients in this collection – *except* when the doctor is a "lady."

It is important to remember that this collection of encounters does not represent a random sample of physicians, patients, or physician–patient exchanges. The data analyzed here were initially collected for purposes of resident training rather than for purposes of my research. Thus, my lack of control over many factors (e.g., length of exchange or past acquaintanceship between doctor and patient) resulted in a non-standardized corpus of materials, involving exchanges of various durations and including doctors and patients with different bases for relationships. Some encounters transpired between parties with well-established relationships of three years' standing, while others constituted the occasions on which physicians and patients met for the first time. Some encounters involved physical examinations, while others were devoted exclusively to verbal interactions. The collection of encounters does not constitute a probability sample of physicians, patients, or medical exchanges, and simple projections from these findings to physicians, patients, or medical encounters generally cannot be justified with the usual logic of statistical inference. The stability of any empirical finding cannot, in any event, be established by a single piece of research. My purpose in presenting these quantitative trends is twofold. First, their consistency offers a rough indication that relations between patients and female physicians constitute a site that merits "drilling for oil" (i.e., through collection of a larger, systematic sample of such interactions). Second, these quantitative data provide a general framework for the detailed qualitative analysis of interruptions that follows.

Interruptions, Dominance and Control

West and Zimmerman's (1977) comparisons of conversations between men and women and interactions between parents and children lead them to suggest that males' use of interruptions may display dominance and control to females (and to any witnesses), just as parents' interruptions communicate aspects of parental control to children and others present. If patients can be likened to children (as proposed by Parsons and Fox, 1952), then we might regard the violations of their speaking rights by male physicians as displays of the physicians' interactional control.

For example, the key to the therapeutic practice of medicine is, for Parsons (1951, 1975), the essential *asymmetry* of the physician–patient relationship. Because, at least within Western cultures, it is the physician who is charged with the legal responsibility for restoring the patient to normality:

> ... The practitioner must have control over the interaction with the patient, ensuring that the patient will comply with the prescribed regimen. If patient compliance is not ensured, then the ability of the practitioner to return the patient to a normal functioning state is undermined. (Wolinsky, 1980: 163, explicating Parsons)

In this view, patients' situational dependency on physicians, physicians' professional prestige and their authority over patients all ensure physicians the necessary leverage for controlling interpersonal encounters. But, if physicians' control is to be exerted in actual exchanges with patients, one would expect some ready vehicle might be available in *any* medical encounter for demonstrating the physician's dominance.

Although medical sociologists place heavy emphasis on social roles as determinants of behaviors (cf. Wilson, 1970: 13–14), the actual behaviors of persons in social roles remain to be enacted in particular situations. Whatever the scripts that may exist for the physician–patient encounter, they must always be negotiated on the basis of the situational exigencies of social life. Fortunately, as Zimmerman (1978: 12) notes, social life is rife with opportunities for enacting them:

> It would surely be odd if a society were designed so that its institutions were partly constructed of role-relationships but lacked any systematic mechanism for articulating societal roles within the features of various interactional settings. [And] stranger still if this articulation were itself not socially organized. Strangest of all would be a state of affairs in which the instantiation of a role in an actual situation had no bearing on the understanding of roles in general, or the sense of "objectivity" and transcendence of the role.

Zimmerman's observations invite us to look more closely at the ways in which the social identities of "doctor" and "patient" are played out in the actual organization of interaction between the two.

Hence, rather than regarding the physician's authority as superimposed *onto* encounters with patients in "well-rehearsed", script-like fashion (cf. Parsons, 1951, 1975; Wilson, 1970), we can examine the dynamics of actual medical exchanges to see how dominance and control are constituted by participants in these social situations. A telling example is offered in the fragment used earlier to display the potential effects of interruption itself. There, a disagreement between a (male) physician and (female) patient was ultimately resolved by the doctor's interruption of the patient's opinion (regarding sleeping pills) with his own contrary view ("They won't help"). In that excerpt, we saw interruption used to advance the physician's (expert) perspective while simultaneously cutting off the patient's (lay) point of view.

Another aspect of the relationship between interruptions and interactional control was first brought to my attention by a friend – in this case, a male physician. Prior to writing up the results of this study, I discussed with him the tendency of male physicians to interrupt patients in these encounters. My friend did not find this trend a surprising one, and explained. "That's because so many patients are still answering your last question when you're trying to ask them the *next* one!" His "explanation" was of interest for two reasons. First, it fails as an explanation on the grounds that answers follow questions, rather than the other way around. Hence, a speaker interrupting an answer with a "next question" is disavowing the obligation to listen to the answer to a prior question. But second, my doctor-friend's explanation was of analytical interest, since I had already begun to notice that a great many physician-initiated interruptions in these data were composed of doctors' questions to their patients.

Consider the following fragment, which shows the staccato pace at which physicians' "next" questions can follow their "last" ones:

(Dyad 20: 053–074)
PATIENT: It us:ually be (1.0) ((she reaches
down to touch her calf with her left
hand)) in: he:ah. You: know, it
jus' ⌈be a li:l   ⌉
PHYSICIAN: ⌊Can y' pull up⌋ yer cuff there
for me? (.6) Duh yuh have the *pain* right no::w?
                    (.2)
PATIENT: *Um*-um. No, it ⌈ha:ppens   ⌉
PHYSICIAN: ⌊It's not happening right now::?⌋
PATIENT: =ss- some- only one: time when ah w⌈as heah.⌉
PHYSICIAN: ⌊Can y ⌋ uh take
yer shoe: off for me please?
                 (.8) ((Patient removes her shoe))
PATIENT: ⌈But I-⌉
PHYSICIAN: ⌊WHU:⌋ :T'RE YUH DO::ING, when yuh *no:tice* the pai:n
            (.4)   ((Physician bends over to touch
                 the patient's legs))
PATIENT: We:ll, I thi:nk that- Well, so:metime I jus' be si:ttin'
theah, (1.0) An' yih: know: ih ji:st- (1.2) ((she
shrugs, holding up both palms)) Then I fee:l a liddul
pai:n in theah, (.2) Yih know, ji:st- gra:dually (.4)
PATIENT: It gradually c⌈ome on. ⌉
PHYSICIAN: ⌊Take thi:s⌋ shoe: off?

We can note here that each of the physician's intrusions into his patient's turn at talk is patently reasonable and warranted by the external constraints of medical examination and treatment. To ask where a patient is feeling pain, how often, when or under what conditions is all justified by, even required for, precise diagnosis of a problem (cf. Cicourel, 1975; 1978). However, when these inquiries cut off what the patient is in the process of saying, particularly when what she is saying is presumably the necessary response to a "prior" needed question, then the physician is not only

violating the patient's rights to speak, but he is also systematically cutting off potentially valuable information *on which he must himself rely* to achieve a diagnosis.[9]

Just below, a similar pattern is evident:

(Dyad 2: 085–099)
((Here, the doctor is inquiring about a recent injury
to the patient's back caused by an auto accident.))
PATIENT: When I'm sitting *up*right. Y'know =
PHYSICIAN: = More so than it
             was even before?
PATIENT: Yay::es =
PHYSICIAN: = Swelling 'r anything like that thet chew've
             no:ticed?
                              (.)
PATIENT: Nuh:o, not the ⎡t I've nodi-   ⎤
PHYSICIAN: ⎣TEN::DER duh the tou⎦ch? Press:ing any?
PATIENT: No::, jus' when it's- si::tting.
PHYSICIAN: Okay: =
PATIENT: = Er lying on it.
PHYSICIAN: Even ly:ing, Stan:ding up? Walking aroun:d? ((sing-song))
PATIENT: No: ⎡jis-   ⎤
PHYSICIAN: ⎣Not so mu:ch.⎦ Jis'- ly:ing on it. Si:tting on it.
             Jis' then.

In this excerpt [. . .] on two occasions, the physician's "next" utterance cuts off the
patient's completion of her answer to his "last" one. The staccato pacing and intrusions into the patient's turnspaces demonstrate that – in essence and in fact – a
simple "yes" or "no" is all this doctor will listen to. Such practices also serve to
demonstrate who is in control in the exchange.

In the case of both excerpts, it appears that the use of interruptions by male
doctors is a *display* of dominance or control to the patient, just as males' and parents'
interruptions (West and Zimmerman, 1977) are employed to communicate control
in cross-sex and parent–child interactions. But also in these exchanges (as in West
and Zimmerman's study), it appears that the use of interruptions is *in fact* a control
device, as the incursions (especially when repeated) disorganize the local construction of conversational topics. Insofar as the over-arching conversational topic is, in
the medical exchange, the state of the patient's health, interruptions in these encounters may have further serious consequences than in casual conversation.

When the doctor is a "lady"

The above analysis notwithstanding, the fact remains that results for four of the 21
exchanges in this collection defy the general pattern. Interactions between female
doctors and female patients display distributions that approximate symmetry. Moreover, encounters between female physicians and male patients show the male patient
(not the female physician) interrupting most (92% of interruptions in one exchange

and 72% in another.) It must be reiterated that there are very few dyads involving female physicians in the collection of materials here analyzed. Thus, attention to these encounters might best be viewed as a variant of case study rather than a survey of such interactions in general. However, since these proportions parallel – rather than contradict – the actual distributions of females in medicine (where women, notes Lorber, are "invisible professionals and ubiquitous patients," 1975), they warrant at least preliminary inspection here.

[. . .]

In our society, Hughes (1945: 353–4) observes, the auxiliary characteristics that have emerged around the status "physician" are "white," "Protestant" and "male." Hence, when persons assuming the powerful status of physician are not properly equipped with whiteness, Protestantism or maleness, there tends to be what Hughes terms a "status contradiction" – or even, a "status dilemma" – both for the individuals themselves and for those with whom they associate.

The "lady doctor" is a case in point, the adjective "lady" (or "woman" or "female") serving to underscore the presumed maleness of the status "physician." Hughes notes that particular statuses (e.g., "Black") operate as "master status-determining traits", i.e., powerful characteristics that outshine any others with which they may be clustered. So, for persons (e.g., women) whose master status conflicts with other very potent statuses (e.g., physician), a dilemma is likely to ensue over whether to treat them as members of the social category "women" *or* as members of the profession "physician."

In the context of these considerations, we are well-advised to remember that the appropriate behaviors of persons occupying social roles remain to be acted out in everyday life. Hughes' (1945) description might lead us to an overly-deterministic perspective that depicts "choices" between two conflicting status-determining characteristics (e.g., "woman" and "physician"), as if the resolution of status dilemmas were an individual matter. However, the issue is more complex than can be described by the "choice" or "nonchoice" of individuals who are caught in status dilemmas, since they must interact with others in their social worlds. For example, the Black man who would "pass" as a white one must rely on others' willingness to read various physical characteristics as constitutive of his "whiteness." Similarly, the woman who would become a physician must rely on others' willingness to honor her displays of professionalism over those of her gender.

While the evidence is far from conclusive, there is reason to believe that Hughes' (1945) analysis is pertinent to my results. Recall, for example, that the four female physicians involved in these encounters were among the first cohort of women ever to enter the residency program at the Family Practice Center. In this sense, they constituted what Hughes terms "a group of some new and peculiar type." Moreover, at the time they began their training at the Center, there was only one woman doctor among the medical faculty members. Hence, there was only one faculty member who might assist these "new and peculiar" entrants into what was formerly an all-male preserve. Even the medical faculty in charge of resident training remarked on the "exceptional" status of the first cohort of women. For example, those who assisted me in my data collection took great pains to include "our new women residents" in the final collection of exchanges.[10] Through such descriptions they helped make gender a salient characteristic of women residents (e.g., not once did I hear a male doctor described as a "man resident").

More telling still were the words of patients themselves. For example, one patient bade her new woman physician farewell, commenting that she had "enjoyed meeting" her since she had never had "a female doctor" before. Another patient, asked by his woman physician if he was having any problems passing urine, responded "You know, the *doctor* asked me that." In this instance, it was difficult to tell who "the doctor" *was*: "the doctor" was *not*, evidently, the female physician who was treating him.

Finally, consider the excerpt below, in which a female physician attempts to provide her professional opinion on a patient's problem:

(Dyad 4: 213–231)
((To this point, the patient has complained about his
weight, and the doctor and patient have been discussing
possible ways for reducing. One suggestion offered by
the physician was to slow down while eating: but the
patient has *just countered* that suggestion with a complaint
– he does not like cold food.))

PATIENT: . . . An' they take twe:nny 'r thirdy minutes

.

.

.

            Tuh eat.
PHYSICIAN: Wull what chew ⌈could DO: ⌉
PATIENT: ⌊An' then by the⌋ time they
            get through: their foo:d is col::d an' uh-
            'ey li:kes it y'know
PHYSICIAN: ⌈engh-hengh-hengh-hengh-hengh⌉ .hh=
PATIENT: ⌊An' th' they enjoy that   ⌋   = but I- I
            'on't *like* cole foo:d.
                        (.2)
PHYSICIAN: One thing yuh could *d* ⌈o::   ⌉
PATIENT: ⌊Spesh'ly⌋ food thet's
            not suhpoze: be col'=
PHYSICIAN: = O:kay .h = is tuh ea:t. say.
            the *meat* firs'. Yuh know:, but if yuh have a
            sal:ad tuh eat, t' sa:ve that till *a*fter yuh eat
            the meat. (.) Cuz the sal:ad's suhpose tuh be
            col:d.

Here, the physician's attempts to advance her solution are interrupted repeatedly by the patient's ongoing elaboration of his (already evident) problem.

In the same encounter, the patient earlier questioned his physician about a medication he is taking for his high blood pressure. He said that he had heard a radio report indicating that this medicine "might" cause cancer, and then another report, indicating that people should continue with use of the drug. Following this, the doctor checked the patient's blood pressure and explained that she had looked into this problem. There was, she said, no alternative medication available, and there was, in her view, no better present alternative than to continue it. At this juncture, the patient shifted to a slightly different complaint:

(Dyad 4: 430–454)

PATIENT: . . . If there wuz any way possible duh git me some
diffrun' type a pill thet li:ke yuh take twi:ce a
da::y instead of three:. .hh an' have th' same
effek with this (allernate) 'n u:h- *wah*dur pi:ll.

PHYSICIAN: OhKa:y, that's egzakly what we: were try:ing
tuh do:: .hh=

PATIENT: =Ah kno:w, but tho:se-
I- (.) heard ⌈what ⌉ th' man sai:d.

PHYSICIAN: ⌊We:ll.⌋
Ay:::e- checked *in*:ta tha:t. oka::y? an:::d-
(1.0) No:t No:t- *exten*sively. I didn' search
all the lidda'chure =

PATIENT: = ((clears throat))
(.4)

PHYSICIAN: .h Bu::t uh:m (.6) ((sniff)) Ah feel *comf*'trable
us:in' thuh dru::g? An' would take it muhself:::
°If I needed tuh. ((Looking directly at the patient))
(6.0)

PHYSICIAN: So it ⌈'s u:p- .hh It's u:p tuh you::   ⌉::=
PATIENT: ⌊But if all they sa:y- if there's *any*-⌋ =Ah
know::w, it's u:h-uh ⌈bud it's u:h- ⌉ Ah'm try:in'
PHYSICIAN: ⌊It's up tuh you:⌋
PATIENT: to: uh- .h ((clears throat)) i:s there: *any other*
ty::pe that chew could u:h fi:gger . . .

To spare readers, I have omitted the next several lines, in which the doctor again asserts that there is nothing else the patient can take and in which the patient again asserts his desire to get around taking this medication. Below, however, is the resolution of their argument:

(Dyad 4: 471–479)

PHYSICIAN: *If I* brought cha some *ar*duhcul(s) saying thet this
wuz Ok*ay*:::, would juh bih*lie*:::*ve* me? .h

PATIENT: Ye:ah, su:re, defin ⌈at'ly. ⌉
PHYSICIAN: ⌊OKa:y.⌋
(.)

PHYSICIAN: O ⌈kay:, ⌉ o::kay =
PATIENT: ⌊But u:h-⌋   = ((clears throat)) .h
Whether I would cha:nge to it 'r no:t, it would
be a diff- y'know, a nuther thi::ng.

Note: the patient might "believe" this woman physician if she brought him some articles supporting her opinions, but whether or not he would follow her advice "would be a nuther thi::ng."

My concern here is *not* with the possible carcinogenic effects of the drug (though important) – nor with the alternatives to it. Rather, I am interested in the way in which this woman physician is "heard" by her (male) patient. As noted earlier, Parsons (1951, 1975) asserts that the therapeutic practice of medicine is predicated on institutionalized asymmetry between physician and patient. In his view, physicians are in a position of situational authority vis-à-vis their patients, since only physicians are possessed of the technical qualifications (and institutional certification) to provide medical care.

Yet these excerpts show that neither technical qualifications (conferred by the training and medical degree) nor personal assurances ("I would take this myself," "I checked into it") are sufficient for the woman physician to have her authority (*as a physician*) respected by the patient. Elsewhere, Hughes (1958) suggests that clients of professionals do not simply grant them authority and autonomy as *faits accompli*. Given a recent history of increasing challenges to medical authority in the United States (cf. Reeder, 1972; Ruzek, 1979; Mendelsohn, 1981), it is entirely possible that patients in general are taking increased initiative in their own health care and questioning physicians more frequently. But, nowhere else in these data did I find a patient who questioned the opinion of a male physician as forcefully or as repeatedly as the case noted here.

Conclusions

These are preliminary findings, based on suggestive but far from definitive results. These data originated in a small and essentially haphazard collection of exchanges between patients and Family Physicians. Thus, generalizations based on them to medical encounters at large cannot be substantiated through quantitative extrapolation. I report them here to call attention to their potential significance for the study of gender, power and interaction.

Encounters between patients and male physicians lend support to conventional descriptions (cf. Parsons, 1951; Parsons and Fox, 1952; Parsons, 1975) of asymmetry in the physician–patient relationship. Face-to-face with one another, male doctors interrupted their patients far more often than the reverse, and they appeared to use interruptions as devices for exercising control over interaction. However, where female physicians were involved, the asymmetrical relationship was exactly reversed: patients interrupted their female doctors as much or more than these doctors interrupted them. Hence, my findings for female physicians conflict with the general pattern.

At this point, any discussion of the implications of this gender-associated difference must be speculative. But, in engaging in such discussion, I hope to eliminate possible misinterpretations of its significance. I am not claiming that female physicians are "better listeners" than their colleagues (although they may be). These preliminary analyses have focused on the distribution of interruptions *between* physicians and patients. While the female physicians in this collection were interrupted disproportionately, it makes as much sense to attribute this finding to their patients' gender-associated "disrespect" as it does to attribute it to the physicians' own communication skills. Neither inference is warranted at this point. What *is* warranted, for the findings reported here, is the suggestion that gender can have primacy over status where women physicians are concerned. These data indicate that gender can amount to a "master" status (Hughes, 1945), even where other power relations are involved.

NOTES

A revised version of this paper was presented at the American Sociological Association Annual Meeting. New York, August 1980.

I wish to thank Sarah F. Berk, Richard M. Frankel, Erving Goffman, Wendy Martyna, Ann Stromberg, and Gilly West for their helpful comments on the earlier versions of this paper. The financial assistance provided by the Southern Regional Educational Board, the Committee on Faculty Research at the University of California, Santa Cruz, and the Organized Research Unit in Institutional Analysis and Social Policy at Santa Cruz (Robert R. Alford, Director) is gratefully acknowledged. Finally, I offer thanks and appreciation to the Department of Family Medicine, Medical University of South Carolina, Charleston.

1   My use of the term *dominant* is not meant in the conventional psychological sense (i.e., as a personality attribute). Rather, I use it sociologically to describe control of and supremacy over one group by another.

2   I use quotation marks around *lady* to illustrate its ironic connotations in this context. For example, Lakoff (1975: 21) contends that this term operates as a euphemism for *woman*:

> Just as we do not call whites "Caucasian-Americans," there is no felt need to refer to men commonly as "gentlemen." And just as there is a need for such terms as "Afro-Americans," there is similarly felt a need for "lady." One might even say that when a derogatory epithet exists, a parallel euphemism is deemed necessary.

> To the extent that *lady* does indeed operate as a euphemism (i.e., rendering the very fact of femaleness less distasteful and more respectable than *woman*), it is especially peculiar to see it coupled with prestigious occupations (e.g., "lady lawyer," "lady doctor" or "lady engineer").

3   Two physicians included in the collection were not residents. One was an alumnus of the training program who continued to see patients at the Center after completing his residency four years earlier; the other was a faculty member who also saw patients there. With regard to the analysis which follows, I found no differences evidenced between these doctors' exchanges with patients and those of resident physicians.

4   In the transcriptions, anything which might identify participants has been altered. Transcription Conventions are given on p. xviii.

5   The criteria for determining a possibly complete utterance, and hence an interrupted turn at talk, are only partially syntactic. For example, the status of a word as a unit-type is also a sequential and thus, social-organizational issue, as where one party says "Yes"

in response to another's question (West and Zimmerman, 1977: 522, fn. 1). However, both syntactic and sequential criteria are fundamentally linked to the above-mentioned characteristic of speech exchange systems, i.e., one party speaks at a time. That this characteristic of talk is seen to describe speech exchange in general, rather than conversation in particular, is of central concern to this paper. For, while Sacks et al.'s (1974) model of turn-taking is intended to account for observed features of actual conversation, it may be that the talk which goes on in medical encounters is not entirely conversational in nature (cf. Frankel, in press).

6   Superscripts to these excerpts denote dyads and line numbers of transcripts in this corpus of materials.

7   To be sure, there are instances of simultaneous speech that appear to ratify – rather than disrupt – the talk of a current speaker, even when they intrude deeply into the current speaker's turnspace (West, 1979: 83). For example, Jefferson (1973) identifies two of these as (1) the emphatic "YEAH" interjected to display recognition of that which is in-the-course-of-being-said, and (2) the display of independent knowledge achieved by saying the same thing at the same time that a current speaker produces it. Following West (1979), I exempted such instances of simultaneous speech from the category, interruptions.

8   I am grateful to Linda Guiffre, who coded these instances of simultaneous speech independently. The categorization of instances involved a detailed coding scheme (West, 1979) designed to distinguish violations of speakers' rights (interruptions) from other types of simultaneity (e.g., errors in transition timing, displays of active listening, simultaneous starts, and continuations of prior incomplete turns). Despite its complexity, the coding scheme yielded substantial inter-coder reliability: in this case 87% between the two coders. Disagreements (typically, over instances of overlap rather than interruption) were resolved by discussion of the individual utterances in question.

9   An anecdote may help to illustrate this point. A friend of mine has suffered all of her life from a chronic but rare lung disorder. Prior to the discovery of sulfa drugs, people died from this disorder: now, it is manageable with routine monitoring and treatment. My friend has traveled around the world and visited numerous physicians for treatment of her condition. Since her disorder is a rare one, she often discovers that she knows more about her problem than the doctors she goes to for treatment. And yet, she observes that most physicians insist on going through a standard battery of questions before they begin to treat her complaints seriously. Thus, suggestions that she tries to raise concerning new ways of coping with her disorder are often aborted by physicians' insistence on a litany of complaints and disorders described in medical textbooks.

10   In passing, it is worth noting Hogan's (1978) contention that the use of personal pronouns in this context ("our new women residents") implies proprietorship rather than collegial relations (e.g., "our girls at the main desk," "my gal at the office," etc.).

REFERENCES

Argyle, Michael, Mansur Lalljee, and Mark Cook (1968) "The effects of visibility on interaction in a dyad." *Human Relations* 21: 3–17.
Braslow, Judith B. and Marilyn Heins (1981) "Women in medical education: a decade of change." *New England Journal of Medicine* 304: 1129–1135.

Cicourel, Aaron V. (1975) "Discourse and text: cognitive and linguistic processes in studies of social structure." *Versus: Quaderni di Studi Semotici* 12: 33–84.

——(1978) "Language and society: cognitive, cultural and linguistic aspects of language use." *Sozialwissenschaftliche Annalen.* Band 2. Seite B25–B58. Vienna: Physica-Verlag.

Eakins, Barbara Westbrook and R. Gene Eakins (1976) *Sex Differences in Human Communication.* Boston: Houghton Mifflin.

Frankel, Richard M. (in press) "Talking in interviews: a dispreference for patient-initiated questions in physician–patient encounters." In G. Psathas (ed.), *Interactional Competence.* New York: Irvington.

Goffman, Erving (1981) *Forms of Talk.* Philadelphia: University of Pennsylvania Press.

Hogan, Patricia (1978) "A woman is not a girl and other lessons in corporate speech." pp. 168–172 in Bette Ann Stead (ed.), *Women in Management.* Englewood Cliffs, N.J.: Prentice-Hall.

Hughes, Everett C. (1945) "Dilemmas and contradictions of status." *American Journal of Sociology* 50: 353–354.

——(1958) *Men and Their Work.* New York: The Free Press.

Hymes, Dell (1974) *Foundations in Sociolinguistics: An Ethnographic Approach.* Philadelphia: University of Pennsylvania Press.

Jefferson, Gail (1973) "A case of precision timing in ordinary conversation: overlapped tag-positioned address terms in closing sequences." *Semiotica* 9: 47–96.

Labov, William and David Fanshel (1977) *Therapeutic Discourse: Psychotherapy as Conversation.* New York: Academic Press.

Lakoff, Robin (1975) *Language and Woman's Place.* New York: Harper Colophon.

Lorber, Judith (1975) "Women and medical sociology: invisible professionals and ubiquitous patients", pp. 75–105 in M. Millman and R. M. Kanter (eds), *Another Voice: Feminist Perspectives on Social Life and Social Science.* Garden City, NY: Anchor Press/Doubleday.

Mattera, Marianne Dekker (1980) "Female doctors: why they're on an economic treadmill." *Medical Economics* (February 18): 98–110.

McMillan, Leslie R., A. Kay Clifton, Diane McGrath, and Wanda S. Gale (1977) "Women's language: uncertainty or interpersonal sensitivity and emotionality?" *Sex Roles* 3: 545–559.

Mendelsohn, Robert S. (1981) *Male Practice: How Doctors Manipulate Women.* Chicago: Contemporary Books.

Natale, Michael, Elliot Entin, and Joseph Jaffee (1979) "Vocal interruptions in dyadic communication as a function of speech and social anxiety." *Journal of Personality and Social Psychology* 37: 865–878.

Octigan, Mary and Sharon Niederman (1979) "Male dominance in conversation." *Frontiers* 4: 50–54.

Parsons, Talcott (1951) *The Social System.* New York: The Free Press.

——(1975) "The sick role and the role of the physician reconsidered." *Millbank Memorial Fund Quarterly* 53: 257–277.

Parsons, Talcott and Renee C. Fox (1952) "Illness, therapy and the modern urban American family." *Journal of Social Issues* 8: 31–44.

Reeder, Leo G. (1972) "The patient-client as a consumer: some observations on the changing professional–client relationship." *Journal of Health and Social Behavior* 13: 406–412.

Ruzek, Sheryl Burt (1979) *The Women's Health Movement.* New York: Praeger.

Sacks, Harvey, Emanuel A. Schegloff, and Gail Jefferson (1974) "A simplest systematics for the organization of turn-taking for conversation." *Language* 50: 696–735.

Scherer, Klaus R. and Howard Giles (eds.) (1979) *Social Markers in Speech.* Cambridge: Cambridge University Press.

West, Candace (1979) "Against our will: male interruptions of females in cross-sex conversation." *Annals of the New York Academy of Sciences* 327: 81–97.

——(1982) "Why can't a woman be more like a man? An interactional note on organizational game-playing for managerial women." *Sociology of Work and Occupations* 9: 5–29.

West, Candace and Don H. Zimmerman (1977) "Women's place in everyday talk: reflections on parent–child interaction." *Social Problems* 24: 521–529.

——(1983) "Small insults: a study of interruptions in cross-sex conversations between unacquainted persons." pp. 86–111 in Barrie Thorne, Cheris Kramarae and Nancy Henley (eds.), *Language, Gender and Society*. Rowley, Mass.: Newbury House.

Willis, Frank N. and Sharon J. Williams (1976) "Simultaneous talking in conversation and sex of speakers." *Perceptual and Motor Skills* 43: 1067–1070.

Wilson, Robert N. (1970) *The Sociology of Health: An Introduction*. New York: Random House.

Wolinsky, Frederic D. (1980) *The Sociology of Health: Principles, Professions and Issues*. Boston: Little, Brown.

Zimmerman, Don H. (1978) "Ethnomethodology." *The American Sociologist* 13: 6–14.

Zimmerman, Don H. and Candace West (1975) "Sex roles, interruptions, and silences in conversation." pp. 105–129 in Barrie Thorne and Nancy Henley (eds.), *Language and Sex: Difference and Dominance*. Rowley, Mass.: Newbury House.

Part VII

Theoretical Debates (2):
Difference or Dominance?

The second debate involves the two major approaches to gender variation in language, the difference approach and the dominance approach. You will have already read several papers relevant to this debate: Part III ('Conversational Dominance') was devoted to work using a dominance perspective, while most of the papers in Part IV ('Same-Sex Talk') took a difference perspective. To put it very simply, research which takes a dominance perspective interprets the differences between women's and men's linguistic usage as reflexes of the dominant–subordinate relationship holding between men and women. Research which takes a difference perspective, by contrast, sees the differences between women's and men's linguistic usage as arising from the different sub-cultures in which women and men are socialized (this approach is sometimes called the sub-cultural or two-cultures approach).

Early work on language and gender took a dominance approach. The reaction against this, and the subsequent flourishing of the difference approach, arose *not* because researchers denied the existence of dominance and oppression in male–female relationships, but because researchers, particularly feminist researchers, became unhappy at the negative portrayal of women in work using the dominance approach. Women's language was described as weak, unassertive, tentative, and women were presented as losers, as victims.

Researchers who began using the difference model in the 1980s argued that the dominance model had become a *deficit* model, that is, a way of interpreting the linguistic facts which represented men's language as the norm and women's language as deviant. The advantage of the difference model, as I said in my introduction to Part IV, is that it allows researchers to show the strengths of linguistic strategies characteristic of women and to celebrate women's ways of talking. For those carrying out research involving mixed talk, the dominance approach provides a useful explanatory framework, but for researchers investigating same-sex talk it seems less appropriate, since dominance and oppression are not obviously helpful categories for the description of all-female talk (or of all-male talk, for that matter, but it is only very recently that sociolinguists have turned their attention to the informal talk of men).

The first paper in this section is the paper which, it can be argued, initiated this debate: Daniel Maltz and Ruth Borker's 'A Cultural Approach to Male–Female Miscommunication'. This paper explicitly claims to present a new (anthropological) framework for discussing gender differences in language. Until 1982, when the paper was published, most researchers had assumed a dominance model, so there is no one paper which sets out the dominance approach (though the papers produced in the 1970s and early 1980s by West and Zimmerman on interruptions could be seen as archetypal – see the paper by them in Part III: 'Women's Place in Everyday Talk'). Maltz and Borker's paper is not based on new data, but rather presents a synthesis of work on gender and language in a variety of fields. Their argument rests on the claim that the 'difficulties' found in cross-sex communication – like the 'difficulties' found in cross-ethnic communication – are the result of cultural difference and should be seen as miscommunication. They argue that boys and girls are socialized largely in same-sex peer groups between the ages of 5 and 15, and that they learn to use language in very different ways. This means that, when male and female speakers interact as adults, they are working with a different set of assumptions about the way interaction works. In the concluding section of their paper, Maltz and Borker make some sensible suggestions about future research in the language and gender field, and summarize the contribution they think a difference approach could offer to language and gender research.

At the time it was published, many sociolinguists found Maltz and Borker's paper refreshing: it certainly gave impetus to those linguists wanting to carry out research into women's talk outside a framework of dominance and oppression. Certainly, for research into talk in single-sex groups, the difference approach had a lot to offer. But, like all frameworks, the difference approach has its limitations. Probably the main problem with the approach is its assumption that all interactional difficulties can be called 'miscommunication'.

However, this idea – the notion that miscommunication was at the heart of male–female problems – had immense popular appeal. This only became evident when Deborah Tannen's book, *That's Not What I Meant!*, published in 1986, sold extremely well, and it became obvious that what readers were most interested in was the chapter on male–female miscommunication. Tannen then wrote a second book aimed at a mass audience, this time focusing exclusively on male–female interaction. This book, *You Just Don't Understand*, became a best-seller and made gender differences in language a topic for discussion in homes all over the English-speaking world. The second paper in this section is the chapter on male–female miscommunication from Tannen's first book. The title – 'Talk in the Intimate Relationship: His and Hers' – suggests she is only discussing interaction in heterosexual couples, but in fact the chapter covers more ground than this, and encapsulates the points she went on to make at greater length in *You Just Don't Understand*. This is the one paper in this Reader which comes from a popular book rather than an academic source. But it is vital for an understanding of the difference–dominance debate to read some of Tannen's work. What Tannen did was to take Maltz and Borker's argument to its logical extreme: women and men belong to different sub-cultures; interactional problems between women and men are cross-cultural miscommunication; if we all take the trouble to understand each other a bit better, these problems can be overcome.

You Just Don't Understand received some of the most critical reviews ever seen in the sociolinguistic world (e.g. Cameron 1992; Freed 1992; Troemel-Ploetz 1991). Theoretical debates do not usually generate such emotional heat, but in this case sociolinguists, particularly feminist linguists, felt very strongly that Tannen's account of gender differences in language misrepresented research findings in the area, as well as over-simplifying the explanatory framework. I've selected as the third paper in this section the fiercest of these reviews, Senta Troemel-Ploetz's 'Selling the Apolitical'.

Troemel-Ploetz articulates the widely held feeling that Tannen has taken the difference approach too far: dominance and power have disappeared from the analysis. Troemel-Ploetz claims that Tannen fails to make clear that women's and men's different ways of talking are *not* different-but-equal, but that men's ways of talking have high status in society while women's talk is denigrated. Moreover, Tannen's book feeds into the genre of self-help books aimed at women which perpetuate the view that, where things aren't working, then it is women who need to adapt (see Cameron 1995; Crawford 1995 for a fuller exposition of this point).

The after-effects of Tannen's book are still being felt: the difference approach is now seen as problematic, because it is associated with a political stance which ignores male dominance. So in one sense it would be true to say that the debate has been resolved in favour of the dominance approach. However, interesting work on same-sex talk continues to be carried out which implicitly draws on a difference or sub-cultural approach. In other ways, the debate has moved on, with researchers assimilating ideas from European social theory, in particular the idea that gender is not a given but is accomplished through talk, and that speakers have available to them a whole range of (often conflicting) discourses (see Coates 1997; Fairclough 1992; Lee 1992; Weedon 1987).

REFERENCES

Cameron, Deborah (1992) Review of Tannen, *You Just Don't Understand. Feminism and Psychology*, 2, 465–8.
Cameron, Deborah (1995) *Verbal Hygiene*. London: Routledge.
Coates, Jennifer (1997) 'Competing discourses of femininity', in Helga Kotthoff and Ruth Wodak (eds) *Communicating Gender*. Amsterdam: John Benjamins.
Crawford, Mary (1995) *Talking Difference: On Gender and Language*. London: Sage.
Fairclough, Norman (1992) *Discourse and Social Change*. Cambridge: Polity Press.
Freed, Alice (1992) 'We understand perfectly: a critique of Tannen's view of cross-sex communication', pp. 144–52 in Kira Hall et al. (eds) *Locating Power. Proceedings of the Second Berkeley Women and Language Conference*. University of California, Berkeley: BWLG.
Lee, David (1992) *Competing Discourses: Perspective and Ideology in Language*. London: Longman.
Tannen, Deborah (1986) *That's Not What I Meant!* London: Dent.

Tannen, Deborah (1990) *You Just Don't Understand: Women and Men in Conversation.* New York: William Morrow.

Troemel-Ploetz, Senta (1991) 'Selling the apolitical'. *Discourse and Society,* 2, 4, 489–502.

Weedon, Chris (1987) *Feminist Practice and Poststructuralist Theory.* Oxford: Blackwell.

RECOMMENDED FURTHER READING

Cameron, Deborah (1995) *Verbal Hygiene.* London: Routledge (esp. ch. 5).

Crawford, Mary (1995) *Talking Difference: On Gender and Language.* London: Sage.

A Cultural Approach to Male–Female Miscommunication

Daniel N. Maltz and Ruth A. Borker

Introduction

This chapter presents what we believe to be a useful new framework for examining differences in the speaking patterns of American men and women. It is based not on new data, but on a reexamination of a wide variety of material already available in the scholarly literature. Our starting problem is the nature of the different roles of male and female speakers in informal cross-sex conversations in American English. Our attempts to think about this problem have taken us to preliminary examination of a wide variety of fields often on or beyond the margins of our present competencies: children's speech, children's play, styles and patterns of friendship, conversational turn-taking, discourse analysis, and interethnic communication. The research which most influenced the development of our present model includes John Gumperz's work on problems in interethnic communication (1982) and Marjorie Goodwin's study of the linguistic aspects of play among black children in Philadelphia (1978, 1980a, 1980b).

Our major argument is that the general approach recently developed for the study of difficulties in cross-ethnic communication can be applied to cross-sex communication as well. We prefer to think of the difficulties in both cross-sex and cross-ethnic communication as two examples of the same larger phenomenon: cultural difference and miscommunication.

The Problem of Cross-Sex Conversation

Study after study has shown that when men and women attempt to interact as equals in friendly cross-sex conversations they do not play the same role in interaction, even when there is no apparent element of flirting. We hope to explore some of these differences, examine the explanations that have been offered, and provide an alternative explanation for them.

The primary data on cross-sex conversations come from two general sources: social psychology studies from the 1950s such as Soskin and John's (1963) research on two young married couples and Strodbeck and Mann's (1956) research on jury deliberations, and more recent sociolinguistic studies from the University of California at Santa Barbara and the University of Pennsylvania by Candace West (Zimmerman and West 1975; West and Zimmerman 1977, reprinted in this volume, p. 165; West 1979), Pamela Fishman (1978), and Lynette Hirschman (1973).

Women's Features

Several striking differences in male and female contributions to cross-sex conversation have been noticed in these studies.

First, women display a greater tendency to ask questions. Fishman (1978: 400) comments that "at times I felt that all women did was ask questions," and Hirschman (1973: 10) notes that "several of the female–male conversations fell into a question–answer pattern with the females asking the males questions."

Fishman (1978: 408) sees this question-asking tendency as an example of a second, more general characteristic of women's speech, doing more of the routine "shitwork" involved in maintaining routine social interaction, doing more to facilitate the flow of conversation (Hirschman 1973: 3). Women are more likely than men to make utterances that demand or encourage responses from their fellow speakers and are therefore, in Fishman's works, "more actively engaged in insuring interaction than the men" (1978: 404). In the earlier social psychology studies, these features have been coded under the general category of "positive reactions" including solidarity, tension release, and agreeing (Strodbeck and Mann 1956).

Third, women show a greater tendency to make use of positive minimal responses, especially "mm hmm" (Hirschman 1973: 8), and are more likely to insert "such comments throughout streams of talk rather than [simply] at the end" (Fishman 1978: 402).

Fourth, women are more likely to adopt a strategy of "silent protest" after they have been interrupted or have received a delayed minimal response (Zimmerman and West 1975; West and Zimmerman 1977: 524).

Fifth, women show a greater tendency to use the pronouns "you" and "we," which explicitly acknowledge the existence of the other speaker (Hirschman 1973: 6).

Men's Features

Contrasting contributions to cross-sex conversations have been observed and described for men.

First, men are more likely to interrupt the speech of their conversational partners, that is, to interrupt the speech of women (Zimmerman and West 1975; West and Zimmerman 1977; West 1979).

Second, they are more likely to challenge or dispute their partners' utterances (Hirschman 1973: 11).

Third, they are more likely to ignore the comments of the other speaker, that is, to offer no response or acknowledgment at all (Hirschman 1973: 11), to respond slowly in what has been described as a "delayed minimal response" (Zimmerman and West 1975: 118), or to respond unenthusiastically (Fishman 1978).

Fourth, men use more mechanisms for controlling the topic of conversation, including both topic development and the introduction of new topics, than do women (Zimmerman and West 1975).

Finally, men make more direct declarations of fact or opinion than do women (Fishman 1978: 402), including suggestions, opinions, and "statements of orientation" as Strodbeck and Mann (1956) describe them, or "statements of focus and directives" as they are described by Soskin and John (1963).

Explanations Offered

Most explanations for these features have focused on differences in the social power or in the personalities of men and women. One variant of the social power argument, presented by West (Zimmerman and West 1975; West and Zimmerman 1977), is that men's dominance in conversation parallels their dominance in society. Men enjoy power in society and also in conversation. The two levels are seen as part of a single social-political system. West sees interruptions and topic control as male displays of power – a power based in the larger social order but reinforced and expressed in face-to-face interaction with women. A second variant of this argument, stated by Fishman (1978), is that while the differential power of men and women is crucial, the specific mechanism through which it enters conversation is sex-role definition. Sex roles serve to obscure the issue of power for participants, but the fact is, Fishman argues, that norms of appropriate behavior for women and men serve to give power and interactional control to men while keeping it from women. To be socially acceptable as women, women cannot exert control and must actually support men in their control. In this casting of the social power argument, men are not necessarily seen to be consciously flaunting power, but simply reaping the rewards given them by the social system. In both variants, the link between macro and micro levels of social life is seen as direct and unproblematic, and the focus of explanation is the general social order.

Sex roles have also been central in psychological explanations. The primary advocate of the psychological position has been Robin Lakoff (1975). Basically, Lakoff asserts that, having been taught to speak and act like "ladies," women become as unassertive and insecure as they have been made to sound. The impossible task of trying to be both women and adults, which Lakoff sees as culturally incompatible, saps women of confidence and strength. As a result, they come to produce the speech they do, not just because it is how women are supposed to speak, but because it fits with the personalities they develop as a consequence of sex-role requirements.

The problem with these explanations is that they do not provide a means of explaining why these specific features appear as opposed to any number of others, nor do they allow us to differentiate between various types of male–female interaction. They do not really tell us why and how these specific interactional phenomena are linked to the general fact that men dominate within our social system.

An Alternative Explanation: Sociolinguistic Subcultures

Our approach to cross-sex communication patterns is somewhat different from those that have been previously proposed. We place the stress not on psychological differences or power differentials, although these may make some contribution, but rather on a notion of cultural differences between men and women in their conceptions of friendly conversation, their rules for engaging in it, and, probably most important, their rules for interpreting it. We argue that American men and women come from different sociolinguistic subcultures, having learned to do different things with words in a conversation, so that when they attempt to carry on conversations with one another, even if both parties are attempting to treat one another as equals, cultural miscommunication results.

The idea of distinct male and female subcultures is not a new one for anthropology. It has been persuasively argued again and again for those parts of the world such as the Middle East and southern Europe in which men and women spend most of their lives spatially and interactionally segregated. The strongest case for sociolinguistic subcultures has been made by Susan Harding from her research in rural Spain (1975).

The major premise on which Harding builds her argument is that speech is a means for dealing with social and psychological situations. When men and women have different experiences and operate in different social contexts, they tend to develop different genres of speech and different skills for doing things with words. In the Spanish village in which she worked, the sexual division of labor was strong, with men involved in agricultural tasks and public politics while women were involved in a series of networks of personal relations with their children, their husbands, and their female neighbors. While men developed their verbal skills in economic negotiations and public political argument, women became more verbally adept at a quite different mode of interactional manipulation with words: gossip, social analysis, subtle information gathering through a carefully developed technique of verbal prying, and a kind of second-guessing the thoughts of others (commonly known as "women's intuition") through a skillful monitoring of the speech of others. The different social needs of men and women, she argues, have led them to sexually differentiated communicative cultures, with each sex learning a different set of skills for manipulating words effectively.

The question that Harding does not ask, however, is, if men and women possess different subcultural rules for speaking, what happens if and when they try to interact with each other? It is here that we turn to the research on interethnic miscommunication.

Interethnic Communication

Recent research (Gumperz 1977, 1978a, 1978b, 1979; Gumperz and Tannen 1978) has shown that systematic problems develop in communication when speakers of different speech cultures interact and that these problems are the result of differences in systems of conversational inference and the cues for signalling speech acts and speaker's intent. Conversation is a negotiated activity. It progresses in large part because of shared assumptions about what is going on.

Examining interactions between English-English and Indian-English speakers in Britain (Gumperz 1977, 1978a, 1979; Gumperz et al. 1977), Gumperz found that differences in cues resulted in systematic miscommunication over whether a question was being asked, whether an argument was being made, whether a person was being rude or polite, whether a speaker was relinquishing the floor or interrupting, whether and what a speaker was emphasizing, whether interactants were angry, concerned, or indifferent. Rather than being seen as problems in communication, the frustrating encounters that resulted were usually chalked up as personality clashes or interpreted in the light of racial stereotypes which tended to exacerbate already bad relations.

To take a simple case, Gumperz (1977) reports that Indian women working at a cafeteria, when offering food, used a falling intonation, e.g. "gravy," which to them indicated a question, something like "do you want gravy?" Both Indian and English workers saw a question as an appropriate polite form, but to English-English speakers a falling intonation signalled not a question, which for them is signalled by a rising intonation such as "gravy," but a declarative statement, which was both inappropriate and extremely rude.

A major advantage of Gumperz's framework is that it does not assume that problems are the result of bad faith, but rather sees them as the result of individuals wrongly interpreting cues according to their own rules.

The Interpretation of Minimal Responses

How might Gumperz's approach to the study of conflicting rules for interpreting conversation be applied to the communication between men and women? A simple example will illustrate our basic approach: the case of positive minimal responses. Minimal responses such as nods and comments like "yes" and "mm hmm" are common features of conversational interaction. Our claim, based on our attempts to understand personal experience, is that these minimal responses have significantly different meanings for men and women, leading to occasionally serious miscommunication.

We hypothesize that for women a minimal response of this type means simply something like "I'm listening to you; please continue," and that for men it has a somewhat stronger meaning such as "I agree with you" or at least "I follow your argument so far." The fact that women use these responses more often than men is in part simply that women are listening more often than men are agreeing.

But our hypothesis explains more than simple differential frequency of usage. Different rules can lead to repeated misunderstandings. Imagine a male speaker who is receiving repeated nods or "mm hmm"s from the woman he is speaking to. She is merely indicating that she is listening, but he thinks she is agreeing with everything he says. Now imagine a female speaker who is receiving only occasional nods and "mm hmm"s from the man she is speaking to. He is indicating that he doesn't always agree; she thinks he isn't always listening.

What is appealing about this short example is that it seems to explain two of the most common complaints in male–female interaction: (1) men who think that women are always agreeing with them and then conclude that it's impossible to tell what a woman really thinks, and (2) women who get upset with men who never seem to be listening. What we think we have here are two separate rules for conversational maintenance which come into conflict and cause massive miscommunication.

Sources of Different Cultures

A probable objection that many people will have to our discussion so far is that American men and women interact with one another far too often to possess different subcultures. What we need to explain is how it is that men and women can come to possess different cultural assumptions about friendly conversation.

Our explanation is really quite simple. It is based on the idea that by the time we have become adults we possess a wide variety of rules for interacting in different situations. Different sets of these rules were learned at different times and in different contexts. We have rules for dealing with people in dominant or subordinate social positions, rules which we first learned as young children interacting with our parents and teachers. We have rules for flirting and other sexual encounters which we probably started learning at or near adolescence. We have rules for dealing with service personnel and bureaucrats, rules we began learning when we first ventured into the public domain. Finally, we have rules for friendly interaction, for carrying on friendly conversation. What is striking about these last rules is that they were learned not from adults but from peers, and that they were learned during precisely that time period, approximately age 5 to 15, when boys and girls interact socially primarily with members of their own sex.

The idea that girls and boys in contemporary America learn different ways of speaking by the age of five or earlier has been postulated by Robin Lakoff (1975), demonstrated by Andrea Meditch (1975), and more fully explored by Adelaide Haas (1979). Haas's research on school-age children shows the early appearance of important male–female differences in patterns of language use, including a male tendency toward direct requests and information giving and a female tendency toward compliance (1979: 107).

But the process of acquiring gender-specific speech and behavior patterns by school-age children is more complex than the simple copying of adult "genderlects" by preschoolers. Psychologists Brooks-Gunn and Matthews (1979) have labelled this process the "consolidation of sex roles"; we call it learning of gender-specific "cultures."

Among school-age children, patterns of friendly social interaction are learned not so much from adults as from members of one's peer group, and a major feature of most middle-childhood peer groups is homogeneity; "they are either all-boy or all-girl" (Brooks-Gunn and Matthews 1979). Members of each sex are learning self-consciously to differentiate their behavior from that of the other sex and to exaggerate these differences. The process can be profitably compared to accent divergence in which members of two groups that wish to become clearly distinguished from one another socially acquire increasingly divergent ways of speaking.[1]

Because they learn these gender-specific cultures from their age-mates, children tend to develop stereotypes and extreme versions of adult behavior patterns. For a boy learning to behave in a masculine way, for example, Ruth Hartley (1959, quoted in Brooks-Gunn and Matthews 1979: 203) argues that:

> both the information and the practice he gets are distorted. Since his peers have no better sources of information than he has, all they can do is pool the impressions and anxieties they derived from their early training. Thus, the picture they draw is over-simplified and overemphasized. It is a picture drawn in black and white, with little or no modulation and it is incomplete, including a few of the many elements that go to make up the role of the mature male.

What we hope to argue is that boys and girls learn to use language in different ways because of the very different social contexts in which they learn how to carry on friendly conversation. Almost anyone who remembers being a child, has worked with school-age children, or has had an opportunity to observe school-age children can vouch for the fact that groups of girls and groups of boys interact and play in different ways. Systematic observations of children's play have tended to confirm these well-known differences in the ways girls and boys learn to interact with their friends.

In a major study of sex differences in the play of school-age children, for example, sociologist Janet Lever (1976) observed the following six differences between the play of boys and that of girls: (1) girls more often play indoors; (2) boys tend to play in larger groups; (3) boys' groups tend to include a wider age range of participants; (4) girls play in predominantly male games more often than vice versa; (5) boys more often play competitive games, and (6) girls' games tend to last a shorter period of time than boys' games.

It is by examining these differences in the social organization of play and the accompanying differences in the patterns of social interaction they entail, we argue, that we can learn about the sources of male–female differences in patterns of language use. And it is these same patterns, learned in childhood and carried over into adulthood as the bases for patterns of single-sex friendship relations, we contend, that are potential sources of miscommunication in cross-sex interaction.

The World of Girls

Our own experience and studies such as Goodwin's (1980b) of black children and Lever's (1976, 1978) of white children suggest a complex of features of girls' play and the speech within it. Girls play in small groups, most often in pairs (Lever 1976; Eder and Hallinan 1978; Brooks-Gunn and Matthews 1979), and their play groups tend to be remarkably homogeneous in terms of age. Their play is often in private or semi-private settings that require participants be invited in. Play is cooperative and activities are usually organized in noncompetitive ways (Lever 1976; Goodwin 1980b). Differentiation between girls is not made in terms of power, but relative closeness. Friendship is seen by girls as involving intimacy, equality, mutual commitment, and loyalty. The idea of "best friend" is central for girls. Relationships between girls are to some extent in opposition to one another, and new relationships are often formed at the expense of old ones. As Brooks-Gunn and Matthews (1979: 280) observe, "friendships tend to be exclusive, with a few girls being exceptionally close to one another. Because of this breakups tend to be highly emotional," and Goodwin (1980a: 172) notes that "the non-hierarchical framework of the girls provides a fertile ground for rather intricate processes of alliance formation between equals against some other party."

There is a basic contradiction in the structure of girls' social relationships. Friends are supposed to be equal and everyone is supposed to get along, but in fact they don't always. Conflict must be resolved, but a girl cannot assert social power or superiority as an individual to resolve it. Lever (1976), studying fifth-graders, found that girls simply could not deal with quarrels and that when conflict arose they made no attempt to settle it; the group just broke up. What girls learn to do with speech is cope with the contradiction created by an ideology of equality and cooperation and a social reality that includes difference and conflict. As they grow up they learn increasingly subtle ways of balancing the conflicting pressures created by a female social world and a female friendship ideology.

Basically girls learn to do three things with words: (1) to create and maintain relationships of closeness and equality, (2) to criticize others in acceptable ways, and (3) to interpret accurately the speech of other girls.

To a large extent friendships among girls are formed through talk. Girls need to learn to give support, to recognize the speech rights of others, to let others speak, and to acknowledge what they say in order to establish and maintain relationships of equality and closeness. In activities they need to learn to create cooperation through speech. Goodwin (1980a) found that inclusive forms such as "let's," "we gonna," "we could," and "we gotta" predominated in task-oriented activities. Furthermore, she found that most girls in the group she studied made suggestions and that the other girls usually agreed to them. But girls also learn to exchange information and confidences to create and maintain relationships of closeness. The exchange of personal thoughts not only expresses closeness but mutual commitment as well. Brooks-Gunn and Matthews (1979: 280) note of adolescent girls:

much time is spent talking, reflecting, and sharing intimate thought. Loyalty is of central concern to the 12- to 14-year old girl, presumably because, if innermost secrets are shared, the friend may have 'dangerous knowledge' at her disposal.

Friendships are not only formed through particular types of talk, but are ended through talk as well. As Lever (1976: 4) says of "best friends," "sharing secrets binds the union together, and 'telling' the secrets to outsiders is symbolic of the 'break-up'."

Secondly, girls learn to criticize and argue with other girls without seeming overly aggressive, without being perceived as either "bossy" or "mean," terms girls use to evaluate one another's speech and actions. Bossiness, ordering others around, is not legitimate because it denies equality. Goodwin (1980a) points out that girls talked very negatively about the use of commands to equals, seeing it as appropriate only in role play or in unequal relationships such as those with younger siblings. Girls learn to direct things without seeming bossy, or they learn not to direct. While disputes are common, girls learn to phrase their arguments in terms of group needs and situational requirements rather than personal power or desire (Goodwin 1980a). Meanness is used by girls to describe nonlegitimate acts of exclusion, turning on someone, or withholding friendship. Excluding is a frequent occurrence (Eder and Hallinan 1978), but girls learn over time to discourage or even drive away other girls in ways that don't seem to be just personal whim. Cutting someone is justified in terms of the target's failure to meet group norms and a girl often rejects another using speech that is seemingly supportive on the surface. Conflict and criticism are risky in the world of girls because they can both rebound against the critic and can threaten social relationships. Girls learn to hide the source of criticism; they present it as coming from someone else or make it indirectly through a third party (Goodwin 1980a, 1980b).

Finally, girls must learn to decipher the degree of closeness being offered by other girls, to recognize what is being withheld, and to recognize criticism. Girls who don't actually read these cues run the risk of public censure or ridicule (Goodwin 1980b). Since the currency of closeness is the exchange of secrets which can be used against a girl, she must learn to read the intent and loyalty of others and to do so continuously, given the system of shifting alliances and indirect expressions of conflict. Girls must become increasingly sophisticated in reading the motives of others, in determining when closeness is real, when conventional, and when false, and to respond appropriately. They must learn who to confide in, what to confide, and who not to approach. Given the indirect expression of conflict, girls must learn to read relationships and situations sensitively. Learning to get things right is a fundamental skill for social success, if not just social survival.

The World of Boys

Boys play in larger, more hierarchically organized groups than do girls. Relative status in this ever-fluctuating hierarchy is the main thing that boys learn to manipulate in their interactions with their peers. Nondominant boys are rarely excluded from play but are made to feel the inferiority of their status positions in no uncertain terms. And since hierarchies fluctuate over time and over situation, every boy gets his chance to be victimized and must learn to take it. The social world of boys is one of posturing and counterposturing. In this world, speech is used in three major ways: (1) to assert one's position of dominance, (2) to attract and maintain an audience, and (3) to assert oneself when other speakers have the floor.

The use of speech for the expression of dominance is the most straightforward and probably the best-documented sociolinguistic pattern in boys' peer groups. Even ethological studies of human dominance patterns have made extensive use of various speech behaviors as indices of dominance. Richard Savin-Williams (1976), for example, in his study of dominance patterns among boys in a summer camp uses the following speech interactions as measures of dominance: (1) giving of verbal commands or orders, such as "Get up," "Give it to me," or "You go over there "; (2) name calling and other forms of verbal ridicule, such as "You're a dolt"; (3) verbal threats or boasts of authority, such as "If you don't shut up, I'm gonna come over and bust your teeth in"; (4) refusals to obey orders; and (5) winning a verbal argument as in the sequence: "I was here first" / "Tough," or in more elaborate forms of verbal duelling such as the "dozens."[2]

The same patterns of verbally asserting one's dominance and challenging the dominance claims of others form the central element in Goodwin's (1980a) observations of boys' play in Philadelphia. What is easy to forget in thinking about this use of words as weapons, however, is that the most successful boy in such interaction is not the one who is most aggressive and uses the most power-wielding forms of speech, but the boy who uses these forms most successfully. The simple use of assertiveness and aggression in boys' play is the sign not of a leader but of a bully. The skillful speaker in a boys' group is considerably more likeable and better liked by his peers than is a simple bully. Social success among boys is based on knowing both how and when to use words to express power as well as knowing when not to use them. A successful leader will use speech to put challengers in their place and to remind followers periodically of their nondominant position, but will not browbeat unnecessarily and will therefore gain the respect rather than the fear of less dominant boys.

A second sociolinguistic aspect of friendly interaction between boys is using words to gain and maintain an audience. Storytelling, joke telling, and other narrative performance events are common features of the social interaction of boys. But actual transcripts of such storytelling events collected by Harvey Sacks (Sacks 1974; Jefferson 1978) and Goodwin (1980a), as opposed to stories told directly to interviewers, reveal a suggestive feature of storytelling activities among boys: audience behavior is not overtly supportive. The storyteller is frequently faced with mockery, challenges and side comments on his story. A major sociolinguistic skill which a boy must apparently learn in interacting with his peers is to ride out this series of challenges, maintain his audience, and successfully get to the end of his story. In Sacks's account (1974) of some teenage boys involved in the telling of a dirty joke, for example, the narrator is challenged for his taste in jokes (an implication that he doesn't know a dirty joke from a non-dirty one) and for the potential ambiguity of his opening line "Three brothers married three sisters," not, as Sacks seems to imply, because audience members are really confused, but just to hassle the speaker. Through catches,[3] put-downs, the building of suspense, or other interest-grabbing devices, the speaker learns to control his audience. He also learns to continue when he gets no encouragement whatever, pausing slightly at various points for possible audience response but going on if there is nothing but silence.

A final sociolinguistic skill which boys must learn from interacting with other boys is how to act as audience members in the types of storytelling situations just discussed. As audience member as well as storyteller, a boy must learn to assert himself and his opinions. Boys seem to respond to the storytelling of other boys not so much with questions on deeper implications or with minimal-response encouragement as with side comments and challenges. These are not meant primarily to interrupt, to change topic, or to change the direction of the narrative itself, but to assert the identity of the individual audience member.

Women's Speech

The structures and strategies in women's conversation show a marked continuity with the talk of girls. The key logic suggested by Kalčik's (1975) study of women's rap groups, Hirschman's (1973) study of students and Abrahams's (1975) work on black women is that women's conversation is interactional. In friendly talk, women are negotiating and expressing a relationship, one that should be in the form of support and closeness, but which may also involve criticism and distance. Women orient themselves to the person they are talking to and expect such orientation in return. As interaction, conversation requires participation from those involved and back-and-forth movement between participants. Getting the floor is not seen as particularly problematic; that should come about automatically. What is problematic is getting people engaged and keeping them engaged – maintaining the conversation and the interaction.

This conception of conversation leads to a number of characteristic speech strategies and gives a particular dynamic to women's talk. First, women tend to use personal and inclusive pronouns, such as "you" and "we" (Hirschman 1973). Second, women give off and look for signs of engagement such as nods and minimal response (Kalčik 1975; Hirschman 1973). Third, women give more extended signs of interest and attention, such as interjecting comments or questions during a speaker's discourse. These sometimes take the form of interruptions. In fact, both Hirschman (1973) and Kalčik (1975) found that interruptions were extremely common, despite women's concern with politeness and decorum (Kalčik 1975). Kalčik (1975) comments that women often asked permission to speak but were concerned that each speaker be allowed to finish and that all present got a chance to speak. These interruptions were clearly not seen as attempts to grab the floor but as calls for elaboration and development, and were taken as signs of support and interest. Fourth, women at the beginning of their utterances explicitly acknowledge and respond to what has been said by others. Fifth, women attempt to link their utterance to the one preceding it by building on the previous utterance or talking about something parallel or related to it. Kalčik (1975) talks about strategies of tying together, filling in, and serializing as signs of women's desire to create continuity in conversation, and Hirschman (1973) describes elaboration as a key dynamic of women's talk.

While the idiom of much of women's friendly talk is that of support, the elements of criticism, competition, and conflict do occur in it. But as with girls, these tend to take forms that fit the friendship idiom. Abrahams (1975) points out that while "talking smart" is clearly one way women talk to women as well as to men, between women it tends to take a more playful form, to be more indirect and metaphoric in its phrasing and less prolonged than similar talk between men. Smartness, as he points out, puts distance in a relationship (Abrahams 1975). The target of criticism, whether present or not, is made out to be the one violating group norms and values (Abrahams 1975). Overt competitiveness is also disguised. As Kalčik (1975) points out, some stories that build on preceding ones are attempts to cap the original speaker, but they tend to have a form similar to supportive ones. It is the intent more than the form that differs. Intent is a central element in the concept of "bitchiness," one of women's terms for evaluating their talk, and it relates to this contradiction between form and intent, whether putting negative messages in overtly positive forms or acting supportive face to face while not being so elsewhere.

These strategies and the interactional orientation of women's talk give their conversation a particular dynamic. While there is often an unfinished quality to particular utterances (Kalčik 1975), there is a progressive development to the overall conversation. The conversation grows out of the interaction of its participants, rather than being directed by a single individual or series of individuals. In her very stimulating discussion, Kalčik (1975) argues that this is true as well for many of the narratives women tell in conversation. She shows how narrative "kernels" serve as conversational resources for individual women and the group as a whole. How and if a "kernel story" is developed by the narrator and/or audience on a particular occasion is a function of the conversational context from which it emerges (Kalčik 1975: 8), and it takes very different forms at different tellings. Not only is the dynamic of women's conversation one of elaboration and continuity, but the idiom of support can give it a distinctive tone as well. Hannerz (1969: 96), for example, contrasts the "tone of relaxed sweetness, sometimes bordering on the saccharine," that characterizes approving talk between women, to the heated argument found among men. Kalčik (1975: 6) even goes so far as to suggest that there is an "underlying esthetic or organizing principle" of "harmony" being expressed in women's friendly talk.

Men's Speech

The speaking patterns of men, and of women for that matter, vary greatly from one North American subculture to another. As Gerry Philipsen (1975: 13) summarizes it, "talk is not everywhere valued equally; nor is it anywhere valued equally in all social contexts." There are striking cultural variations between subcultures in whether men consider certain modes of speech appropriate for dealing with women, children, authority figures, or strangers; there are differences in performance rules for story-telling and joke telling; there are differences in the context of men's speech; and there are differences in the rules for distinguishing aggressive joking from true aggression.

But more surprising than these differences are the apparent similarities across sub-cultures in the patterns of friendly interaction between men and the resemblances between these patterns and those observed for boys. Research reports on the speaking patterns of men among urban blacks (Abrahams 1976; Hannerz 1969), rural New-foundlanders (Faris 1966; Bauman 1972), and urban blue-collar whites (Philipsen 1975; LeMasters 1975) point again and again to the same three features: storytelling, arguing and verbal posturing.

Narratives such as jokes and stories are highly valued, especially when they are well performed for an audience. In Newfoundland, for example, Faris (1966: 242) comments that "the reason 'news' is rarely passed between two men meeting in the road – it is simply not to one's advantage to relay information to such a small audience." Loud and aggressive argument is a second common feature of male–male speech. Such arguments, which may include shouting, wagering, name-calling, and verbal threats (Faris 1966: 245), are often, as Hannerz (1969: 86) describes them, "debates over minor questions of little direct import to anyone," enjoyed for their own sake and not taken as signs of real conflict. Practical jokes, challenges, put-downs, insults, and other forms of verbal aggression are a third feature of men's speech, accepted as normal among friends. LeMasters (1975: 140), for example, describes life in a working-class tavern in the Midwest as follows:

> It seems clear that status at the Oasis is related to the ability to "dish it out" in the rapid-fire exchange called "joshing": you have to have a quick retort, and preferably one that puts you "one up" on your opponent. People who can't compete in the game lose status.

Thus challenges rather than statements of support are a typical way for men to respond to the speech of other men.

What Is Happening in Cross-Sex Conversation

What we are suggesting is that women and men have different cultural rules for friendly conversation and that these rules come into conflict when women and men attempt to talk to each other as friends and equals in casual conversation. We can think of at least five areas, in addition to that of minimal responses already discussed, in which men and women probably possess different conversational rules, so that miscommunication is likely to occur in cross-sex interaction.

(1) There are two interpretations of the meaning of questions. Women seem to see questions as a part of conversational maintenance, while men seem to view them primarily as requests for information.

(2) There are two conventions for beginning an utterance and linking it to the preceding utterance. Women's rules seem to call for an explicit acknowledgment of what has been said and making a connection to it. Men seem to have no such rule and in fact some male strategies call for ignoring the preceding comments.

(3) There are different interpretations of displays of verbal aggressiveness. Women seem to interpret overt aggressiveness as personally directed, negative, and disruptive. Men seem to view it as one conventional organizing structure for conversational flow.

(4) There are two understandings of topic flow and topic shift. The literature on storytelling in particular seems to indicate that men operate with a system in which topic is fairly narrowly defined and adhered to until finished and in which shifts between topics are abrupt, while women have a system in which topic is developed progressively and shifts gradually. These two systems imply very different rules for and interpretations of side comments, with major potential for miscommunication.

(5) There appear to be two different attitudes towards problem sharing and advice giving. Women tend to discuss problems with one another, sharing experiences and offering reassurances. Men, in contrast, tend to hear women, and other men, who present them with problems as making explicit requests for solutions. They respond by giving advice, by acting as experts, lecturing to their audiences.[4]

Conclusions

Our purpose in this paper has been to present a framework for thinking about and tying together a number of strands in the analysis of differences between male and female conversational styles. We hope to prove the intellectual value of this framework by demonstrating its ability to do two things: to serve as a model both of and for sociolinguistic research.

As a model *of* past research findings, the power of our approach lies in its ability to suggest new explanations of previous findings on cross-sex communication while linking these findings to a wide range of other fields, including the study of language acquisition, of play, of friendship, of storytelling, of cross-cultural miscommunication, and of discourse analysis. Differences in the social interaction patterns of boys and girls appear to be widely known but rarely utilized in examinations of sociolinguistic acquisition or in explanations of observed gender differences in patterns of adult speech. Our proposed framework should serve to link together these and other known facts in new ways.

As a model *for* future research, we hope our framework will be even more promising. It suggests to us a number of potential research problems which remain to be investigated. Sociolinguistic studies of school-age children, especially studies of the use of speech in informal peer interaction, appear to be much rarer than studies of young children, although such studies may be of greater relevance for the understanding of adult patterns, particularly those related to gender. Our framework also suggests the need for many more studies of single-sex conversations among adults, trying to make more explicit some of the differences in conversational rules suggested by present research. Finally, the argument we have been making suggests a number of specific problems that appear to be highly promising lines for future research:

(1) A study of the sociolinguistic socialization of "tomboys" to see how they combine male and female patterns of speech and interaction;

(2) An examination of the conversational patterns of lesbians and gay men to see how these relate to the sex-related patterns of the dominant culture;

(3) An examination of the conversational patterns of the elderly to see to what extent speech differences persist after power differences have become insignificant;

(4) A study of children's cultural concepts for talking about speech and the ways these shape the acquisition of speech styles (for example, how does the concept of "bossiness" define a form of behavior which little girls must learn to recognize, then censure, and finally avoid?);

(5) An examination of "assertiveness training" programs for women to see whether they are really teaching women the speaking skills that politically skillful men learn in boyhood or are merely teaching women how to act like bossy little girls or bullying little boys and not feel guilty about it.

We conclude this paper by reemphasizing three of the major ways in which we feel that an anthropological perspective on culture and social organization can prove useful for further research on differences between men's and women's speech.

First, an anthropological approach to culture and cultural rules forces us to reexamine the way we interpret what is going on in conversations. The rules for interpreting conversation are, after all, culturally determined. There may be more than one way of understanding what is happening in a particular conversation and we must be careful about the rules we use for interpreting cross-sex conversations, in which the two participants may not fully share their rules of conversational inference.

Second, a concern with the relation between cultural rules and their social contexts leads us to think seriously about differences in different kinds of talk, ways of categorizing interactional situations, and ways in which conversational patterns may function as strategies for dealing with specific aspects of one's social world. Different types of interaction lead to different ways of speaking. The rules for friendly conversation between equals are different from those for service encounters, for flirting, for teaching, or for polite formal interaction. And even within the apparently uniform domain of friendly interaction, we argue that there are systematic differences between men and women in the way friendship is defined and thus in the conversational strategies that result.

Third and finally, our analysis suggests a different way of thinking about the connection between the gender-related behavior of children and that of adults. Most discussions of sex-role socialization have been based on the premise that gender differences are greatest for adults and that these adult differences are learned gradually throughout childhood. Our analysis, on the other hand, would suggest that at least some aspects of behavior are most strongly gender-differentiated during childhood and that adult patterns of friendly interaction, for example, involve learning to overcome at least partially some of the gender-specific cultural patterns typical of childhood.

NOTES

1   The analogy between the sociolinguistic processes of dialect divergence and genderlect divergence was pointed out to us by Ron Macaulay.
2   In the strict sense the term "dozens" refers to a culturally specific form of stylized argument through the exchange of insults that has been extensively documented by a variety of students of American black culture and is most frequently practiced by boys in their teens and pre-teens. Recently folklorist Simon Bronner (1978) has made a convincing case for the existence of a highly similar but independently derived form of insult exchange known as "ranking," "mocks," or "cutting" among white American adolescents. What we find striking and worthy of note is the tendency for both black and white versions of the dozens to be practiced primarily by boys.
3   "Catches" are a form of verbal play in which the main speaker ends up tricking a member of his or her audience into a vulnerable or ridiculous position. In an article on the folklore of black children in South Philadelphia, Roger Abrahams (1963) distinguishes between catches which are purely verbal and tricks in which the second player is forced into a position of being not only verbally but also physically abused as in the following example of a catch which is also a trick:

> A: Adam and Eve and Pinch-Me-Tight
> Went up the hill to spend the night.
> Adam and Eve came down the hill.
> Who was left?
> B: Pinch-Me-Tight
> [A pinches B]

What is significant about both catches and tricks is that they allow for the expression of playful aggression and that they produce a temporary hierarchical relation between a winner and loser, but invite the loser to attempt to get revenge by responding with a counter-trick.
4   We thank Kitty Julien for first pointing out to us the tendency of male friends to give advice to women who are not necessarily seeking it, and Niyi Akinnaso for pointing out that the sex difference among Yoruba speakers in Nigeria in the way people respond verbally to the problems of others is similar to that among English speakers in the U.S.

REFERENCES

Abrahams, R. (1963) "The 'Catch' in negro Philadelphia". *Keystone Folklore Quarterly*, 8(3), 107–11.

Abrahams, R. (1975) "Negotiating respect: patterns of presentation among black women", in C. Farrar (ed.) *Women in Folklore*. Austin: University of Texas Press.

Abrahams, R. (1976) *Talking Black*. Rowley, MA: Newbury House.

Bauman, R. (1972) "The La Have Island General Store: sociability and verbal art in a Nova Scotia community". *Journal of American Folklore*, 85, 330–43.

Bronner, S. (1978) "A re-examining of white dozens". *Western Folklore*, 37(2), 118–28.

Brooks-Gunn, J. and Matthews, W. (1979) *He and She: How Children Develop Their Sex-Role Identity*. Englewood Cliffs, NJ: Prentice-Hall.

Eder, D. and Hallinan, M. (1978) "Sex differences in children's friendships", *American Sociological Review*, 43, 237–50.

Faris, J. (1966) "The dynamics of verbal exchange: a Newfoundland example", *Anthropologica (Ottawa)*, 8(2), 235–48.

Fishman, P. (1978) "Interaction: the work women do", *Social Problems*, 25(4), 397–406.

Goodwin, M. (1978) Conversational Practices in a Peer Group of Urban Black Children. Doctoral dissertation, University of Pennsylvania, Philadelphia.

Goodwin, M. (1980a) "Directive–response speech sequences in girls' and boys' task activities", in S. McConnell-Ginet, R. Borker and N. Furman (eds) *Women and Language in Literature and Society*. New York: Praeger.

Goodwin, M. (1980b) "He-said-she-said: formal cultural procedures for the construction of a gossip dispute activity", *American Ethnologist*, 7(4), 674–95.

Gumperz, J. (1977) "Sociocultural knowledge in conversational inference", in M. Saville-Troike (ed.) *Linguistics and Anthropology (Georgetown University Round Table on Languages and Linguistics)*. Washington, DC: Georgetown University Press.

Gumperz, J. (1978a) "The conversational analysis of interethnic communication", in E. Lamar Ross (ed.) *Interethnic Communication*. Athens, GA: University of Georgia Press.

Gumperz, J. (1978b) "Dialect and conversational inference in urban communication", *Language in Society*, 7(3), 393–409.

Gumperz, J. (1979) "The sociolinguistic basis of speech act theory", in J. Boyd and S. Ferrara (eds) *Speech Act Ten Years After*. Milan: Versus.

Gumperz, J. (1982) *Discourse Strategies*. Cambridge: Cambridge University Press.

Gumperz, J., Agrawal, A. and Aulakh, G. (1977) *Prosody, Paralinguistics and Contextualisation in Indian English*. MS, Language Behavior Research Laboratory, University of California, Berkeley.

Gumperz, J. and Tannen, D. (1978) "Individual and social differences in language use", in W. Wang and C. Fillmore (eds) *Individual Differences in Language Ability and Language Behavior*. New York: Academic Press.

Hass, A. (1979) "The acquisition of genderlect", in J. Orasanu, M. Slater and L. Adler (eds) "Language, Sex and Gender: Does La Différence Make a Difference?" *Annals of the New York Academy of Sciences*, 327, 101–13.

Hannerz, U. (1969) *Soulside*. New York: Columbia University Press.

Harding, S. (1975) "Women and words in a Spanish village", in R. Reiter (ed.) *Toward an Anthropology of Women*. New York: Monthly Review Press.

Hirschman, L. (1973) Female–Male Differences in Conversational Interaction. Paper presented at Linguistic Society of America, San Diego.

Jefferson, G. (1978) "Sequential aspects of storytelling in conversation", in J. Schenker (ed.) *Studies in the Organisation of Conversational Interaction*. New York: Academic Press.

Kalčik, S. (1975) "'. . . Like Anne's gynaecologist or the time I was almost raped': personal narratives in women's rap groups", in C. Farrar (ed.) *Women in Folklore*. Austin: University of Texas Press.

Lakoff, R. (1975) *Language and Woman's Place*. New York: Harper & Row.

LeMasters, E. (1975) *Blue Collar Aristocrats: Life-Styles at a Working-Class Tavern*. Madison: University of Wisconsin Press.

Lever, J. (1976) "Sex differences in the games children play", *Social Problems*, 23, 478–83.

Lever, J. (1978) "Sex differences in the complexity of children's play and games", *American Sociological Review*, 43, 471–83.

Meditch, A. (1975) "The development of sex-specific speech patterns in young children", *Anthropological Linguistics*, 17, 421–33.

Philipsen, G. (1975) "Speaking 'like a man' in Teamsterville: cultural patterns of role enactment in an urban neighbourhood", *Quarterly Journal of Speech*, 61, 13–22.

Sacks, H. (1974) "An analysis of the course of a joke's telling in conversation", in R. Bauman and J. Sherzer (eds) *Explorations in the Ethnography of Speaking*. Cambridge: Cambridge University Press.

Savin-Williams, R. (1976) "The ethnological study of dominance formation and maintenance in a group of human adolescents", *Child Development*, 47, 972–9.

Soskin, W. and John, V. (1963) "The study of spontaneous talk", in R. Barker (ed.) *The Stream of Behavior*. New York: Appleton-Century-Crofts.

Strodbeck, F. and Mann, R. (1956) "Sex role differentiation in jury deliberations", *Sociometry*, 19, 3–11.

West, C. (1979) "Against our will: male interruptions of females in cross-sex conversation", in J. Orasanu, M. Slater and L. Adler (eds) "Language, Sex and Gender: Does La Différence Make a Difference?" *Annals of the New York Academy of Sciences*, 327, 81–100.

West, C. and Zimmerman, D. (1977) "Women's place in everyday talk: reflections on parent–child interaction", *Social Problems*, 24(5), 521–9.

Zimmerman, D. and West, C. (1975) "Sex roles, interruptions, and silences in conversation", in B. Thorne and N. Henley (eds) *Language and Sex: Difference and Dominance*. Rowley, MA: Newbury House.

28

Talk in the Intimate Relationship: His and Hers

Deborah Tannen

Male–female conversation is always cross-cultural communication. Culture is simply a network of habits and patterns gleaned from past experience, and women and men have different past experiences. From the time they're born, they're treated differently, talked to differently, and talk differently as a result. Boys and girls grow up in different worlds, even if they grow up in the same house. And as adults they travel in different worlds, reinforcing patterns established in childhood. These cultural differences include differing expectations about the role of talk in relationships and how it fulfils that role. [. . .]

To see how male–female differences in conversational style can cause misunderstandings that lead to complementary schismogenesis – a mutually aggravating spiral – in close relationships, let's start by seeing what some of those differences are.

He Said/She Said: His and Her Conversational Styles

Everyone knows that as a relationship becomes long-term, its terms change. But women and men often differ in how they expect them to change. Many women feel, 'After all this time, you should know what I want without my telling you.' Many men feel, 'After all this time, we should be able to tell each other what we want.'

These incongruent expectations capture one of the key differences between men and women. Communication is always a matter of balancing conflicting needs for involvement and independence, but although everyone has both these needs, women often have a relatively greater need for involvement, and men a relatively greater need for independence. Being understood without saying what you mean gives a payoff in involvement, and that is why women value it so highly.

If you want to be understood without saying what you mean explicitly in words, you must convey meaning somewhere else – in how words are spoken, or by metamessages. Thus it stands to reason that women are often more attuned than men to the metamessages of talk. When women surmise meaning in this way, it seems mysterious to men, who call it 'women's intuition' (if they think it's right) or 'reading things in' (if they think it's wrong). Indeed, it could be wrong, since metamessages are not on record. And even if it is right, there is still the question of scale: how significant are the metamessages that are there?

Metamessages are a form of indirectness. Women are more likely to be indirect, and to try to reach agreement by negotiation. Another way to understand this preference is that negotiation allows a display of solidarity, which women prefer to the display of power (even though the aim may still be the same – getting what you want). Unfortunately, power and solidarity are bought with the same currency. Ways of talking intended to create solidarity have the simultaneous effect of framing power differences. When they think they're being nice, women often end up appearing deferential and unsure of themselves or of what they want.

When styles differ, misunderstandings are always rife. As their differing styles create misunderstandings, women and men try to clear them up by talking things out. These pitfalls are compounded in talks between men and women because of their different ways of going about talking things out, and their different assumptions about the significance of going about it.

Women Listen for Metamessages

Sylvia and Harry celebrated their golden wedding anniversary at a country club. Some of the guests were there for the whole weekend, most just for the evening of the celebration: a cocktail party followed by dinner. During dinner, the headwaiter approached Sylvia. 'Since we have a rich dessert tonight, and everyone has already eaten at the cocktail party, perhaps you would prefer to cut the anniversary cake at lunch tomorrow?' Sylvia asked the advice of the others at her table. All the men agreed: 'Yes, that makes sense. Save the cake for tomorrow.' All the women disagreed. 'No, the party is tonight. Have the cake tonight.' The men were focusing on the message: the cake as food. The women were thinking of the metamessage: serving a special cake frames an occasion as a celebration.

Why are women more attuned to metamessages? Because they are more focused on involvement, that is, on relationships among people, and it is through metamessages that relationships among people are established and maintained. If you want to take the temperature and check the vital signs of a relationship, the barometers to check are its metamessages: what is said and how.

Everyone can see these signals, but whether or not we pay attention to them is another matter – a matter of being sensitized. Once you are sensitized, you can't roll your antennae back in; they're stuck in the extended position.

When interpreting meaning, it is possible to pick up signals that weren't intentionally sent out, like an innocent flock of birds on a radar screen. The birds are there – and the signals women pick up are there – but they may not mean what the interpreter thinks they mean. For example, Mary looks at Larry and asks, 'What's wrong?' because his brow is furrowed. Since he was only thinking about lunch, her expression of concern makes him feel under scrutiny.

The difference in focus on messages and metamessages can give men and women different points of view on almost any comment. Harriet complains to Mark, 'Why don't you ask me how my day was?' He replies, 'If you have something to tell me, tell me. Why do you have to be invited?' The reason is that she wants the metamessage of interest: evidence that he cares how her day was, regardless of whether or not she has something to tell.

A lot of trouble is caused between women and men by, of all things, pronouns. Women often feel hurt when their partners use 'I' or 'me' in a situation in which they would use 'we' or 'us'. When Mark announces, 'I think I'll go for a walk,' Harriet feels specifically uninvited, though Mark later claims she would have been welcome to join him. She felt locked out by his use of 'I' and his omission of an invitation: 'Would you like to come?' Metamessages can be seen in what is not said as well as what is said.

It's difficult to straighten out such misunderstandings because each one feels convinced of the logic of his or her position and the illogic – or irresponsibility – of the other's. Harriet knows that she always asks Mark how his day was, and that she'd never announce, 'I'm going for a walk', without inviting him to join her. If he talks differently to her, it must be that he feels differently. But Mark wouldn't feel unloved if Harriet didn't ask about his day, and he would feel free to ask, 'Can I come along', if she announced she was taking a walk. So he can't believe she is justified in feeling responses he knows he wouldn't have.

Messages and Metamessages in Talk Between . . . Grown Ups?

These processes are dramatized with chilling yet absurdly amusing authenticity in Feiffer's *Grown Ups*. To get a closer look at what happens when men and women focus on different levels of talk in talking things out, let's look at what happens in this play.

Jake criticizes Louise for not responding when their daughter, Edie, called her. His comment leads to a fight, even though they're both aware that this one incident is not in itself important.

JAKE: Look, I don't care if it's important or not, when a kid calls its mother the mother should answer.
LOUISE: Now I'm a bad mother.
JAKE: I didn't say that.
LOUISE: It's in your stare.
JAKE: Is that another thing you know? My stare?

Louise ignores Jake's message – the question of whether or not she responded when Edie called – and goes for the metamessage: his implication that she's a bad mother, which Jake insistently disclaims. When Louise explains the signals she's reacting to,

Jake not only discounts them but is angered at being held accountable not for what he said but for how he looked – his stare.

As the play goes on, Jake and Louise replay and intensify these patterns:

LOUISE: If I'm such a terrible mother, do you want a divorce?
JAKE: I do not think you're a terrible mother and no, thank you, I do not want a divorce. Why is it that whenever I bring up any difference between us you ask me if I want a divorce?

The more he denies any meaning beyond the message, the more she blows it up, the more adamantly he denies it, and so on:

JAKE: I have brought up one thing that you do with Edie that I don't think you notice that I have noticed for some time but which I have deliberately not brought up before because I had hoped you would notice it for yourself and stop doing it and also – frankly, baby, I have to say this – I knew if I brought it up we'd get into exactly the kind of circular argument we're in right now. And I wanted to avoid it. But I haven't and we're in it, so now, with your permission, I'd like to talk about it.
LOUISE: You don't see how that puts me down?
JAKE: What?
LOUISE: If you think I'm so stupid why do you go on living with me?
JAKE: *Dammit! Why can't anything ever be simple around here?!*

It can't be simple because Louise and Jake are responding to different levels of communication. [. . .] Jake tries to clarify his point by overelaborating it, which gives Louise further evidence that he's condescending to her, making it even less likely that she will address his point rather than his condescension.

What pushes Jake and Louise beyond anger to rage is their different perspectives on metamessages. His refusal to admit that his statements have implications and overtones denies her authority over her own feelings. Her attempts to interpret what he didn't say and put the metamessage into the message make him feel she's putting words into his mouth – denying his authority over his own meaning.

The same thing happens when Louise tells Jake that he is being manipulated by Edie:

LOUISE: Why don't you ever make her come to see you?
          Why do you always go to her?
JAKE: You want me to play power games with a nine year old? I want her to know I'm interested in her. Someone around here has to show interest in her.
LOUISE: You love her more than I do.
JAKE: I didn't say that.
LOUISE: Yes, you did.
JAKE: You don't know how to listen. You have never learned how to listen. It's as if listening to you is a foreign language.

Again, Louise responds to his implication – this time, that he loves Edie more because he runs when she calls. And yet again, Jake cries literal meaning, denying he meant any more than he said.

Throughout their argument, the point to Louise is her feelings – that Jake makes her feel put down – but to him the point is her actions – that she doesn't always respond when Edie calls:

LOUISE: You talk about what I do to Edie, what do you think you do to me?
JAKE: This is not the time to go into what we do to each other.

Since she will talk only about metamessages, and he will talk only about messages, neither can get satisfaction from their talk, and they end up where they started – only angrier:

JAKE: That's not the point!
LOUISE: It's *my* point.
JAKE: It's hopeless!
LOUISE: Then get a divorce.

Conventional wisdom (and many of our parents and English teachers) tell us that meaning is conveyed by words, so men who tend to be literal about words are supported by conventional wisdom. They may not simply deny but actually miss the cues that are sent by how words are spoken. If they sense something about it, they may nonetheless discount what they sense. After all, it wasn't said. Sometimes that's a dodge – a plausible defence rather than a gut feeling. But sometimes it is a sincere conviction. Women are also likely to doubt the reality of what they sense. If they don't doubt it in their guts, they nonetheless may lack the arguments to support their position and thus are reduced to repeating, 'You said it. Yes you did.' Knowing that metamessages are a real and fundamental part of communication makes it easier to understand and justify what they feel.

'Talk to Me'

An article in a popular newspaper reports that one of the five most common complaints of wives about their husbands is 'He doesn't listen to me any more.' Another is 'He doesn't talk to me any more.' Political scientist Andrew Hacker noted that lack of communication, while high on women's lists of reasons for divorce, is much less often mentioned by men. Since couples are parties to the same conversations, why are women more dissatisfied with them than men? Because what they expect is different, as well as what they see as the significance of talk itself.

The Strong Silent Type

One of the most common stereotypes of a 'real' man is the strong silent type. Jack Kroll, writing about Henry Fonda on the occasion of his death, used the phrases 'quiet power', 'abashed silences', 'combustible catatonia', and 'sense of power held in check'. He explained that Fonda's goal was not to let anyone see 'the wheels go around', not to let the 'machinery' show. According to Kroll, the resulting silence was effective on stage but devastating to Fonda's family.

The image of a silent father is common and is often the model for the lover or husband. But what attracts us can become flypaper to which we are unhappily stuck. Many women find the strong silent type to be a lure as a lover but a lug as a husband. Nancy Schoenberger begins a poem with the lines, 'It was your silence that hooked me,/so like my father's.' Adrienne Rich refers in a poem to the 'husband who is frustratingly mute'. Despite the initial attraction of such quintessentially male silence, it may begin to feel, to a woman in a long-term relationship, like a brick wall against which she is banging her head.

In addition to these images of male and female behaviour – both the result and the cause of them – are differences in how women and men view the role of talk in relationships as well as how talk accomplishes its purpose. These differences have their roots in the settings in which men and women learn to have conversations: among their peers, growing up.

Growing Up Male and Female

Children whose parents have foreign accents don't speak with accents. They learn to talk like their peers. Little girls and little boys learn how to have conversations as they learn how to pronounce words: from their playmates. Between the ages of five and fifteen, when children are learning to have conversations, they play mostly with friends of their own sex. So it's not surprising that they learn different ways of having and using conversations.

Anthropologists Daniel Maltz and Ruth Borker (e.g. this volume, p. 417) point out that boys and girls socialize differently. Little girls tend to play in small groups or, even more common, in pairs. Their social life usually centres around a best friend, and friendships are made, maintained, and broken by talk – especially 'secrets'. If a little girl tells her friend's secret to another little girl, she may find herself with a new best friend. The secrets themselves may or may not be important, but the fact of telling them is all-important. It's hard for newcomers to get into these tight groups, but anyone who is admitted is treated as an equal. Girls like to play cooperatively; if they can't cooperate, the group breaks up.

Little boys tend to play in larger groups, often outdoors, and they spend more time doing things than talking. It's easy for boys to get into the group, but not everyone is accepted as an equal. Once in the group, boys must jockey for their status in it. One of the most important ways they do this is through talk: verbal display such as telling stories and jokes, challenging and sidetracking the verbal displays of other boys, and withstanding other boys' challenges in order to maintain their own story – and status. Their talk is often competitive talk about who is best at what.

From Children to Grown Ups

Feiffer's play is ironically named *Grown Ups* because adult men and women struggling to communicate often sound like children. 'You said so!' 'I did not!' The reason is that when they grow up, women and men keep the divergent attitudes and habits they learned as children – which they don't recognize as attitudes and habits but simply take for granted as ways of talking.

Women want their partners to be a new and improved version of a best friend. This gives them a soft spot for men who tell them secrets. As Jack Nicholson once advised a guy in a movie: 'Tell her about your troubled childhood – that always gets 'em.' Men expect to *do* things together and don't feel anything is missing if they don't have heart-to-heart talks all the time.

If they do have heart-to-heart talks, the meaning of those talks may be opposite for men and women. To many women, the relationship is working as long as they can talk things out. To many men, the relationship isn't working out if they have to keep working it over. If she keeps trying to get talks going to save the relationship, and he keeps trying to avoid them because he sees them as weakening it, then each one's efforts to preserve the relationship appear to the other as reckless endangerment.

How to Talk Things Out

If talks (of any kind) do get going, men's and women's ideas about how to conduct them may be very different. For example, Diana is feeling comfortable and close to Tom. She settles into a chair after dinner and begins to tell him about a problem at work. She expects him to ask questions to show he's interested; reassure her that he understands and that what she feels is normal; and return the intimacy by telling her a problem of his. Instead, Tom sidetracks her story, cracks jokes about it, questions her interpretation of the problem, and gives her advice about how to solve it and avoid such problems in the future.

All of these responses, natural to men, are unexpected to women, who interpret them in terms of their own habits - negatively. When Tom comments on side issues or cracks jokes, Diana thinks he doesn't care about what she's saying and isn't really listening. If he challenges her reading of what went on, she feels he is criticizing her and telling her she's crazy, when what she wants is to be reassured that she's not. If he tells her how to solve the problem, it makes her feel as if she's the patient to his doctor – a metamessage of condescension, echoing male one-upmanship compared to the female etiquette of equality. Because he doesn't volunteer information about his problems, she feels he's implying he doesn't have any.

Complementary schismogenesis can easily set in. His way of responding to her bid for intimacy makes her feel distant from him. She tries harder to regain intimacy the only way she knows how – by revealing more and more about herself. He tries harder by giving more insistent advice. The more problems she exposes, the more incompetent she feels, until they both see her as emotionally draining and problem-ridden. When his efforts to help aren't appreciated, he wonders why she asks for his advice if she doesn't want to take it.

'You're Not Listening to Me'

The other complaint wives make about their husbands is, 'He doesn't listen to me any more.' The wives may be right that their husbands aren't listening, if they don't value the telling of problems and secrets to establish rapport. But some of the time men feel unjustly accused: 'I *was* listening.' And some of the time, they're right. They were.

Whether or not someone is listening only that person can really know. But we judge whether or not we think others are listening by signals we can see – not only their verbal responses but also their eye contact and little listening noises like 'mhm,' 'uh-huh', and 'yeah'. These listening noises give the go-ahead for talk; if they are misplaced along the track, they can quickly derail a chugging conversation.

Maltz and Borker also report that women and men have different ways of showing that they're listening. In the listening role, women make – and expect – more of these noises. So when men are listening to women, they are likely to make too few such noises for the women to feel the men are really listening. And when women are listening to men, making more such listening noises than men expect may give the impression they're impatient or exaggerating their show of interest.

Even worse, what women and men mean by such noises may be different. Does 'uh-huh' or 'mhm' mean you agree with what you heard, or just that you heard and you're following? Maltz and Borker contend that women tend to use these noises just to show they're listening and understanding. Men tend to use them to show they agree. So one reason women make more listening noises may be that women are listening more than men are agreeing with what they hear.

In addition to problems caused by differences in how many signals are given, there is bound to be trouble as a result of the difference in how they're used. If a woman cheers a man on in his talk by saying 'mhm' and 'yeah' and 'uh-huh' all over the place, and it later comes out that she disagrees with what he said, he may feel she misled him (thereby reinforcing his stereotype of women as unreliable). Conversely, if a man sits through a woman's talk and follows all she says but doesn't agree, he's not going to shower her with 'uh-huh's' – and she's going to think he's not paying attention.

Notice that the difference in how women and men use listening noises is in keeping with their focus in communication. Using the noises to show 'I'm listening; go on' serves the relationship level of talk. Using them to show what one thinks of what is being said is a response to the content of talk. So men and women are being stylistically consistent in their interactive inconsistency.

'Why Don't You Talk About Something Interesting?'

Sometimes when men and women feel the other isn't paying attention, they're right. And this may be because their assumptions about what's interesting are different. Alison gets bored when Daniel goes on and on about the stock market or the world soccer match. He gets bored when she goes on and on about details of her daily life or the lives of people he doesn't even know.

It seems natural to women to tell and hear about what happened today, who turned up at the bus stop, who called and what she said, not because these details are important in themselves but because the telling of them proves involvement – that you care about each other, that you have a best friend. Knowing you will be able to tell these things later makes you feel less alone as you go along the lone path of a day. And if you don't tell, you are sending a metamessage about the relationship – curtailing it, clipping its wings.

Since it is not natural to men to use talk in this way, they focus on the inherent insignificance of the details. What they find worth telling are facts about such topics as sports, politics, history, or how things work. Women often perceive the telling of facts as lecturing, which not only does not carry (for them) a metamessage of rapport, but carries instead a metamessage of condescension: I'm the teacher, you're the student. I'm knowledgeable, you're ignorant.

A *New Yorker* cartoon shows a scene – probably the source of a thousand cartoons (and a million conversations) – of a breakfast table, with a husband reading a newspaper while the wife is trying to talk to him. The husband says, 'You want to talk? Get a newspaper. We'll talk about what's in the newspaper.' It's funny because everyone knows that what's in the newspaper is not what the wife wants to talk about.

Conversations About Conversations

When women talk about what seems obviously interesting to them, their conversations often include reports of conversations. Tone of voice, timing, intonation, and wording are all re-created in the telling in order to explain – dramatize, really – the experience that is being reported. If men tell about an incident and give a brief summary instead of re-creating what was said and how, the women often feel that the essence of the experience is being omitted. If the woman asks, 'What exactly did he say?', and 'How did he say it', the man probably can't remember. If she continues to press him, he may feel as if he's being grilled.

All these different habits have repercussions when the man and the woman are talking about their relationship. He feels out of his element, even one down. She claims to recall exactly what he said, and what she said, and in what sequence, and she wants him to account for what he said. He can hardly account for it since he has forgotten exactly what was said – if not the whole conversation. She secretly suspects he's only pretending not to remember, and he secretly suspects that she's making up the details.

One woman reported such a problem as being a matter of her boyfriend's poor memory. It is unlikely, however, that his problem was poor memory in general. The question is what types of material each person remembers or forgets.

Frances was sitting at her kitchen table talking to Edward, when the toaster did something funny. Edward began to explain why it did it. Frances tried to pay attention, but very early in his explanation, she realized she was completely lost. She felt very stupid. And the indications were that he thought so too.

Later that day they were taking a walk. He was telling her about a difficult situation in his office that involved a complex network of interrelationships among a large number of people. Suddenly he stopped and said, 'I'm sure you can't keep track of all these people.' 'Of course I can,' she said, and she retraced his story with all the characters in place, all the details right. He was genuinely impressed. She felt very smart.

How could Frances be both smart and stupid? Did she have a good memory or a bad one? Frances's and Edward's abilities to follow, remember, and recount depended on the subject – and paralleled her parents' abilities to follow and remember. Whenever Frances told her parents about people in her life, her mother could follow with no problem, but her father got lost as soon as she introduced a second character. 'Now who was that?' he'd ask. 'Your boss?' 'No, my boss is Susan. This was my friend.' Often he'd still be in the previous story. But whenever she told them about her work, it was her mother who would get lost as soon as she mentioned a second step: 'That was your tech report?' 'No, I handed my tech report in last month. This was a special project.'

Frances's mother and father, like many other men and women, had honed their listening and remembering skills in different areas. Their experience talking to other men and other women gave them practice in following different kinds of talk.

Knowing whether and how we are likely to report events later influences whether and how we pay attention when they happen. As women listen to and take part in conversations, knowing they may talk about them later makes them more likely to pay attention to exactly what is said and how. Since most men aren't in the habit of making such reports, they are less likely to pay much attention at the time. On the other hand, many women aren't in the habit of paying attention to scientific explanations and facts because they don't expect to have to perform in public by reciting them – just as those who aren't in the habit of entertaining others by telling jokes 'can't' remember jokes they've heard, even though they listened carefully enough to enjoy them.

So women's conversations with their women friends keep them in training for talking about their relationships with men, but many men come to such conversations with no training at all – and an uncomfortable sense that this really isn't their event.

'What Do You Mean, My Dear?'

Most of us place enormous emphasis on the importance of a primary relationship. We regard the ability to maintain such relationships as a sign of mental health – our contemporary metaphor for being a good person.

Yet our expectations of such relationships are nearly – maybe in fact – impossible. When primary relationships are between women and men, male–female differences contribute to the impossibility. We expect partners to be both romantic interests and best friends. Though women and men may have fairly similar expectations for romantic interests, obscuring their differences when relationships begin, they have very different ideas about how to be friends, and these are the differences that mount over time.

In conversations between friends who are not lovers, small misunderstandings can be passed over or diffused by breaks in contact. But in the context of a primary relationship, differences can't be ignored, and the pressure cooker of continued contact keeps both people stewing in the juice of accumulated minor misunderstandings. And stylistic differences are sure to cause misunderstandings – not, ironically, in matters such as sharing values and interests or understanding each other's philosophies of life. These large and significant yet palpable issues can be talked about and agreed on. It is far harder to achieve congruence – and much more surprising and troubling that it is hard – in the simple day-to-day matters of the automatic rhythms and nuances of talk. Nothing in our backgrounds or in the media (the present-day counterpart of religion or grandparents' teaching) prepares us for this failure. If two people share so much in terms of point of view and basic values, how can they continually get into fights about insignificant matters?

If you find yourself in such a situation and you don't know about differences in conversational style, you assume something's wrong with your partner or you, or you for having chosen your partner. At best, if you are forward-thinking and generous-minded, you may absolve individuals and blame the relationship. But if you know about differences in conversational style, you can accept that there are differences in habits and assumptions about how to have conversation, show interest, be considerate, and so on. You may not always correctly interpret your partner's intentions, but you will know that if you get a negative impression, it may not be what was intended – and neither are your responses unfounded. If he says he really is interested even though he doesn't seem to be, maybe you should believe what he says and not what you sense.

Sometimes explaining assumptions can help. If a man starts to tell a woman what to do to solve her problem, she may say, 'Thanks for the advice but I really don't want to be told what to do. I just want you to listen and say you understand.' A man might want to explain, 'If I challenge you, it's not to prove you wrong; it's just my way of paying attention to what you're telling me.' Both may try either or both to modify their ways of talking and to try to accept what the other does. The important thing is to know that what seem like bad intentions may really be good intentions expressed in a different conversational style. We have to give up our conviction that, as Robin Lakoff put it, 'Love means never having to say "What do you mean?"'

29

Selling the Apolitical

Senta Troemel–Ploetz

Review of Deborah Tannen's *You Just Don't Understand* (New York: Ballantine Books, 1990).

Reading Tannen's *You Just Don't Understand* – the lamentation of the title alone places it squarely into the profuse relationship literature à la Ann Landers, along with books of the caliber of Norwood's *Women Who Love Too Much* and selling as well – one might believe feminism had never happened in this country.

This is a book for the present period of restoration, undoing the upsetting politics of the last three decades, adjusting and accommodating to those in power, namely men, providing appeasement for the male chauvinist backlash so that it does not hurt the wrong women, and appealing to readers who have lived through these decades untouched and untroubled by the analyses of social and economic injustice all around them. That such a deeply reactionary book should appeal to so many readers informs us, disconcerting as it may be, that what is non-threatening to the status quo sells better than critical analysis.

This is a dishonest book precisely because of its non-engaged and apolitical stance. It veils and conceals the political analysis to which women have given their energy during the last 30 years, and the changes they have brought about with the help of fair men. It waters down our insights; it equalizes where differences have to be acknowledged; it hardly ever talks about inequity – and never with real concern; it again and again stops short of drawing any political inferences that would suggest that significant changes are needed in the communication and relationships between women and men.

The author shields her readers also from linguistic knowledge. Thus if one did not know, one would never find out that there is an enormous body of feminist literature presenting a critical analysis of the differences in power and access to power between women and men, on all levels, public and private, and in all areas – work, pay, family, sexuality, the professions, the institutions, e.g. medicine, the court system, even academia (where Tannen is located), and even conversational analysis (which is her field).

The main thesis of Tannen's book is that women's and men's conversation *is* (not even *is patterned like*) cross-cultural communication (pp. 18, 42, 47). This is entirely unsupported and unproven. What Tannen claims, that 'if adults learn their ways of speaking as children growing up in separate social worlds of peers, then conversation between women and men is cross-cultural communication' (p. 47), simply does not follow. Even if it were true that girls and boys grow up in different linguistic worlds, it would not follow. Girls and boys, women and men (always remaining within the white middle class) live together in shared linguistic worlds, be it in the family, in schoolrooms, in the streets, in colleges, in jobs; they are probably spending more time in mixed-sex contexts than in single-sex contexts, and, above all, they are not victims of constant misunderstandings. On the contrary, they understand each other quite well. They know who is allowed to use dominant speech acts, like commands, orders, explanations, contradiction, doubts, advice, criticism, evaluations, definitions, punishment, attacks, challenges, accusations, reproaches; and who has to apologize, defend, ask for favors, beg, request permission, justify herself, agree, support, adjust, accommodate, and accept someone else's definition of the situation.

By using these speech acts to a large extent asymmetrically, a conversational reality is being constructed in which men claim more authority and autonomy for themselves, and women become more dependent and non-autonomous. We are acting out our social roles and producing, via our speech acts, a conversational world in which our social reality is reflected and corroborated: men have power, women submit.

Consequently, we find two conversational cultures or two different styles that are not equal. Men, the speakers of the dominant style, have more rights and privileges. They exhibit their privileges and produce them in every conversational situation. Men are used to dominating women; they do it especially in conversations: they set the tone as soon as they enter a conversation, they declare themselves expert for almost any topic, they expect and get attention and support from their female conversational partners, they expect and get space to present their topics and, above all, themselves – their conversational success is being produced by the participants in that conversation. Women are trained to please; they have to please also in conversations, i.e. they will let men dominate and they will do everything not to threaten men: not set the tone, not insist on their own topics or opinions, package opposing views pleasantly, not refuse support, not take more space than men, i.e. let men win conversationally and renounce their own conversational success and satisfaction in the process.

Men also exhibit and produce their conversational rights: the right to dominate, the right to self-presentation or self-aggrandizement at the expense of others, the right to have the floor and to finish one's turn, the right to keep women from talking (by disturbance or interruption), the right to get attention and consideration from women, the right to conversational success. Women, on the other hand, have conversational obligations: they must not disturb men in their dominating and imposing behavior; they must support their topics, wait with their own topics, give men attention, take them seriously at all times, and, above all, listen and help them to their conversational success. By assuming, attributing and reconstructing men's rights and privileges and women's obligations in every conversation, status differences between women and men are being confirmed and produced in most mixed-sex interactions – the social hierarchy remains intact.

Reading through what a German critic called Professor Tannen's 'chatter', one searches in vain for concepts like dominance, control, power, politics of gender, sexism, discrimination, and finds two of them mentioned after 200 pages but not explored, borrowed probably from another author. Concepts like feminism or patriarchy never occur, being evidently far too radical for the author. Tannen is selling political naïveté, but neither is sociology quite so naïve nor linguistics quite as apolitical as Tannen would have us believe. In both fields women have, long before Tannen started publishing on mixed-sex communication, given political analyses of their data and introduced new concepts from a feminist perspective that suggested a revision of the existing male models, e.g. Labov's model of the male storyteller as the protagonist; Labov's model of the language of youth which was neither the language of youth nor of black youth but the language of male black youth; Sacks' and Schegloff's turn-taking model, etc.

Significantly, the feminist literature in her own field is not even mentioned by Tannen or, where mentioned en passant, as in the case of Aries, Edelsky, Goodwin, Spender, it is reduced in such a way that its spark is neutralized and its critical impetus watered down so as not to offend anyone or lead him to think. But we do not hear about Lee Jenkins (1981, 1982) who first worked on story-telling in a women's group concentrating on women's competence and their high degree of cooperation, in the process doing away with the stereotypes of women's style found in linguistics as elsewhere. We do not hear about new work done on women's discourse, work on women's friendships, women's professional style, emphasizing the competence of women whose style lends itself very well to all kinds of verbal endeavors, from psychotherapy to teaching to management, and whose success is appreciated independently in these fields. Conspicuous by its absence too is the work of the psychologists of the Stone Center at Wellesley, although Tannen is tampering in relationships.

All these works, apparently, would be far too feminist to be considered by Tannen, since they attack the principle of male superiority and male dominance. Even staying within sociolinguistics, however, there is no mention of the important work by Sue Fisher and Alexandra Todd (Fisher, 1984, 1986; Fisher and Todd, 1983, 1986; Todd, 1984, 1989) who analyzed medical discourse as an unequal power contest where male doctors use their power at the expense of women and their organs. We do not hear about the analysis by Candace West (1984), looking at female doctors and male and female patients respectively, and corroborating the asymmetries as we know them in mixed-sex conversations, even where the doctor is a woman and the patient male. We do not hear about West's interesting result, the construction of symmetry – with respect to interruptions – between the woman doctor and her female patients, giving the first indication that women use power differently than men. We do not hear about Pamela Fishman's work on couples in private conversations which shows male dominance and points out that, when dominance is threatened, the man has recourse to verbal and physical violence. Of course, we do not hear about sexual antagonism (Whitehead, 1976), sexual harassment or verbal insults – Tannen stays with polite conversation.

But even discussing certain topics, e.g. gossip, the powerful analyses of Reiter (1975) and Harding (1975) are missing; in talking about body language, there is no reference to the important *Body Politics* by Henley; the discussion of jokes (pp. 90, 140) is done without using the extensive literature on the politics of humor which shows at whose expense the jokes are made, and who does the work to construct the success of the jokers.

Tannen chooses to ignore all this work because it takes a political stand, because it is looking at interactions between women and men in terms of mechanisms of control and exertion of power, in terms of unequal rights. It is informed by a sense of justice and its authors, each in her own field, are committed to social change. Only an author who is not in touch with the women in her field could write a book in 1990 on conversations between women and men without understanding that women cannot simply adopt the male style and be powerful, too; and also that men will not voluntarily give up their style and be powerless like women. Of course, Tannen never considers such a radical option as men giving up their style to adopt a more humane one; she suggests 'mutual adjustment'. Reading some of the women in her field, understanding the criticism of her work as it is offered in Henley/Kramarae (1991) might have helped her to avoid the superficial dilettantism of her analysis.

Unfortunately, Tannen is also not in touch with other professional women, e.g. women in law, in politics, in journalism, who are fighting for their credibility and their status. The work of these women depends entirely on language as their instrument. Acting in their professions is nothing but speaking. They are trained like the men; they speak with authority – still their experience in their professions is very different from that of men. Tannen has no explanation for this and apparently is unfamiliar with the concept of status dilemma – I return to this point later.

And as to linguistics, readers who do not know will not learn, in this book written by a linguist, that speaking has been analyzed since Austin (1962) as a social act in a social context. Utterances are acts that reflect as well as construct differences in status and power among speakers, and as such they can hurt and degrade another, they can decrease respect for and credibility of another, they can ignore, diminish, ridicule, i.e. discriminate against others. They can do this quite without conscious intention by their speakers. But, of course, as social beings situated in a certain cultural context, we have the obligation to inform ourselves about which acts are seen as discriminatory, i.e. as sexist or racist or both, by our hearers and we have to guarantee that our speech acts are such that they are not offensive if we do not want to offend. If we do not want to exclude someone, we have to guarantee that our advertisement or invitation is such that they feel included. If we want to comfort someone, we have to speak in such a way that the hearer can accept it as comfort. If we fail to follow the conventions of our language to address or comfort someone then our speech acts do not succeed, they 'misfire', as Austin said. We are responsible for how we speak. We cannot arbitrarily produce speech acts and claim idiosyncratic intentions for them – there is a limit to how an utterance can be both understood and misunderstood.

This has to be kept in mind when reading Tannen where again and again what is meant by one speaker and what is understood by another is described as having merely the most tenuous connection. Tannen's linguistically innocent stance gives us no clue that speakers, when talking, are active in a social exchange that can legitimate and produce the domination of men and the subordination of women, and that their interaction just as well could undo social inequality by not reproducing utterances and acts that discriminate, by producing fairer language and more symmetric conversations.

Here may be the reason why Tannen's book is without passion, even 'linguistic' passion as we find it in Labov or Chomsky or Lakoff (Robin Lakoff, of course). Its author does not envisage change anywhere, she does not allow herself linguistic passion or political passion. She is writing in the service of the male research perspective, not making any value judgements, especially none that would threaten the existing hierarchies, i.e. the status quo. However, in selling the status quo, her by-intention apolitical book becomes a highly political act. As such, it is not even in the tradition of American linguistics which all in all has had a deep political and social concern embodied foremost in Chomsky, but also in Labov, who in the 1960s salvaged Black English from primitive status by showing it as a creative endeavor with complex linguistic practices that white standard speakers could not dream to match. Even the anthropologist-linguists of old were more political than Tannen and more concerned with equality. They defended Native American languages (called Indian languages, then) as just as good and just as rich to express the relevant concerns of Native American life as was Standard English with respect to the concerns of its speakers. But none of these linguists would have dismissed the power differences between the speakers of Native American languages or Black English and standard speakers.

Turning away now from academia and her colleagues, to the women and men who are the subjects of Tannen's *You Just Don't Understand*, it is difficult to believe that they could feel their communication adequately described. The plaintive reproach of the title is obviously a woman's utterance, resigned to not being understood instead of insisting on being understood. This is indicative of what is to come. As a critic wrote: 'Tannen's wailing lament about male conversational behaviour is bound to frustrate frustrated women even more' (*Spiegel* 18, 1991: 223). Women are being told that men who are unempathic, who do not care about women's feelings or their wishes, who are selfish and self-centered, speak a different language, called a language of report, and are interested in a different goal, namely the solution of problems. This will not comfort the women who think that men should also be able to communicate on an emotional level and who want to educate men to their emotional culture. Are they to give up the idea of a loving heterosexual relationship based on mutual sharing?

Take for instance the woman who had a breast operation and felt she had been cut into and that the seam of the stitches 'had changed the contour of her breast' (p. 49).

Her husband replies with only one sentence to his wife's distress: 'You can have plastic surgery to cover up the scar and restore the shape of your breast' (p. 49). Then the following dialogue evolves (p. 50):

WOMAN: I'm not having any more surgery! I'm sorry you don't like the way it looks.
MAN: I don't care. It doesn't bother me at all.
WOMAN: Then why are you telling me to have plastic surgery?
MAN: Because you were saying *you* were upset about the way it looked.

Note that in this dialogue the man has the last word and the woman afterwards 'felt like a heel'. We hear a lot about her feelings – e.g. she felt guilty about snapping at him – but we hear nothing about his feelings, only that he was reacting to her complaint by reassuring her that there is something she could do about it. Tannen concludes: 'Eve wanted the gift of understanding, but Mark gave her the gift of advice. He was taking the role of problem-solver, whereas she simply wanted confirmation of her feelings' (p. 50). Tannen's analysis ends here.

It is interesting to see who gets their needs fulfilled. The man solved a problem and presented his solution – he did what he needed to do. The woman did not get what she needed in her situation. There is not the slightest suggestion that especially in a difficult situation of that kind the man should perhaps for once not react to his wife with the usual unempathic, unconcerned, cold, problem-solving response. Is this woman to accept that even when she most needs compassion and empathy (a word that does not occur in Tannen's book), she is not going to get it? And should she believe Tannen's explanation that her husband did not *understand* what she wanted?

Many women know that men just do not *want* to be interested in what they need and it often shows most dramatically in situations where a woman is sick or pregnant or becomes disabled or gets old. It is not that men do not understand what women want and, if they only knew, they would generously give it. Neither women nor men are as dumb as Tannen wants us to believe: 'Many men honestly do not know what women want, and women honestly do not know why men find what they want so hard to comprehend and deliver' (p. 81). Many men, however, must appreciate Tannen's analysis – they do not have to find out what women want and, above all, they do not have to change. My thesis is that men understand quite well what women want but they give only when it suits them. In many situations they refuse to give and *women cannot make them give*.

To claim, as Tannen does, that women want comfort and do not want advice or solution of problems, and that men can give only the latter but not the former, is simply ridiculous. Women also want advice and solutions to problems and men also want empathy. What is wrong is that most of the time men are getting both from women, and women often (as in the case of Tannen's Eve) get neither.

Conversations between women and men are not as superficial as suggested by this book, and they do not fail because of miscommunication. Dialogues also do not stop where they do in this book; often women and men do go on to inquire what went wrong. They both know that they are not just expressing their caring, loving, selfless thoughts in two different ways, but that they are doing essentially different things: women care for, and support, men; empathize with them, comfort them, and especially work for men in conversations and relationships, at home and at work; men take women's energy and work, and use it for themselves (what Tannen calls their love of independence and autonomy), and return when and what and if they feel like returning. The majority of relationships between women and men in our society are fundamentally asymmetrical to the advantage of men. If they were not, we would not need a women's liberation movement, women's commissions, houses for battered women, legislation for equal opportunity, antidiscrimination laws, family therapy, couple therapy, divorce. We would not even need Tannen's book.

To pursue the subjects of Tannen's book a bit further – just like Eve, other women in her examples have to submit to male domination: The woman who came out of the hospital early and 'had to move around more' (p. 50) (obviously because her husband was not doing for her what strange nurses did for her in the hospital), was told by her husband: 'Why didn't you stay in the hospital where you would have been more comfortable?' (p. 50). A perfectly reasonable answer 'to her complaint about the pain she was suffering' from the person closest to her? Tannen herself surely would have taken such a response in her stride, understanding her husband's suggestion just as it was intended. Or the woman who, when she braked, extended her right arm to protect the man beside her from falling forward (p. 35), an automatic gesture which infuriated this man, who thought she should keep both hands on the wheel. This woman ends up 'training herself to resist this impulse with Maurice to avoid a fight, but *she felt sadly constrained* by what she saw as his irrational reaction' (p. 50, my emphasis). Or the woman who had asked her husband 'Would you like to stop for a drink?', and he said 'no', whereupon they did not stop (p. 15). Now, apart from the fact that even a very dense man can infer the indirect meaning of a request from this question, it is again interesting to see who did what he wanted to do, and who accommodated to his wishes and did not do what she wanted to do.

Although women are submitting, annoyed, hurt and losing out in one example after the other, and men are getting their needs fulfilled, Tannen ends up rescuing the men. She explains them to us so we can perceive them as they should be perceived: in their puzzlement, confusion, frustration, while they all get their way.

However, at one point Tannen's explanation stops: men don't talk to their heterosexual partners, Tannen claims, but she does not tell us why. She fails to explain why men who talk all day long, whose business is talk, including talk of a high degree of indirectness, in politics, law, advertising, sales, journalism, on school boards, in academia, cannot say two sentences to their wives at home. Take the man who cannot answer his wife's question 'What's new with X?' and says 'Nothing' (p. 80). Do you think if his boss asked him the same question about the same X, he would say 'nothing'? And if he did indeed, and his boss reacted in anger, would he not know why? As a native speaker he knows that his answer means not only there is nothing new about X but also that it has an indirect message of 'I don't care to talk with you now', and is a refusal to enter into further conversation. But how is it that a man, when talking to his female boss, knows more about indirect meaning and indirect speech acts than when he talks with his wife? Because he can afford to. He *has to* supply information to his boss, but at home *his wife has to* work at drawing information out of him and he gives it only when he is good and ready.

So let us now look at the men in Tannen's book. So far, we have learned that although they are emotionally retarded and impoverished, morose and taciturn – Tannen calls it 'hampered by their style' (p. 146) – they always have the best of intentions. To be sure, they are being sold for stupid as far as their proficiency in their native language is concerned, but that does not matter since they can maintain their privileges. Take the man who is moving out of the house and wants to tell his 12-year-old son (pp. 146–7). He ends up talking about wars and politics instead of the new situation and his feelings, not to mention his son's feelings and fears. Tannen considers him handicapped by his style. Did he get his need to lecture fulfilled, did the boy get his needs fulfilled? Should we accept that men are total emotional illiterates even when it comes to their children? Should we accept that they do not have to be knowledgeable about emotions, not even their own? That it is just their style which makes them know more about wars than about their relationships with the most important people in their lives? And so they can lecture forth about wars and weapons, and Japan and Russia, but not say one empathic comforting word to their children or their wives when they are in distress.

Is it a matter of style that men in this country spend three minutes a day talking to their small children?

Has anyone found out how much time they spend talking to their wives?

Should we really believe what Tannen tells us about men not talking at home, namely 'many men are deeply frustrated by feeling they have disappointed their partners, without understanding how they failed or how else they could have behaved' (p. 82).

If men were that frustrated, they would change, and talk to their wives. If women could make them talk, they would, but women accommodate because that is all they can do. Those who do not accommodate get to feel the consequences. Women even accommodate where it is not necessary because of their family, job, or economic situation, i.e. they allow themselves to be dominated even when they could walk out of a doctor's office or tell a man to shut up, without negative consequences.

A beautiful case in point is the author (Tannen) herself who, after giving a talk in a bookstore for an audience of mainly women, found that 'the discussion was being conducted by men in the audience. At one point', to follow her insightful description, 'a man sitting in the middle was talking at such great length that several women in the front rows began shifting in their seats and rolling their eyes at me. Ironically, what he was going on about was how frustrated he feels when he has to listen to women going on and on about topics he finds boring and unimportant' (p. 76). Again, the story ends here. There is no comment on the fact that a man dominated all the women in the audience, including the speaker; no comment on her letting the man 'conduct the discussion' at the expense of the women present. These poor women learned the lesson over that they already know: who talks and who listens, who feels disappointed and frustrated, and who feels satisfied. Only this time they learned it from the expert, by her shining example.

If you leave out power, you do not understand any talk, be it the discussion after your speech, the conversation at your own dinner-table, in a doctor's office, in the back yards of West Philadelphia, in an Italian village, on a street in Turkey, in a courtroom or in a day-care center, in a women's group or at a UN conference. It is like saying Black English and Oxford English are just two different varieties of English, each valid on its own; it just so happens that the speakers of one variety find themselves in high-paying positions with a lot of prestige and power of decision-making, and the others are found more in low-paying jobs, or on the streets and in prisons. They don't always understand each other, but they both have the best intentions; if they could only learn a bit from each other and understand their differences as a matter of style, all would be well.

I prefer an analysis that has more descriptive and explanatory adequacy – and also more passion, an analysis like that of Henley/Kramarae (1991: 20) that takes into consideration that 'Hierarchies determine whose version of the communication situation will prevail; whose speech style will be seen as normal; who will be required to learn the communication style, and interpret the meaning, of the other; whose language style will be seen as deviant, irrational, and inferior; and who will be required to imitate the other's style in order to fit into the society' (p. 20); or that views US culture as 'requiring (and teaching through popular magazines) females, not males, to learn to read the silence, lack of emotional expression, or brutality of the other sex as not only other than, but more benign than, it appears' (p. 23). Tannen's book is such a product of US culture, quite comparable to popular magazines and teaching just that.

In my own research (Troemel-Ploetz, 1981, 1982) I have shown that the gender hierarchy is stronger than the hierarchy created by social status. Thus even when women have a high social status, i.e. when they have experience and expertise, age and high professional position, younger or less-qualified men often succeed in constructing a higher conversational status for themselves.

Tannen supplies us with several examples where her expertise is questioned by men who contradict, doubt or challenge her, but she seems to have no problem with these male attempts to construct a higher status for themselves. She takes such challenges as an invitation to show her expertise (p. 145), and presumably submits, just like she let herself and her women audience be dominated by a few men. Professional women, women in politics, the women doctors of West (1984), the judges and attorneys in reports on *Women in the Courts* (1984 to present), usually arrive at different interpretations in similar situations. They know that they are questioned more because they are women, and they are challenged in ways men would not be. They would laugh at Tannen's naïve suggestion that a man's challenge is 'a sign of respect and equal treatment' (pp. 128–9), or that they are 'misinterpreting challenges as personal attacks on their credibility' (p. 129). But significantly, professional women, working women, intellectual women hardly occur in Tannen's book. The women she describes do not even read the paper (pp. 80–2). The women she describes do not talk about politics or professional matters, but about 'who was at the bus stop, who called, what they said, how they made them feel' (p. 80). Her women are the adjusting, begging, nagging, wailing women, who regularly eat the chicken back (p. 184), and keep complying, but who are, in spite of all their efforts, just not understood.

But take a woman judge who can insist on being understood in the courtroom. She still must construct her professional competence against male attempts to deconstruct it. Kathryn Stechert describes in *Sweet Success* (1986: 185) the efforts of a female justice of the peace to demonstrate power so she can use it. The judge does this by 'maintaining a sense of awe' in the courtroom, by a stern facial expression, by raising her voice at times, by being very cold. The judge says: 'I think of it as acting and it does have an effect on people'. Stechert concludes: 'with other accoutrements of power, the black robe, the gavel, and court room bench, that place her higher than the lawyers and litigants who come before her, she retains the power that goes with her position' (p. 185).

Or take a woman attorney, who depends on making herself understood and is competent to do so. In one of the reports of *Women in the Courts*, an attorney stated that when she came up to the bar in a child custody suit, the male judge asked her: 'Are you the child?' I wonder if Tannen would analyze this insult as the male judge's 'different habitual style' or as his 'creating an imbalance'. Telling the woman attorney that 'the real problem is conversational style', 'women and men have different ways of talking', 'men are handicapped by their style', or 'hurtful and unjustified misinterpretations can be avoided by understanding the conversational styles of the other gender' (p. 95) would not be very helpful in this situation.

Fortunately, some American lawyers believe more in the power of words than the linguist Deborah Tannen does. They would throw out immediately Tannen's wishy-washy explication: 'The culprit then is not an individual man or even men's styles alone, but the difference between women's and men's styles. If that is the case, then both can make adjustments' (p. 95). They would point out to Tannen that men do not voluntarily make adjustments and women should not have to. Feminist lawyers actually did something about the 'different ways of talking' men use in the courtroom and they *made* men change *their* way of talking. They found that it was quite systematic talk used by men, to and about women, to violate women's credibility and professionalism. They defined such talk as sexist, and have shown that sexist bias against women is damaging to women on all levels in the court system, as accused and as witnesses, as jurors and court personnel, as lawyers and secretaries and judges; it does not make for justice.

Whereas Tannen tries to explain away male insensitivity, many sensitive men have been taking a stand during the last ten years, looking critically at themselves and their colleagues. They have supported feminist lawyers, instituted task forces in one US state after the other to identify discriminatory verbal behavior in the courts; they have worked for change. Ironically, Tannen's understanding of the social and political function of language falls below what sensitive and reasonable men in high positions know, without being linguists. To quote one of them, Robert N. Wilentz, Chief Justice of New Jersey:

> There's no room for gender bias in our system . . . there's no room for the funny joke
> and the not-so-funny joke, there's no room for conscious, inadvertent, sophisticated,
> clumsy, or any other kind of gender bias, and certainly no room for gender bias that
> affects substantive rights.
>   There's no room because it hurts and it insults. It hurts female lawyers psycholo-
> gically and economically, litigants psychologically and economically, and witnesses,
> jurors, law clerks and judges who are women. It will not be tolerated in any form
> whatsoever. (The First Year Report of the New Jersey Supreme Court Task Force on
> *Women in the Courts*, June 1984)

I do not think this man will change his politics to a watered-down stance about
men's different style of communication. I hope other self-critical and fair men will
also refuse Tannen's thesis, recognizing it for what it aims at: the cementation of
patriarchy.

Knowledge gained about discourse in the courtroom or in medical practice can
easily be extended to private conversations, for what is going on in this arena is, after
all, not that different. The repertoire of speech acts is quite the same; the construction of dominance and superiority is quite similar. The difference is that private talk
among lovers or wife and husband *could* be symmetrical. Hierarchy in private relationships is not as formalized as in the court system. Private talk has a chance
courtroom interaction, unless there is an enlightened judge, does not have. (How
could the attorney who was called a child demand and construct symmetry?)

This is why Tannen's book is so depressing. In one example after the other she is
trying to make the man's responses understandable, to explain his ignorance, his dis-
interest, selfishness or rudeness. She is telling women who have gained insight into
the power politics of talk that men and women do not understand each other (without
her explanation). She completely misses the point that conversations are constructed,
that people don't 'fall into differences of their interactional habits' (p. 125) or 'find
themselves arrayed in an asymmetrical alignment' (p. 125), but that we produce equality or inequality, symmetry or asymmetry in every conversation, only it is usually the
more powerful who have the choice to give up some of their privileges and rights,
and the less powerful who cannot just demand equality or symmetry and get it.

To tell professional women, who have worked for two decades in rape crisis
centers, with domestic violence, in universities and state women's commissions with
sexual harassment, defining it on a scale from verbal utterance to date rape or
acquaintance rape, to tell women lawyers and doctors who have worked with sexual
abuse of girls and baby girls at home by fathers and male relatives, that 'the real
problem is conversational style' (p. 79) or 'misunderstandings arise because the
styles are different' (p. 47), or 'that men have a different way of showing they care'
(p. 298), is more than absurd. These women know that underlying the conversational politics and the body politics is the power politics of female–male relationships
where men have social control of women and, if need be, recourse to violence. There
are many other manifestations of the power relationship between the sexes, e.g. an
analysis of women's and men's economics shows men earn 90 percent of the world
income, own 99 percent of the world property, while doing only one-third of the

world's work (UN Report of 1980 – with the growing poverty of women also in the USA, these figures have probably changed for the worse in the last decade).

I hope Tannen's readers will see through her 'explanations', will not be kept at the naïve level of ignorance the author assigns them to. The chances are good, because many of the women readers are giving the book to their husbands to read (p. 85). A follow-up study showing that all husbands now put down their paper at breakfast and talk, talk, talk empathically will (against all of Tannen's predictions) not be forthcoming.

I hope Tannen's readers will not stay in their place. I hope they will see through the patterns of domination in their exchanges with men. I hope they will see that *their* understanding the masculine style does not help them (p. 123) and that nothing changes if men just *understand* female style without valuing it as more humane and changing their style to become more empathic and caring. I hope they test Tannen's claim of the good intentions in males and insist on symmetry – if they are listening supportively to a man's problem, they should get the same, if they are freely giving information, they should get it just as freely, if they are open, their partner should also open up. I hope they know that the 'hope for the future' (p. 148) does not lie in *their* changing their style, but in men being less dominant, and learning from women.

This book trivializes our experience of injustice and of conversational dominance; it disguises power differences; it conceals who has to adjust; it veils differences again and again and equalizes with a leveling mania any distinction in how we experience women and men.

REFERENCES

Allen, Sheila and Barker, Diana Leonard, eds (1976) *Dependence and Exploration in Work and Marriage*. London: Longman.

Austin, John L. (1962) *How to Do Things with Words*. Oxford: Clarendon.

Coupland, Nikolas, Giles, Howard and Wiemann, John M., eds (1991) *'MisCommunication' and Problematic Talk*. Newbury Park, CA: Sage.

Fisher, Sue (1984) 'Was Ärzte sagen – was Patientinnen sagen: Die Mikropolitik des Entscheidungsprozesses im medizinischen Gespräch', in Senta Troemel-Ploetz (1984).

Fisher, Sue (1986) *In the Patient's Best Interest*. New Brunswick, NJ: Rutgers University Press.

Fisher, Sue and Todd, Alexandra, eds (1983) *The Social Organization of Doctor–Patient Communication*. Washington, DC: The Center for Applied Linguistics.

Fisher, Sue and Todd, Alexandra, eds (1986) *Discourse and Institutional Authority: Medicine, Education, Law*. Norwood, NJ: Ablex Publishing Corporation.

Harding, Susan (1975) 'Women and Words in a Spanish Village', in Rayna R. Reiter (1975).

Henley, Nancy M. and Kramarae, Cheris (1991) 'Gender, Power and Miscommunication!', in Nikolas Coupland et al. (1991).

Jenkins, Lee (1981) 'The Development and Structure of Stories in a Women's Rap Group', Paper presented at Speech Communication Association, Anaheim, CA.

Jenkins, Lee (1982) 'Stories Women Tell: An Ethnographic Study of Personal Experience Narratives in a Women's Rap Group', Paper given at the 10th World Congress of Sociology, Mexico City, Mexico.

Reiter, Rayna R., ed. (1975) *Toward an Anthropology of Women*. New York: Monthly Review Press.

Todd, Alexandra (1984) ' "Die Patientin hat nichts zu sagen": Kommunikation zwischen Frauenärzten und Patientinnen', in Senta Troemel-Ploetz (1984).

Todd, Alexandra (1989) *Intimate Adversaries: Cultural Conflict between Doctors and Women Patients*. Philadelphia: University of Pennsylvania Press.

Troemel-Ploetz, Senta (1981) ' "Sind Sie angemessen zu Wort gekommen?": Zur Konstruktion von Status in Gesprächen', Paper presented at the 3rd Annual Conference of the German Society for Linguistics, University of Regensburg, March 1981. Published in Senta Troemel-Ploetz (1982).

Troemel-Ploetz, Senta (1982) *Frauensprache: Sprache der Veränderung*. Frankfurt: Fischer Taschenbuch Verlag.

Troemel-Ploetz, Senta (1982) 'The Construction of Conversational Differences in the Language of Women and Men', Paper presented at the 10th World Congress of Sociology, Mexico City, August 1982. Published in Senta Troemel-Ploetz (1984).

Troemel-Ploetz, Senta, ed. (1984) *Gewalt durch Sprache: Die Vergewaltigung von Frauen in Gesprächen*. Frankfurt: Fischer Taschenbuch Verlag.

West, Candace (1984) *Routine Complications: Troubles with Talk between Doctors and Patients*. Bloomington: Indiana University Press.

Whitehead, Ann (1976) 'Sexual Antagonism in Herefordshire', in Sheila Allen and Diana Leonard Barker (1976).

Women in the Courts:

The First Year Report of the New Jersey Supreme Court Task Force on *Women in the Courts*, June 1984.

The Second Report of the New Jersey Supreme Court Task Force on *Women in the Courts*, June 1986.

Report of the New York Task Force on *Women in the Courts*, March 1986. Published in *Fordham Urban Law Journal* XV (1), 1986–8: 11–198.

See also:

Lynn Hecht Schafran (1987) 'Documenting Gender Bias in the Courts: The Task Force Approach', *Judicature* 70 (5), February–March: 280–90.

Gail Diane Cox (1990) 'Reports Track Discrimination: Fourteen Volumes Chronicle How Women Are Treated in Court', *The National Law Journal* no. 12, 26 November.

Part VIII

Looking to the Future

This last section consists of three papers, each of which should provoke you into reconsidering the ways you think about language and gender. But these three papers are positioned very differently in relation to current knowledge. The first takes a relatively accepting view of existing research and of existing theoretical frameworks. The second paper is more critical, arguing that researchers in the language and gender field have taken refuge in abstractions and need to look more carefully at the ways in which gender is daily constructed. The last paper queries the value of the term 'gender' altogether, and so is explicitly critical of earlier research.

The first of these papers is Janet Holmes's 'Women's Talk: The Question of Sociolinguistic Universals'. Holmes draws attention to the fact that some of the linguistic features associated with women's talk seem to be shared by women in very different speech communities. She claims that some of the generalizations which can be made from published research findings could be regarded as potential sociolinguistic universals. Her paper provides a very useful summary of research in the language and gender area to date, dividing it up in terms of four dimensions of analysis: function, solidarity, power, status. She clarifies the areas where research evidence is thin or missing, and in this way points to likely directions for future research.

By contrast, the second paper, Penelope Eckert and Sally McConnell-Ginet's 'Communities of Practice', urges researchers to *avoid* generalizing, to *avoid* abstractions. Eckert and McConnell-Ginet's slogan is 'Think practically and look locally'. In particular, they urge researchers to work in terms of *communities of practice*, a concept which they adopt to assert the dynamism of living communities, and to underscore the fact that who we are is not constructed in a vacuum, but in the many communities of practice each of us belongs to. Gender, one aspect of who we are, is not a given, but is constantly created and recreated in social interaction with others in these communities of practice. Moreover, gender is complex: there are many different ways of being a woman or a man.

The complexity of gender is the starting point of the final paper of the section, Janet Bing and Victoria Bergvall's 'The Question of Questions: Beyond Binary

Thinking'. In this paper, Bing and Bergvall query the simplistic binary model of gender that most research in this area tacitly draws on. Gender has been used as a non-linguistic variable in sociolinguistic studies as if the division into two sub-categories – women and men, feminine and masculine – were unproblematic. They argue that language and gender research should ask questions which challenge rather than reinforce gender polarization, and which move away from binary thinking to an acceptance of diversity.

Since the late 1980s, sociolinguists have begun to come to terms with 'the complex system of intersecting social relations that supports linguistic variation' (Cameron and Coates 1989: 24). The field of sociolinguistic research focusing on language and gender has become increasingly popular, and researchers are now starting to ask more sophisticated questions about language and about gender. These three papers show us some of the directions future research might take.

REFERENCE

Cameron, Deborah and Coates, Jennifer (1989) 'Some problems in the sociolinguistic explanation of sex differences', pp. 13–26 in J. Coates and D. Cameron (eds) *Women in Their Speech Communities*. London: Longman.

RECOMMENDED FURTHER READING

The following volumes are all very recent collections of work in the field.

Bergvall, Victoria, Bing, Janet and Freed, Alice (eds) (1996) *Rethinking Language and Gender Research: Theory and Practice*. London: Longman.

Bucholtz, Mary, Liang, Anita, Sutton, Laurel and Hines, Caitlin (eds) (1994) *Cultural Performances. Proceedings of the Third Berkeley Women and Language Conference, 1994*. Berkeley, CA: BWLG cooperative.

Hall, Kira and Bucholtz, Mary (eds) (1995) *Gender Articulated. Language and the Socially Constructed Self*. London: Routledge.

Johnson, Sally and Meinhof, Ulrike Hanna (eds) (1997) *Language and Masculinity*. Oxford: Blackwell.

Livia, Anna and Hall, Kira (eds) (1997) *Queerly Phrased*. New York: Oxford University Press.

Mills, Sara (ed.) (1995) *Language and Gender: Interdisciplinary Perspectives*. London: Longman.

30

Women's Talk: The Question of Sociolinguistic Universals

Janet Holmes

There are many myths and stereotypes about women's talk, some longstanding and well-established, some more recent. One widely held stereotype is that women talk too much and they won't let you get a word in edgeways. Proverbs from a range of different communities attest to the extensiveness of this view of women.

> *Women's tongues are like lambs' tails – they are never still* [English proverb].
> *Foxes are all tail, and women are all tongue* [English proverb].
> *The North Sea will sooner be found wanting in water than a woman at a loss for words*
>   [Jutland proverb].
> *Nothing is so unnatural as a talkative man or a quiet woman* [Scottish proverb].
> *The tongue is the sword of a woman and she never lets it become rusty* [Chinese proverb].
> *A woman's tongue is the last thing about her that dies* (Jespersen, 1922, p. 253; Kramarae,
>   1982, p. 87; Coates, 1993, p. 16).

Another widely held view is that women don't know their own minds; they hedge and qualify everything they say. Lakoff, an American linguist, comments:

> it is among the mysogynistic stereotypes in our culture that women cannot follow the rules of conversation: that a woman's discourse is necessarily indirect, repetitious, meandering, unclear, exaggerated – the antithesis of every one of Grice's principles – while of course a man's speech is clear, direct, precise and to the point. (1975, p. 73)

There are related claims that women never say what they mean; they are indirect and devious. The list could go on and on.

Some of these stereotypes are very widespread and can be found in many cultures. What of the reality? Are there generalisations about the way women speak that apply to all societies? Are there features of women's talk which can be found in all speech communities? Is it possible to formulate sociolinguistic universals or at least identify universal tendencies relating to women's talk? There is abundant, widely accepted evidence of developmental differences between women and men in the area of language (for example, Maccoby & Jacklin, 1974). It is also widely accepted that women and men use language differently (for example, Thorne, Kramarae, & Henley, 1983; Cameron, 1992; Coates, 1993). One could formulate this least contentious sociolinguistic universal as follows:

*Women and men develop different patterns of language use.

But do the same kinds of differences turn up in culturally contrasting communities? How far can claims about specific features of women's language be regarded as sociolinguistic universals?

I should state at the outset that this paper is largely exploratory. I simply want to propose some possible contenders for the status of sociolinguistic universal tendencies in the area of language and gender, and explore some of the evidence for and against them. I hope that the discussion may stimulate other researchers to test out my suggestions against data they are familiar with.

As a framework for the discussion, I will use four dimensions of analysis that have proved very useful in a range of research settings, and which are sociolinguistic universals in that they can be used to analyse language in use in any speech community (see Holmes, 1992).

Function: what is the purpose of the talk?
Solidarity: how well do the participants relate to each other?
Power: who's in charge?
Status: how does speech indicate social status?

Function

Example 1
Context: Two colleagues passing each other at work
PAT: Hi Chris. How's things?
CHRIS: Hi! How are you? Great day eh!

Example 2
Here is the forecast for the Wellington district until midnight Tuesday issued by the meteorological service at 6 o'clock on Monday evening. It will be rather cloudy overnight with some drizzle, becoming fine again on Tuesday morning. The outlook for Wednesday – a few morning showers then fine.

One fundamental distinction which can be made in analysing the function of talk is the distinction between *affective* or interpersonal meaning and *referential* or informative meaning. Example 1 provides a clear instance of talk which is primarily affective, while example 2 is referential talk: its main purpose is to convey information.

In Western speech communities, there is some evidence that women tend to be more oriented to affective meaning when they are talking to others, while men tend to focus more readily on the referential meaning of the talk. When someone speaks, women tend to be sensitive to what their talk tells about how they are feeling, as well as the information being conveyed, while men tend to focus on the information and give only secondary attention to the affective function of the talk. The generalisation can be formulated as follows:

Women tend to focus on the affective functions of an interaction more often than men do.

I observed a recent example of this when a couple I know, Helen and John, were talking to a friend, Harry, who is a school principal. He was describing the problems that schools face in adjusting to the new competitive environment and describing the increase in stress this involved for teachers. In the course of the conversation he mentioned in passing some severe physical symptoms of stress that he had been experiencing. At this point Helen's attention was entirely directed to concern for his physical health, and as soon as there was an opportunity she asked, 'but are you OK now? have you seen a doctor?'. John's almost simultaneous comment continued the philosophical discussion about education policy: 'but this is a clear example of intensification of work and it's always the effect of pressure for increased efficiencies'. Harry's response to Helen's concern for his health was very brief and even a little impatient, suggesting her question was irrelevant, and this was reinforced as he picked up the discussion with John. When I questioned them later, both men remembered the incident and both argued that Helen's concern for Harry was inappropriate and distracting at that point in the discussion, even though they were all close friends.

Example 3

Context: Motor camp. Man is fiddling with car radio. Woman is passing by with washing.
WOMAN: You've got a radio there then
MAN: Yes (pause) I'm trying to get the weather
WOMAN: I've been trying on mine but I can't get a thing
MAN: mm
WOMAN: We really need to know before we leave (pause) we're on bikes you see
MAN: mm
WOMAN: I've got a handicapped kiddie too (pause) we're from
Hamilton and we're cycling to Taupo (pause) where are you going then?
MAN: Taupo

After this conversation, the man reported he thought the woman was genuinely interested in hearing the weather forecast, whereas I, who had overheard it from inside our tent, was confident that she had been just wanting to make social contact and have a chat.

This difference in orientation can lead to misunderstandings between partners. Often the woman wants to share how she is feeling about a problem and she is looking for a sympathetic response, but the man seems unaware of this and focusses on the facts or looks for ways of solving the problem. Here is a conversation which took place between Ann and her husband Bob after dinner one evening.

Example 4
Context: Husband and wife at dinner table
ANN: That meeting I had to go to today was just awful.
BOB: Where was it?
ANN: In the NLC building. People were just so aggressive.
BOB: Mm. Who was there?
ANN: Oh the usual representatives of all the government departments. I felt really put down at one point, you know, just so humiliated.
BOB: You should be more assertive dear. Don't let people trample all over you and ignore what you say.

This looks like a pleasant and polite interchange – and in some respects it was. The woman, however, felt at the end of it that she hadn't really been heard, and that her husband had missed her main message. He had undoubtedly been responsive – asking about where, and who, and proffering advice to help resolve her problem. But she had been conveying an affective message, rather than simply exchanging information; her point was to share how she had felt at the meeting with the aim of eliciting sympathy and understanding from her spouse. He, on the other hand, scanned her communication for information and facts, and elicited more to fill out his picture of her experience.

This tendency for male communication to focus on content or information, while females are more often orientated to feelings, seems to be remarkably widespread. The pattern illustrated by this example is certainly familiar to many English-speaking women in Western societies, as attested by the success of Tannen's (1990a) book *You Just Don't Understand*, which provides many more examples of such 'miscommunications' between women and men.

But is it a potential sociolinguistic universal, or at least a universal tendency? Does the pattern occur in all cultures? Are men in non-Western cultures more concerned than women with facts, information, and solving problems? Do women in other cultures focus more often than men on the affective content of an interaction? It is difficult to know since we have only just begun to explore these patterns in Western societies. There is evidence, for instance, that men tend to talk about things and activities, while women focus more on relationships and feelings (Aries, 1976; Aries & Johnson, 1983; Haas & Sherman, 1982; Tannen, 1990a, 1990b; Wodak, 1981). There is evidence that women pay more compliments than men, especially to other women (Holmes, 1988a; Herbert, 1990), and women tend to apologise more often than men (Holmes, 1989). All this supports the suggestion that women pay more attention than men to the feelings of their addressees (their 'face needs' in Goffman's [1967] terms). But there is little evidence on the extent to which these patterns generalise to other cultures. This is an obvious area for further research.

Solidarity

Focussing on the feelings of the person they are talking to is one way in which women express solidarity (or positive politeness) in their interactions, especially in informal and intimate contexts. Example 5 illustrates some of the strategies women use to achieve this.

Example 5
Context: Two friends talking over a coffee at Max's place
MAX: I got a phone call from Pat's mother saying you/c- you're a complete bastard Pat's told us what you did to her//you're so inconsiderate/   especially when she's
NELL: oh dear
MAX: been under such stress//well what was I supposed to say /what did they want
NELL: mm/tricky/did [you ask her   ]
MAX: [I didn't know] what to say/I mean I have no idea what story Pat had told them//   she's got a
NELL: mm
MAX: vivid imagination when she gets started who knows w-/who knows what fabrication they had been treated to
NELL: well she was pretty stressed out/maybe they were just over-reacting from worry [about her d'you think]
MAX: [not them not them   ] they just hate my guts//any excuse to abuse me/I'm not good enough for their daughter
[The words within the square brackets were uttered simultaneously.]

This is intimate talk. Max is letting off steam to Nell who is listening sympathetically. It appears to be a good example of a male expressing affective meaning and using talk to establish solidarity. Note, however, that Max expresses frustration because he does not see the point of Pat's mother's call. What was her message? What did she expect him to do? What, in other words, was the referential meaning of the interaction? Nell's encouraging responses (*oh dear, mm*) are neatly placed to be non-disruptive. Her questions seem designed to encourage Max's train of thought. She is focussing on Max's feelings and expressing solidarity towards him in his distress. Though short, this interchange proves remarkably typical of patterns of interaction between women and men in informal and intimate contexts.

There is extensive evidence, for instance, that women provide more encouraging supportive feedback or positive minimal responses (for example, *mm, mhm, uh-huh, yeah*) than men in informal interaction. This has been demonstrated in conversations between couples (Fishman, 1980, 1983), in management discussion groups (Schick-Case, 1988), in political debates (Edelsky & Adams, 1990), as well as in interactions between women and men in laboratory or studio conditions (Hirschman, 1974; Leet-Pellegrini, 1980; Preisler, 1986). All these studies support a view of women as cooperative and facilitative conversationalists, concerned for their partner's positive face needs. Women value solidarity and their linguistic behaviour reflects this.

Another way in which concern for the addressee can be expressed is by the use of facilitative devices which invite the addressee to contribute to the conversation. In the 1970s, Lakoff identified a number of linguistic features including tag questions like *isn't it*, *didn't she*, and phrases such as *you know*, and *sort of*, which she labelled 'hedges'. She suggested these forms were used more by women than by men, and that they give the impression that the speaker does not know her own mind. She regarded them as signals of uncertainty and tentativeness. A number of researchers subsequently confirmed that, at least in some contexts, women did indeed use more of the forms that Lakoff had identified as characterising 'women's language' (for example, Crosby & Nyquist, 1977; McMillan et al., 1977; Baumann, 1979; Hartman, 1979; Preisler, 1986; Coates, 1989, reprinted in this volume, p. 226).

I was interested in these claims and I began to examine these so-called 'hedges' more carefully. In every case they turned out to be much more complicated in meaning than the label 'hedge' suggests. I therefore prefer the term 'pragmatic particle'. It is not so loaded with value judgments. Take tag questions as an example. It is true, as Lakoff suggests, that a tag may express uncertainty, as example 6 illustrates.

Example 6
Context: Husband and wife at dinner table
                                        /
JOHN: Fay Weldon's lecture is at eight isn't it?
PAM: Yeah
JOHN: That's good/it was just that Max seemed to think it started at 7.30

The speaker is asking for confirmation of a fact he is uncertain about. Alternatively, however, a tag question can be used to invite participation in the conversation, as in (7).

Example 7
Context: Host to guest at a dinner party
                                /
you've got a new job, Tom, haven't you?

In this case, the speaker is not at all unsure of her facts. She is giving Tom an opportunity to join in the conversation. The tag acts as a facilitative device not as a signal of uncertainty. In (8), the tag is used for yet another function – to soften a critical comment.

Example 8
Context: Wife to husband viewing flood on kitchen floor
                                        \
well that wasn't the best bit of plumbing you've ever done was it?

These examples show that tags are complex in form (the intonation varies, for example), as well as in meaning. Analyses which treat them as monolithic linguistic forms expressing uncertainty clearly distort the reality of the interactions they examine.

Exactly the same point can be made for *you know, sort of,* and for the High Rising Terminal (HRT) which has been identified in the speech of New Zealanders (Britain, 1992), Australians (Guy & Vonwiller, 1984; Guy et al., 1986), and North Americans (Ching, 1982; Cruttenden, 1986; James et al., 1989; McLemore, 1991). These forms can be used to convey friendliness and informality as well as uncertainty. *You know,* for example, may signal the speaker's confidence that she shares the same attitudes and values as the people she is speaking to, as example 9 demonstrates.

Example 9
Context: Mother to daughter
well he was a good man/you know/always ready with a helping hand.

The mother is not expressing doubt. Rather she is referring to shared values, confident that her daughter understands the kind of characteristics she is alluding to. An HRT can similarly 'claim common ground' (Brown & Levinson, 1987, p. 103) as illustrated in this example taken from the data collected for the Wellington social dialect survey (↑ marks the HRT).

Example 10
Context: Maori male interviewee
Joe: I like the closeknitness of the en- of um/of the locals, you know? um i- it's a real
           secure sort of feeling/just knowing everybody, I think eh/and and the fact that
           i- you know your kids can pretty much walk around here and feel fairly safe. ↑

Joe uses three different devices here to signal he is assuming common ground with his addressee: *you know* at the end of the first clause, the invariant tag *eh* at the end of the second, and an HRT at the end of the third clause (Britain, 1992, p. 81). These three devices are all ways of reducing the distance between the speaker's and listener's point of view.

Examining data which was carefully matched in quantity and context revealed that women used these forms more often than men to express a facilitative meaning and friendliness. In fact it was the men, not the women as Lakoff had claimed, who were using tags more often to express uncertainty (Holmes, 1984). And the men used *you know* almost twice as often to express uncertainty, compared to expressing confidence and friendliness, while women use *you know* equally often for both functions (Holmes, 1986). The fact that women's tags are labelled as expressions of uncertainty indicates that it is male norms which predominate; women's talk is filtered and interpreted through male perceptions.

In other cultures, too, it seems that women use more of these softening forms than men (for example, Brown, 1980, reprinted in this volume, p. 81; Ide, 1982; Wetzel, 1988, reprinted in this volume, p. 388). Brown, for example, reports on the usage of these forms by Mayan Indian women. Overall, the women used more pragmatic particles than the men in this Mayan community. Similar observations have been made about Japanese women's speech (Ide, 1982; Wetzel, 1988; Smith, 1992). Mayan

Indian men speaking to men used fewest particles of all. They used a relatively direct and unmodified style.

Facilitative pragmatic devices are clear examples of devices which express solidarity in interaction. Supportive feedback and compliments are further obvious ways in which speakers express a positive orientation to their addressees. The evidence from a wide range of research – largely but not entirely based on Western societies – suggests, then, that women tend to use linguistic devices such as these, which focus on the feelings of the addressee, and express solidarity and friendliness more often than men do. The generalisation may be formulated in the following way.

> *Women tend to use linguistic devices that stress solidarity more often than men do.

There is evidence from a range of cultures suggesting that this generalisation may be a robust one. Mayan Indians (Brown, 1980, 1990), Javanese (Smith-Hefner, 1988), Japanese (Ide, 1982), Mendi women of the Papua New Guinea Highlands (Lederman, 1984), and Nepalese speakers of Maithili (Singh, 1989), to name but a few, appear to conform to this pattern. Nevertheless, the generalisation needs testing further, of course, not only in a variety of cultures but also in a range of contexts. Most of the evidence to date comes from relatively informal contexts. It would be interesting to examine more formal contexts such as meetings and formal interviews, since I suspect that the generalisation will hold in such contexts too.

By contrast, the interactive devices which men use more than women tend to express dominance or power and seem to be more oriented to the speaker's status in relation to the addressee than to expressing solidarity.

Power

There is a widespread belief that women tend to dominate the talking time, that they interrupt more often than men, and that men find it difficult to get a word in when women are talking. As illustrated at the beginning of this paper, this view tends to be expressed in many different cultures. How true is it?

Let's look again at example 5. Note that in this interaction, despite the widespread stereotype that women will not let men get a word in, it is Max who talks most. He not only talks more than Nell, he also interrupts her twice, and at one point he baldly contradicts her suggestion (*not them not them*). These are the kinds of linguistic devices which are often used by powerful communicators to keep control of an interaction. They are certainly not solidarity oriented, affiliative interaction strategies.

Interruption

The research evidence suggests that, once again, this example proves not atypical of interaction in Western societies. Despite the stereotype, there is evidence that it is

Table 1 Features of turn-taking (based on Zimmerman and West, 1975: 116)

	1st speaker	2nd speaker
Twenty same-sex pairs		
Overlaps	12	10
Interruptions	3	4
Eleven mixed-sex pairs		
Overlaps	9	0
Interruptions	14	2

much more common for men to interrupt women than for women to interrupt men. The most widely quoted study is undoubtedly that of Zimmerman & West (1975), which showed a very dramatic pattern, as table 1 demonstrates.

This is a contentious area, and there has been a great deal of debate over the appropriate methodology and the definition of terms like 'interruption'. It is clearly important, for instance, to distinguish a mistimed unintended overlap, or an over-enthusiastic supportive comment with no 'take-over-the-floor' intention (see, for example, Coates, 1989; Swann, 1989, reprinted in this volume, p. 185) from a deliberately disruptive interruption.

Overall, however, now that the dust seems to have settled a little on such issues, the balance of evidence from the methodologically sounder research tends to confirm the view that, where there are gender differences, men disruptively interrupt others more often than women do, and that, more specifically, men interrupt women more than women interrupt men (McMillan et al., 1977; Natale, Entin, & Jaffe, 1979; Octigan and Niederman, 1979; Eakins & Eakins, 1979; Leet-Pellegrini, 1980; Brooks, 1982; West & Zimmerman, 1983; Mulac et al., 1988; Schick-Case, 1988; cf. James & Clarke, 1992). And, interestingly, at least in Western speech communities, this pattern appears to hold regardless of status, since doctors (West, 1984, reprinted in this volume, p. 396) and managers (Woods, 1989) were much more likely to be interrupted if they were female than if they were male.

There is little doubt that a disruptive interruption is an effective control device and a way of asserting power in an interaction. An interruption denies the speaker the right to finish their turn. Children are interrupted by adults far more often than the reverse, for instance. A disruptive interruption is a dominance strategy and generally reflects the power relations in an interaction.

Amount of talk

In example 5, Max talked more than Nell, refuting the stereotype that women dominate talking time. How representative is the example? Interestingly, the evidence in this area reveals very different patterns according to the formality of the context. Let's look first at formal contexts. There is a substantial body of evidence that challenges

Table 2   Amount of talk by TV interviewers (Franken, 1983)

Total words Interviewer sex	1		2		3	
	No.	*%*	*No.*	*%*	*No.*	*%*
F1 (front-person)	243	17.4	181	11.6	244	24.3
F2	289	20.7	540	34.5	263	26.2
F3	865	61.9	843	53.9	497	49.5
TOTAL	1397	100	1564	100	1004	100

the claim and provides adequate justification for feminists' complaints about the in-accuracy of the negative stereotype of the garrulous woman encoded in the proverbs of many societies. Males dominate the talk in seminar contributions and committee meetings (Eakins & Eakins, 1979; Swacker, 1979; Edelsky, 1981; Holmes, 1988b; Bashiruddin, Edge, & Hughes-Pélégrin, 1990), in television debates (Edelsky & Adams, 1990; Troemel-Ploetz, 1992), and in classrooms at all levels (for example, Karp & Yoels, 1976; Safilios-Rothschild, 1979; Spender, 1980a, 1980b, 1982; Swann, 1989; Gass & Varonis, 1985).

An example from New Zealand illustrates not only this pattern, but also women's sensitivity to the appropriate amount of talk for a particular context. Franken (1983) examines the distribution of talk in three television interviews. The interviewee in each case was a well-known male, and in each program there were three interviewers: the front-person, who was a woman, and two invited guests – different people in each interview – one male and one female. It was reasonable to expect that the males being interviewed should dominate the talking time available, as indeed they did. In an interview the interviewee has the responsibility to do most of the talking. Any-thing else would have been anomalous. One must take account of the context and people's social roles when considering who talks most.

The role of the interviewers, however, was quite different. Their job was to elicit talk, to encourage the interviewee to contribute in an interesting way. There was no reason why any one of them should have talked more than any other, though perhaps the front-person, as the person responsible for the program, might legitimately have been expected to contribute more than her two guest assistants. The distribution of talk, however, revealed a very different pattern, as can be seen in table 2. In a situation where each of the interviewers was entitled to a third, at most, of the talking time, the males in each of the three television programs in fact appropriated at least half. In this formal context, then, the men unfairly dominated the talking time. Public talk is highly valued and generally attracts positive attention. It seems possible that men tend to dominate the talk when this offers potential advantages, such as status enhancement.

This suggestion is further supported by our experience of social dialect interview-ing for the Wellington Social Dialect Survey (Holmes, Bell, & Boyce, 1991). As far as we were concerned, the more talk the better. But, in these private, informal interviews, the men, and especially the young Pakeha men, were generally much less talkative than the women. They answered every question as briefly as possible, and in many cases monosyllabically. This despite the fact that they were being interviewed by a young man of similar age and background – a point that we had thought would help people feel comfortable. (Interviewers were matched in ethnicity and gender with the people they were to interview.) Example 11 was typical for this group.

Example 11

Context: I, the interviewer, talking to Trevor, a young Pakeha man.
I: how long you lived here?
T: about a year and a half
I: what was it like/has it changed since you've been here?
T: nah
I: what are the people like// are they friendly?
T: oh some of them
I: um you remember the story reading about the passage in the boat and that um?
T: yeah
I: um somebody getting into danger and that you ever exp- + put yourself in a position where you thought you might c- + not come out of it alive//kill yourself or anything//
T: nah
I: um/have you had any really bad accidents?/
T: nah

One might even suggest that this constitutes sociolinguistic incompetence – a suggestion I will return to below. By contrast, most of the women were willing to talk at length (as were older men). None produced anything like the kind of monosyllabic responses illustrated above, and some checked out regularly with their interviewer whether they were providing a satisfactory response.

Example 12

Context: Female interviewee to interviewer
Jo: Is this the sort of thing you want like/I'm just rabbiting on here/are you sure this is what you want?

It seems that men are prepared to talk when there is some obvious advantage to them in terms of achieving a goal, controlling the situation, or status enhancement, but they are not so talkative in other contexts. This interpretation is further supported by research which looks at interactions between couples in private. A number of American studies suggest men are much less forthcoming in intimate contexts (for example, Soskin & John, 1963; Fishman, 1978, 1983; DeFrancisco, 1991, reprinted in this volume, p. 176). When they were alone with their wives, the men in these studies contributed much less talk than the women. The women, on the other hand, worked hard to get a conversation going and keep it going; the women did the lion's share of keeping the conversation alive (Fishman, 1983; Soskin & John, 1963). By contrast with their behaviour in more public settings, when the only audience was an intimate partner, men did not talk even as much as their partners would have liked.

The generalisation, then, may be that women and men contribute differently in different contexts because they have different communicative aims. The amount that each sex talks will differ according to what they perceive as the function of the talk. Men appear to regard public formal contexts as opportunities for display, but they seem to be more reticent in private interactions with another individual. Women tend to regulate their talk according to their perceptions of the needs of others. In other words, women tend to put more weight on behaviour which will maintain and increase solidarity, while men tend to focus on action-oriented or status-oriented behaviour.

Overall, then, what seems to be apparent from studies of the ways women and men interact is that women focus more often on the solidarity dimension, while men are more concerned with power and status. Women behave in ways that indicate concern for the feelings of their addressees and attention to the positive face needs of their addressees, while men tend to use linguistic strategies which reflect a greater concern with their own presentation of face. Women provide more encouraging feedback than men; they use facilitative pragmatic devices more than men; they pay compliments and apologise more often than men. Men, on the other hand, disruptively interrupt others more than women, and contribute talk to different situations in ways which will enhance their status or signal their power. The generalisation could be formulated in this way:

> *Women tend to interact in ways which will maintain and increase solidarity, while (especially in formal contexts) men tend to interact in ways which will maintain and increase their power and status.

Is this a plausible sociolinguistic universal? Does it need qualification according to different cultural as well as social contexts? It seems clear that generalisations about women's and men's talk need to be formulated as context sensitive rules. Many patterns which have been observed in women's and men's talk are valid only in certain types of context. The generalisations I have discussed, for instance, concerning the affective and referential functions of talk, apply much more often to personal interactions in informal private contexts than they do to public talk in formal contexts. It is rarely appropriate to focus on affective meaning in a formal ceremony or a news report. On the other hand, men tend to dominate the talking time in more formal contexts.

These are obvious areas for further research. Do these patterns apply in non-Western speech communities? Smith-Hefner (1988, p. 541) reports that the pattern of less talk in intimate family contexts can be observed in Java: 'Javanese men tend to speak less than women, especially within the family'. A review of a wide range of non-Western speech communities by Sherzer (1987) suggests that the pattern of men dominating the talk in status-enhancing contexts may be reasonably robust. Though he insists on the importance of looking at 'the diversity of voices' and the differences between superficially similar patterns (1987, p. 119), he nevertheless provides ample evidence that men tend to dominate the talk in public political contexts in a wide range of communities. (It is also interesting to note that he proposes a distinction between different styles of politeness [an oratorical allusive style vs a face-oriented style], which resolves the apparent contradiction between Keenan's [1974] Malagasy data on men's linguistic behaviour and data from other societies [Sherzer, 1987, pp. 114–15].)

Status

How does speech indicate social status?

One sociolinguistic generalisation which has proved particularly robust is the widely cited social dialect finding that women use more standard forms than men from the same social group (for example, Labov, 1972; Trudgill, 1983; Chambers, 1992). This generalisation was clearly supported by the data from our social dialect research on New Zealand English. Wellington women used more instances of the standard form *-ing* rather than the vernacular *-in'*, in words like walking and swimming, for example, compared to men. Women dropped fewer instances of initial *h-* in words like house and help than men did (Holmes, Bell, & Boyce, 1991).

Though this is a widely attested generalisation, some researchers have suggested that there may be exceptions to this pattern. Hudson (1980) and Labov (1982), for example, refer to communities where it seems the men use more standard forms than the women of the same social group in the same contexts. These are all communities where women's roles are extremely circumscribed.

> It appears that where women have not traditionally played a major role in public life, cultural expectations will lead them to react less strongly to the linguistic norms of the dominant culture. (Labov, 1982, p. 79)

The status of these exceptions has recently been challenged, however, by Ibrahim (1986), who points out that, in such cases, the relevant norms need to be carefully established. The norms on which the counter-examples are based are often the norms of a super-imposed variety (for example, the high variety in a diglossic situation) or are external norms (for example, based on British English in India, as described by Khan, 1991). It seems possible, then, that here we have a strong contender for the status of a sociolinguistic universal tendency.

> *Women use more standard forms than men from the same social group in the same social context.

Standard pronunciations are used by those from higher social groups. More standard forms are associated with higher social status. So, superficially, this generalisation seems to suggest that, at least in features of their speech such as pronunciation, women put more weight on appearing socially statusful than men – a finding which would contradict my interpretation of the evidence of gender differences in other aspects of verbal interaction, where I suggested men put more weight on status-enhancement.

There are, however, many ways in which an interpretation of this pattern as an indication of women's concern with status can be challenged (see, for example, Holmes, 1992; Coates, 1993). I will mention here just two closely related points which suggest that such an interpretation would be inaccurate. Firstly, it is possible to interpret the women's behaviour in a way which is entirely consistent with the data on patterns of verbal interaction discussed above. The interviewers in most social dialect surveys have been middle class academics. There is little doubt that in a formal interview with a person they did not know well they would use a relatively high percentage of standard forms. The fact that women use more standard forms than men in such contexts could, then, be interpreted as evidence of their greater sensitivity to their addressee's patterns of use. This would then provide further evidence of the pattern discussed earlier that women tend to be more sensitive than men to the face needs of their addressees. It would also be consistent with evidence from research on accommodation theory examining how people adjust to each other's speech. In a number of studies women accommodated to their addressees' style of speech more than men did (for example, Bilous & Krauss, 1988; Mulac et al., 1988). In other words, the women adapted their own speech patterns in the direction of the addressee's patterns more than men did. Women's use of standard form in social dialect interviews may well reflect their sensitivity to their addressee's speech norms.

Secondly, the pattern may equally reflect women's awareness of the appropriate style of speech for such an interview, and their greater ability to adapt to such a context. The context in which most social dialect data has been collected has generally been some kind of interview between people who do not know each other well, and who may even be complete strangers. This is a relatively formal context and it is well established that most speakers move towards more formal styles in such contexts. There is good evidence, however, from a range of social dialect research, that women tend to control a wider stylistic range than men (see Milroy, 1987; Labov, 1972, 1990; Chambers, 1992, pp. 196, 199), and they are therefore more able to adapt their speech to different situations more sensitively.

> The empirical evidence clearly shows women as much more able performers than men in the whole spectrum of sociolinguistic situations . . . they command a wider range of linguistic variants . . . they have the linguistic flexibility to alter their speech as social circumstances warrant. (Chambers, 1992, p. 199)

So, the second point is that women may use more standard forms than men because they are better able than men to produce such forms in the formal interview context where they judge them appropriate. The discussion has thus led to the final generalisation I want to propose for consideration as a potentially interesting socio-linguistic universal tendency.

*Women are stylistically more flexible than men.

The empirical evidence for this generalisation comes mainly from social dialect surveys which testify to the stylistic range exhibited by women in social dialect interviews (Labov, 1990; Chambers, 1992). However, the Wellington Social Dialect Survey suggested a number of caveats and qualifications that might need to be made to such a generalisation. We found that the pattern did not hold for all variables, but rather seemed to vary according to whether the variable was a stable one, or was involved in linguistic change. In other words, gender differences in stylistic flexibility varied from one sound to another. (For the stable variable ING, the men shifted very much more than the women as they moved from careful reading style to relaxed conversation. For the more volatile variable, EAR/AIR, which is currently involved in change, the women showed more style shifting.)

Another factor which was an obvious influence on the degree to which people shifted style within the interview was how comfortable they felt in the interview situation, and to what extent they relaxed during the interview. Overall, the most style shifting within the interview occurred among the Maori men and the older Pakeha men. They seemed much more comfortable, for instance, than the young Pakeha males mentioned above. Perhaps because of their maturity and experience, these men told good stories and generally seemed at ease in the interview situation. So generalisations about style shift need to take careful account of contextual factors such as these.

This suggests that we need to treat with caution Chambers's (1992) suggestion that women control a wider stylistic repertoire and develop a greater diversity of interactional skills than men. Care is necessary if we are to avoid simply propagating yet another inaccurate stereotype of women's speech.

It should also be noted that a social dialect interview is a relatively restricted social context. Our data suggests that the conditions which the interviewer creates may encourage some interviewees to style shift more than others. It would be useful to test this generalisation across a much wider range of natural contexts. Moreover, generalisations about stylistic flexibility may be a more accurate description of the behaviour of some social groups than others. Women in the second highest status groups illustrate the pattern more clearly than any others in British and American research, for example. And there is very little current research on other cultures which would enable us to test this generalisation more widely.

The cross-cultural evidence with which I am familiar also seems rather mixed, and certainly in need of a sophisticated interpretation. Japanese women, for example, are required to express themselves with more deference than men, and Ide (1982) demonstrates that they therefore use a wider and more complex range of honorifics than men, and that they are very responsive to contextual factors (see also Ide et al., 1986). Javanese women are also expected to express deference to males, but Smith-Hefner (1988) points out that Javanese men use the same forms with considerable skill in public to signal superior status or authority. It is interesting to note, too, that Javanese women are responsible for the socialisation of the children, including developing their sociolinguistic competence, a role which clearly demands control of a range of styles including the 'honorific baby-talk register', a very specialised style. Javanese women do the shopping and bargaining (Smith-Hefner, 1988, p. 538), a pattern also reported by Keenan (1974) in Madagascar. Thus, Javanese women appear to control a wide stylistic repertoire, even if all the component styles are not recognised and valued.

In Madagascar, women demonstrate their stylistic skills most obviously in less formal and less socially valued styles. Keenan (1974) contrasts the direct and open style of women with the indirect, allusive style of men, and her analysis of Malagasy speech repertoires appears to contradict the claim that, in general, women control a wider range of styles than men. It is clear, however, that Malagasy women are better at arguing, bargaining, and confronting others than men; they demonstrate superior skill in these areas. But these speech styles are not valued, and so it is men's speech that is regarded as better, subtler, and more skilled. The fact that women control less valued styles means their skills in these styles are discounted (cf. Hill, 1987). In Guyana, too, working class women appear to be the experts in the language of abuse (Edwards, 1979). Yet there, at least their skills in *busin* mean they are feared and respected.

Traditional Maori society appears to provide another counter-example to the generalisation concerning women's control of a wider range of styles, since it is Maori men who control the more formal oratorical speech styles or *whaikorero*. In most tribes, *whaikorero* is the prerogative of men. Men's linguistic skills are apparent in the most public, formal, and highly respected contexts of talk, a pattern which was apparent in the earlier discussion of public and private talk. Maori women have traditionally controlled a range of speech styles, too. But there is little research on the linguistic repertoire of Maori women, and the contexts in which women contribute most are less public and attract less overt high valuation than those in which men perform. (See Sherzer [1987] for a discussion of this pattern in a wide range of different cultures. Lederman [1984] illustrates it for the Mendi, a tribe of Highland Papua New Guinea. See Philips, Steele, & Tanz [1987] for further examples.)

All this suggests that testing the generalisability of universals relating to style, solidarity, and status will require a great deal more cross-cultural research into the stylistic repertoires of women and men. We especially need investigations of the range of styles used in less formal contexts, which are often less valued and may therefore be ignored, overlooked, or even denied. (Compare Ferguson's [1959] comments on people's denial of knowledge of L in diglossia situations.)

Explanations

I have identified a number of potential sociolinguistic universal tendencies and suggested they need to be thoroughly tested, not only across different cultures, but also across different contexts within the culture from which they arose. In this concluding section, I will briefly examine three different explanations which have been suggested for some of the patterns described in this paper: a cultural explanation appealing to different patterns of socialisation; a power-based explanation which focuses on women's subordinate status; and a biological explanation.

The cultural explanation for differences in the way women and men use language points to the fact that women and men are socialised differently. As a result, it is claimed, they belong to different sub-cultures. Their ways of interacting are determined in their childhood same-sex play groups, and the patterns established in those early years persist into adulthood (Maltz & Borker, 1982, reprinted in this volume, p. 417).

Tannen's (1990a) book is the most recent and most fully-developed exposition of this position:

> The chief commodity that is bartered in the boys' hierarchical world is status . . . The chief commodity that is bartered in the girls' community is intimacy. (1990a, p. 47)

The results of these different socialisation patterns are that boys and girls develop different cultures with different norms for interaction:

> If adults learn their ways of speaking as children growing up in separate social worlds of peers, then conversation between women and men is cross-cultural communication. (1990a, p. 47)

Though it is offered as an explanation of differences in male and female patterns of interaction, it is important to note that it addresses the *means* by which males and females develop different communicative norms, rather than the reasons why they do so. It is a convincing account of *how* females and males develop different patterns of interaction, but it does not explain *why* the socialisation of women leads them to behave in supportive, affiliative, context-sensitive ways which focus on maintaining and enhancing solidarity, while that of men leads to competitive, unsupportive verbal behaviour which makes few concessions to the addressee, and seems aimed at maintaining power and enhancing status.

A second explanation attributes differences in the communicative patterns of women and men to differences in power between the sexes. Men are the power brokers in most speech communities. Women are subordinate. Consequently, the patterns of interaction which distinguish the sexes reflect male dominance and female subordination. Men can dominate the talking time, interrupt, and use a narrower range of speech variants because they don't need to worry about pleasing their interlocuters, especially when the addressee is a woman. Women by contrast need to be supportive and non-aggressive and must be linguistically flexible in order to survive in societies where they are not in control. Henley & Kramarae (1991) present this argument very convincingly. Men are the socially and politically dominant group in most societies, and male discourse patterns reflect and enact this power and control. Men's linguistic patterns are regarded as ways in which they display power, 'a power based in the larger social order but reinforced and expressed in face-to-face interaction with women' (Maltz & Borker, 1982, pp. 198–99). Male dominance is demonstrated through male control in a wide variety of spheres, including the sphere of female–male interaction (West & Zimmerman, 1987).

The third explanation, which points to biology as a contributing factor in female–male linguistic differences, is the most controversial. Chambers (1992) argues that females have a genetic head-start over men which they use to their advantage to develop greater sociolinguistic skills. He points out that women have an innate neurological advantage (based on brain lateralisation differences between females and males) which provides the basis for the development of further advantages in the area of verbal skills:

> There is, in the psychological literature, a long record of evidence of female verbal superiority. Over many years, women have demonstrated an advantage over men in tests of fluency, speaking, sentence complexity, analogy, listening, comprehension of both written and spoken material, vocabulary, and spelling [see the summary in Maccoby & Jacklin, 1974, p. 75]. (Chambers, 1992, p. 199)

And

> female precocity in verbal skills beginning in infancy predisposes them to apply their verbal skills to all kinds of situations as they grow up. (Chambers, 1992, p. 201)

He notes that this biological advantage is a slight one, but a real one, and suggests that it may provide enough of an initial advantage for women to build on and develop further.

It seems likely that all three of these explanations contribute something to a proper understanding of linguistic gender differences. An initial slight genetic advantage may provide the basis on which females build. The reasons they develop this advantage may well relate to their subordinate position in the society. A subordinate group needs to develop survival techniques such as sociolinguistic and stylistic flexibility, and sensitivity to contextual factors, including the linguistic behaviour of their addressees (cf. Carli, 1990; LaFrance, 1992). It is also clear that, as Maltz & Borker (1982) outline, the socialisation process through which boys and girls proceed is different. Girls learn to be accommodating, compliant, and polite, while a greater degree of assertiveness, competitiveness, and aggressive linguistic behaviour is tolerated from boys. Overall, then, it seems possible that biology, power relationships, and the acculturation process all contribute to accounting for gender-differentiated patterns in communities where women demonstrate more context-sensitive pragmatic skills and a wider sociolinguistic repertoire than men.

I have identified in this paper a number of sociolinguistic generalisations, and I have examined some of the evidence for them. I have suggested that some at least deserve further consideration as potential sociolinguistic universals. There is enough evidence in some cases to suggest that the patterns observed in Western cultures may generalise to other cultures too. In other cases, I have suggested we need to be wary of perpetuating stereotypes and myths which result from the over-simplification of complex data.

In conclusion, I would emphasise that it is important to recognise that gender-differentiated patterns of linguistic behaviour will reflect the particular interaction of biological, social, and psychological factors in any society. The particular manifestations of this interaction will not be identical from one community to another. Socio-linguistic universals in the area of gender will therefore take the form of universal tendencies which reflect the predominant patterns in the relationships between women and men in different cultures. There is clearly much work to be done in exploring these patterns in a wide range of speech communities as well as in more social contexts in familiar communities.

NOTE

An earlier version of this paper was presented at the national conference of the Australian Communication Association, Melbourne, 7 July 1993. It has benefited from discussion at the conference, and from the comments of Allan Bell and Miriam Meyerhoff.

REFERENCES

Aries, E. (1976). Interaction patterns and themes of male, female and mixed groups. *Small Group Behaviour*, *7*(1), 7–18.

Aries, E. J., & Johnson, F. L. (1983). Close friendship in adulthood: Conversational content between same-sex friends. *Sex Roles*, *9*(12), 1183–1196.

Bashiruddin, A., Edge, J., & Hughes-Pélégrin, E. (1990). Who speaks in seminars? Status, culture and gender at Durham University. In R. Clark, N. Fairclough, R. Ivanic, N. McLeod, J. Thomas, & P. Meara (Eds.). *Language and power* (pp. 74–84). London: Centre for Information on Language Teaching.

Baumann, M. (1979). Two features of 'women's speech'. In B-L. Dubois & I. M. Crouch (Eds.). *The sociology of the languages of American women* (pp. 32–40). San Antonio, Texas: Trinity University Press.

Bilous, F. R., & Krauss, R. M. (1988). Dominance and accommodation in the conversational behaviours of same- and mixed-gender dyads. *Language and Communication*, *8*(3/4), 183–94.

Britain, D. (1992). Linguistic change in intonation: The use of high rising terminals in New Zealand English. *Language Variation and Change*, *4*(1), 77–104.

Brooks, V. R. (1982). Sex differences in student dominance behaviour in female and male professors' classrooms. *Sex Roles*, *8*, 683–90.

Brown, P. (1980). How and why are women more polite: Some evidence from a Mayan community. In S. McConnell-Ginet, R. Borker, & N. Furman (Eds). *Women and language in literature and society* (pp. 111–36). New York: Praeger.

——. (1990). Gender, politeness, and confrontation in Tenejapa. *Discourse Processes*, *13*, 123–41.

Brown, P., & Levinson, S. (1987). *Politeness: Some universals in language usage*. Cambridge: Cambridge University Press.

Cameron, D. (1992). *Feminism and linguistic theory* (2nd ed.). London: Macmillan.

Carli, L. L. (1990). Gender, language and influence. *Journal of Personality and Social Psychology, 59*(5), 941–51.

Chambers, J. C. (1992). Linguistic correlates of gender and sex. *English World-Wide, 13*(2), 173–218.

Ching, M. (1982). The question intonation in assertions. *American Speech, 57*, 95–107.

Coates, J. (1989). Gossip revisited: Language in all-female groups. In J. Coates & D. Cameron (Eds.). *Women in their speech communities* (pp. 94–121). London: Longman.

——. (1993). *Women, men and language* (2nd ed.). London: Longman.

Crosby, F., & Nyquist, L. (1977). The female register: An empirical study of Lakoff's hypotheses. *Language in Society, 6*(3), 313–22.

Cruttenden, A. (1986). *Intonation*. Cambridge: Cambridge University Press.

DeFrancisco, V. L. (1991). The sounds of silence: How men silence women in marital relations. *Discourse and Society, 2*(4), 413–23.

Eakins, B., & Eakins, G. (1979). Verbal turn-taking and exchanges in faculty dialogue. In B-L. Dubois & I. Crouch (Eds.) *The sociology of the languages of American women* (pp. 53–62). San Antonio, Texas: Trinity University Press.

Edelsky, C. (1981). Who's got the floor? *Language in Society, 10*, 383–421.

Edelsky, C., & Adams, K. (1990). Creating inequality: Breaking the rules in debates. *Journal of Language and Social Psychology, 9*(3), 171–90.

Edwards, W. F. (1979). Speech acts in Guyana: Communicating ritual and personal insults. *Journal of Black Studies, 10*(1), 20–39.

Ferguson, C. A. (1959). Diglossia. *Word, 15*, 325–40.

Fishman, P. M. (1978). Interaction: The work women do. *Social Problems, 25*(4), 397–406.

——. (1980). Conversational insecurity. In H. Giles, P. Robinson, & P. M. Smith (Eds.). *Language: Social psychological perspectives* (pp. 127–32). Oxford: Pergamon.

——. (1983). Interaction: The work women do. In B. Thorne, C. Kramarae, & N. Henley (Eds). *Language, gender and society* (pp. 89–101). Rowley, Mass.: Newbury House.

Franken, M. (1983). Interviewers' strategies: How questions are modified. Unpublished manuscript, Victoria University, Wellington, New Zealand.

Gass, S. M., & Varonis, E. M. (1985). Sex differences in NNS/NNS interactions. In D. Day (Ed.). *Conversation in second language acquisition*. Rowley, Mass.: Newbury House.

Goffman, E. (1967). *Interaction ritual*. New York: Anchor Books.

Guy, G., Horvath, G., Vonwiller, J., Daisley, E., & Rogers, I. (1986). An intonational change in progress in Australian English. *Language in Society, 15*(1), 23–52.

Guy, G., & Vonwiller, J. (1984). The meaning of an intonation in Australian English. *Australian Journal of Linguistics, 4*(1), 1–17.

Haas, A., & Sherman, M. A. (1982). Reported topics of conversation among same-sex adults. *Communication Quarterly, 30*(4), 332–42.

Hartman, M. (1979). A descriptive study of the language of men and women born in Maine around 1900. In B-L. Dubois & I. Crouch (Eds.). *The sociology of the languages of American women* (pp. 81–90). San Antonio, Texas: Trinity University Press.

Henley, N. M., & Kramarae, C. (1991). Gender, power and miscommunication. In N. Coupland, H. Giles, & J. W. Wiemann (Eds.). *'Miscommunication' and Problematic Talk* (pp. 18–43). London: Sage.

Herbert, R. K. (1990). Sex-based differences in compliment behaviour. *Language in Society, 19*, 201–24.

Hill, J. H. (1987). Women's speech in modern Mexico. In S. U. Philips, S. Steele, & C. Tanz (Eds.). *Language, gender and sex in comparative perspective* (pp. 121–60). Cambridge: Cambridge University Press.

Hirschman, L. (1974). *Analysis of supportive and assertive behaviour in conversations.* Paper given at meeting of the Linguistic Society of America, San Francisco.

Holmes, J. (1984). Hedging your bets and sitting on the fence: Some evidence for hedges as support structures. *Te Reo, 27*, 47–62.

———. (1986). Functions of you know in women's and men's speech. *Language in Society, 15*(1), 1–22.

———. (1988a). Paying compliments: A sex-preferential positive politeness strategy. *Journal of Pragmatics, 12*(3), 445–65.

———. (1988b). Sex differences in seminar contributions. *BAAL Newsletter, 31*, 33–41.

———. (1989). Sex differences and apologies: One aspect of communicative competence. *Applied Linguistics, 10*(2), 194–213.

———. (1992). *An introduction to sociolinguistics.* London: Longman.

Holmes, J., Bell, A., & Boyce, M. (1991). *Variation and change in New Zealand English: A social dialect investigation.* Project report to the Social Sciences Committee of the Foundation for Research, Science and Technology, Victoria University, Wellington, New Zealand.

Hudson, R. A. (1980). *Sociolinguistics.* Cambridge: Cambridge University Press.

Ibrahim, M. H. (1986). Standard and prestige language: A problem in Arabic sociolinguistics. *Anthropological Linguistics, 28*, 115–26.

Ide, S. (1982). Japanese sociolinguistics: Politeness and women's language. *Lingua, 57*, 357–85.

Ide, S., Hori, M., Kawasaki, A., Ikuta, S., & Haga, H. (1986). Sex differences and politeness in Japanese. *International Journal of the Sociology of Language, 58*, 25–36.

James, D., & Clarke, S. (1992). Interruptions, gender and power: A review of the literature. In K. Hall, M. Bucholtz, & B. Moonwomon (Eds.). *Locating power: Proceedings of the second Berkeley women and language conference, April 4 & 5, 1992*: Vol. 1 (pp. 286–99). Berkeley, California: Berkeley Women and Language Group, University of California.

James, E., Mahut, C., & Latkiewicz, G. (1989). The investigation of an apparently new intonation pattern in Toronto English. *Information Communication, 19*, 11–17.

Jespersen, O. (1922). *Language: Its nature, development and origins.* London: Allen and Unwin.

Karp, D. A., & Yoels, W. C. (1976). The college classroom: Some observations on the meanings of student participation. *Sociology and Social Research, 60*, 421–39.

Keenan, E. (1974). Norm-makers, norm-breakers: Uses of speech by men and women in a Malagasy community. In R. Baumann & J. Sherzer (Eds.). *Explorations in the ethnography of speaking* (pp. 125–43). Cambridge: Cambridge University Press.

Khan, F. (1991). Final consonant cluster simplification in a variety of Indian English. In J. Cheshire (Ed.). *English around the world: Sociolinguistic perspectives* (pp. 288–98). Cambridge: Cambridge University Press.

Kramarae, C. (1982). Gender how she speaks. In E. Bouchard-Ryan & H. Giles (Eds.). *Attitudes towards language variation* (pp. 84–98). London: Edward Arnold.

Labov, W. (1972). *Sociolinguistic patterns.* Philadelphia, Pa.: University of Pennsylvania Press.

———. (1982). Building on empirical foundations. In W. P. Lehmann & Y. Malkiel (Eds.). *Perspectives on historical linguistics* (pp. 79–92). Amsterdam and Philadelphia: Benjamins.

———. (1990). The intersection of sex and social class in the course of linguistic change. *Language Variation and Change, 2*, 205–54.

LaFrance, M. (1992). Gender and interruptions: Individual infraction or violation of the social order? *Psychology of Women Quarterly, 16*, 497–512.

Lakoff, R. (1975). *Language and woman's place*. New York: Harper & Row.

Lederman, R. (1984). Who speaks here? Formality and the politics of gender in Mendi, Highland Papua New Guinea. In D. L. Brenneis & F. R. Myers (Eds.). *Dangerous Words* (pp. 85–107). New York: New York University Press.

Leet-Pellegrini, H. M. (1980). Conversational dominance as a function of gender and expertise. In H. Giles, P. Robinson, & P. Smith (Eds.). *Language: Social psychological perspectives* (pp. 97–104). Oxford: Pergamon.

Maccoby, E. E., & Jacklin, C. N. (1974). *The psychology of sex differences*. Stanford: Stanford University Press.

Maltz, D. N., & Borker, R. A. (1982). A cultural approach to male–female miscommunication. In J. J. Gumperz (Ed.). *Language and social identity* (pp. 196–216). Cambridge: Cambridge University Press.

McLemore, C. (1991). The interpretation of L*H in English. *Texas Linguistic Forum, 32*, 175–96.

McMillan, J. R., Clifton, A. K, McGrath, D., & Gale, W. S. (1977). Woman's language: Uncertainty or interpersonal sensitivity and emotionality? *Sex Roles, 3*(6), 545–59.

Milroy, L. (1987). *Language and social networks* (2nd ed.). Oxford: Blackwell.

Mulac, A., Wiemann, J. M., Widenmann, S., & Gibson, T. (1988). Male/female language differences and effects in same sex and mixed-sex dyads: The gender-linked language effect. *Communication Monographs, 55*(4), 315–35.

Natale, M., Entin, E., & Jaffe, J. (1979). Vocal interruptions in dyadic communication as a function of speech and social anxiety. *Journal of Personality and Social Psychology, 37*, 865–78.

Octigan, M., & Niederman, S. (1979). Male dominance in conversations. *Frontiers, 4*(1), 50–4.

Philips, S. U., Steele, S., & Tanz, C. (Eds.) (1987). *Language, gender and sex in comparative perspective*. Cambridge: Cambridge University Press.

Preisler, B. (1986). *Linguistic sex roles in conversation*. Berlin: Mouton de Gruyter.

Safilios-Rothschild, C. (1979). *Sex role, socialisation and sex discrimination: A synthesis and critique of the literature*. Washington, D.C.: National Institute of Education.

Schick-Case, S. (1988). Cultural differences, not deficiencies: An analysis of managerial women's language. In S. Rose & L. Larwood (Eds.). *Women's careers: Pathways and pitfalls* (pp. 41–63). New York: Praeger.

Sherzer, J. (1987). A diversity of voices: Men's and women's speech in ethnographic perspective. In S. U. Philips, S. Steele, & C. Tanz (Eds.). *Language, gender and sex in comparative perspective* (pp. 95–120). Cambridge: Cambridge University Press.

Singh, U. N. (1989). How to honour someone in Maithili. *International Journal of the Sociology of Language, 75*, 87–107.

Smith, J. S. (1992). Linguistic privilege: 'Just stating the facts' in Japanese. In K. Hall, M. Bucholtz, & B. Moonwomon (Eds.). *Locating power: Proceedings of the second Berkeley women and language conference, April 4 & 5, 1992: Vol. 2* (pp. 540–48). Berkeley, California: Berkeley Women and Language Group, University of California.

Smith-Hefner, N. J. (1988). Women and politeness: The Javanese example. *Language in Society, 17*(4), 535–54.

Soskin, W. F., & John, V. P. (1963). The study of spontaneous talk. In R. Barker (Ed.). *The stream of behaviour* (pp. 228–87). New York: Appleton-Century-Crofts.

Spender, D. (1980a). *Man made language*. London: Routledge and Kegan Paul.

——. (1980b). Talking in class. In D. Spender & E. Sarah (Eds.), *Learning to lose*. London: The Women's Press.

——. (1982). *Invisible women*. London: The Women's Press.

Swacker, M. (1979). Women's verbal behaviour at learned and professional conferences. In B-L. Dubois & I. Crouch (Eds.). *The sociology of the languages of American women* (pp. 155–60). San Antonio, Texas: Trinity University Press.

Swann, J. (1989). Talk control: An illustration from the classroom of problems in analysing male dominance of conversation. In J. Coates & D. Cameron (Eds.). *Women in their speech communities* (pp. 122–40). London: Longman.

Tannen, D. (1990a). *You just don't understand: Women and men in conversation*. New York: William Morrow.

——. (1990b). Gender differences in topical coherence: Creating involvement in best friends' talk. *Discourse Processes, 13*, 73–90.

Thorne, B., Kramarae, C., & Henley, N. (Eds.). (1983). *Language, gender and society*. Rowley, Mass.: Newbury House.

Troemel-Ploetz, S. (1992). The construction of conversational equality by women. In K. Hall, M. Bucholtz, & B. Moonwomon (Eds.). *Locating power: Proceedings of the second Berkeley women and language conference* (pp. 581–89). Berkeley, California: Berkeley Women and Language Group, University of California.

Trudgill, P. (1983). *On dialect* (Chapter 9). Oxford: Blackwell.

West, C. (1984). When the doctor is a 'lady'. *Symbolic Interaction, 7*(1), 87–106.

West, C., & Zimmerman, D. H. (1983). Small insults: A study of interruptions in cross-sex conversations between unacquainted persons. In B. Thorne, C. Kramarae, & N. Henley (Eds.). *Language, gender and society* (pp. 102–17). Rowley, Mass.: Newbury House.

——. (1987). Doing gender. *Gender and Society, 1*, 125–51.

Wetzel, P. J. (1988). Are 'powerless' communication strategies the Japanese norm? *Language in Society, 17*(4), 555–64.

Wodak, R. (1981). Women relate, men report: Sex differences in language behaviour in a therapeutic group. *Journal of Pragmatics, 5*, 261–85.

Woods, N. (1989). Talking shop: sex and status as determinants of floor apportionment in a work setting. In J. Coates & D. Cameron (Eds.). *Women in their speech communities* (pp. 141–57). London: Longman.

Zimmerman, D. H., & West, C. (1975). Sex roles, interruptions and silences in conversation. In B. Thorne & N. Henley (Eds.). *Language and sex: Difference and dominance* (pp. 105–29). Rowley, Mass.: Newbury House.

31

Communities of Practice: Where Language, Gender, and Power All Live

Penelope Eckert and Sally McConnell-Ginet

Introduction: Too Much Abstraction Spoils the Broth

Studies of language and gender in the past twenty years have looked at many different dimensions of language use and have offered a rich variety of hypotheses about the interaction between gender and language and especially about the connection of power to that interaction. On the one hand, language has been seen as supporting male dominance; on the other, it has been seen as a resource for women resisting oppression or pursuing their own projects and interests. We have all learned a lot by thinking about such proposals, most of which have been supported by interesting and often illuminating observations. But their explanatory force has been weakened by the absence of a coherent theoretical framework within which to refine and further explore them as part of an ongoing research community.

The problem is not an absence of generalizations. Our diagnosis is that gender and language studies suffer from the same problem as that confronting sociolinguistics and psycholinguistics more generally: too much abstraction. Abstracting gender and language from the social practices that produce their particular forms in given communities often obscures and sometimes distorts the ways they connect and how those connections are implicated in power relations, in social conflict, in the production and reproduction of values and plans. Too much abstraction is often symptomatic of too little theorizing: abstraction should not substitute for theorizing but be informed by and responsive to it. Theoretical insight into how language and gender interact requires a close look at social practices in which they are jointly produced. What we want to do in this paper is to sketch the main outlines of a theoretical perspective on language, gender, and power that can help us continue to make progress toward a productive community of language–gender scholars who hold themselves accountable both to one another's work and to relevant developments in linguistics, social theory, and gender studies.

Why is abstraction so tempting and yet so dangerous? It is tempting because at some level and in some form it is irresistible, an inevitable part of theoretical inquiry. People and their activities, including their use of language, are never viewed in completely concrete or particularistic terms. With no access to abstract constructs like linguistic systems and social categories and relations like class and race and gender, we could not hope to engage in any kind of illuminating investigation into how and why language and gender interact. The danger, however, is that the real force and import of their interaction is erased when we abstract each uncritically from the social practices in which they are jointly produced and in which they intermingle with other symbolic and social phenomena. In particular, if we view language and gender as self-contained and independent phenomena, we miss the social and cognitive significance of interactions between them. Abstraction that severs the concrete links between language and gender in the social practices of communities kills the power that resides in and derives from those links.

The notions of "women" and "men," for example, are typically just taken for granted in sociolinguistics. Suppose we were to take all the characterizations of gender that have been advanced to explain putatively gender-differentiated linguistic behavior. Women's language has been said to reflect their (our) conservatism, prestige consciousness, upward mobility, insecurity, deference, nurturance, emotional expressivity, connectedness, sensitivity to others, solidarity. And men's language is heard as evincing their toughness, lack of affect, competitiveness, independence, competence, hierarchy, control. Linguists are not, of course, inventing such accounts of gender identities and gender relations out of whole cloth. Not only commonplace stereotypes but also social-scientific studies offer support for the kinds of characterizations linguists offer in explanation of language use. But the social-science literature must be approached critically: the observations on which such claims about women and men are based have been made at different times and in different circumstances with different populations from those whose linguistic behavior they are being used to explain.

The problem is too much or at least too-crude abstraction. Gender is abstracted whole from other aspects of social identity, the linguistic system is abstracted from linguistic practice, language is abstracted from social action, interactions and events are abstracted from community and personal history, difference and dominance are each abstracted from wider social practice, and both linguistic and social behavior are abstracted from the communities in which they occur. When we recombine all these abstractions, we really do not know what we have. Certainly we don't seem to find real women and men as sums of the characteristics attributed to them.

What we propose is not to ignore such abstract characterizations of gender identities and relations but to take responsibility for connecting each such abstraction to a wide spectrum of social and linguistic practice in order to examine the specificities of its concrete realization in actual communities. This can happen only if we collectively develop a community of analytic practice that holds itself responsible for language and gender writ large.

This means that we are responsible to linguistic theory and research beyond the areas of our particular specializations. Furthermore, we cannot excuse our inattention to social theory and gender studies on the grounds that we are "just linguists," not if we hope to make responsible claims about language and gender interactions. And perhaps the most important implication is that we cannot abandon social and political responsibility for how our work is understood and used, especially given what we know about sexism and racism and elitism and heterosexism in so many of the communities where our research might be disseminated.

Our major aim is to encourage a view of the interaction of gender and language that roots each in the everyday social practices of particular local communities and sees them as jointly constructed in those practices: our slogan, "Think practically and look locally." To think practically and look locally is to abandon several assumptions common in gender and language studies: that gender works independently of other aspects of social identity and relations, that it "means" the same across communities, and that the linguistic manifestations of that meaning are also the same across communities. Such assumptions can be maintained only when the language–gender partnership is prematurely dissolved by abstraction of one or both partners.

Language, Power, and Gender Viewed Locally

Becoming language users and becoming gendered members of local communities both involve participating with other members in a variety of practices that often constitute linguistic, gender, and other social identities and relations at one and the same time. Many such activities have been described in the papers in Hall et al., 1992: instigating or taking the plaintiff or defendant role in a he-said-she-said dispute (Goodwin, 1992), providing sexy talk on the 900 lines (Hall, 1992), participating in "Father Knows Best" dinnertime dramas (Ochs & Taylor, 1992), taking a police report from a bleeding woman (McElhinny, 1992, reprinted in this volume, p. 309), joining in a debate about rape and race and responsibility on the walls of a bathroom stall (Moonwomon, 1992), smiling at the boss's "Sleazy bitch" (Case, 1992), silencing a planned anecdote during a conference paper when you note its (male) protagonist in the audience (Lakoff, 1992), criticizing or defending a colleague's bestseller (Freed, 1992).

In the course of engaging with others in such activity, people collaboratively construct a sense of themselves and of others as certain kinds of persons, as members of various communities with various forms of membership, authority, and privilege in those communities. In all of these, language interacts with other symbolic systems – dress, body adornment, ways of moving, gaze, touch, handwriting style, locales for hanging out, and so on. And the selves constructed are not simply (or even primarily) gendered selves: they are unemployed, Asian American, lesbian, college-educated, post-menopausal selves in a variety of relations to other people. Language is never encountered without other symbol systems, and gender is always joined with real people's complex forms of participation in the communities to which they belong (or have belonged or expect to join).

Individuals may experience the language–gender interface differently in the different communities in which they participate at a given time or at different stages of their lives. Using *Mrs. Jones* may be important for avoiding the condescension of

Mary when a professionally employed woman addresses the woman who cleans her house; for that professional woman, receiving address as *Mrs. Smith* (particularly from her colleagues) may seem to emphasize her subordination to a husband and to deny her individual identity as Joan Doe, who (as she sees it) simply happens to be married to John Smith. On the other hand, acquiring a new name of *Mrs. John Smith* upon marriage may have functioned thirty years ago for the young Joan Doe as a mark of her achieving fully adult status as a married woman (a possibility denied her lesbian sister who rejects marriage). And the woman who with a tolerant smile receives *Mary* from the six-year-old daughter of her employer may insist in her local residential community on *Mrs. Jones* from her own daughter's friends.

Exploring any aspect of the language–gender interface requires that we address the complexities of its construction within and across different communities: what *Mrs. Jones* means, what social work is done by the use of that title, can be understood only by considering its place in the practices of local communities (and in the connections among those communities). Analysts not only jump too readily from local observations to global claims; they/we also too often ignore the multiple uses of particular linguistic resources in the practices of a given community. We can see the confusion that results by trying to put together some of the general claims about the social and psychological underpinnings of language use common in the variation literature with claims about gender such as those common in interaction studies.

A methodological cornerstone of variation studies is the notion that all speakers step up the use of vernacular variants when they are at their most emotional. It is also generally accepted that vernacular variants function to establish solidarity. If women are more emotional than men or more interested in promoting solidarity, as so many interactionists have claimed, the variationists might be expected to predict that vernacular variants typify women's rather than men's language. But the general claim in variation studies has been that men's language exemplifies the vernacular whereas women's aspires toward standard or prestige variants. The explanation offered is not men's emotionality or greater interest in social connections but women's supposed prestige-consciousness and upward mobility (often accompanied by claims of women's greater conservatism). Even in situations in which some vernacular variant is more frequent in women's than men's speech, analysts do not consider how their explanations relate to their own claims about the social meanings of vernaculars. There are many other tensions and potential contradictions when we try to put together all the different things said about language, gender, and power. The standard or prestige variants are associated with the speech of those who have economic and political power, the social elite; at the same time, standard speech is associated with women and "prissiness," and the vernacular is heard as tough and "macho." Once we take seriously the connections among gender characterizations and the various aspects of language that we study and try to develop a coherent picture, it quickly becomes apparent that the generalizations to be found cannot be integrated with one another as they now stand. This suggests serious difficulties in adopting as our primary goal the search for generalizations about "women" and "men" as groups with some kind of global sociolinguistic unity that transcends social practices in local communities.

Statements like "Women emphasize connection in their talk whereas men seek status" may have some statistical support within a particular community. Statistics being what they are, there is, of course, no guarantee that the actual women and men whose behavior supports one such generalization will overlap very much with those supporting another – say, that women prefer standard and men vernacular variants in everyday talk with their peers – and this is true even if our statistics come from a single community. The more serious problem, however, is that such generalizations are seldom understood as simple reports of statistics.

Most American women are under five feet nine inches tall and most American men are over five feet six inches tall, but it would sound odd indeed to report these statistical facts by saying, "Women are under five feet nine inches tall" and "Men are over five feet six inches tall" without some explicit indicator of generalization like *most*. Although unmodified claims about "women" and "men" do allow for exceptions, such claims, which we have certainly made ourselves, often seem to imply that individuals who don't satisfy the generalization are indeed exceptional "as women" or "as men," deviants from some normative model (perhaps deviants to admire but nonetheless outsiders in some sense). This is especially true when women and men are being characterized as "different" from one another on some particular dimension. But if gender resides in difference, what is the status of the tremendous variability we see in actual behavior within sex categories? Too often dismissed as "noise" in a basically dichotomous gender system, differences among men and among women are, in our view, themselves important aspects of gender. Tomboys and goody-goodies, homemakers and career women, body-builders and fashion models, secretaries and executives, basketball coaches and French teachers, professors and students, grandmothers and mothers and daughters – these are all categories of girls and women whose mutual differences are part of their construction of themselves and each other as gendered beings. When femaleness and maleness are differentiated from one another in terms of such attributes as power, ambition, physical coordination, rebelliousness, caring, or docility, the role of these attributes in creating and texturing important differences among very female identities and very male identities becomes invisible.

The point here is not that statistical generalizations about the females and the males in a particular community are automatically suspect. But to stop with such generalizations or to see finding such "differences" as the major goal of investigations of gender and language is problematic. Correlations simply point us toward areas where further investigation might shed light on the linguistic and other practices that enter into gender dynamics in a community. An emphasis on difference as constitutive of gender draws attention away from a more serious investigation of the relations among language, gender, and other components of social identity; it ignores the ways difference (or beliefs therein) function in constructing dominance relations. Gender can be thought of as a sex-based way of experiencing other social attributes like class, ethnicity, or age (and also less obviously social qualities like ambition, athleticism, and musicality). To examine gender independently as if it were just "added on" to such other aspects of identity is to miss its significance and force. Certainly, to interpret broad sex patterns in language use without considering other aspects of social identity and relations is to paint with one eye closed. Speakers are not assembled out of separate independent modules: part European American, part female, part middle-aged, part feminist, part intellectual. Abstracting gender away from other aspects of social identity also leads to premature generalization even about normative conceptions of femaleness and maleness. While most research that focuses on sex difference is not theoretically committed to a universalizing conception of women or of men, such research has tended to take gender identity as given at least in broad strokes at a relatively global level.

Too much abstraction and too-ready generalization are encouraged by a limited view of theorizing as aimed at accounts of gender difference that apply globally to women and men. In the interests of abstraction and global generalization, William Labov has argued that ethnographic studies of language and society must answer to the results of survey studies – that generalized correlations reflect a kind of objective picture that must serve as the measure of any locally grounded studies. Others cite the objectivity of controlled experimental studies. We argue instead that ethnographic studies must answer to each other, and that survey and experimental studies in turn must answer to them (see Eckert, 1990). Surveys typically examine categories so abstracted from social practice that they cannot be assumed to have independent status as sociolinguistically meaningful units, and they rely heavily on interviews, a special kind of social activity. Experimental studies also abstract in ways that can make it hard to assess their relevance to the understanding of naturally occurring social practice, including cognition. To frame abstractions so that they help explain the interaction of language and social practice, we need a focus of study and analysis that allows us to examine them each on something like an equal footing. This requires a unit of social analysis that has explanatory power for the construction of both language and gender. It is mutual engagement of human agents in a wide range of activities that creates, sustains, challenges, and sometimes changes society and its institutions, including both gender and language, and the sites of such mutual engagement are communities. How the community is defined, therefore, is of prime importance in any study of language and gender, even those that do not use ethnographic methods (e.g., survey or experimental studies).

Language, Gender, and Communities of Practice

Sociolinguists have located linguistic systems, norms, and social identities within a loosely defined construct, the *speech community*. Although in theory sociolinguists embrace John Gumperz's (1982) definition of a speech community as a group of speakers who share rules and norms for the use of language, in practice community studies have defined their populations on the basis of location and/or population. Differences and relations among the speakers who people sociolinguists' speech communities have been defined in terms of abstracted characteristics: sex, age, socio-economic class, ethnicity. And differences in ways of speaking have been interpreted on the basis of speculative hypotheses about the relation between these character-istics and social practice. Sociolinguistic analysis, then, attempts to reconstruct the practice from which these characteristics, and the linguistic behavior in question, have been abstracted. While participation in community practice sometimes figures more directly into classification of speakers, sociolinguists still seldom recognize explicitly the crucial role of practice in delineating speech communities and more generally in mediating the relation between language, society, and consciousness.

To explore in some detail just how social practice and individual "place" in the community connect to one another, sociolinguists need some conception of a com-munity that articulates place with practice. For this reason, we adopt Jean Lave and Etienne Wenger's notion of the *community of practice*.[1] The community of practice takes us away from the community defined by a location or by a population. Instead, it focuses on a community defined by social engagement – after all, it is this engage-ment that language serves, not the place and not the people as a collection of individuals.

A community of practice is an aggregate of people who come together around mutual engagement in some common endeavor. Ways of doing things, ways of talk-ing, beliefs, values, power relations – in short, practices – emerge in the course of their joint activity around that endeavor. A community of practice is different as a social construct from the traditional notion of community, primarily because it is defined simultaneously by its membership and by the practice in which that membership engages. Indeed, it is the practices of the community and members' differentiated participation in them that structures the community socially.

A community of practice might be people working together in a factory, regulars in a bar, a neighborhood play group, a nuclear family, police partners and their ethnographer, the Supreme Court. Communities of practice may be large or small, intensive or diffuse; they are born and they die, they may persist through many changes of membership, and they may be closely articulated with other commun-ities. Individuals participate in multiple communities of practice, and individual identity is based in the multiplicity of this participation. Rather than seeing the individual as some disconnected entity floating around in social space, or as a loca-tion in a network, or as a member of a particular group or set of groups, or as a bundle of social characteristics, we need to focus on communities of practice. Such a focus allows us to see the individual as an actor articulating a range of forms of participation in multiple communities of practice.

Gender is produced (and often reproduced) in differential membership in com-munities of practice. People's access and exposure to, need for, and interest in different communities of practice are related to such things as their class, age, and ethnicity, as well as their sex. Working-class people are more likely on the whole than middle-class people to be members of unions, bowling teams, close-knit neighbor-hoods. Upper-middle-class people, on the other hand, are more likely than working-class people to be members of tennis clubs, orchestras, professional organizations.

Men are more likely than women to be members of football teams, armies, and boards of directors. Women, on the other hand, are more likely to be members of secretarial pools, aerobics classes, and consciousness-raising groups.

And associated with differences in age, class, and ethnicity are differences in the extent to which the sexes belong to different communities of practice. Different people, for a variety of reasons, will articulate their multiple memberships differently. A female executive living in a male-dominated household will have difficulty articulating her membership in her domestic and professional communities of practice, unlike a traditional male executive "head of household." A lesbian lawyer "closeted" within the legal community may also belong to a women's community whose membership defines itself in opposition to the larger heterosexual world. And the woman who scrubs toilets in the household "managed" by the female executive for her husband and also in the home of the lesbian lawyer and her artist lover may be a respected lay leader in her local church, facing a different set of tensions than either of her employers does in negotiating multiple memberships.

Gender is also produced and reproduced in differential forms of participation in particular communities of practice. Women tend to be subordinate to men in the workplace, women in the military do not engage in combat, and in the academy, most theoretical disciplines are overwhelmingly male with women concentrated in descriptive and applied work that "supports" theorizing. Women and men may also have very different forms of participation available to them in single-sex communities of practice. For example, if all-women groups do in fact tend to be more egalitarian than all-men groups, as some current literature claims (e.g., Aries, 1976), then women's and men's forms of participation will be quite different. Such relations within same-sex groups will, of course, be related in turn to the place of such groups in the larger society.

The relations among communities of practice when they come together in overarching communities of practice also produce gender arrangements. Only recently, for example, have female competitive sports begun to receive significant recognition, and male sports continue to bring far greater visibility, power, and authority both to the teams and to the individual participants in those teams. The (male) final four is the focus of attention in the NCAA basketball world every spring, with the women's final four receiving only perfunctory mention. Many a school has its Bulldogs and Lady Bulldogs, its Rangers and Rangerettes. This articulation with power and stature outside the team in turn translates into different possibilities for relations within. The relation between male varsity sports teams and female cheerleading squads illustrates a more general pattern of men's organizations and women's auxiliaries. Umbrella communities of this kind do not offer neutral membership status. And when several families get together for a meal prepared by the women who then team up to do the serving and clearing away while the men watch football, gender differentiation (including differentiation in language use) is being reproduced on an institutional level.

The community of practice is where the rubber meets the road – it is where observable action and interaction do the work of producing, reproducing, and resisting the organization of power in society and in societal discourses of gender, age, race, etc. Speakers develop linguistic patterns as they engage in activity in the various communities in which they participate. Sociolinguists have tended to see this process as one of acquisition of something relatively "fixed" – the linguistic resources, the community, and the individual's relation to the two are all viewed as fixed. The symbolic value of a linguistic form is taken as given, and the speaker simply learns it and uses it, either mechanically or strategically. But in actual practice, social meaning, social identity, community membership, forms of participation, the full range of community practices, and the symbolic value of linguistic form are being constantly and mutually constructed.

And so although the identity of both the individual and the individual community of practice is experienced as persistent, in fact they both change constantly. We continue to adopt new ways of talking and discard some old ways, to adopt new ways of being women and men, gays and lesbians and heterosexuals, even changing our ways of being feminists or being lovers or being mothers or being sisters. In becoming police officers or psychiatrists or physicists or professors of linguistics, we may change our ways of being women and perhaps of being wives or lovers or mothers. In so doing, however, we are not negating our earlier gendered sociolinguistic identities; we are transforming them, changing and expanding forms of femininity, masculinity, and gender relations. And there are many more unnamed ways of thinking, being, relating, and doing that we adopt and adapt as we participate in different ways in the various communities of practice to which we belong.

What sociolinguists call the *linguistic repertoire* is a set of resources for the articulation of multiple memberships and forms of participation. And an individual's ways of speaking in a particular community of practice are not simply a function of membership or participation in that community. A way of speaking in a community does not simply constitute a turning on of a community-specific linguistic switch, or the symbolic laying of claim to membership in that community, but a complex articulation of the individual's forms of participation in that community with participation in other communities that are salient at the time. In turn, the linguistic practices of any given community of practice will be continually changing as a result of the many saliencies that come into play through its multiple members.

The overwhelming tendency in language and gender research on power has been to emphasize either speakers and their social relations (e.g., women's disadvantage in ordinary conversations with men) or the meanings and norms encoded in the linguistic systems and practices historically available to them (e.g., such sexist patterns as conflating generic human with masculine in forms like *he* or *man*). But linguistic forms have no power except as given in people's mouths and ears; to talk about meaning without talking about the people who mean and the community practices through which they give meaning to their words is at best limited.

Conclusion: A Scholarly Community of Practice

Susan Gal (1992) has called for the integration of the wide range of endeavors that come under the rubric of language and gender. [. . .] Mary Talbot (1992) shows us how a teen magazine attempts to create an imaginary community around the consumption of lipstick. It provides many of the requirements of a community of practice – knowledge, membership, history, practices – inviting the readers to become engaged in lipstick technology and to form their own real communities of practice around the consumption of lipstick. Many people studying gender dynamics in everyday conversation may not immediately see the relation between their work and studies of the discourses of gender as revealed in teen magazines. But just as gender is not given and static, it is also not constructed afresh in each interaction or each community of practice. Those of us who are examining the minutiae of linguistic form need to build detailed understanding of the construction of gender in the communities of practice that we study. But part of the characterization of a community of practice is its relation to other communities of practice and to the wider discourses of society. Thus while we do our close examination, we need to work within a consciously constructed broader perspective that extends our own necessarily limited view of the communities we study.

Significant advances in the study of language and gender from now on are going to have to involve integration on a level that has not been reached so far. The integration can come only through the intensive collaboration of people in a variety of fields, developing shared ways of asking questions and of exploring and evaluating possible answers. Language and gender studies, in fact, require an interdisciplinary community of scholarly practice. Isolated individuals who try to straddle two fields can often offer insights, but real progress depends on getting people from a variety of fields to collaborate closely in building a common and broad-based understanding. We will cease to be a friendly but scattered bunch of linguists, anthropologists, literary critics, etc., when we become mutually engaged in the integration of our emerging insights into the nexus between language, gender, and social practice.

Sometimes our mutual engagement will lead us to controversy. And some researchers have been concerned about the development of controversy over the cultural-difference model. It is true that argument that is not grounded in shared practice can reduce to unpleasant and *ad feminam* argument. But rich intellectual controversy both requires and enhances mutual engagement. Without sustained intellectual exchange that includes informed and detailed debate, we will remain an aggregate of individuals with vaguely related interests in language and gender. With continued engagement like that begun in works such as Hall et al. (1992) we may become a productive scholarly community.

NOTES

Many of the ideas expressed in this paper have appeared also in Penelope Eckert and Sally McConnell-Ginet (1992).

1   See Etienne Wenger (1990 and forthcoming); and Jean Lave and Etienne Wenger (1991).

REFERENCES

Aries, Elizabeth (1976). Interaction patterns and themes of male, female, and mixed groups. *Small Group Behaviour* 7: 7–18.

Case, Susan (1992). Organizational inequity in a steel plant: A language model. In Hall et al. (eds).

Eckert, Penelope (1990). The whole woman: Sex and gender differences in variation. *Language Variation and Change* 1: 245–67.

Eckert, Penelope, & Sally McConnell-Ginet (1992). Think practically and look locally: Language and gender as community-based practice. *Annual Review of Anthropology* 21: 461–90.

Freed, Alice F. (1992). We understand perfectly: A critique of Tannen's view of cross-sex communication. In Hall et al. (eds).

Gal, Susan (1992). Language, gender, and power: An anthropological view. In Hall et al. (eds).

Goodwin, Marjorie Harness (1992). Orchestrating participation in events: Powerful talk among African American girls. In Hall et al. (eds).

Gumperz, John J. (1982). *Discourse strategies*. Cambridge: Cambridge University Press.

Hall, Kira (1992). Women's language for sale on the fantasy lines. In Hall et al. (eds).

Hall, Kira, Mary Bucholtz & Birch Moonwomon (eds) (1992) *Locating Power. Proceedings of the 2nd Berkeley Women and Language Conference*. Berkeley, CA: Berkeley Women & Language Group.

Lakoff, Robin Tolmach (1992). The silencing of women. In Hall et al. (eds).

Lave, Jean, & Etienne Wenger (1991). *Situated learning: Legitimate peripheral participation*. Cambridge: Cambridge University Press.

McElhinny, Bonnie S. (1992). "I don't smile much anymore": Affect, gender, and the discourse of Pittsburgh police officers. In Hall et al. (eds).

Moonwomon, Birch (1992). Rape, race, and responsibility: A graffiti text political discourse. In Hall et al. (eds).

Ochs, Elinor, & Carolyn Taylor (1992). Mothers' role in the everyday reconstruction of "Father knows best." In Hall et al. (eds).

Talbot, Mary (1992). A synthetic sisterhood: False friends in a teenage magazine. In Hall et al. (eds).

Wenger, Etienne (1990). *Toward a theory of cultural transparency*. Palo Alto: Institute for Research on Learning. (Also forthcoming, Cambridge: Cambridge University Press.)

32

The Question of Questions:
Beyond Binary Thinking

Janet M. Bing and Victoria L. Bergvall

The Continuum of Experience

Just as we rarely question our ability to breathe, so we rarely question the habit of dividing human beings into two categories: females and males. At the birth of a child we ask almost automatically 'Is it a boy or a girl?'. The question carries important messages about both biological and cultural differences; the two categories seem natural and the differences between them obvious.

However, much of our experience does not fit neatly into binary categories, and is better described as a continuum with indistinct boundaries. People relaxing at dusk experience the gradual change from day to night with no concern or precise word for the exact moment when day becomes night. Linguists travelling from village to village understand that there are no clear boundaries dividing one dialect or language from another. Berlin and Kay (1969) and Kay and McDaniel (1978) show that although basic colours have a universal biological basis, the variation across languages and individuals is so great that boundaries between colours can be identified only with fuzzy logic, a logic based on probabilities. In a study investigating how subjects distinguish between cups, bowls, mugs, and vases, Labov (1973: 353) points out that although language is essentially categorical, 'in the world of experience all boundaries show some degree of vagueness, and any formal system which is useful for semantic description must allow us to record, or even measure, this property'. Because language is discrete and biased towards dichotomy and clear boundaries, the scalar values and unclear boundaries of reality are sometimes difficult to recognize and to accept; we must continually remind ourselves that reality and language can conflict. The many real-world continua hidden by language suggest a question: is our automatic division of humans into female and male as justified as we think? Are the boundaries between them as clear as the words *female* and *male* suggest?

We have reconsidered other binary distinctions that are no longer defensible. English speakers readily use categories such as Black and White (or, in the USA, African American and European American) to classify individuals with a wide range of skin colour, despite the fact that there are no definitive biological criteria for sorting human beings into races (Omi and Winant 1994). Terms such as *mulatto* or *mixed race* are rarely used, possibly because of their negative connotations and possibly because of laws stipulating that even individuals with only small percentages of 'negro blood' are classified as *Black* on their birth certificates (West and Fenstermaker 1995: 34). Even the popular press has noted the difficulty of treating all people of colour as a homogeneous group. The 13 February 1995 issue of *Newsweek* graphically illustrated its cover story 'What Color is Black?' with a series of photos showing the wide range of hues of those of African American descent. The accompanying stories note the injustice of classifying citizens by race, a practice which results in the restriction of individual rights. Despite an obvious continuum of skin colour, however, the Black–White dichotomy persists in language and in public discourse about race.

Feminist scholars have pointed out that although the majority of human beings can be unambiguously classified as either female or male, there are actually more than two sexes and/or sexualities; a binary division fails to predict purportedly sex-based phenomena such as behaviour, sexual orientation, and even physiology. Because the terms *female* and *male* insufficiently categorize our experience, English also includes *tomboy, sissy, bisexual, gay, lesbian, hermaphrodite, androgyne, transvestite, transsexual, transgendered individual*, etc. The negative connotations often associated with these words suggest that although such a multiplicity exists, these are aberrations and departures from a basic dichotomy: *female* and *male*. The simple belief in 'only two' is not an experiential given but a normative social construction.

In the past, linguists have used the term *gender* to refer to grammatical word categories based on, but independent of, sex differences. The words *sex* and *gender* have traditionally referred to biological and linguistic classifications, respectively. When feminist scholars pointed out in the 1960s and 1970s that feminine and masculine behaviours were prescriptively divided into two mutually exclusive sets which do not necessarily correspond to female and male, theorists borrowed the term *gender* from linguists to refer to behaviour that was socially acquired rather than biologically innate (McConnell-Ginet 1988; Nicholson 1994). Identifying gendered behaviour as independent of biological sex has raised new questions in a number of disciplines, including psychology, sociology, anthropology, and linguistics. One of these questions is, 'Can all humans be divided into only two biological categories?'

Recently, Butler (1990, 1993), Epstein (1990), Bem (1993), Nicholson (1994), and others have claimed that, like gender, sex is socially constructed and better described as a continuum rather than a dichotomy. In what are often called Western (meaning industrialized) countries, biological sexual variance is now surgically corrected to fit binary categories (Epstein 1990), in contrast to cultures that recognize more than two biological categories, as well as more than two social and linguistic categories (Jacobs and Cromwell 1992; Hall and O'Donovan 1996). Even discussions of gender have often assumed innate biological differences between females and males, but this 'biological foundationalism' (Bem 1993) is now being challenged. Butler, Bem, Nicholson, and Epstein do not assume dichotomies in either sex or gender and their work is encouraging those in other disciplines to examine the consequences of looking for and finding dichotomies.

Traditional Questions about Language and Gender

Current researchers on language and gender are increasingly troubled by many of the preconceptions and presuppositions inherent in the questions traditionally asked about the language of women and men and are beginning to question the division of speech on the basis of a binary division of gender or sex. For example, the articles in Bergvall, Bing and Freed (1996) investigate speech communities without presupposing differences between women and men and show the diverse ways in which traditional ideas about sex and gender have influenced questions asked about language. Not surprisingly, these authors raise some important new questions, including the following:

1 Why are questions that strengthen the female–male dichotomy so frequently asked, while those that explore other types of variation evoke much less interest?

2 How much of this apparent dichotomy is imposed by the questions themselves?

Although researchers studying language and gender are generally sensitive to the power of language, the traditional questions have tended to reinforce rather than to weaken the prevailing female–male dichotomy. Researchers asking the question, 'How do men and women speak differently?' (Lakoff 1975; Maltz and Borker 1982, reprinted in this volume, p. 417; Tannen 1990) not only presuppose that women and men do speak differently, but have too often found the language of women deficient (Jespersen 1922; Lakoff 1975), reinforcing the perception of *women* as deficient (see Cameron 1996).

A second question, 'How does language reflect, construct, and maintain male dominance?' represents another major strand of language and gender research. Feminists such as Shulamith Firestone, Catherine MacKinnon, Alison Jaggar, and Mary Daly have shown how social systems limit women's freedom of choice and action (for a summary, see Tong 1989); feminists interested in exploring how dominance is achieved through language explore how interruptions, topic control, use of generic pronouns and nouns, polite forms, and formal and informal speech all constitute evidence that language not only reflects power relationships, but helps maintain them (Zimmerman and West 1975; Fishman 1983; West and Zimmerman 1983; James and Clarke 1992; Bing 1994, etc.). Such studies challenge the rights of males to control language, but as a result of asking questions that presuppose a dichotomy, they also reinforce the predominant assumption that females and males are essentially different.

The recognition that gender roles are socially constructed has brought about a reframing of the traditional question from 'How do women and men speak differently?' to 'How are women and men *taught* to speak differently?' Those who study culture and language have always insisted that difference and inferiority are not the same, and scholars such as Maltz and Borker (1982) and Tannen (1990) emphasize parallels between gender differences and cultural differences. Although researchers adopting a cultural-difference approach do not deny male dominance nor necessarily assume an essential biological difference between women and men, those writing for a wider, popular audience, such as Gray (1992) *Men Are from Mars, Women Are from Venus* and Tannen (1990) *You Just Don't Understand*, emphasize differences, minimize similarities, and largely ignore unequal power or status. As Freed (1992) argues, such books reinforce stereotypes and mask the fact that female and male language and behaviour form an overlapping continuum rather than two distinct categories.

The Persistence of Dichotomies

Linguists have documented extensively how individual speakers command a range of styles with situationally appropriate competence (Chafe 1985; Tannen 1985; Chafe and Danielewicz 1987; Biber 1988; West 1995; Freed 1996; Greenwood 1996). Researchers such as Tannen (1981, 1982, 1984) and Labov (1972) emphasize ethnic variation and functional or social variation in some of their research but in other work seem to imply that women share a common language different from the common language of men (Tannen 1990; Labov 1991). For example, the question of why women use more prestige forms presupposes that women do use more prestige forms, despite studies that show that not all and not only women use such forms (James 1996).

There is considerable evidence that variables such as race, social class, culture, discourse function, and setting are as important as gender and not additive or easily separated (Keenan 1974; Gal 1989, 1992; hooks 1990; Goodwin 1980, 1990; Ochs 1992; West and Fenstermaker 1995; Freed and Greenwood 1996; Bucholtz 1996; Polanyi and Strassmann 1996). Eckert and McConnell-Ginet (1992a, reprinted in this volume, p. 484; 1992b; 1995) have argued against taking gender as natural or given and have advocated grounding the study of gender and language in investigations of the social and linguistic activities of specific groups, such as the communities of high school jocks and burnouts (Eckert 1989). The research of O'Barr and Atkins (1980, reprinted in this volume, p. 377) challenges the assumption that there is a women's language different from that of men, arguing that differences attributed to sex are actually differences between powerful or powerless styles of language used by both men and women. In examining how children construct arguments, Goodwin and Goodwin (1987: 205) report, 'Though there are some differences in the ways in which girls and boys organize their arguing . . . the features they use in common are far more pervasive. Were one to focus just on points where girls and boys differ, the activity itself would be obscured.' Ochs (1992: 340) observes, 'In relating sociocultural constructions of gender to social meaning of language, an issue of importance emerges: *few features of language directly and exclusively index gender'* (emphasis in the original). Evidence of this kind is often overlooked. Researchers can accept evidence that shows that gender is a social construct and that language is learned behaviour. However, because they accept a biological female–male dichotomy, they often assume that language reflects this dichotomy. Studies that reinforce female–male differences continue to capture the interest and imagination of both scholars and the general public, thus further reinforcing the presupposed dichotomy.

Certain ideas (including ideas about female–male differences) persist in the face of contradictory evidence, while other ideas just never seem to gain wide interest or attention. Facts and arguments that challenge conventional wisdom tend to be overlooked or forgotten. For example, in spite of frequent efforts to debunk the belief that Eskimos have 100 words for snow (Pullum 1989), the general public is unlikely to abandon this myth. As Pullum (1989: 277) notes, 'the lack of little things like verisimilitude and substantiation are not enough to stop a myth'. Similarly, despite the observations of researchers like O'Barr and Atkins (1980), Goodwin and Goodwin (1987), and Eckert (1989), there will probably be no decline in the number of students who begin their term-paper research with the question, 'How is the language of men and women different?' Such questions strengthen deeply held certainties that mere facts cannot dislodge. The belief that there are separate women's and men's ways of speaking reinforces the social myth that males and females are fundamentally and categorically different.

Both language and traditional social practice suggest that there are clear boundaries between biological females and males. However, if the boundaries are not problematic, it is curious that so much energy is expended to reinforce them and to render invisible large numbers of people, including homosexuals, bisexuals, eunuchs, hermaphrodites, transvestites, transsexuals, transgendered and intersexed individuals, and others who assume social and sexual roles different from those that their cultures legitimize. Anthropologists, psychologists, and sociologists have long accepted the idea that gender roles are learned and arbitrary and that conventional feminine and masculine behaviour varies from culture to culture. Despite the evidence provided by Butler (1990, 1993), Bem (1993), Nicholson (1994), and many others, the claim that not only gender, but the category of sex itself is also socially constructed is usually greeted with disbelief or scepticism.

Individuals who fail to fit the strict female–male dichotomy are either ignored or subject to boundary policing. Groups that inhabit or stretch the boundaries of restrictive gender roles either become taboo (unmentioned and unmentionable) or are labelled aberrant. Thus, assertive women may be nudged back into their approved roles by being labelled *aggressive bitches*, and nurturing men may be reminded of their deviance by being labelled *wimp*, *sissy*, *fag*, or *pussy-whipped*. Like the dichotomies *day* and *night* and *Black* and *White*, the categories *female* and *male* are used and reinforced daily, whereas words such as *invert* or *intersexed* (words that describe hermaphrodites and ambiguously sexed individuals) are rare and likely to evoke disbelief or confusion.

The Emergence of Dichotomy

It is important to examine the debate between those who view sexual differentiation as innate and those who argue that both sex and gender are socially constructed. An analysis of this debate will help us understand how predominant the belief in biological essentialism is and how the female–male dichotomy helps strengthen the conviction that anatomy is destiny. By understanding how dichotomy is enforced, we may recognize that we inadvertently contribute to it. It is particularly important to look at definitions and note who does the defining. A good place to begin is with the definitions and the definers of the words *female* and *male*.

Over time, scientists have had many ways to account for differences between women and men. Citing Hippocrates, many early writers 'scientifically' accounted for sex differences as a distinction between *complexions*; that is, the balance of the qualities hot, cold, moist, and dry. Because men were believed to have greater heat than women, they were judged to be superior (Cadden 1993: 171). Edward Clarke's (1873) *Sex in Education* used the concept of *vital force* to argue against the education of women, for if the nervous system has a fixed amount of energy, any energy spent in the development of a woman's brain would be diverted from her reproductive organs and, hence, would be harmful to her health (Bem 1993: 10). However, the idea that female and male bodies are fundamentally different is relatively new. Historically, women's sexual organs were believed to be the same as, but less developed than, those of men.

Thomas Laqueur (1990) identifies the historical shift in the eighteenth century from a one-sex view of the body to a two-sex view. Just as studies such as Jespersen's identified women's language as an inferior form of men's, so until relatively recently, the female body was seen as an inferior version of the male's, and the 'less-developed' female sexual organs had the same names as those of males. Prior to the eighteenth century, philosophers and physicians assumed the incapacity and dependency of women and children since both were incomplete or underdeveloped men (Cadden 1993: 181). Under this view, the fact that all embryos have tissue for both female and male genitalia and reproductive organs (Bem 1993: 23) was not problematic for defenders of the status quo.

Both the Church and Aristotle provided traditional reasons why males should rule females, but with the decline of their authority, the single-sex hypothesis became a potential threat to the social order, making it necessary to justify the limitation of women's rights by defining women as *essentially* different. If women were the same, they might ask for the same privileges enjoyed by men. The boundaries between the sexes needed to be reinforced; intersexed individuals ceased to be acknowledged and became redefined as a medical problem. With the shift to the two-sex view of the body, differences rather than similarities became emphasized, organs such as the vagina were given names of their own (Nicholson 1994: 87), and hermaphrodites subsequently became pseudo-hermaphrodites whose 'true' sex had to be discovered by doctors (Epstein 1990: 100).

Medical Enforcement: Fixing Nature's 'Mistakes'

The medical categorization of intersexed individuals shows that the distinction between female and male is an issue that is not only linguistic and cultural but is also medical. Julia Epstein (1990: 104) quotes a 1964 medical textbook that states, 'There is no standard legal or medical definition of sex.' Biological sex results from variations in chromosome combinations (such as XX, XY, XO, XXX, and XXY), internal gonad structure, external gonad structure, hormonal dominance, secondary sexual characteristics, apparent sex, psychological sex, and sex of rearing. In the majority of human births, the combinations of these factors lead to clearly sexed males and females, but they can also result in as many as seventy different types of intersexed individuals (Epstein 1990: 105). Such intersexed individuals are not as rare as most people believe. Duckett and Baskin (1993: S80) report that the incidence of intersex is approximately 1 in 30,000 newborns, of which about 10 percent are true hermaphrodites. The more common pseudo-hermaphroditism results from a number of causes, including hormonal variations. Although the birth of intersexed individuals is not rare, it *is* unmentionable, even in tabloids that regularly report such outrageous topics as copulation with extraterrestrials and the reappearance of Elvis.

The assignment of intersexed individuals to the categories of female and male is complex and partly dependent on the biases of particular physicians. Although chromata are often an important factor in determining sex, they are not always the deciding factor. For example, in the case of Androgen Insensitivity Syndrome (testicular feminization), individuals with XY chromatin patterns and normal androgen levels appear to be female at birth and are generally raised as females. Referring to a summary of studies on true hermaphrodites, Krob et al. (1994: 4–5) note that although hermaphrodites are generally 'assigned' a female sex, those with a Y chromosome are made female as often as those with an X chromosome are made male. As Kessler (1990: 21) notes, for some physicians, chromosomes are less relevant in determining sex than penis size; that is, *male* is defined neither by the genetic condition of having one Y and one X chromosome nor by the production of sperm, but by the aesthetic condition of having an appropriately large penis.

Evidence in the medical literature suggests that different physicians use different criteria for assigning sex. If the primary physician for an intersexed child is a pediatric endocrinologist, the child is more likely to be classified as female, but if the decision is made by a urologist, the same child is more likely to be classified as male (Kessler 1990: 12). As one endocrinologist noted, urologists 'like to make boys' (p. 21). It is worth noting that physicians recognize and emphasize to parents of intersexed children that sex as well as gender is socially constructed, but this is rarely discussed in public domains. One pediatric endocrinologist reports '[I] try to impress upon them [the parents] that there's an enormous amount of clinical data to support the fact that if you sex-reverse an infant . . . the majority of the time the alternative gender identity is commensurate with the socialization, the way that they are raised, and how people view them, and that seems to be the most critical' (p. 17).

Thus, just as language and society enforce the division between genders, the medical profession enforces a binary division into two sexes, suppressing the diversity of gender positions. Intersexed individuals (who were previously treated as monsters) are now defined as 'treatable', with physicians reconstructing the body as either female or male with surgery and/or hormones. The possibility of *not* 'curing' these individuals is never considered. Although determining a true sex sometimes takes as long as two or three months, the pretence remains that all humans are born female or male, but never both, neither, or indeterminate. Despite relatively large numbers of babies born intersexed and an extensive medical literature on the subject, references to intersexed or ambiguously sexed individuals are uncommon in public discourse. Since most intersexed individuals are 'cured' as infants, even those individuals who are most affected are often unaware of their previous biological status, one enforced by silence. Similarly, until quite recently, gays, lesbians, cross-dressers, and other groups at the boundaries of gender were also treated with silence, and in many situations they still are.

Supernumerary Categories

Sex and gender polarizations are widespread, but also culture-specific. The way different societies define homosexuality and intersexed individuals suggests that 'compulsory heterosexuality' (Rich 1980) is not universal. Many cultures recognize supernumerary genders, categories that describe roles other than feminine and masculine; the most widely cited are the Native American *berdache* (Martin and Voorhies 1975; Whitehead 1981). In most Native American tribes, the berdache had well-defined and sometimes respected status (Whitehead 1981). In most cases, the supernumerary terms refer to gender roles rather than to sex, as in the case of North Piegan women who became *ninauposkitzipxpe*, 'manly-hearted women' (Martin and Voorhies 1975: 101).

However, some societies also have common names for intersexed individuals. Although the Pokot of Kenya usually put intersexed individuals to death as monsters, they use a common word, *serrer*, to refer to 'male and female yet neither male nor female' (Jacobs and Cromwell 1992: 50; Martin and Voorhies 1975: 89). Similarly, the *hijras* are a visible and socially recognized part of society in India (Hall and O'Donovan 1996). The Navajo call the intersexed *nadle*, and distinguish between real nadle (presumably hermaphrodites) and those with either female or male genitals who pretend they are nadle. Both categories have well-defined and respected status in Navajo society, and the roles of both are sanctioned by Navajo mythology (Martin and Voorhies 1975: 93). The existence of four genders in tribes such as the Pima (males, females, males who act like females, and females who act like males) is a direct recognition by the society that not all people fit into just two categories. The mythologies of the Navajo, Pima, Mojave, and other Native American groups recognize that intersexuals, homosexuals, and transgendered individuals have always existed.

[...]

Difference Is Not the Problem

One important fact cannot be overlooked: there are clear biological differences between most women and most men. Nobody denies this, although some writers suggest that feminists *do* deny it and are being irrational when they criticize findings that emphasize female–male differences. Noting that in higher math, 'the topmost ranks are thronged with male minds', Nicholas Wade (1994: 32) says, 'Some feminist ideologues assert that all minds are created equal and women would be just as good at math if they weren't discouraged in school'. He discounts the effect of bias and cites an expert who 'concludes that boys' superiority at math is mostly innate'.

The issue, of course, is not difference, but oversimplification and stereotyping. One obvious oversimplification is that of using statistical differences between two groups as proof that all members of one group have certain characteristics shared by no members of the other group (and vice versa). This oversimplification has traditionally been used to limit choices and opportunities for girls and women. Contrary to what Wade suggests, the point is not that everyone is created equal, but that everyone should be allowed equal opportunity. Even if scientists were to discover some correlation between sex and innate superiority at certain math skills, this would not necessarily be problematic unless it were used as an excuse to ignore biased behaviour in the classroom (such as teachers interpreting statistical differences as categorical and telling their students that girls are no good at math). However, the average performance of a group is too often used to restrict the opportunities of individuals, such as girls who just happen to excel at math; their performance can then be labelled exceptional, thus further reinforcing lowered expectations for other girls.

Wade might have considered similar evidence from other fields. The top-ranked chefs are also mostly male; does this suggest that cooking is also an innate ability better left to men? Doreen Kimura (1992: 125) judges females to be less suitable than men for the fields of engineering and physics. Does this suggest that colleges should train *no* female engineers or physicists, regardless of prior achievement? Does this justify the androcentric bias in engineering programmes described by Bergvall (1996)? As Gould (1984: 7) notes, biological determinism is a 'theory of limits', and theories which treat all members of a group as identical impose real limits on real people.

The issue is not difference, but *gender polarization*, 'the ubiquitous organization of social life around the distinction between male and female' (Bem 1993: 2). Bem observes:

> It is thus not simply that women and men are seen to be different but that this male–female difference is superimposed on so many aspects of the social world that a cultural connection is thereby forged between sex and virtually every other aspect of human experience, including modes of dress and social roles and even ways of expressing emotion and experiencing sexual desire. (p. 2)

As Bem shows, the problem with gender polarization is not that there are differences, but that these differences define mutually exclusive scripts for being female and male (p. 80).

Gender polarization makes it easier to limit opportunities and exclude girls and women from education, public office, and the military and easier to deny them legal protection and highly paid positions. For example, in a court case claiming employer discrimination against women, representatives defending the retail corporation, Sears, argued 'that "fundamental" differences between the sexes (and not its own actions) explained the gender imbalances in its labour force' (Scott 1988: 39). The plaintiff's attorneys provided statistical evidence to show that women were not being hired in commission sales jobs. Sears contended that differences could be accounted for not by discrimination against women, but by *natural* difference. By treating women as a homogeneous group and establishing this group as *different*, Sears won its case. Apparently 'women' did not want the more lucrative positions, in spite of the fact that it was women who sued.

The issue is not difference, but the denial of any differences within or across groups. In the United States, individual rights are fiercely defended, so it is ironic that women are so often treated as members of a group and not as individuals. Exclusion on the basis of sex is not uncommon. For example, in the United States, until recently, women have been excluded from some state-supported military academies (the Citadel and the Virginia Military Institute) despite outstanding achievement of women at others; the top graduate from West Point in 1995 was Rebecca Elizabeth Marier.

The case of Debra DiCenso, an amateur bodybuilder, provides another reminder of how much variation there is within the categories *women* and *men*, as well as a striking example of how strongly gender polarization is still enforced. Ms DiCenso was arrested for working out in the men's weight room in a Boston gym. She was there because the heaviest dumbbells in the women's weight room were 34 pounds too light for her workout. This would not be a problem for most women, but for the 'crime' of working out in the men's weight room (not forbidden by any gym rules) and for refusing to leave when asked, this woman was 'handcuffed, driven to the police station and booked' (Associated Press 1995: A6). Debra DiCenso's crime was that of disobeying the unspoken rules of gender polarization. For her, the problem was not difference; she's different not only from most men but also from most women. For Debra DiCenso, the problem was inequality of opportunity.

Difference, Diversity, and Gender Polarization

Some aspects of difference are positive. Feminists have sometimes emphasized difference in order to show that women's speech, bodies, and work are valuable (Scott 1988; Hess 1990; Tannen 1990; West and Fenstermaker 1995). But for many feminists, the word *difference* is a problem because, when it is used, the power differential between groups is usually ignored. Attempts to prove difference are often attempts at gender polarization and one way to rationalize limiting the opportunities of women. For those who perceive no inequality of opportunity, *difference* does not signal an underlying pattern of dominance. Trudgill (1974: 95), for example, states: 'Thus geographical, ethnic group, and social-class varieties [of language] are, at least partly, the result of social *distance*, while sex varieties are the result of social *difference*.' Many feminists would disagree, arguing that sex, class and ethnicity all involve social distance (difference in status) and not simply difference (McIntosh 1988; Bing 1994).

The word *diversity* also has different meanings for different people. For many feminists and people of colour, the word *diversity* implies equality of opportunity for traditionally excluded groups and the recognition of individual differences within groups. Gender polarization is a failure to accept diversity. As Scott (1988: 45) says of gender polarization: 'In effect, the duality this opposition creates draws one line of difference, invests it with biological explanations, and then treats each side of the opposition as a unitary phenomenon. Everything in each category (male/female) is assumed to be the same; hence, differences within either category are suppressed.'

For members of privileged groups, diversity is often unwelcome. Although difference can be used to justify the status quo, diversity challenges it. To some people, diversity, like affirmative action, does not suggest equal opportunity, but another false dichotomy: They ask, 'Do we give a woman an opportunity, or do we choose the best candidate, that is, someone who is qualified?' The simplifications of such dichotomies not only hide the genuine complexities of experience, but also provide justification for the exclusion of individuals. Critics, such as Wade (1994), who chastise 'feminist ideologues' for pointing out the dangers of emphasizing difference, should address the question of what it is that they find so threatening about diversity. After all, isn't diversity just a more complex and accurate understanding of difference?

Beyond Dichotomy

It would be ironic if feminists interested in language and gender inadvertently reinforced gender polarization and the myths of essential female–male difference. By assuming a female–male dichotomy and by emphasizing language which reflects the two categories, linguists may be reinforcing biological essentialism, even if they emphasize that language, like gender, is learned behaviour. Unfortunately, there are indications that the work of linguists is being co-opted. In a chapter called 'Speculations on the Evolution of Mind, Woman, Man, and Brain', Joseph (1992) cites the work of a number of linguists, including Tannen (1990), to underscore what he believes are essential female–male differences. Linguists must realize that when they publish answers to the question, 'How do women and men speak differently?', their discoveries of difference may be used for the purpose of strengthening gender polarization. [. . .]

If we are interested in undermining rather than reinforcing gender polarization, in addition to asking different questions, we need to create new metaphors to help us think about sex, gender, and language. Nicholson (1994: 100) suggests that we compare *women* to a tapestry unified by 'overlapping threads of color', noting that 'no one particular color is found throughout the whole'. This metaphor suggests a 'complicated network of criss-crossing intersecting similarities and differences' (Nicholson 1994: 100). Nicholson also borrows the well-known game metaphor from Wittgenstein; just as there is no single feature common to all games, there is also no characteristic common to all women, but any two individuals in a group will share some common trait. West and Fenstermaker (1995) suggest a visual metaphor to account for interactions of gender, class, and race; they propose a number of inter-secting circles to capture the fact that different members of groups share some, but not all, characteristics.

To comprehend the complexity of experience, most people need some way to simplify it, and these new metaphors suggest ways to simplify and think about gen-der while still acknowledging individual differences within and across groups; these new metaphors emphasize diversity rather than dichotomy. By refusing to accept dichotomy and by asking new questions, we can abandon the tired old question 'How do women and men speak differently?', remembering that every time we seek and find differences, we also reinforce gender polarization.

The deficit, difference, and dominance models often presupposed by language and gender researchers all suggest dichotomies separated by clear boundaries. In order to move beyond binary thinking to an acceptance of diversity, we need to examine the presuppositions that underlie our questions, seek new metaphors and new models, and study different communities of practice without preconceived ideas about language and gender. Simple 'innocent' questions, such as 'Is it a boy or a girl?' or 'How do men and women speak differently?' may seem harmless. However, as an old Persian saying notes, 'Drop by drop, a river is made.' Rivers can produce deep grooves and repeated questions can produce habitual ways of thinking. Let us now abandon the binary models and move on to a new diversity model and begin to ask *new* questions about language and gender.

NOTE

This is a slightly revised version of the first chapter of Bergvall, Bing and Freed (1996) *Rethinking Language and Gender Research: Theory and Practice*, which also included introduc-tions to the chapters in the book. We would like to thank John Broderick, Mary Bucholtz, Susan Ehrlich, Alice Freed, Dana Heller, Charles Ruhl and Craig Waddell for their helpful comments on earlier versions and Anita Fellman, Ethel Pollack and Kathy Pearson for helping us find sources. Any inaccuracies or misrepresentations are, of course, our own.

REFERENCES

Associated Press (1995) (3 June) Woman is arrested for not being a guy. *Virginian Pilot-Ledger Star*, p. A6.
Bem, Sandra (1993) *The Lenses of Gender: Transforming the Debate on Sexual Inequality*. Yale University Press, New Haven.

Bergvall, Victoria (1996) Constructing and enacting gender through discourse: negotiating multiple roles as female engineering students. In Victoria Bergvall, Janet Bing, Alice Freed (eds) pp. 173–201.

Bergvall, Victoria, Bing, Janet and Freed, Alice (eds) (1996) *Rethinking Language and Gender Research: Theory and Practice*. Longman, London.

Berlin, Brent and Kay, Paul (1969) *Basic Color Terms: Their Universality and Evolution*. University of California Press, Berkeley.

Biber, Douglas (1988) *Variation Across Speech and Writing*. Cambridge University Press, Cambridge.

Bing, Janet (1994) Friendly deception: status and solidarity. In Mary Bucholtz et al. (eds) pp. 44–9.

Bucholtz, Mary (1996) Black feminist theory and African American women's linguistic practice. In Victoria Bergvall, Janet Bing, Alice Freed (eds) pp. 267–90.

Bucholtz, Mary, Liang, Anita, Sutton, Laurel and Hines, Caitlin (eds) (1994) *Cultural Performances: Proceedings of the Third Berkeley Women and Language Conference*. Berkeley Women and Language Group, Berkeley, CA.

Butler, Judith (1990) *Gender Trouble: Feminism and the Subversion of Identity*. Routledge, New York.

Butler, Judith (1993) *Bodies that Matter: On the Discursive Limits of 'Sex'*. Routledge, New York.

Cadden, Joan (1993) *Meanings of Sex Difference in the Middle Ages: Medicine, Science, and Culture*. Cambridge University Press, Cambridge.

Cameron, Deborah (1996) The language–gender interface: challenging co-optation. In Victoria Bergvall, Janet Bing, Alice Freed (eds) pp. 31–53.

Chafe, Wallace (1985) Linguistic differences produced by differences between speaking and writing. In David Olson, Nancy Torrance, Angela Hildyard (eds) pp. 105–23.

Chafe, Wallace and Danielewicz, Jane (1987) Properties of spoken and written language. In Rosalind Horowitz and S. Jay Samuels (eds) *Comprehending Oral and Written Language*. Academic Press, New York, pp. 83–113.

Clarke, Edward H. (1873) *Sex in Education, or, A Fair Chance for Girls*. J. S. Osgood, Boston.

Duckett, John and Baskin, Laurence (1993) Genitoplasty for intersex anomalies. *European Journal of Pediatrics* 152 [Suppl. 2]: S80–S84.

Eckert, Penelope (1989) *Jocks and Burnouts: Social Categories and Identity in the High School*. Teacher's College Press, New York.

Eckert, Penelope and McConnell-Ginet, Sally (1992a) Communities of practice: where language, gender, and power all live. In Kira Hall, Mary Bucholtz, Birch Moonwomon (eds) pp. 89–99.

Eckert, Penelope and McConnell-Ginet, Sally (1992b) Think practically and look locally: language and gender as community-based practice. *Annual Review of Anthropology* 21: 461–90.

Eckert, Penelope and McConnell-Ginet, Sally (1995) Constructing meaning, constructing selves: snapshots of language, gender and class from Belten High. In Kira Hall and Mary Bucholtz (eds) *Gender Articulated: Language and the Socially Constructed Self*. Routledge, London and New York, pp. 469–507.

Epstein, Julia (1990) Either/or–neither/both: sexual ambiguity and the ideology of gender. *Genders* 7: 99–142.

Fishman, Pamela (1983) Interaction: the work women do. In Barrie Thorne, Cheris Kramarae, Nancy Henley (eds) pp. 89–101.

Freed, Alice (1992) We understand perfectly: a critique of Tannen's view of cross-sex communication. In Kira Hall, Mary Bucholtz, Birch Moonwomon (eds) pp. 144–52.

Freed, Alice F. (1996) Language and gender research in an experimental setting. In Victoria Bergvall, Janet Bing, Alice Freed (eds) pp. 54–76.

Freed, Alice and Greenwood, Alice (1996) Women, men and type of talk: what makes the difference? *Language in Society* 25: 1–26.

Gal, Susan (1989) Between speech and silence: the problematics of research on language and gender. *Papers in Pragmatics* 3.1: 1–38.

Gal, Susan (1992) Language, gender, and power: an anthropological view. In Kira Hall, Mary Bucholtz, Birch Moonwomon (eds) pp. 153–61.

Goodwin, Marjorie Harness (1980) Directive–response speech sequences in girls' and boys' task activities. In Sally McConnell-Ginet, Ruth Borker, Nelly Furman (eds) pp. 157–73.

Goodwin, Marjorie Harness (1990) *He-Said-She-Said*. Indiana University Press, Bloomington.

Goodwin, Marjorie Harness and Goodwin, Charles (1987) Children's arguing. In Susan Philips, Susan Steele, Christine Tanz (eds) *Language, Gender and Sex in Comparative Perspective*. Cambridge University Press, Cambridge, pp. 200–48.

Gould, Stephen Jay (1984) (12 Aug.) Similarities between the sexes. (Review of Bleier, Ruth (1984) *Science and Gender: A Critique of Biology and Its Theories on Women*. Pergamon Press, New York.) *The New York Times Book Review*, p. 7.

Gray, John (1992) *Men Are from Mars, Women Are from Venus: A Practical Guide for Improving Communication and Getting What You Want in Your Relationships*. Harper Collins, New York.

Greenwood, Alice (1996) Floor management and power strategies in adolescent conversation. In Victoria Bergvall, Janet Bing, Alice Freed (eds) pp. 77–97.

Hall, Kira, Bucholtz, Mary and Moonwomon, Birch (eds) (1992) *Locating Power: Proceedings of the Second Berkeley Women and Language Conference*. Berkeley Women and Language Group, Berkeley, CA.

Hall, Kira and O'Donovan, Veronica (1996) Shifting gender positions among Hindi-speaking hijras. In Victoria Bergvall, Janet Bing, Alice Freed (eds) pp. 228–66.

Hess, Beth (1990) Beyond dichotomy: drawing distinctions and embracing differences. *Sociological Forum* 5.1: 75–93.

hooks, bell (1990) (Jul./Aug.) Feminism and racism: the struggle continues. *Z Magazine* 3.7: 41–3.

Jacobs, Sue-Ellen and Cromwell, Jason (1992) Visions and revisions of reality: reflections on sex, sexuality, gender, and gender variance. *Journal of Homosexuality* 23.4: 43–69.

James, Deborah (1996) Women, men, and prestige speech forms: a critical review. In Victoria Bergvall, Janet Bing, Alice Freed (eds) pp. 98–125.

James, Deborah and Clarke, Sandra (1992) Interruptions, gender, and power: a critical review of the literature. In Kira Hall, Mary Bucholtz, Birch Moonwomon (eds) pp. 286–99.

Jespersen, Otto (1922) The woman. In *Language: Its Nature, Development and Origins*. Allen & Unwin, London, pp. 237–54.

Joseph, Rhawn (1992) *The Right Brain and the Unconscious: Discovering the Stranger Within*. Plenum Press, New York.

Kay, Paul and McDaniel, C. K. (1978) The linguistic significance of the meanings of basic color terms. *Language* 54: 610–46.

Keenan, Elinor Ochs (1974) Norm-makers and norm-breakers: uses of speech by men and women in a Malagasy community. In Richard Bauman and Joel Sherzer (eds) *Explorations in the Ethnography of Speaking*. Cambridge University Press, New York, pp. 125–43.

Kessler, Suzanne J. (1990) The medical construction of gender: case management of intersexed infants. *Signs: Journal of Women in Culture and Society* 16.1: 3–26.

Kimura, Doreen (1992) (Sept.) Sex differences in the brain. *Scientific American* 267: 119–25.

Krob, G., Braun, A. and Kuhnle, U. (1994) True hermaphroditism: geographical distribution, clinical findings, chromosomes and gonadal histology. *European Journal of Pediatrics* 153: 2–10.

Labov, William (1972) The isolation of contextual styles. In *Sociolinguistic Patterns*. University of Pennsylvania Press, Philadelphia, PA, pp. 70–109.

Labov, William (1973) The boundaries of words and their meanings. In Charles-James Bailey and Roger Shuy (eds) *New Ways of Analyzing Variation in English*. Georgetown University Press, Washington, DC, pp. 340–73.

Labov, William (1991) The intersection of sex and social class in the course of linguistic change. *Language Variation and Change* 2.2: 205–54.

Lakoff, Robin (1975) *Language and Woman's Place*. Harper & Row, New York.

Laqueur, Thomas (1990) *Making Sex: Body and Gender from the Greeks to Freud*. Harvard University Press, Cambridge, MA.

Maltz, Daniel and Borker, Ruth (1982) A cultural approach to male–female miscommunication. In John J. Gumperz (ed.) *Language and Social Identity*. Cambridge University Press, Cambridge, pp. 196–216.

Martin, M. Kay and Voorhies, Barbara (1975) *Female of the Species*. Columbia University Press, New York.

McConnell-Ginet, Sally (1988) Language and gender. In Frederick J. Newmeyer (ed.) *Linguistics: The Cambridge Survey*, vol. IV: *Language: The Sociocultural Context*. Cambridge University Press, Cambridge, pp. 75–99.

McConnell-Ginet, Sally, Borker, Ruth and Furman, Nelly (eds) (1980) *Women and Language in Literature and Society*. Praeger, New York.

McIntosh, Peggy (1988) White privilege and male privilege: a personal account of coming to see correspondences through work in women's studies. *Wellesley College Working Paper no. 189*. Wellesley College Center for Research on Women, Wellesley, MA.

Nicholson, Linda (1994) Interpreting gender. *Signs: Journal of Women in Culture and Society* 20.1: 79–105.

O'Barr, William and Atkins, Bowman K. (1980) 'Women's language' or 'powerless language'? In Sally McConnell-Ginet, Ruth Borker, Nelly Furman (eds) pp. 93–110.

Ochs, Elinor (1992) Indexing gender. In Alessandro Duranti and Charles Goodwin (eds) *Rethinking Context: Language as an Interactive Phenomenon*. Cambridge University Press, Cambridge, pp. 335–58.

Olson, David, Torrance, Nancy and Hildyard, Angela (eds) (1985) *Literacy, Language, and Learning: The Nature and Consequences of Reading and Writing*. Cambridge University Press, Cambridge.

Omi, Michael and Winant, Howard (1994) *Racial Formation in the United States: From the 1960s to the 1990s*. Routledge, New York.

Polanyi, Livia and Strassmann, Diana (1996) Storytellers and gatekeepers in economics. In Victoria Bergvall, Janet Bing, Alice Freed (eds) pp. 126–52.

Pullum, Geoffrey (1989) The great Eskimo vocabulary hoax. *Natural Language and Linguistic Theory* 7: 275–81.

Rich, Adrienne (1980) Compulsory heterosexuality. *Signs: Journal of Women in Culture and Society* 5: 631–60.

Scott, Joan (1988) Deconstructing equality-versus-difference: or, the uses of poststructuralist theory for feminism. *Feminist Studies* 14.1: 33–50.

Tannen, Deborah (1981) New York Jewish conversational style. *International Journal of the Sociology of Language* 30: 133–49.

Tannen, Deborah (1982) Ethnic style in male–female conversation style. In John J. Gumperz (ed.) *Language and Social Identity*. Cambridge University Press, Cambridge, pp. 217–31.

Tannen, Deborah (1984) *Conversational Style: Analyzing Talk Among Friends*. Ablex, Norwood, NJ.

Tannen, Deborah (1985) Relative focus on involvement in oral and written discourse. In David Olson, Nancy Torrance, Angela Hildyard (eds) pp. 124–47.

Tannen, Deborah (1990) *You Just Don't Understand: Women and Men in Conversation*. Morrow, New York.

Thorne, Barrie, Kramarae, Cheris and Henley, Nancy (1983) *Language, Gender, and Society*. Newbury House, Rowley, MA.

Tong, Rosemarie (1989) *Feminist Thought: A Comprehensive Introduction*. Westview Press, Boulder, CO.

Trudgill, Peter (1974) *Sociolinguistics: An Introduction*. Penguin, Harmondsworth.

Wade, Nicholas (1994) (12 June) Method and madness: how men and women think. *New York Times Magazine*, p. 32.

West, Candace (1995) Women's competence in conversation. *Discourse and Society* 6.1: 107–31.

West, Candace and Fenstermaker, Sarah (1995) Doing difference. *Gender and Society* 9.1: 8–37.

West, Candace and Zimmerman, Don (1983) Small insults: a study of interruptions in cross-sex conversations between unacquainted persons. In Barrie Thorne, Cheris Kramarae, Nancy Henley (eds) pp. 102–17.

West, Candace and Zimmerman, Don (1987) Doing gender. *Gender and Society* 1.2: 125–51.

Whitehead, Harriet (1981) The bow and the burden strap: a new look at institutionalized homosexuality in native North America. In Sherry B. Ortner and Harriet Whitehead (eds) *Sexual Meanings: The Cultural Construction of Gender and Sexuality*. Cambridge University Press, Cambridge, pp. 80–115.

Zimmerman, Don and West, Candace (1975) Sex roles, interruptions and silences in conversation. In Barrie Thorne and Nancy Henley (eds) *Language and Sex: Difference and Dominance*. Newbury House, Rowley, MA, pp. 105–29.

Index

Sources

8 Janet Holmes 'Complimenting: A Positive Politeness Strategy'.
   'What a lovely tie! Compliments and positive politeness strategies' in J. Holmes (1995) Women, Men and Politeness *(London: Longman), pp. 115–53.*

9 Marjorie Harness Goodwin 'Cooperation and Competition Across Girls' Play Activities'.
   'Cooperation and competition across girls' play activities' in A. Dundas Todd & S. Fisher (eds) (1988) Gender and Discourse: The Power of Talk *(Norwood, NJ: Ablex), pp. 55–94.*

10 Susan Gal 'Peasant Men Can't Get Wives: Language Change and Sex Roles in a Bilingual Community'.
   'Peasant men can't get wives: language change and sex roles in a bilingual community', Language in Society *7 (1978), 1–16.*

Part III   Conversational Dominance in Mixed Talk

11 Candace West & Don H. Zimmerman 'Women's Place in Everyday Talk'.
   'Women's place in everyday talk', Social Problems *24 (1977), 521–29.*

12 Victoria Leto DeFrancisco 'The Sounds of Silence: How Men Silence Women in Marital Relations'.
   'The sounds of silence: how men silence women in marital relations', Discourse and Society *2 (4) (1991), 413–24.*

13 Joan Swann 'Talk Control: An Illustration from the Classroom of Problems in Analysing Male Dominance of Conversation'.
   'Talk control: an illustration from the classroom of problems in analysing male dominance of conversation' in J. Coates & D. Cameron (eds) (1989) Women in their Speech Communities *(London: Longman), pp. 123–40.*

14 Susan C. Herring et al. 'Participation in Electronic Discourse in a "Feminist" Field'.
   'Participation in electronic discourse in a "feminist" field' in K. Hall et al. (eds) (1992) Locating Power. Proceedings of the 2nd Berkeley Women and Language Conference *(Berkeley: BWLG), pp. 250–62.*

Part IV   Same-Sex Talk

15 Fern L. Johnson & Elizabeth J. Aries 'The Talk of Women Friends'.
   'The talk of women friends', Women's Studies International Forum, *6 (4) (1983), pp. 353–61.*

16 Jennifer Coates 'Gossip Revisited: Language in All-Female Groups'.
   'Gossip revisited: language in all-female groups' in J. Coates & D. Cameron (eds) (1989) Women in Their Speech Communities *(London: Longman), pp. 94–122.*

17 Jane Pilkington '"Don't try and make out that I'm nice!" The Different Strategies Women and Men Use when Gossiping'.
   '"Don't try and make out that I'm nice!" The different strategies women and men use when gossiping', Wellington Working Papers in Linguistics 5 (1992), pp. 37–60.

18 Deborah Cameron 'Performing Gender Identity: Young Men's Talk and the Construction of Heterosexual Masculinity'.
   'Performing gender identity: young men's talk and the construction of heterosexual masculinity' in S. Johnson & U. Meinhof (eds) (1997) Language and Masculinity *(Oxford: Blackwell)*, pp. 47–64.

19 Koenraad Kuiper 'Sporting Formulae in New Zealand English: Two Models of Male Solidarity'.
   'Sporting formulae in New Zealand English: two models of male solidarity' in J. Cheshire (ed.) (1991) English around the World *(Cambridge: Cambridge University Press)*, pp. 200–209.

Part V   Women's Talk in the Public Domain

20 Katsue Akiba Reynolds 'Female Speakers of Japanese in Transition'.
   'Female speakers of Japanese in transition' in S. Ide & N. McGloin (eds) (1991) Aspects of Japanese Women's Language *(Tokyo: Kurosio Publishers)*, pp. 129–46.

21 Bonnie S. McElhinny '"I don't smile much any more": Affect, Gender and the Discourse of Pittsburgh Police Officers'.
   '"I don't smile much any more": affect, gender and the discourse of Pittsburgh police officers' in K. Hall et al. (eds) (1992) Locating Power. Proceedings of the 2nd Berkeley Women and Language Conference *(Berkeley: BWLG)*, pp. 386–403.

22 Candace West '"Not just doctor's orders": Directive–Response Sequences in Patients' Visits to Women and Men Physicians'.
   '"Not just doctor's orders": directive–response sequences in patients' visits to women and men physicians', Discourse & Society 1 (1) (1990), pp. 85–112.

23 Marie Wilson Nelson 'Women's Ways: Interactive Patterns in Predominantly Female Research Teams'.
   'Women's ways: interactive patterns in predominantly female research teams' in B. Bate & A. Taylor (eds) (1988) Women Communicating: Studies of Women's Talk *(New Jersey: Ablex)*, pp. 199–232.

Part VI   Theoretical Debates (1) Gender or Power?

24 William M. O'Barr & Bowman K. Atkins '"Women's Language" or "Powerless Language"?'
   '"Women's language" or "powerless language"?' in S. McConnell-Ginet et al. (eds) (1980) Women and Language in Literature and Society *(New York: Praeger)*, pp. 93–110.

Part VII Theoretical Debates (2) Difference or Dominance?

Part VIII Looking to the Future